W0049917

THE NIAM INFORMATION ANALYSIS METHOD

The NIAM Information Analysis Method

Method

Theory and Practice

J.J.V.R. WINTRAECKEN

Houtvesterstraat 8, 5241 JX Rosmalen

CONTROL
DATA

Kluwer Academic Publishers

Dordrecht / Boston / London

Library of Congress Cataloging-in-Publication Data

Wintraecken, J. J. V. R.
    [Informatie-analyse volgens NIAM. English]
    The NIAM information analysis method : theory and practice /
J.J.V.R. Wintraecken.
        p.   cm.
    Translation of: Informatie-analyse volgens NIAM.
    Bibliography: p.
    ISBN-13:978-94-010-6687-7   e-ISBN-13:978-94-009-0451-4
    DOI: 10.1007/978-3-94-009-0451-4

    1. System design.   2. System analysis.
    QA76.9.S88W56   1989
    003--dc20   89-32243

ISBN-13:978-94-010-6687-7

(translated from Dutch by the author)
(Dutch title: Informatie-analyse volgens NIAM
subtitle: in theorie en praktijk)

Published by Kluwer Academic Publishers,
P.O. Box 17, 3300 AA Dordrecht, The Netherlands

Kluwer Academic Publishers incorporates
the publishing programmes of
D. Reidel, Martinus Nijhoff, Dr W. Junk and MTP Press.

Sold and distributed in the U.S.A. and Canada
by Kluwer Academic Publishers,
101 Philip Drive, Norwell, MA 02061, U.S.A.

In all other countries, sold and distributed
by Kluwer Academic Publishers Group,
P.O. Box 322, 3300 AH Dordrecht, The Netherlands.

Printed on acid-free paper

TABLE OF CONTENTS

AUTHOR'S PREFACE

About information analysis

Everywhere people are working, they are communicating or exchanging information about their work. Unless they come to reasonable agreements about this communication, i.e., agreements describing the "language" of their communication so that they can understand each other's information, sooner or later there will be such a "Tower of Babel" that their goal of communication will be doomed to failure.

There are a lot of places where some of the communication between people working together is being carried out via an information system. In these cases too, a clear agreement about communication must be made, so that people communicating via an information system can understand each other at all times. In such an agreement, it is determined which data may be exchanged with the information system and the meaning everyone should assign to that data. For communication taking place via an information system, such an agreement is called a "grammar" or a "conceptual schemea" of this information system.

"Information analysis" is that field and also that phase of development of an information system in which the grammar or the conceptual schemea of the information system is determined. The grammar or the conceptual scheme is an essential part of the specifications of present-day information systems.

About NIAM

The "Nijssen Information Analysis Method" (NIAM) is a formal method in support of information analysis which has been developed under the direction of Prof.Dr.Ir. G.M. Nijssen since 1975. This method has a solid theoretical basis and has been successfully applied in the past in various practical situations.

In recent years, NIAM has figured prominently in many publications and conferences (see e.g., Reference 8).

A proposal of the International Standards Organization (ISO) in the field of conceptual schemata and databases contains a number of concepts and terms and a formal method of describing conceptual schemata characteristic of, for example, NIAM (see Reference 1).

In the last few years, interest in and use of NIAM has been steadily increasing. However, the lack of a textbook on the subject of NIAM up to now has been considered by many as a serious deficiency.

In this book, I have tried to bring together into one volume the knowledge about NIAM dispersed over a wide range of syllabuses, articles and other publications. This book aims at providing insight into the basic concepts of NIAM and at setting down practical guidelines for applying this method.

About this book

This book is intended for anyone involved or interested in this field or in NIAM, whether they are experts in the field of information science or laypeople.

In light of the broad range of this target group, I have tried to keep the text as readable and as easy to understand as possible, while simultaneously attempting to convey NIAM's theoretical basis as clearly as possible. I have avoided the use of technical terms from information science and automation wherever possible. The more technical concepts are concentrated in Appendix 1.

This book has been organized intuitively rather than formally. Consequently, formal cogency should not be sought in every page of the text; some of the concepts and definitions are, strictly speaking, not always purely formal, although they are intuitively clear and easy to comprehend.

In selecting concepts and terminology for this book, I have stuck as closely as possible to the proposals of the ISO.

The term "universe of discourse" has been replaced by the term "reality." Although this is, strictly speaking, not the customary formal term, I am convinced that it is sufficiently clear within the intuitive nature of this book. The term "conceptual schema" has been replaced in the text by the more intuitive term "grammar," which is often encountered in NIAM circles. And instead of "methodology," I have used the term "method."

The layout of this book

The theoretical and practical parts of this book have been put into separate chapters. The theory is constructed stepwise with the aid of concrete examples. The concepts, rules, and graphical symbols used in this process are summarized at the end of the relevant sections.

The "practically oriented" chapters deal with the application of NIAM in practice, and are likewise based on concrete examples. These chapters gradually develop a stepwise plan that can be used as a "cookbook" or "checklist" when NIAM is applied in practice.

All of the examples used in the book involve one particular context.

Appendix 1 explains how the results of the NIAM method of information analysis can be used to determine the representation of information in an information system and to design the data storage structure. Although in my opinion it can be read by everyone, this explanation is necessarily more technical in nature than the other chapters of the book, and is primarily intended for those involved or interested in the technical side of developing information systems.

Appendix 2 consists of a summary of the foremost concepts, graphical symbols, and rules and the steps in the NIAM method of information analysis, along with the number of the page on which they appeared for the first time. This appendix is consequently a list of definitions, an index, and a guideline for applying NIAM in practice, all in one.

The "References and Bibliography" contain an enumeration of the publications referred to in the text and a number of publications which have in some way, in my opinion, influenced the contents of this book.

Acknowledgements

Of all of the persons to whom I owe a debt of gratitude for the realization of this book, I wish to mention first Prof.Dr.Ir.G.M. Nijssen and the staff of Control Data's former International Center for Information Analysis Services in Brussels. Without their inspiration and enthusiasm, NIAM and consequently this book would probably never have been written.

Rijswijk, July 1985   *Jean-Jacques Wintraecken*

1 THE NIAM METHOD OF INFORMATION ANALYSIS

This first chapter begins with a definition of what we mean by "information analysis" in this book, what has to be done during information analysis, and what the results of its application should be. This chapter serves as a framework and reference point for upcoming chapters.

1.1 Knowledge, information, and communication

The concepts "knowledge," "information," and "communication" play an important role in information analysis. We start right off in this section by defining these basic concepts. The concepts "information" and "communication" can be derived from the general concept "knowledge." *Knowledge* is everything that someone knows about a certain subject or area. Knowledge can be generated by transferring or communicating it to others, or it can be generated on the basis of experience and in many cases on the basis of intuition and feeling. An example of the transfer or communication of knowledge is a learning process such as taking a course or reading a book. In general, only part of someone's knowledge can be communicated to someone else. Knowledge which is based purely on experience, intuition, or feeling can usually be only partially communicated. Knowledge can only be communicated when it can be structured and made explicit.

In this book, we shall call that part of general knowledge about a certain subject or area which can be communicated to others *information*.

We shall call any exchange of information *communication*. Knowledge is transferred by means of communication. Communication is realized via a specific communication medium. The information to be transferred is physically represented in the communication medium and passed on through it. Some examples of communication media are:

- A book for written forms of communication.
- The spoken word for oral forms of communication.
- A sheet with a sketch or a drawing for communication forms in which the information to be transferred is represented by means of a diagram.

We shall call the representation of information within a communication medium *data*. Some examples of data are the words of a written text or an oral conversation, or a drawing when diagrams are the means of communication.

Data must be interpreted in a certain way in order to deduce the information they represent and thus their meaning. For example, to understand the words of an English text, we must know the English language, that is, the language constructs that are allowed in English and their meanings. To be able to interpret a technical drawing, we must know the meanings of the drawing technique and the symbols used. Data have no meaning in themselves. The meaning and therefore the information or knowledge they represent is derived from the data by interpreting them on the basis of certain agreements and rules.

We shall explain this by means of an example. This book is the means by which I wish to transfer my knowledge of the NIAM method of information analysis to you. To this end, I have structured my knowledge of this subject, made it explicit, and then written it down. For you, this book contains information about NIAM, that is, knowledge about this subject which is communicated to you via this book. Because I am transferring this knowledge to you, we are communicating via this book. This book is the means by which our communication is realized. The information that I want to transfer to you is presented in this book by means of the vocabulary and constructs of the English language. These words and constructs constitute the data in the comunication process between you and me. You attach a meaning to this book by interpreting these data on the basis of the rules and agreements that are valid for the English language. These are laid down by the grammar of the English language. This grammar consists of a description of the agreements and rules which prescribe which English words and constructs are allowed and what their meaning is. For my part, I have complied with the grammatical rules of English while writing. Should you be unable to read English, or should you not be familiar with English grammar, you would be unable to understand me. The communication process between you and me via this book would then not function.

Just as in this example, those involved in a communication process must reach an agreement about which data may be used for the information to be communicated and what their meaning is. They must stick to this agreement in order for the communication process to take place without any disturbances. Those transmitting information may only use data permitted by the agreement and must assign to it the meaning that was agreed to. In interpreting the data, the recipients of transmitted information must not assign any meaning to the data other than what was agreed to. If they do not abide by the agreements made in the communication process, they run a risk of not being able to understand each other, that is, of having disturbances occur in the communication process.

In analogy to our example of this book as a medium of communication, we will call the description of the agreement which has to be made in every communication process the *grammar* of this communication process. Every communication process occurs on the basis of a specific grammar. The grammar is there to see to it that those involved in a communication process understand each other as well as possible, or in other words, that as few disturbances as possible occur in the communication.

The area or the topics about which information is exchanged during communication, form a part of some real or abstract world. Hereafter, we shall call that part of the real or abstract world to which a certain communication process is related the *reality* (in the literature, the term *"Universe of Discourse"* is commonly used for this concept). Every communication process is related to a reality specific for this communication process. For example, the reality for the communication taking place via this book consists of everything that has something to do with information analysis.

In the process of communication there is often not only an exchange of information in space, i.e., over a certain distance, but also in time. Probably, you are reading this book in another place than that in which I wrote it. What's more, you are most certainly reading it at another time than that at which I wrote it. By generalizing this to arbitrary communication processes, it follows that a communication medium must be able to transfer information in space and sometimes in time as well.

In this section, we have defined a number of concepts which will play a significant role in the remainder of this book. These definitions are summarized below:

Knowledge:
Everything that someone knows about a certain subject or a certain area.

Information:
Knowledge that can be physically communicated.

Communication:
Exchange or transfer of information.

Reality (Universe of Discourse):
That part and those aspects of a real or abstract world to which the information exchanged during communication is related.

Data:
The representation of information in a communication medium.

Grammar:
The description of the agreement prescribing which data may be used for the information to be communicated and what their meaning is.

Information analysis, in the broadest sense, is the activity in which the information to be exchanged during communication processes is analyzed and in which, on the basis of that analysis, a grammar of these processes is formulated.

The NIAM method of information analysis is restricted to processes in which an information processing system is used as a communication medium. In the following section, we will go more deeply into communication processes by means of information processing systems.

1.2 The information system

Communication processes take place wherever people are working together. In the previous section, we defined a number of concepts related to general communication processes. From now on, we will restrict ourselves to communication processes in which an information processing system, or an *information system*, for short, is used as the medium of communication.

People who are working together are generally executing and/or controlling a certain process. Examples of this can be found particularly in organizations or companies. For instance, in a public library, the employees in the Loan Department are responsible for the execution and control of the process "lending books." Every large company has staff in its Personnel Department who are responsible for such things as the execution and control of the process "maintaining personnel data." In an industrial setting, one of the responsibilities of the staff in the Research and Development Department is the execution and control of the process "researching and developing new products and production methods."

The general situation in which people are executing and controlling a process is illustrated in Figure 1.1.

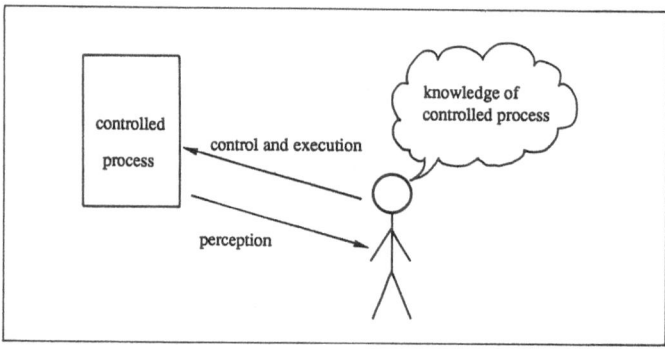

Figure 1.1.

The process being controlled and executed is called the *controlled process*. People control and execute this process by means of controlling and executing activities, with which they influence the operation of the process. They carry out these activities on the basis of their knowledge of the controlled process. This consists of general knowledge about the process and of specific knowledge about the state the process is in at the moment of control or execution. One of the ways people obtain this knowledge is by observing the process and its state.

When several people control and execute the same process, they must transfer their knowledge of this process to each other, which means that communication takes place between them (see Figure 1.2). This communication concerns the controlled process and related matters. The controlled process is thus part of the reality of this communication process.

In some cases, particularly when the controlled process is complex or when many people have to control or execute it, the communication can be more effective if an information system is used. This situation is illustrated in Figure 1.3.

People transfer information to the information system, which then stores this information. Some time later, people request the same information, or information derived from it, and use this in their control and execution activities. The information system contains the knowledge of the controlled process which all the users have in common as well as of the state it is in at the moment of control and execution. An information system is therefore an information processing system that:

– receives information and requests for information from its users and provides them with information and answers to their requests.
– can store information in time.
– can derive new information from given information.

The representation or description of all of the information stored by the information system is called the *information base* of the information system.

The people who add information to the information system are not necessarily those who in turn retrieve this information from the system. A comparison of Figure 1.2 with Figure 1.3 shows that the communication between the people involving the process to be controlled and executed now proceeds via the information system. In this situation the information system is the communication medium, the means by which the people communicate with each other.

Because the information system stores the information added to it, in this type of communication process information is not only transferred in space, but also in time. After all, the information which is added to the system can be consulted at a later point.

Just as for all communication processes, a grammar needs to be prescribed for this type of communication process as well. This grammar contains a specification of the data that may be used in the information exchange with the information system and the rules for interpreting these data. All of the users of the information system must be familiar with this grammar and are obliged to abide by these rules during the information exchange with the information system. Henceforth, we shall call the grammar of a communication process taking place by means of an information system, the *grammar* of the information system, or for short, the grammar. The information system may only accept data which may be exchanged on the basis of the grammar.

As we have seen, not only is general information about the controlled process being exchanged with the information system, but also information about the state this process is in at a certain moment. Consequently, the rules of the grammar

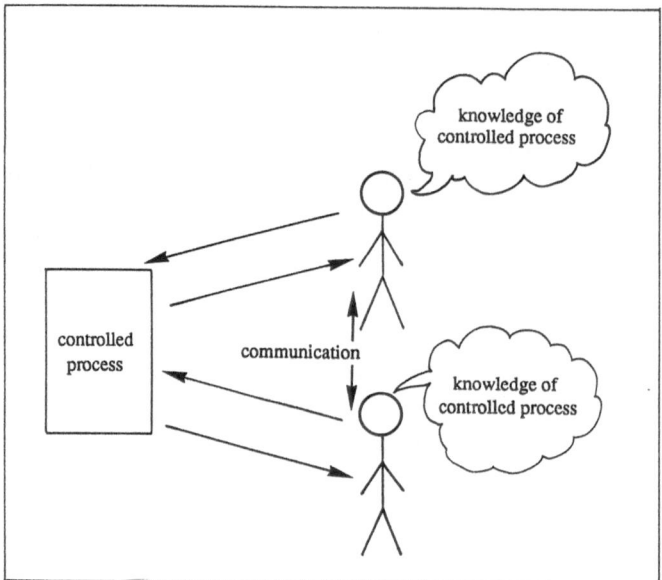

Figure 1.2.

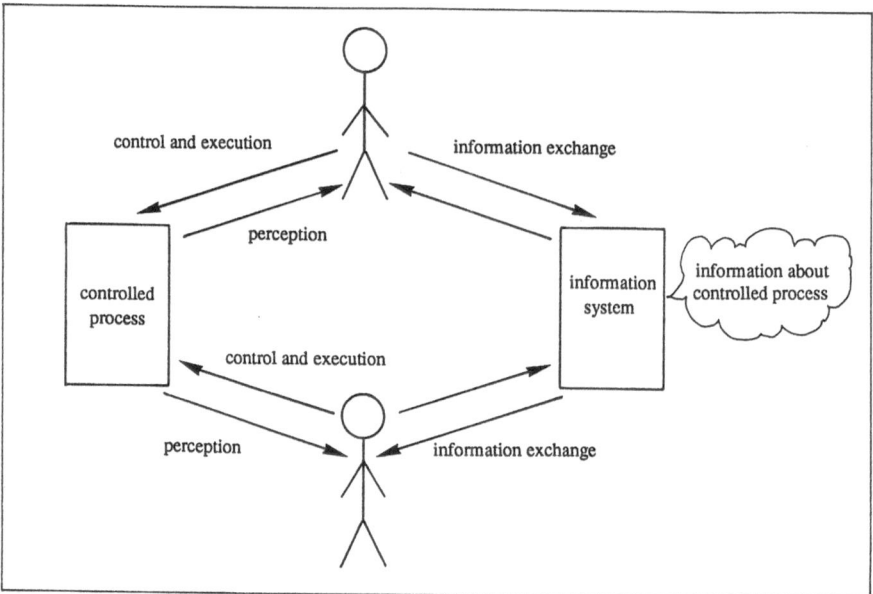

Figure 1.3.

must be formulated such that the information being exchanged with the information system can only describe states of the controlled process which are **possible** on the basis of the rules and laws valid for this process. Should it, for example, be impossible for an employee in a certain company to work for more than one department, the grammar of the information system handling the process "maintaining personnel data" must express the fact that no information describing a state in which a certain employee works for more than one department may be exchanged with the system. In addition, the grammar can exclude states of the controlled process which may occur in reality, but which may not occur in the communication about this reality. To understand this book properly, it is important to remember that the grammar of an information system contains a description of the rules which are valid for the **communication** about the reality via the information system and not rules which are valid for the reality itself. Naturally, the rules of the grammar should exclude at least those states which are impossible in reality.

The people who make use of an information system to control and execute a process are called the *users* of the information system. The relation between the controlled process, the information system, and its users is represented in Figure 1.4.

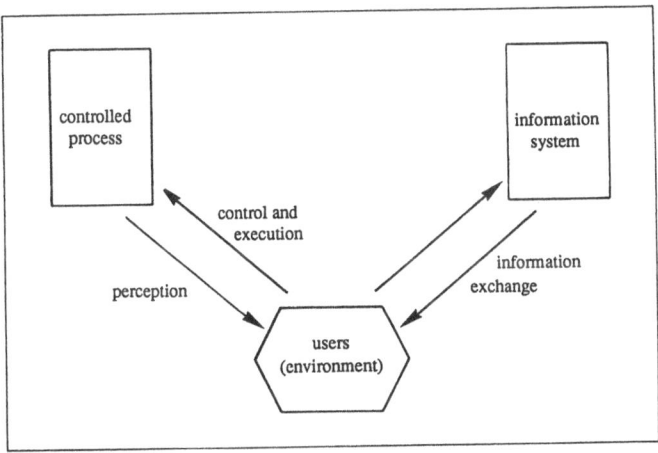

Figure 1.4.

The users of an information system are represented by a hexagon. We use this symbol because the users of an information system do not necessarily have to be people, but could be, for example, process control equipment or even another information system. Because the users as such belong to the environment of the information system rather than to the system itself, one often speaks in terms of the *"environment"* of a system rather than its "users." Both terms will be used in this book. A fundamental difference between an information system and its environment is that the behavior of an information system by definition always is deterministic. By this we mean that the information system always produces the same output for a same given input. Or stated differently, the information system always reacts to a given stimulus with the same response. Or stated yet another way, the behavior of an information system is predictable and repeatable, and can always be described exactly and formally. Consequently, the information system appears to the outside world to perform like an automaton. On the contrary, the behavior of the environment of the information system is not by definition deterministic. This is the reason why the information system and its environment are denoted by different symbols in Figure 1.4. The entity formed by the process, the information system, and its environment is called the *object system*.

In this section, we have taken a look at communication processes in which an information system is used as a communication medium. A summary of the most important concepts is given below.

Controlled process:
A process from a real or an abstract world which is controlled and executed by one or more persons and/or equipment.

Information system:
An information processing system that:

- receives information and requests for information from its environment and provides information and answers to requests to its environment.
- can store information in time.
- can derive new information from given information.

Environment:
That which does not belong to the information system and which exchanges information with the information system. The environment can be considered as the set of all of the the users of the information system. Unlike the behavior of an information system, the behavior of the environment is not by definition deterministic.

Information base:
The description of all the information which is stored by the information system.

Grammar:
The description of all the rules that prescribe which data may be exchanged with the information system and how these data must be interpreted by the users of the information system.

Object system:
The entity formed by the controlled process, the information system, and its environment.

During information analysis, the information which the users wish to exchange with their information system is determined and analyzed, and the grammar of the information system is formulated on the basis of this analysis.
In the next section, we shall show the general developmental stages of an information and the place of information analysis in this process.

1.3 The development of an information system

The information system is the communication medium by which its users communicate with each other in order to control and execute the controlled process. As such, the information system functions as an aid for its users. Like any aid, the information system must first be designed and then manufactured. That is to say, specifications have to be provided about what the system is supposed to do and what requirements it has to meet. Then the information system has to be designed based on these specifications and after that it has to be produced according to this design. These stages are no different than those customary for the development of machines, buildings, etc. In this section, we shall take a closer look at the general stages involved in the development of an information system and indicate how information analysis fits into this scheme. Roughly speaking, an information system is developed in two phases: *analysis* and *realization*.

During the analysis phase, the specifications of the information system are drawn up. In other words, it is determined what the system has to do, how it has to behave to the outside world, and which demands it has to meet. In the realization phase, the way in which these specifications are to be realized is described and the system is then implemented according to these specifications.

The specifications drawn up during the analysis phase have only to do with the "what" of the information system: they describe **what** the information system must do. During the realization phase, only the "how" of the information system is considered: **how** the specifications must be realized. The "what" is considered to belong to the *conceptual aspects* of the information system, and the "how" to the *realization aspects*. Only the conceptual aspects are described during the analysis phase. In this phase, one thus abstracts from how the information system could be realized. On the contrary, in the realization phase only the realization aspects are considered.

The conceptual and realization aspects of an information system are kept separate primarily to ensure that the thinking going on during the analysis phase is not influenced by solution-oriented considerations and that the specifications are not initially restricted or influenced by any (incidental) restrictions implied by the solutions and techniques to be applied. One of the consequences of this is that the specifications should be checked after the analysis phase, to see whether they can be realized technically and how they might have to be adapted to make technical realization possible.

Another consequence of abstracting from any realization aspects in the analysis phase is that no decision can be taken during this phase as to the extent to which the specified information system can be automated (with the aid of computers). How much it can be automated is determined in part by technical feasibility. During the analysis phase, the information system is specified independently of the question of whether it is to be realized as an automated system, a manual administrative system or a combination of these. In practice, an information system is often realized as a combination of both manual and automated systems. After the analysis phase, one thus has to determine which parts of the system must be realized by automation and which by manual administrative procedures.

Because the realization aspects are abstracted from during the analysis phase, future users of the information system, who are generally not experts in the technical realization aspects of information systems, can be involved in the analysis or can carry it out themselves.

1.3.1 Object system analysis and information analysis

The analysis phase usually falls into two parts: *object system analysis* and *information analysis*.

During object system analysis, the object system, which includes the information system and its users, is studied as a whole. During this analysis phase the controlled process is determined, the activities by which this process is controlled and executed are ascertained, the information system is defined within the object system, and the type of information which has to be exchanged with the information system is determined.

Exactly which data may be exchanged with the information system and how these data are to be interpreted by the users, is determined during the information analysis phase. We have called the description of this the grammar of the information system. The grammar is therefore one of the specifications to be produced during the analysis phase. The information system which is produced during the realization phase must behave according to these specifications. As far as the grammar is concerned, this means that the information system may only accept data which may be exchanged with the system on the basis of this grammar. Moreover, the grammar serves as an agreement about how all the users are to interpret the data exchanged with the information system. Sometimes the grammar of an information system is called the *information model* or the *conceptual schema* as well.

Object system analysis lies outside the scope of the NIAM method of information analysis, and thus of this book as well. To facilitate understanding, we will briefly highlight some matters that are relevant for the NIAM method of information analysis.

During object system analysis, the controlled process is determined and defined. The controlling and executing activities which the users have to perform to control and execute this process are defined and described.

Furthermore, it is determined what kind of information supporting these controlling and executing activities has to be exchanged with the future information system. In this way the information system is delimited and defined: it is determined what the boundaries of the information system within the object system are, what kind of information the information system has to exchange with its environment, and how the users are to work with the information system. In this connection, the information system is considered a "black box" whose boundaries and interaction with its environment are defined, but whose internal construction is not (yet) relevant. The general performance demands for the information system thus defined are usually formulated as well.

The term *"business analysis"* is sometimes used instead of object system analysis. This is a correct designation when the controlled process is a company or organization, or part of one.

1.3.2 Design and construction

During realization, the automated part of the information system is realized technically, and the nonautomated part is implemented by means of specifying manual administrative procedures, any relevant organizational measures, and other solutions. The realization lies outside the scope of information analysis and thus outside the scope of this book. However, to further understanding, we will give a general and brief survey of the realization of the automated part of an information system.

This part of the realization can usually be divided into two phases, *design* and *construction*.

During the design phase it is determined how the data to be exchanged with the information system must be represented externally for the users, how these data must be represented internally in the information system to ensure efficient processing, and what processing the system has to perform to transform these internal data representations into external representations, and vice versa. The external data representations can be specified by means of command languages, screen layouts, report layouts, potential dialogues between the users and the system, etc.

The internal data representation is described by the design of the files which are to store the data. In addition, the processing efficiency and the efficiency of the data storage are taken into account.

During the design phase, the meaning of the data is no longer considered. This belongs to the conceptual aspects which are analyzed during the information analysis phase. In the design phase, the representation of the data is determined, independently of their meaning.

In the design of an information system, the grammar is one of the foundations.

The information system should be designed such that it will only accept data that may be exchanged with it on the basis of the grammar.

In Appendix 1, we shall point out the role played by the grammar in the design of data files and/or databases.

Once the information system has been designed, it can be constructed during the construction phase. During this phase, the design of the information system is represented in terms of the physical structures of the hardware and software environments in which the information system is to be implemented. The specification of the external data representation is translated into screen definitions, reports and other external data carriers. The specification of the internal data representation is translated into definitions of data files. This translation is carried out manually or semi-automatically by means of supporting software. The specification of the process necessary to transform the internal data representation into external data representations and vice versa, and the process necessary to interpret command languages and carry out dialogues between the system and its users, is represented in terms of physical process structures (programs, etc.). Such representation is accomplished by manual coding, automatic code generation by supporting software, or a combination of these. The definitions and program code obtained in this way are (generally automatically) translated into machine code which can be executed by the computer equipment to be used. The resulting parts of the information system are tested separately and then integrated.

In this section, we have briefly described the general stages in the development of an information system, and indicated the role of information analysis in these stages. The definitions of the concepts used in this section are summarized below.

Conceptual aspects of an information system:
Everything concerned with what the information system must do and the non-technical demands it must meet.

Realization aspects of an information system:
Everything concerned with how the information system must be realized and the technical demands it must meet.

Analysis:
The phase in the development of an information system in which the specifications of the information system are formulated. These are exclusively concerned with the conceptual aspects of the information system. The grammar of the information system is one of its specifications. During the analysis phase, only the conceptual aspects of the information system are considered.

analysis
realization

Figure 1.5.

Realization:
The phase in the development of an information system in which the information system is realized according to its specifications. During the realization phase, only the realization aspects of the information system are considered. Not only the automated part of the information system, but also the nonautomated part, is realized during the realization phase by specifying manual administrative procedures, relevant organizational measures, and any other solutions.

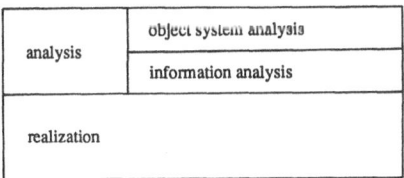

Figure 1.6.

Object system analysis:
The analysis phase in which the object system as a whole (which encompasses the controlled process, and the information system and its environment) is analyzed and described. During object system analysis the following items are defined and described:

- the controlled process.
- the controlling and executing activities being carried out for this process.
- the type of information that the users exchange while performing these activities.
- the type of information which, in support of the controlling and executing activities, must be exchanged with the information system.

In object system analysis, emphasis is placed on how the users have to make use of the information exchanged with the information system to control and execute the controlled process, and thus on how they are to work with the information system.

analysis	object system analysis
	information analysis
realization	design
	construction

Figure 1.7.

Information analysis:
The analysis phase in which the information that is to be exchanged with the information system, is analyzed and described. During information analysis, the data which may be exchanged with the information system and their meanings (i.e., how these data are to be interpreted by the users) are described. This description is the grammar of the information system.

Design:
The realization phase of the automated part of an information system in which it is determined:

- how the data to be exchanged with the information system must be represented externally for the users.
- how these data are to be represented internally to ensure efficient processing in the information system.
- how these data are to be processed in order to transform the internal data representation into the external data representation and vice versa.

Construction:
The realization phase in which the automated part of the information system is realized on the basis of the design.

NIAM is a **method** and a **technique** for supporting information analysis. Object system analysis and realization fall outside the actual sphere of activity of NIAM, and thus outside the scope of this book. In Chapter 3, we will take up a practical example in order to illustrate the results which must be achieved through object system analysis for information analysis according to NIAM. An example of a method supporting object system analysis and any related activities can be found in Reference 2.

Because the realization of information systems lies outside the information analysis field, this book will not deal with subjects connected to realization.

Neither will it take up the subject of how the general developmental stages which we handled in this section can be refined, how these stages can be synchronized, how the development of an information system can be planned and managed, what type of people ought to be brought into which developmental phases, what documentation ought to result at the end of which phase, what quality standards this documentation ought to meet, etc. These and other topics belong to the field "methods of system development," an example of which can be found in Reference 4.

The developmental stages outlined above roughly indicate how the NIAM method of information analysis proceeds along the general course of development of information systems. NIAM can be applied as a method and a technique in every system development method and every project based on the general developmental stages outlined in this section.

1.4 The main principles of the NIAM method of information analysis

Up to now in this chapter we have shown what we mean by the NIAM method of information analysis. The two main principles which form the foundations for the remainder of this book will be summarized in this section.

The first of those two principles expresses the fact that the grammar of an information system is exclusively related to its conceptual aspects, i.e., during analysis only the conceptual aspects of the information system are described. We shall call this principle the *conceptual principle*. It can be formulated as follows:

The grammar exclusively describes the **conceptual** aspects of the information exchange with the information system.

The grammar exclusively describes the meaning of the data which may be exchanged with the information system. The grammar does not describe any realization aspects of the information system and does not contain any elements involving external or internal data representation. In accordance with this principle, no single term or concept dealing with the realization aspects of information systems or with computer technology will be used in this book (with the exception of Appendix 1).

The conceptual principle prescribes what must exclusively be described by the grammar and thus also what **must never** be described by the grammar. The following principle prescribes what **must always** be described by the grammar:

The grammar describes **all** of the conceptual aspects of the information exchange with the information system.

The data that may be exchanged with the information system and their meanings are described one hundred percent by the grammar. For this reason, we shall call this second principle the *100% principle*. It follows from the 100% principle that no data other than that described by the grammar may be exchanged with the information system.

It follows further from the 100% principle that the grammar must completely describe the meaning of the data which may be exchanged with the information system. This means that all of the users of the information system who are interpreting these data may only make use of the interpretation rules which are described in the grammar. Knowledge about the reality may never be assumed to be implicitly known by the users. The grammar must describe the knowledge communicated via the information system completely and explicitly. During information analysis, everything that is implicitly (and perhaps partly unconsciously) present "in the heads of the users" has to be described in the grammar explicitly (consciously) and completely.

In forms of communication other than that by means of an information system, oral communication for example, certain data (a certain word or a certain language construct) can often be interpreted in more than one way. The correct interpretation is partly determined by the context of the conversation or by knowledge assumed implicitly by the communication partners. This would not be acceptable for communication by means of an information system, because so many different people can be involved and because these people must communicate with each other over long intervals of time. Consequently, in this form of communication it is essential that the grammar be specified so precisely that any data based on this grammar can only be interpreted in one single way.

The conceptual principle and the 100% principle form the very heart of the NIAM method of information analysis.

1.5 Summary

In this chapter we have given some idea of what we mean by information analysis. In Section 1.1, we went into the concept of general communication processes and in Section 1.2 we showed that the NIAM method of information analysis involves communication processes using an information system. In this connection, we stated that the information which may be exchanged with the information system is determined and analyzed during information analysis, and that a grammar for the information system is specified on the basis of this analysis. Then, in Section 1.3, we showed the general developmental stages an information system undergoes in the process of realization, and the place of information analysis in these stages. Lastly, in Section 1.4 we summarized the foregoing into two main principles, the conceptual principle and the 100% principle, which form the basis of the NIAM method of information analysis.

2 AN INFORMATION SYSTEM MODEL

In the previous chapter, we saw that the objective of the NIAM method of information analysis is the specification of the grammar. Before taking up the question of how the grammar has to be specified, we must first get an idea of how the information exchange with the information system takes place. Therefore, in this chapter we will take a look at how an information system works in general and what its functional components are. These components and their mutual relations then form a model of an arbitrary information system. In setting up this model, we use the main principles of the NIAM method of information analysis, the conceptual principle and the 100% principle, as our starting point. One of the consequences of this is that only the conceptual aspects, and not the realization aspects, of an information system are described. That is, this model only indicates **what** the information system and its components must do, and not **how** they could be realized in practice. That is the reason we talk about a conceptual model of information systems. In fact, the conceptual model forms the specification of an arbitrary information system. During information analysis, we will assume that every information system behaves as is described by the conceptual model.

We repeat, perhaps unnecessarily, that information analysis is not directed exclusively toward an automated information system, and that the conceptual model consequently describes an arbitrary information system. This can be an automated system, a non-automated system, or a combination of both of these. In the following sections we will construct the conceptual model step by step.

2.1 The message exchange with the environment

Studying the object system as a whole is the subject of object system analysis. This is, as stated before, not part of the NIAM method of information analysis, and thus beyond the scope of this book. In subsequent sections and chapters we will therefore only take a look at the information system, its environment, and the exchange of information between them. In doing this, we will assume that the reality involved in the information exchange has been determined and delineated earlier. The controlled process is part of this reality, and will as such not be considered separately.

In the previous chapter, we defined an information system as an information processing system that:

- receives information and requests for information from its environment and provides information and answers to requests to its environment.
- can store information in time.
- can derive new information from the information given.

The information system receives information and requests for information from its environment and provides information and answers to requests to the environment. To accomplish this, the information system and the environment exchange messages with each other.

This message exchange is represented in Figure 2.1 by message flows i1 and i2. Flow i1 represents messages going from the environment to the information

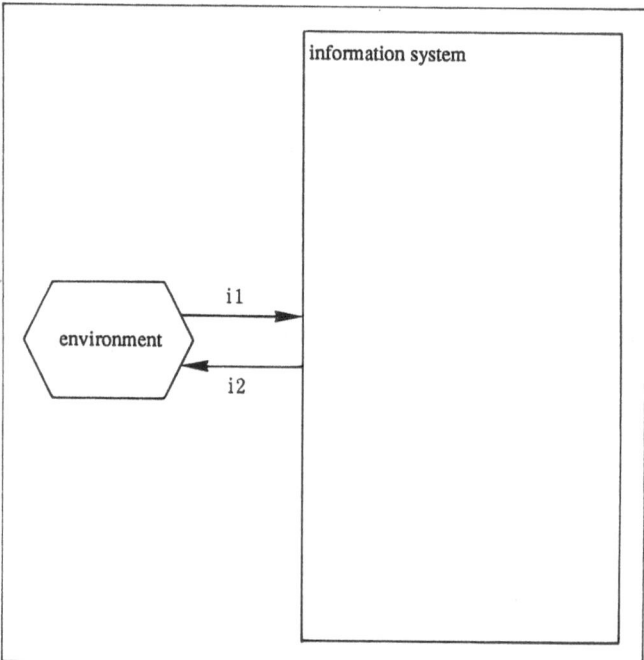

Figure 2.1.

system. These messages consist of questions from the users about the information that is stored by the system, or requests to the information system to add certain information to the system or to delete certain information from it. Flow i2 represents messages going from the information system to the environment. These messages contain answers to requests from the users, or questions and/or messages from the information system to the users. By this means, the information system requests more information when the question or the request from the users is not clear, or reports to the users that for one reason or another the question cannot be answered or the request cannot be executed. The information which can be exchanged between the users and the information system via message flows i1 and i2 thus always concerns the information which is stored by the information system.

2.2 The information base

In the previous chapter, we called the description of all information which is stored by the information system the information base of the information system. All information which is exchanged between the users and the information system via message flows i1 and i2 concerns the information stored by the information system, and thus the information base. This information base is, of course, part of the information system, as represented in Figure 2.2.

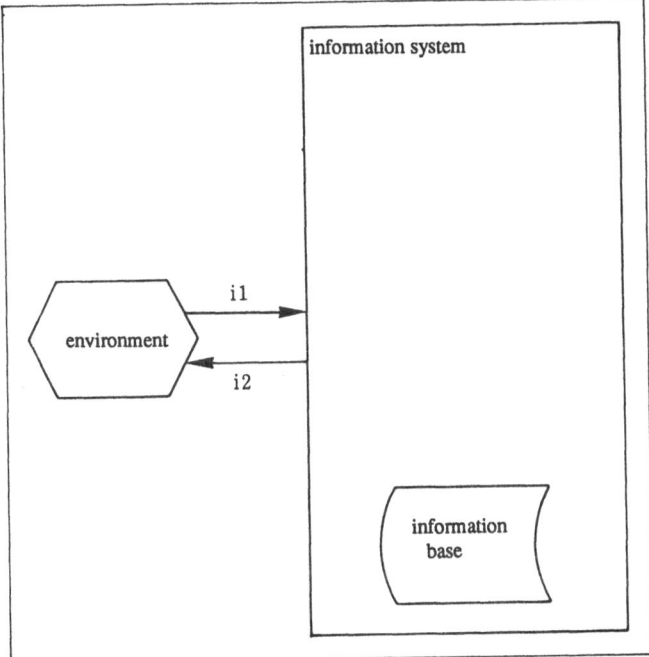

Figure 2.2.

As already remarked in the introduction to this chapter, the conceptual model of an information system is only concerned with the conceptual aspects of an information system, and not with its realization aspects. Consequently, the information base must not, in spite of the symbol with which we wish to represent it, be viewed as a data file or a database. The information base is considered to be the **description** of all the information stored by the system. How this can be technically realized is (still) irrelevant for information analysis. From the viewpoint of information analysis, it is not relevant whether this takes place by means of, for example, automated data files, "manual" files, or a combination of these. Likewise, from the viewpoint of information analysis, it is not important whether all the information in the information base is actually being stored or whether it is derived from other information when a request is made.

We were able to see in the foregoing chapter that the users of an information system can communicate with each other about a certain reality by means of the information system. The information which is being exchanged at a given moment is therefore concerned with the state which the reality is in at that particular moment.

The state which the reality is in at a given moment changes as a consequence of events taking place within that reality. When an event is sufficiently relevant, the users request the information system to change the information base in such a way that it describes the new state of the reality resulting from that event. The information base does not have to describe at every moment the state of the reality valid at that moment, but only those states which the users wish to communicate to each other via the information system and consequently wish to register in the information base.

In terms of time, the contents of the information base will change at the request of the users. We call the contents of the information base at a given moment the *state* of the information base. Each time the information system changes the contents of the information base at the request of the users, the state of the information base changes, and the previous state goes to a new state. We label this an *information base state transition*. Although the contents of the information base do not have to describe at every moment the state of the reality valid at that moment, it may never describe an impossible state of the reality. Therefore, not all possible or conceivable states of the information base are allowed. Further, an information base state transition may never correspond to an impossible change in the state of the reality. As a consequence, not all possible or conceivable information base state transitions are allowed.

2.3 The grammar

As the grammar of an information system plays an essential role in information analysis, we will assume that it is an integral component of the information system. This is illustrated in Figure 2.3.

The grammar contains a description of the rules which determine the communication allowed between the users and the information system. As the users must be able to see at any moment whether their communication with the information system satisfies the rules of the grammar, the description of these rules must be available at any moment and thus must be stored. To denote this, we have assigned the grammar a symbol that is analogous but not the same as the information base symbol. We wish to emphasize that the grammar and the information base are different and thus separate components of the information system.

In the previous section, we saw that **all** information that is exchanged with the information system (via message flows i1 and i2) concerns the information contents (the state) of the information base and that the users can request the information system to change the information contents (the state) of the information base. It follows from the facts that:

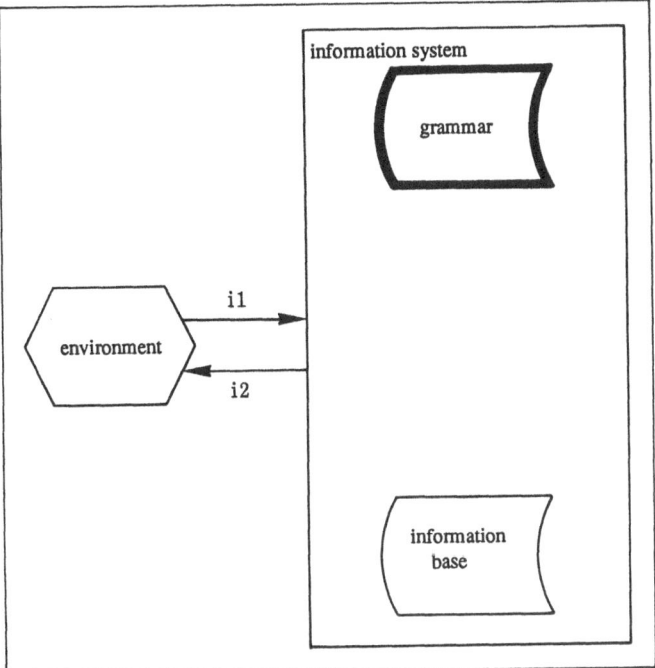

Figure 2.3.

- the grammar describes the information which may be exchanged with the information system,
- all of this information concerns the information contents of the information base, and
- the state of the information base can change as a consequence of the messages exchanged between the information system and the environment,

that the grammar prescribes which states and which information base state transitions may occur.

For these reasons, we tighten the definition of the grammar as follows:

The grammar is the description of all the rules which prescribe which information base states and state transitions may occur and the meaning of the data stored in the information base.

We note once more that the grammar is a description of the rules which are valid for the **communication** (via the information system) about a certain reality, and not of the rules which are valid for the reality itself.

In general, the reality will change with time, and likewise, the rules which are valid for the communication about this reality can change as well. The grammar of an information system will therefore, in general, change with time. For the time being, we will assume that the grammar does not change, as this will help to make things clearer.

2.4 The information processor

The model of an information system as we have constructed it thus far, represented by Figure 2.3, is not yet complete. The information system should contain a function that interprets, and subsequently answers or executes, the questions and requests that the users address to the information system by means of message flow i1. We shall call this function the *conceptual information processor*, or the *information processor* for short. The information processor must answer the questions and execute the requests of the users in such a way that they do not violate the rules of the grammar. If it did not do this, the communication between the users of the information system might no longer meet the agreed upon rules of the grammar, leading to communication disturbances. Should the users of the information system request a change in the contents of the information base, the information processor may only execute this request if the resulting state transition and new state of the information base are allowed on the basis of the rules of the grammar. The information processor answers the questions of the users and executes their requests, and sees to it that the rules of the grammar are not violated. Thus, the information processor guarantees that at any given moment the communication between the users of the information system satisfies the rules of the grammar.

In Figure 2.4, we have added the information processor to the model and also added lines connecting message flows i1 and i2 to the information processor. Further, we have indicated how the information processor communicates with the information base when answering the questions and executing the requests of the users.

The information processor receives a message from the users via message flow i1. When this involves a request to add information to the information base or delete information from it, the information processor verifies whether the new contents of the information base and the resulting state transition are allowed by the rules of the grammar. To do this, the information processor interprets the rules of the grammar via i5 and the existing state of the information base via i4. If the rules of the grammar allow the new contents of the information base and the change from the old state to the new, the information processor executes the requested change via i3, and the information base goes into a new state. The information processor then reports to the users via i2 that the request has been executed and that the new state of the information base has been realized. If, however, the rules of the grammar do not allow the new contents of the information base or the transition from the old state to the new, the information processor does not execute the requested change. It then reports to the users via i2 that their

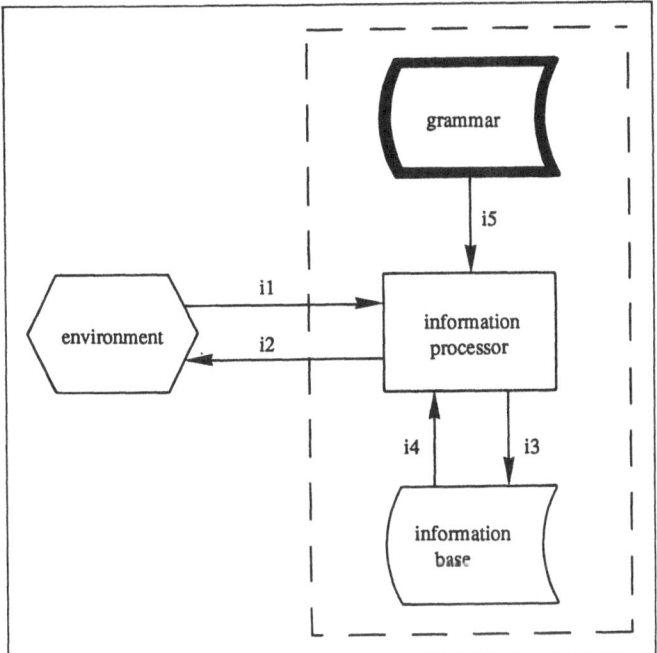

Figure 2.4.

request has not been executed (listing the grammatical rules violated) and that the old state of the information base remains in effect.

When the message that the information processor receives from the users via i1 involves a question, the information processor fetches via i4 the information needed to answer the question from the information base. On the basis of the rules of the grammar, the information processor determines via i5 what information is involved in the question or how the requested information can be derived from the information described by the information base. Sometimes the questions of the users are related solely to the rules of the grammar. Then the information processor provides the users with the answers to the questions via i2.

The information base and the grammar are the passive components of the information system, while the information processor and the environment are active components. The information processor and the environment send, receive and process each other's messages, and pose questions and provide each other with answers. By definition, the environment is nondeterministic, while the information processor is.

The operation of an information system is completely described by Figure 2.4. In this figure, all the conceptual components of an information system are represented in their entirety. To indicate that the constituent components of an information system have now been laid bare, we have represented the information system itself in Figure 2.4 by means of broken lines.

2.5 Summary

In this chapter, we have constructed a conceptual model of information systems. The information system that was considered as a "black box" in the previous chapter has now been decomposed into its constituent components and its operation has been described. Below we repeat the definitions of the most important concepts that were used.

Messages:
The information exchange between the users and the information system is accomplished by means of messages. These messages involve:

- questions the users have about the information described by the information base or the grammar.
- requests from the users to change the information base.
- answers and questions from the information system in response to the questions and requests of the users.

Information base state:
The contents of the information base at a certain moment.

Information base state transition:
A change in the contents of the information base.

Grammar:
The description of all the rules which prescribe which information base states and information base state transitions may occur and the meaning of the data stored in the information base.

Information processor:
The active component of an information system which:

- interprets and executes the questions and requests of the users.
- addresses questions and answers to the users.
- sees to it in carrying out these operations that the rules of grammar are not violated.

3 FROM OBJECT SYSTEM ANALYSIS TO INFORMATION ANALYSIS

In this chapter we shall show the connection between object system analysis and information analysis. By means of an example, we shall give a short survey of the results of object system analysis and of the way in which these results should be used during information analysis. At the same time, we will roughly survey what should occur during object system analysis, as far as this is relevant for information analysis. Many aspects of object system analysis will necessarily be left out of consideration.

As stated earlier, object system analysis actually lies beyond the scope of this book. The treatment in this chapter merely serves as a means of getting some idea of object system analysis, and is therefore incomplete and informal.

The example that we will use in this chapter is an imaginary public library in a likewise imaginary large city. All the examples which will be used in the remainder of this book will deal with this library and will therefore have the character of a case study. Henceforth, we shall be talking about the "library case," for short. In preparation for subsequent chapters, the reader will be made familiar in this chapter with this case study.

We begin this chapter by taking a look at the way in which our library is organized.

3.1 The organization of the library

Because the library is located in a large city, it has a sizeable collection and a fairly extensive organization. The main purpose of the library is to lend books to its members. Anyone can become a member of this library by paying an annual subscription fee. A second important purpose of the library is to provide all the information available about the books in its possession to members and nonmembers. The library regularly purchases new books to replace worn-out copies or to expand its collection.

Figure 3.1 schematically depicts the organization of the library. Every department is represented in it by a rectangle. The connecting lines denote their hierarchical structure.

At the head of the library is the management. The Personnel Department is charged with personnel management, managing the personnel data of the library employees, and advising the management as to its personnel policy. There are two main departments or sectors: Executive and Support Services. The Executive Department is charged with implementing the policy as formulated by management in accordance with the aims of the library, and Support Services with providing the support necessary to carry out this policy.

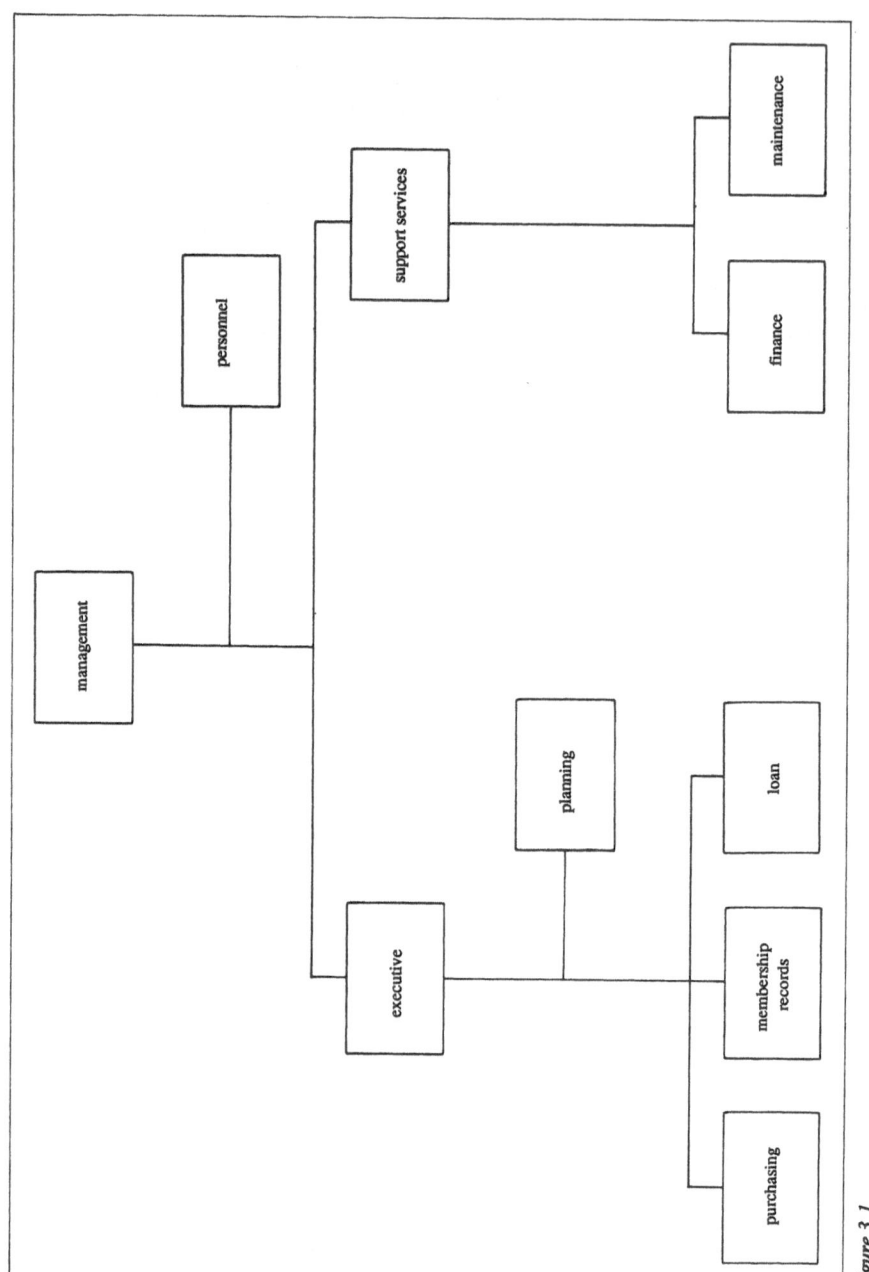

Figure 3.1.

The main Executive Department is composed of the Planning, Purchasing, Membership Records, and Loan subdepartments. The Planning Department advises the managers of the main Executive Department with respect to the planning of the work of this department. To this end, it maintains statistical data about such things as the lending of books to library members. The Purchasing Department is charged with the acquisition of new books. The management decides, on the basis of information from the Planning and Loan Departments and on the basis of the wishes and ideas of the library members, which books the Purchasing Department should purchase. The Membership Records Department maintains the records of members and sees to it that they pay their subscription fees on time. The Loan Department is charged with lending books to members, keeping records of these loans, and providing information about the books in the library.

The main Support Services department is composed of the sub-departments Finance and Maintenance. The Finance Department maintains financial data, coordinates the drawing up of the budgets of the various library departments, and monitors these budgets. The Maintenance Department is in charge of the building in which the library is housed and of its contents.

Because of the large number of library members, the great number of books they borrow, and the numerous requests for information, the Loan Department, with its current staffing, can barely manage to do its work. Consequently, the management wants to investigate whether the effectiveness and efficiency of this department can be increased by using an information system to support its work.

The investigation consists of an analysis of the library and of the Loan Department within it as an object system. In the course of this object system analysis, it is checked to see whether the work of the Loan Department can be arranged more efficiently and effectively and what role an information system might play.

The object system analysis begins with a description of the present arrangement of the work in the library in general, and the Loan Department in particular, in order to determine what approach to take to bring about a change. The following section gives an overview of this.

3.2 The activity diagram

From the above description of the library organization, it follows that the following activities are being carried out:

- managing the library
- managing personnel and maintaining the personnel records
- planning loans
- purchasing books
- maintaining the membership records
- lending books

- providing information about books in the library
- maintaining and monitoring budgets
- maintaining the financial data
- maintaining the building and its contents.

Figure 3.2 roughly represents how the library employees work with each other to carry out these activities and how they communicate by exchanging goods and information with each other. Note that we have left out the activities "managing the library," "managing personnel and maintaining the personnel records," "maintaining and monitoring budgets," and "maintaining the building and its contents," as these activities are not of direct importance to the analysis of the Loan Department.

The activities that the library employees carry out are represented in Figure 3.2 by hexagons. The bold lines represent the objects or other material goods which are exchanged or passed on during these activities: the *material flows* in the library. The remaining lines represent the information that is exchanged or passed on during these activities. These lines represent the *information flows* that occur in the library. The arrows indicate the direction in which the goods or information are passed on. An arrow on both sides of the material or information flows means that there is an exchange of these goods or information in both directions. The round symbols (containing the labels "members" and "publishers") denote the *environment* of the library, in other words, everything that does not belong to the library itself.

The hexagons represent the **persons** who carry out the relevant activities (the library employees). These persons can be distinguished from each other only on the basis of the activities they carry out, and not by their position or function within the library. The material and information flows represent the way in which people work together and communicate with each other when carrying out their work.

A more detailed description of the activity "lending books" and the material and information flows that play a role in it are given below. This description can be followed in Figure 3.2.

Books are loaned out to members of the library at their request. To prevent books being loaned to someone who is not a library member or has not paid a subscription fee, membership data is consulted during check-out. Upon request, the due date can be extended. If a book is brought back after the due date, a fine has to be paid. When all the copies of a book have been checked out, library members can ask for a book to be reserved. Books which have been loaned out and then brought back to the library are collected by the activity "lending books." This activity also provides statistical data concerning the loans, renewals, and reservations to the activity "planning loans." The activity "lending books" provides additional information about the fines paid by the members to the activity "maintaining financial data."

The remaining flows of information and goods in Figure 3.2 speak for themselves.

The diagram in Figure 3.2 gives a very general picture of the library as an object

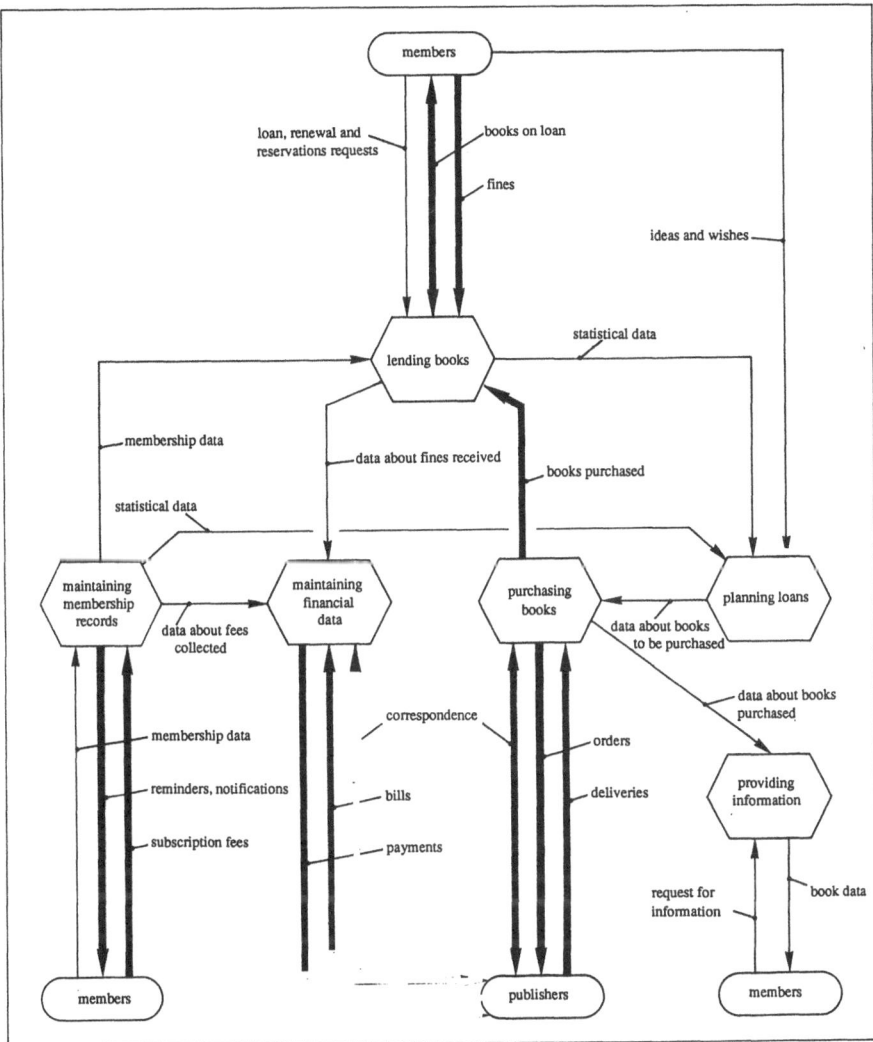

Figure 3.2.

system and therefore contains only the primary activities and material and information flows. This diagram is, of course, incomplete; it serves mainly to provide the reader with an overview and a picture of the activities.

Naturally, the diagram in Figure 3.2 should be made more detailed. As we know, our object system analysis concerns the work of the Loan Department. Consequently, in going into more detail, we need only concentrate on the activities which are performed within that department (primarily the activities "lending books" and "providing information") and on the connection between those activities and the general activities represented in Figure 3.2.

We have represented this more detailed description in Figure 3.3.

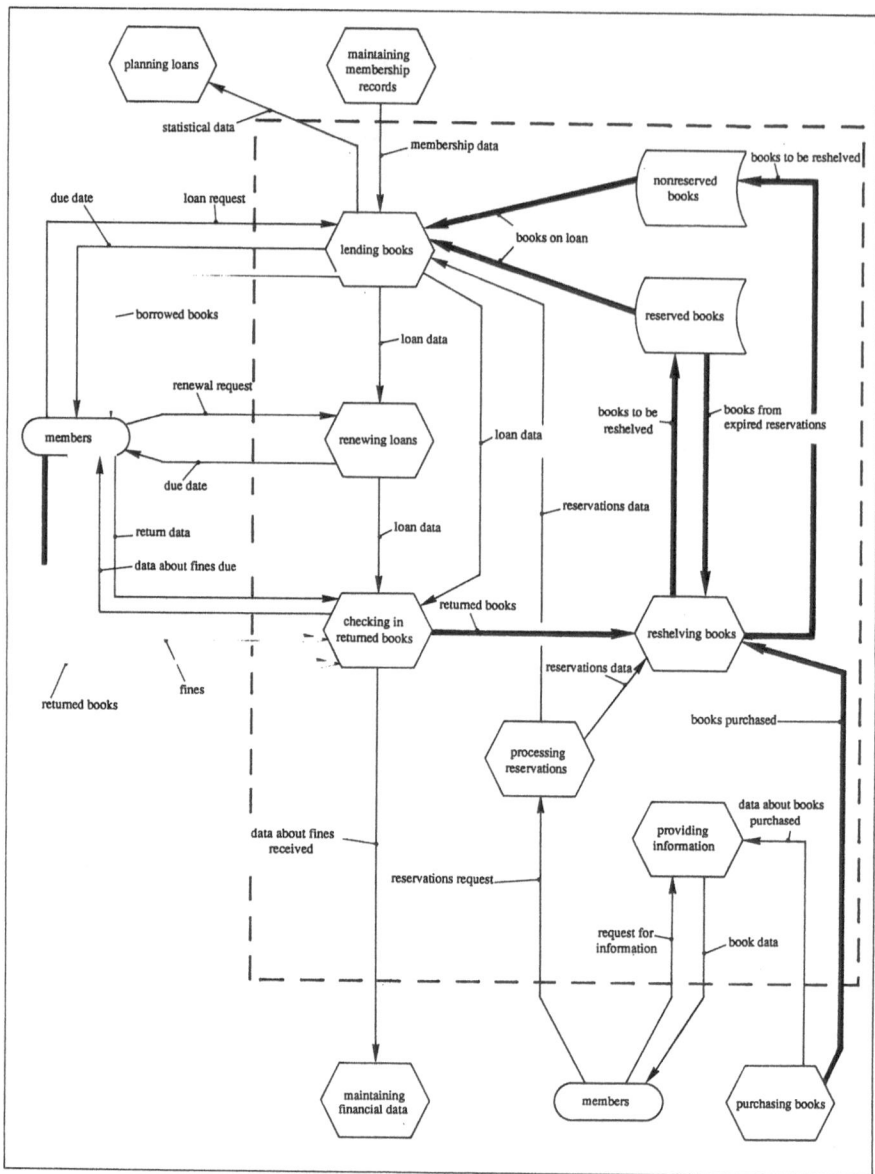

Figure 3.3.

As we can see, the activities "lending books" and "providing information" have now been supplemented with the following activities:

- renewing loans
- checking in returned books
- processing reservations
- reshelving books.

The activities lying within the rectangle formed by the broken lines are a detailed description of or addition to the activities in the general diagram of Figure 3.2. The area inside this rectangle can be considered an "enlargement" of the area around the activities "lending books" and "providing information" which were given in the diagram of Figure 3.2. We can use this rectangle to investigate the connection with the diagram of Figure 3.2.

Below is a description of the activities and material and information flows of Figure 3.3 which do not occur in the general diagram of Figure 3.2.

The actual lending of books is performed by the activity "lending books." When a book is loaned out, the member is informed of the "due date." This is the last possible date by which the book has to be returned to the library.

At the request of the member, the due date can be extended by the activity "renewing loans." The member is informed of the new due date when the period is extended. However, the due date cannot be extended if, in the meantime, another member has reserved the book.

Books which have been borrowed and brought back by members are checked in by the activity "checking in returned books." The "return data" consists of an identification of the loan involved. Where necessary, the fines to be paid are determined and it is seen to that the fine is paid by the member concerned.

While extending due dates and checking in returned books, the relevant data is looked up and processed such that the extension or termination of the loan is expressed in them.

When all the available copies of a particular book are loaned out, any member wishing to borrow a copy can reserve the book. This takes place through the activity "processing reservations." The first copy of the reserved book that is brought back to the library is then loaned out to the member who reserved it. This member receives a notification from the library as soon as a copy of the reserved book is returned.

All the books which are returned to the library as well as all the newly purchased books are put back on the shelves through the activity "reshelving books." The books are shelved in the reading room in stacks. Anyone wanting to check out a book has to fetch it from the relevant stack and proceed to the check-out desk. To prevent a book reserved for a member from being loaned out to someone else, all the reserved books brought back to the library are kept in a separate cupboard by the check-out desk for one week. In order to determine whether a book brought back to the library ought to be put away in this cupboard, the reservations data needs to be inspected by the activity "reshelving books" in order to determine whether this book is reserved.

When a reserved book has not been picked up by the member who reserved it within one week, the reservation is canceled and the book is brought back to the stacks in the reading room through the activity "reshelving books."

When a member comes to pick up a reserved book, the reservations data is checked by the activity "lending books."

The following symbol:

represents a collection of information and material goods which are to be stored
in time. This symbol represents the fact that the books which have not been loaned
out, are stored in the library, and that the reserved and nonreserved books need
to be stored separately. Because the collections "nonreserved books" and
"reserved books" concern flows of material goods, it is clear that these are
collections of material goods.

From now on, we shall call such diagrams as those of Figures 3.2 and 3.3
activity diagrams. An activity diagram represents the way in which the communication and the cooperation within an object system take place by an exchange of
information and goods.

With respect to information anlysis, only the information flows are important.
In object system analysis, in which the operation of the object system is studied
as a whole (including potentially the information system), the information flows
and the material flows clearly play an equally important role.

3.3 The information system within the object system

The diagram of Figure 3.3 represents the main lines of the work routine of the Loan
Department. As stated earlier, the work of this department ought to be arranged
more effectively and efficiently. An improvement is represented in Figure 3.4, in
which use is made of an information system. This diagram depicts the way in
which the library employees need to work and communicate with each other in
the new situation, using the information system.

In this diagram, the information system is represented by means of a rectangle.
Unlike the activities, the information system is by definition a "process" which is
subject to formalization and which processes only information.

The users of the information system communicate with each other via the
information system by means of information flows which begin or end in the
information system.

During information analysis, a grammar, which prescribes exactly which information may be found in these information flows, must be specified, along with the
way in which this information is to be interpreted by all the users of the information
system.

The users of the information system are represented by means of the activities
which they perform and in whose support they use the information system. The
manner of drawing in Figure 3.4 conforms with that which we used in Figure 1.4
(Chapter 1) to illustrate the operation of an arbitrary information system.

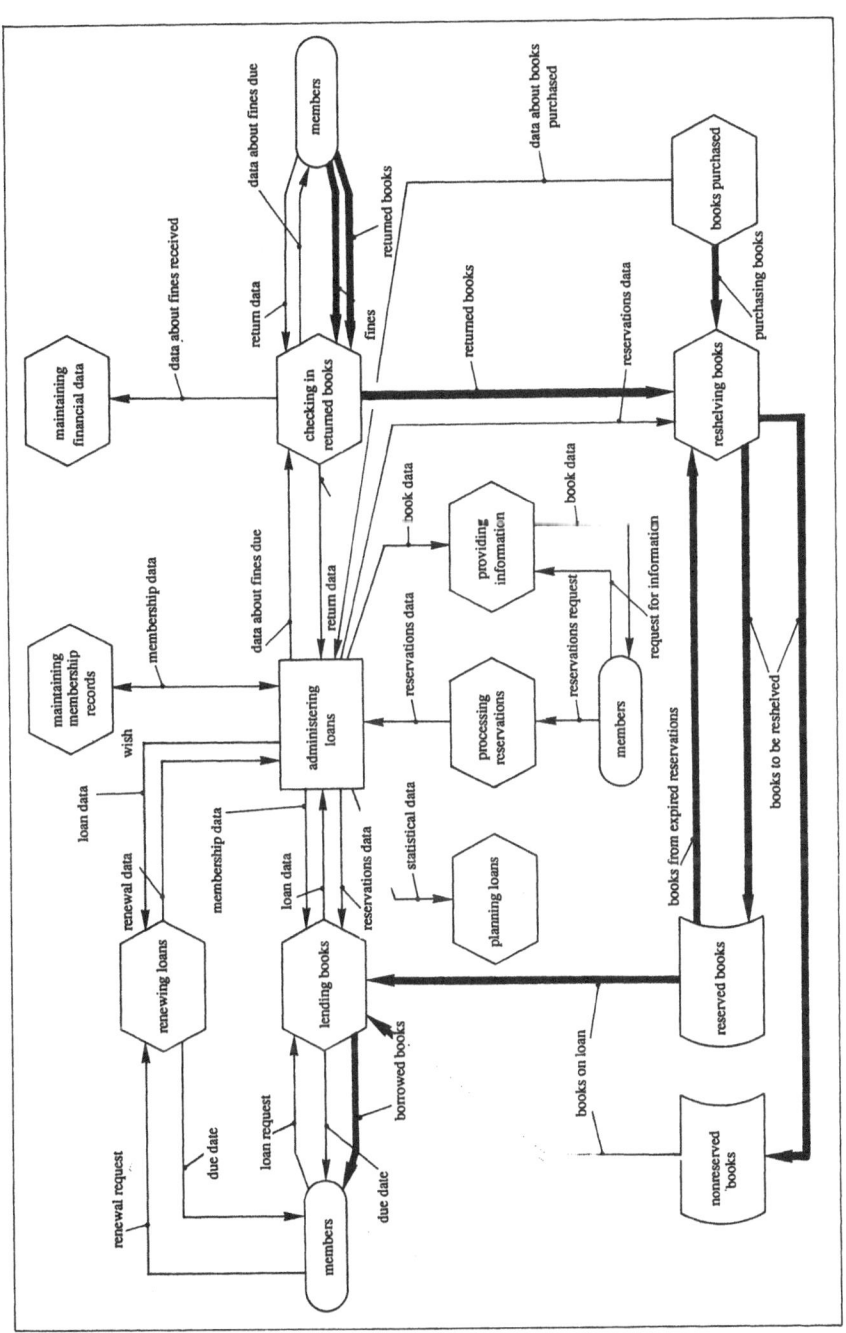

Figure 3.4.

A more detailed description of the information system of Figure 3.4 follows below.

The information system stores data about the books in the library (book data), the loans (loan data), the reservations (reservations data), and the members (membership data). The book data are used for the activity "providing information." These book data are updated with the data about newly purchased books through the activity "purchasing books." The loan data are updated with the renewal data through the activity "renewing loans" and with the return data through the activity "checking in returned books." The reservations data are used by the activity "reshelving books" to determine whether a book returned to the library must be saved by the checkout desk because it has been reserved. Further, the reservations data are used to check whether someone has come to check out the book he or she has reserved through the activity "lending books." The data dealing with the fines to be paid and the statistical data for the activity "planning loans" are derived from the loan and reservations data.

3.4 From object system analysis to information analysis

Activity diagrams, such as the diagrams of Figures 3.2, 3.3, and 3.4, are typical results of object system analysis. During object system analysis, there is an investigation into and description of the activities which have to be carried out within the object system, how these activities must be carried out, and which material goods and/or information then need to be exchanged in which way within the object system or with its environment. Object system analysis can concern an existing situation, but, as is the case in this example, it usually concerns a nonexistent but desirable situation that has yet to be realized.

When the description of the object system contains an information system by whose means part of the communication within the object system ought to take place, object system analysis is followed by information analysis and the realization of an information system. When no information system occurs in the ultimate result of object system analysis, apparently a solution has been found in which no use has to be made of an information system. In this case, naturally, no information system is developed, and thus information analysis does not take place.

The results of object system analysis are usually described to a large extent in some kind of graphical form, such as the activity diagrams used here. The graphical means of representation used varies with the methods and techniques used in support of object system analysis. References [2] and [3] give an example of a couple of other often-used graphical means of representation which, roughly speaking, have the same effect as the activity diagrams used here. The activity diagrams used in this chapter must be seen as examples of a **possible** graphical means of representation of part of the results of object system analysis.

For the NIAM method of information analysis, exactly which graphic or other kind of technique is used for object system analysis is not important, provided that the description meets the following demands:

- On the basis of the description, there must be a clear delineation between the information system and the activities. (This is one of the reasons we have used different symbols in the activity diagrams to represent the information system and the activities.)
- On the basis of the description, it must be clear which information has to be exchanged with the information system. It must be possible to describe this information by means of concrete examples.

During information analysis, the information contents of the information flows which begin or end in the information system are investigated and described. To do this, one starts with concrete examples, as we shall see in the upcoming chapters. This is why the level of detail in the description of the object system is sufficient for information analysis if concrete examples of the contents of every information flow which begins or ends in the information system can be given. If this is not possible, the description of the object system needs to be described in more detail by decomposing one or more activities into subactivities, or by adding one or more attendant activities and/or information flows to the description of the object system.

Coming up with a description of the object system is by definition part of object system analysis. Still, some people count the creation of the description of the last level of detail as part of information analysis. There are those who, for example, consider the transition from Figure 3.3 to Figure 3.4 as one of the first steps in information analysis. This sometimes occurs because the distinction between the "subjects" or "disciplines" ("object system analysis" and "information analysis") is not always sharp or because the **phase** "information analysis" within a project is confused with the **subject** or the **discipline** "information analysis." The last steps of object system analysis and the first steps of information analysis often take place more or less simultaneously. Clearly, the last phases of object system analysis and the first phases of information analysis can influence each other and are therefore often carried out iteratively and cyclically. In many cases, the last phases of object system analysis are carried out by those who are performing the information analysis as well.

Our starting point will be that object system analysis and information analysis are, formally speaking, different activities and therefore represent different "disciplines" or "subjects."

In object system analysis, the object system is seen as a *system*, consisting of processes working together and communicating with each other. On the contrary, information analysis (as defined in this book) considers the object system as the **reality** with which the information to be exchanged via the information system is concerned. This reality is thus conceived of as a set of objects having certain relations to each other. Object system analysis and information analysis thus consider the object system from different viewpoints. In practice, these different viewpoints complement each other.

3.5 The information flow diagram

In our example, information analysis can be started on the basis of the information flows in Figure 3.4 which begin or end in the information system.

The library case, however, is a relatively simple example. In many real practical situations, so many different information flows will begin or end in the information system that a diagram like that of Figure 3.4 will very quickly be too difficult to read, too inaccurate, and not explicit enough for information analysis. As a consequence, it is usually necessary to divide the information system into a number of functional parts, as we have done in Figure 3.5.

In this figure, each rectangle stands for a functional part of the information system. Only the information exchange between the activities and these functional parts of the information system are represented in this diagram. Its connections to the remaining activities within the object system follow from the activity diagram of Figure 3.4.

The functional parts of the information system depicted in Figure 3.5 are called the *functions* of the information system. In light of the fact that no technical aspects are taken into account during the analysis by virtue of the conceptual principle, the functions must only be seen as **functional** or **logical** components of the information system, rather than as **technical** components.

The rectangle within the broken lines indicates that all together the functions of Figure 3.5 form the information system of Figure 3.4. The rectangle within the broken lines can be considered an "enlargement" of the information system of Figure 3.4. The connection between Figures 3.4 and 3.5 can be investigated by means of this rectangle.

The symbol

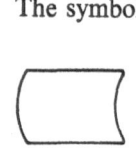

represents the set of all information which is to be stored by the information system. In the previous chapter, we called this the *information base*. As we began by assuming that all the information which is exchanged with the information system is stored by the information system, the functions of the information system may only communicate with each other via the information base.

Figure 3.5 represents the loan data being updated with the renewal data and the return data more clearly and explicitly than did the activity diagram. This example reveals that a diagram such as that of Figure 3.5 can provide a more exact and explicit representation of matters than an activity diagram can.

A diagram like that of Figure 3.5 is called an *information flow diagram*. This is sometimes abbreviated to "IFD."

An information flow diagram represents the communication between the activities and the functions of the information system, separate from the remainder of the object system. It is created on the basis of an activity diagram or a similar description. Our starting point will be that the users always communicate with the information base via a function, thus never directly. For this reason, every information flow must always begin or end in a function, even when the information is merely "passed on" by this function. Further, for every function there must be at least one information flow which ends in this function (this describes the input information of that function) and at least one information flow which begins in this function (this describes the output information of that function).

A function, an information flow, or the information base may be drawn in more than one place in an information flow diagram because of drawing limitations or to achieve a better presentation, and an information flow diagram can be spread over more than one drawing.

Just like activity diagrams, information flow diagrams are only **static** descriptions of the possible information flows. With the aid of information flow diagrams, no causal connections to events taking place inside or outside the object system and no mutual order of execution of the functions can be represented.

In the NIAM method of information analysis, our starting point is an activity diagram such as in Figure 3.4 (or an equivalent description of an object system) or an information flow diagram such as in Figure 3.5. We begin, in particular, with an information flow diagram if the activity diagram (or the equivalent description of the object system) is too difficult to read, too inaccurate, or not explicit enough.

The creation of an information flow diagram is, in most cases, the first step in information analysis.

When only an activity diagram (or an equivalent description of the object system) is available, the desired information contents of all the information flows which begin or end in the information system are analyzed and described during information analysis.

When an information flow diagram is available, the desired information contents of **all** the information flows of that information flow diagram are analyzed and described during information analysis.

In the upcoming chapters, we shall analyze the desired information contents of the information flows "book data," "reservations data," and "membership data." The information flows "renewal data," "return data," and "data about fines to be paid" will not be analyzed separately because these contain, as will appear later, part of the information contents of the information flow "loan data." The information flow "statistical data" will remain outside our consideration.

Interested readers are referred to References [2] and [3] for examples of other often-used graphical means of representation which can be compared to information flow diagrams. These and other means of drawing can equally serve as the starting point of information analysis, provided the information exchange taking place between the environment of the information system and its functions is expressed satisfactorily.

Naturally, information flow diagrams of different levels of detail can be created by decomposing functions further into their constituent functions or by adding

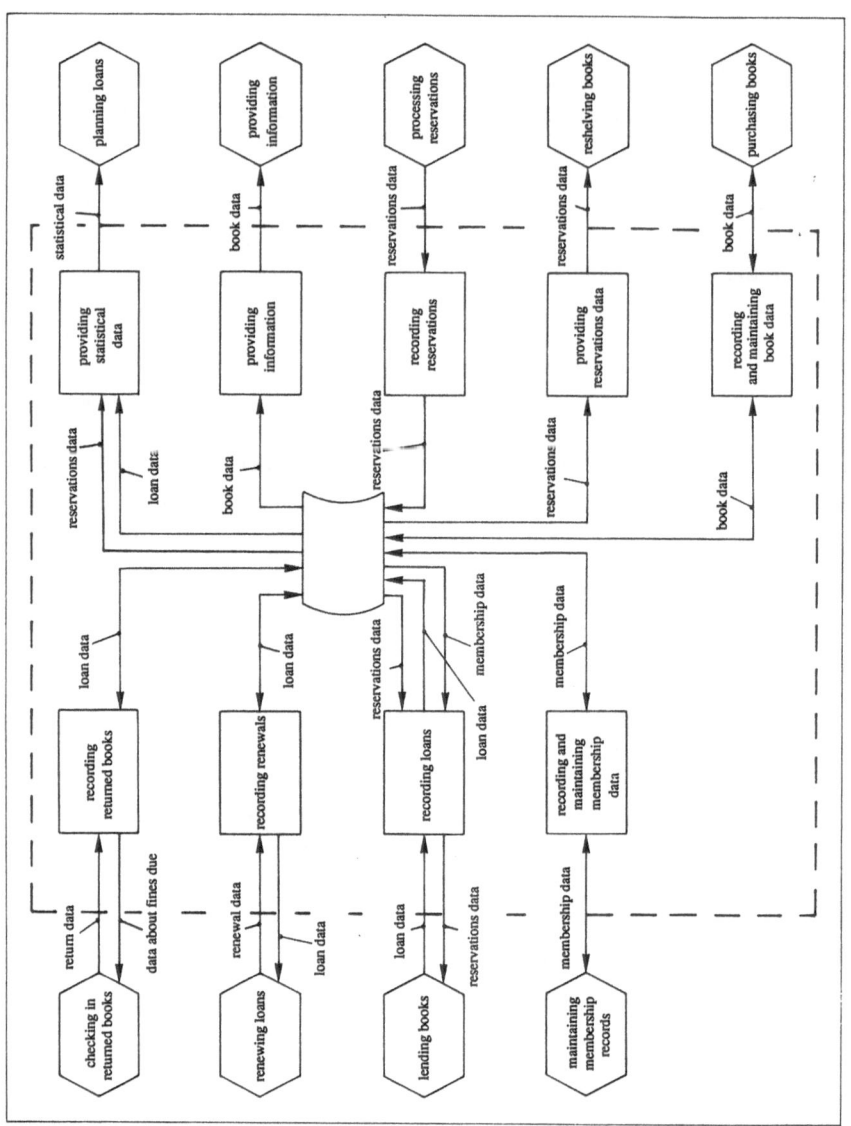

Figure 3.5.

new functions and/or information flows to an information flow diagram.   It holds here as well that the level of detail for information analysis is sufficient if concrete examples of the desired information contents of the information flows in the information flow diagram can be given.

If we had decided to support not only the activities of the Loan Department but also those of other departments (for example, the Membership Records Department) by means of an information system, this would have resulted in an activity diagram in which, in addition to the information system "administering loan data," a second information system (for example, "administering membership data") would appear. For the purposes of information analysis, it doesn't matter whether this is seen as two separate information systems or as separate functions of one general information system.

The NIAM method of information analysis consists, properly speaking, of specifying the grammar of an information system on the basis of an activity diagram (or an equivalent description of the object system) or of an information flow diagram.

The description of the object system and/or the information flow diagram serve to get in a structered way to a specification of the grammar.

4 THE STRUCTURE OF INFORMATION

In Chapter 1, we saw that the aim of information analysis is to specify the grammar of an information system. The rules of the grammar prescribe the information of which the information base may consist at any moment and the information base state transitions which may occur. Before we can indicate how the grammar of an information system can be specified, we must first give a more detailed description of information or communicable knowledge.

In this chapter, we will give a more specific definition of information and we will show how information is built up, or structured. At the same time, we will develop a graphical representation of information step by step. The conceptual principle takes a central position in all of this. That is, we will only take a look at the **meaning** of information, and will not go into its external and internal forms of representation. We will only indicate how information is built up **conceptually** and how information can be described **conceptually** by means of a graphical representation.

The way in which the grammar of an information system can be described will be treated in Chapter 5.

The most important concepts in the NIAM method of information analysis will be discussed in this chapter.

4.1 A more detailed definition of information

In Chapter 1, we defined information as knowledge about a certain reality which can be communicated to others. This reality consists of that part and those aspects of a real or abstract world which are relevant for this knowledge. From now on, we shall consider the reality as a set of real or abstract matters, called **objects** or *entities*, to which this knowledge is related. When, for example, the reality concerns a public library, the employees and the various library departments belong to the objects of this reality. Information or communicable knowledge about the library is concerned with these objects, and thus with its employees and departments.

Henceforth, we shall conceive of communicable knowledge or information about a certain reality as *assertions* (also called *propositions*) about objects in this reality which we **know** or **suppose** are true at the moment we are in possession of that knowledge. These propositions express the assertion or supposition that at that moment certain facts related to the reality exist.

In our example, where the reality is concerned with a public library, part of our communicable knowledge or information about this library could consist of the following propositions:

In this company, there are employees and departments. Employees have last names and departments have department names. Employees can only work for one department. Johnson and Peterson work for the Purchasing Department and King works for the Personnel Department. A department may not consist of more than 10 employees.

Figure 4.1.

The text of Figure 4.1 represents a number of propositions about the library's employees and departments. Together, these propositions form communicable knowledge or information about this library. The library is the reality concerning this knowledge. The employees and the departments to which the propositions are related are objects belonging to this reality. The propositions express certain facts related to the library.

Propositions can always be expressed by means of a natural language, as was done in the above example. When we wish to communicate our knowledge of a certain reality to others, we usually do it by expressing the propositions containing this (communicable) knowledge by means of a natural language. Because we conceive of communicable knowledge or information as a number of propositions about the objects of a certain reality, and because propositions can always be expressed by means of a natural language, there is a strong relationship between information and sentences in a natural language. We shall look into this further in the next chapter.

In this section, we have defined the concepts "reality" and "information" more accurately. Below is a summary of the most important concepts in this section. The concept "assertion (proposition)" is considered here as a nondefined concept.

Object or entity:
A matter or object from a real or abstract world or part of one.

Reality (Universe of Discourse):
A set of objects which are relevant for a certain knowledge.

Information or communicable knowledge:
Propositions about objects in a reality which we know or assume to be true at a particular moment.

4.2 Elementary propositions

The text of Figure 4.1 in the previous section is an example of information about a certain public library. Most of the propositions which are represented in this text express more than one fact about the reality (the library). Thus, the proposition "Johnson and Peterson work for the Purchasing Department and King works for the Personnel Department" expresses three facts, namely:

- The fact that Johnson works for the Purchasing Department.
- The fact that Peterson works for the Purchasing Department.
- The fact that King works for the Personnel Department.

Propositions that express exactly one fact will henceforth be called *elementary propositions*. Propositions that express more than one fact will be called *non-elementary propositions*. A non-elementary proposition can always be split into a number of elementary propositions which together express the same facts as the original proposition. An elementary proposition, on the other hand, cannot be split without losing the fact it expresses.

Thus, in the above example, the proposition "Johnson and Peterson work for the Purchasing Department and King works for the Personnel Department" is a non-elementary proposition. This can be split into the following elementary propositions:

- Johnson works for the Purchasing Department.
- Peterson works for the Purchasing Department
- King works for the Personnel Department.

Each of these propositions expresses exactly one fact and cannot be split further into smaller propositions without losing the facts. If we were to try to split the proposition "Johnson works for the Purchasing Department" into smaller propositions, something like "Johnson works for a department" and "somebody works for the Purchasing Department" would result. The fact that Johnson works for the Purchasing Department – the relationship between Johnson and the Purchasing Department – has been lost.

In the previous section, we stated that information about a certain reality consists of propositions about objects in that reality. This can be elementary or non-elementary propositions. In this section, we have seen that non-elementary propositions can always be split into elementary propositions that together express the same facts or information. We can conclude that information about a certain reality always consists of **elementary** propositions about objects in that reality.

All the propositions of Figure 4.1 have been split into elementary propositions in Figure 4.2.

All of these propositions describe one single fact and are thus elementary propositions. Together they describe the same information as the non-elementary propositions of Figure 4.1.

(P1) There are employees.

(P2) There are departments.

(P3) Employees work for departments.

(P4) An employee may only work for one department.

(P5) There are last names.

(P6) There are department names.

(P7) Employees are denoted by their last names.

(P8) Johnson is the last name of a certain employee.

(P9) Peterson is the last name of a certain employee.

(P10) King is the last name of a certain employee.

(P11) Departments are referred to by department names.

(P12) Purchasing is the department name of a certain department.

(P13) Personnel is the department name of a certain department.

(P14) Johnson works for the Purchasing Department.

(P15) Peterson works for the Purchasing Department.

(P16) King works for the Personnel Department.

(P17) A department may not contain more than 10 employees.

Figure 4.2.

The most important concepts in this section are:

Elementary proposition:
A proposition that expresses one single fact. Elementary propositions cannot be split into smaller propositions, without having the facts expressed by them get lost.

Non-elementary proposition:
A proposition that can be split into elementary propositions. These elementary propositions express the same information or facts as the original proposition.

Information, communicable knowledge:
Elementary propositions about objects in a reality which we know or assume to be true at a particular moment.

4.3 Lexical and non-lexical objects

The elementary propositions of Figure 4.2 concern the following objects: employees, departments, last names, department names, Johnson, Peterson, King, Purchasing, Personnel.

The objects "Johnson," "Peterson," "King," "Purchasing," and "Personnel" are used in these propositions as **names** for other objects, namely employees and departments. Thus, the object "Johnson" is used as a name for a certain employee, and the object "Purchasing" is used as a name for a certain department.

These names belong, just like the objects they name, to the reality related to this information or communicable knowledge. The fact that we **know** that a certain object can be used as a name for or reference to another object is, after all, part of our knowledge of this reality. The objects of a certain reality are thus either objects which can be used as names for other objects, or objects which themselves are named by other objects or to which other objects refer. Reality consists of two kinds of objects:

- objects which can be used as names for or references to other objects
- objects which are named or referred to by objects of the first kind

We shall call objects of the first kind *lexical objects* and objects of the second kind *non-lexical objects*. The term "lexical" is derived from the concept "lexicon." A lexicon is a list of names of all the objects which occur in a certain reality. The objects which are named by the lexical objects, those to which the lexical objects refer, are called non-lexical objects.

Because they are **names**, lexical objects consist of letters, numbers, symbols and/or other characters. These objects can therefore always be uttered, written down, or represented in some other way.

Our starting point is that all objects from the reality being considered, which can be uttered, written down, or otherwise represented are by definition lexical objects. All objects for which this is impossible are, by definition, non-lexical objects.

When we wish to communicate knowledge about certain non-lexical objects to someone else, we must concretely designate these non-lexical objects by means of lexical objects which can be uttered, written down, or otherwise represented. These are then used as names or designations for the non-lexical objects.

When, for example, we know that a certain employee works for a certain department and we wish to communicate this knowledge to another person, we must denote this employee and this department (non-lexical objects) explicitly by means of lexical objects, for example "Johnson" and "Purchasing." Because these lexical objects can be uttered, written down, or otherwise represented, we can communicate this knowledge verbally, in writing, or in some other form.

In a reality to which certain **communicable** knowledge or information is related, **every** non-lexical object can be referred to by means of one or more lexical objects.

If this was not possible for one non-lexical object, we would not be able to communicate our knowledge about this non-lexical object to someone else, and we would be dealing with non-communicable knowledge and thus not with information.

The reality to which the example of the present and previous sections is related is schematically depicted in Figure 4.3. The broken line indicates the distinction

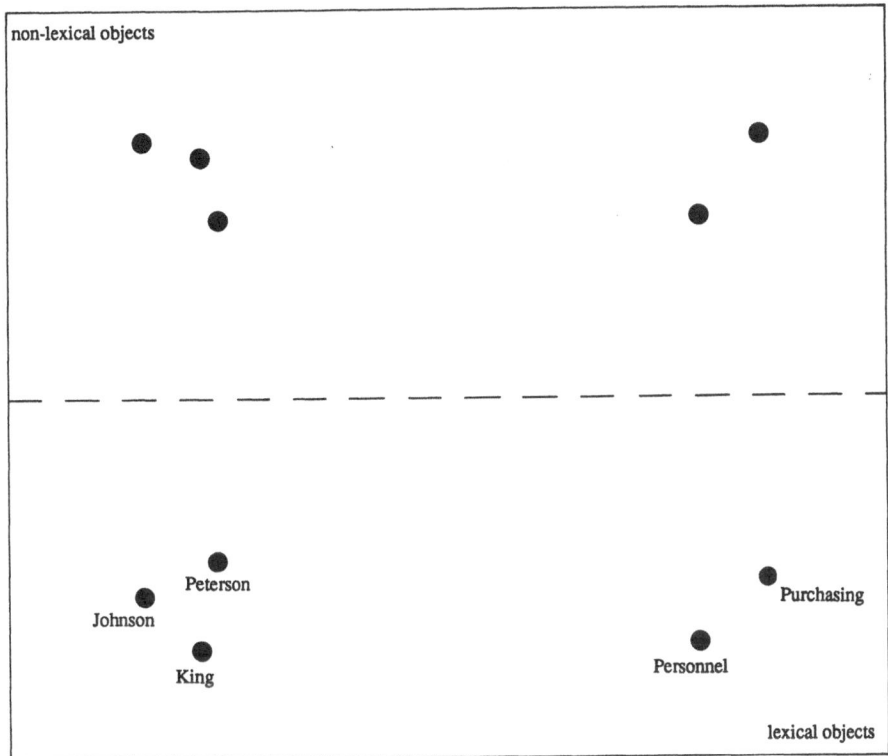

Figure 4.3.

between lexical and non-lexical objects, with the non-lexical objects above the line and the lexical objects below it. The reality consists, as it were, of two separate "worlds": the "world" of the lexical objects and the "world" of the non-lexical objects. Together, the lexical and the non-lexical objects form the reality under consideration.

A summary of the concepts "lexical object" and "non-lexical object" is given below:

Lexical object (label):
An object in a certain reality which can be uttered, written down, or otherwise represented. Lexical objects always consist of letters, numbers, symbols and/or

other characters. Lexical objects can be used as names for or references to other objects.

Non-lexical object (entity):
An object in a certain reality which cannot be uttered, written down, or otherwise represented. Non-lexical objects must be named by lexical objects or referred to by means of lexical objects.

4.4 Facts, ideas, and bridges

In Figure 4.4, we have repeated a number of the elementary propositions of Figure 4.2.

(P8)   Johnson is the last name of a certain employee.

(P9)   Peterson is the last name of a certain employee.

(P10) King is the last name of a certain employee.

(P12) Purchasing is the department name of a certain department.

(P13) Personnel is the department name of a certain department.

(P14) Johnson works for the Purchasing Department.

(P15) Peterson works for the Purchasing Department.

(P16) King works for the Personnel Department.

Figure 4.4.

Each one of these elementary propositions expresses a certain relationship between objects in the reality being considered.

From now on, we shall call elementary propositions about a certain reality which express relationships between objects in that reality *facts*. Facts express the proposition or supposition that these relationships exist at a particular moment in the reality. The propositions in Figure 4.4 are therefore examples of facts. The facts of Figure 4.4 are represented graphically in Figure 4.5. This figure was created by connecting the objects in Figure 4.3 with each other. Each connection of two objects in Figure 4.5 is the graphical representation of one fact in Figure 4.4. For clarity, the numbers of these facts are given next to their respective connecting lines.

Figure 4.5 is a representation of information (communicable knowledge) about the reality under consideration, and thus of that which we know or think we know about this reality. It is not a direct representation of the reality itself.

For clarity, we shall for the time being limit ourselves to facts in which only two objects occur. In Chapters 12 and 14 we will extend what has been handled up to that moment to facts in which either one single object or more than two objects occur. Facts which concern exactly two objects are called **binary facts**.

We note in Figure 4.5 that there are two kinds of facts:

– facts which are only concerned with non-lexical objects.
– facts which are concerned with one non-lexical and one lexical object.

The facts which are expressed by Propositions P14, P15, and P16 are examples of facts which only concern non-lexical objects. The facts which are expressed by Propositions P8, P9, P10, P12, and P13 are examples of facts which are concerned with one non-lexical and one lexical object each. We shall assume that there are no facts which only concern lexical objects, because these kinds of facts can always be expressed by means of the first two kinds of facts.

Henceforth, we shall call those facts which concern one non-lexical and one lexical object **bridges**. This name has been selected because the facts of this kind connect objects from the two "worlds" in which we mentally divided the reality

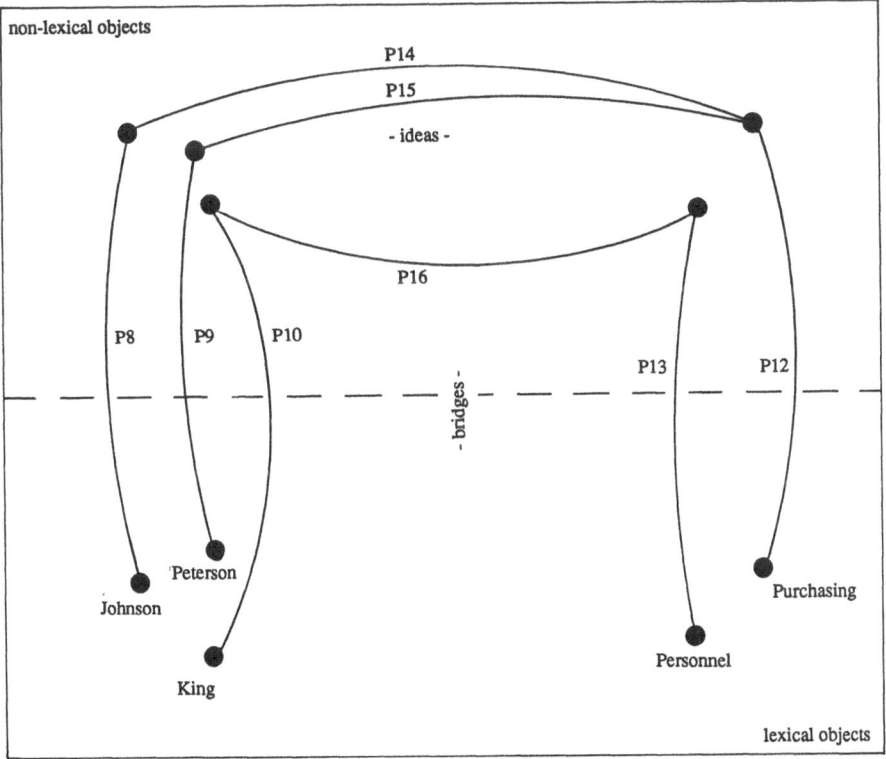

Figure 4.5.

(the "world" of the lexical objects and the "world" of the non-lexical objects). The bridges indicate which lexical objects refer to which non-lexical objects or which lexical objects represent certain characteristics of which non-lexical objects. Thus, the bridges in Figure 4.4 express the knowledge or information that there are three employees who are called "Johnson," "Peterson," and "King" and that there are two departments which are called "Purchasing" and "Personnel." Bridges are by definition binary facts, because they always deal with one non-lexical and one lexical object.

Hereafter, we shall call those facts which concern only non-lexical objects *ideas*. We selected this name because the facts of this kind represent our (communicable) knowledge about the non-lexical objects themselves, separate from the knowledge which we have about any possible names of these objects. The "ideas" represent that part of our knowledge that on its own can exist only in our thoughts. If we wish to inform someone else of an idea, we must express every object involved in that idea by means of a name which can be uttered, written down, or otherwise represented.

The ideas in our example represent the knowledge that the employees "Johnson" and "Peterson" work for the department "Personnel" and that employee "King" works for the department "Purchasing." Ideas which involve exactly two non-lexical objects are called *binary ideas*.

A summary of the most important concepts in this section is given below:

Fact:
An elementary proposition that expresses a relationship between objects in a certain reality. A fact expresses the proposition or supposition that this relationship exists at a certain moment in the reality.

Binary fact:
A fact that involves exactly two objects.

Bridge:
A fact that concerns one non-lexical and one lexical object. A bridge indicates how a lexical object refers to a non-lexical object or which lexical object represents a certain characteristic of which non-lexical object. A bridge is by definition a binary fact.

Idea:
A fact that involves only non-lexical objects.

Binary idea:
An idea that involves exactly two non-lexical objects.

4.5 Non-lexical and lexical object types

Figure 4.5 graphically depicts part of the information which is expressed by the elementary propositions of Figure 4.2. A comparison of both figures shows that not all the information which is expressed by the propositions in Figure 4.2 is represented in Figure 4.5. Propositions P1 and P2 of Figure 4.2 are not represented in Figure 4.5.

(P1)   There are employees.

(P2)   There are departments.

Figure 4.6.

These propositions express the knowledge or information that there are two sets or classes of objects, namely **employees** and **departments**. If we next bring these into relation to the facts given in Figure 4.7,

---

(P8)   Johnson is the last name of a certain employee.

(P9)   Peterson is the last name of a certain employee.

(P10) King is the last name of a certain employee.

(P12) Purchasing is the department name of a certain department.

(P13) Personnel is the department name of a certain department.

Figure 4.7.

it appears that:

- The **non-lexical** objects to which the lexical objects "Johnson," "Peterson," and "King" refer belong to the set or class "employees."
- The **non-lexical** objects which are referred to by the lexical objects "Purchasing" and "Personnel" belong to the set or class "departments."

The sets "employees" and "departments" are thus sets of non-lexical objects. Objects which belong to a same class or set are of the same kind or type. The non-lexical objects which belong to the set "employees" are of the kind or type "employee." The non-lexical objects which belong to the set "departments" are of the kind or type "department." From now on, we shall call a set or class of non-lexical objects which are of the same kind or **type** a *non-lexical object type*. Because this concept occurs frequently, we often use the abbreviation NOLOT (from **NOn-Lexical Object Type**). A non-lexical object type, or NOLOT, is a set or class of equivalent non-lexical objects. Propositions P1 and P2 express the knowledge that there is a non-lexical object type "employee" and a non-lexical object type "department," respectively.

It is customary in set theory to graphically represent a set of objects by means of an ellipse or a circle, and the objects which belong to this set by means of dots or points within these circles or ellipses. Figure 4.8 is, for example, a graphical representation of an arbitrary set A, to which the objects a1, a2, and a3 belong.

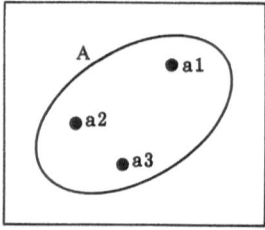

Figure 4.8.

In this way, we could represent the non-lexical object type "employee" (the set of all employees) and the non-lexical object type "department" (the set of all departments) graphically as is done in Figure 4.9.

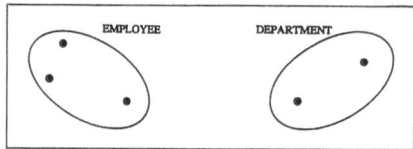

Figure 4.9.

The dots within the circles represent the three employees and the two departments in the library. Applying this method of drawing to Figure 4.5 results in Figure 4.10. This is a representation of part of our communicable knowledge about the reality being considered. Propositions P1 and P2 are now represented in this figure as well.

If we next compare Figure 4.10 with the elementary propositions in Figure 4.2, it appears once again that not all of the information which is expressed by the propositions of Figure 4.2 are given in Figure 4.10.

Propositions P5 and P6 are not represented in this figure.

(P5) There are last names.

(P6) There are department names.

Figure 4.11.

These propositions express the knowledge or information that there are two sets or classes of objects, namely **last names** and **department names**.

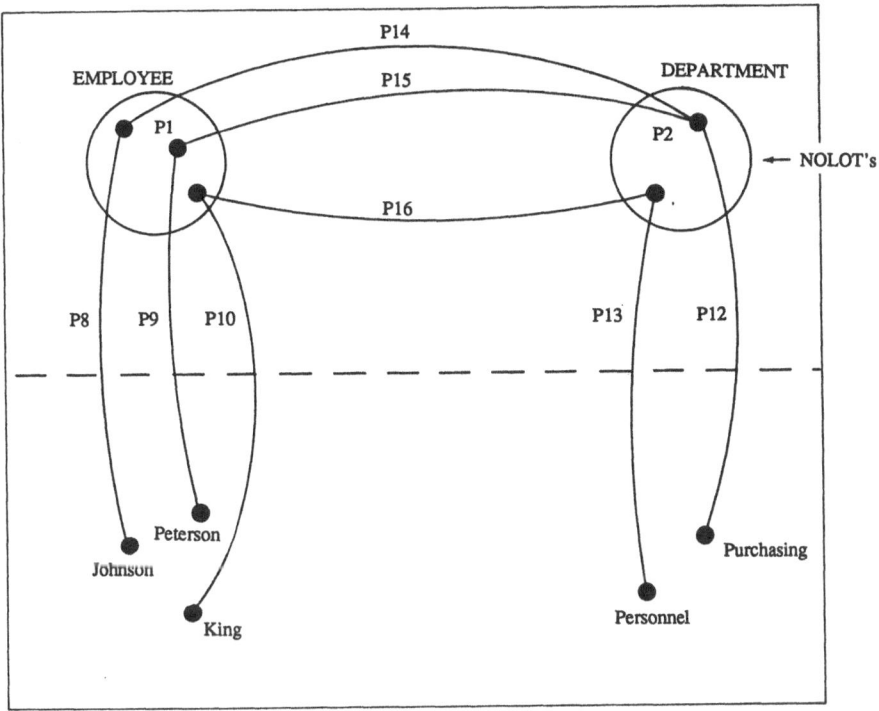

Figure 4.10.

If we then bring this into relationship to Figure 4.7, it appears that:

- the **lexical objects** "Johnson," "Peterson," and "King" belong to the set or class "last names."
- the **lexical objects** "Purchasing" and "Personnel" belong to the set or class "department names."

The sets "last names" and "departments" are thus sets of lexical objects. Lexical objects which belong to a same class or set are of the same kind or type. The lexical objects which belong to the set "last names" are of the kind or type "last name," and the lexical objects which belong to the set "department names" are of the kind or type "department name." From now on, we shall call a set or class of lexical objects which are of the same kind or **type** a *lexical object type*. Because this concept occurs frequently, the abbreviation LOT (from Lexical Object Type) is often used. A lexical object type, or LOT, is a set or class of equivalent lexical objects. Propositions P5 and P6 express the knowledge that there is a lexical object type "last name" and a lexical object type "department name," respectively.

If we want to represent the lexical object type "last name" (the set of all last names) and the lexical object type "department name" (the set of all department names) in the same way as we did the non-lexical object types, represented in Figure 4.10, we wind up with Figure 4.12. Propositions P5 and P6 are now represented in this figure as well.

In this figure, we have left out the broken line that separates the "world" of the non-lexical objects and the "world" of the lexical objects. Because we still wish to express the difference between lexical and non-lexical objects, we will represent the non-lexical object types from now on by means of solid circles or ellipses and the lexical object types by means of broken circles or ellipses. As will appear later, a strict separation between non-lexical and lexical objects is one of the most fundamental characteristics of the NIAM method of information analysis.

The objects which belong to a certain object type at a certain moment form a so-called *population* of this object type. Therefore, in our example the lexical objects "Johnson," "Peterson," and "King" form a population of the lexical object type "last name," and the lexical objects "Purchasing" and "Personnel" form a population of the lexical object type "department name." The employees with the last names "Johnson," "Peterson," and "King" form a population of the non-

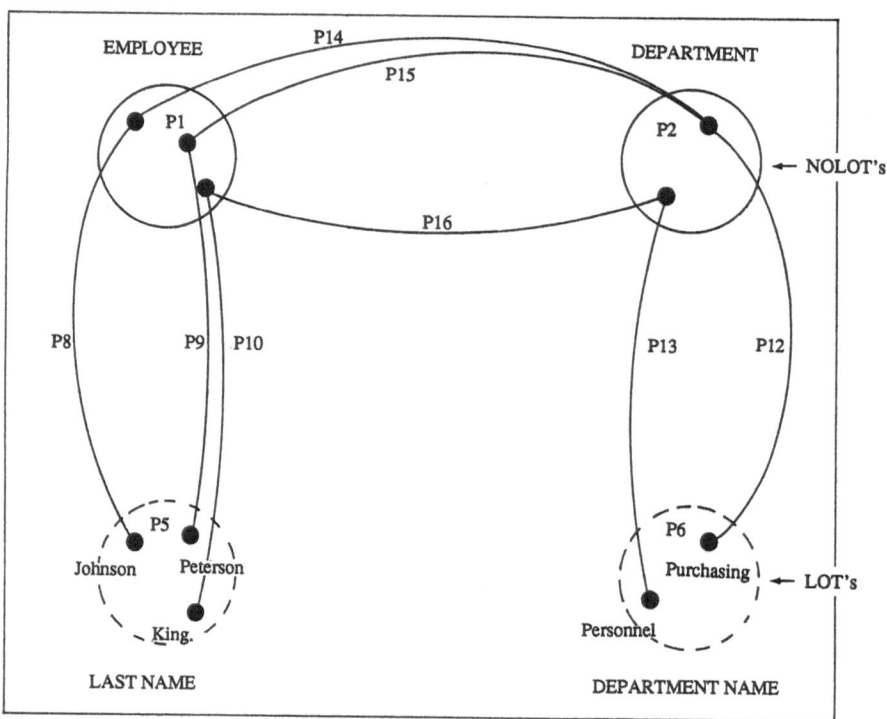

Figure 4.12.

lexical object type "employee" and the departments with the department names "Purchasing" and "Personnel" form a population of the non-lexical object type "department."

A summary of the most important concepts in this section is given below.

Non-lexical object type (entity category), NOLOT:
A set or class of equivalent non-lexical objects.

Lexical object type (label category), LOT:
A set or class of equivalent lexical objects.

Object type population:
The objects which belong at a given moment to an object type.

In this section we have used the following graphical symbols:

non-lexical object type

lexical object type

4.6 Fact types, idea types, and bridge types

Figure 4.12 is a graphical representation of part of the information which is expressed by the elementary propositions of Figure 4.2.

Proposition P3 of Figure 4.2 is not represented in Figure 4.12.

(P3) Employees work for departments.

Figure 4.13.

This proposition expresses the knowledge that there is a set or class of facts which concern the non-lexical objects of the type "employee" and the non-lexical objects of the type "department." All of these facts express the same kind of knowledge or information, namely that a certain employee works for a certain department, and are therefore in this respect of the same kind or type. We shall call a set or class of facts which express the same kind of information a *fact type*. Proposition P3 expresses the knowledge that there is a fact type whose individual facts express the knowledge or information that certain employees work for certain departments. Facts P14, P15, and P16 belong to this fact type.

In set theory, sets or classes of equivalent relationships between elements of sets (so-called relations) are often represented by means of tables, in which the related elements of these sets are placed next to each other. A relation between the elements of two sets A and B is, for example, represented as in Figure 4.14.

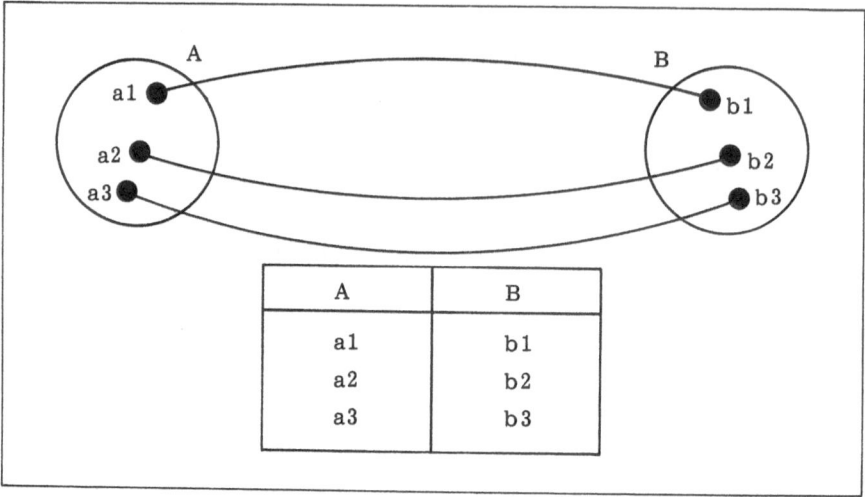

Figure 4.14.

Using this kind of representation, we can depict the fact type that is expressed by Proposition P3 as is done in Figure 4.15.

Naturally, we have denoted the non-lexical objects in this table by means of the associated lexical objects (their names), because lexical objects can by definition be written down and non-lexical objects cannot.

Henceforth, we shall represent a fact type graphically by connecting the associated object types by means of the symbol:

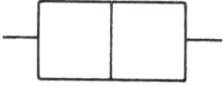

We have selected this symbol because it is a symbolic representation of a table. By this means, we wish to express that a fact type is a **set** of facts. The results of applying this kind of representation to Figure 4.12 can be seen in Figure 4.16.

Proposition P3 has now been represented in this figure too.

The facts which belong to a certain fact type at a certain moment form a *population* of this fact type. A fact type and any of its possible populations can

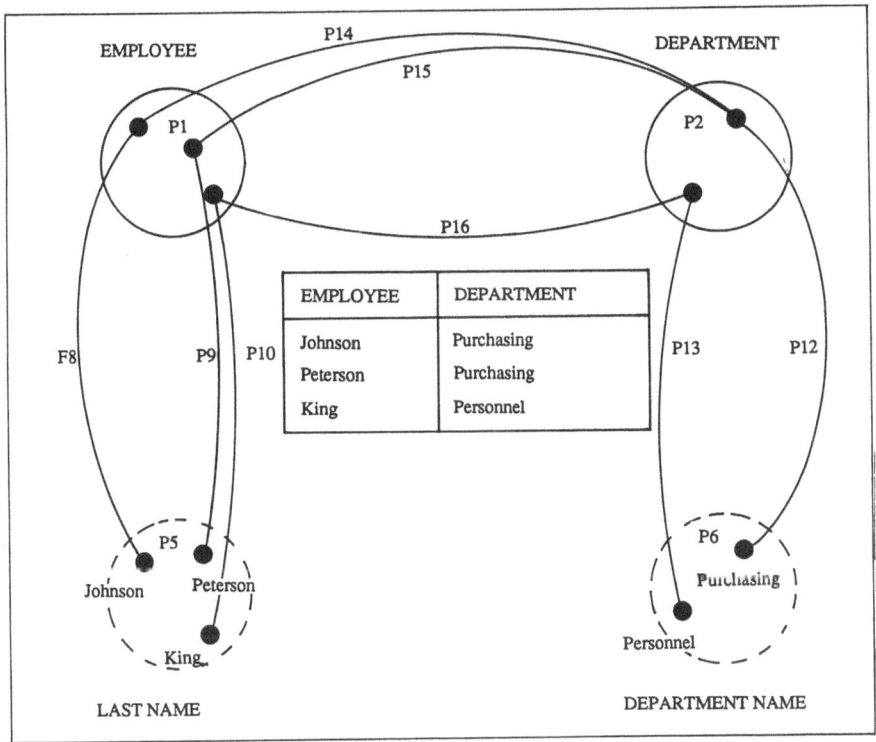

Figure 4.15.

be graphically depicted by combining the table method of representing a fact type with the method used in Figure 4.16. This has been done in Figure 4.17.

A diagram like the one in Figure 4.17 is called a ***population diagram***. A population diagram is a graphical representation of a fact type and one of its possible populations. In the following chapters we shall see that population diagrams are a powerful tool when practising the NIAM method of information analysis.

A population diagram is a representation of the facts of a certain fact type, whose descriptions belong to the information base at a certain moment. Clearly, the description of one and the same fact can only be stored once in the information base. One particular fact (one particular combination of objects) is therefore always represented in a population diagram only once. A population diagram thus never contains a repetition of one and the same fact (of one and the same combination of objects). We shall call this last fairly self-evident rule the ***singularity rule*** for population diagrams.

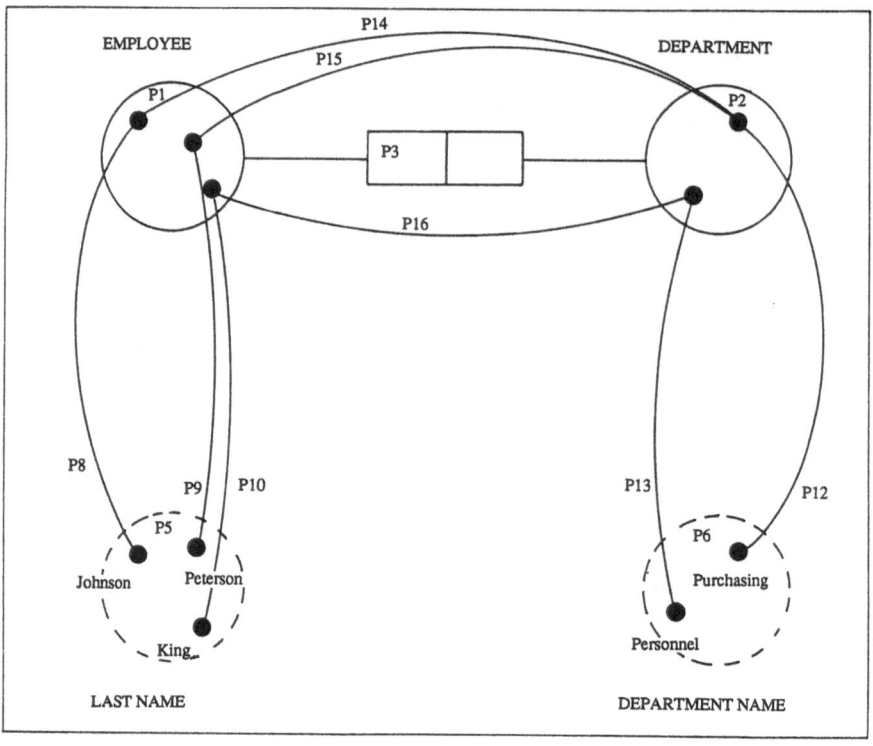

Figure 4.16.

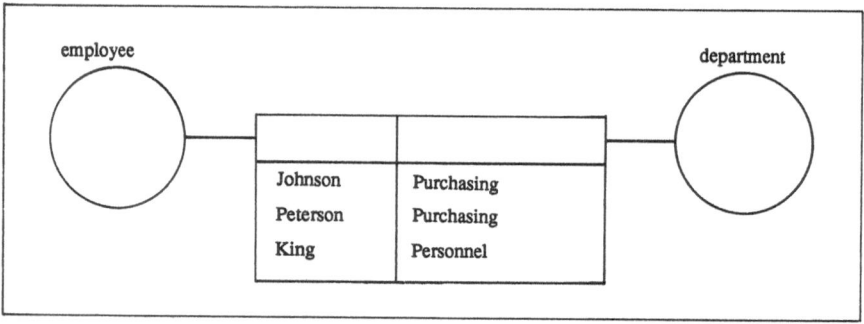

Figure 4.17.

The population diagram in Figure 4.18 does not satisfy this rule, because the fact that Johnson works for Purchasing (the combination of the employee "Johnson" and the department "Purchasing") is given here twice. Repeating one and the same fact in a population diagram is always redundant.

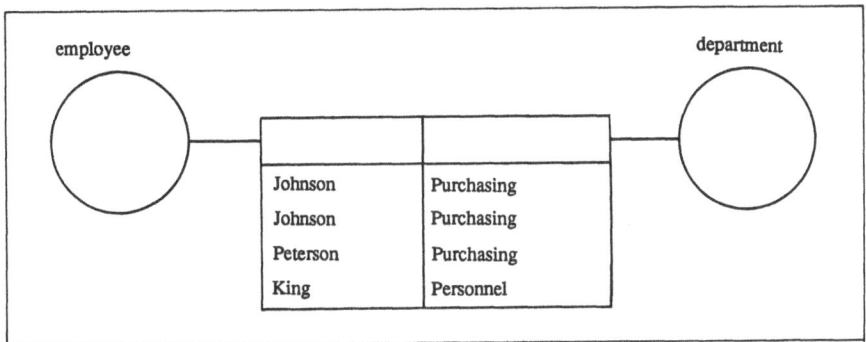

Figure 4.18.

Facts are, as we have seen, propositions about the existence of relationships between objects in a reality. Every object plays a certain role in each of these relationships. The columns in a population diagram correspond to these roles. The columns in a population diagram of a fact type are therefore also called the *roles* of this fact type.

Propositions P7 and P11 in Figure 4.2 have not yet been represented in Figure 4.16.

(P7) Employees are denoted by their last names.

(P11) Departments are referred to by department names.

Figure 4.19.

Proposition P7 expresses the knowledge that there is a set or class of facts which are related to the non-lexical objects of the type "employee" and the lexical objects of the type "last name", which state that employees are denoted by their last names. Because these facts express the same kind of information, they are of the same kind or type. Proposition P7 describes, therefore, a fact type related to the non-lexical object type "employee" and the lexical object type "last name." Facts P8, P9, and P10 form a population of this fact type. Proposition P11 expresses the knowledge that there is a set or class of facts related to the non-lexical objects of the type "department," and the lexical objects of the type "department name," which express that departments are referred to by means of department names. These facts express the same kind of information and are thus of the same kind or type. Consequently, Proposition P11 describes a fact type related to the non-lexical object type "department" and the lexical object type "department name." Facts P12 and P13 form a population of this fact type. We have added the last two fact types to Figure 4.16, resulting in Figure 4.20.

Propositions P7 and P11 are now also represented in this figure. All of the fact

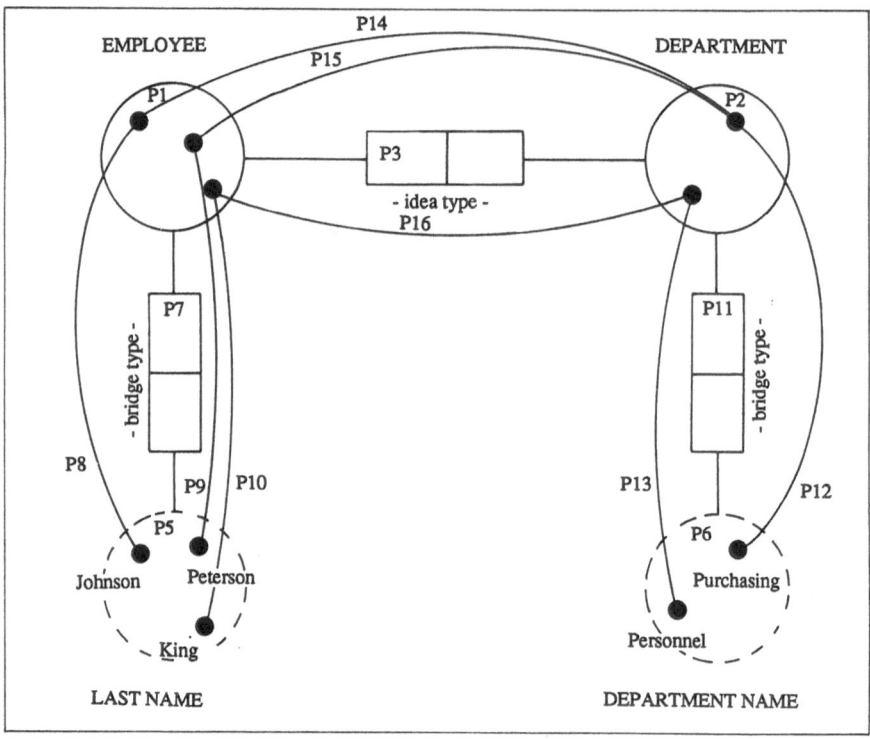

Figure 4.20.

types of Figure 4.20 involve two object types. A fact type that involves exactly two object types is called a **binary fact type**. A population of a binary fact type always consists of binary facts.

In the previous section we separated facts into two kinds, namely ideas and bridges. Ideas are facts which only involve non-lexical objects, and bridges are facts which involve one non-lexical and one lexical object. In just the same way, we will distinguish fact types into two kinds:

– Fact types which are exclusively related to non-lexical object types and whose populations thus consist of ideas are called **idea types**.
– Fact types which are related to one non-lexical object type and one lexical object type and whose populations thus consist of bridges are called **bridge types**.

In general, idea types can be related to more than two or even to one single non-lexical object type. For convenience, we shall limit ourselves, however, to binary idea types until Chapter 12. By definition, bridge types are always related to **two** object types, namely one non-lexical and one lexical object type, and are thus always binary.

Below we give a summary of the most important concepts in this section.

Fact type:
A set or class of facts which express the same kind of information.

Fact type population:
The facts which belong at a given moment to a fact type.

Population diagram:
A graphical representation of a fact type and one of its possible populations.

Role:
A column in a population diagram of a fact type.

Binary fact type:
A fact type that involves exactly two object types.

Idea type:
A fact type that exclusively involves non-lexical object types and whose populations thus consist of ideas.

Bridge type:
A fact type that involves one non-lexical object type and one lexical object type and whose populations thus consist of bridges.

Every population diagram must satisfy the **singularity rule:**
In a population diagram, every fact (every combination of objects) is only represented once.

In this section we have defined the following graphical symbols:
idea type

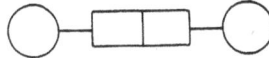

bridge type

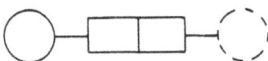

population diagram

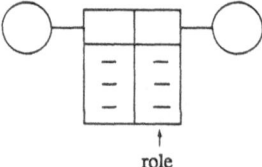

role

4.7 Facts and rules

All the propositions in Figure 4.2, with the exception of Proposition P4 ("an employee may only work for one department") and Proposition P17 ("a department may not contain more than 10 employees"), have now been represented in Figure 4.20. Propositions P8, P9, P10, P12, P13, P14, P15, and P16 are facts.

Figure 4.21.

(P8) Johnson is the last name of a certain employee.

(P9) Peterson is the last name of a certain employee.

(P10) King is the last name of a certain employee.

(P12) Purchasing is the department name of a certain department.

(P13) Personnel is the department name of a certain department.

(P14) Johnson works for the Purchasing Department.

(P15) Peterson works for the Purchasing Department.

(P16) King works for the Personnel Department.

Facts are elementary propositions about the existence of certain relationships between objects in a reality. All the remaining propositions are called ***rules***. Propositions P1, P2, P3, P4, P5, P6, P7, P11, and P17 are rules.

(P1) There are employees.

(P2) There are departments.

(P3) Employees work for departments.

(P4) An employee may only work for one department.

(P5) There are last names.

(P6) There are department names.

(P7) Employees are denoted by their last names.

(P11) Departments are referred to by department names.

(P17) A department may not contain more than 10 employees.

Figure 4.22.

Rules are elementary propositions which are not facts. Rules determine which facts can and cannot be part of the communicable knowledge or information about a certain reality.

Thus, rules P1, P2, P5, and P6 in Figure 4.22 prescribe that all the facts which belong to the communicable knowledge about the reality in our example must be related to objects of the types "employee," "department," "last name," and "department name." These propositions form the definitions or the specifications of these object types.

Rules P3, P7, and P11 prescribe the fact types to which all the facts which in our example are part of the communicable knowledge about the reality must belong. These propositions form the definitions or specifications of these fact types.

Rules P4 ("an employee may only work for one department") and P17 ("a department may not contain more than 10 employees") restrict the possible facts which are allowed on the basis of the other rules. For example, the following two facts together are in agreement with all the rules in Figure 4.22, with the exception of rule P4:

"Johnson works for the Purchasing Department"
"Johnson works for the Personnel Department"

Because Johnson works for more than one department, these facts do not satisfy rule P4, so they may not **both simultaneously** belong to the communicable knowledge about the reality in our example. In this sense, Proposition P4 as well as Proposition P17 restricts the facts which may occur on the basis of the other rules. Rules such as P4 and P17 are called *constraints*.

To summarize:

Rules are elementary propositions which are not facts.

Rules involve the facts which are part of the communicable knowledge or information about a certain reality and can express:

- that the objects to which these facts are related should belong to certain object types, such as Propositions P1, P2, P5, and P6. These rules form the specifications of these object types.
- that these facts should belong to certain fact types, such as Propositions P3, P7, and P11. These rules form the specifications of these fact types.
- that there are further limitations for the facts which are allowed on the basis of the previous rules, such as Propositions P4 and P17. These rules are called constraints.

In this and the previous section, we pointed out how information is, in general, built up or structured. In Figure 4.23, we have depicted this general structure of information schematically. One of the starting points of the NIAM method of information analysis is that information is generally built up as is depicted in this figure.

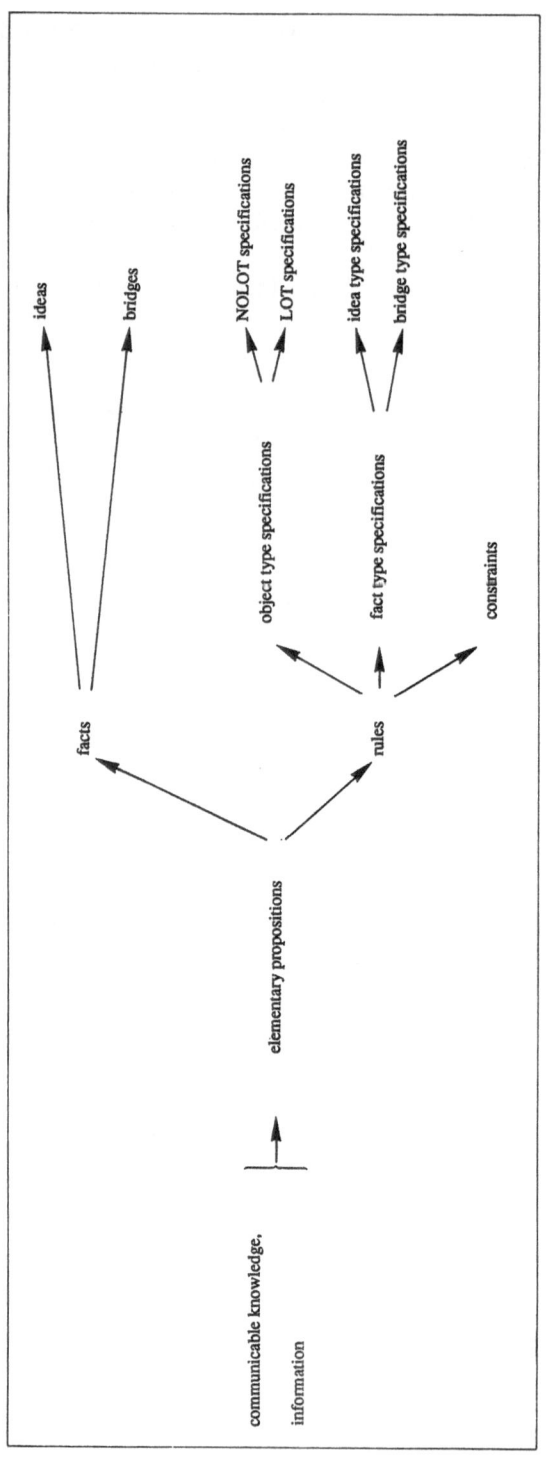

Figure 4.23.

Facts represent part of our (communicable) knowledge of a certain reality. The knowledge that we possess at a certain moment generally changes as time goes by. This happens because our knowledge increases or decreases as time passes, or because the reality itself changes. In terms of time, new facts can come into being in our knowledge, and already-existing facts can pass out of it.

Rules are propositions which are valid for all existing and new facts. In this sense, rules are more general in character than facts. They represent our knowledge about the general rules and laws which hold within the reality. Rules prescribe which facts can be part of our communicable knowledge of the reality and which cannot.

Facts and rules **together** form communicable knowledge or information about a certain reality.

Because the reality changes with time, in general the rules will also change with time: new rules can be added and existing rules can be dropped.

In the previous chapters, we have defined the information base of an information system as the description of all information which is stored by the information system. The grammar of an information system has been defined as the description of all the rules which prescribe which information base states and transitions may occur. In light of what has been dealt with in this chapter, we can refine these definitions as follows:

- The information base and the grammar **together** describe the communicable knowledge or information which we possess about a certain reality at a given moment, in so far as this knowledge is to be registered by the information system.
- The **information base** contains the description of all the **facts** which belong to this knowledge.
- The **grammar** contains the description of all the **rules** which belong to this knowledge.

We have seen earlier that information analysis consists of specifying the grammar of an information system. From the above, it follows that this amounts to specifying the **rules** which belong to the communicable knowledge or information which is to be registered by the information system.

In the upcoming chapters, we shall see that during information analysis according to NIAM, the rules of the grammar are determined according to a stepwise method by:

- verbally describing the communicable knowledge about the reality on the basis of concrete examples, as has been done in Figure 4.1.
- transforming the propositions resulting from these verbal descriptions into elementary propositions, as has been done in Figure 4.2.
- separating these elementary propositions into facts and rules.
- formally describing these rules.

In the following chapter we will summarize what has been treated above into a general principle, and from it derive a way of formally describing the rules which belong to the communicable knowledge of a certain reality.

To summarize:

Rules:

Elementary propositions which are not facts. Together facts and rules constitute communicable knowledge or information about a certain reality.

Constraints:

Rules which are not specifications of object types and fact types. Constraints restrict the facts which are allowed on the basis of the definitions of object types and fact types.

Information base:

The description of all the facts which belong at a certain moment to the communicable knowledge or information about a certain reality, in so far as this knowledge is to be registered by the information system.

Grammar:

The description of all the rules which belong at a certain moment to the communicable knowledge or information about a certain reality, in so far as this knowledge is to be registered by the information system.

4.8 State rules and transition rules

It follows from the fact that the grammar prescribes which states and which state transitions may occur in the information base that there are two kinds of rules:

- rules which prescribe which **states** may occur in the information base.
- rules which prescribe which **state transitions** may occur in the information base.

Rules which prescribe which states may occur in the information base are called *state rules*, and rules which prescribe which state transitions may occur in the information base are called *transition rules*.

State rules prescribe which facts may be described by the information base at any moment, and therefore always involve one single information base state. Transition rules prescribe which changes may occur in the information base, and

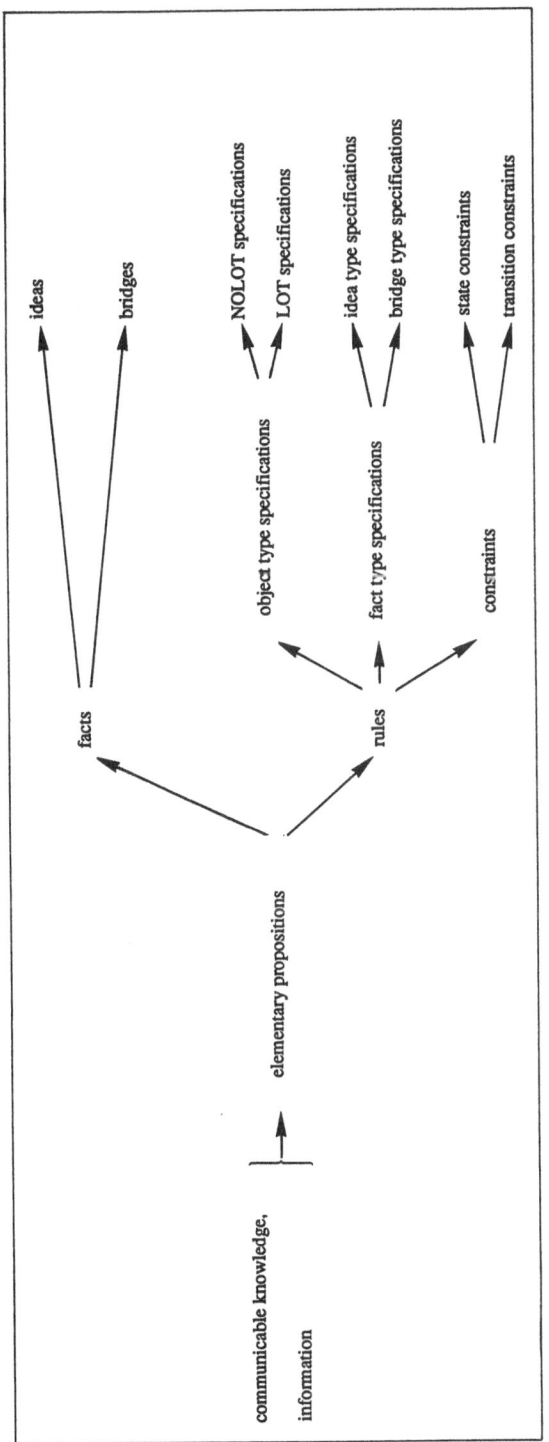

Figure 4.24.

therefore always involve the transition from one information base state to another state.

The specifications of the object and fact types prescribe to which fact types the facts being described by the information base at any moment should belong, and they are therefore state rules. Constraints can involve one single information base state or an information base state transition. Rules which are concerned with one single information base state are called *state constraints*. State constraints prescribe which facts may occur at any moment in the fact type populations. Constraints that are concerned with an information base state transition are called transition constraints. These prescribe which changes may occur in the fact type populations.

In Figure 4.24, we have taken the general structure of information one step further by separating the rules into state and transition constraints.

To summarize:

State constraints:
Constraints which involve one single information base state. State constraints prescribe which facts may be found at any moment in the fact type populations described by the other rules.

Transition constraints:
Constraints which describe the information base transition states allowed. Transition constraints prescribe which changes may occur in the fact type populations described by the other rules.

5 DESCRIBING INFORMATION

We stated earlier that during information analysis the grammar of an information system is described. In this chapter we shall look at how information in general, and the grammar of an information system in particular, can be described.

In the previous chapter, we studied how information is built up, and saw that information consists of facts and rules. At any moment, the information base of an information system contains the facts which are then valid, and the grammar contains a description of the rules which hold for these facts.

In this chapter, we will point out how information, and therefore also the facts and rules from which information is built, can be described. As the grammar of an information system contains a description of the rules, we will indicate at the same time the manner in which the grammar can be described.

The starting point in the previous chapter was the conceptual principle. The general structure of the information given there was therefore concerned only with the conceptual aspects of information. That is, it was concerned only with those aspects which were related to the meaning of information and not with its possible representations. The conceptual principle will also be our starting point in this chapter. The way in which information in general, and the grammar in particular, will be described will also be related only to the conceptual aspects – to the meaning of information. In addition to the conceptual principle, we will also use the 100% principle as a starting point in this chapter. The 100% principle states that the grammar completely describes **all** of the conceptual aspects. That is, all of the knowledge which is necessary to understand the data in the information base and to interpret the grammar has to be described completely, exactly, and explicitly. Implicit knowledge may never be assumed, and the data in the information base may be interpreted in only one way.

For these reasons, we shall describe information in such a way that the meaning of this information appears from the description to be complete, unambiguous and exact. In the next section, we will formulate a principle that will serve as the starting point for the way in which we will describe information, one which complies with the conceptual principle and the 100% principle, one of the main principles of the NIAM method of information analysis. In the subsequent sections we will, on the basis of this principle, first point out how information in general, and then the grammar of an information system in particular, can be described. Lastly, we will show that an important part of the grammar can be described by means of the graphical representations which we have developed in the previous chapter, exemplified by Figure 4.20.

5.1 The natural language principle

Our starting point in the previous chapter was that information consists of elementary propositions about a certain reality. We then saw that propositions can always be described by means of sentences in a natural language. Thus, all the elementary propositions occurring in Figure 4.2 are described by means of sentences in the English language.

It follows from the fact that information consists of propositions about a reality and that propositions can always be described by means of sentences in a natural language that information can always be described by means of sentences in a natural language.

Sentences in a natural language which describe **elementary** propositions are called *elementary sentences*. Elementary sentences describe one single fact and, like elementary propositions, cannot be split into smaller sentences without losing the information described by the original sentences. Figure 4.1 in the previous chapter contains a number of non-elementary sentences. These are the descriptions of a number of non-elementary propositions. Figure 4.2 contains only elementary sentences, each of which describes one elementary proposition.

It follows from the fact that information is built up from elementary propositions and that elementary propositions can always be described by elementary sentences in a natural language that information can always be described by means of elementary sentences in a natural language. We shall call this the *natural language principle*:

Information can always be described by means of elementary sentences in a natural language.

(This is a temporary formulation of this principle; in one of the upcoming sections, we will refine this formulation.)

This principle, along with the conceptual principle and the 100% principle, is one of the starting points of the NIAM method of information analysis.

Sentences in a natural language only reflect the meaning – the conceptual aspects – of the information they describe. By starting with the natural language principle, we shall arrive at a method of describing the grammar of an information system (the rules) which is based on sentences in a natural language and which therefore reflects only the conceptual aspects of information. The natural language principle is thus in line with the conceptual principle. It is a specialisation of this principle for information analysis. The grammar of an information system can be specified in many different ways such that only the conceptual aspects of information are described by it. In the NIAM method of information analysis, we start, by virtue of the natural language principle, with the idea that the grammar is described in a way based on sentences in a natural language.

We shall also bring the 100% principle into our reasoning. This principle states that the grammar of an information system must completely describe **all** of the conceptual aspects of the information to be exchanged with the information system, and that on the basis of the grammar, only one interpretation of the information to be exchanged with the information system is possible. In other words, the grammar must be described in such a way that it completely and explicitly reflects the meaning of the information to be exchanged. In determining this meaning, one may never appeal to any implicitly assumed knowledge which is not explicitly reflected in the description of the grammar. This can only be ensured if the grammar is described in a formal manner. The natural language principle, as we have temporarily formulated it above, offers too few opportunities to do this. The number of possible elementary sentence structures in a natural language is, after all, too large. Most of the words and structures in a natural language can be interpreted in different ways. The correct interpretation is very often dependent on the context and is therefore based on implicitly supposed prior knowledge of this context. To stay in line with the 100% principle, the elementary sentences used to describe information ought to be restricted to a well-defined subset of the language structures which are possible in a natural language. The elementary sentences belonging to this subset ought to describe the meaning of the information completely, exactly and unambiguously. Consequently, these sentences must have a fixed and unequivocal structure.

For these reasons, in describing information, we shall begin with a special kind of elementary sentence which always have a fixed structure and which completely reflect the meaning of the information they describe. In the course of this chapter, we will have refined the natural language principle to the statement that information can always be described by means of these kinds of sentences. In its ultimate form, the natural language principle will fit in with both the conceptual principle and the 100% principle.

In this section, we introduced the concept "elementary sentence."

Elementary sentence:
A sentence in a natural language which forms the description of one elementary proposition.

In the next section, we will attempt to represent the structure of elementary sentences by means of a general structural formula. To do this, we will derive a restricted kind of elementary sentence which always have a fixed structure and which fully reflect the meaning of the information described.

5.2 A general structural formula for elementary sentences

In the last chapter, we described one of the elementary propositions (P16) in Figure 4.2 by means of the following elementary sentence: "King works for the Personnel Department." This elementary sentence consists of the lexical objects "King" and "Personnel Department" and of the phrase "works for." A phrase such as "works for" is called a *sentence predicate*, or a *predicate* for short. The construction of this elementary sentence is represented in Figure 5.1.

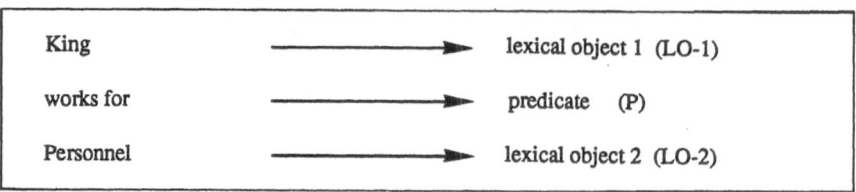

Figure 5.1.

The elementary proposition which is described by this elementary sentence expresses an association between the non-lexical objects to which the lexical objects "King" and "Personnel Department" refer, namely the employee with the last name "King" and the department with the department name "Personnel." The predicate is a **name** for this association.

In set theory, an association A between the elements a and b of two sets A and B, such as depicted in Figure 5.2, is sometimes notated in the form of a formula, such as: A(a,b).

In analogy to this method of notation, we can represent the construction of the elementary sentence of Figure 5.1 by the following structural formula:

ES = P(LO-1, LO-2)

where ES stands for elementary sentence and P for the predicate of this sentence, and where LO is the abbreviation for "lexical object." The predicate is a name for the association which is described by the elementary sentence.

As already noted in the last chapter, we will for the time being limit ourselves, for the sake of clarity, to elementary propositions, and therefore to elementary sentences which are concerned with **two** objects. In general, elementary propositions and thus elementary sentences may concern one, two, or more objects. In the chapters to come, we will encounter some examples of these. Therefore, we shall expand the above structural formula for elementary sentences into the following (temporary) general form:

ES = P(LO-1, ...)

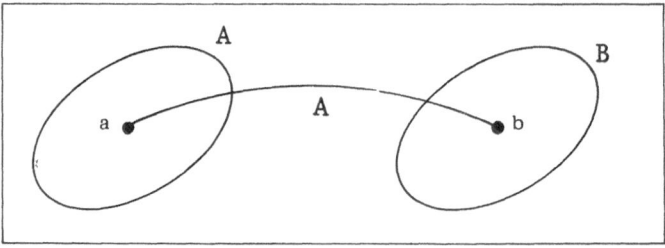

Figure 5.2.

In this section, we have introduced the concept of a "predicate" of an elementary sentence.

Predicate of an elementary sentence.
A name for the association between the objects in a certain reality which are described by the elementary sentence.

In the upcoming sections, we shall show that elementary sentences built according to the structural formula of Figure 5.3 do not completely, explicitly, and unequivocally reflect the information they describe, and thus do not satisfy the demands of the 100% principle. Subsequently, we will extend the structural formula for elementary sentences to a form such that the elementary sentences structured by this formula do satisfy the demands of the 100% principle.

5.3 Elementary deep structure sentences

Actually, we are only capable of interpreting the sentence "King works for the Personnel Department" correctly because in the course of reading this book we have become familiar with the context of this sentence, or because we make certain suppositions about its possible context. We know, or suppose, that "King" is the name of an employee and that "Personnel Department" is the name of a department. In interpreting this sentence, we thus use knowledge which is not explicitly reflected in the formulation of the sentence, but which is implicitly assumed.

This becomes clearer if we take a look at the following elementary sentence: "K731 works for D006." The chance that we will not understand this sentence is greater, because we must know that employees can be denoted not only by their last names but also by personnel numbers, that departments can not only have department names but also department numbers, and that "K731" is a personnel number and "D006" is a department number. This knowledge is not explicitly expressed in the sentence, but is implicitly assumed. If we do not possess this implicitly assumed knowledge, we cannot interpret the sentence in the correct manner.

It appears from this that the elementary sentences which satisfy the structural formula of Figure 5.3 do not, in general, fit the 100% principle. After all, for our purposes (namely, the specification of the grammar of an information system), the 100% principle requires that information be described in such a way that all the knowledge which is necessary to understand the information be explicitly and completely expressed in the description.

To understand the sentence "K731 works for D006," we must know that employees can be denoted by personnel numbers, that departments can be denoted by department numbers, and that "K731" is a personnel number and "D006" a department number. When we express this knowledge explicitly in the formulation of the sentence, the formulation turns out as follows:

"The employee with personnel number K731 works for the department with the department number D006."

Only now can this sentence be interpreted and understood in just one way by everybody who is confronted with it.

To interpret this sentence, no more implicit knowledge is assumed. Such a formulation of elementary sentences consequently fits the 100% principle.

If we take a closer look at the above formulation of our sentence, we see that "personnel number" is the **name** of the lexical object type (the LOT name) to which the lexical object "K731" belongs. "Employee" is the **name** of the non-lexical object type (the NOLOT name) to which the non-lexical object referred to by the lexical object "K731" belongs. Thus, the "department number" is the **name** of the lexical object type (the LOT name) to which the lexical object "D006" belongs. "Department" is the **name** of the non-lexical object type (the NOLOT name) to which the non-lexical object referred to by the lexical object "D006" belongs. We have represented this in Figure 5.4.

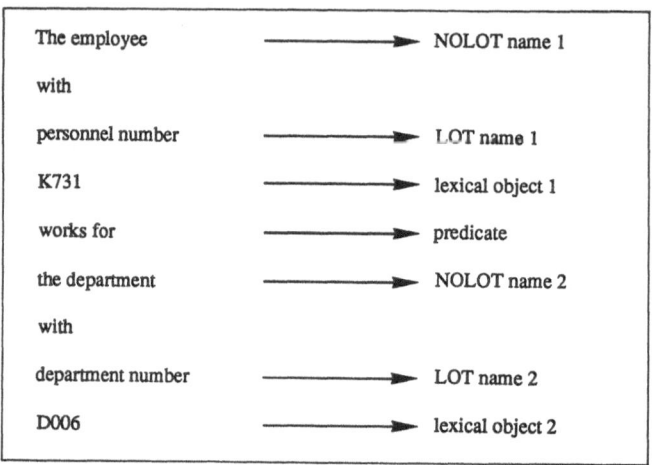

Figure 5.4.

When an elementary sentence is formulated in this way, the meaning of the sentence is expressed completely in the formulation itself. A sentence structure in which the meaning has been expressed completely is called a *deep structure* of a sentence. A sentence structure, such as that in Figure 5.3, in which the meaning of the sentence is not completely expressed and which only gives an association between lexical objects, is conversely called a *surface structure* of a sentence. From now on, we shall call *elementary* sentences which show the structure of Figure 5.4 *elementary deep structure sentences*.

We can represent this sentence structure in a structural formula as follows:

EDS = P($\langle$NOLOT name 1,LOT NAME 1,LO-1$\rangle$,$\langle$NOLOT name 2,LOT name 2,LO-2$\rangle$)

where EDS stands for elementary deep structure sentence. What is expressed in this formula is that an elementary deep structure sentence describes an association of which the predicate P is the name and in which the terms are an ordered triad, each of which consists of the name of a non-lexical object type, the name of a lexical object type, and a lexical object. Because elementary sentences can generally concern one, two, or more objects, the general structural formula for elementary deep structure sentences is as follows:

EDS = P(<NOLOT name 1,LOT name 1,LO-1>,...)

Figure 5.5.

It is necessary to include in the formulation of an elementary sentence the names of the lexical object types to which any lexical objects which appear in the sentence belong, in order to express the meaning of the sentence completely and explicitly. For example, the meaning of the sentence "Employee K731 works for department D006" (in which the names of the lexical object types are not expressed) is not absolutely one hundred percent clear if we do not know that K731 is a personnel number and D006 a department number. This point can be made clearer by the following example.

If we know that the products which are developed by a company can be denoted by means of an internal research number or an external commercial code (which for different products may coincidentally have the same value), the meaning of the sentence "The department whose name is Research and Development develops product X007" is not clear. We don't know, after all, which product is meant: the product with research number "X007" or another product which coincidentally bears the commercial code "X007." The meaning of this sentence is then only completely clear when we include the name of the lexical object type to which the lexical object "X007" belongs explicitly in the formulation: "The department with the department name Research and Development develops the product with **research number** X007."

Because elementary deep structure sentences, as descriptions of information, satisfy the demands which arise from the 100% principle as well as the conceptual principle, we shall assume from now on that information can be described by means of elementary deep structure sentences. Consequently, we shall refine the natural language principle as follows:

Information can always be described by means of elementary deep structure sentences in a natural language.

Not all of the sentence structures that are possible in a natural language satisfy the structural formula for elementary deep structure sentences. Elementary deep structure sentences therefore form a restricted and well-defined subset of all the possible sentence structures in a natural language. The NIAM method of information analysis is based on the assumption that information that has to be exchanged with an information system can always be described by means of elementary deep structure sentences.

To summarize:

Elementary deep structure sentence:
An elementary sentence which is formulated such that it completely and explicitly represents all the knowledge which is necessary to understand this sentence.

An elementary deep structure sentence is by definition constructed according to the following structural formula:

$$EDS = P(\langle NOLOT \text{ name } 1, LOT \text{ name } 1, LO\text{-}1 \rangle, ...)$$

EDS: elementary deep structure sentence
P: predicate
LO: lexical object

The natural language principle:

> Information can always be described by means of elementary deep structure sentences in a natural language.

In the following section, we shall see that elementary deep structure sentences can be divided into sets or classes of sentences which describe the same kind of information.

5.4 Elementary sentence types

In Figure 5.6, we have described Propositions P14, P15, and P16 from Figure 4.2 by means of elementary deep structure sentences.

P14: The employee with the last name Johnson works for the department with the department name Purchasing.
P15: The employee with the last name Peterson works for the department with the department name Purchasing.
P16: The employee with the last name King works for the department with the department name Personnel.

Figure 5.6.

What catches our attention is that all of these elementary deep structure sentences contain the predicate "works for," the NOLOT names "employee" and "department," and the LOT names "last name" and "department name." These three sentences are therefore concerned with the same non-lexical object types, the same lexical object types, and describe the same kind of associations between the objects of these types. In other words, these sentences describe the same kind of information. We shall call a set or class of elementary deep structure sentences which describe the same kind of information and are consequently of the same type an *elementary deep structure sentence type*, or an *elementary sentence type* for short.

The elementary deep structure sentences which at a certain moment belong to the same elementary sentence type form a *population* of that elementary sentence type.

To summarize:

Elementary sentence type:
A set or class of elementary deep structure sentences which describe the same kind of information.

Elementary sentence type population:
The elementary deep structure sentences which belong at a given moment to this elementary sentence type.

In the following section, we shall show that it is possible to have elementary deep structure sentences with different predicates, even though they describe the same kind of information and consequently belong to the same elementary sentence type.

5.5 Sentences of the same type with different predicates

In the following elementary deep structure sentences we have printed the predicates in bold to enhance the clarity:

"The employee with the last name Johnson **works for** the department with the department name Purchasing." (1)
"The employee with the last name Johnson **is employed by** the department with the department name Purchasing." (2)
The employee with the last name Johnson **is part of** the department with the department name Purchasing." (3)
The department with the department name Purchasing **employs** the employee with the last name Johnson." (4)
"The department with the department name Purchasing **gives work to** the employee with the last name Johnson." (5)

Because all of these elementary deep structure sentences contain different predicates, they are by definition different sentences. Still, all of these sentences describe exactly the same information, namely the fact that there is a certain association between the employee with the last name Johnson and the department with the department name Purchasing. The predicates of these sentences are different names for a same association. Because all of these sentences describe the same information (and thus the same kind of information), they all belong to the same elementary sentence type. It appears from this that elementary deep structure sentences which belong to a same elementary sentence type can have different predicates.

If we compare sentences 1, 2, and 3 with sentences 4 and 5, we see that the order in which the objects (the employee with the last name Johnson and the department with the department name Purchasing) occur in these sentences is different. It follows from this that the order of objects in elementary deep structure sentences which belong to a same elementary sentence type, and which thus describe the same kind of information, can be different. Two elementary deep structure sentences which describe the same information, but in which the order of the objects is different (such as, for example, sentences 3 and 4 above) always have different predicates.

5.6 Population tables

The information which is described by the elementary deep structure sentences of a same sentence type can be represented by means of a table, thanks to the fixed structure of these sentences. Such a table forms a "shortened notation" for the elementary deep structure sentences of a same sentence type. Figure 5.7 depicts what such a table could look like.

employee	department
last name	department name
works for	employs
Johnson	Purchasing
Peterson	Purchasing
King	Personnel

Figure 5.7.

This table represents the information which is described by the elementary deep structure sentences of Figure 5.6.

The "headings" are written above the double line in the table. These contain successively the names of the non-lexical object types, the names of the lexical object types, and two of the possible predicates of the elementary deep structure sentences of the sentence type under consideration. The entries in the table are found below the double line. The lexical objects which occur in the different sentences are listed on each line. These lexical objects are, of course, noted below the corresponding LOT names. The fact that the order of the objects in the individual sentences of this sentence type can differ is taken into account: every column lists one of the possible predicates of the elementary deep structure sentences, beginning with an object of the type belonging to the column. We can read these sentences directly from the table. Beginning with the left column, the first entry calls forth the sentence: "The employee with the last name Johnson **works for** the department with the department name Purchasing." And starting from the right column brings forth the sentence: "The department with the department name Purchasing **employs** the employee with the last name Johnson." As we have seen, both sentences describe the same information.

The headings describe the characteristics which all of the sentences of that particular elementary sentence type have in common. The entries describe the specific characteristics of the individual sentences of this sentence type. The headings reflect the **meaning** of the data described by the individual sentences of that particular sentence type. The entries reflect the **data** themselves.

A table like that of Figure 5.7 represents the population of an elementary sentence type and is therefore called a sentence population table, or a *population table* for short. In general, an elementary deep structure sentence can involve one, two, or more objects. Every population table contains as many columns as there are objects in the elementary deep structure sentences of that sentence type.

Naturally, only a few of the several possible predicates of the elementary deep structure sentences of the relevant sentence type can be noted in a population table. For example, in the left-hand column of the population table in Figure 5.7, the predicates "is working for" or "is part of" could have also been included, and the predicate "gives work to" could have been in the right-hand column.

A population **table** should not be confused with a population **diagram**, as was defined in the previous chapter (Section 4.6), exemplified by Figure 4.17:

- A population table is a representation in **table form** of an elementary sentence type and one of its possible populations.
- A population diagram is a **graphical** representation of a fact type and one of its possible populations.

Just as with population diagrams, every fact (every combination of objects) is only represented once in a population table.

Both population tables and population diagrams are important aids which can be used when putting the NIAM method of information analysis into practice.

The foremost concept from this section is:

Population table:
A representation in table form of an elementary sentence type and one of its possible populations.

In the next section, we will derive a general structural formula for elementary sentence **types**.

NOLOT name 1	. . .	. . .
LOT name 1	. . .	. . .
predicate 1	. . .	. . .
LO-1	. . .	. . .
. . .	. . .	. . .
. . .	. . .	. . .

Figure 5.8.

5.7 A general structural formula for elementary sentence types

As we have seen, an elementary sentence type describes equivalent associations between objects in a reality. These objects play a certain role in the associations. The columns of a population table of an elementary sentence type correspond to these roles. These columns are therefore called the *roles* of such sentence types. The predicates which are recorded in each of these columns are called the *role names* of the sentence type. The role names of an elementary sentence type are thus also the predicates of the elementary deep structure sentences which belong to this elementary sentence type. In Figure 5.9, we have adapted the general method of notation for a population table (Figure 5.8) to correspond to this arrangement.

NOLOT name 1	. . .	. . .
LOT name 1	. . .	. . .
role name 1	. . .	. . .
LO-1	. . .	. . .
. . .	. . .	. . .
. . .	. . .	. . .

Figure 5.9.

The predicates of elementary deep structure sentences should not be confused with the role names of elementary sentence types.

We talk about role names in connection with sentence types. Elementary sentences have predicates. The role names of an elementary sentence type are also the predicates of individual elementary sentences of this type. In one of the previous sections, we saw that the elementary deep structure sentences of one and the same sentence type generally have many different predicates. Because all of these predicates are also used as names for roles of the relevant sentence type, the elementary sentence type roles generally have many different names. Only a few of these possible role names are noted in the columns of a population table.

Elementary sentence types which are concerned with exactly two object types and which consequently consist of exactly two roles are called *binary sentence types*. In general, elementary sentence types can involve one, two or more object types. However, until Chapter 12, we will restrict ourselves to binary sentence types only.

When we consider a certain role in a **binary** sentence type, the other role is called the *co-role* of the sentence type. Therefore, in the elementary sentence type illustrated in Figure 5.7, the role "employs" is called the co-role of the role "works for," and the role "works for" is called the co-role of the role "employs."

We can now derive a general structural formula from the structure of the population table in Figure 5.9. This structural formula describes the characteristics of an elementary sentence type. By this we mean the characteristics which all elementary sentences of this type have in common. The general structural formula for elementary sentence **types** is given in Figure 5.10.

EST = (<NOLOT name 1,LOT name 1, role name 1>,...)

Figure 5.10.

In this formula, EST stands for "elementary sentence type."

What this structural formula expresses is that an elementary sentence type is a relation, in which the terms are an ordered triad, each of which consists of the name of a non-lexical object type, the name of a lexical object type, and a role name.

To summarize:

Elementary sentence type role:
A column in a population table of an elementary sentence type.

Binary sentence type:
An elementary sentence type that involves exactly two object types.

Co-role:
The other role in a binary sentence type.

The general method of notation in a population table is:

NOLOT name 1	• • •	• • •
LOT name 1	• • •	• • •
role name 1	• • •	• • •
lexical object 1	• • •	• • •
• • •	• • •	• • •
• • •	• • •	• • •

↑
role

The general structural formula for an elementary sentence type is:

EST = ($\langle$ NOLOT name 1,LOT name 1,role name 1 $\rangle$,...)

EST: elementary sentence type.

In the section below, we shall show that thanks to their fixed and unequivocal structure, elementary deep structure sentences can be represented graphically. To do this, we shall use the diagrams that we developed in the previous chapter to represent objects and facts.

5.8 A graphical representation for elementary deep structure sentences

In the last chapter, we took a look at what information is and how it is structured. We have shown that the structure of information can be represented by means of a graph, such as in Figure 4.20. In this chapter, we have shown that information can be described by means of elementary deep structure sentences. The population table of Figure 5.7 is a representation of three elementary deep structure sentences which belong to the same elementary sentence type. These three sentences describe the same information as those whose structure was depicted by Figure 4.20. Figure 5.11 combines the diagram of Figure 4.20 and the population table of Figure 5.7.

The diagram and the table describe precisely the same information. This information is, as we have seen, concerned with equivalent associations between two types of objects, namely an employee and a department. In these associations, the objects play a particular role. These roles are illustrated in the population table by the elementary sentence type roles (the columns of the population table), and in the graphical representation by the fact type roles connecting the object types "employee" and "department." The elementary sentences described by the population table are a description of the facts belonging to this fact type. Consequently, in Figure 5.11 we have assigned to these fact type roles the names of the corresponding elementary sentence type roles. As we have seen, these are two of the many possible names for the roles of the elementary sentence type.

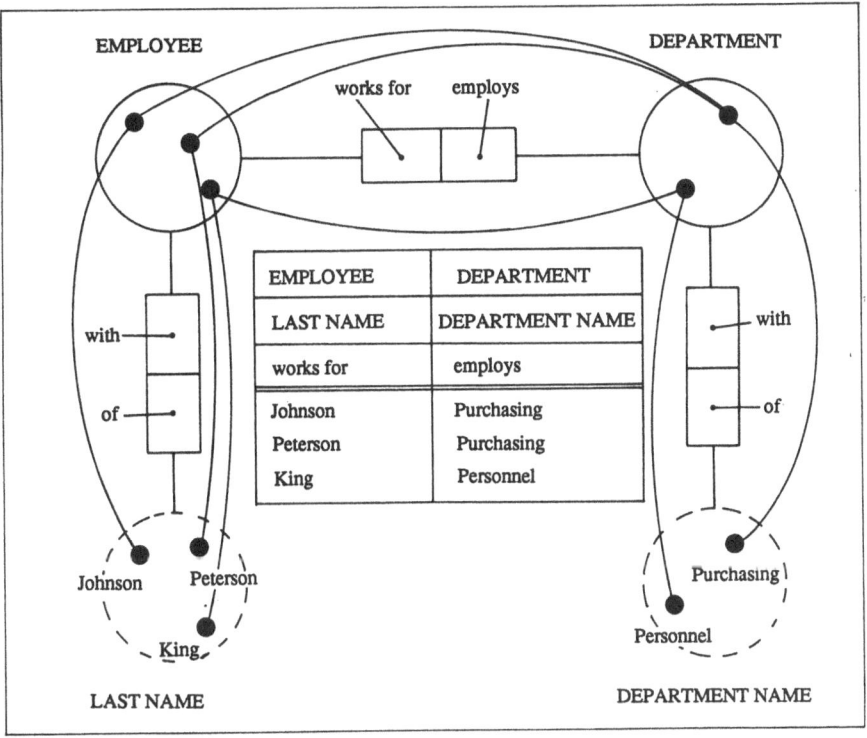

Figure 5.11.

We saw earlier that the knowledge that a lexical object is a name of or reference to a certain non-lexical object is in itself information or communicable knowledge as well. For that reason, we are going to take a look at the following two elementary sentences:

"There is an employee **with** the last name Johnson."
"Johnson is the last name **of** an employee."

Both sentences express the knowledge or information that the lexical object "Johnson" (belonging to the lexical object type "last name") denotes a non-lexical object of the type "employee." The same information is represented in Figure 5.11 by means of the bridge connecting the lexical object "Johnson" to the non-lexical object of the type "employee." The above two elementary sentences describe exactly the same information. Both sentences therefore belong to the same elementary sentence type. The predicates "with" and "of" in these elementary sentences are two of the possible names for the roles of this sentence type. These roles are depicted graphically in Figure 5.11 by the bridge type roles connecting the non-lexical object type "employee" with the lexical object type "last name." Just as we did for the idea type roles, in Figure 5.11 we have assigned to these bridge type roles the names of the corresponding elementary sentence type roles.

The population table and the graphical representation in Figure 5.11 describe the same information. By adding the role names, the graphical representation has become a direct representation of the elementary deep structure sentences described by the population table.

This can be explained best with the aid of Figure 5.12.

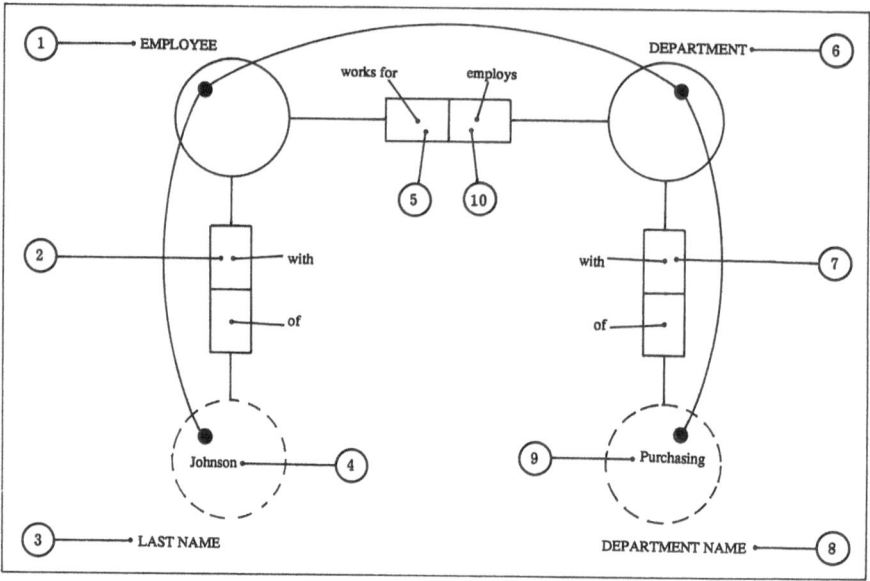

Figure 5.12.

The elements from which this diagram is built are: non-lexical object types, lexical object types, lexical and non-lexical objects, and fact type roles. The non-lexical object types are designated by NOLOT names, the lexical object types by LOT names, and the idea and bridge type roles by role names. The role names of an elementary sentence type are also predicates of elementary deep structure sentences of this type. NOLOT names, LOT names, predicates, and lexical objects are the building blocks - the language elements - from which elementary deep structure sentences are built, as we have shown by means of the general structural formula for elementary deep structure sentences (Figure 5.5). Elementary deep structure sentences and diagrams such as those of Figure 5.12 contain building blocks having the same names. In the diagram of Figure 5.12, these building blocks are numbered. We can immediately read the following two elementary deep structure sentences from this diagram:

1 The employee	(NOLOT name)
2 with	(role name or predicate)
3 the last name	(LOT name)
4 Johnson	(lexical object)

5	works for	(role name or predicate)
6	the department	(NOLOT name)
7	with	(role name or predicate)
8	the department name	(LOT name)
9	Purchasing	(lexical object)

and:

6	The department	(NOLOT name)
7	with	(role name or predicate)
8	the department name	(LOT name)
9	Purchasing	(lexical object)
10	employs	(role name or predicate)
1	the employee	(NOLOT name)
2	with	(role name or predicate)
3	the last name	(LOT name)
4	Johnson	(lexical object)

The diagram of Figure 5.12 is therefore a direct representation of these elementary deep structure sentences. It is an even more exact representation of these deep structure sentences than the population table because the bridge types in the diagram are expressed explicitly, the bridge type roles are designated explicitly, and the diagram represents the structure of the information described more explicitly and in more detail than does the population table. From now on, we shall therefore describe information by such diagrams.

5.9 A graphical representation for elementary sentence types

The diagram of Figure 5.12 graphically represents the elementary deep structure sentences which belong to a same elementary sentence type. When we omit the individual objects from this diagram, this elementary sentence **type** is represented graphically, as in Figure 5.13.

This diagram is built up of non-lexical object types, lexical object types, and fact type roles. The non-lexical object types are designated by NOLOT names, the lexical object types by LOT names, and the roles by role names. NOLOT names, LOT names, and role names are also the building blocks - the language elements - out of which elementary sentence types are built, as we have shown by means of the structural formula for elementary sentence types (Figure 5.10). Thus, elementary sentence types and diagrams such as those in Figure 5.13 contain building blocks with the same names. These kinds of diagrams are therefore direct representations of elementary sentence types. Such diagrams represent not only idea types but also bridge types, and the structure of the sentence types is more explicitly represented than in population tables. Henceforth, we shall describe elementary sentence types by means of this kind of diagram.

In the previous chapter (Figure 4.24), we have seen that information is built up from facts and rules which are valid for these facts. These rules consist of:

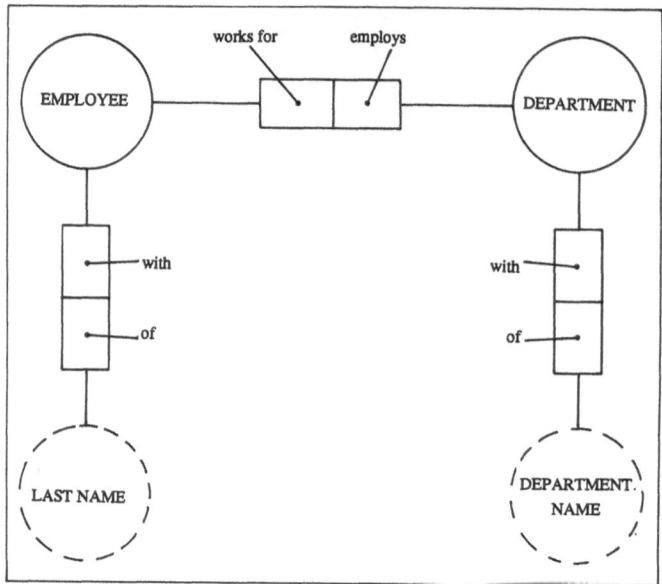

Figure 5.13.

- the specifications of the object types to which the objects must belong and
  to which the facts are related,
- the specifications of the fact types to which the facts themselves must belong,
  and
- the specifications of the constraints.

It appears from the structural formula for elementary sentence types (Figure
5.10) that elementary sentence types are determined by:

- the names of the object types to which the objects involving the elementary
  sentences of the relevant type should belong, and
- the role names (also the predicates of the individual elementary sentences of
  the relevant type).

The roles of the elementary sentence types describe the fact type roles.
Therefore, object types and fact types are described by elementary sentence
types. Elementary sentence types are consequently a description of all the rules,
with the exception of the constraints.

We are now at the point where we can deal in the next section with how the
grammar of an information system can be specified.

5.10 Describing the grammar of an information system

We saw earlier that the information base contains a description of the facts from which the information stored in the information system is built up. The grammar contains a description of the rules which hold for these facts. The rules describe which facts (which information) can be exchanged with the information system and what they mean.

It follows from the natural language principle that facts can be described by elementary deep structure sentences and that the rules holding for these facts with the exception of the constraints can be described by elementary sentence types. Based on the natural language principle, our starting points are:

– the information base of an information system can be described by means of elementary deep structure sentences.
– the grammar of an information system, with the exception of the constraints, can be described by the specifications of the elementary sentence types to which these elementary deep structure sentences must belong.

A description of the constraints needs to be added to the description of the grammar of an information system by elementary sentence types. We will get back to this in Section 5.14.

We saw in the previous section that a diagram, such as the one in Figure 5.13, is a graphical representation of an elementary sentence type. It follows from this that we can describe the grammar of an information system (excepting the constraints) by means of these kinds of diagrams. From now on, we shall call such diagrams *information structure diagrams*. "Information structure diagram" is sometimes abbreviated to "ISD."

In this section, we have further refined the definition of the grammar of an information system as follows:

Grammar:
A specification of:

– the elementary sentence types to which the elementary deep structure sentences describing the contents of the information base must belong.
– the constraints.

Information structure diagram (ISD):
A graphical representation of elementary sentence types and thus of part of the grammar of an information system. Together, the information structure diagram and the specifications of the constraints describe the grammar of an information system.

In the following section, we shall take a closer look at the information structure diagram.

5.11 The information structure diagram

In Section 5.3 of this chapter, we supposed that the library employees could be denoted not only by their last names, but by personnel numbers as well. In Figure 5.14, we have extended the information structure diagram of Figure 5.13 to include this aspect. We have added to it the lexical object type "personnel number" and a bridge type which connects this lexical object type to the non-lexical object type "employee."

In an information structure diagram, the object type names and the role names are given in or next to the symbols for the object types and the roles. One of the possible role names is given for every role. The name of a role of an object type is always one of the predicates of the elementary sentences which begin with an object of this object type and which belong to the elementary sentence type that describes the fact type belonging to this role. We shall call this the "role name rule."

In the information structure diagram of Figure 5.14, the roles of the bridge types all have the name "with" or "of." In practice, different roles may have the same

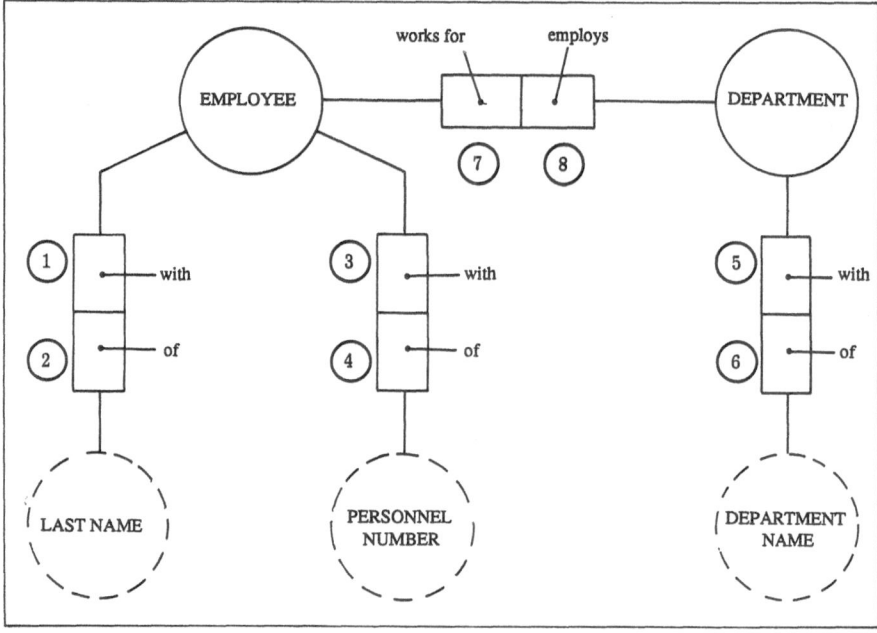

Figure 5.14.

name. To indicate a role uniquely, we shall, for fact types consisting of two roles (binary fact types), agree to the following rule:

A role of a binary fact type can be uniquely denoted (identified) by combining the name of the object type of that role, the role name itself, and the name of the object type of the other role (the co-role) of that fact type.

We shall call this rule the "role identification rule." Bear in mind that this rule only holds for roles of **binary** fact types.

In Figure 5.14, we have numbered the fact type roles. These roles are uniquely denoted, on the basis of the role identification rule, by the following expressions:

1 Employee with last name
2 Last name of employee
3 Employee with personnel number
4 Personnel number of employee
5 Department with department name
6 Department name of department
7 Employee works for department
8 Department employs employee

This method of unique denotation of roles fits with what we are used to in natural languages. In an information structure diagram, different roles, in which the combinations of the names of the object type of these roles, the role names themselves, and the names of the object types of the co-roles are equal, may not occur.

In practice, many bridge type roles have the fairly meaningless names "with" and "of." Because these "standard names" occur often, we shall hereafter adopt the following simplifying rule:

If no role name is listed by a bridge type, we will assume that the role of the non-lexical object type has the name "with," and that the role of the lexical object type has the name "of."

Only those names of bridge type roles which deviate from these names must be explicitly listed in the information structure diagram. The names of the **idea** type roles must always be explicitly listed.

For convenience, we shall remember this as the "with/of rule."

Below is a summary of the rules for information structure diagrams dealt with in this section.

The role name rule:
The name of a role of an object type is one of the predicates of the elementary sentences which begin with an object of this object type and which belong to the

elementary sentence type that describes the fact type belonging to that role.

The role identification rule:
A role of a binary fact type is uniquely denoted by combining the name of the object type of that role, the role name itself, and the name of the object type of the other role (the co-role) of that fact type.

The with/of rule:
If no role name is listed by a bridge type, it is assumed that the role of the non-lexical object type has the standard name "with," and that the role of the lexical object type has the standard name "of."

In the following two sections, we shall show that on the basis of the role identification rule, there are expressions closely resembling natural language which can refer to roles, role populations, and their subsets. This is so because role names are also predicates of sentences in a natural language. The expressions by which we will refer to role populations and their subsets are based on elementary deep structure sentences, and are therefore well-defined subsets of a normal natural language. We shall show that the expressions of this "reference language" are crucial for specifying constraints when putting the NIAM method of information analysis into practice.

One of the characteristics of the NIAM method of information analysis is that the expressions for referring to roles and role populations and for specifying constraints are very close to natural language, so that they can also be formulated and understood by persons who are not information system specialists. In the upcoming chapters, we shall see that the NIAM method of information analysis begins by describing information by means of natural language, then "transforms" this description into elementary deep structure sentences, and finally derives an information structure diagram from it.

5.12 References to roles and role populations

The role identification rule treated in the previous section states that for every role in an information structure diagram the combination of the names of the object type of that role, of the role itself, and of the object type of its co-role must be unique. From now on, we shall call such a combination of object type names and of a role name which refers in a unique way to a certain role, a *reference* to that role. Because role names are also predicates of elementary sentences, references to roles are, in general, more or less readable expressions. Thus the expression "employee works for department" is, for example, a reference to the role of the object type "employee" in the fact type which connects this object type with the object type "department."

In a reference to a role, the name of the object type of that role is always found to the left of the role name, and the name of the object type of its co-role to the right.

We saw earlier that a role can have different names. The role to which the above expression refers could have not only the name "works for," but also, for example, the names "is working for," "is part of," or "working for." Thus, the slightly more readable expression "employee working for department" refers to the same role of the object type "employee" as the former expression.

Part of the contents of the information base in our example can be represented with the aid of the population diagram of Figure 5.15.

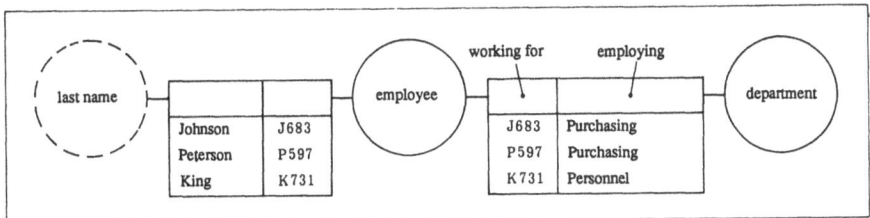

Figure 5.15.

In this population diagram, we have depicted the employees by their (unique) personnel numbers and the departments by their (unique) department names, in order to eliminate ambiguity.

We shall now assume that a reference to a role refers not only to the role itself, but also to its population. Thus, the expression "employee working for department" refers to one of the roles of the information structure diagram of Figure 5.14 and at the same time to the population of this role. In the population diagram of Figure 5.15, this population consists of the employees with personnel numbers J863, P597, and K731.

To improve the readability of references to roles and to bring them somewhat closer to natural language, it is permitted to add "fillers," such as "the," "that," "which," "a," "an," "is," "are," "all," etc. Furthermore, plurals may also be used for the object names.

Therefore, the reference:

"employee working for department" (1)

is equal to:

"the *employees working for* a *department."*

or to:

"employees working for departments."

When the fillers and plurals are omitted, a valid reference to a role has to be left over. A valid reference to a role consists, as we have seen, of the name of the object type, the name of this object type's role, and the name of the object type of its co-role. An automated system which "is familiar with" an information structure diagram could interpret the above expressions by skipping over the fillers and plurals, so that only object type names and role names are left behind.

Henceforth, for the sake of clarity, we shall print in bold the object type names and role names in all of the references to roles. This allows us to "follow" these expressions in the information structure diagram.

The following expression refers to the role "of" of the object type "last name," and thus to the last names of all the employees about which something is known at a given moment in the information base:

"last name of employee." (2)

A reference to a role or to its population can consist of a combination of more than one object type name and role name. Therefore, the following expression refers to the last names of all the employees who are known to work for a department (it does not have to be known for all of the employees whose last names are known whether they also work for a department):

"last name of employees working for a department." (3)

This expression was formed by connecting the above expressions (2) and (1) with each other via the object type "employee." The object type occurs in expression (1) as well as in expression (2). In these kinds of "compound" sentences as well, there is to the left of every role name the name of the object type of this role and to the right the name of the object type of its co-role. When we "follow" this reference in the information structure diagram of Figure 5.14, we see that it determines a "path" or "route" through the diagram. A reference to a role or to a role population generally consists of an array of object type names and role names, in which every role name is preceded by the name of the object type of that role and followed by the name of the object type of its co-role.

If we allow the word "not" to precede the role name when we are referring to a role, the result is a reference to the objects which do not occur in the population of that role, but do occur in the population of another role of this object type. Thus, the expression *"employees not working for a department"* refers to all the employees who do not occur in the population of the role "working for" of the object type "employee," but do occur in the population of another role of this object type. In this example, therefore, that would be all the employees whose last name or personnel number is known, but of whom it is not known whether they work for a department. In the population of Figure 5.15 there are no employees who satisfy this reference.

We repeat below the definition of a reference to a role:

A reference to a role:
An array of object type names and role names, where the name of the object type of the role appears to the left of each role name and the name of the object type of its co-role appears to the right of the role name. A reference to a role determines a connected path of object types and fact types in the information structure diagram and refers to a role and its population. "Fillers" can be added to references to a role when this is thought desirable, and plurals can be used.

In the next section we shall derive expressions which refer to subsets or combinations of role populations. We shall handle these expressions in an intuitive manner on the basis of concrete examples, rather than on the basis of strict rules.

5.13 References to subsets and combinations of role populations

A subset of the population of a role can be referred to by adding a restrictive condition to the reference to this role. Therefore, the following expression refers to the employees who work for the Purchasing Department:

"the *employees working for* the *department with department name* = Purchasing."

This reference has been created by adding the restrictive condition " = Purchasing" to the expression:

"the *employees working for* a *department with* a *department name*"

(all employees who work for a department whose department name is known). Only those employees who work for a department whose department name is equal to the lexical object (the "value") "Purchasing" satisfy this expression. In the population table of Figure 5.15, the employees with the personnel numbers J683 and P597 satisfy this expression. The restrictive condition is added to the reference **after the name of a lexical object type**. The " = " sign can be left out if this is easier and if it improves the readability. The above expression is thus equivalent to:

"the *employees working for* the *department with department name* Purchasing."

In the restrictive conditions that are added to references to roles, we can make use of not only the sign " = " (equal to), but also the signs " > " (greater than), " < " (smaller than), " ≥ " (greater than or equal to), " ≤ " (smaller than or equal to), and " ≠ " (not equal to). These mathematical signs are used to compare lexical objects (values) with each other. As they are only related to **lexical objects**, they must always be placed immediately after the name of the lexical object type concerned. The " = " sign is the only one which may be left out.

The expression

"the *employees working for* the *departments with department name* ≠ Personnel"

refers to the employees who do not work for the Personnel Department (but for another department). In the population depicted in Figure 5.15, these are the employees with the personnel numbers J683 and P597.

The expression

"the *employees with personnel number* > J683"

refers to employees whose personnel numbers are greater than J683 (irrespective of whether this would be meaningful in practice). "Greater than" must be interpreted in this case according to the so-called lexicographical ordering. This is the ordering or arrangement of combinations of alphabetical and numerical symbols on the basis of a mutual ordering of letters, numbers, and other symbols, such as that used in telephone books or dictionaries, for example.

Instead of the symbols ">," "<," "⩾," "⩽," "=," and "≠," the following descriptions may be used respectively to enhance the readability: "greater than," "smaller than," "greater than or equal to," "smaller than or equal to," "equal to," and "not equal to."

The expression

"the *employees working for* the *departments with department name* ≠ Personnel"

is therefore equivalent to

"the *employees working for* the *departments with department name not equal to* Personnel."

And likewise the expression

"the *employees with personnel number* > J683"

is equivalent to

"the *employees with personnel number greater than* J683."

When there is only one bridge type for a non-lexical object type, the name of the role of the non-lexical object type and the name of the lexical object type of this bridge type can be omitted in expressions using the equal sign (" = "). Because the non-lexical object type "department" has only one bridge type, the expression:

"the *employees working for* the *department with department name* Purchasing"

is equivalent to:

"the *employees working for* the *department* Purchasing."

This expression has been created by omitting the role name "with" and the name of the lexical object type "department name" in the first expression. Because there is only one bridge type that belongs to the non-lexical object type "department," it is clear that the elements of the role population of the lexical object type of this bridge type (namely, the lexical object type "department name") must be compared with the value "Purchasing."

We remind you that this rule only holds for expressions having the equal sign ("="). This rule is not valid for the remaining signs (">," "<," "⩾," "⩽," and "≠").

The restrictive conditions can be combined by means of "and" and "or." The following expression refers to all employees who work for the Purchasing or the Personnel Department:

"*employees working for* the *department with department name* = Purchasing *or with department name* = Personnel."

It is not necessary in these kinds of expressions to repeat such references as "with department," so that the above expression can also be given as:

"*employees working for* the *department with department name* = Purchasing *or* = Personnel."

The equal sign " = " can also be omitted, as we have seen earlier. The above expression is therefore equivalent to:

"*employees working for* the *department with department name* Purchasing *or* Personnel."

And as there is only one bridge type for the non-lexical object type "department," the role name of the non-lexical object type and the name of the lexical object type of this bridge type may also be omitted:

"*employees working for* the *department* Purchasing *or* Personnel."

In the population of Figure 5.15, the employees with the personnel numbers J683, P597, and K731 satisfy this expression.

The following expressions, equivalent to one another, refer to the employees who work for the Purchasing Department as well as for the Personnel Department:

"employees working for the *department with department name* = Purchasing *and with department name* = Personnel."

"employees working for the *department with department name* = Purchasing *and* = Personnel."

"employees working for the *department with department name* Purchasing *and* Personnel."

"employees working for the *department* Purchasing *and* Personnel."

In the population of Figure 5.15, none of the employees satisfies these expressions. The expression

"employees with personnel number greater than J000 *and smaller than* P999"

refers to all employees whose personnel number lies between the numbers J000 and P999 according to the lexicographical ordering. All employees in the population of Figure 5.15 satisfy this expression.

By using "and" and "or" to combine references to roles, one can refer to objects which simultaneously occur in the populations of more than one role, or in the populations of some of the roles. Some examples of this follow below.

The expression:

"employees working for a *department and with* a *last name"*

refers to all employees who work for a department and whose last names are known in the information base. All the employees in the population diagram of Figure 5.15 satisfy this expression.

The expression:

"the *employees working for* a *department and with last name* Johnson"

refers to the employees about whom it is known that they work for a department and whose last name is "Johnson." In the population of Figure 5.15, only one employee, J683, satisfies this expression.

The expression:

"employees with last name Johnson *and working for* the *department* Personnel"

refers to the employees with the last name Johnson who also work for Personnel. None of the employees in the population diagram of Figure 5.15 satisfies this expression.

Naturally restrictive conditions can be added as well to "compound" references, such as, for example, expression (3) in the previous section ("last name of employees working for a department").

Therefore, the expression:

"last name of employees working for the *department* Purchasing"

refers to the last names of the employees who work for the Purchasing Department. In the population of Figure 5.15, these are the last names "Johnson" and "Peterson."

The combination or union of the populations of **all** the roles of a certain object type are referred to by an expression which consists only of the name of that object type. Thus, the expression *"employee"* or (should the filler "all" be added) "all *employees*" refers to the union of the populations of all the roles of the object type "employee." This means all the employees about whom something is known at that particular moment in the information base.

Below is a short summary of the "rules" for references to subsets and combinations of role populations. These rules are not formal and exhaustive, but are intuitive and sufficient for the NIAM method of information analysis in practice.

A subset of a role can be referred to by adding a restrictive condition to the reference to that role **directly after the name of a lexical object type**. The restrictive condition consists of a mathematical sign and a lexical object (a "value") to which the objects of the lexical object type concerned must be compared.

The following mathematical signs are allowed:

= or "equal to"
> or "greater than"
< or "smaller than"
⩾ or "greater than or equal to"
⩽ or "smaller than or equal to"
≠ or "not equal to"

The " = " may be left out, if so desired.

When a non-lexical object type has only one bridge type, the name of the role of the non-lexical object type of this bridge type and the name of the lexical object type can be omitted in expressions using the equal signs (" = ").

In a reference to a role, several restrictive conditions can be combined by means of "and" and "or."

References to roles can be combined by means of "and" and "or." This creates expressions which refer to the union or to the intersection of several role populations.

A reference which consists only of the name of an object type refers to the union of the populations of all roles of this object type.

5.14 Graphical and non-graphical constraints

We have seen that on the basis of the natural language principle, the contents of the information base of an information system can be described by means of elementary deep structure sentences in a natural language, and that the grammar, with the exception of the constraints, can be described by specifying the elementary sentence types to which these elementary deep structure sentences must belong. Elementary sentence types, and thus part of the grammar, can be graphically represented by means of an information structure diagram. The information structure diagram describes the object types and the fact types to which the facts (information) exchanged with the information system must belong. A description of the grammar in the form of an information structure diagram, however, needs to have a specification of the constraints added to it.

Constraints restrict the populations of the fact type roles which are allowed on the basis of the information structure diagram. Constraints are thus always concerned with fact type **roles**, and can consequently be specified with the aid of references to roles. For example, rule P17 in Figure 4.2 (a department may not contain more than 10 employees) can be formally described as follows:

for every department d *holds: number employees working for* d ⩽ 10.

This must be read as: for every department, say d, it holds that the number of employees that work for d may be maximally equal to 10.

For the most frequently occurring kinds of constraints, a graphical symbol by which these constraints can be represented directly in the information structure diagram, has been defined. An example is rule P4 from Figure 4.2 (an employee may only work for one department). This rule restricts the population of the role "working for" in the information structure diagram of Figure 5.14. After all, in a population of this role, an employee may not appear two or more times with different departments. These kinds of constraints are graphically represented by placing the symbol "↔" next to that role, as has been done in Figure 5.16:

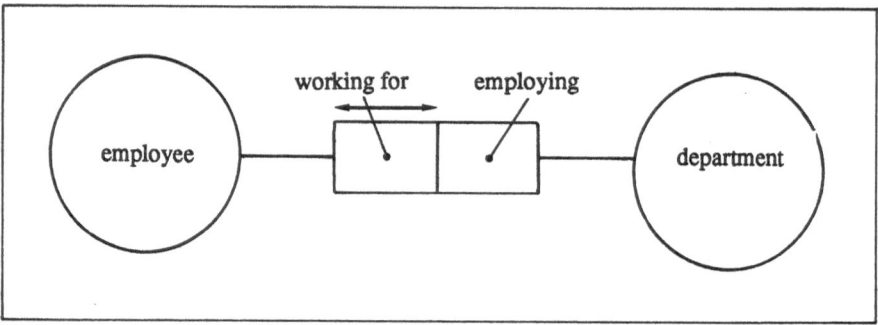

Figure 5.16.

Because constraints constitute restrictions on role populations, the graphical symbols representing constraints always involve **roles**.

The constraints which can be represented by graphical symbols in the information structure diagram are called *graphical constraints*. Those which cannot be so represented are called *non-graphical constraints*.

Graphical constraints are represented in an information structure diagram, and thus belong to this diagram. Non-graphical constraints must be described separately. The grammar is described by the information structure diagram **and** the specifications of all the non-graphical constraints.

The specification of the necessary constraints constitutes one of the most essential parts of the NIAM method of information analysis. This is because the constraints, together with the definition of the necessary fact types and object types, determine the meaning of the data which is exchanged with the information system. The remainder of this book will consequently deal mainly with the specification of constraints.

5.15 The operation of an information system

We developed a general model for information systems in Chapter 2. We have now reached the point where we can describe how, based on this model, the communication between the users and the information system takes place. The model for information systems dealt with in Chapter 2 indicates, in line with the conceptual principle, only what an information system is supposed to do, without going into the technical realization aspects of this. In the same way, in this section we will only point out how the information system should behave to the outside world, without indicating how certain things should technically be realized. One of the starting points of the NIAM method of information analysis is the model for information systems and the description of its operation. In the process of information analysis, we will assume that every information system behaves as was described in Chapter 2 and worked out in more detail in this section.

We have depicted the general model for information systems once again in Figure 5.17.

The users address their requests for changes in the information base or questions regarding the information base or the grammar to the information processor. The information processor executes these requests and answers these questions. A request to change the information base is only executed if the resulting new state of the information base and the transition from the old to the new state are allowed by the rules of the grammar. In this way, the information processor guarantees that the information exchange between the users and the information system satisfies the rules of the grammar at every moment.

Because we assumed that the information which is exchanged between the users and the information system can be described by means of **elementary** deep structure sentences, it is sufficient to suppose that the users can address only two kinds of requests for change to the information processor:

- requests to add the information which is described by one elementary deep structure sentence to the information base.
- requests to delete the information which is described by one elementary deep structure sentence from the information base.

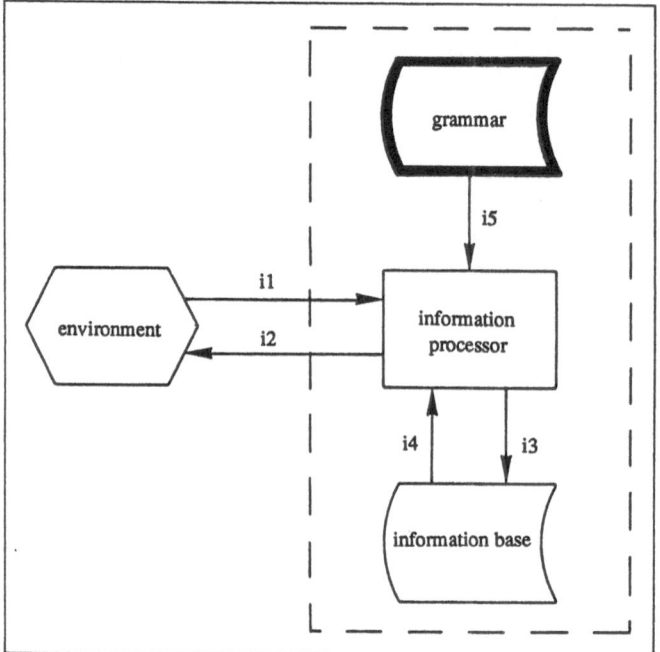

Figure 5.17.

A request to update the information which is described by one elementary deep structure sentence always consists of a request to delete this information and then to add it again in an altered form.

We shall describe a request to add information to the information base by the verb *"add"*, followed by an elementary deep structure sentence which describes the information to be added.

We shall describe a request to delete information from the information base by the verb *"delete"*, followed by an elementary deep structure sentence which describes the information to be deleted.

The elementary deep structure sentences which reflect the information to be added or deleted have to belong to those elementary sentence types which are described by the grammar, and thus also by the information structure diagram.

We will illustrate the interaction between the users and the information system by means of a few examples.

Let us assume that the grammar is partially described by the information structure diagram of Figure 5.14, and that at a given point in time the information base is "empty," that is, it contains no information.

A request to add to the information base the fact that the employee with the personnel number J683 has the last name Johnson is then described as follows:

    add: the *employee with personnel number* J638 *with last name* Johnson.

The elementary deep structure sentence which describes the information which is to be added to the information base is located after the verb "add." This elementary deep structure sentence has to belong to one of the elementary sentence types which are defined in the grammar (and thus also in the information structure diagram), and is therefore expressed by means of the object type names and the role names of these elementary sentence types.

The information processor now verifies:

- whether this elementary sentence belongs to one of the elementary sentence types which are defined in the grammar.
- whether the new state resulting from this change in the information base is allowed according to the rules of the grammar (in other words, whether any state constraints have been violated by the change).
- whether the transition from the old to the new state in the information base is allowed according to the rules of the grammar (in other words, whether any transition rules have been violated by the change).

Because no rules of the grammar are violated in this case, the information processor reports back to the users:

request executed

signaling in this way that the request has been executed and that the new state has been realized in the information base.

The new information base state can be represented by means of the population diagram of Figure 5.18.

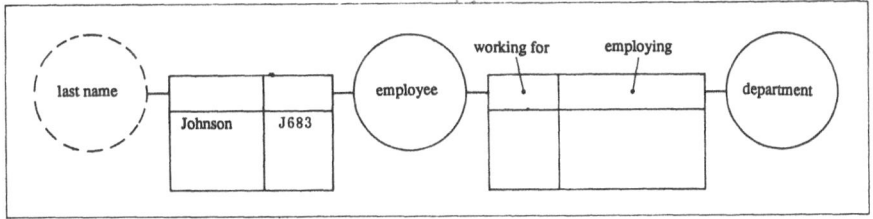

Figure 5.18.

The request to add the fact that there is a department with the department name Personnel is described as follows:

add: the ***department with the department name*** Personnel.

Because no rules of the grammar are violated, the information processor responds again with:

request executed.

The request to add the fact that employee J683 works for Personnel and the information processor's response are described as follows:

add: the **employee with personnel number** J683 **working for** the **department** Personnel

request executed.

The new information base state resulting from this is depicted in Figure 5.19.

We see that the interactions between the users and the information system are described by means of the expressions which refer to populations and subsets of role populations, which we have dealt with in Sections 5.12 and 5.13 of this chapter.

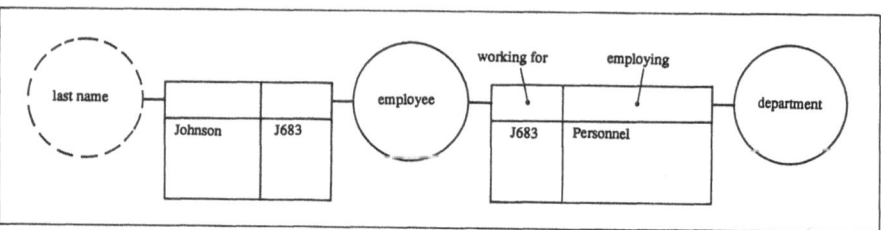

Figure 5.19.

Let us next suppose that a user adds the fact that there is a Purchasing Department to the information base:

add: the **department with department name** Purchasing

the information processor responds again with:

request executed.

If a user were then to address the following request to the information processor:

add: the **employee with personnel number** J683 **working for** the **department** Purchasing

in the resulting information base state, employee J683 would work for two departments, namely Personnel and Purchasing. This is in conflict with rule P4 of Figure 4.2 (an employee may only work for one department). In this case, the information processor responds as follows:

Request not executed because of violation of rule P4 (an employee may only work for one department).

In this way, the information processor tells that the request has not been executed and gives the reason why it has not.

When the user concludes that employee J683 ought to work for Purchasing rather than for Personnel, he first has to delete the fact that employee J683 works for Personnel from the information base:

delete: the *employee with personnel number* J683 *working for* the *department* Personnel
request executed

and then has to add the fact that this employee works for Purchasing:

add: the *employee with personnel number* J683 *working for* the *department* Purchasing
request executed.

These two requests result in the new information base state illustrated in Figure 5.20.

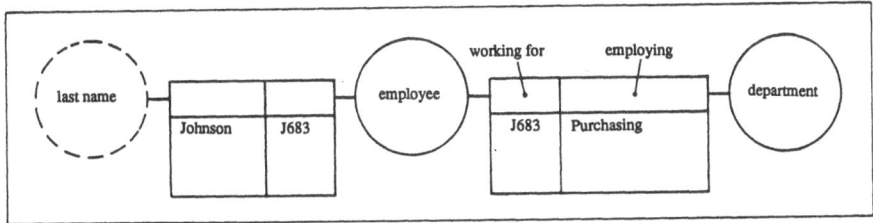

Figure 5.20.

The users can, if they wish, add **multiple facts** to the information base or delete them in one single request. For example, the user can combine the previous two requests for change into one single request:

begin
add: the *employee with personnel number* J683 *working for* the *department* Purchasing
delete: the *employee with personnel number* J683 *working for* the *department* Personnel
end.

From now on, we shall call a request to add or delete one single fact to or from the infomation base an *elementary request*. A request to add or delete more than one fact to or from the information base will henceforth be called a *non-elementary*, or *compound*, *request*. A compound request always consists of a number of elementary requests. We shall describe a compound request by preceding the first elementary request by "begin" and following the last elementary request by "end."

We shall assume that the information processor first executes each of the individual requests in a compound request and then verifies whether the new information base state and the resulting transition from the old to the new state satisfy the rules of the grammar. It is possible that one or more of the individual requests bring the information base to a state or cause a state transition that does not meet the rules of the grammar, while the final result of executing all of the individual requests is in agreement with the rules of the grammar. The information processor verifies these rules only after all the individual requests of a compound request have been executed. The information processor thus only checks the final result of a compound request, and never the interim result.

When the final result of a compound request does not satisfy one of the rules of the grammar, the information processor annuls it and restores the information base state which was valid just before the compound request was executed. It also reports to the users that the request was not executed and gives the reason why this was not done.

After having executed the first elementary request in the above compound request (add: the employee with personnel number J683 working for the department Purchasing), the information base is in a state which conflicts with one of the rules of the grammar. Employee J683 now works for two departments, Personnel and Purchasing. This state, however, is immediately rectified by the second elementary request (delete: the employee with personnel number J683 working for the department Personnel), so that the final result of the compound request agrees with the rules of the grammar. The information processor then responds to this compound request with:

request executed.

In subsequent chapters, we shall see that in many cases it is not possible to alter the information base state in agreement with the rules of the grammar without combining at least a few of the requests for change into a compound request.

Let us assume that, after a number of requests for change, the information base has reached the state described by the population diagram of Figure 5.21.

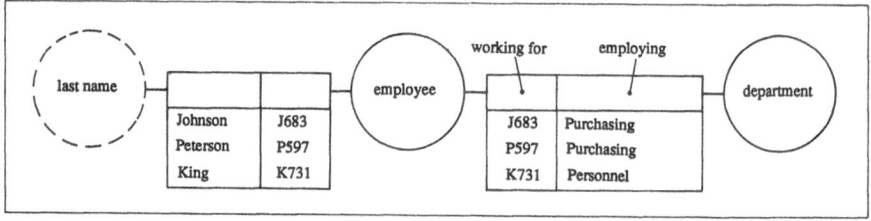

Figure 5.21.

The users can ask the information processor any questions regarding the information base by referring directly to the role populations of the sentence types involved.

If a user wishes, for example, to know the last names of all the employees who work for a department, the following question must be addressed to the information processor:

Last name of employees working for a department?

or, after having added a few "fillers":

Give me the *last name of* every *employee working for* a *department.*

The information processor then answers:

Johnson, Peterson, King.

The following question yields the personnel numbers of all the employees about whom something is known in the information base:

Personnel numbers of all employees?

The answer to this is:

J683,P597,K731.

The expressions used to pose questions to the information processor must, of course, be valid references to role populations. That is, they must, except for any possible "fillers," exclusively contain object type names and role names which are defined in the grammar. The information processor can then "look up" in the grammar exactly what information is being requested.

Every question must always result in lexical objects, because (by definition) only lexical objects can be physically represented and can therefore be passed on to the users by means of messages. Thus, for example, the question: *"Employees working for a department?"* is invalid, because the information processor can only communicate by means of lexical objects, in this case personnel numbers or last names, which employees satisfy the reference. In this case, the information processor does not "know" whether the answer to this question should consist of personnel numbers or of last names.

The above question must, for example, be formulated as follows:

Personnel numbers of employees working for a department?

The expressions used by the users to pose questions to the information processor must therefore always refer to roles of **lexical object types**.

In this section, we have defined the concepts "elementary request" and "compound request."

Elementary request:

A request from the users to the information processor to add or delete one single fact to or from the information base.

Compound request:

A request from the users to the information processor to add or delete more than one fact to or from the information base. A compound request consists of two or more elementary requests. The information processor first executes these elementary requests and then verifies whether the resulting state transition and new information base state are in agreement with the rules of the grammar.

6 THE NIAM METHOD OF INFORMATION ANALYSIS IN PRACTICE - 1

This is the first of a number of practically oriented chapters in which, after one or more chapters on theory, we shall keep coming back to the practice of the NIAM method of information analysis. Little by little, we will construct a stepwise plan that can be used as a "cookbook" or checklist for applying NIAM.

The practically oriented chapters are more informal in nature than the theoretical chapters. The rules formulated in these chapters are practical rules. That is, they have the character of general practical advice, rather than of formal rules.

As we already stated in Chapter 3, our starting point in the NIAM method of information analysis is a model (usually graphical), in which the information which is to be exchanged with the information system is represented in the form of information flows. Several of this model's information flows describe the information exchange with the information system or parts of it; these flows always begin or end in the information system or part (a function) of it. When applying the NIAM method of information analysis, the grammar of the information system is built up in a stepwise fashion by determining and describing the allowable information contents of each of these information flows.

This is done by successively analyzing the information contents of one or more information flows. The fixed analysis steps in this process will come up for discussion in the practically oriented chapters. Every execution of these analysis steps for one information flow or a group of them is called an *analysis cycle*. An information structure diagram is generated in this way in the first analysis cycle. In the analysis cycles which follow, the fact types and constraints identified at that moment are added to the diagram. Thus, the information structure diagram grows with every analysis cycle. When all the information flows which begin or end in the information system or a part of it have been analyzed in this way, the information analysis is at an end. In this chapter, the following analysis steps will be dealt with:

- Select or devise an example of the contents of the information flow(s) to be analyzed.
- Describe the example in natural language.
- Describe the example by means of one or more population tables.
- Determine the elementary sentence types.
- Add the fact types which are described by these sentence types to the information structure diagram.

In the practically oriented chapters which are to follow, we will successively expand this stepwise plan with further steps. The analysis steps must be seen as a tool in the application of NIAM. We advise anyone with little experience with the NIAM method of information analysis or anyone faced with a complex analysis problem to follow this stepwise plan carefully. As you gain more and more experience, you will automatically begin to gradually combine a number of steps or execute them implicitly.

6.1 The catalog card

We have repeated a portion of the information flow diagram of the library case in Figure 6.1. We shall now explain each of the above analysis steps for one of the information flows in this diagram.

1. Select or devise an example of the contents of the information flow(s) to be analyzed.

In the NIAM method of information analysis, we **always** begin with **concrete** examples of the information which is to be exchanged with the information system by means of the information flows. The information contents of the information flows desired by the future users of the information system, i.e., the "information needs" of the users, can, after all, be described most clearly by concrete examples of the desired information contents. By concrete examples, we mean such things as:

- output reports, input documents, examples of screen layouts, etc. of an existing or a not yet existing automated information system.
- completed forms, statements, overviews, etc. of an existing or a not yet existing manual administrative system.
- diagrams, sketches, drawings, tables, etc. which describe examples of the relevant information.

Naturally, we prefer it when these kinds of examples are already in existence. Usually, however, these examples are not there, because we are dealing with an information system (manual or automatic) which has yet to exist. In such cases, examples of the **desired** output reports, input documents, screen layouts, forms, statements, overviews, etc. have to be drawn up.

Very often, those involved in the information analysis are used to communicating by means of diagrams, sketches, or drawings, or diagrams or drawings are available which are sufficiently accurate examples of the contents of some information flows. In such cases, the analysis of the information flows is based on these diagrams, sketches, and drawings.

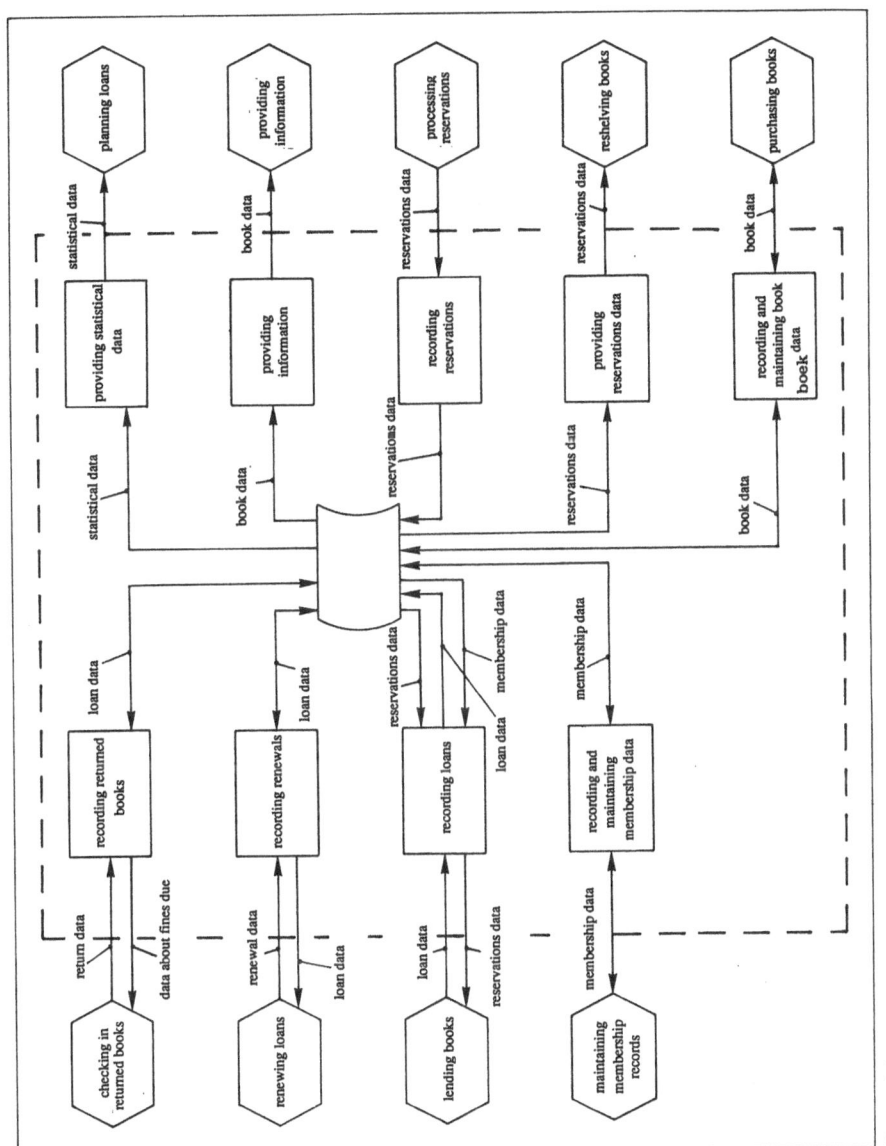

Figure 6.1.

All of the examples which are used must be as concrete, accurate, and complete as possible, or must contain as few as possible obscure or vague items.

If concrete examples have not been found or cannot be devised, or if those involved prefer or find it easier to express themselves verbally, you can begin with a written verbal description of the information. The verbal description can, for example, be a written report of an interview or a conversation about the subject. In these verbal descriptions, a few concrete examples must be included, in a descriptive form if necessary. When use is made of verbal descriptions, this first information analysis step is skipped, and the analysis cycle begins with the subsequent step.

Sometimes in the process of information analysis, the information structure diagram is drawn directly, without beginning with concrete examples. Such a diagram then grows gradually in size as more object types and fact types are "thought up." This is, in general, bad practice, because the information analysis proceeds in too unstructured a way, because too few concrete examples are used, and because the actual information needs of the future users of the system is often bypassed. These information needs are initially represented by the concrete examples of the contents of the information flows. As there are too few concrete points of departure, the process of information analysis in such cases cannot sufficiently be checked and often takes up a lot of unnecessary time.

We will apply this first step in the NIAM method of information analysis to the information flow "book data" in the information flow diagram of the library case. So as not to make our example too complex, we will assume that our library already has a manual administrative system and that the information system aimed at must back up this manual system. As we remarked earlier, this is a simplification of what is encountered in practice. In practice, we are often faced with administrative systems that still have to be designed and thus not with existing examples of the desired information exchange.

In the library, the most important data are listed on cards. The book data, the contents of the information flow we are going to analyze, are listed for each book on catalog cards, one of which is illustrated in Figure 6.2.

The example resulting from this step is described orally or in writing in the second step of the NIAM method of information analysis. When a description of the contents of the information flow is obtained instead of a concrete example, the analysis cycle begins directly with step 2.

2. Describe the example in natural language.

In this second step, the example obtained from step 1 is described in normal natural language. What is involved here is the **meaning** of the information illustrated by the example. This description can be oral or written, for example, a report of a conversation or interview.

A description of the information illustrated by the catalog card for one of the books in our library (Figure 6.2) follows below.

```
┌─────────────────────────────────────────────────────────────────────┐
│  CATALOG CARD                                                         │
│                                                                       │
│  Johnson J.H., Peterson P.                    ISBN   90 6233 134 3    │
│  Public library management                                            │
│  The Publishing Co. - Amsterdam - 1981                  1st edition   │
│                                                                       │
│                                                                       │
│  A practical manual for public library management. Contains a detailed practical case and several exercises │
│  with answers.                                                        │
│  textbook  Eng                                                        │
│                                                                       │
│                                                                       │
│                                                                       │
│                                                                       │
│                                                                       │
│                                                                       │
│                                                                       │
└─────────────────────────────────────────────────────────────────────┘
```

Figure 6.2.

There is a catalog card for every book in the library. The number "90 6233 134 3" is the International Standard Book Number, usually abbreviated to ISBN. This is an internationally regulated code, by which all participating countries and publishers uniquely denote every book. The names "Johnson J.H." and "Peterson P." are the names of the authors of the book in our example. The text "Public library management" is the book's title. "The Publishing Co." is the name of the publisher of the book. "Amsterdam" is the place where the book was published. The year "1981" is the year of publication. "1st" refers to the edition number of the book. The various editions of a certain book are numbered consecutively by the publisher. When a new edition of a book appears, thus changing the edition number, the ISBN number likewise changes, and one talks in terms of "another" book. The text "A practical...answers" is a brief description of the contents of the book. "Textbook" is the kind of book to which this particular book belongs. Some other examples of these kinds of books are: novel, science fiction, and thriller. "Eng." (meaning "English") is a code for the language in which the book is written or into which it has been translated.

When an example is extensive, for example, an output report of several dozen lines, a portion of this example which is as representative as possible has to described.

3. Describe the example by means of one or more population tables.

In this step, we construct population tables which represent the information contents of our example. These population tables describe the information contents independently of the external representation of the data and form the basis of the analysis which follows in subsequent steps.

This step consists of the following substeps:

– Determine the lexical objects and name the lexical object types.
– Create one or more population tables listing the lexical objects and the names of the lexical object types.
– Determine the non-lexical object types and note their names in the population table(s).

We shall now take up each of these substeps one by one.

3.1 Determine the lexical objects and name the lexical object types.

In this substep, it is determined which lexical objects (texts, values, signs, symbols, etc.) in the example describe the actual information contents of the information flow(s) involved (and therefore play a role in the subsequent information analysis), and which elements serve only for the external representation of the data (and therefore have no further role in the subsequent information analysis). The lexical objects which are relevant for information analysis are separated in this way from those matters which have only to do with the presentation, the arrangement, etc. of the data. Non-variable texts and values, for example, the fixed "ISBN" and "edition," should be allocated to the external representation and thus not to the information to be analyzed. Next, it is determined to which lexical object **types** these lexical objects belong. The lexical objects are therefore classified into lexical object types. Lastly, these lexical object types are provided with a name.

We begin this step by circling in the example (or in a verbal description) the lexical objects which are relevant for the analysis. The name of the particular lexical object type is listed next to each circled lexical object. In doing this, we stick as closely as possible to the verbal description of the example obtained in the previous step. The names of the lexical object types can usually be recognized immediately in this text. When we do this for the catalog card in the library, Figure 6.3 results.

As stated earlier, the texts "ISBN" and "edition" on the catalog card only serve to present the data, and consequently have no further role to play in the information analysis.

We can conclude from the fact that the author's initials belong to what we have

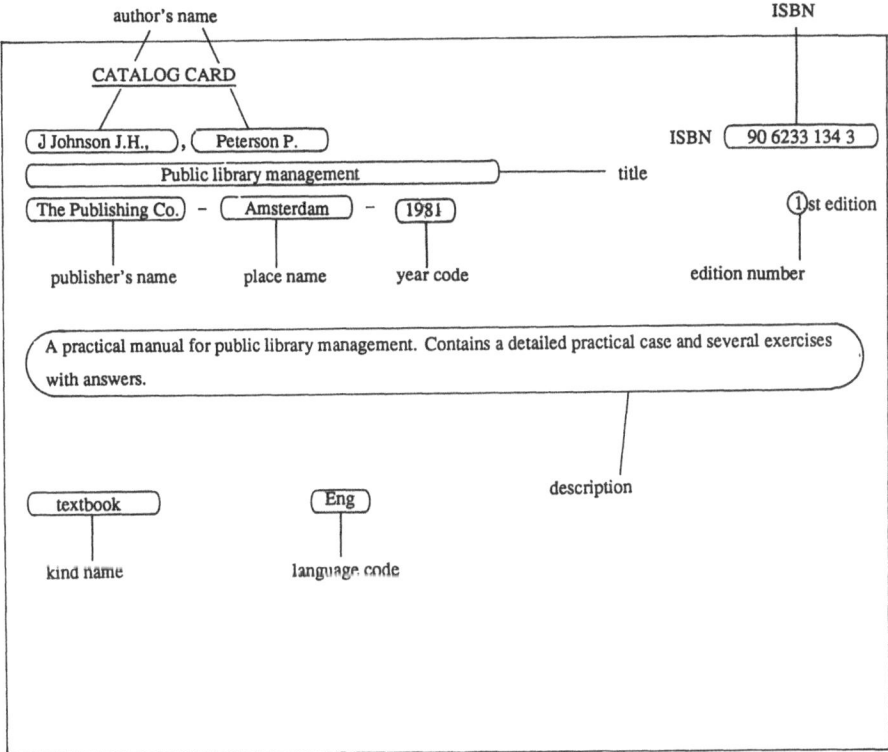

Figure 6.3.

called the "author's name" that we have decided (at least within this analysis) not to distinguish between the author's initials and his actual name. Because we have considered the whole ISBN as one lexical object rather than its parts as separate lexical objects, we shall (within this analysis) not take any notice of the internal structure of the ISBN. We shall conceive of the whole ISBN as one single number.

It appears from these remarks that, in determining the relevant lexical objects in this step, some decisions have to be made which can be decisive for the development of the information system yet to come.

When the example to be analyzed is extensive, the lexical objects and the lexial object types are determined on the basis of a portion of the example which is as representative and complete as possible.

3.2 Create one or more population tables listing the lexical objects and the names of the lexical object types.

In this substep, the lexical objects and the names of the lexical object types determined in the previous step are put into a population table. This has been done for the library catalog card in Figure 6.4.

There is a column in the population table for each lexical object type. The name of each of these lexical object types is given above each column. In the spaces for the entries, all or some of the lexical objects from the example are given.

The book whose data is listed on our sample catalog card has been written by two authors. The columns in a population table are per definition never combined. To be able to indicate which two authors have written this book, we must necessarily include the remaining data of this book twice.

When the example is extensive, we create several population tables which together describe the same information as the example.

3.3 Determine the non-lexical object types and note their names in the population table(s).

In this substep, the non-lexical object types concerned with the information described by our example are determined. In doing this, we ask ourselves for every lexical object type in the population table whether the objects of this type are a name or designation of or a reference to certain non-lexical objects. For the lexical object types where this is the case, the names of the non-lexical object types are written above the column associated with them. Naturally, there can be lexical object types in the table which are "independent," that is, the objects of which do not refer to certain non-lexical objects.

In Figure 6.5, the population table of Figure 6.4 has been extended with the names of the non-lexical object types.

The ISBN clearly indicates a book. The title likewise denotes a book. The lexical objects of the types "ISBN" and "title" thus refer to non-lexical objects of the same type, namely books. When, as in this case, different lexical object types correspond to the same non-lexical object type, we write the name of this non-lexical object type above the **combination** of the columns of the corresponding lexical object types. Therefore, we have listed the name of the non-lexical object type "book" in our population table above the combination of the columns of the lexical object types "ISBN" and "title." Every non-lexical object type is thus only included once in a population table.

The determination of the remaining non-lexical object types on the catalog card is fairly trivial.

An author's name indicates an author. A publisher's name refers to a publisher or publishing company. The name of a place denotes a city or town. The year code denotes a certain year. The kind name refers to a kind.

A description is a lexical object which does not directly denote a certain non-lexical object, but which refers to itself, and which is, in this sense, "independent." There is no non-lexical object type which directly corresponds to the lexical object type "description." The column "description" in the population table therefore does not contain the name of a certain non-lexical object type.

The non-lexical object types are determined as far as possible on the basis of

ISBN	title	author's name	publisher's name	place name	year – code	edition no.	kind name	language code	description
90 6233 134 3	Public library management	Johnson, J.H.	The Publishing Co.	Amsterdam	1981	1	textbook	Eng	a practical...
90 6233 134 3	Public library management	Peterson, P.	The Publishing Co.	Amsterdam	1981	1	textbook	Eng	a practical...

Figure 6.4.

book		author	publisher	place	year	edition	kind	language	description
ISBN	title	author's name	publisher's name	place name	year – code	edition no.	kind name	language code	description
90 6233 134 3	Public library management	Johnson, J.H.	The Publishing Co.	Amsterdam	1981	1	textbook	Eng	a practical...
90 6233 134 3	Public library management	Peterson, P.	The Publishing Co.	Amsterdam	1981	1	textbook	Eng	a practical...

Figure 6.5.

the verbal or written description of the example, which has been constructed in step 2. Sometimes the names of the non-lexical object types occur explicitly in this description, and sometimes they are implied by the description and have to be determined by reasoning and analysis.

4. Determine the elementary sentence types.

The population table or tables stemming from the previous step usually describe a number of **non-elementary** deep structure sentences. In this step, these **non-elementary** deep structure sentences are broken down into **elementary** sentences. It is determined which combinations of columns in a population table describe elementary deep structure sentences of the same sentence type and thus "belong together." These columns are connected by lines, as has been done in Figure 6.6. At the same time, the role names of these elementary sentence types are added to the population table. This filling in of the role names can aid in finding the elementary sentence types. By attempting to fill in the role names, we sometimes come up "automatically" with the right elementary sentence type. (Bear in mind here that the role name which is to be filled in in a certain column of a population table is always one of the predicates of the elementary sentences which begin with an object of the type belonging to that column.)

The elementary sentence types are determined as much as possible on the basis of the verbal or written description of the example produced in step 2. By listening carefully to a verbal description made by yourself or others and paying attention to the predicates used, you can often directly "hear" the sentence types which occur. By closely analyzing a written description and tracking down the predicates, we can discover the sentence types or run across clues which could lead to them. Language elements such as "and," "that," "which," etc. point out the non-elementary sentences. These can be mentally broken down into elementary sentences by omitting these language elements and similarly adapting the text.

It follows from the description of the catalog card that:

- a **book** has a certain **title**
- a **book** is written by an **author**
- a **book** is published by a **publisher**
- a **book** is published in a certain **place**
- a **book** is published in a certain **year**
- a **book** is of a certain **edition**
- a **book** is of a certain **kind**
- a **book** is written in a certain **language**
- a **book** has a certain **description**.

The relationships between the columns in a population table, which determine the elementary sentence types as well as clues to possible role names, follow directly from this.

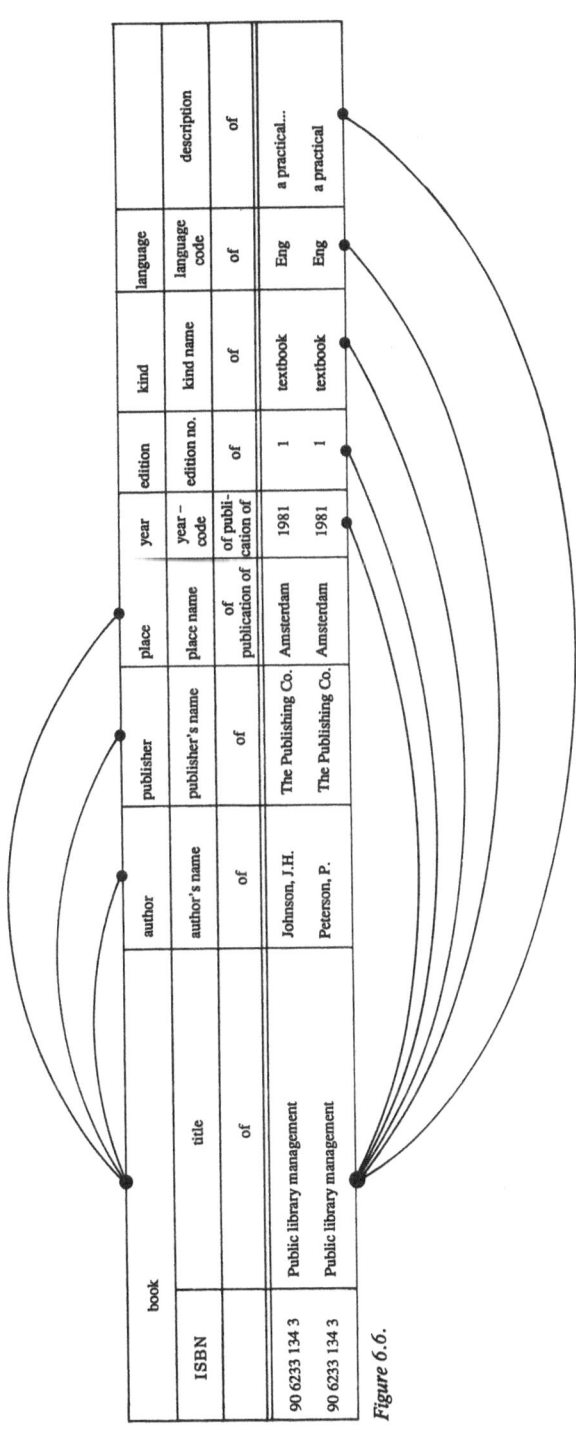

Figure 6.6.

By assuming that a book is published in a certain place (that there is a relationship between "book" and "place" and not between "publisher" and "place"), we have decided that "place" generally does not have to be the domicile of the publisher, and that it is possible for a book to be published in a place other than the publisher's domicile. In practice, these kinds of decisions or assumptions must be verified.

Because we have agreed to deal with only binary sentence types for the time being (until Chapter 12), we need only look for binary sentence types in this and subsequent practically oriented chapters. However, in general, one must take into account the fact that not all elementary sentence types are binary, which somewhat complicates the determination of the elementary sentence types. We will be getting back to this in Chapters 12 and 13.

5. Add the fact types which are described by these sentence types to the information structure diagram.

The elementary sentence types determined in the previous step are described in an information structure diagram by means of fact types. In this step, these (new) fact types are added to the information structure diagram. When the analysis cycle is executed for the first time, there is obviously no information structure diagram. In that case, we begin with an information structure diagram which only contains the fact types corresponding to the sentence types determined in the previous step. In the following analysis cycles, new fact types are gradually added on to the diagram.

The fact types describing the elementary sentence types correspond to the "horizontal relationships" (idea types or bridge types) between the columns of the population table (in the last step, we denoted these by lines connecting the columns) and the "vertical relationships" (bridge types) between the lexical and the non-lexical object types within one column.

To make things clear, we have drawn the information structure diagram below in two steps. Figure 6.7 contains only those fact types which correspond to the "horizontal relationships" between the columns in the population table. In Figure 6.8, we have added the bridge types which correspond to the "vertical relationships" between the lexical and non-lexical object types within one column of the population table.

The role names of most of the bridge types have not been filled in. By virtue of the "with/of rule," these get the standard names "with" (for the role of the non-lexical object type) and "of" (for the role of the lexical object type). For the role names of the remaining fact types, we have selected possible predicates of the elementary sentences of the corresponding sentence types:

– The book **with** the title "Public library management" is **written by** the author **with** the author's name "Johnson, J.H."

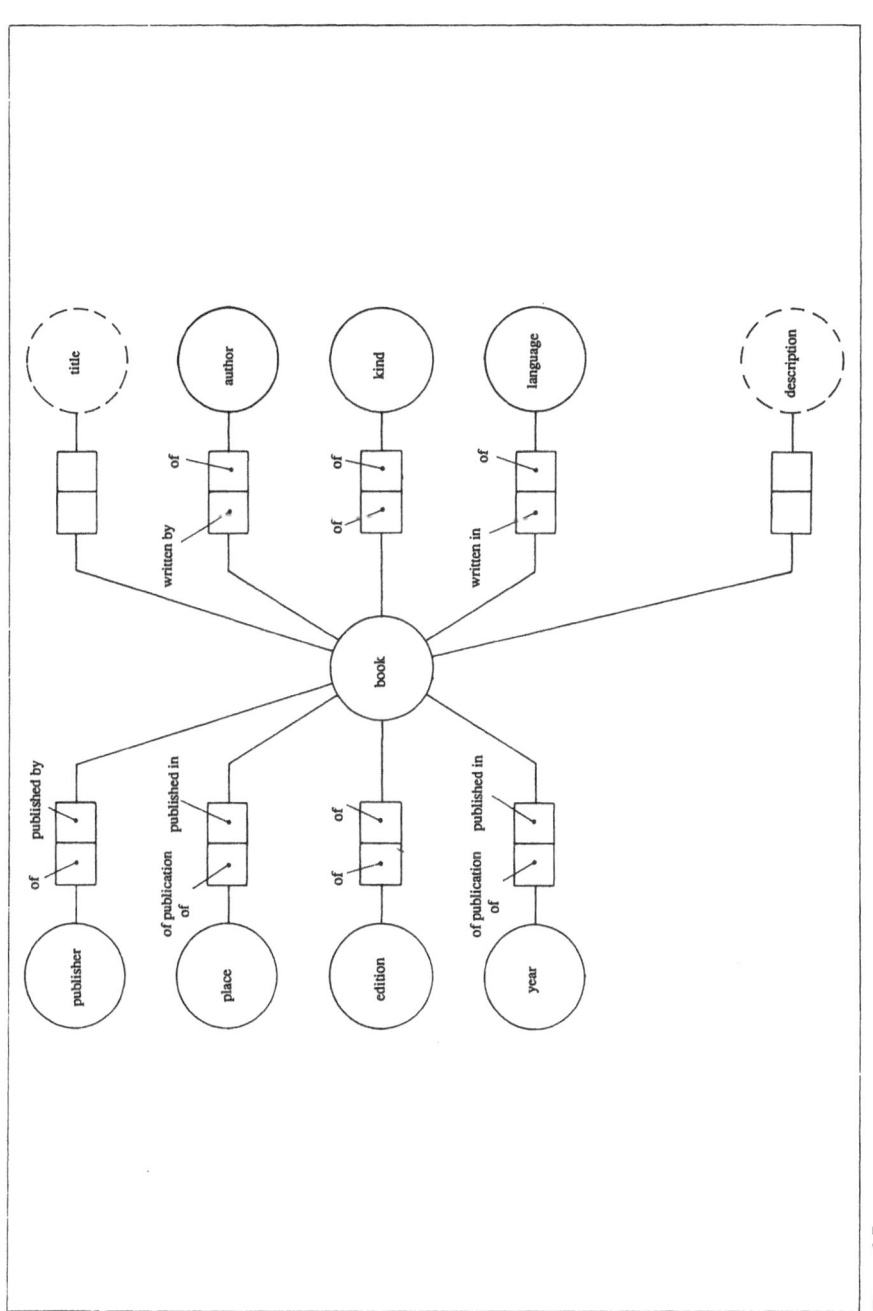

Figure 6.7.

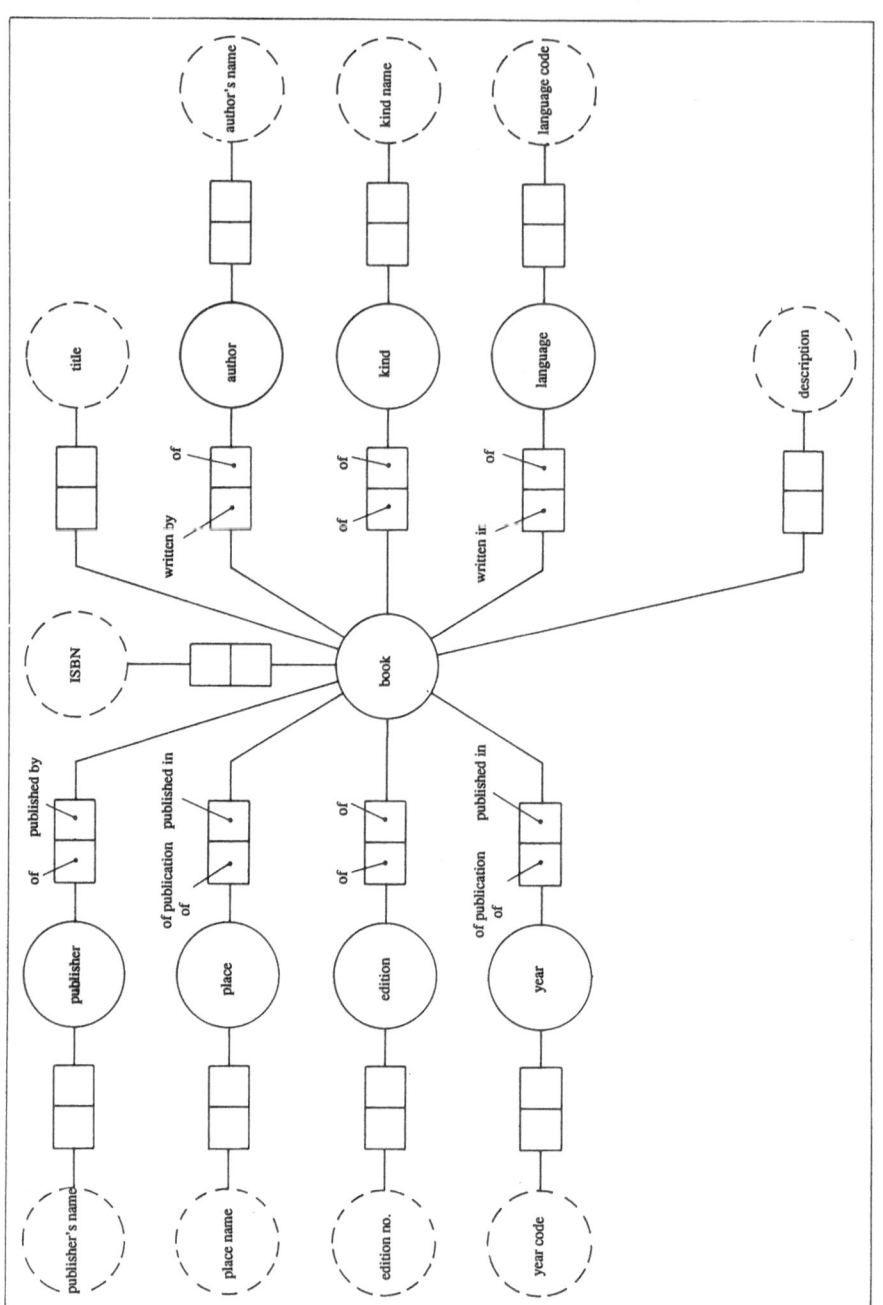

Figure 6.8.

– "Johnson, J.H." is the author's name **of** of the author **of** the book **with** the title "Public library management."
– The book **with** the title "Public library management" is **published in** the year **with** the year code "1981."
– "1981" is the year code **of** the year **of publication of** the book **with** the title "Public library management."
– The book **with** the title "Public library management" is **written in** the language **with** the language code "Eng."
– "Eng" is the language code **of** the language **of** the book **with** the title "Public library management."
– The book **with** the title "Public library management" is **of** the kind **with** the kind name "textbook."
– "Textbook" is the kind name **of** the kind **of** the book **with** the title "Public library management."

The predicates (in bold) in these elementary deep structure sentences have been selected, with the exception of the "fillers" such as "the" and "is," as role names for the corresponding fact types. Consequently, these elementary deep structure sentences can be "read" directly from the information structure diagram. If we were to ask someone to describe in detail the catalog card of Figure 6.2, the same sentences or sentence derivations could be heard in the description, although the predicates might differ. This illustrates once again how close an information structure diagram is to natural language, thanks to the natural language principle, and why, in constructing this diagram, we started with a detailed verbal or written description in natural language. Because an information structure diagram is so closely allied to the natural use of language, the NIAM method of information analysis can be carried out by everyone involved in the information system-to-be, specialists and (to a certain degree) nonspecialists alike. An information structure diagram, in particular, is a good medium of communication between specialists and nonspecialists. Thanks to the fact that a NIAM information model lies very close to the natural use of language, it is still, by virtue of the 100% principle, exact and sufficiently formal.

6.2 The first addition to the catalog card

In this second section, we will again run through the steps of the NIAM method of information analysis that we have dealt with so far. For this purpose, we have added a little bit to the catalog card of Figure 6.2, resulting in the version depicted in Figure 6.9.

When the example on which the analysis is based is extensive and complex, it is often advisable to first analyze a portion of the example and to successively add to this in one or more subsequent analysis cycles. In the previous section, we analyzed a portion of the catalog card in this way, and we are now going to extend

CATALOG CARD

Johnson J.H., Peterson P.   ISBN 90 6233 134 3

Public library management

The Publishing Co. - Amsterdam - 1981   1st edition

A practical manual for public library management. . Contains a detailed practical case and several exercises

with answers.

textbook   Eng

C30960   1981
C43728   1981
C31604   1985

Figure 6.9.

the analysis in this section. In the practically oriented chapters which are to follow, we will extend the catalog card even further and then analyze these additions.

We shall now carry out the analysis steps treated above for the additions shown in Figure 6.9.

1. Select or devise an example of the contents of the information flow(s) to be analyzed.

See Figure 6.9.

2. Describe the example in natural language.

Of course, we will only describe the portion that was added to the original example. This description follows below:

The library acquires one or more copies of a book (identified by an ISBN, with a certain title, published by a certain publisher, etc.). Every copy is uniquely denoted by a copy number. "C30960," "C43728" and "C31604" are copy numbers of the three copies of the book whose data are reported on the catalog card. The year that the copy was acquired by the library is given next to every copy number. "1981" is the year that copies "C30906" and "C43728" were purchased, and "1985" the year copy "C31604" was bought.

3.1 Determine the lexical objects and name the lexical object types.

In Figure 6.10, we have circled the new lexical objects and listed the names of their object types on the catalog card.

From the description of the example, it appears that the lexical objects "C30906," "C43728" and "C31604" are copy numbers and thus belong to the lexical object type "copy number." "1981" and "1985" are year codes of the years in which the copies were acquired. These codes are presented in exactly the same

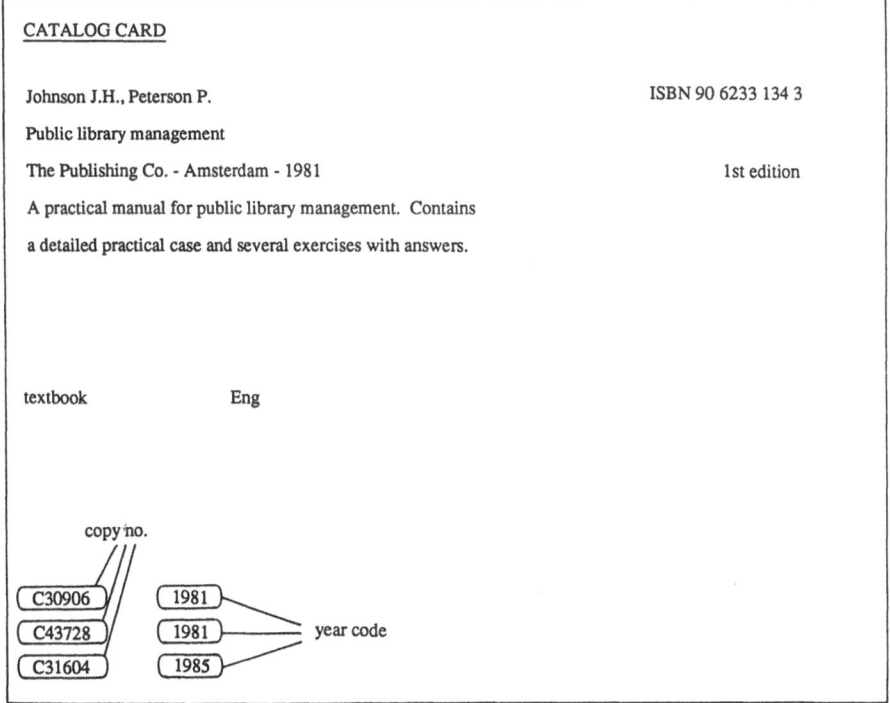

Figure 6.10.

way as for the year of the book's publication, and cannot be distinguished from them. Consequently, they belong to the same lexical object type "year code."

In practice, we begin with the assumption that lexical objects whose representations cannot be distinguished from one another belong to the same lexical object type.

3.2 Create one or more population tables listing the lexical objects and the names of the lexical object types.

Because the copy numbers and the year codes of the years of acquisition have to do with the copies of the book whose data is listed on the catalog card, and because the ISBN is unique for this book, we have included the copy numbers and the years together with the ISBN in a population table, represented in Figure 6.11.

As we already know, the columns of a population table are always single rather than compound. To still be able to indicate which copy numbers belong to which book, we have had to include the book's ISBN three times in the population table.

3.3 Determine the non-lexical object types and note their names in the population table(s).

We already know from the analysis in the first part of this example (Section 1 of this chapter) that the ISBN refers to a book and the year code refers to a year, so that in the corresponding population table we have to fill in "book" above the name "ISBN" and the "year" above "year code." Determining the non-lexical objects to which the copy numbers refer is somewhat more difficult. Initially, we are inclined to think that a copy number, like an ISBN, refers to a book. An analysis of the example and descriptions of it, however, illustrates that this is not tenable. The data listed on the catalog card are only concerned with one particular **book**. There are apparently three copy numbers which "belong" to this book, and the year codes "belong" **to each** of these copy numbers. It is natural to conclude that these year codes have something to do with an object other than the book. This object is denoted by a copy number and in turn has something to do with that book. It appears from this that the library makes a distinction between "books" and "copies." A "book" is apparently a nonphysical object with such characteristics as an ISBN, a title, a publisher, an author and so on. A "copy," or defined even more closely a "book copy," is the physical object that is purchased by the library, placed in the reading room, and can be checked out and taken along. A "copy" belongs to a particular book. It is a physical copy of a book. All copies are uniquely denoted in the library by copy numbers. It appears from the fact that the catalog card lists several copy numbers that the library can purchase several copies of a particular book. Each of these copies has been acquired in a certain year. The year of acquisition is listed next to every copy number on the catalog card.

After this analysis, it is clear that a (lexical) copy number denotes a (non-lexical) copy and that the name "copy" thus has to be placed above the name "copy number" in the population table of Figure 6.11. See Figure 6.12.

ISBN	copy no.	year code
90 6233 134 3	C 30 960	1981
90 6233 134 3	C 43 728	1981
90 6233 134 3	C 31 604	1985

Figure 6.11.

book	copy	year
ISBN	copy no.	year code
90 6233 134 3	C 30 960	1981
90 6233 134 3	C 43 728	1981
90 6233 134 3	C 31 604	1985

Figure 6.12.

The foregoing illustrates that determining the lexical and non-lexical object types is far from being trivial in all cases and that, particularly in the early practice of applying NIAM, it is advisable to follow the NIAM information analysis steps carefully. To determine the lexical and non-lexical object types as well as (in the next step) the elementary sentence types, you have to listen carefully to a description of the example, whether verbal or written, in order to analyze it meticulously. You have to look carefully for the object type names and predicates in this description. Should a written description of the example be available, it is advisable to denote the revelant object type names and predicates, for example by underlining or highlighting them.

4. Determine the elementary sentence types.

It appears from the layout of the catalog card, the above description of it, and the foregoing analysis that a copy belongs to a particular book and that a year of acquisition belongs to a copy. After all, the library acquires "copies" rather than "books." The relationship between a book and a copy can be concluded from the fact that a catalog card is concerned with one particular book and that more than one copy number appears on the catalog card. The relationship between a copy and the year of acquisition also appears from the fact that the year codes indicating the years of acquisition are listed next to the copy numbers on the catalog card. We have denoted these relationships as well as the role names of the corresponding elementary sentence types in the population table of Figure 6.13.

book	copy	year
ISBN	copy no.	year code
	of	acquired in
90 6233 134 3	C 30 960	1981
90 6233 134 3	C 43 728	1981
90 6233 134 3	C 31 604	1985

Figure 6.13.

5. Add the fact types which are described by these sentence types to the information structure diagram.

Some of the things the population table describes are:

– the relationship between a book and a copy
– the relationship between a copy and a year (of acquisition)
– the relationship between a copy and a copy number.

We have added in Figure 6.14 the three new fact types obtained in this way to the information structure diagram.

In this information structure diagram, the object type "year" plays two roles, namely:

– year **of publication** of a book
– year **of acquisition** of a copy.

If we were to play strictly according to the rules, the solution of Figure 6.15 would also be correct:

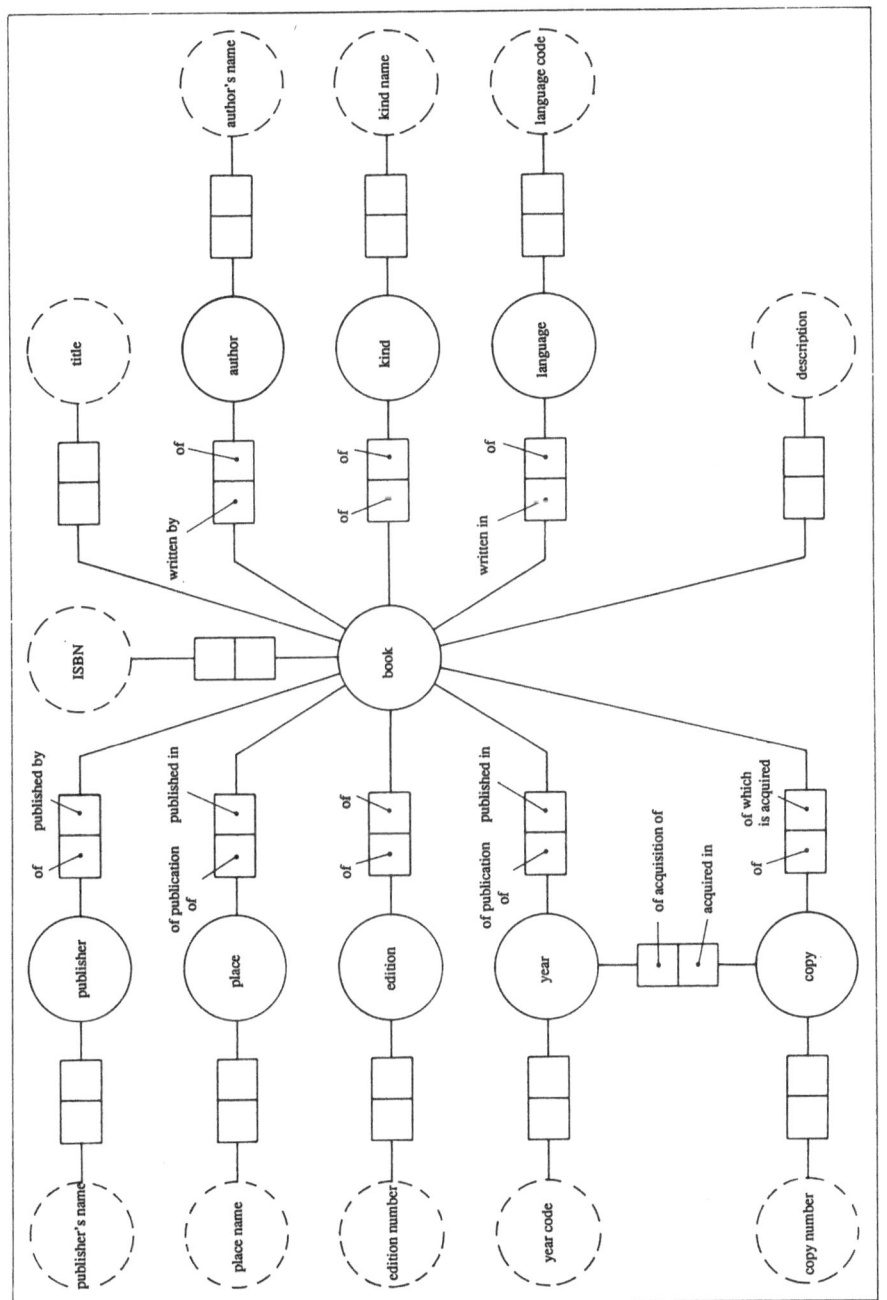

Figure 6.14.

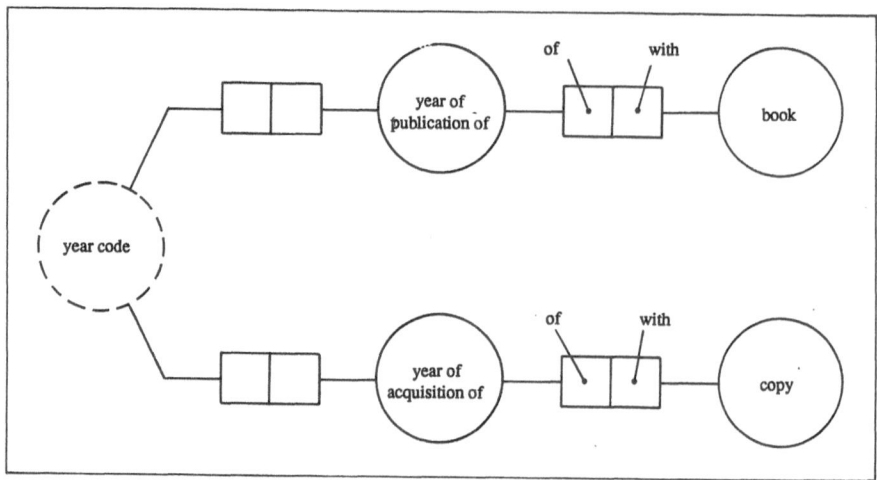

Figure 6.15.

Although, strictly speaking, this solution is correct, the concepts of "role" and "object type" are confused with each other. To the outside world, the "year of publication of a book" cannot be distinguished from a "year of acquisition of a copy." Both are represented by the same lexical object "year code." Actually, it is a question of having one object type (one concept), "year," which can occur in two different roles (two different "capacities"), namely in the role of "year of publication of a book" and in the role of "year of acquisition of a copy." In the solution of Figure 6.15, the lexical object type "year code" occurs in two bridge types, namely in the bridge type of "year of publication" and in the bridge type of "year of acquisition." In practice, an information structure diagram is clearest when, as far as is possible, every lexical object type only occurs in one bridge type. Consequently, we formulate the following **practical rule**:

Aim towards having, as far as is possible, every lexical object type occur in only one bridge type. In every case where this is not possible, check whether the non-lexical object types belonging to different bridge types of the same lexical object type describe the same concept, so that they can be combined into one non-lexical object type.

Bear in mind that this is not a formal but a practical rule. Because the lexical object type "year code" occurs in two different bridge types in Figure 6.15, we need, by virtue of this rule, to check whether the non-lexical object types of these bridge types (the object types "year of publication" and "year of acquisition") describe one and the same concept, so that they can be combined into one single object type. "Year of publication" and "year of acquisition" indeed describe the same concept "year," which occurs in two different roles (two different "capacities"): on the one side the role of "year of publication of a book" and on the other side the role of "year of acquisition of a copy." These two object types therefore need to be combined into one object type, resulting in the solution of Figure 6.14.

6.3 Summary

Below is an overview of the analysis steps dealt with thus far.

Repeat the following steps for one or more information flows which begin or end in the information system or part of it.

1. Select or devise an example of the contents of the information flow(s) to be analyzed.

2. Describe the example in natural language.

3. Describe the example by means of one or more population tables.

   3.1 Determine the lexical objects and name the lexical object types.

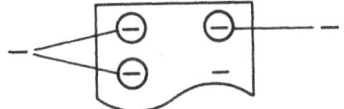

   3.2 Create one or more population tables listing the lexical objects and the names of the lexical object types.

   3.3 Determine the non-lexical object types and note their names in the population table(s).

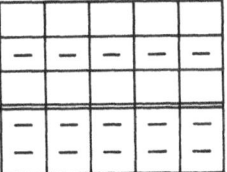

4. Determine the elementary sentence
   types.

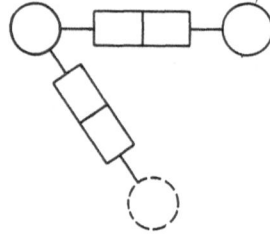

5. Add the fact types which are described by these sentence types to the
   information structure diagram.

7 GRAPHICAL CONSTRAINTS INVOLVING ONE FACT TYPE

As we noted at the end of Chapter 5, a significant portion of the remainder of this book deals with constraints. In this chapter, we will begin by taking a look at two graphical constraint types which limit the populations of one single fact type.

7.1 Uniqueness constraints

We have repeated the elementary propositions which formed the starting points of Chapter 4 and the information structure diagram of Chapter 5 in Figures 7.1 and 7.2.

(P1) There are employees.

(P2) There are departments.

(P3) Employees work for departments.

(P4) An employee may only work for one department.

(P5) There are last names.

(P6) There are department names.

(P7) Employees are denoted by their last names.

(P8) Johnson is the last name of a certain employee.

(P9) Peterson is the last name of a certain employee.

(P10) King is the last name of a certain employee.

(P11) Departments are referred to by department names.

(P12) Purchasing is the department name of a certain department.

(P13) Personnel is the department name of a certain department.

(P14) Johnson works for the Purchasing Department.

(P15) Peterson works for the Purchasing Department.

(P16) King works for the Personnel Department.

(P17) A department may not contain more than 10 employees.

Figure 7.1.

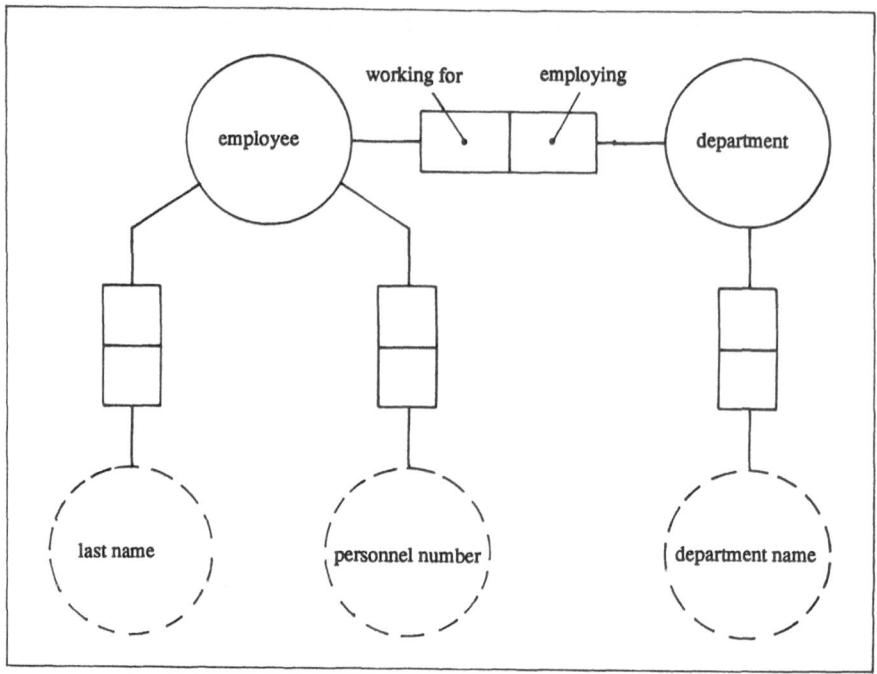

Figure 7.2.

In Chapter 5, we saw that Proposition P4 of Figure 7.1 ("An employee may only work for one department") is a description of a constraint, and consequently was not (yet) represented in the information structure diagram. Figure 7.3 shows a population of the information base which is allowed solely on the basis of the object types and the fact types of this information structure diagram. To avoid ambiguity, we have represented the employees in this population diagram by means of a unique personnel number.

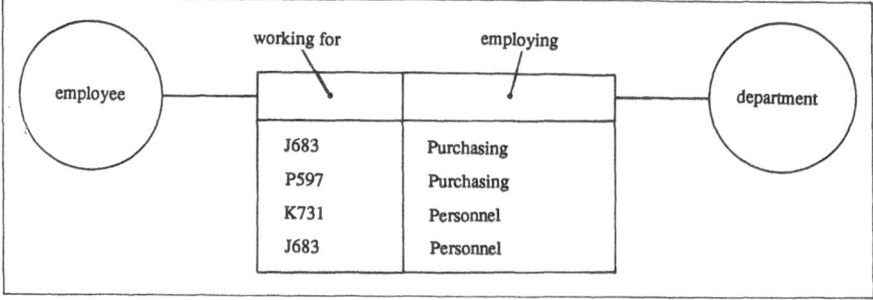

Figure 7.3.

However, in this population employee J683 works for two different departments, namely Purchasing and Personnel. This conflicts with the constraint described by Proposition P4.

The above population can only satisfy this rule when the fact that employee J683 works for Purchasing or the fact that J683 works for Personnel or both of them are deleted from the population. In Figure 7.4, we have dropped the fact that employee J683 works for Personnel.

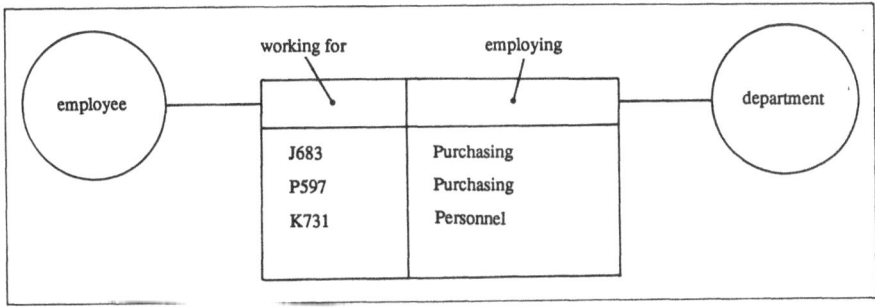

Figure 7.4.

The population of Figure 7.4 now satisfies the constraint described by Proposition P4. Unlike Figure 7.3, in Figure 7.4 each employee occurs only once in the population of the role "employee working for department." It follows from this that rule P4 is the equivalent of:

Every employee may only occur once in the population of the role "employee working for department."

This rule is a translation of rule P4 in terms of role populations of fact types, i.e., in terms of the components of an information structure diagram. Both rules mean exactly the same thing; they express the same knowledge.

A role in which an object may only occur once in each population, such as the role "employee working for department," is called a **unique role**. The constraint described by Proposition P4 expresses the uniqueness of this role, and is therefore called a **uniqueness constraint.**

A department may, of course, contain several employees, and may consequently occur more than once in the population of the role "department employing employee." Thus, as the Purchasing Department contains two employees, it occurs twice in the population of the role "department employing employee." This role is therefore not unique.

From now on, we shall denote unique roles in the information structure diagram by means of the symbol "↔," as we have done in Figure 7.5.

The role "employee working for department" is unique. Each employee occurs only once in the population of this role. The uniqueness symbol ("↔") which has been drawn along the role "employee working for department" expresses the uniqueness of this role and is a graphical representation of the uniqueness constraint expressed by Proposition P4. We have extended the information structure diagram with this uniqueness constraint in Figure 7.6.

The information processor checks whether a constraint is violated every time there is a request to add a fact to the information base. Suppose that the population diagram of Figure 7.5 describes part of the information base at a given moment and that at that moment a user addresses the following request to the information processor:

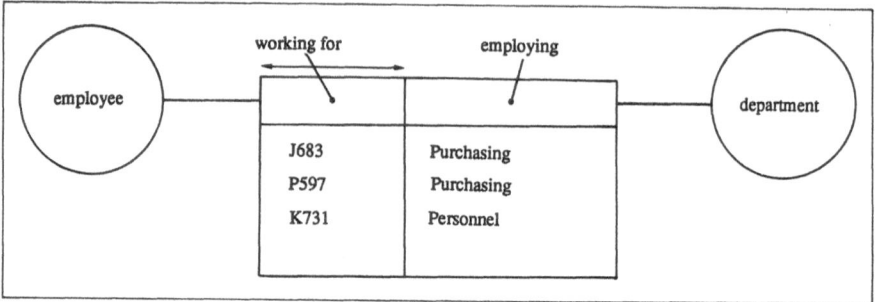

Figure 7.5.

> **add** : the **employee with personnel number** J683 **working for** the **department**
> Personnel.

Then the information processor responds as follows:

> **Request not executed** because of violation of rule P4 (an employee may only work for one department).

The user then has to refrain from adding this new fact or first delete the fact that employee J683 works for Purchasing.

When the user addresses the following compound request to the information processor:

> **Begin Delete** : the **employee with personnel number** J683 **working for** the **depart-**
> **ment** Purchasing.
> **Add** :   the **employee with personnel number** J683 **working for** the **depart-**
> **ment** Personnel.
> **End**

the uniqueness constraint is not violated after these two requests are executed.

If requested to, the information processor can, by virtue of the uniqueness constraint of Figure 7.6, conclude from the fact that employee J683 works for the Purchasing Department that this employee is not working for another department.

To summarize:

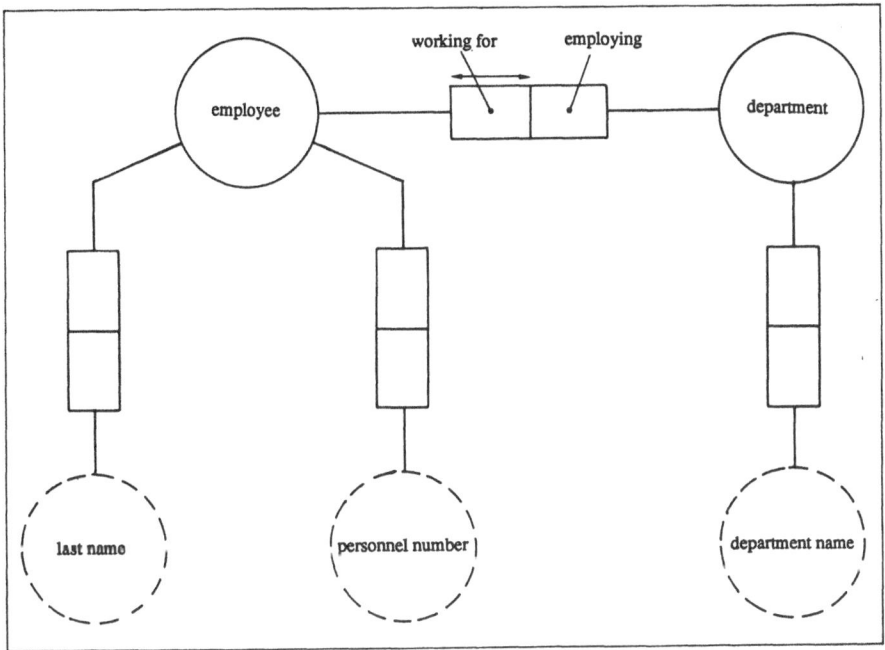

Figure 7.6.

A unique role:
A role in which every object of the object type of that role may only occur once in every population.

Uniqueness constraint:
A constraint which expresses the uniqueness of a role.

Uniqueness symbol:
The graphical representation of a uniqueness constraint.

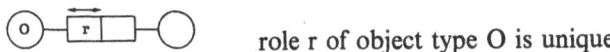   role r of object type O is unique

7.2 Some examples of uniqueness constraints

In this section, we shall give some other examples of uniqueness constraints. To do this, we shall elaborate on the library case. We shall assume that the library makes use of a system of job tracking. In such a system, the work that the employees in the various departments have to do over a certain period is divided up into a number of "activities." Each of these activities is assigned to one or more employees. The population diagram of Figure 7.7 illustrates the relation between the employees and the activities assigned to them. In this population diagram, we have represented the employees by a (unique) personnel number and the activities by a (likewise unique) activity number.

Let us assume that the following two rules are valid:

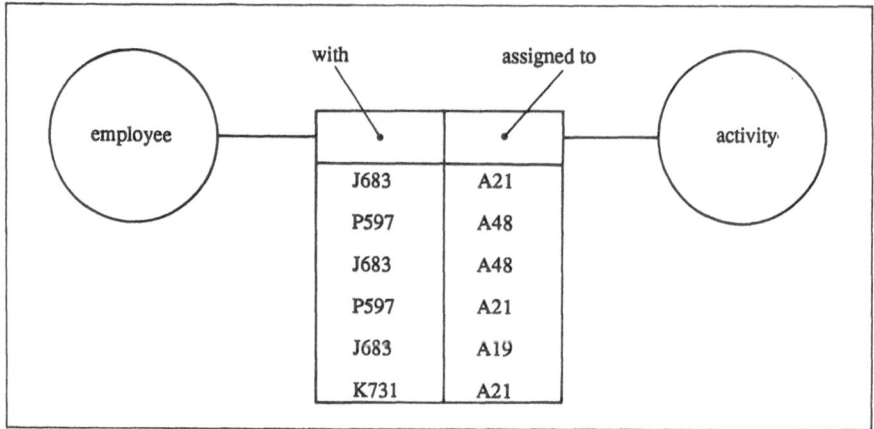

Figure 7.7.

R1: An employee can only be assigned one activity.
R2: An activity can only be assigned to one employee.

Both rules restrict the populations which are allowed purely on the basis of the object types and the fact types of Figure 7.7. The population of this figure does not satisfy these rules, because employees J683 and P597 have been assigned to more than one activity, and because activities A21 and A48 are each assigned to more than one employee.

Both rules R1 and R2 are uniqueness constraints. R1 expresses the uniqueness of the role "employee with activity": every employee may only occur once in the population of this role. R2 expresses the uniqueness of the role "activity assigned to employee": each activity may only occur once in the population of this role. We have included both uniqueness constraints along with a valid population in Figure 7.8. (For the sake of clarity, we have listed the numbers of the above two rules next to the uniqueness symbols involved.)

Every employee now occurs only once in the population of the role "employee with activity," and each activity occurs only once in the population of the role "activity assigned to employee."

This is an example of a fact type in which two roles are unique.

Let us now suppose that only uniqueness constraint R2 is valid. That is, an activity can only be assigned to one employee, but an employee can be assigned more than one activity. This uniqueness constraint is depicted in Figure 7.9, along with a valid population.

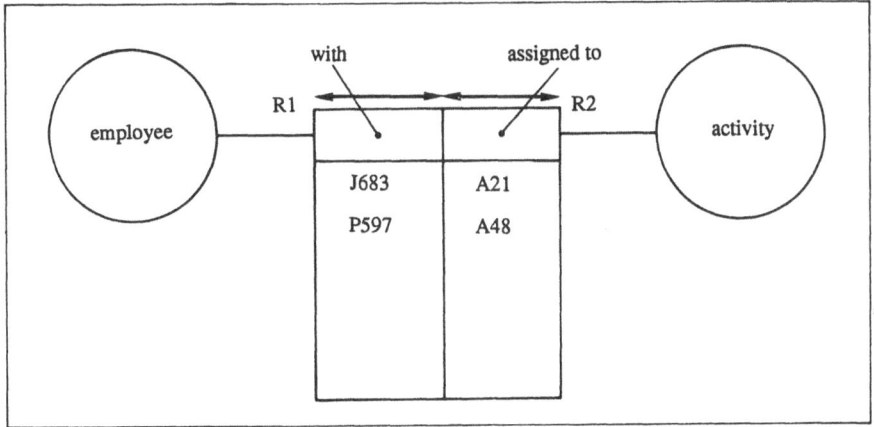

Figure 7.8.

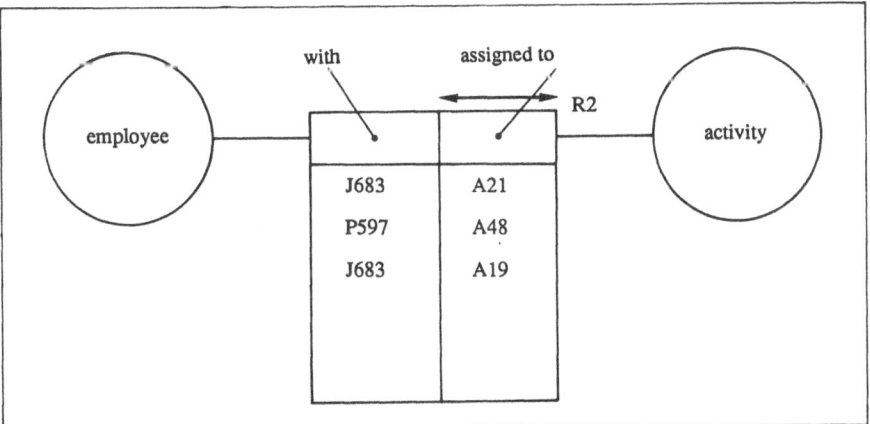

Figure 7.9.

This time, only the role "activity assigned to employee" is unique. Each activity may occur only once in the population of this role. The role "employee with activity" is now not unique. More than one activity may be assigned to every employee, and each employee may consequently appear more than once in the population of this role. Thus, two activities have been assigned to employee J683. As a result, this employee appears twice in the population of the role "employee with activity."

Let us next suppose the reverse, that only uniqueness constraint R1 is valid. That is, every employee may only be assigned one activity, but each activity may be assigned to more than one employee. This uniqueness constraint has been represented in Figure 7.10, along with a valid population.

This time, the role "employee with activity" is unique. Every employee may occur only once in the population of this role. The role "activity assigned to

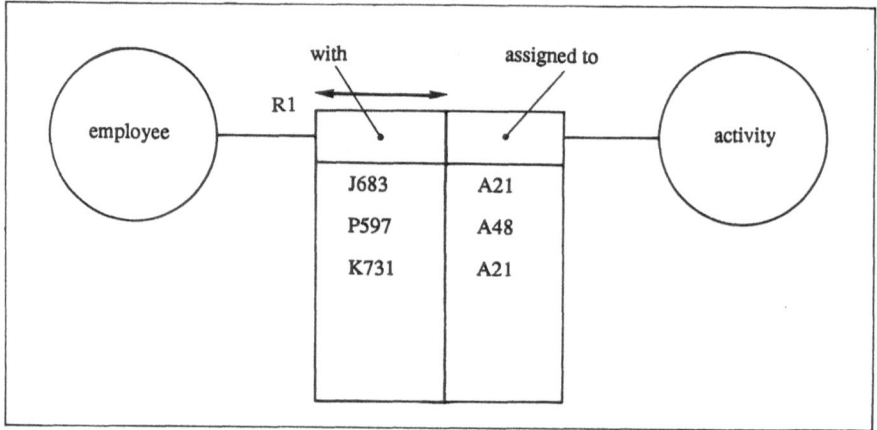

Figure 7.10.

employee" is not unique. Each activity may be assigned to more than one employee, so that each activity may appear more than once in the population of this role. Thus, activity A21 has been assigned to two employees. This activity consequently appears twice in the population of the role "activity assigned to employee."

Lastly, let us suppose that neither rule R1 nor R2 is valid. Every employee may then be assigned more than one activity, and every activity may be assigned to more than one employee. In short, every possible combination of employees and activities belongs in this case to a valid population. The population of Figure 7.7 is then a valid population.

We have seen earlier that, by virtue of the singularity rule, every fact, every combination of objects, may occur only once.

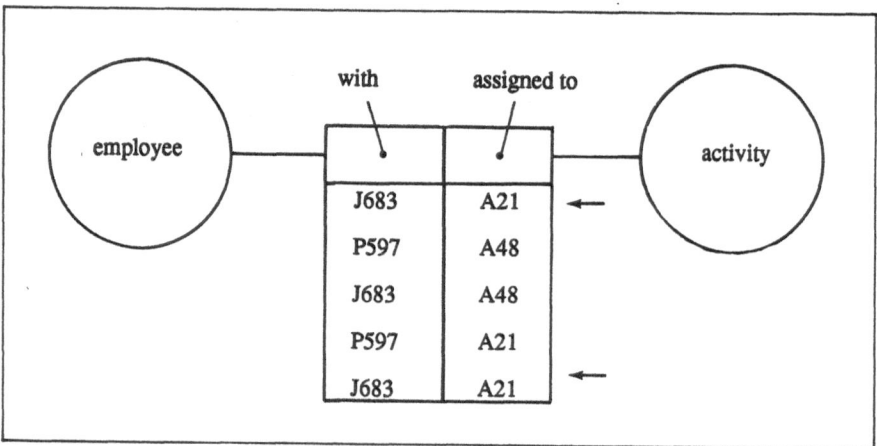

Figure 7.11.

The population of Figure 7.11 does not satisfy the singularity rule, because the fact that activity A21 is assigned to employee J683 (the combination J683-A21) is represented twice in the population diagram.

We can make use of the uniqueness symbol to explicitly represent the singularity rule, as has been done in Figure 7.12.

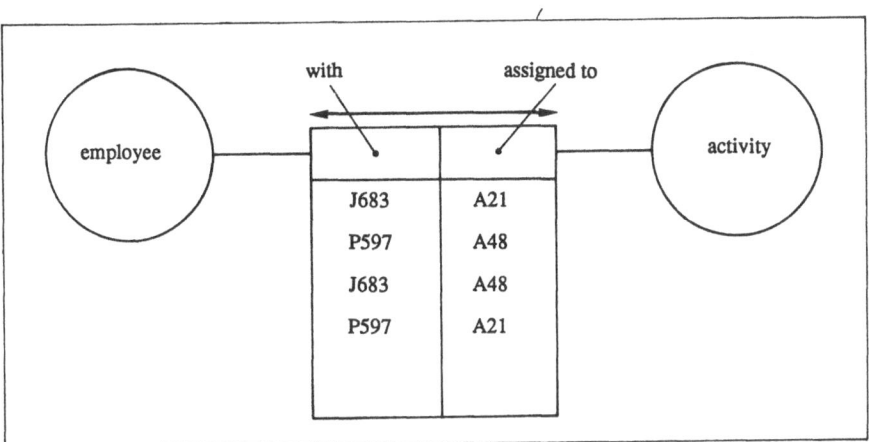

Figure 7.12.

We have now drawn the uniqueness symbol along all the fact type roles. This expresses the fact that the **combination** of all the fact type roles is unique; in other words, that every possible combination of objects may occur only once in this fact type population.

The above is a graphical representation of the singularity rule. We can now reformulate this rule as follows:

The **combination** of **all** roles of a fact type is always unique.

In concrete terms, this means that if neither of the individual roles of a binary fact type is unique, the **combination** of both roles is in any case unique, by virtue of the singularity rule.

When neither of the **individual** roles of a binary fact type is unique (thus, when no uniqueness symbol can be drawn along the individual roles), this will be explicitly denoted from now on by drawing a uniqueness symbol along **both** roles of this fact type (as has been done in Figure 7.12). In Chapter 12, we shall make a similar agreement for non-binary fact types.

As a consequence of this agreement, we have to draw at least one uniqueness symbol by every fact type in an information structure diagram. We will draw a uniqueness symbol along all roles when there are no uniqueness constraints on the individual roles. Because we have to draw a uniqueness symbol explicitly by each fact type, we are forced to make a decision about the uniqueness of all the fact type roles in the information structure diagram. The above agreement is therefore primarily of practical value.

The examples of uniqueness constraints dealt with above have been summarized in Figure 7.13.

A binary fact type is **always** accompanied by a uniqueness symbol:

- placed along one of the roles, when one of the roles is unique (such as in cases
  2 and 3 in Figure 7.13)
- placed along both roles, when each of the roles is unique (such as in case 1
  in Figure 7.13)
- placed along the **combination** of both roles, when neither of these two roles
  is unique (such as in case 4 in Figure 7.13).

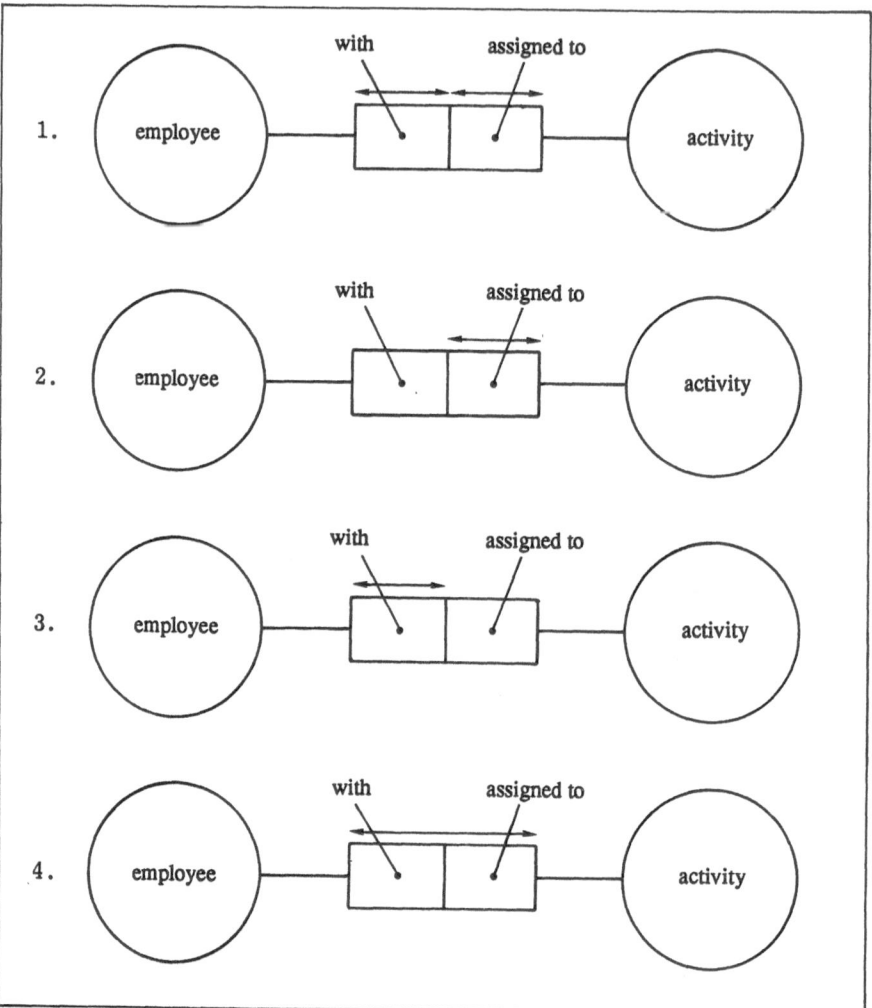

Figure 7.13.

Sometimes it is difficult to remember the meaning of a uniqueness symbol correctly. The mnemonic which follows may help you to remember this.

A uniqueness symbol is always placed next to a unique role. When "reading" one of the elementary sentences in the information structure diagram, add to the sentence the words "only one" immediately behind the name of this unique role. In this way, you get (somewhat depending on the role name chosen) an assertion that expresses the uniqueness constraint. If we do this for, for example, case 1 in Figure 7.13, we get the following two propositions:

"An employee (is) with **only one** activity."
"An activity (is) assigned to **only one** employee."

In this section, we have made use of population diagrams to explain uniqueness constraints. In the following chapter, we shall see that when putting information analysis into practice, population diagrams play a significant role in determining and verifying constraints.

To summarize:

The singularity rule:
The **combination** of **all** roles of a fact type is always unique.

The four possible uniqueness constraints in binary fact types are:

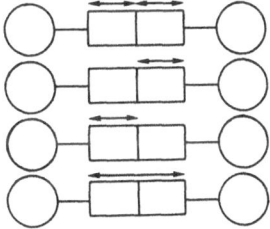

In this section, we have talked about the different uniqueness constraints involved in one (binary) fact type. As we already know, a fact type can be an idea type or a bridge type. In the upcoming section, we will zero in on uniqueness constraints involving bridge types.

7.3 Uniqueness constraints involving bridge types

We saw earlier that bridges, just like ideas, express certain facts or characteristics about non-lexical objects, and that, in addition, lexical objects can serve to denote non-lexical objects or to refer to them. In this section, we will go into the consequences for uniqueness constraints in bridge types when lexical objects are

used to denote non-lexical objects. To that end, we will add the following rules
to the library case:

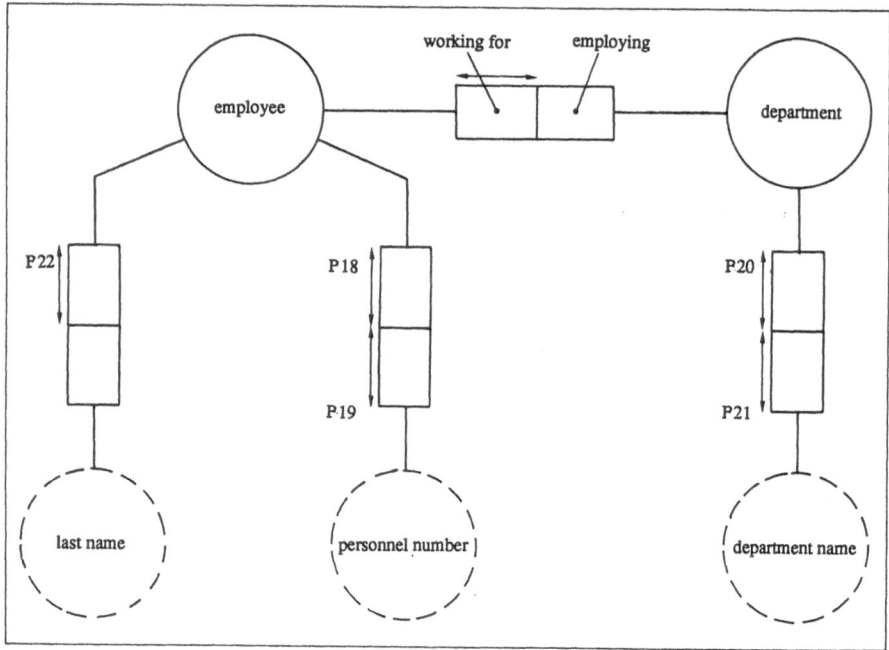

Figure 7.14.

P18 : An employee has precisely one personnel number.
P19 : A personnel number belongs to only one employee.
P20 : A department has precisely one department name.
P21 : A department name belongs to only one department.
P22 : An employee has precisely one last name.

These propositions express the uniqueness of the bridge type roles in the
information structure diagram and are therefore constraints. In Figure 7.14, we
have added these constraints to the information structure diagram. To make
things clear, we have put the numbers of the propositions next to the uniqueness
symbols to which they refer.

Both roles of the bridge type expressing the relation between employees and
their personnel numbers are unique: an employee has precisely one personnel
number, and every personnel number belongs to precisely one employee. Therefore, there is one and only one employee with personnel number J683, and
personnel number J683 belongs to one and only one employee. In other words,
there is precisely one employee who satisfies the reference:

"the ***employee with personnel number J683***"

and this one employee has precisely one personnel number, namely number J683. The above expression therefore refers in a one-to-one way to an employee. Consequently, the above expression is called a one-to-one reference to a non-lexical object of the type "employee."

In the above rules, it is stated that an employee has only one last name, but **not** that a certain last name belongs to only one employee. The role "last name of employee" has therefore not been provided with a uniqueness symbol. This bridge type has been provided in Figure 7.15 with a population diagram in which the employees are denoted by unique personnel numbers.

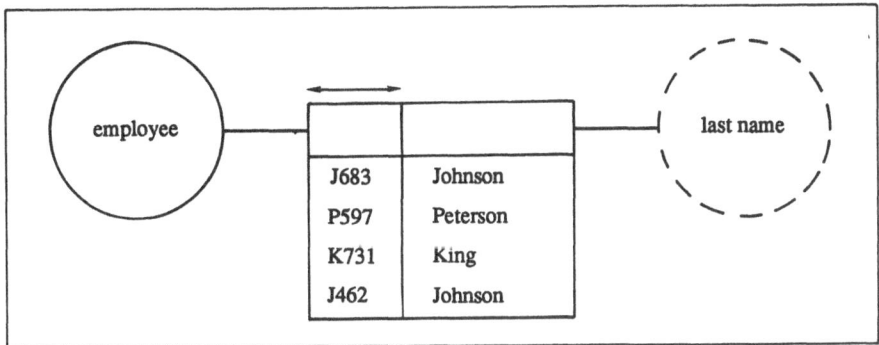

Figure 7.15.

In line with rule P22, every employee in this population has precisely one last name, while Johnson is an example of a last name which two different employees have, namely employees J683 and J462. A last name can therefore belong to one or more employees and can consequently not be used to uniquely denote an employee. There can be several employees that satisfy the reference:

"the *employee with last name* Johnson"

while each of these employees has only one last name, namely the last name Johnson. This expression consequently does not refer uniquely to an employee.

Figure 7.16 contains an example of a bridge type in which only the role of the lexical object type is unique.

This bridge type expresses the knowledge that employees can have nicknames. An employee can have more than one nickname, but every nickname always belongs to only one employee. So employee J683 has two nicknames, namely "Donald Duck" and "Garfield." Because a nickname always refers to exactly one employee, it can be used to uniquely denote an employee. There is precisely one employee who satisfies the reference:

"the *employee with nickname* Donald Duck"

while this one employee can have several nicknames. These nicknames refer to

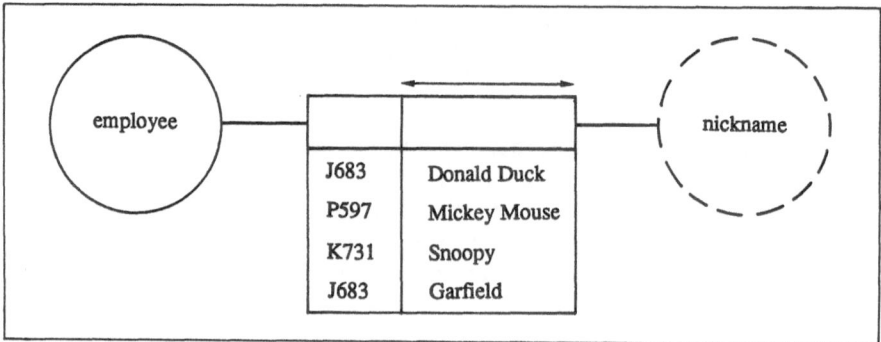

Figure 7.16.

the same employee and are in this sense each other's synonyms. The above expression is consequently called a *synonymous reference* to a non-lexical object of the type "employee." A synonymous reference is always unique, as the above example illustrates.

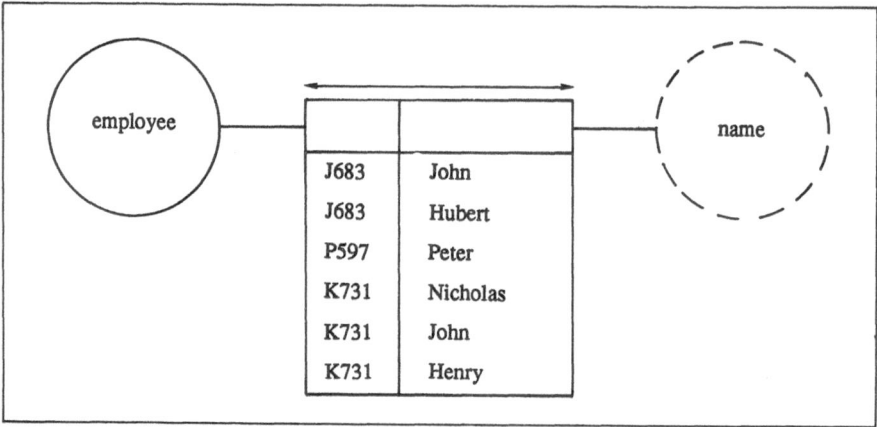

Figure 7.17.

Lastly, Figure 7.17 contains an example of a bridge type in which neither of the two roles is unique and which is therefore, as agreed in the previous section, provided with a uniqueness symbol along both roles.

This bridge type expresses the knowledge that the employees can have several names and that each name can belong to more than one employee. Employee K731, for example, has the first and middle names "Nicholas," "John" and "Henry," while "John" is also the first name of employee J683. Clearly, lexical objects of the type "name" cannot be used to refer uniquely to non-lexical objects of the type "employee."

The four possible ways uniqueness constraints can occur in bridge types are summarized below.

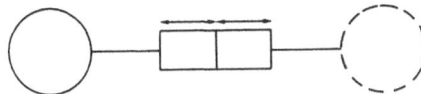

The lexical objects of this lexical object type refer, via the bridge type, in a one-to-one way (and thus **uniquely**) to the non-lexical objects of the non-lexical object type.

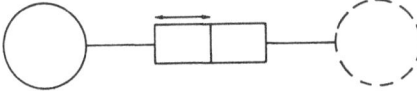

The lexical objects of this lexical object type refer, via the bridge type, **non-uniquely** to the non-lexical objects of the non-lexical object type.

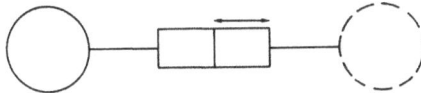

The lexical objects of this lexical object type refer, via the bridge type, **uniquely** to the non-lexical objects of the non-lexical object type.

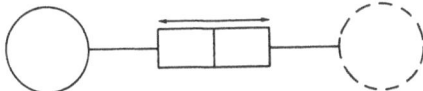

The lexical objects of this lexical object type refer, via the bridge type, **non-uniquely** to the non-lexical objects of the non-lexical object type.

7.4 Totality constraints

We next add to our example the following rule concerning the organization of the library:

P23 : **Every** department must employ one or more employees.

Thus, no information about departments which do not contain employees can occur in the information base. Figure 7.18 illustrates part of the information structure diagram with a possible population.

This population is allowed purely on the basis of the object types and the fact types of the information structure diagram. Because the department "Maintenance" does not actually contain any employees, this population does not satisfy Proposition P23. This proposition restricts the populations which are allowed in

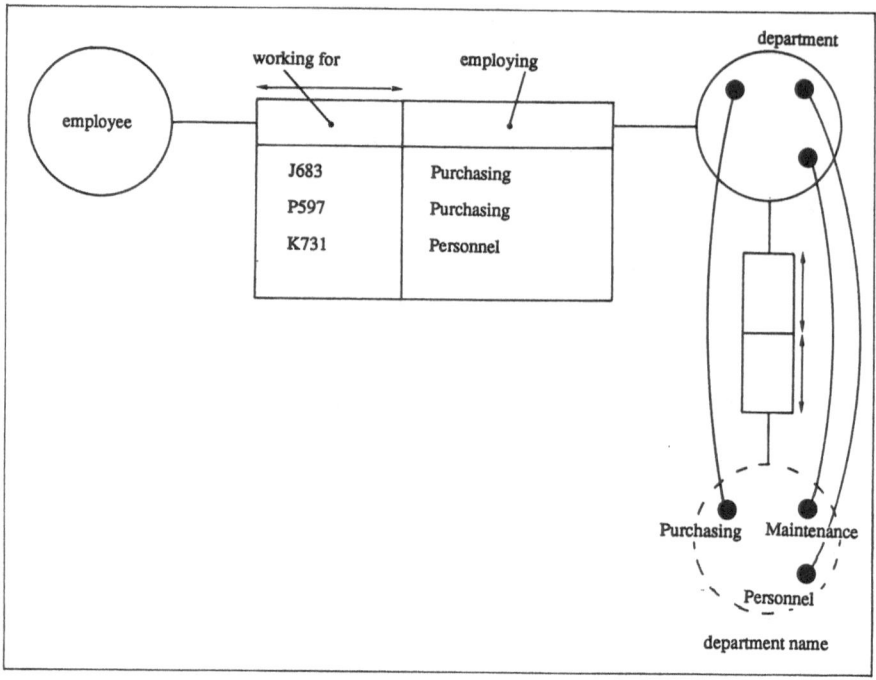

Figure 7.18.

the information structure diagram on the basis of the object types and the fact types, and is therefore a constraint. The population of Figure 7.18 only satisfies this constraint if the department "Maintenance" is deleted from the population of the object type "department" or if this department is included in the fact type population with at least one employee. The latter has been done in Figure 7.19.

The population of Figure 7.19 now satisfies the constraint described by Proposition P23. Unlike the population in the previous figure, **every** object of the object type "department" now occurs in the population of the role "department employing employee." It follows from this that rule P23 is equivalent to the following rule:

> **Every** object of the object type "department" must occur in the population of the role "department employing employee."

This rule is a translation of rule P23 in terms of fact type roles, and therefore in terms of the components of an information structure diagram. Both rules mean exactly the same thing; both express the same knowledge. A role in which every object must occur in every population, such as the role "department employing employee," is called a mandatory role or *total role*. As the constraint which is described by Proposition P23 expresses the totality of this role, it is called a *totality constraint*. From now on, we will denote total roles by placing the symbol "A" on the line connecting the role with its object type. This has been done in Figure 7.20.

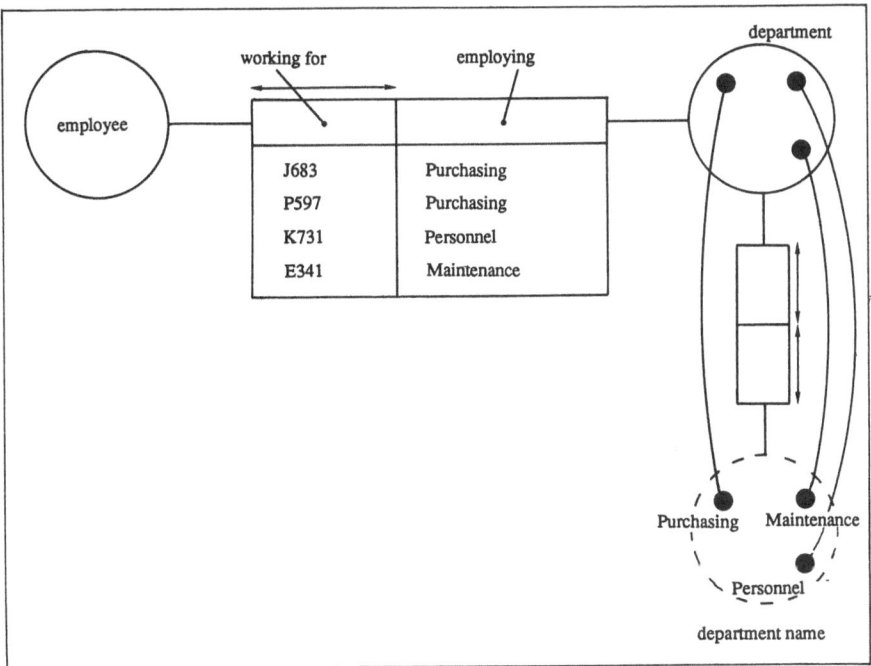

Figure 7.19.

The symbol "A" is an abbreviation of "for All."

The role "department employing employee" is total. **Every** department must occur in the population of this role. The totality symbol expresses the totality of this role and is a graphical representation of the totality constraint described by Proposition P23.

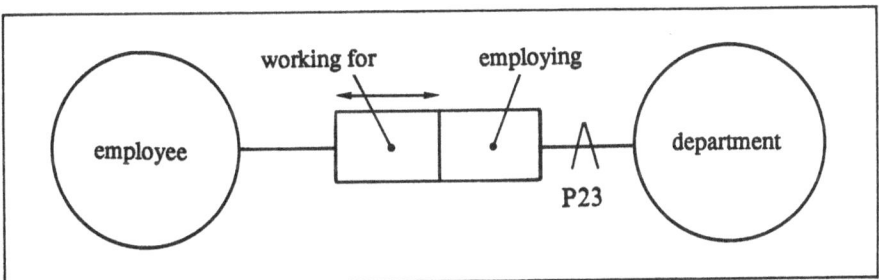

Figure 7.20.

The totality constraint discussed here has been added to the information structure diagram in Figure 7.21.

The role "employee working for department" is not total. Apparently, not every employee who is recorded in the information base has to work for a department. We can indeed imagine that the data of an employee who has just been hired or

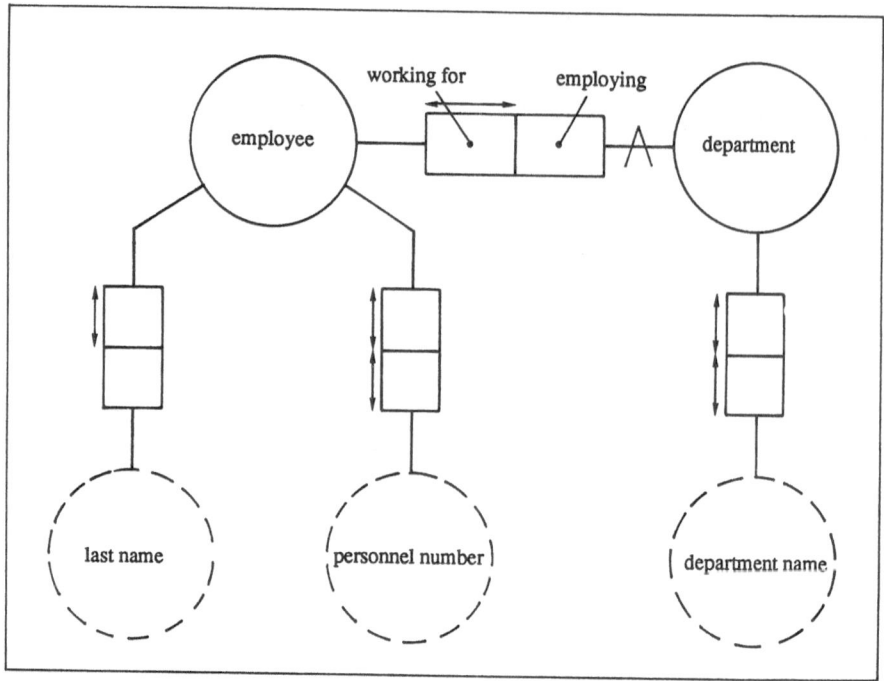

Figure 7.21.

who has yet to be hired are already recorded in the information base and that this employee is later added to a department.

The information processor checks to see whether a totality constraint is violated every time it receives a request to add a fact to the information base or to delete one from it.

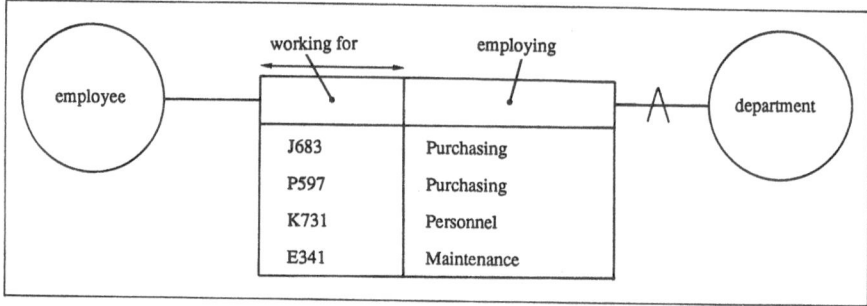

Figure 7.22.

Let us suppose that the population diagram in Figure 7.22 describes part of the information base at a given moment and that the user at that moment addresses the following request to the information processor:

Delete: the **employee with personnel number** E341 **working for** the **department** Maintenance.

The result of this would be that the Maintenance Department would no longer contain any employees.

The information processor would respond as follows:

Request not executed because of violation of rule P23 (Every department must contain one or more employees).

Then the user must either not delete the fact that employee E341 works for Maintenance, or first add another employee to the Maintenance Department.

When the user addresses the following compound request to the information processor:

Begin Delete: the **employee with personnel number** E341 **working for** the **department** Maintenance.
      Delete: the **department** Maintenance.
End

the totality constraint is not violated once the two individual requests have been executed. When the user addresses, on the basis of the population of Figure 7.22, the following request to the information processor:

Add: the **department** Loan

the information processor responds as follows:

Request not executed because of violation of rule P23 (Every department must contain one or more employees).

However, when the user addresses the following compound request to the information processor:

Begin Add: the **department** Loan.
      Add: the **employee with personnel number** F759 **working for** the **department** Loan.
End

the totality constraint is not violated once the two individual requests have been executed.

To summarize:

Total role (mandatory role):
A role in which every object of the object type of that role must occur in every population.

Totality constraint:
A constraint which expresses the totality of a role.

Totality symbol:
The graphical representation of a totality constraint.

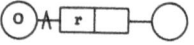   role r of object type O is total.

7.5 Totality constraints involving bridge types

We add the following rules to our example:

P24 : Every employee must have a personnel number.
P25 : Every employee must have a last name.
P26 : Every department must have a department name.

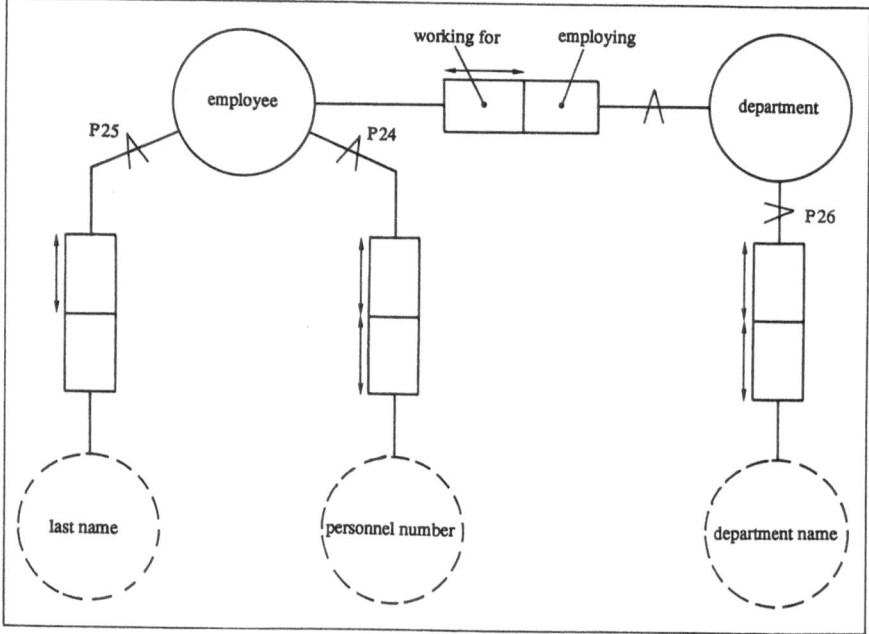

Figure 7.23.

These rules express the totality of the bridge type roles and are thus totality constraints. In Figure 7.23, we have added these totality constraints to the information structure diagram.

7.6 Referenceability

The grammar and therefore also the information structure diagram describe information, or, stated differently, **communicable** knowledge. Knowledge is only communicable if every non-lexical object involved in this knowledge can be **uniquely** denoted by one or more lexical objects. When a non-lexical object cannot be denoted or cannot be denoted uniquely, the knowledge about this non-lexical object is not communicable and therefore this knowledge is, by definition, not information. When, for example, employees can only be denoted by their last names, others may not be clear about to whom certain knowledge about an employee "Johnson" refers, because there can be more than one employee with that name. This knowledge is consequently noncommunicable and is thus, by definition, not information.

It follows from this that:

An information structure diagram must be such that, on the basis of this diagram, **every** non-lexical object can always be referred to **uniquely**.

From now on, we shall call this the *referenceability rule*. An information structure diagram that satisfies this rule is considered *referenceable*. Formulated somewhat differently, the referenceability rule reads:

An information structure diagram must be referenceable.

An information structure diagram that is not referenceable does not describe information (communicable knowledge) in every possible case and is therefore incorrect. Consequently, it is not even, by definition, an **information** structure diagram.

We shall next show a few examples of referenceable and non-referenceable information structure diagrams.

Let us suppose that an information structure diagram consists of only the bridge type of Figure 7.24.

In this figure, the personnel numbers are one-to-one references to employees, but as not **every** employee has a personnel number, this diagram is not referenceable. In Figure 7.24, there is, for example, a non-lexical object of the type "employee" without a personnel number. In this population there is no lexical object by which this employee might be uniquely denoted, and therefore no knowledge about this employee can be communicated. This information structure diagram is only referenceable when **every** employee has a personnel number or,

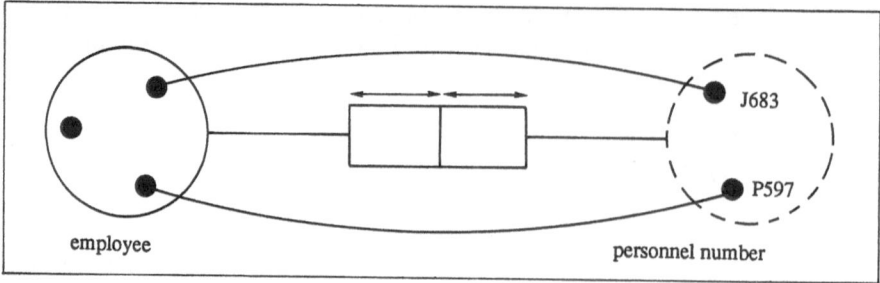

Figure 7.24.

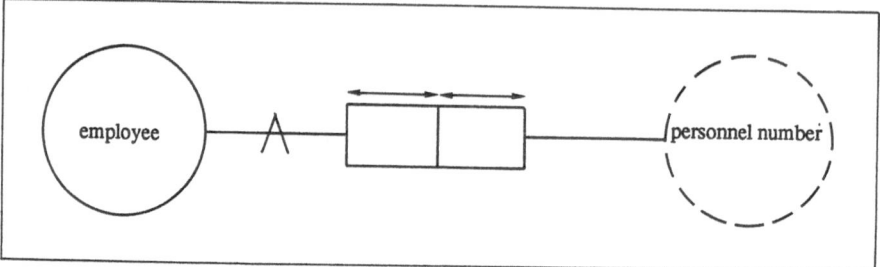

Figure 7.25.

stated differently, if the role of the non-lexical object type in the bridge type is total, as is the case in Figure 7.25.

In this information structure diagram, **every** employee can be uniquely referred to by means of a personnel number. This information structure diagram is therefore referenceable.

The information structure diagram of Figure 7.26 is referenceable. Because the role of the object type "employee" is total, **every** employee has a nickname, and because the role of the object type "nickname" is unique, every nickname refers to precisely one employee.

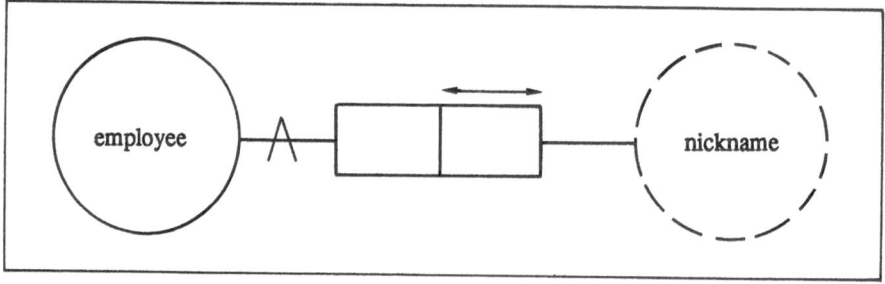

Figure 7.26.

Although there is no bridge type for the non-lexical object type "department," the information structure diagram of Figure 7.27 is still referenceable. A nickname belongs to precisely one employee, and if an employee works for a department, he then works for precisely one department. A department can thus be referred to uniquely by one of the nicknames of one of the employees who work for this department. Because **every** department contains an employee and **every** employee has a nickname, **every** department can be **uniquely** referred to by a nickname of one of its employees, and the information structure diagram is thus referenceable. For example, the expression "The department employing the employee with the nickname Donald Duck" refers to precisely one department. Because a department can be uniquely denoted by **several** nicknames (namely, all the nicknames of all the employees who work for this department), the above expression is a synonymous reference to a department.

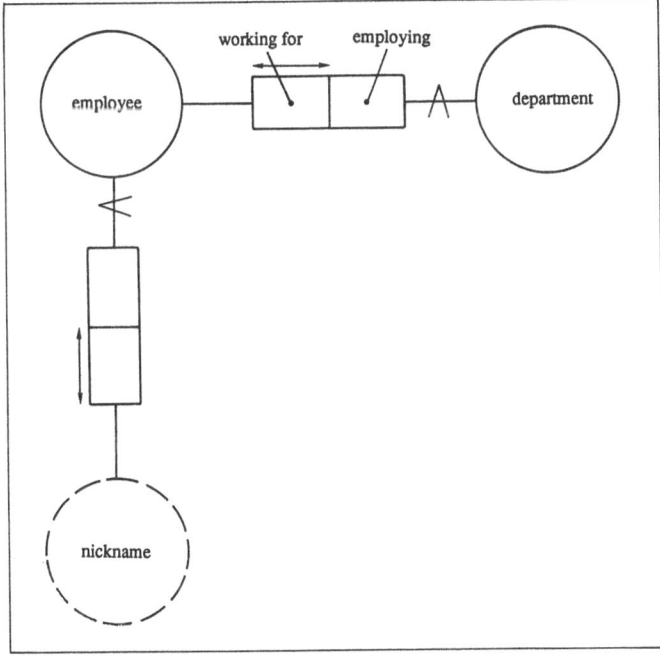

Figure 7.27.

In the information structure diagram of Figure 7.28, a last name can refer to more than one employee, so that an employee cannot be uniquely denoted by a last name. This information structure diagram is consequently not referenceable, and is not acceptable in this form as an information structure diagram. The information structure diagram of Figure 7.29 is not referenceable for the same reason.

It is only possible to demonstrate or verify constraints with the aid of population diagrams if every non-lexical object is represented in these population diagrams

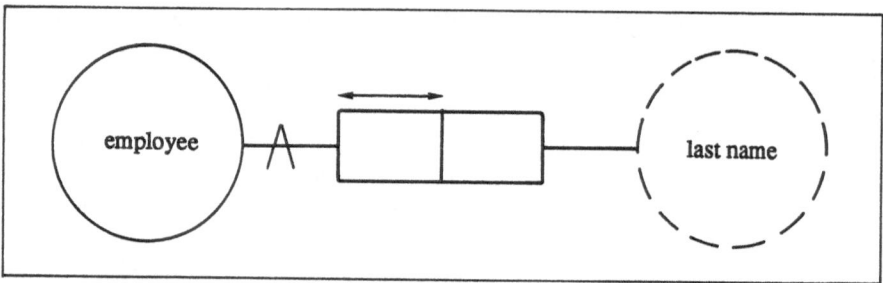

Figure 7.28.

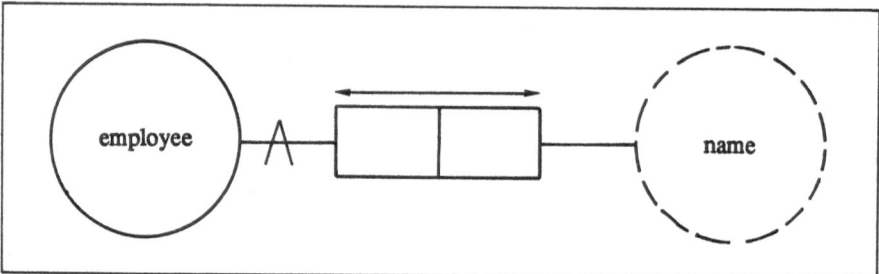

Figure 7.29.

by one or more lexical objects which refer **uniquely** to this non-lexical object. This is always possible in a referenceable information structure diagram.

To summarize:

A referenceable information structure diagram:
An information structure diagram in which every non-lexical object can always be referred to uniquely.

The referenceability rule:
An information structure diagram must be referenceable.

7.7 An abridged notation for bridge types

The bridge types in Figure 7.23 involving "employee" and "personnel number" as well as "department" and "department name" satisfy each two characteristics:

- both roles are unique
- the role of the non-lexical object type is total.

Bridge types with these characteristics occur frequently in practice. For this reason, there is an "abridged notation" for these bridge types, which can keep an information structure diagram from becoming too extensive in practice. This abridged notation means that, for example, the bridge type involving "employee" and "personnel number" can be drawn as in Figure 7.30.

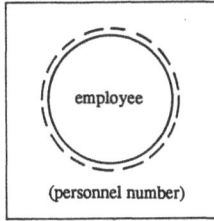

Figure 7.30.

The symbol of the lexical object type is drawn around the symbol of the non-lexical object type, and the name of the lexical object type is noted between parentheses. This abridged notation has been carried out in the information structure diagram of Figure 7.31.

Bear in mind that this abridged notation is **only** allowed for bridge types in which:

– both roles are unique
– the role of the non-lexical object type is total.

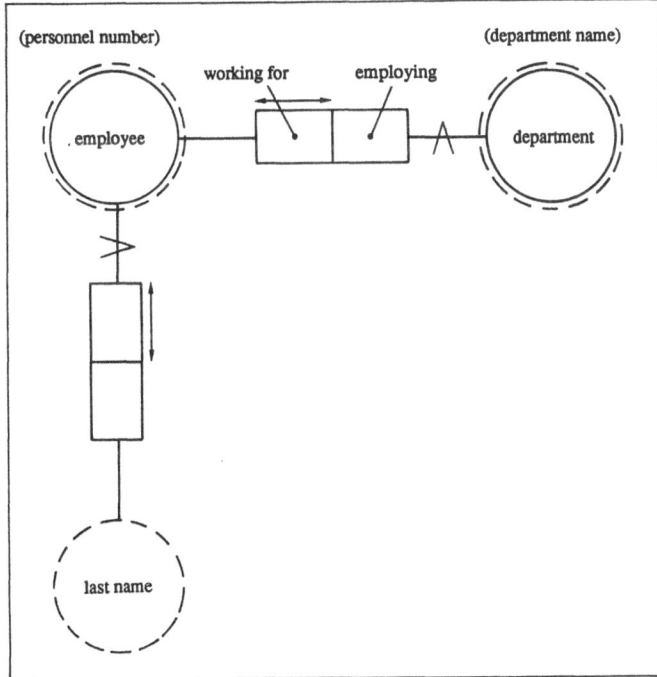

Figure 7.31.

8 THE NIAM METHOD OF INFORMATION ANALYSIS IN PRACTICE - 2

In this chapter, we shall add the following two steps to the stepwise plan of the NIAM method of information analysis:

> 6. Determine the uniqueness constraints and totality constraints with respect to the individual fact types.

> 11. Verify the information structure diagram.

The steps in between these will come up for discussion in the next practical chapters.

In Figure 8.1, we have repeated part of the information structure diagram of the library case. We shall now carry out the above steps for this part of the information structure diagram.

6. Determine the uniqueness constraints and totality constraints with respect to the individual fact types.

In this step, the uniqueness constraints and, where applicable, the totality constraints are determined for each of the fact types added to the information structure diagram in the previous step. To make things clearer, we will divide this step into two substeps:

- Determine the uniqueness constraints with respect to the individual fact types.
- Determine the totality constraints with respect to the individual fact types.

6.1 Determine the uniqueness constraints with respect to the individual fact types.

In this substep, we look into which roles are unique for every fact type. When this is not immediately clear for a certain fact type, the various possibilities are analyzed with the aid of a population diagram by using **concrete examples** (preferably those obtained in practice). When, for example, it is not immediately clear or directly obvious which fact type roles involving the object types "book" and "kind" are unique, we use population diagrams to analyze which populations are allowed for these roles. See Figure 8.2.

It appears that the third line of the population diagram is not allowed, because the book with ISBN "90 6233 134 3" is, according to the catalog card of Figure

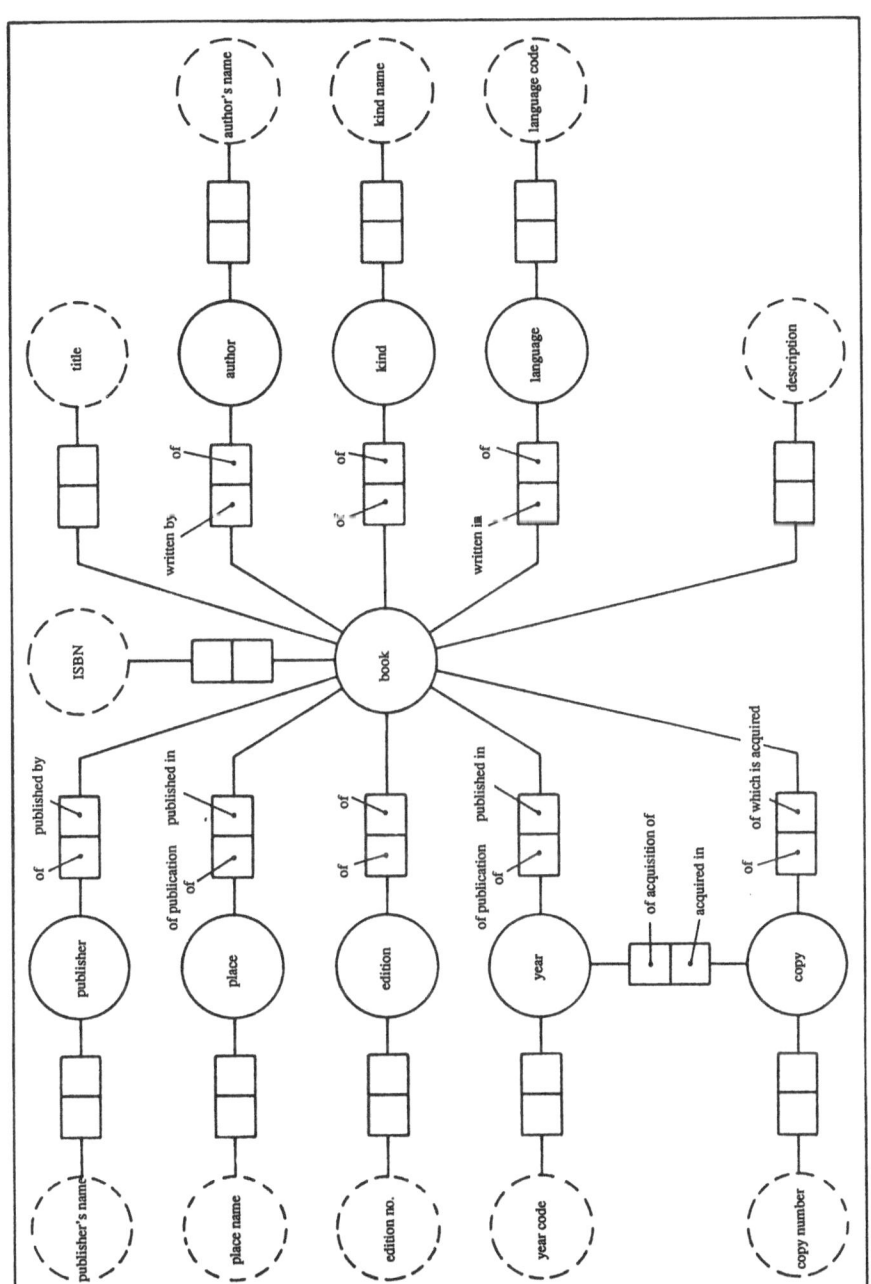

Figure 8.1.

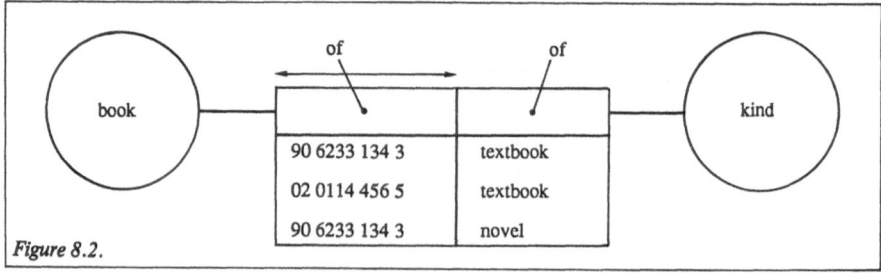

Figure 8.2.

6.2, of the kind "textbook" and cannot simultaneously be a textbook and a novel. In general, every book can only belong to one kind, so that the role "book of the kind" is unique. We have indicated this in the population diagram with a uniqueness symbol. There are generally more books of one particular kind, so that the role "kind of book" is certainly not unique.

The catalog card of Figure 6.2 contains an example of a book that has been written by two authors. But, can one certain author be the writer of more than one book? Let us suppose that we have looked through the catalog card file and found a few concrete examples which we have illustrated in the population diagram of Figure 8.3.

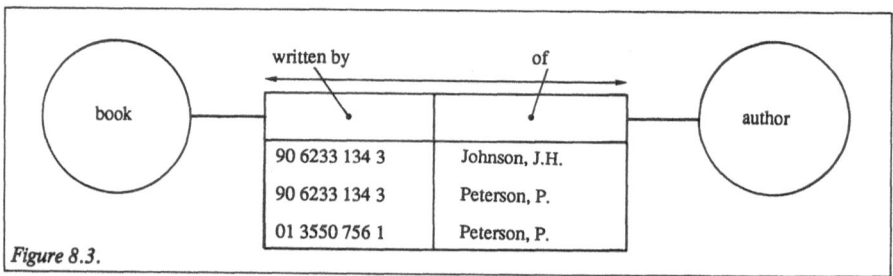

Figure 8.3.

It appears that Peterson, P. is not only one of the authors of the book with ISBN "90 6233 134 3," but that he is also the author of another book. In the population diagram both a book and an author appear twice, so that apparently neither of the roles is unique. We have denoted this, as agreed in the previous chapter, by drawing a uniqueness symbol along both roles of this fact type.

When it is not immediately clear or directly obvious whether roles of a certain fact type are unique, it is more efficient and effective to "try out" various possibilities by using actual or imaginary examples in a population diagram, and then to come to a decision on the basis of these, rather than to think and reason (often for too long) without any concrete examples and points of departure.

Next, we analyze the uniqueness of the roles of the remaining fact types in the information structure diagram (Figure 8.1). The uniqueness constraints determined this way are given in Figure 8.4.

We shall begin by assuming that a book can have only one title. We have then

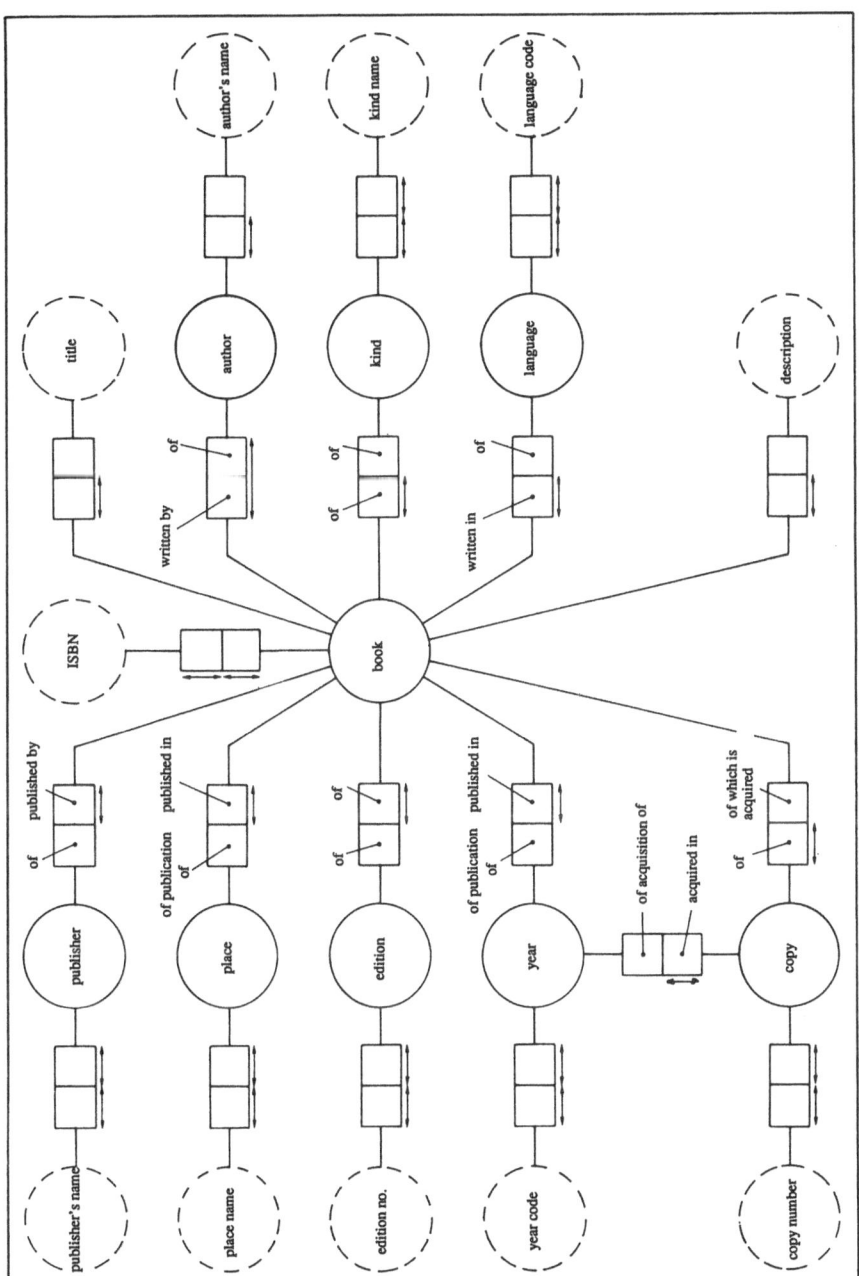

Figure 8.4.

decided not to record subtitles as such. The role "book with title" is therefore unique. Sometimes, a title can belong to more than one book. There are for example several books in the library with the very common title "History of the art of printing." The role "title of book" is therefore certainly not unique.

Every book is written in only one language. The role "book written in language" is therefore unique. Naturally there are several books in the library which are written in one particular language, so that the role "language of book" is not unique.

Only one description can be included on the catalog card per book, so that the role "book with description" is apparently unique. Some descriptions are so general that they can occur for more than one book. There are, for example, several books with the very common description: "This book provides a historical overview of the development of the art of printing." It follows from this that the role "description of book" is not unique.

Every book is published by one publisher, in one place of publication and in one year of publication. The roles "book published by publisher," "book published in place," and "book published in year" are therefore unique. A publisher generally publishes more than one book, and more than one book can be published in a certain place and in a certain year. The roles "publisher of book," "place of publication of book," and "year of publication of book" are therefore not unique.

For every book, there is only one edition number on the catalog card. The role "book of edition" is consequently unique. We have previously stated that when a new edition of a book is published (when the edition number changes), the book is considered to be a new book that is identified by a new ISBN. Obviously, several books can have the same edition number, so that the role "edition of book" is not unique.

It appears from the catalog card of Figure 6.2 that there can be several copies of one book. Of course, every copy can be the copy of only one book. The role "book of which is acquired copy" is therefore not unique, while the role "copy of book" is.

A copy can only be acquired in one single year, while in one particular year, several copies can be acquired. The role "copy acquired in year" is therefore unique, and the role "year of acquisition of copy" is not.

We assume that every author has one author's name. We therefore do not take various pseudonymns and such into account. A certain author's name can, however, belong to different authors, just like the last name of a person. It follows from this that the role "author with author's name" is unique, and that the role "author's name of author" is not unique.

Furthermore, we assume that a kind name refers in a one-to-one way to a kind, a language code refers in a one-to-one way to a language, a publisher's name refers in a one-to-one way to a publisher, a place name refers in a one-to-one way to a place, an edition number refers in a one-to-one way to an edition, a year code refers in a one-to-one way to a year and, lastly, that a copy number refers in a one-to-one way to a copy. It follows from this that both roles of each of these bridge types are unique.

6.2 Determine the totality constraints with respect to the individual fact types.

We begin by assuming that for each book that is recorded, the title, the author, the publisher, the place of publication, the edition, and the year of publication must always be known, while the remaining data need not always be known. It is, for example, possible that a book has no description or that it has not (yet) been classified into a kind.

This means concretely that the roles "book with title," "book written by author," "book published by publisher," "book published in place," "book of edition," and "book published in year" are total.

For every copy, the book associated with it must be known. The year of acquisition, on the other hand, does not have to be known for every copy. In other words, the role "copy of book" is total.

Further, we assume that each book has an ISBN, each author an author's name, each kind a kind name, each language a language code, each publisher a publisher's name, each place a place name, each edition an edition number, each year a year code, and each copy a copy number. This means that the roles "book with ISBN," "author with author's name," "kind with kind name," "language with language code," "publisher with publisher's name," "place with place name," "edition with edition number," "year with year code," and "copy with copy number" are total.

We have represented all of these totality constraints in Figure 8.5.

We remind the reader that the populations of a total role must contain, **at every moment,** all the objects of the relevant object type about which something is known in the information base at that moment. Because, for example, the role "book published in year" is total, the year of publication of every book must **always** be known. The rule that the year of publication of a book does not have to be known in the information base at every moment, but only under certain circumstances, would not be a totality constraint, but another kind of constraint.

In Figure 8.6, we have replaced all the bridge types in which both roles are unique and in which the role of the non-lexical object type is total by the shortened method of notation for bridge types agreed to in the previous chapter. This makes the information structure diagram less extensive.

11. Verify the information structure diagram.

In this step, the correctness of the information structure diagram is verified. This takes place in the following substeps:

- Verify the information structure.
- Verify the constraints.
- Verify the referenceability.

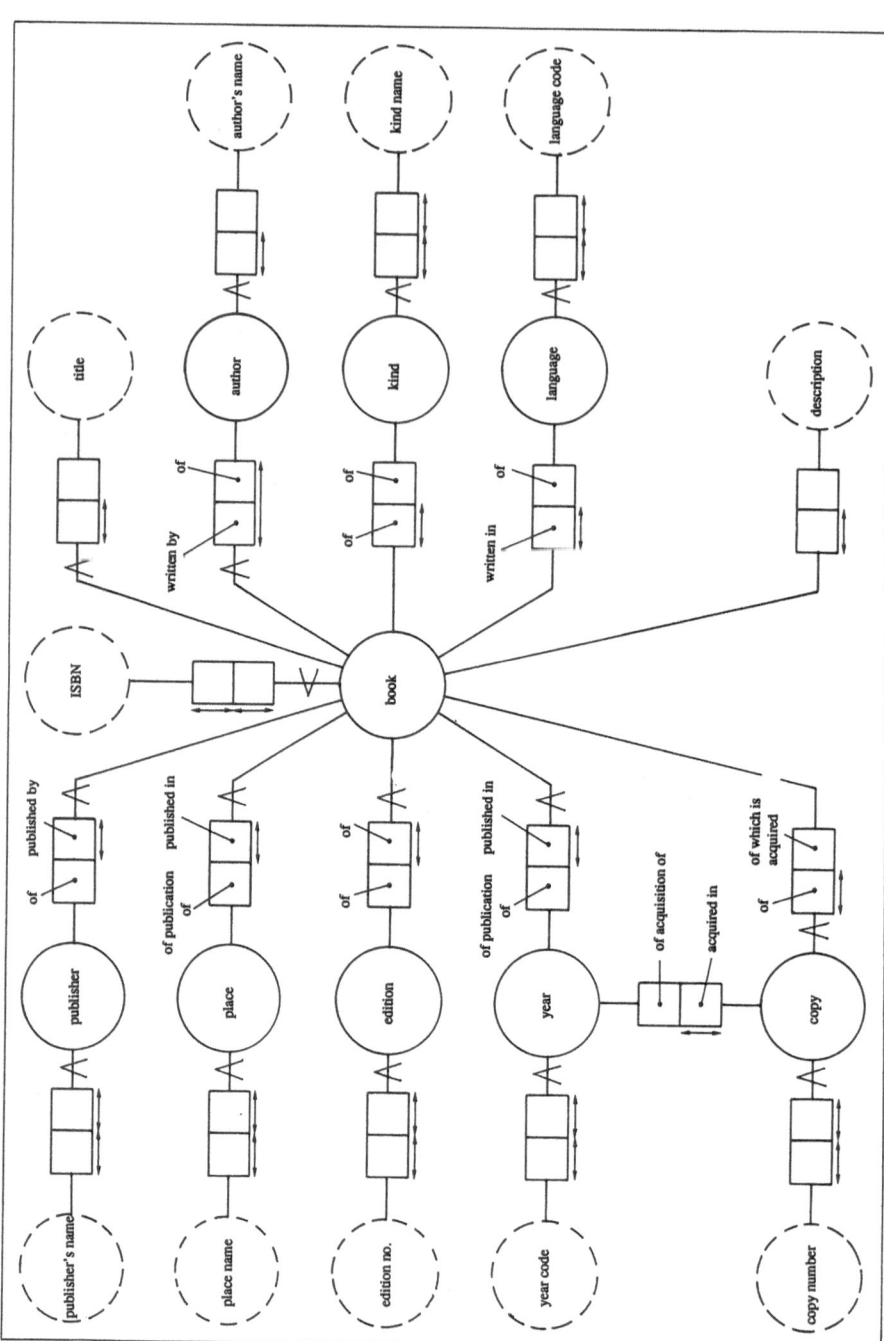

Figure 8.5.

11.1 Verify the information structure.

We could consider the information base as a collection of tables, each of which corresponds to one fact type and whose allowable contents are restricted by the constraints. In this step, it is verified whether it is possible with all due consideration of the constraints to transfer the entire contents of the original population table(s), on the basis of which the information structure diagram is constructed, to (imaginary) tables which each correspond to one fact type in the information structure diagram. This verification step can be done mentally, or more tangibly on paper, or by using computerized aids (should these be available). In the library case, we thus need to verify whether the information base, as it is described by the diagram in Figure 8.6, can be "filled," while considering the constraints, with the original population tables of Figures 6.5 and 6.12. If this does not succeed, it is a sign of an analysis error made earlier.

Next, we look into whether the original population tables can be reconstructed, with all due consideration of the constraints, from the (imaginary) tables described by the information structure diagram. This is likewise done mentally, or more tangibly on paper, or by using computerized aids. Should this fail, it is a sign of an analysis error made earlier in the process.

We leave the reader to carry out this substep for the library case on his or her own.

11.2 Verify the constraints.

In this substep, the correctness and completeness of all the constraints are checked, in particular whether:
- all the necessary constraints have been specified completely
- any constraints have been included which are redundant, because they are implied by other constraints
- there are any constraints which are in conflict with each other.

Later in this book, when we take up the subject of other kinds of constraints, the necessity of this step will automatically become clear.

11.3 Verify the referenceability.

In this substep, we check to see whether the information structure diagram is referenceable. That is, we look to see whether, on the basis of the diagram, **every** non-lexical object can be **uniquely** denoted by one or more lexical objects.

If we take another look at the information structure diagram of Figure 8.6, and

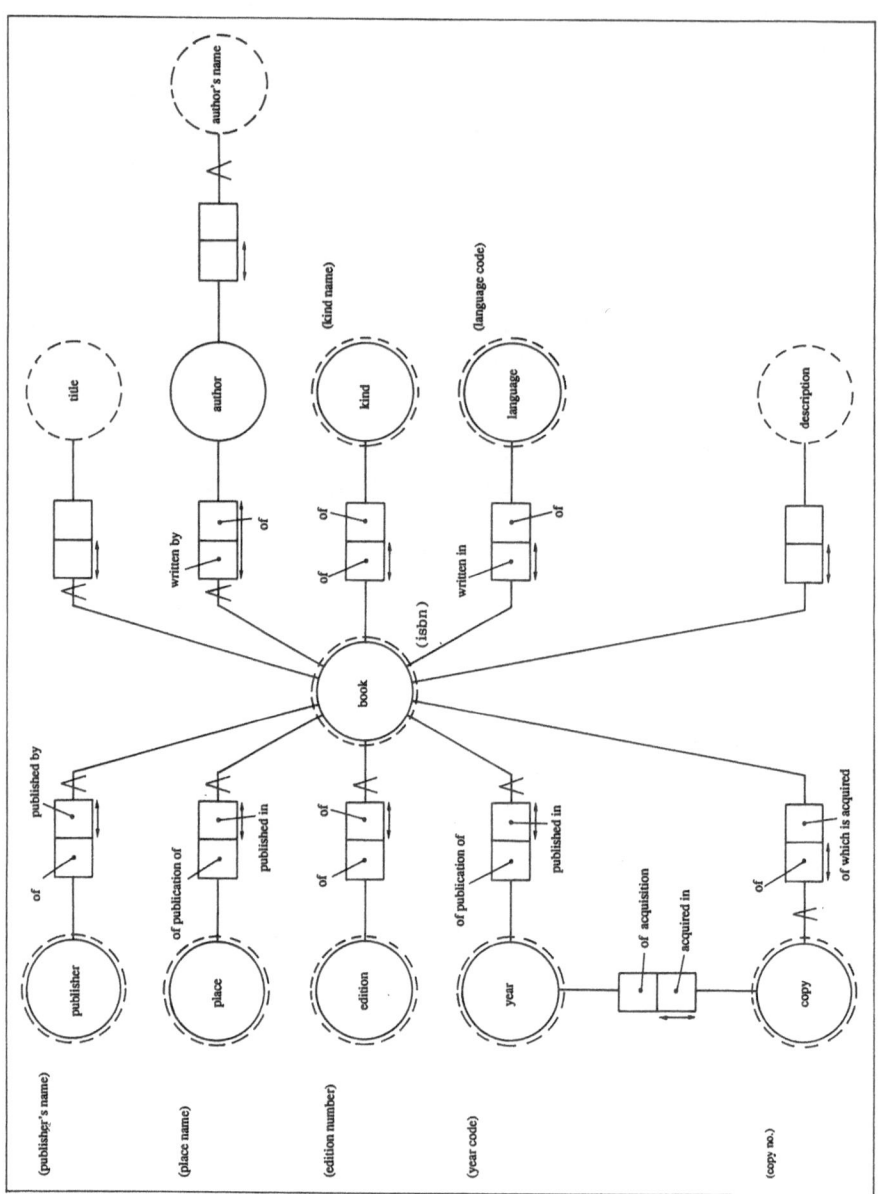

Figure 8.6.

in particular at the object type "author," we see that we have run into a few snags at this point. While it is true that every author has an author's name, one particular author's name can, in principle, belong to more than one author. Therefore, an author's name does **not** in all cases refer uniquely to an author. Because the object type "author" has only one bridge type, the non-lexical objects of the type "author" cannot in general be uniquely denoted by lexical objects. The information structure diagram is consequently not referenceable.

As a nonreferenceable information structure digram is not acceptable, we will have to adapt the diagram such that it does become referenceable.

We could consider coming up with a new lexical object type "author code" or "author number," in which the lexical objects would each refer uniquely or perhaps even in a one-to-one way to an author. However, in practice, we should never, or only very rarely, add to the information structure diagram object types which do not occur in the population tables on which this diagram has been based. After all, these population tables have been constructed on the basis of the examples reflecting the information needs of the future users of the information system. According to the examples used here, there is no need in the library for an "author code" or an "author number." "Author code" or "author number" are not viable concepts in the library, making it incorrect to introduce such alien or artificial concepts to the future users via the information analysis process.

In such situations, we should rather ask ourselves whether our analysis up to this point perhaps contains errors or imperfections. Let us take another look at the catalog card (Figure 6.2) and at the lexical object on this card which we have called "author's name." In fact, it is impossible to distinguish an author's name, as it is given on the catalog card, from the last name of a member of the library or one of its employees. If it is impossible to distinguish between lexical objects, there is no practical reason to classify these objects into different lexical object types. In our analysis of the loan management up to now, we have introduced the concept "author's name," without realizing that this is the same as "last name," because the authors' names, as used on the catalog cards, can in practice not be distinguished from last names as used elsewhere in the library. Our conclusion is that last names are listed on catalog cards rather than authors' names. These last names appear on the catalog cards in the **role** of last names of authors. "Last name" is a lexical object type that (thus far) occurs in two different bridge types, namely as the last name of an author on the one hand, and as the last name of a member on the other hand.

In Figure 8.7, we have adapted the information structure diagram in this sense. This diagram is now referenceable.

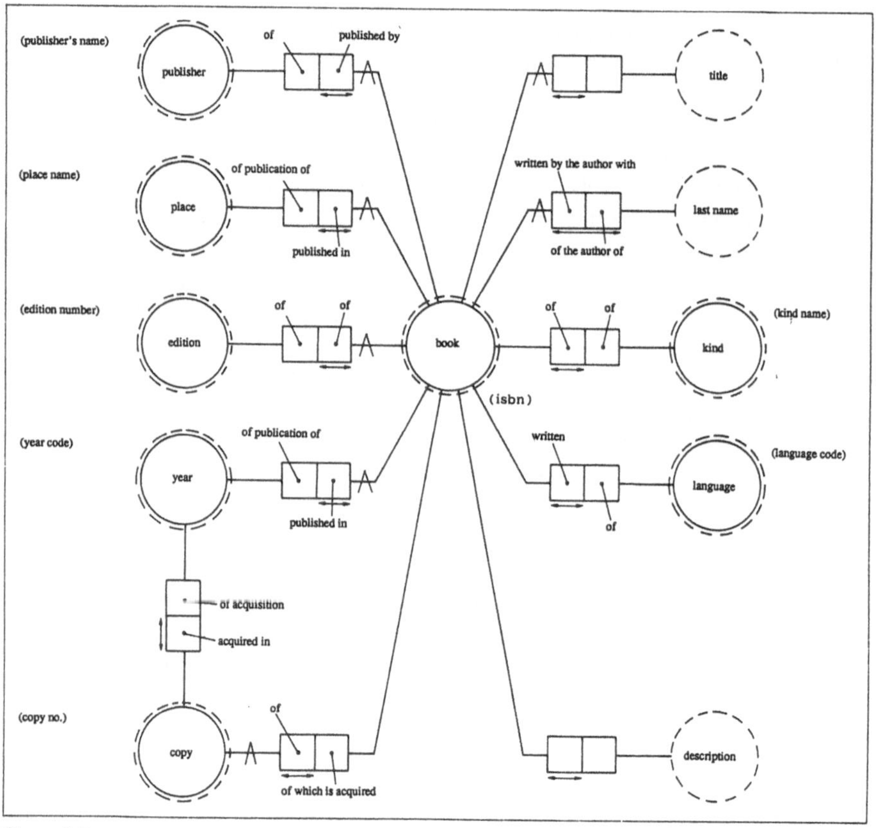

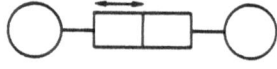

Figure 8.7.

Summary

Below is a summary of the analysis steps in the NIAM method of information analysis dealt with in this chapter.

6. Determine the uniqueness constraints and totality constraints with respect to the individual fact types.

   6.1 Determine the uniqueness constraints with respect to the individual fact types.

6.2 Determine the totality constraints with respect to the individual fact types.

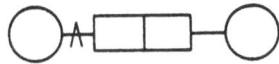

11. Verify the information structure diagram.

    11.1 Verify the information structure.

        – Verify, with all due consideration of the constraints, whether (imaginary) tables, each corresponding to one fact type in the information structure diagram, can be "filled" with the contents of the original population tables.

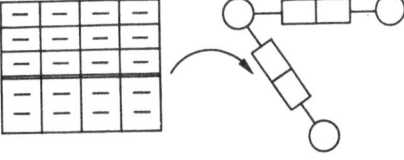

        – Verify, with all due consideration of the constraints, whether the original population tables can be reconstructed from (imaginary) tables, each corresponding to one fact type in the information structure diagram.

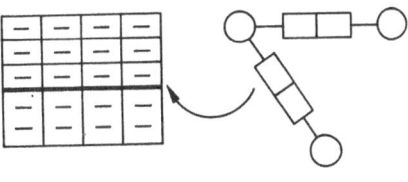

    11.2 Verify the constraints:

        – Have all the necessary constraints been specified completely?

        – Are there any constraints which are implied by other constraints and are therefore redundant?

        – Are there any constraints which are in conflict with each other?

    11.3 Verify the referenceability:

        – Can every non-lexical object be referred to uniquely by a lexical object or by a combination of lexical objects?

9 GRAPHICAL CONSTRAINTS INVOLVING MULTIPLE FACT TYPES

In Chapter 7, we took a look at graphical constraints which restrict the role populations of one single fact type. In the upcoming sections we shall investigate graphical constraints which restrict the role populations of two or more fact types. Just as in Chapter 7, these constraints will be illustrated by the library case. To do this, we will be adding to the library case in each section.

9.1 Equality constraints

We shall assume that the library employees have been assigned organizational functions, which are denoted in a one-to-one way by function names. It is possible that an employee who has not definitely been hired or who has just started, has not yet been assigned a function. An employee can, in principle, be assigned more than one function. Further, the employees are divided up into salary groups, which are denoted in a one-to-one way by salary codes. Every employee can be classified into only one salary group. Every employee can only be classified into a salary group if he or she has been assigned a function. Conversely, an employee can only be assigned a function if his or her salary group is known.

This additional knowledge about the library is summarized by the following rules:

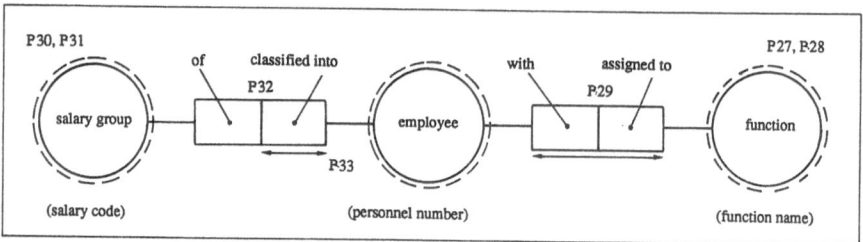

Figure 9.1.

P27 : There are functions.
P28 : Every function is referred to in a one-to-one way by a function name.
P29 : Functions can be assigned to employees.
P30 : There are salary groups.
P31 : Every salary group is referred to in a one-to-one way by a salary code.
P32 : Employees can be classified into salary groups.
P33 : An employee can only be classified into one salary group.
P34 : An employee classified into a salary group must be assigned a function

and, conversely, an employee assigned a function must be classified into a salary group.

Propositions P28 and P31 are not elementary. These propositions each describe a one-to-one bridge type in which the role of the non-lexical object type is total and to which the shortened method of notation for bridge types can therefore be applied.

The above rules are described by the part of the information structure diagram that is represented in Figure 9.1. So that we can compare the above rules with the diagram, we have written the rule numbers next to the symbols to which they refer.

Because the role "employee with function" is not unique, an employee can be assigned, in line with the description given above, more than one function. In this diagram all of the above rules are represented except for rule P34. This is clearly a constraint. The population of Figure 9.2 is allowed purely on the basis of the object types, the fact types, and the uniqueness constraints in the diagram of Figure 9.1.

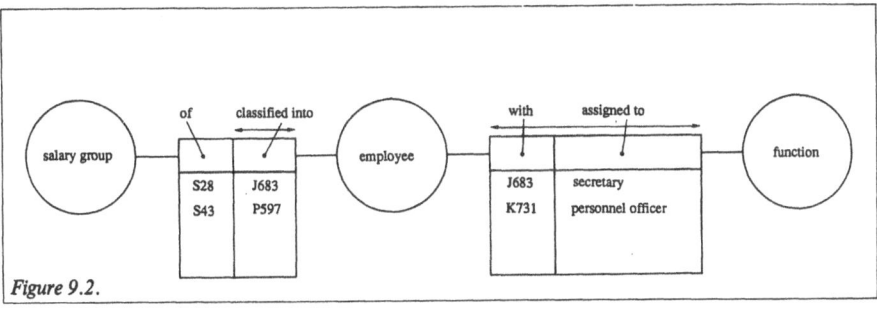

Figure 9.2.

In this population, employee K731 indeed has a function, but is not classified into a salary group, while employee P597 is classified into a salary group but has no function. This is in conflict with the constraint described by Proposition 34. The population of Figure 9.2 only satisfies this constraint if either the fact that employee K731 is assigned a function and the fact that employee P597 is classified into a salary group are deleted, or if employee K731 is put in a certain salary group and employee P597 is assigned a certain function. The latter has been done in Figure 9.3.

This population now satisfies the constraint described by Proposition P34. Every employee assigned a function is classified into a salary group, and every employee classified into a salary group is assigned a function. Unlike Figure 9.2, every employee who occurs in the population of the role "employee with function" also occurs in the population of the role "employee classified into salary group," and vice versa. The populations of these two roles are thus equal. It follows from this that rule P34 is equivalent to the following rule:

The populations of the roles "employee with function" and "employee classified into salary group" must always be equal.

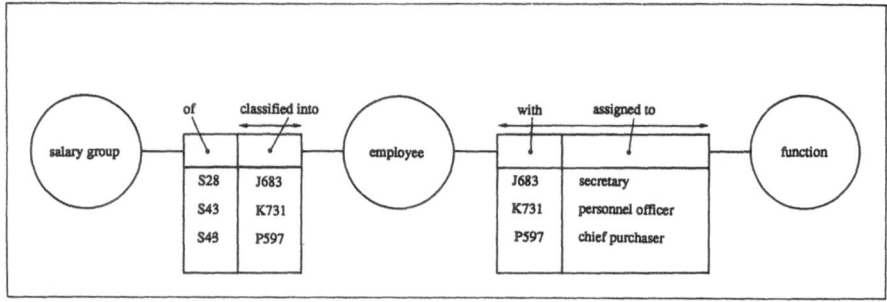

Figure 9.3.

This rule is a translation of rule P34 in terms of role populations of fact types. Both rules mean exactly the same thing; they both express the same knowledge.

Two roles whose populations are equal at any moment, such as the roles "employee with function" and "employee classified into salary group," are called *equal roles*. The constraint described by Proposition P34 expresses the equality of two roles, and is consequently called an *equality constraint*. We shall denote equal roles in an information structure diagram by using the symbol E, for Equal, to connect these roles. We have carried this out in Figure 9.4.

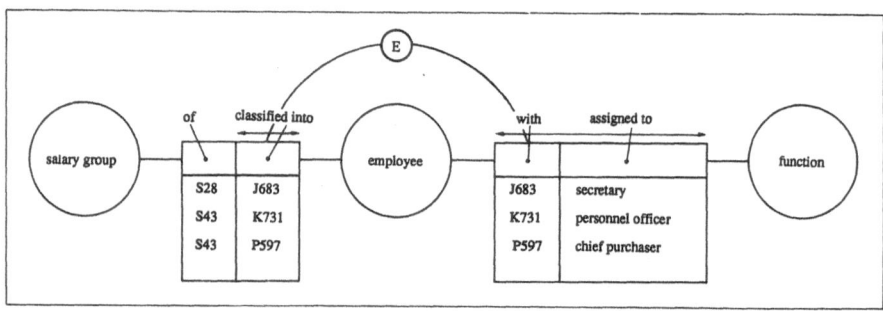

Figure 9.4.

The roles "employee with function" and "employee classified into salary group" are equal. Every employee occurring in the population of the role "employee with function" also occurs in the population of the role "employee classified into salary group," and vice versa. The symbol connecting these two roles expresses their equality, and is a graphical representation of the equality constraint described by Proposition P34.

In the following population, two functions are assigned to employee K731, namely that of "personnel officer" and "legal advisor."

Consequently, this employee now appears twice in the population of the role "employee with function" and only once in the population of the role "employee classified into salary group." Even so, every employee who occurs in the population of the role "employee with function" also occurs in the population of the role "employee classified into salary group," and vice versa. This makes the two **populations,** by definition, equal. Two role populations are equal if every object

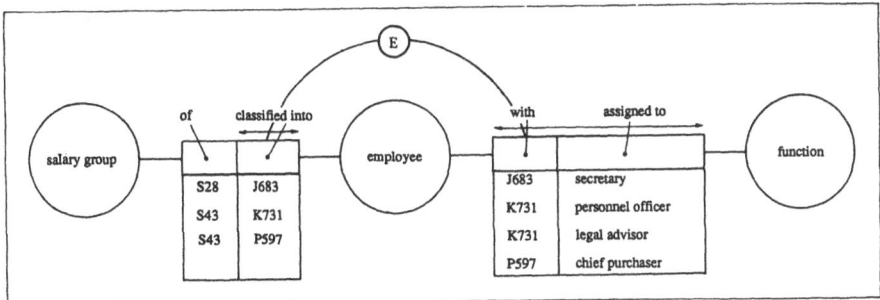

Figure 9.4.

that occurs in one population also occurs in the other population, regardless of how often each object appears individually in both populations. Role populations are, after all, considered as sets. The sets {J683,K731,P597} and {J683,K731,K731,P597} contain the same elements and are therefore by definition equal. The above population thus satisfies the equality constraint.

In Figure 9.5, we have added the new fact types introduced in this section and the equality constraint discussed here to the information structure diagram.

Whether the populations of two roles are equal can only be determined when the elements of these populations can be compared to each other. This can be done only when these elements are of the same type. That is, they can only be compared when their roles involve the same object type. Therefore the role populations of **different** object types, can never be said to "be equal."

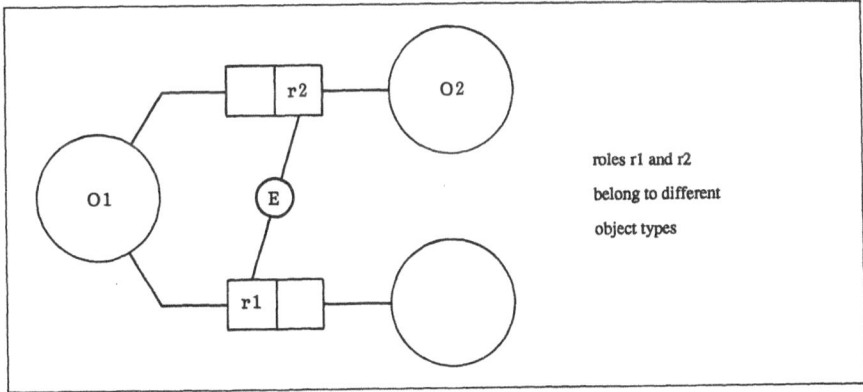

Figure 9.6.

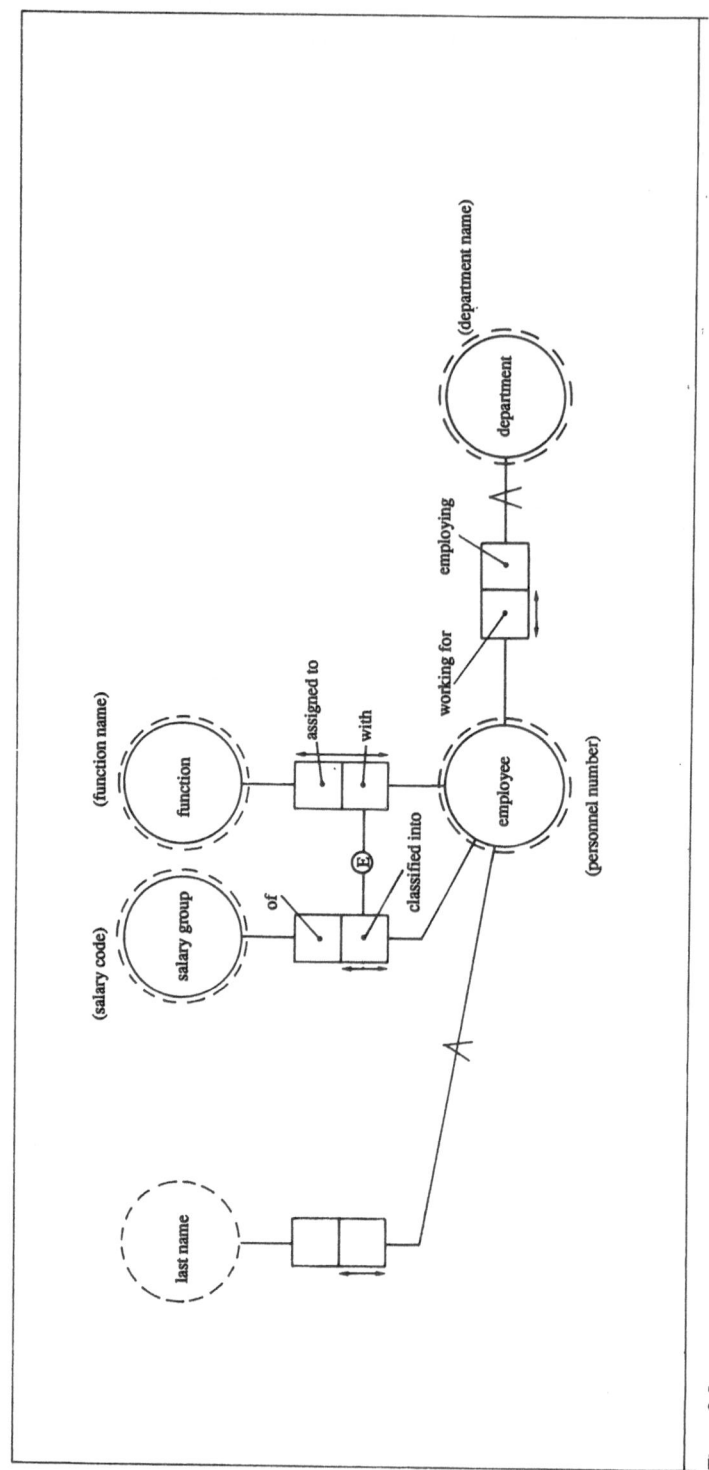

Figure 9.5.

For this reason, the information structure diagram of Figure 9.6 is not correct and is consequently not acceptable as an information structure diagram.

The information processor checks whether an equality constraint is violated every time there is a request to add a fact to the information base or to delete one. Let us suppose that the population diagram of Figure 9.4 describes part of the information base at a given moment, and that a user addresses the following request to the information processor at that moment:

Add : *Employee with personnel number* E341 *with function* janitor.

This would result in a population in which employee E341 has a function but is not classified into a salary group, which is in conflict with the equality constraint. The information processor then responds to this request as follows:

Request not executed because of violation of rule P34 (an employee classified into a salary group must be assigned a function, and conversely, an employee assigned a function must be classified into a salary group).

It does not help to first add the fact that employee E341 is classified into a certain salary group in order to then be able to add the fact that this employee is assigned a certain function, because this employee would still not have a function after the first addition, which is in conflict with the equality constraint. Both requests must therefore, as a consequence of the equality constraint, be executed in one single compound request:

Begin Add : *Employee with personnel number* E341 *with function* janitor.
    Add : *Employee with personnel number* E341 is *classified into salary group* S39.
End

After execution of this compound request, the equality constraint is not violated. After execution of the request:

Delete : The *employee with personnel number* J683 is *classified into salary group* S28.

employee J683 would (assuming the population of Figure 9.4) no longer be classified into a salary group, but would have a function, which is once more in conflict with the equality constraint.

In this case as well, the request is only executed if the fact that employee J683 is assigned the function of secretary is simultaneously deleted:

Begin Delete : The *employee with personnel number* J683 is *classified into salary group* S28.

> *Delete*: The *employee with personnel number* J683 *with function* secretary
> *End*

Facts belonging to fact types whose roles are equal must always be added or deleted simultaneously in one compound request.

If requested to, the information processor can, by virtue of the equality constraint dealt with here, conclude from the fact that a certain employee is classified into a salary group that this employee is assigned a function, and vice versa.

To summarize:

Equal roles:
Roles of the same object type whose populations are always equal.

Equality constraint:
A constraint which expresses the equality of two roles of a same object type.

Equality symbol:
The graphical representation of an equality constraint.

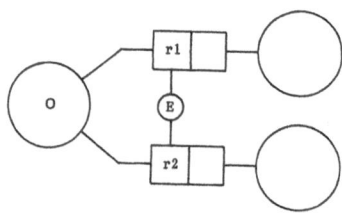

Roles r1 and r2
of object type O are equal

9.2 Subset constraints

We will now add the fact that the library employees earn a certain salary to the library case. Naturally, every employee earns only one salary. A salary can only be assigned to employees who are classified into a salary group.

We have summarized this additional knowledge of the library in the following rules:

P35: There is an "amount of money."

P36: An employee can earn a certain amount of money as salary.

P37: An employee can only earn one salary.

P38: An employee may only earn a salary if that employee is classified into a salary group.

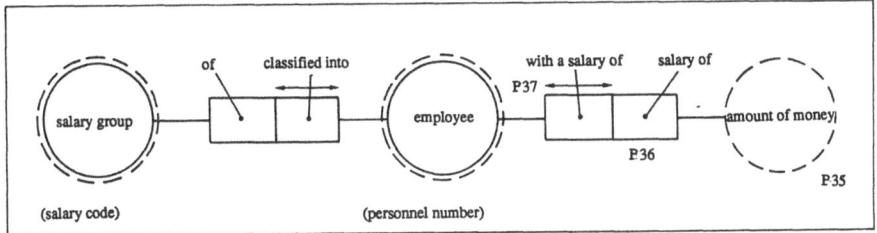

Figure 9.7.

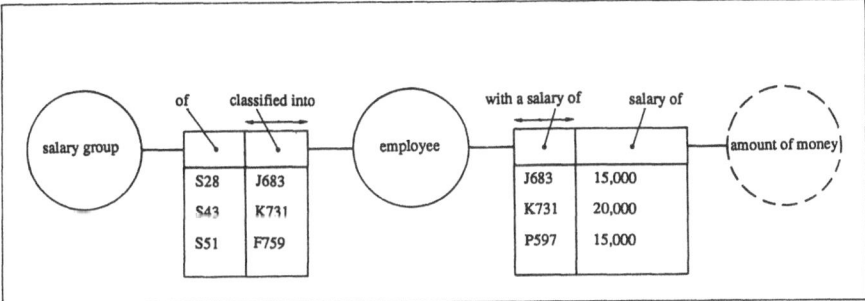

Figure 9.8.

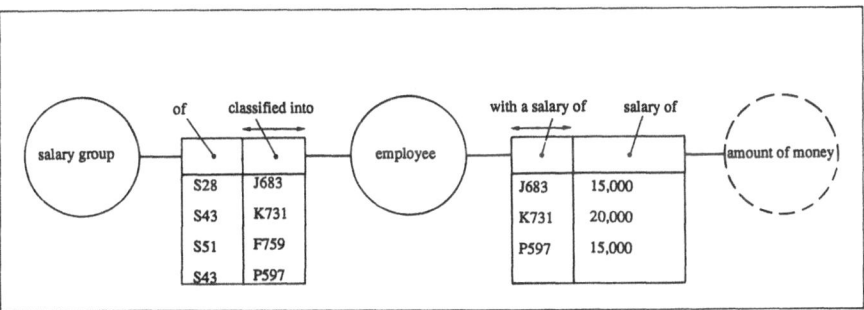

Figure 9.9.

These rules are described by the portion of the information structure diagram that is represented in Figure 9.7.

All of the above rules are depicted in this diagram, except for rule P38. This is clearly a constraint.

The population of Figure 9.8 is allowed purely on the basis of the object types, the fact types and the uniqueness constraints in the diagram of Figure 9.7.

In this population, employee P597 earns a salary but is not classified into a salary group. This conflicts with the constraint that is described by Proposition P38. The population of Figure 9.8 only satisfies this rule when either the fact that employee P597 earns a certain salary is deleted, or if this employee is put in a certain salary group. The latter has been done in Figure 9.9.

This population now satisfies the constraint described by Proposition P38. Every employee who earns a salary is also classified into a salary group. Unlike Figure 9.8, every employee who occurs in the population of the role "employee with a salary of amount of money" also occurs in the population of the role "employee classified into salary group." The population of the role "employee with a salary of amount of money" thus forms a subset of the population of the role "employee classified into salary group."

In set theory, set A is a subset of set B if every element of set A is also an element of set B.

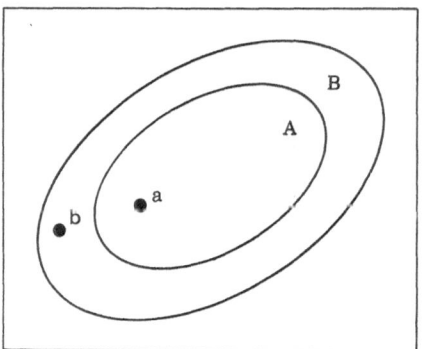

Figure 9.10.

In Figure 9.10, set A is a subset of set B. Every element of set A, for example the element a, is also an element of set B. But not every element of set B, for example the element b, belongs to set A. Set A "lies completely inside" set B. Or stated differently, set B "contains" set A. The fact that an element a of set A also belongs to set B is sometimes notated as:

$(a \in A) \rightarrow (a \in B)$

This should be read as: "If an element a belongs to set A, then this element also belongs to set B" (the reverse, of course, need not hold, as is, for example, the case for element b in Figure 9.10). In line with this notation, the fact that a set A is a subset of a set B is sometimes notated as:

$A \rightarrow B$

The arrow always points to the set which contains the other set. The arrow points from the "smallest" set to the "largest" set.

In Figure 9.9, the population of the role "employee with a salary of amount of money" has three elements (namely the employees J683, K731, and P597), and the population of the role "employee classified into salary group" has four elements (namely employees J683, K731, F759, and P597). All elements of the population of the role "employee with a salary of amount of money" also belong to the population of the role "employee classified into salary group." The population of the role "employee with a salary of amount of money" is therefore a subset of the population of the role "employee classified into salary group." It appears from this that rule P38 is equivalent to the following rule:

The population of the role "employee with a salary of amount of money" must always be a subset of the population of the role "employee classified into salary group."

This last rule is a "translation" of rule P38 in terms of populations of fact type roles. Both rules have exactly the same meaning; both of them express the same knowledge.

A *role* is a *subset of another role* if the population of the first role always forms a subset of the population of the second role, such as is the case with the roles "employee with a salary of amount of money" and "employee classified into salary group." The constraint which is described by Proposition P38 expresses the fact that a role is a subset of another role, and is consequently called a *subset constraint*.

Borrowing the notation A→B (for a set A which forms a subset of a set B), we shall denote the fact that a role is a subset of another role by using an arrow to connect these roles. The arrow points to the role whose population contains the population of the other role. We have done this in Figure 9.11.

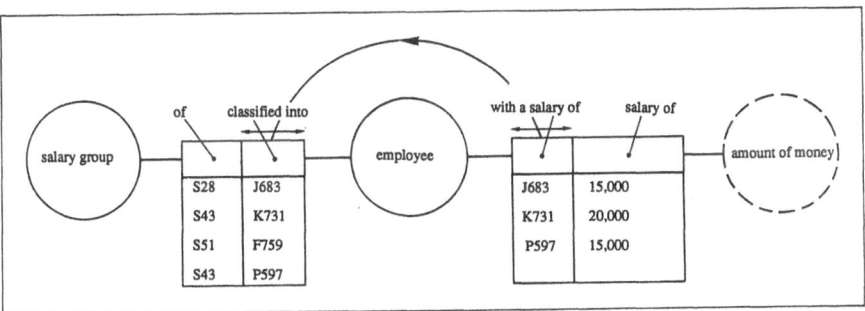

Figure 9.11.

The role "employee with a salary of amount of money" is a subset of the role "employee classified into salary group." Every employee who occurs in the population of the role "employee with a salary of amount of money" must also occur in the population of the role "employee classified into salary group." The arrow connecting both roles expresses this, and is a graphical representation of the subset constraint described by Proposition P38.

In the population of Figure 9.11, the employee F759 is classified into a salary group, but has no salary. This is not in conflict with the subset constraint. Every employee with a salary must also be classified into a salary group. But the reverse

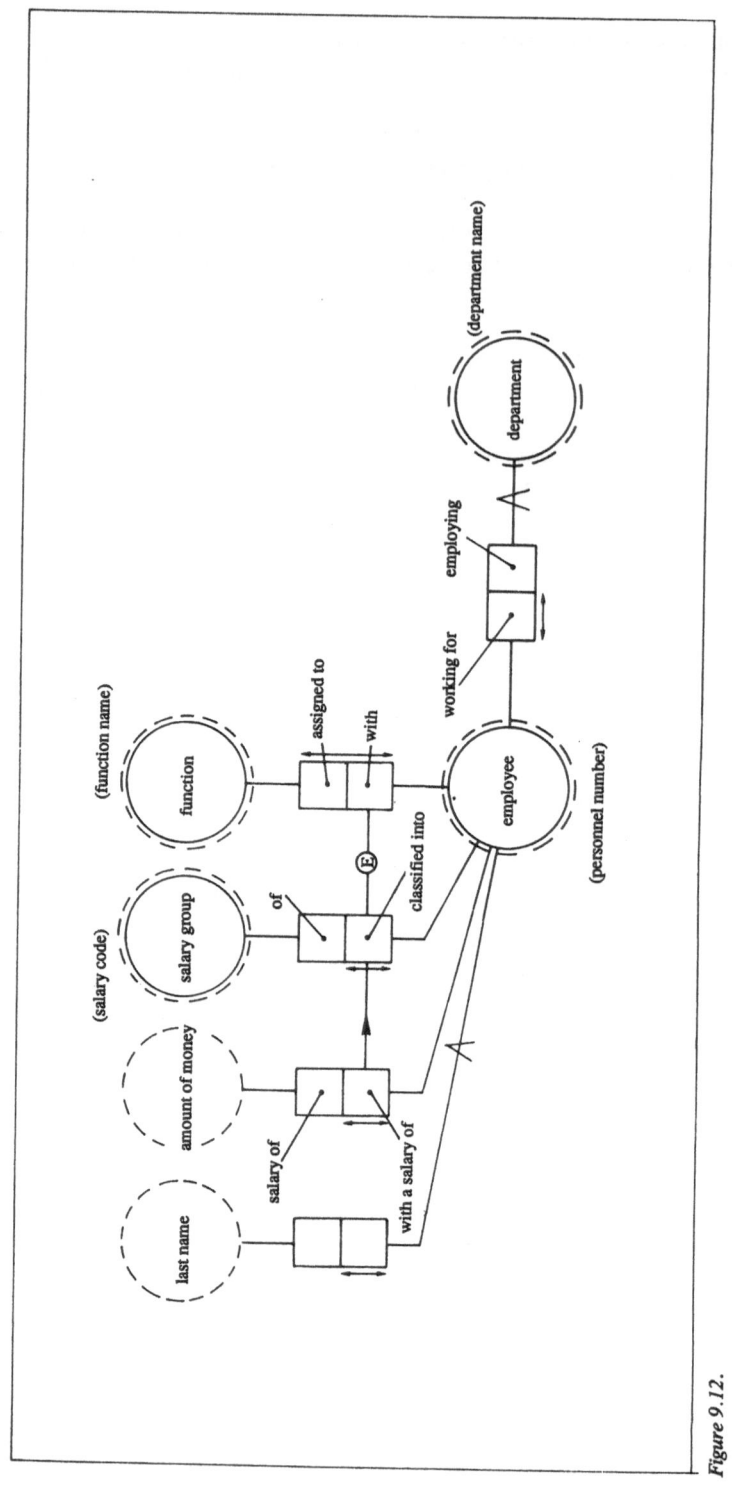

Figure 9.12.

does not have to hold. There can be employees who are classified into a salary group, but who do not (yet) have a salary, such as is the case for employee F759.

In Figure 9.12, we have added the new fact type introduced in this section and the subset constraint discussed here to the information structure diagram.

One can only determine whether one population of a role is a subset of another when the elements of these populations can be compared to each other. This can only be done if the elements are of the same type. That is, they can only be compared when the roles involve the same object type. When two sets have elements that are not of the same type and therefore cannot be compared, such as the populations of roles of **different** object types, it can never be said that "one set is a subset of the other set."

For this reason, the following information structure diagram is not correct, and is therefore not acceptable as an information structure diagram:

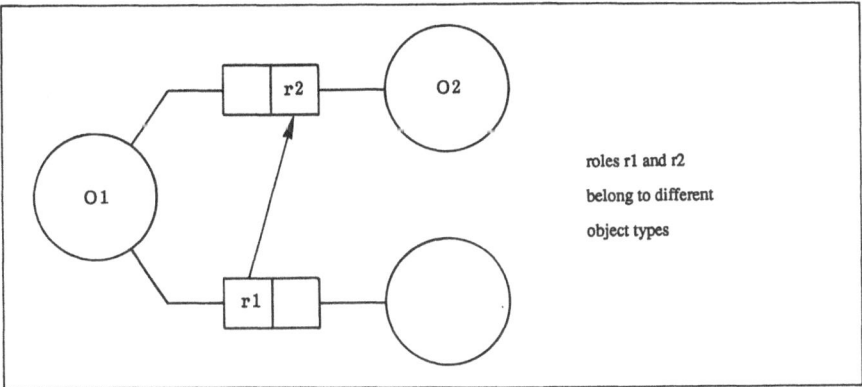

Figure 9.13.

The information processor checks whether a subset constraint is violated every time there is a request to add a fact to the information base or to delete one. Let us suppose that the population diagram of Figure 9.11 describes part of the information base at a given moment, and that the user addresses the following request to the information processor at that moment:

Add : The *employee with personnel number* E341 *with a salary of $15,000.*

This would result in a population in which employee E341 would earn a salary but would not be classified into a salary group, which conflicts with the subset constraint. The information processor then responds to the request as follows:

Request not executed because of violation of rule P38 (an employee may only earn a salary if that employee is classified into a salary group).

The user must then either not add that fact, or must **first** add the fact that employee E341 is classified into a certain salary group. In the latter case, this employee would (temporarily) be classified into a salary group without a salary, which, as we have seen, is not in conflict with the subset constraint.

If the user, assuming the population of Figure 9.11, were to address the following request to the information processor:

> *Delete*: The **employee with personnel number** J683 is **classified into salary group** S28.

the result would be that employee J683 would earn a salary without being classified into a salary group, which is in conflict with the subset constraint. This request is therefore not executed.

The user must then either not delete this fact, or **first** delete the fact that employee J683 earns a salary of $15,000. In the latter case, this employee would be classified into a salary group, but would not earn a salary, which does not conflict with the subset constraint.

It appears from the foregoing that subset constraints determine the order in which facts having roles involved in a subset constraint can be individually added or deleted.

When the user addresses one of the following two compound requests to the information processor:

> *Begin Add*: The **employee with personnel number** E341 **with a salary of** $15,000.
> *Add*: The **employee with personnel number** E341 **classified into salary group** S28.

End

or

> *Begin Delete*: The **employee with personnel number** J683 **classified into salary group** S28.
> *Delete*: The **employee with personnel number** J683 **with a salary of** $15,000.

End

the subset constraint is not violated after either of these compound requests have been executed.

If requested to, the information processor can, by virtue of the subset constraint dealt with here, conclude from the fact that a certain employee earns a salary that this employee is classified into a salary group.

To summarize:

A role of an object type is a subset of another role of the same object type:

If the population of the first role always forms a subset of the population of the second role.

Subset constraint:
A constraint expressing the fact that a role of an object type is a subset of another role of the same object type.

Subset constraint symbol:
The graphical representation of a subset constraint:

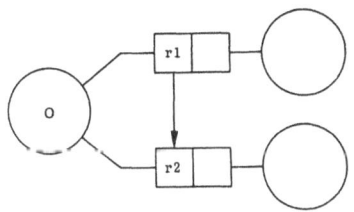

Role r1 of object type O
is a subset of role r2
of this object type.

9.3 Exclusion constraints

We are going to add just a little bit more to our example of the organization of the library. Up to now we have only been able to indicate which employees generally work for a department on the basis of the information structure diagram. We shall now adapt the information structure diagram in such a way that we can indicate which employees manage a department as department heads and which employees are part of a department as staff members.

Every department has one department manager. The department managers are all employees of the library. An employee who is a department manager can only be manager of one department, and he or she cannot at the same time be a staff member of this or any other department. An employee may be a staff member of only one department, and each department must contain at least one staff member. We have summarized this additional knowledge about the library in the following rules:

P39: Employees can be staff members of a department.
P40: An employee can be a staff member of only one department.
P41: Every department has staff members.
P42: Employees can be department manager.
P43: An employee can be manager of only one department.
P44: A department has exactly one department manager.
P45: Every department has a department manager.

P46 : An employee who is manager of a department cannot be a staff member of this or any other department.

These rules are described by the part of the information structure diagram depicted in Figure 9.14.

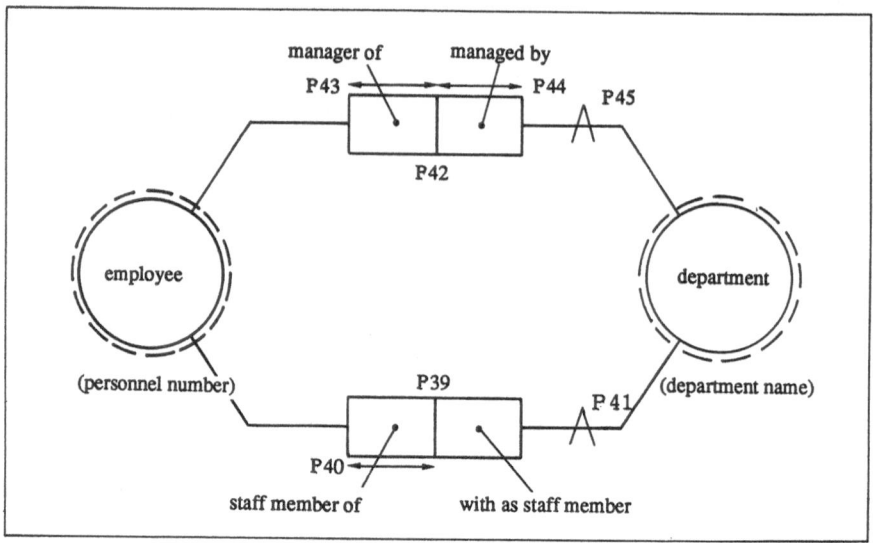

Figure 9.14.

There are now two different fact types related to the object types "employee" and "department." These two fact types describe two different kinds of information about the objects of these object types.

All of the above rules are depicted in the diagram of Figure 9.14, except for rule B46, which is clearly a constraint. The population of Figure 9.15 is allowed purely on the basis of the object types, the fact types and the uniqueness and totality constraints in the diagram of Figure 9.14.

To enhance the presentation, we have drawn the object type "department" twice in this population diagram. In general, object types and fact types may be drawn more than once to aid presentation. Even though they are represented in more than one place, the object types remain the same.

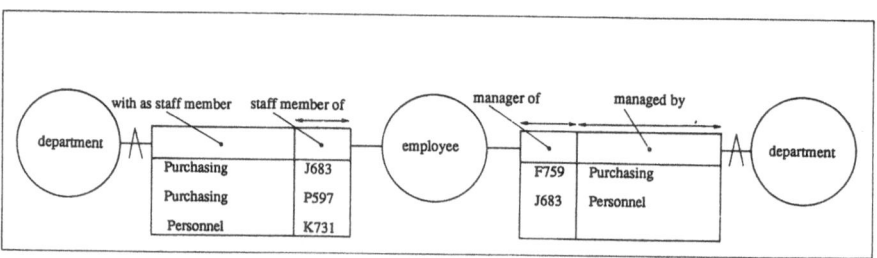

Figure 9.15.

In the population of Figure 9.15, employee J683 is both a staff member in a department (namely the Purchasing Department) and manager of a department (namely the Personnel Department). This is in conflict with the constraint described by Proposition P46. The population of Figure 9.15 only satisfies this rule when the fact that employee J683 is manager of Personnel or the fact that this employee is a staff member in Purchasing, or both facts, are deleted. In Figure 9.16, we have deleted the fact that employee J683 is manager of Personnel and put in another employee as head of this department.

This population now satisfies the constraint described by Proposition P46. Any employee who is a staff member in a department is not manager of this or any other department. Unlike Figure 9.15, no employee who occurs in the population of the role "employee staff member of department" occurs simultaneously in the population of the role "employee manager of department." The populations of these two roles do not contain any common elements and are therefore non-overlapping sets.

In set theory, sets which have no elements in common and which therefore do not overlap are called *exclusive* or *disjoint* sets.

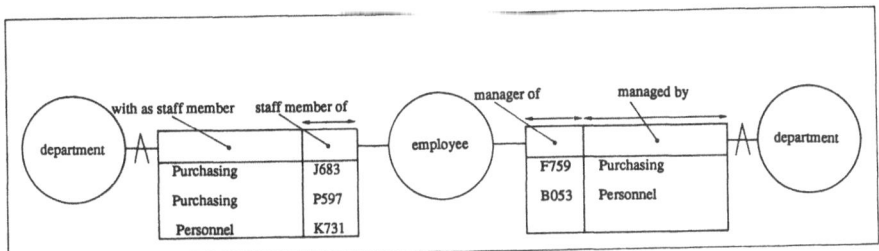

Figure 9.16.

In Figure 9.17, sets A and B have no elements in common. These sets do not overlap, and therefore exclude each other.

In Figure 9.16, the populations of the roles "employee staff member of department" and "employee manager of department" do not contain any common elements, do not overlap, and therefore exclude each other.

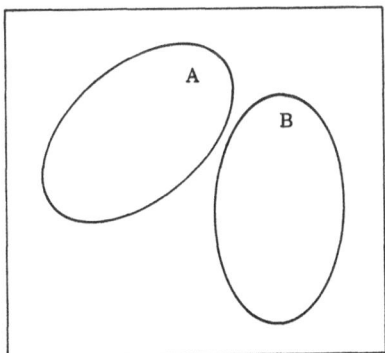

Figure 9.17.

It follows from this that rule P46 is equal to the following rule:

The populations of the roles "employee staff member of deparment" and "employee manager of department" must always exclude each other.

This last rule is a translation of rule P46 in terms of populations of fact type roles. Both rules have exactly the same meaning; they both express the same knowledge. If the populations of two roles always exclude each other, we say they are *exclusive roles*. The constraint described by Proposition P46 expresses the fact that two roles exclude each other and is therefore called an *exclusion constraint*. We shall denote exclusive roles in an information structure diagram by using the symbol X, which stands for eXclusive, to connect these roles. This has been done in Figure 9.18.

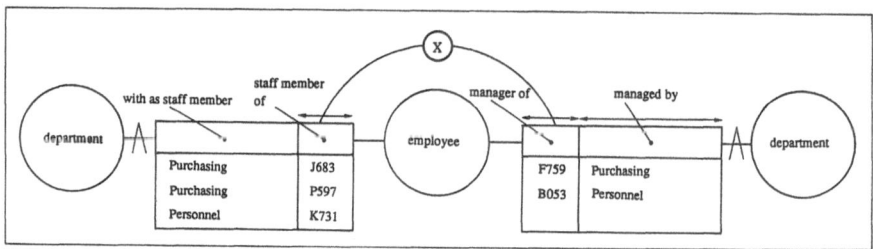

Figure 9.18.

An employee who occurs in the population of the role "employee staff member of department" may not also occur in the population of the role "employee manager of department." The populations of these two roles must exclude each other. The symbol connecting these roles expresses this and is a graphical representation of the exclusion constraint described by Proposition P46.

In Figure 9.19, we have added the new fact types introduced in this section and the constraint dealt with here to the information structure diagram. We have replaced the original fact type denoting which employees work for which departments by two new fact types indicating which employees are staff members or managers of which departments.

It can only be determined whether the populations of roles exclude each other if these populations can be compared to each other. This can only be done if these elements are of the same type. That is, they can only be compared if the roles involve the same object type. Sets which have elements that are not of the same type and therefore cannot be compared, such as the role populations of different object types, can never be said to "exclude each other."

For this reason, the information structure diagram of Figure 9.20 is not correct, and is therefore not acceptable as an information structure diagram.

The information processor checks whether an exclusion constraint is violated whenever there is a request to add a fact to the information base or to delete one. Let us assume that the population diagram of Figure 9.18 describes part of the

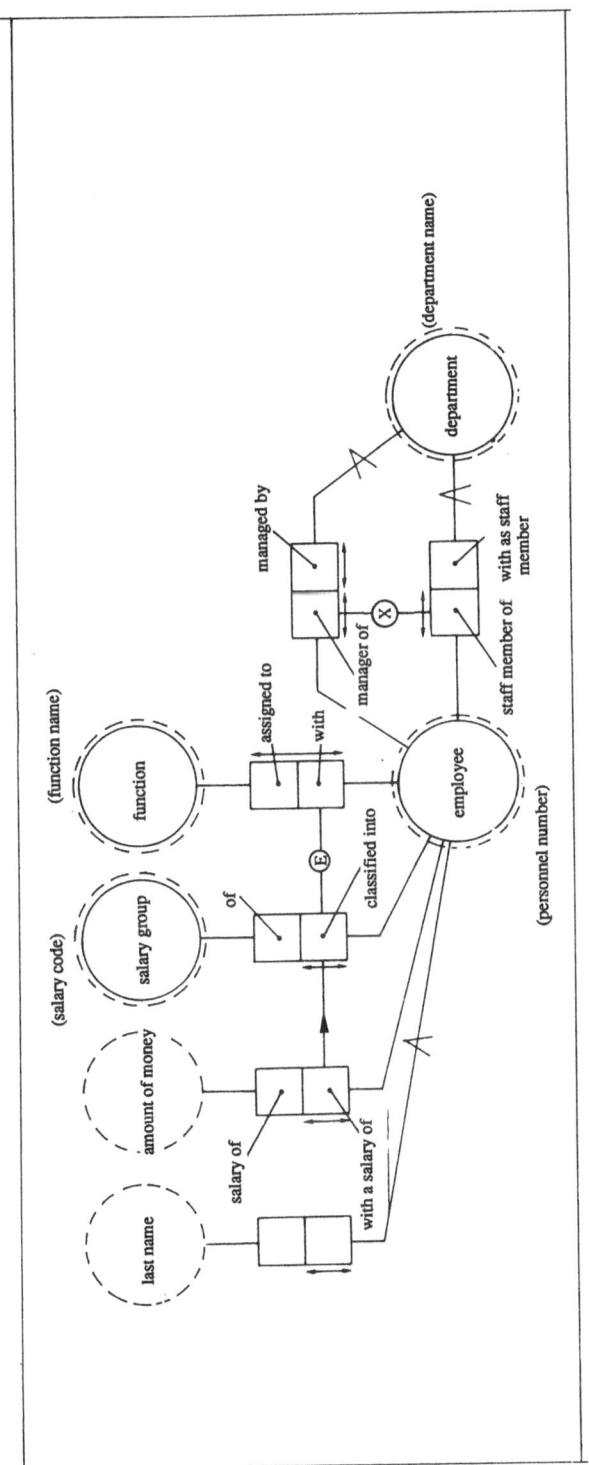

Figure 9.19.

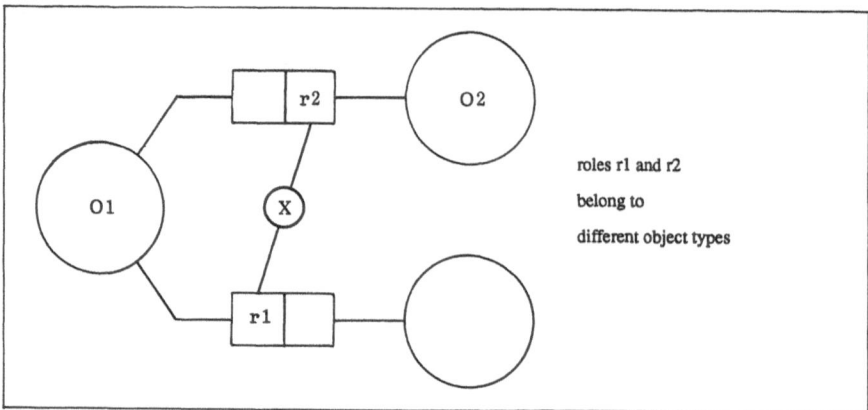

Figure 9.20.

information base at a given moment and that the user addresses the following request to the information processor at that moment:

Add : The *employee with employee number* J683 is *manager of* the *department* Personnel.

This would result in a population in which employee J683 is both manager and staff member of a department, which is in conflict with the exclusion constraint. The information processor then responds to this request as follows:

Request not executed because of violation of rule P46 (an employee who is manager of a department cannot be a staff member of this or any other department).

The user must then either refrain from adding this fact, or **first** delete the fact that employee J683 is a staff member in Purchasing.

In contrast, when the user addresses the following compound request to the information processor:

Begin Delete : The *employee with personnel number* J683 is *staff member of* the *department* Purchasing.
   Add :   The *employee with personnel number* J683 is *manager of* the *department* Personnel.
 End

the exclusion constraint is not violated once this compound request has been executed.

If requested to, the information processor can, by virtue of the exclusion constraint dealt with here, conclude from the fact that a certain employee is a staff member of a department that this employee is not manager of this or any other department.

An exclusion constraint does not necessarily have to be restricted to two roles of the same object type, but can in general also be concerned with three or more roles of the same object type. In what follows, we give an example of an exclusion constraint involving three roles. We assume that some of the library employees have an expense account with a certain limit. The employees who have an expense account may not at the same time be department manager or department staff member. This situation is described in the information structure diagram of Figure 9.21.

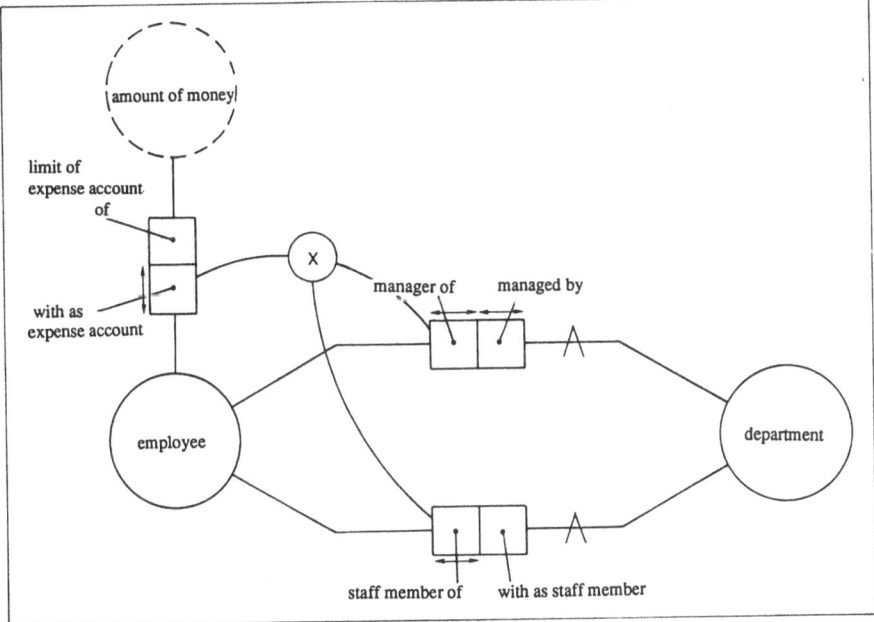

Figure 9.21.

To summarize:

Exclusive roles:
Roles of the same object type whose populations exclude each other (which have no elements in common, which do not overlap).

Exclusion constraint:
A constraint that expresses the fact that certain roles of the same object type exclude each other.

Exclusion symbol:
The graphical representation of an exclusion constraint.

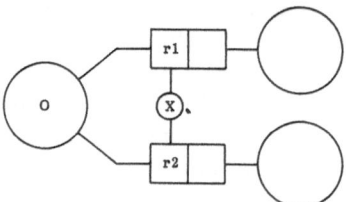

Roles r1 and r2 of object type O
exclude each other.

9.4 Implied equality and subset constraints

Part of the information structure diagram and a possible population have been
depicted in Figure 9.22.

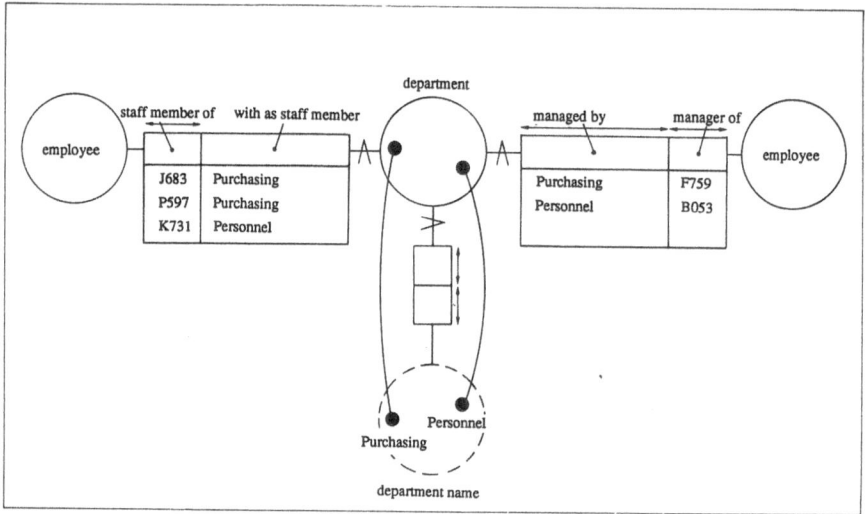

Figure 9.22.

The roles "department with as staff member employee" and "department
managed by employee" are total. That is, every department about which something
is known in the information base must occur in the populations of these two roles.
Because at any moment the populations of both roles contain **all** departments
about which something is known in the information base, the populations of these
two roles are equal. We have represented this in Figure 9.23 by using an equality
symbol to connect the two roles.

We have used broken lines to draw this equality symbol because the equality
of these two roles follows directly from (is implied by) the fact that both roles are
total. Consequently, the equality symbol as such is redundant. The following
general rule follows from this:

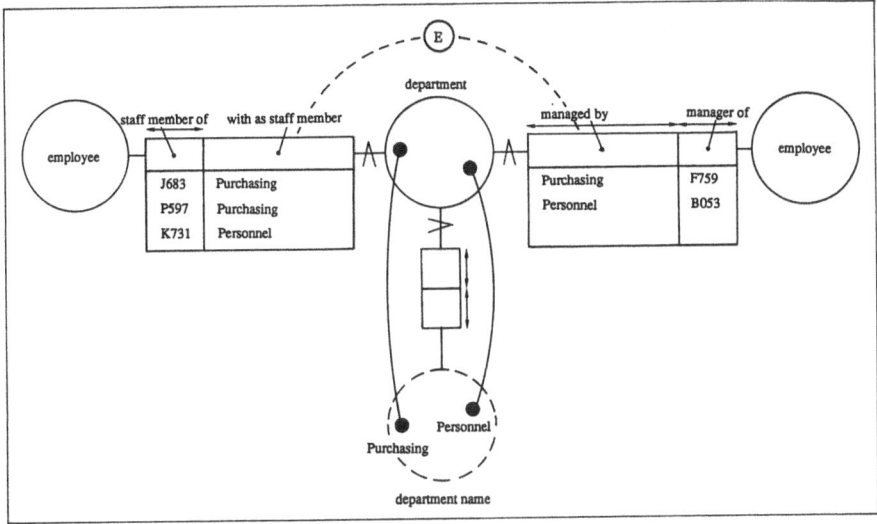

Figure 9.23.

Total roles of a same object type are always equal.

Equality constraints that are implied by totality constraints are not explicitly drawn in an information structure diagram.

Figure 9.24 contains another part of the information structure diagram together with a possible population.

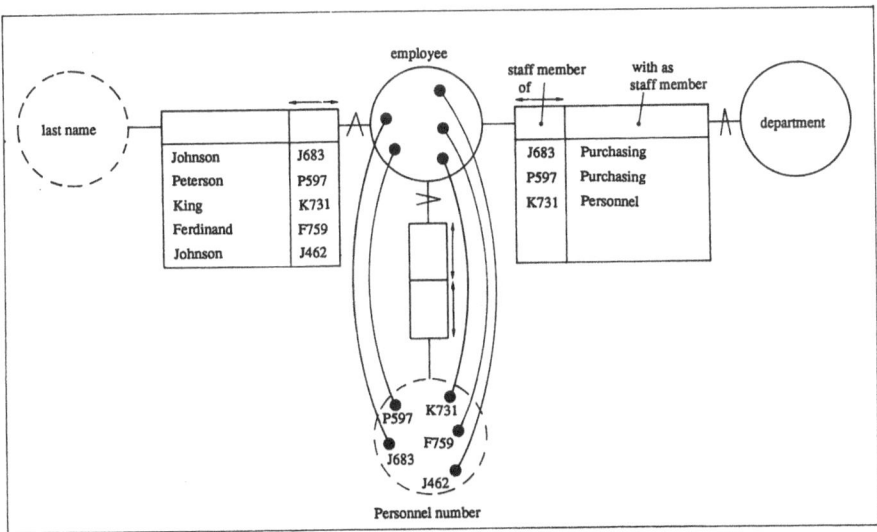

Figure 9.24.

The role "employee staff member of department" is not total, while the role "employee with last name" is. Therefore, not every employee about whom something is known in the information base must occur in the population of the role "employee staff member of department," while the population of the role "employee with last name" always contains all employees about who something is known in the information base. As a consequence, the population of the role "employee staff member of department" is a subset of the population of the role "employee with last name." We have represented this in Figure 9.25 by connecting these two roles by a subset symbol.

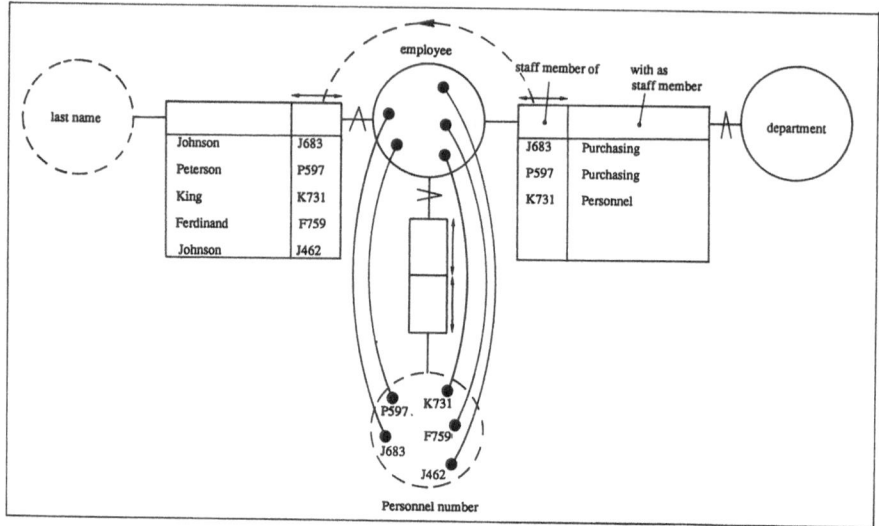

Figure 9.25.

We have used broken lines to draw this subset symbol because the fact that the role "employee staff member of department" is a subset of the role "employee with last name" is a direct consequence of (is implied by) the fact that the former role is not total, while the latter is. Consequently, the subset symbol as such is redundant. The following general rule follows from this:

Non-total roles of an object type are always subsets of total roles of this object type.

Subset constraints that are implied by totality constraints are not explicitly drawn in an information structure diagram.

10 GRAPHICAL CONSTRAINTS INVOLVING COMBINATIONS OF ROLES

In this chapter, we shall show that graphical constraints can also involve **combinations of roles of different fact types**.

In Sections 10.1 through 10.4, the subset, exclusion, uniqueness and totality constraints involving combinations of roles of different fact types will successively come up for discussion.

In Section 10.5, we will investigate the consequences of uniqueness constraints involving combinations of roles of different fact types in terms of the referenceability of an information structure diagram.

In Section 10.6, we will show two examples to illustrate fact types whose roles involve one single object type.

10.1 Subset constraints involving combinations of roles

We shall add the following to our example of the organization of the library:

The library departments each have one or more departmental secretaries. A departmental secretary can only work for one department and is a staff member of that particular department. We have summarized this additional knowledge about the library in the following rules:

P47 : An employee can work for a department as a departmental secretary.
P48 : An employee can be departmental secretary of only one department.
P49 : Every department has a departmental secretary.
P50 : Any employee who is departmental secretary of a department must be a staff member of that department.

These rules are described by the part of the information structure diagram that is depicted in Figure 10.1.

All of the above rules are represented in this diagram, except for rule P50, which is clearly a constraint. The population of Figure 10.2 is allowed purely on the basis of the object types, the fact types, and the uniqueness and totality constraints of the diagram in Figure 10.1.

In this population, employee E341 is departmental secretary of the Purchasing Department, although she is not a staff member of this department, and employee J683 is departmental secretary of the Personnel Department, although she is a staff member of another department, namely the Purchasing Department. This is in conflict with rule P50. The population of Figure 10.3, on the other hand, does satisfy this rule.

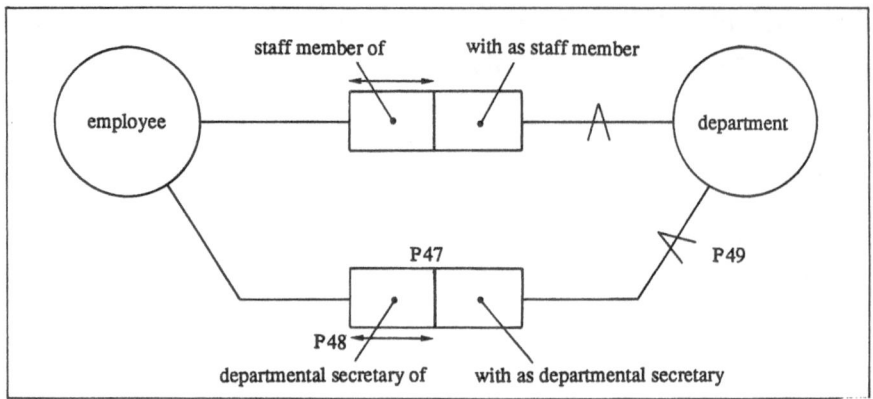

Figure 10.1.

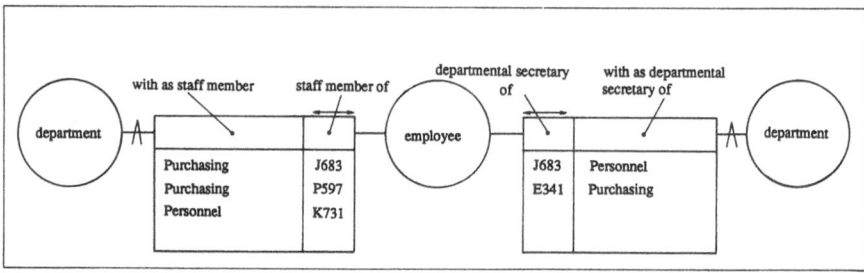

Figure 10.2.

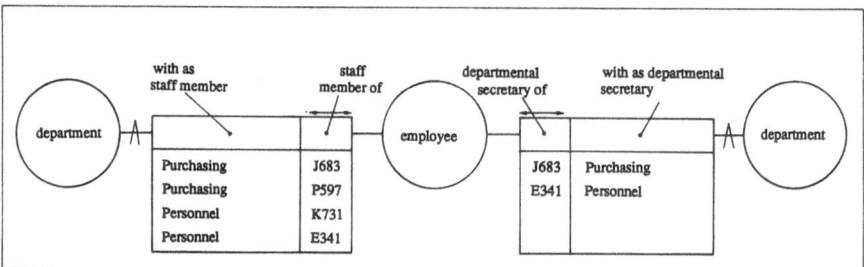

Figure 10.3.

We have altered the previous population in such a way that employee J683 is now departmental secretary of the Purchasing Department and employee E341 is both departmental secretary and staff member of the Personnel Department. Every employee who is departmental secretary of a department is now also a staff member of that same department. If we compare Figures 10.3 and 10.2, we see that in Figure 10.3, unlike Figure 10.2, every employee and every department which occur in the population of the **combination** of the roles "employee departmental secretary of department" and "department with as departmental secretary employee" also occur in the population of the **combination** of the roles "employee staff member of department" and "department with as staff member employee." The reverse does not have to be the case; for example, employee P597 and the Purchasing Department belong to the population of the combination of the roles "employee staff member of department" and "department with as staff member employee," but not to the population of the combination of the roles "employee departmental secretary of department" and "department with as departmental secretary employee." It follows from this that rule P50 is equivalent to the assertion that the population of the **combination** of the roles "employee departmental secretary of department" and "department with as departmental secretary employee" must always be a subset of the population of the **combination** of the roles "employee staff member of department" and "department with as staff member employee."

Rule P50 therefore expresses the fact that the population of the **combination** of two roles must be a subset of the population of the **combination** of two other roles, and is consequently a subset constraint. It appears from this that a subset constraint can involve two **individual** roles of one and the same object type (such as in Section 9.2) or two **combinations** of roles of the same object types (as is the case here).

Subset constraints involving combinations of roles are represented in an information structure diagram by using a subset symbol to connect these combinations of roles, as has been done in Figure 10.4.

In Figure 10.5, we have added the new fact types introduced in this section and the subset constraint dealt with here to the information structure diagram.

In Figure 10.6, we have drawn next to each other a subset constraint involving two individual roles and a subset constraint involving two combinations of roles, in order to emphasize the difference.

Just as with subset constraints involving individual roles, it is only possible to determine whether the populations of two **combinations** of roles form a subset if their elements can be compared to each other. This can only be done if these elements are of the same type. It follows from this that the roles of combinations involving a subset constraint must belong to **the same** object types.

For this reason, the information structure diagram of Figure 10.7 is not correct, and is therefore not acceptable as an information structure diagram.

To conclude this section, we have expanded below the definitions given in Section 9.2:

A role of an object type, or a combination of roles of object types, is a **subset** of another role of the same object type or of another combination of roles of the same object types, if the population of the first role or of the first combination of roles always forms a subset of the population of the second role or of the second combination of roles.

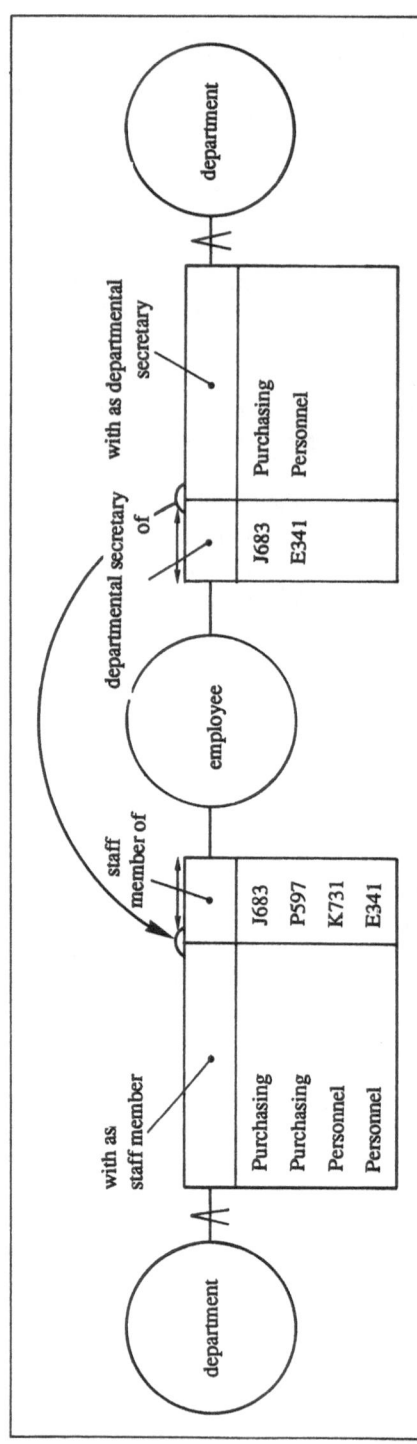

Figure 10.4.

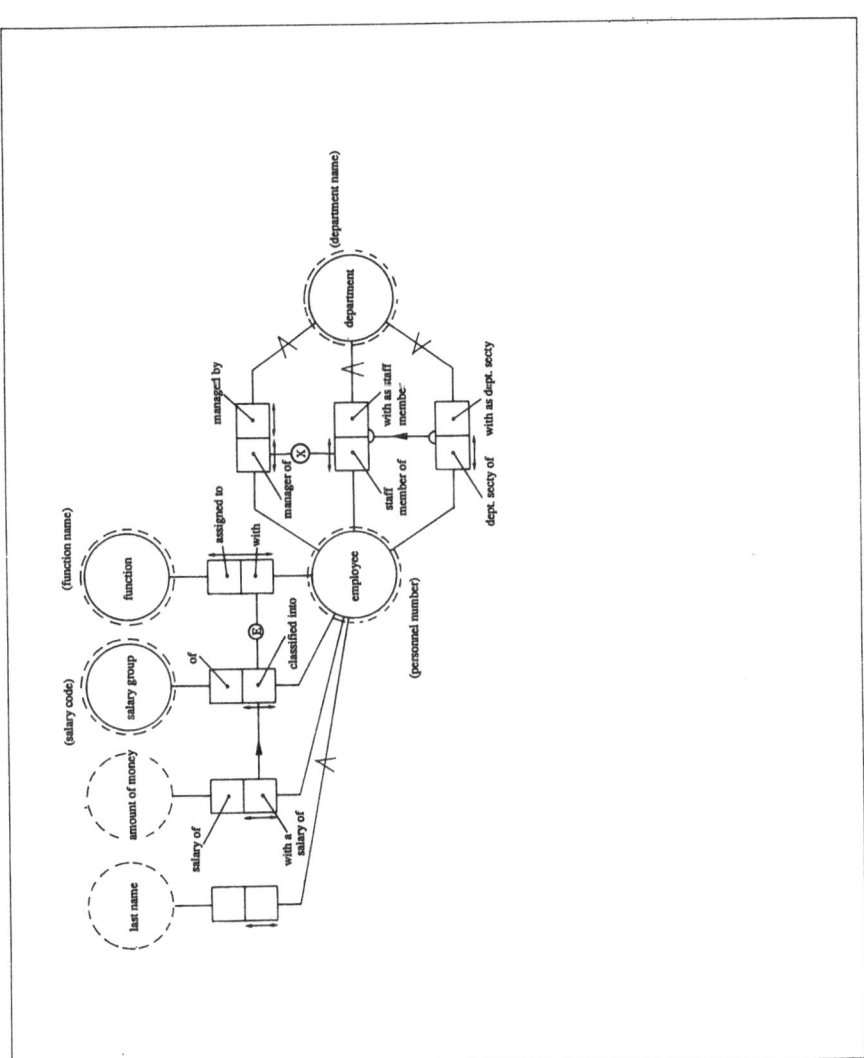

Figure 10.5.

194

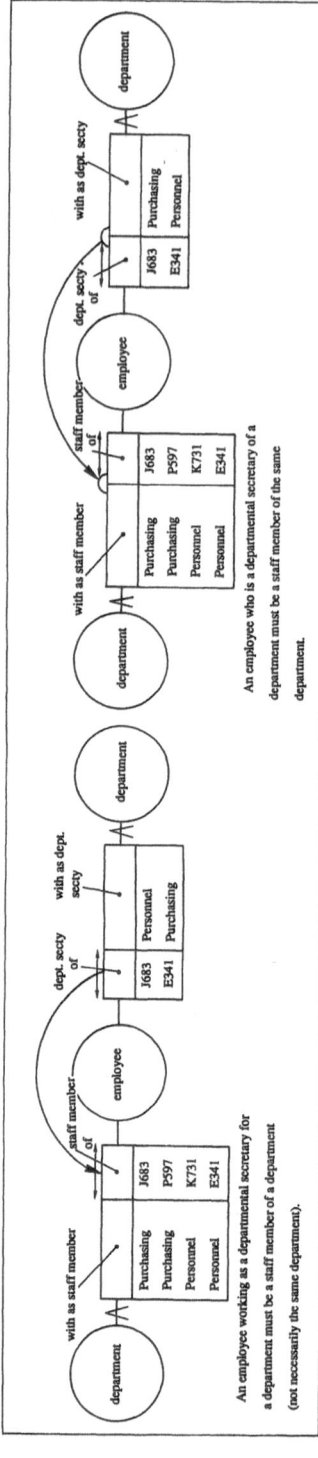

Figure 10.6.

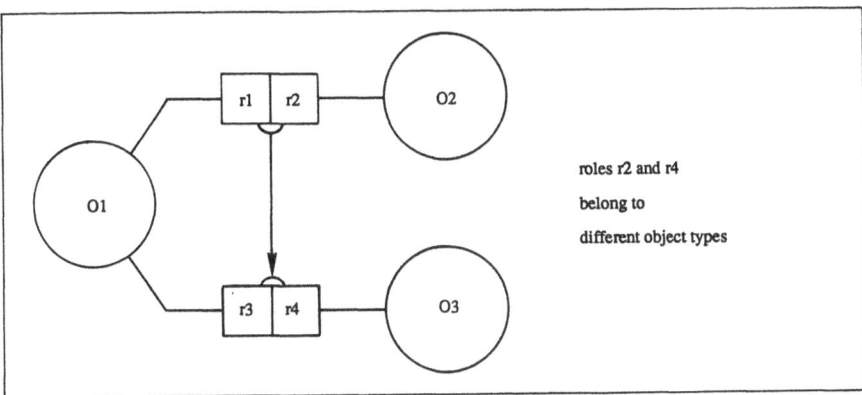

Figure 10.7.

Subset constraint:
A constraint which expresses the fact that a role of an object type or of a combination of roles of object types is a subset of another role of the same object type or of another combination of roles of the same object types.

Subset symbol:
The graphical representation of a subset constraint.

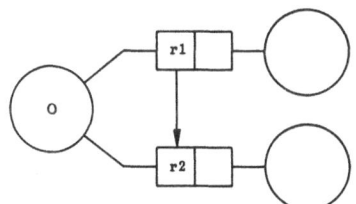

Role r1 of object type O
is a subset of role r2
of this object type.

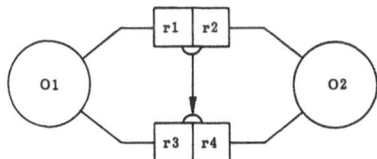

The combination of roles r1 and r2
of object types O1 and O2
is a subset of
the combination of roles r3 and r4
of these object types.

10.2 Exclusion constraints involving combinations of roles

In this section, we will show an example of an exclusion constraint involving combinations of roles of different fact types. To this end, we will once again add to the library case.

Sometimes, the library carries out projects in which employees of different departments may work together. An employee can, in principle, work on more than one project at a time. One of the employees assigned to a project is the project manager of that particular project. An employee can be project manager and staff member of **different** projects, but never project manager and staff member of **the same** project. Every project is identified in a one-to-one way by a project number. We have summarized this additional knowledge about the library in the following rules:

P51 : There are projects.
P52 : Every project is denoted in a one-to-one way by a project number.
P53 : Employees can be staff members of projects.
P54 : Employees can be project managers of projects.
P55 : A project can have only one project manager.
P56 : An employee cannot be staff member and project manager of **the same** project.

These rules are described by the part of the information structure diagram that is depicted in Figure 10.8.

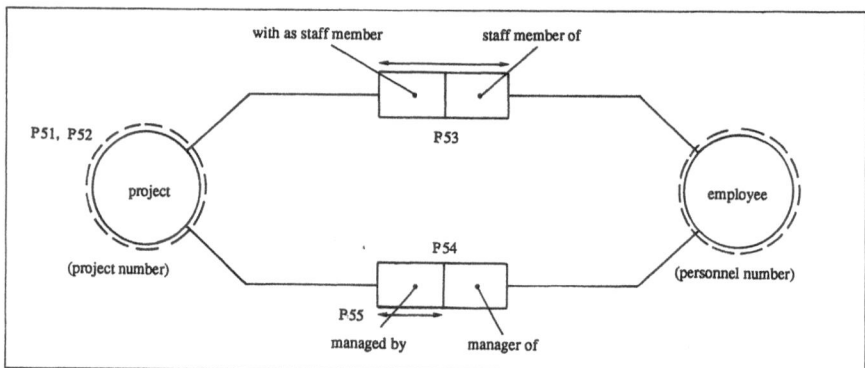

Figure 10.8.

All of the above rules are represented in this diagram, except for rule P56, which is clearly a constraint. The population of Figure 10.9 is allowed purely on the basis of the object types, the fact types and the uniqueness constraints in the diagram of Figure 10.8.

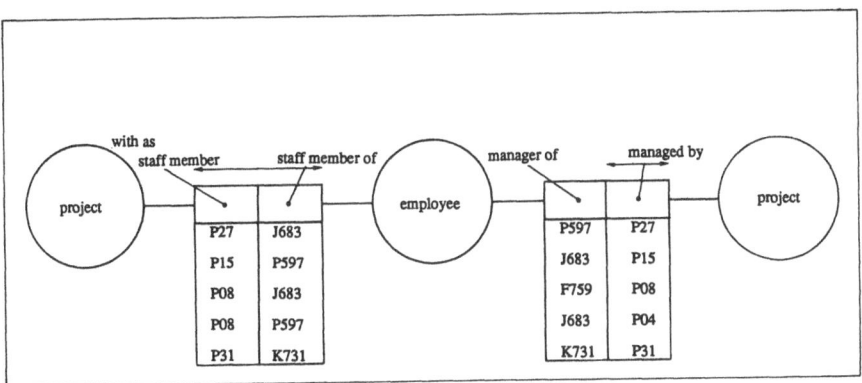

Figure 10.9.

Because employee K731 is both staff member and project manager of the same project (namely project P31), this population does not satisfy rule P56. The population of Figure 10.10, on the other hand, does satisfy this rule.

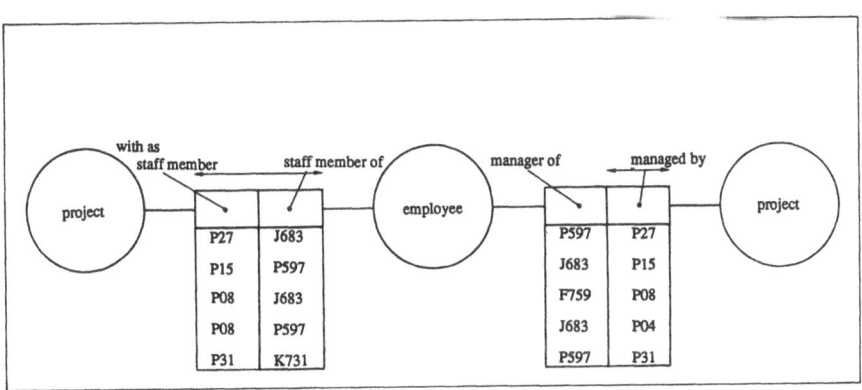

Figure 10.10.

Employee P597 is now project manager of project P31 instead of employee K731. Unlike Figure 10.9, in Figure 10.10 the populations of the **combination** of the roles "employee staff member of project" and "project with as staff member employee" and of the **combination** of the roles "employee manager of project" and "project managed by employee" do not contain any elements in common. The **combinations** of these roles therefore exclude each other. Rule P56 indicates that the populations of the **combination** of the roles "employee staff member of project" and "project with as staff member employee" and of the **combination** of the roles "employee manager of project" and "project managed employee" have to exclude each other, and is therefore an exclusion constraint. It appears from this that an exclusion constraint can involve individual roles of an object type (such as in Section 9.3) or combinations of roles of the same object types (such as is the case here).

Exclusion constraints involving combinations of roles are represented in the information structure diagram by using the exclusion symbol to connect these combinations of roles, as has been done in Figure 10.11.

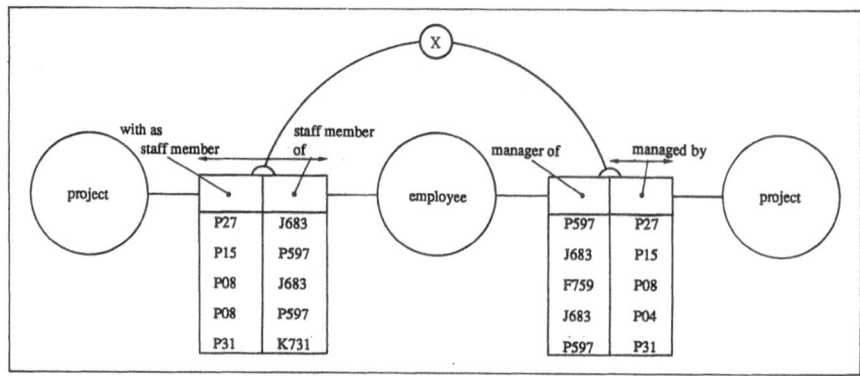

Figure 10.11.

In Figure 10.12, we have added the new fact types introduced in this section and the exclusion constraint dealt with here to the information structure diagram.

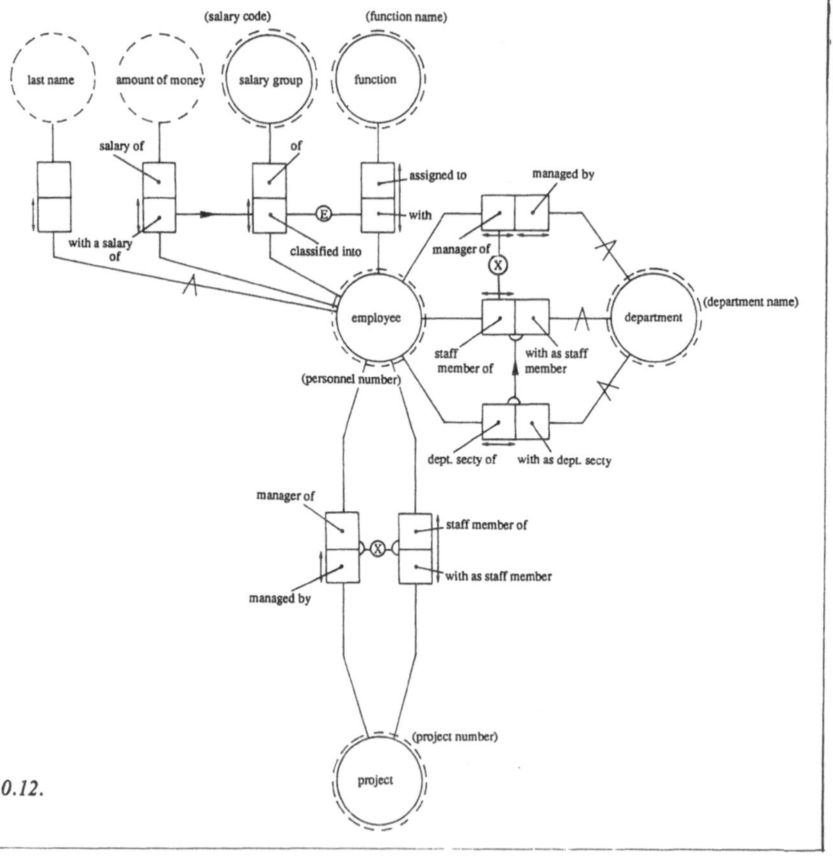

Figure 10.12.

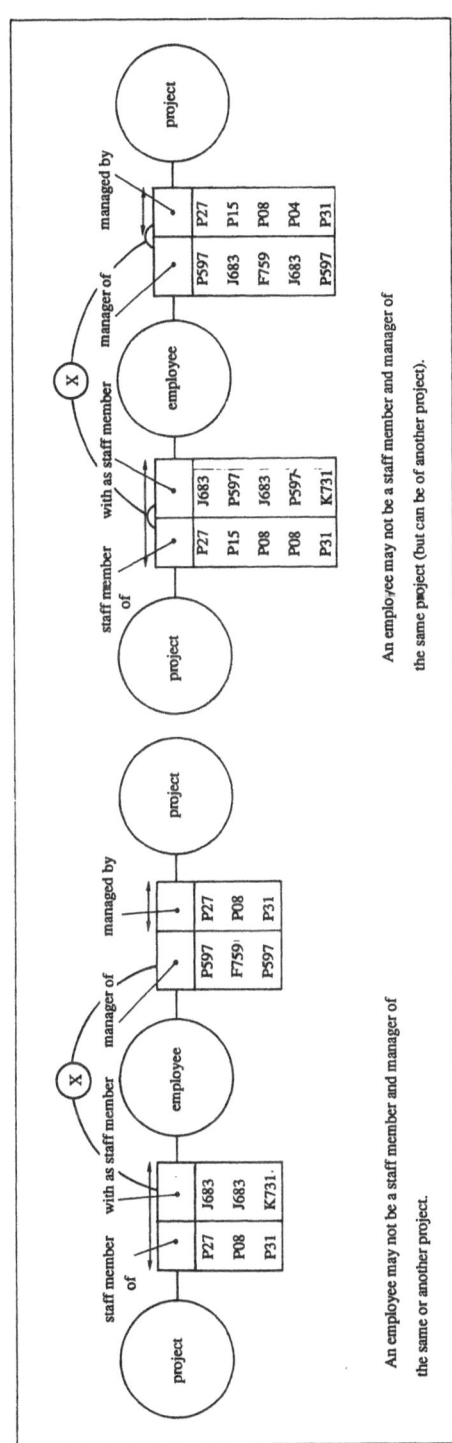

Figure 10.13.

In Figure 10.13, we have drawn an exclusion constraint involving two individual roles and an exclusion constraint involving two combinations of roles next to each other, in order to emphasize the difference.

Just as with exclusion constraints involving individual roles, it is only possible to determine whether populations of **combinations** of roles exclude each other if their elements can be compared to each other. This can only be done if these elements are of the same type. It follows from this that the roles of combinations involved in an exclusion constraint have to belong to **the same** object types.

For this reason, the information structure diagram of Figure 10.14 is not correct, and is consequently not acceptable as an information structure diagram.

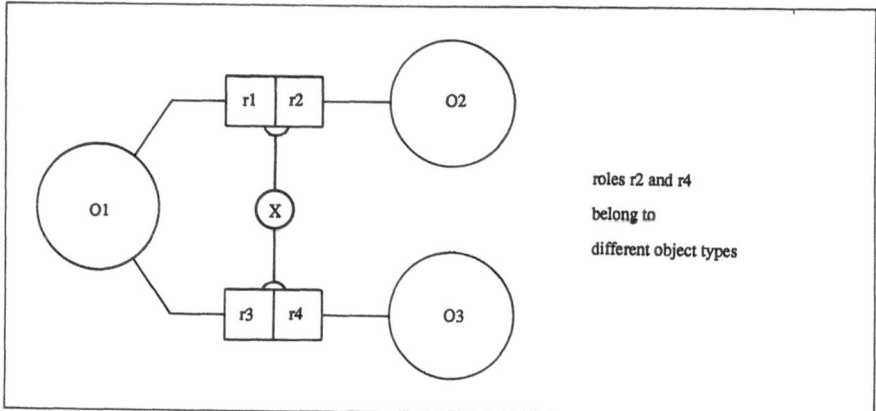

Figure 10.14.

An **equality constraint** can only involve individual roles and never combinations of roles.

On the basis of the equality constraint, the populations of the two fact types of Figure 10.15 are always equal. Consequently, both fact types describe exactly the same information, and are therefore, by definition, equal to each other. In the

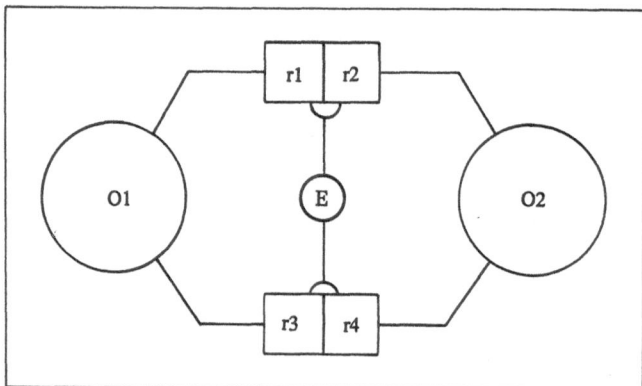

Figure 10.15.

information structure diagram of Figure 10.15, the same fact type has apparently been depicted twice. When such situations occur in practice, we are faced with fact types which are erroneously seen as being different.

To conclude this section, the definitions given in Section 9.3 are expanded below.

Exclusive roles:
Roles of the same object type or combinations of roles of the same object types whose populations exclude each other.

Exclusion constraint:
A constraint which expresses the fact that roles of the same object type or combinations of roles of the same object types exclude each other.

Exclusion symbol:
The graphical representation of an exlusion constraint.

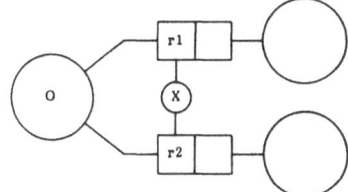

Roles r1 and r2 of object type O exclude each other.

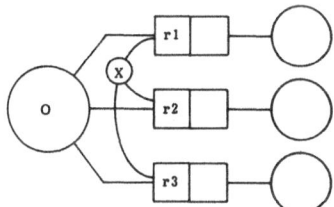

Roles r1, r2 and r3 of object type O exclude each other.

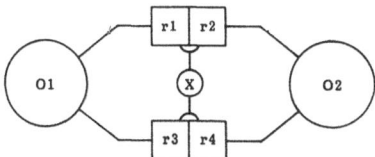

The combinations of roles r1 and r2 and r3 and r4 of object types O1 and O2 exclude each other.

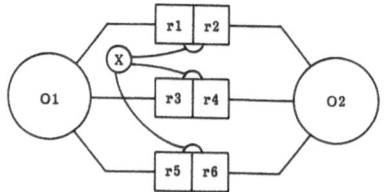

The combinations of
roles r1 and r2, r3 and r4 and r5 and r6
of object types O1 and O2
exclude each other.

10.3 Uniqueness constraints involving roles of different fact types

In this section we show an example of a uniqueness constraint involving a combination of roles of different fact types. We begin by adding to the library case.

The library employees are situated in one or more rooms within the library building. Every room is identified in a one-to-one way by a room number. One or more mailboxes are found in every room. These mailboxes are numbered consecutively per room. Consequently, only the mailboxes within one room can be distinguished from one another. The mailboxes in different rooms can not be distinguished from one another with this numbering system. Every employee has one or more of these mailboxes. Yet each box is assigned per room to only one employee. For every employee a room and a mailbox number must be known. We have summarized this additional knowledge about the library in the following rules:

P57 : There are rooms.

P58 : There are room numbers.

P59 : Every room is denoted in a one-to-one way by a room number.

P60 : There are mailbox numbers.

P61 : An employee is situated in one or more rooms.

P62 : Every employee is situated in at least one room.

P63 : Every employee is assigned one or more mailbox numbers.

P64 : Every employee is assigned at least one mailbox number.

P65 : Each mailbox number is assigned per room to only one employee.

These rules are described by the part of the information structure diagram depicted in Figure 10.16.

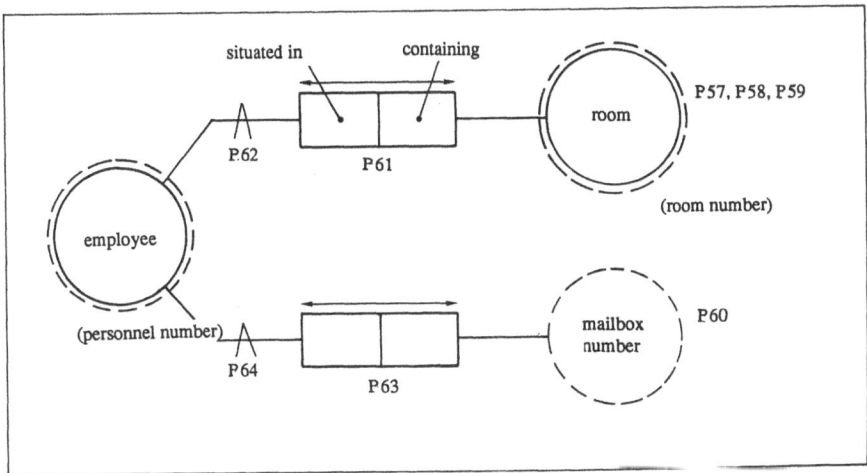

Figure 10.16.

All of the above rules are represented in this diagram, except for rule P65. This is clearly a constraint.

The population of Figure 10.17 is allowed purely on the basis of the object types, the fact types, and the uniqueness and totality constraints of the diagram of Figure 10.16.

In this population, however, mailbox number 6 has been assigned in room 211 to two different employees (namely employees J683 and F759). This is in conflict with rule P65.

The population of Figure 10.18, on the other hand, does satisfy this rule.

We have changed the previous population such that employee F759 has now been assigned in room 211 another mailbox number, namely mailbox number 3. If we compare Figures 10.17 and 10.18 with each other, we see that in Figure

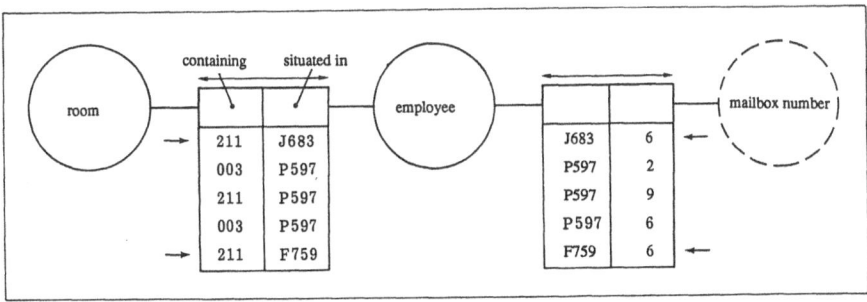

Figure 10.17.

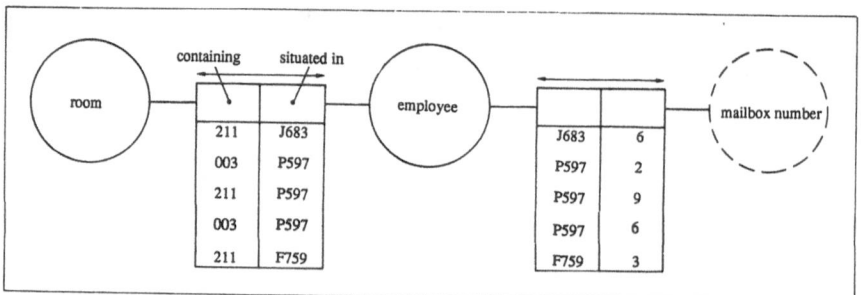

Figure 10.18.

10.18, unlike Figure 10.17, each combination of a room and a mailbox number occurs for only one employee.

This becomes even more clear if we combine the populations of the two fact types into one combined population table, in which the object type "employee" occurs once. (This combined table, of course, no longer describes an elementary sentence type.) Figure 10.17 then results in the combined population table of Figure 10.19.

employee	room	
personnel number	room number	mailbox number
	containing	of
J683	211	6
P597	003	2
P597	211	9
P597	003	6
F759	211	6

Figure 10.19.

We can now clearly see that in room 211, mailbox number 6 has been assigned to two different employees or, stated differently, that the combination of room 211 and mailbox 6 occurs more than once in this combined population table. As we have already seen, the population of this table is in conflict with rule P65.

Figure 10.18, on the other hand, results in the combined table of Figure 10.20.

The population of this table does agree, as we have seen, with rule P65. In this population, a mailbox number has been assigned to exactly one employee per room, or stated differently, every **combination** of a room and a mailbox number occurs only once in this combined table.

A **combination** of two or more roles in each population of which every possible **combination** of objects may only occur once, is called a ***unique combination*** of roles. In the combined population table of Figure 10.20, the combination of the roles of the object types "room" and "mailbox number" is unique. Because this combined table has been created by combining the two binary tables of the population diagram of Figure 10.18, the combination of these roles is naturally unique in this diagram as well; every possible combination of objects of the type "room" and "mailbox number" occurs only once in the population of the combination of these two roles.

employee	room	
personnel number	room number	mailbox number
	containing	of
J683	211	6
P597	003	2
P597	211	9
P597	003	6
F759	211	3

Figure 10.20.

Rule P65 expresses the uniqueness of the **combination** of the roles "room containing employee" and "mailbox number of employee," and is therefore a uniqueness constraint. Uniqueness constraints can involve individual roles, combinations of roles of one fact type (such as was the case in Chapter 7), or combinations of roles of different fact types (such as is the case here).

Uniqueness constraints involving combinations of roles of **different** fact types (such as rule P65) are graphically represented by using the symbol U, standing for Unique, to connect these roles. We have done this in Figure 10.21.

The **combination** of the roles "room containing employee" and "mailbox number of employee" is unique. Every possible combination of objects of the type "room" and "mailbox number" may only occur once in each population of the combination of these two roles. The symbol connecting these roles expresses this uniqueness, and is a graphical representation of the uniqueness constraint described by Proposition P65. In Figure 10.22, we have added the new fact types introduced in this section and the uniqueness constraint dealt with here to the information structure diagram.

Of course, a uniqueness constraint can involve a combination of more than two roles of different fact types. In the following chapter, we will provide an example of this.

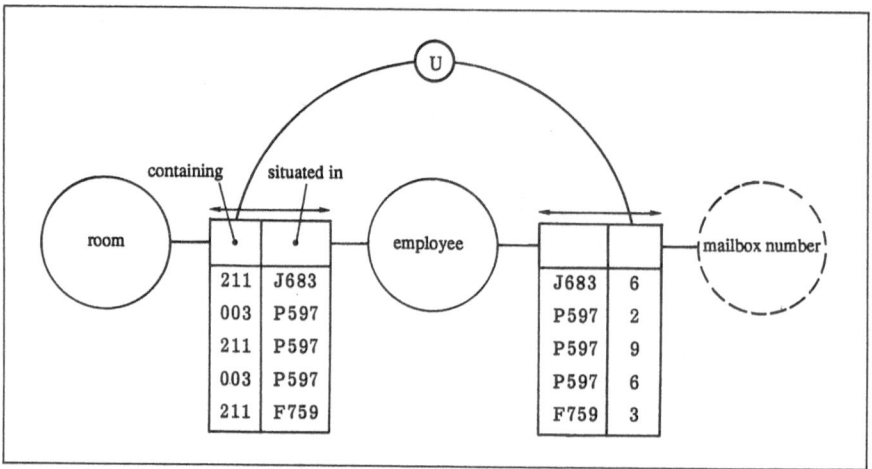

Figure 10.21.

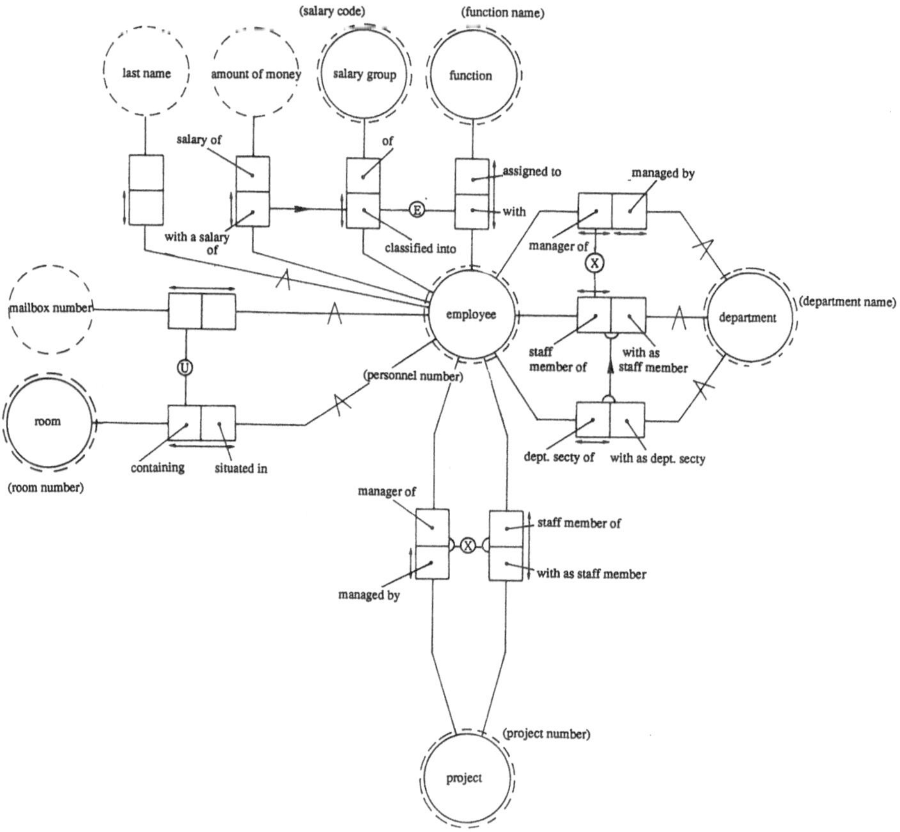

Figure 10.22.

In Figure 10.23, we have drawn examples of uniqueness constraints involving an individual role and combinations of roles of the same or of different fact types next to each other, in order to emphasize the difference.

To conclude this section, a few definitions taken from Chapter 7 are expanded below.

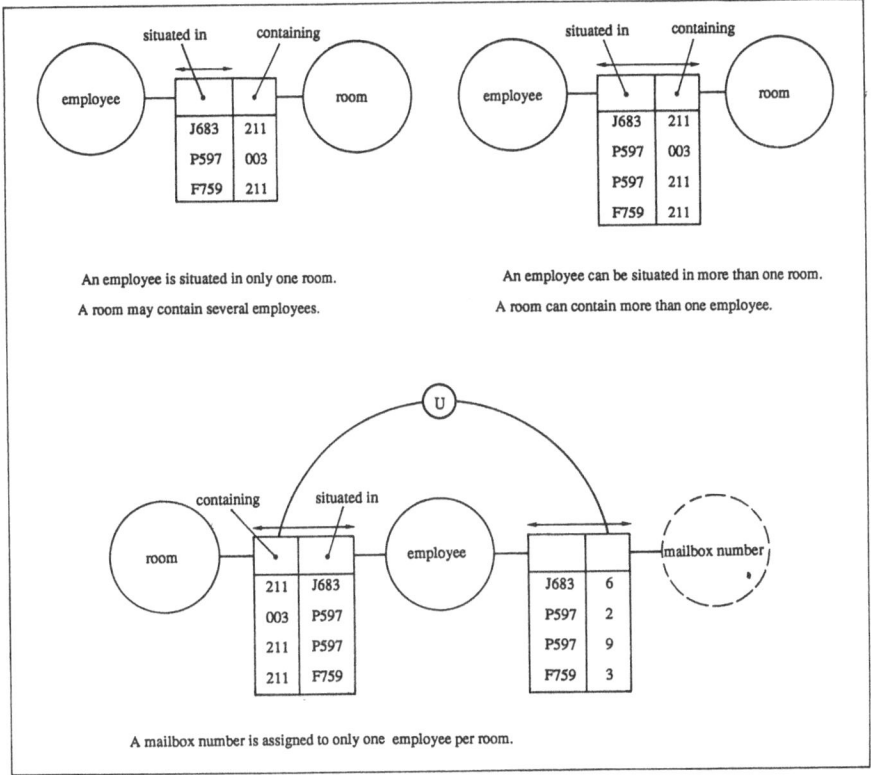

Figure 10.23.

A unique role or a unique combination of roles:
A role or a combination of roles in every population of which every object or every possible combination of objects may occur only once.

Uniqueness constraint:
A constraint which expresses the uniqueness of a role or of a combination of roles.

Uniqueness symbol:
The graphical representation of a uniqueness constraint.

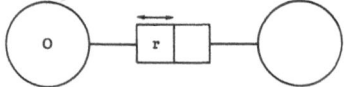

Role r of object type O is unique.

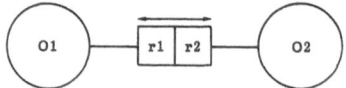

The combination of roles r1
of object type O1 and r2
of object type O2 is unique.

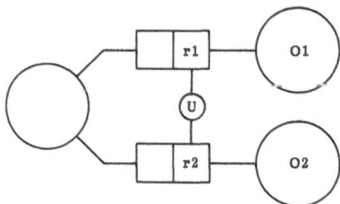

The combination of roles r1
of object type O1 and r2
of object type O2 is unique.

10.4 Totality constraints involving combinations of roles

In this section, we shall give an example of a totality constraint involving a combination of roles. To do this, we shall add the following rule to the library case:

P66 : Every employee is either a staff member or manager of a department.

This rule is not represented in the information structure diagram as it now appears, and is thus clearly a constraint.

The population of Figure 10.24 is allowed purely on the basis of this information structure diagram.

However, because employees K731 and B053 are neither staff members nor managers of a department, this population does not satisfy rule P66. The population of Figure 10.25, on the other hand, does satisfy this rule.

In this figure, we have added the facts that employee K731 is a staff member of the Personnel Department and that employee B053 is manager of this depart-

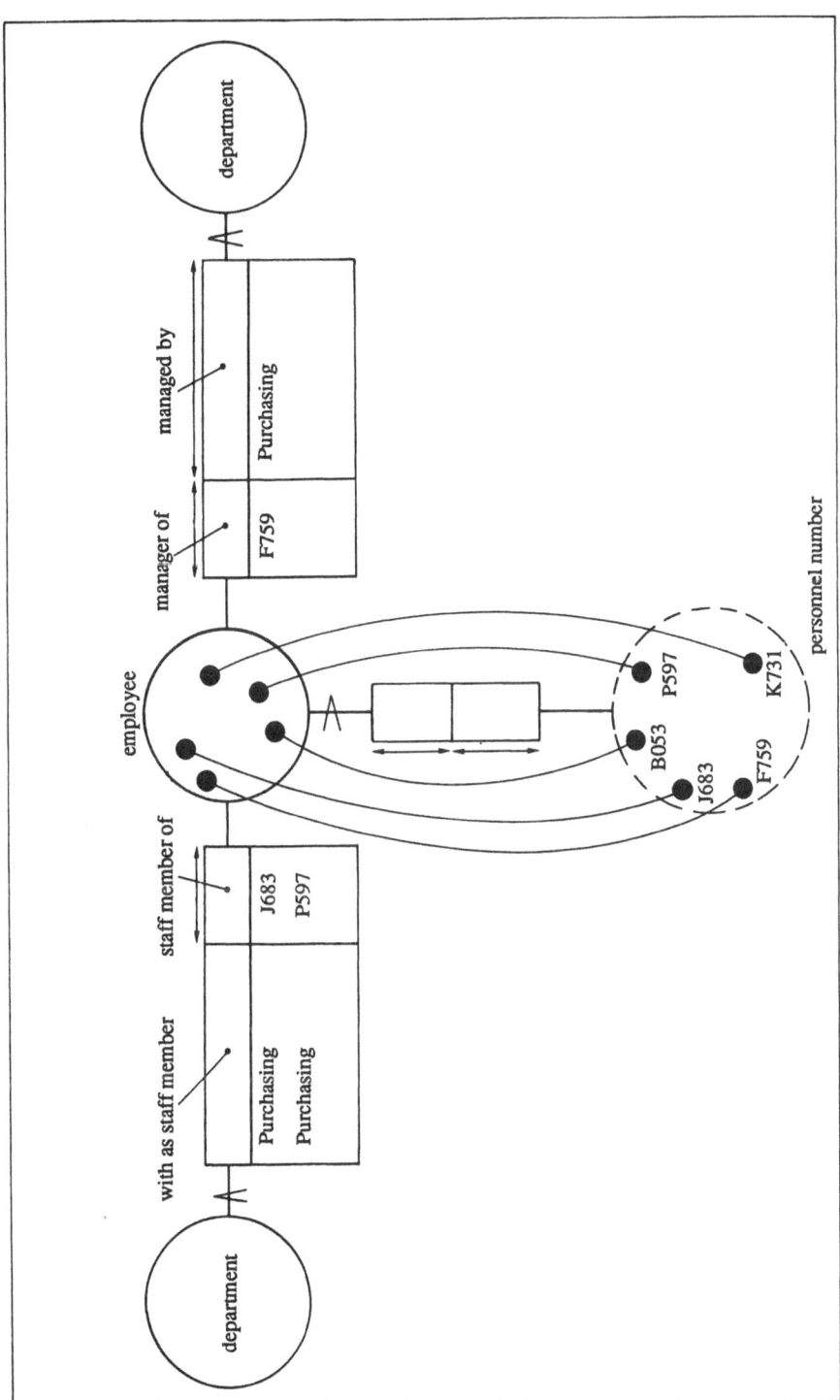

Figure 10.24.

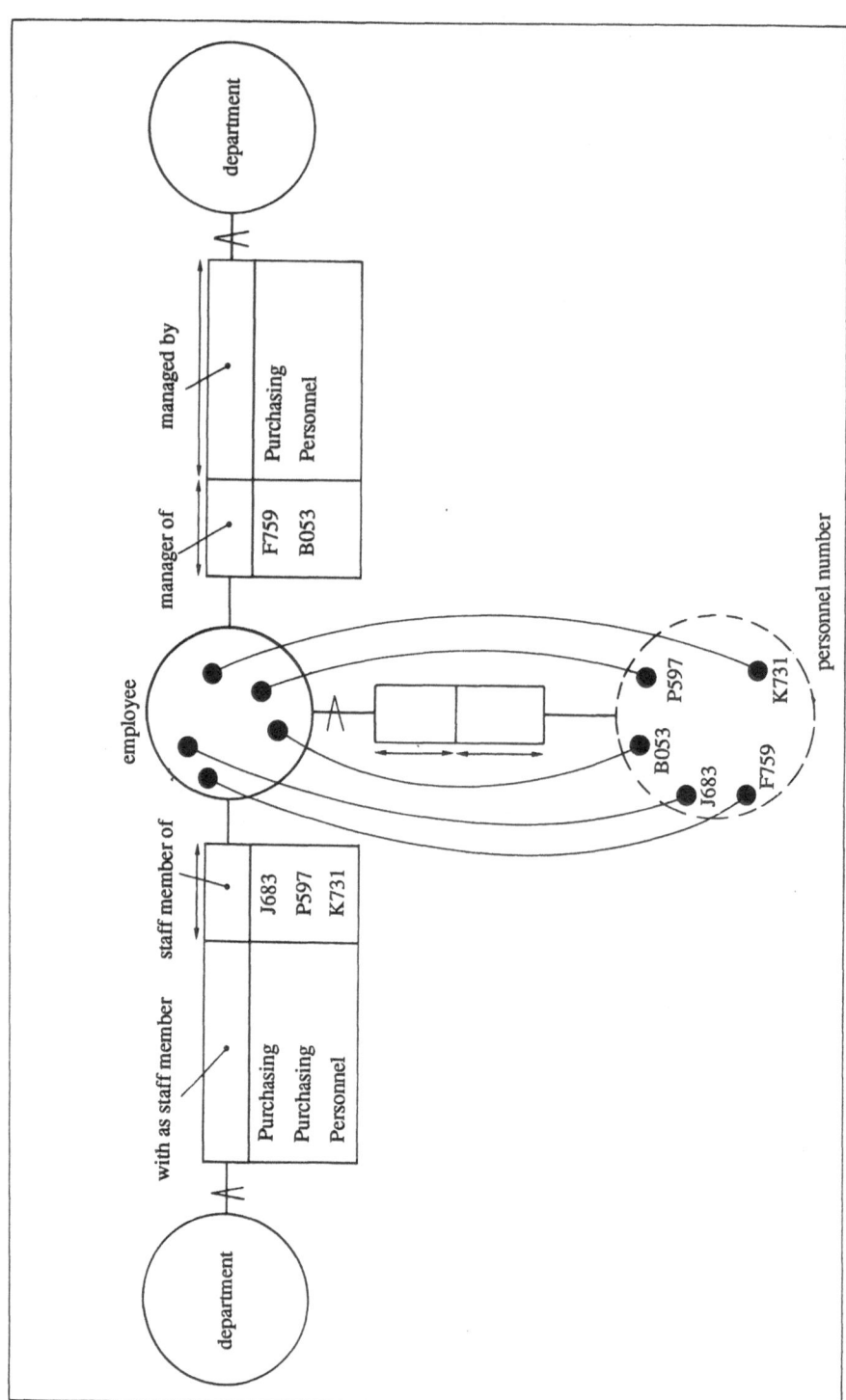

Figure 10.25.

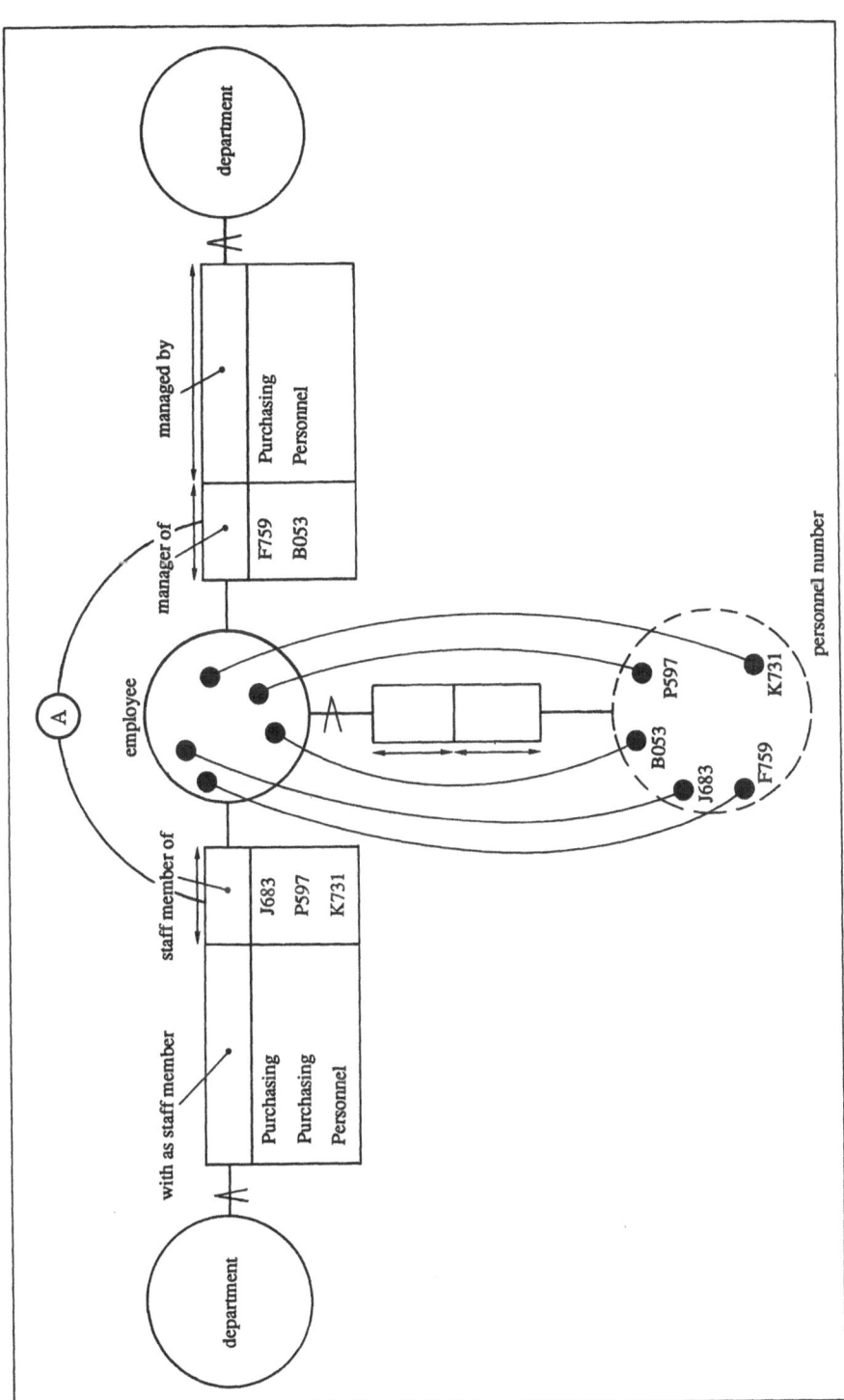

Figure 10.26.

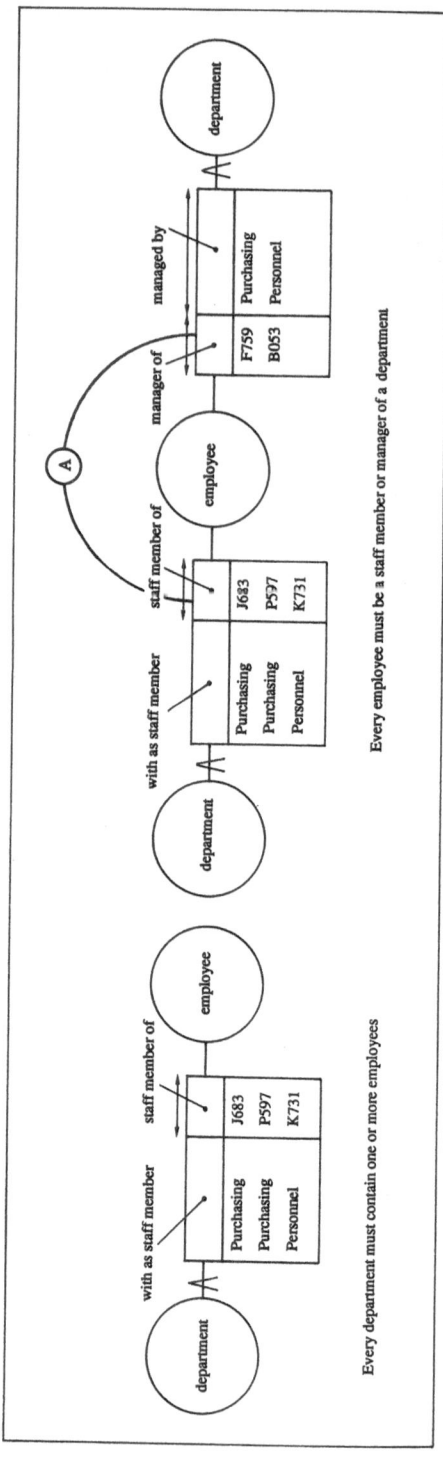

Figure 10.27.

ment, so that in this population every employee is either a staff member or manager of a department. Unlike Figure 10.24, in Figure 10.25 every employee occurs in the population of at least one of the roles "employee staff member of department" or "employee manager of department."

A **combination** of roles of an object type is considered *total* when each object of this object type must occur in at least one of the roles of this combination. Rule P66 expresses the totality of the **combination** of the roles "employee staff member of department" and "employee manager of department," and is therefore a totality constraint. Totality constraints can involve individual roles (such as was the case in Chapter 7) and **combinations** of roles of one object type (such as is the case here).

Totality constraints involving a **combination** of roles of an object type are represented in the information structure diagram by using the symbol A to connect these roles, as we have done in Figure 10.26. Just like the symbol for the totality of individual roles, this symbol is an abbreviation of: for All.

The **combination** of the roles of the object type "employee" is total. Every employee must occur in the population of at least one of the two roles. The symbol connecting these roles expresses this totality, and is a graphical representation of the totality constraint described by Proposition P66.

In Figure 10.27, we have drawn a totality constraint involving an individual role and a totality constraint involving a combination of two roles next to each other, in order to emphasize the difference.

We were able to see in Chapter 9 that the roles "employee staff member of department" and "employee manager of department" exclude each other (an employee cannot be both a staff member and a manager of a department). We have included this exclusion constraint in Figure 10.28.

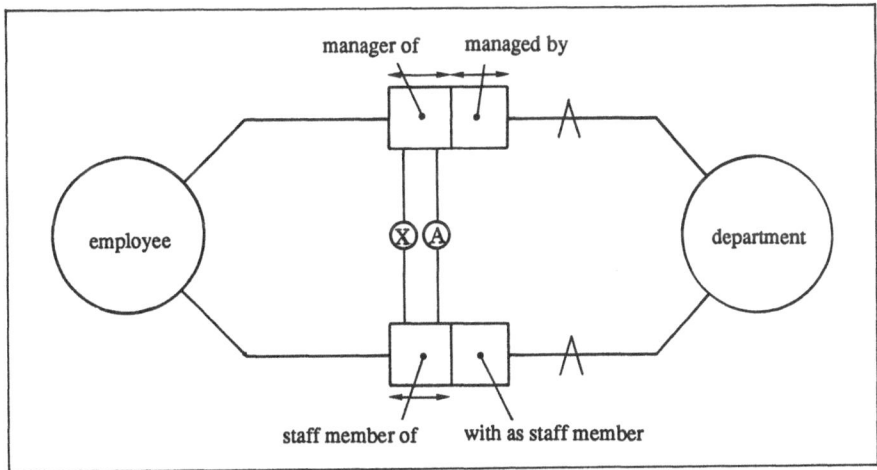

Figure 10.28.

The roles "employee staff member of department" and "employee manager of department" exclude each other **and** their combination is total. Because it often occurs in practice that two roles exclude each other and their combination is total, we shall represent a combined exclusion and totality constraint involving the same roles by the symbol X/A, as we have done in Figure 10.29.

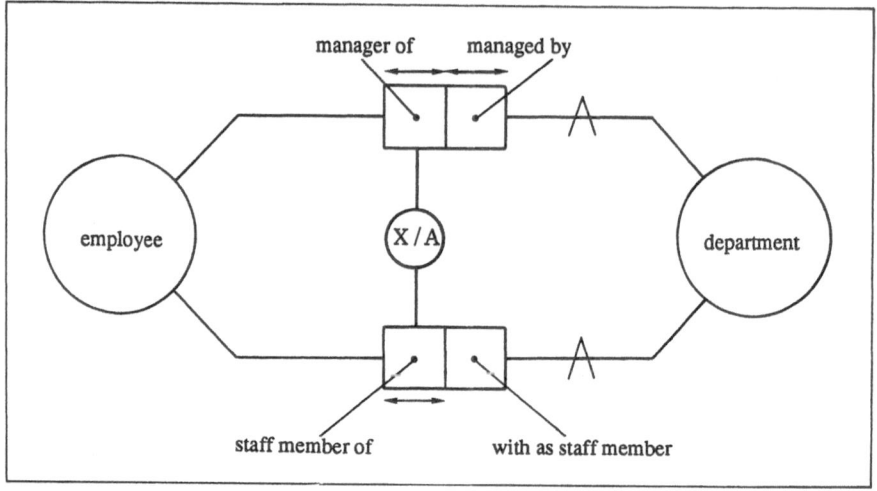

Figure 10.29.

The symbol X/A is an abridged representation of **two** constraints: an exclusion constraint and a totality constraint involving two (or more) roles of the same object type. In Figure 10.30 we have added the totality constraint dealt with in this section to the information structure diagram.

Of course, the roles of a total combination have to belong to the same object type. For this reason, the information structure diagram of Figure 10.31 is not correct, and is therefore not acceptable as an information structure diagram.

Totality constraints do not need to be restricted to a combination of two roles, but can involve three or more roles. Below, we show an example of a totality constraint involving three roles. To do this, we assume once again that some of the employees have an expense account with a certain limit. Every employee must either have an expense account, or be a staff member of a department or manager of a department. This situation is described by the information structure diagram of Figure 10.32.

We saw in Chapter 9 that the same three roles exclude each other. In Figure 10.33, we have depicted the totality constraint and the exclusion constraint involving these three roles in combined form.

Some of the definitions in Chapter 7 are expanded below.

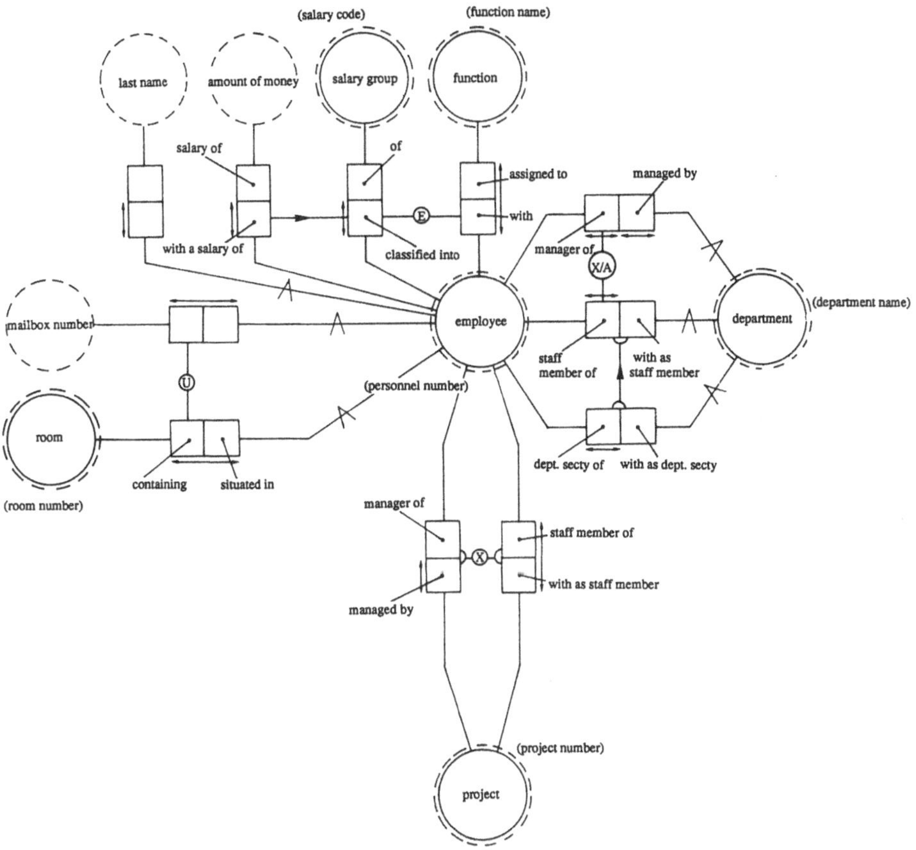

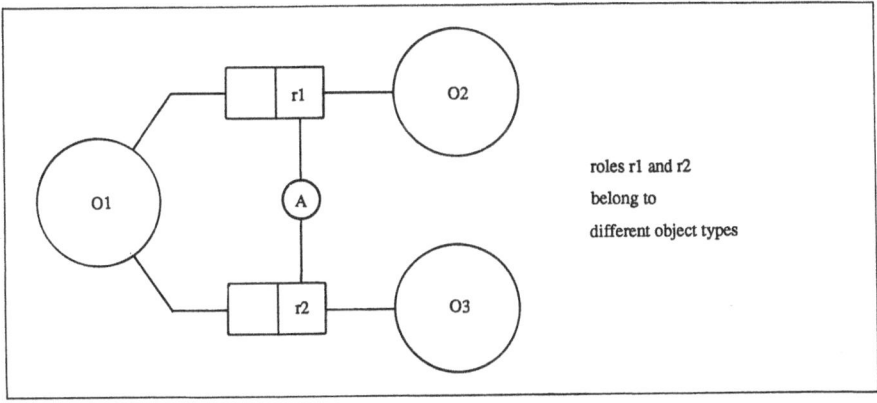

Figure 10.30.

Figure 10.31.

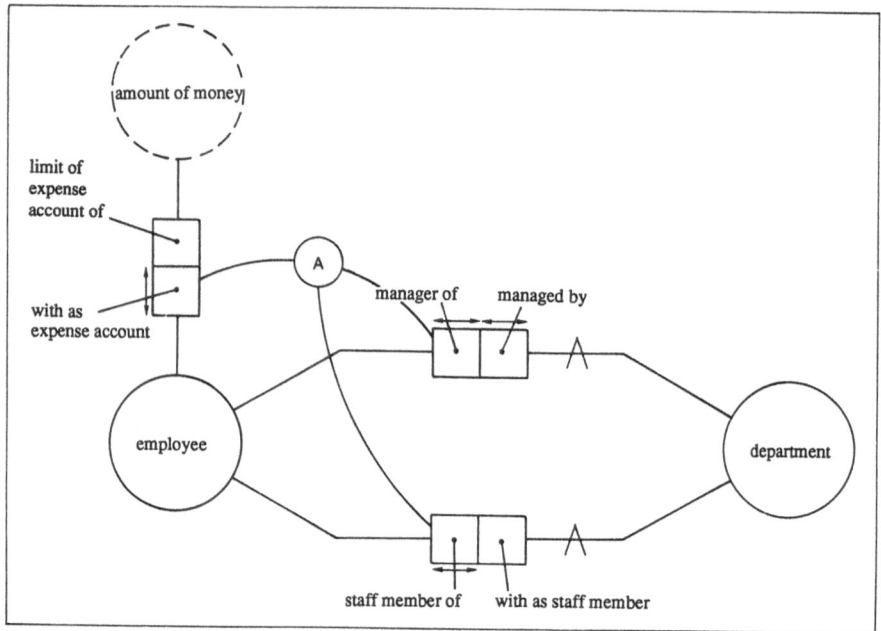

Figure 10.32.

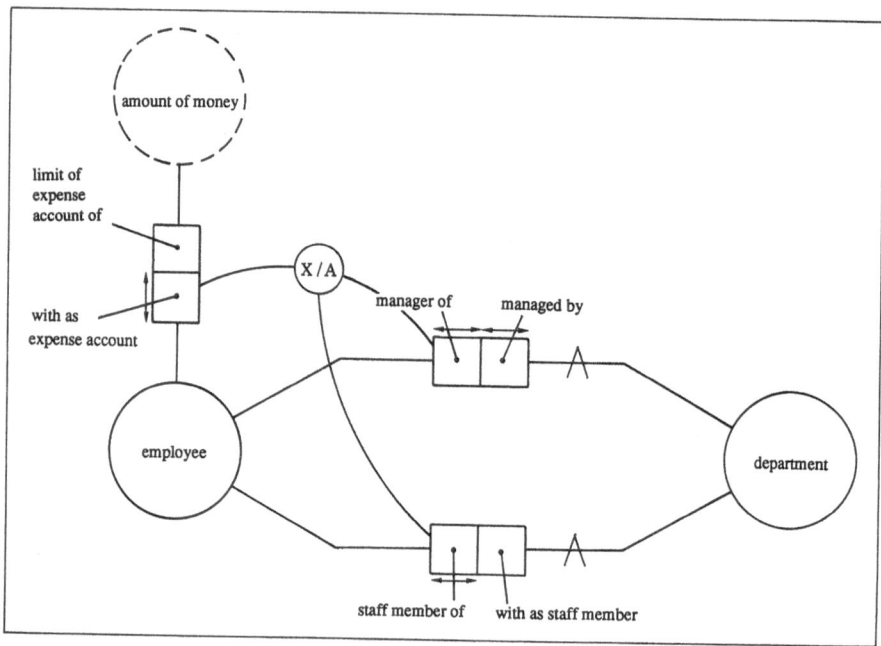

Figure 10.33.

A total role or a total combination of roles:
A role or a combination of roles of one object type with the characteristic that each object of this object type must occur in the population of this role or in the population of at least one of the roles of this combination.

Totality constraint:
A constraint which expresses the totality of a role or of a combination of roles.

Totality symbol:
The graphical representation of a totality constraint.

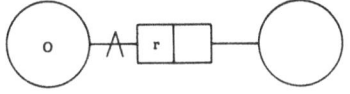

Role r of object type O is total

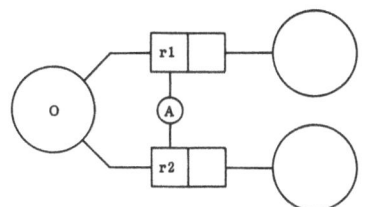

The combination of roles r1 and r2
of object type O is total

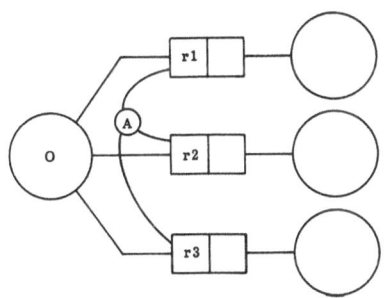

The combination of roles r1, r2 and r3
of object type O is total

A totality constraint combined with an exclusion constraint is notated as follows:

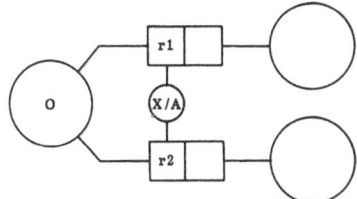

Roles r1 and r2 of object type O
exclude each other
and their combination is total

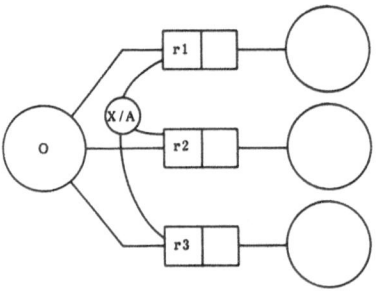

Roles r1, r2 and r3
of object type O exclude each other
and their combination is total

10.5 Referenceability

We saw in Chapter 7 that an information structure diagram must be referenceable. That is to say, it must be possible on the basis of the diagram to denote every non-lexical object uniquely by one or more lexical objects. In this section, we shall show that uniqueness constraints involving combinations of roles have an important role to play in references to non-lexical objects. To do this, we will again add to the library case.

We saw earlier that every library employee is situated in one or more rooms. These rooms are denoted in a one-to-one way by room numbers. In what follows, we will stop using the room numbers to denote rooms, and come up with another way to refer uniquely to the rooms.

The rooms are located on different floors of the building, and we will assume that they are provided with a "room sequence number" which runs consecutively from the lowest to the highest number **per floor**. A room can only be located on one floor and has only one room sequence number. In general, a floor contains one or more rooms and there are rooms (necessarily on different floors) with the same room sequence number. For every room sequence number, there is only one room **per floor**. (Another way of saying this is that for every possible combination of floor and room sequence number there is exactly one room.) Every floor is identified in a one-to-one way by a floor number.

We have summarized this in the underlying, fairly obvious, rules:

P67: There are floors.

P68: Every floor is denoted in a one-to-one way by a floor number.

P69: There are room sequence numbers.

P70 : A room is located on a floor.

P71 : A room is located on only one floor.

P72 : Every room is located on a floor.

P73 : A room has a room sequence number.

P74 : A room has only one room sequence number.

P75 : Every room has a room sequence number.

P76 : A room sequence number belongs to only one room **per floor**.

These rules are described by the part of the information structure diagram that is represented in Figure 10.34.

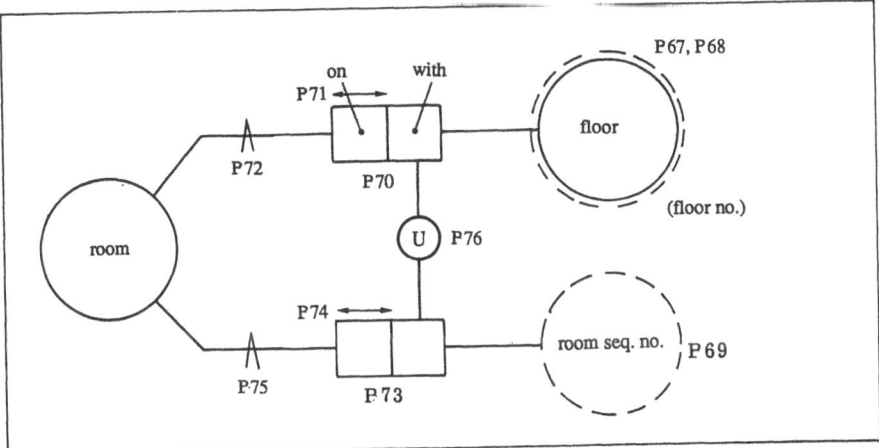

Figure 10.34.

The question is whether the information structure diagram is still referenceable, in spite of its missing a bridge type with respect to the object type "room."

Because of uniqueness constraint P76, there is exactly one room belonging to the combination of a floor and a room sequence number. This combination therefore refers **uniquely** to a room. Because of the totality constraints P72 and P75, there has to be a floor and a room sequence number for **every** room, so that **every** room can be uniquely denoted by using the combination of a floor and a room sequence number. Every floor can be uniquely referred to by a floor number. It follows from all of this that the information structure diagram is referenceable.

Because of the uniqueness constraints P71 and P74, only one floor and one room sequence number, and thus also only one combination of a floor and a room sequence number belongs to every room. It follows from this that a combination of a floor and a room sequence number refers not just uniquely, but even in a one-to-one way, to a room.

The expression:

"The *room on floor* 2 *and with room sequence number* 8"

refers to exactly one room. On the other hand, this room is located on the second floor only and has the room sequence number 8 only. The above expression is consequently an one-to-one reference to a non-lexical object of the type "room." Every room can be unambiguously referred to by means of such an expression.

In general, references proceed through an information structure diagram via "paths" formed by one or more fact types. Thus, in Figure 10.34, the reference to the non-lexical objects of the type "room" proceeds via a "path" that consists of the bridge type involving "floor number" and "floor," the idea type involving "room" and "floor," and the bridge type involving "room sequence number" and "room." These "paths" generally have the structure of a tree.

For the sake of our example let us now assume, contrary to what was determined in previous sections, that there are no personnel numbers. The question is then whether the information structure diagram (part of which is depicted in Figure 10.35) is still referenceable.

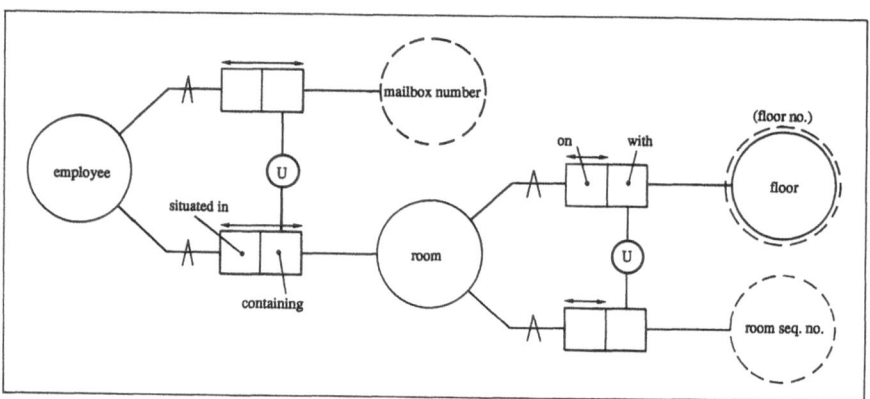

Figure 10.35.

Because of the uniqueness constraint involving the combination of the roles "mailbox number of employee" and "room containing employee," every combination of a mailbox number and a room refers uniquely to an employee. Since a mailbox number and a room belong to **every** employee, **every** employee can be uniquely referred to by a combination of these objects. We have seen that every room can uniquely be referred to by a combination of a floor and a room sequence number. It follows from this that, even though the personnel number is missing, the information structure diagram is still referenceable.

Because an employee can be assigned more than one mailbox number and can be situated in more than one room, several combinations of a mailbox number and a room can belong to one employee. All of these combinations refer uniquely to the same employee. It follows from this that a combination of a mailbox number and a room refers synonymously to an employee. The expression:

"the *employee with mailbox number* 6 *situated in* the *room (on floor* 2 *and with room sequence number* 11)"

refers to exactly one employee. On the other hand, this employee can be in possession of several mailboxes and can be situated in several rooms. The above expression is therefore a synonymous reference to a non-lexical object of the type "employee."

(In the above expression, we have used parentheses to indicate that "room sequence number 11" is related to the room and not to the "employee." In practice, one must often use parentheses to indicate how a particular expression must be read.)

In this case, the reference to the non-lexical object of the type "employee" proceeds via a "path" that consists of:

– the bridge type involving room sequence number and room
– the bridge type involving floor number and floor
– the idea type involving floor and room
– the idea type involving room and employee
– the bridge type involving mailbox number and employee.

Figure 10.36 contains the same information structure diagram as Figure 10.35, except that, in the latter, the roles "employee with mailbox number" and "employee

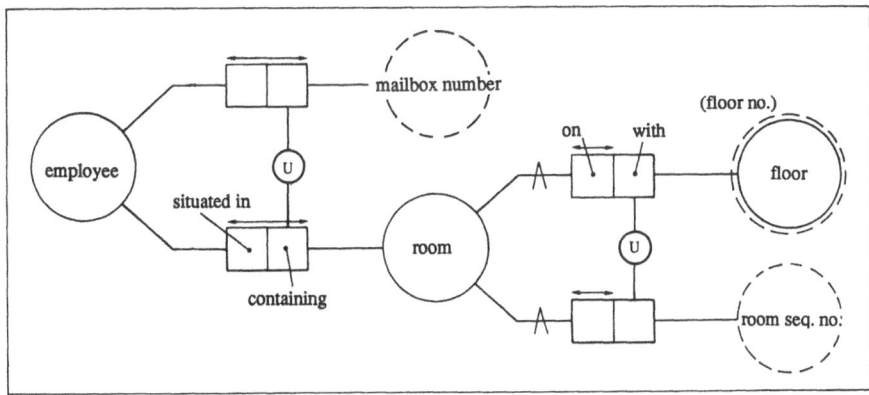

Figure 10.36.

situated in room" are not total. An employee can still be denoted uniquely by a combination of a mailbox number and a room. But because not **every** employee has a mailbox number and a room, not **every** employee can be denoted by a combination of these objects. This means that the information structure diagram of Figure 10.36 is not referenceable, and is as such not acceptable as an information structure diagram.

We have seen in the above example that objects belonging to populations of unique combinations of roles refer uniquely to objects of another type. For example, every combination of objects of the type "room" and "mailbox number" refers uniquely to an object of the type "employee," and every combination of objects of the type "floor" and "room sequence number" refers uniquely to an object of the type "room."

In general, it holds that objects belonging to populations of unique combinations of roles always refer uniquely to other objects of a certain type. On the basis of the 100% principle, this object type must be explicitly represented in the information structure diagram. The co-roles of the roles whose combination is unique always involve this object type.

As a result, the co-roles of roles the combination of which is unique and which belong to different fact types, must always belong to the same object type.

In Figure 10.35 the combination of the roles "room containing employee" and "mailbox number of employee" is unique. The co-roles of these roles (the roles "employee situated in room" and "employee with mailbox number," respectively) involve the same object type (namely the object type "employee"). Similarly, the combination of the roles "floor with room" and "room sequence number of room" is unique. The co-roles of these roles (the roles "room on floor" and "room with room sequence number," respectively) involve the same object type, namely the object type "room."

For the same reason, the information structure diagram of Figure 10.37 is not correct, and is therefore not acceptable as an information structure diagram.

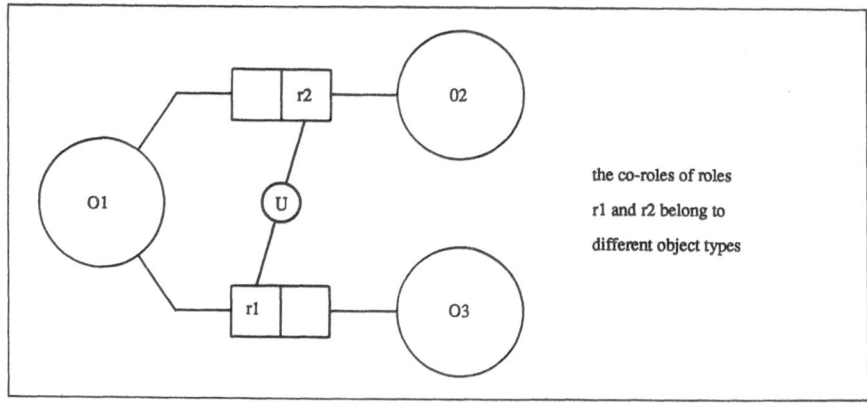

Figure 10.37.

It is assumed in Figure 10.38 that the employees can be denoted in a one-to-one way by a personnel number **and/or** a salary number. The salary number, used in payroll records, is not the same kind of number as a personnel number. Every employee has a personnel number or a salary number or both. That is, every employee occurs in the population of at least one of the roles "employee with personnel number" and "employee with salary number." Every employee can thus be uniquely denoted by a personnel or a salary number. It follows from this that this information structure diagram is referenceable. The expressions

"the *employee with personnel number* J683"

and

"the *employee with salary number* 5218"

each refer to precisely one employee. It is possible for both expressions to refer to the same or to different employees.

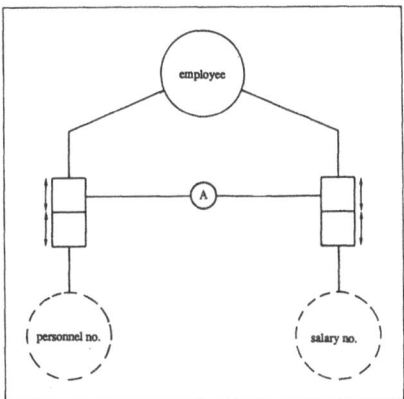

Figure 10.38.

In Figure 10.39, we have added the object types, the fact types and the constraints of Figure 10.35 to the information structure diagram.

Figure 10.40 is the representation of a population table illustrating the rooms in which some of the library employees are situated.

This population table could conceivably have arisen from a concrete example of the contents of the information flows and could belong to the tables on which the information structure diagram is based.

We note that the fact that the combination of a floor and a room sequence number forms a reference to a room is expressed in the population table by adding an extra heading to the table. In this extra "heading," the object type name "room" is put above the **combination** of the columns of the object types "floor" and "room

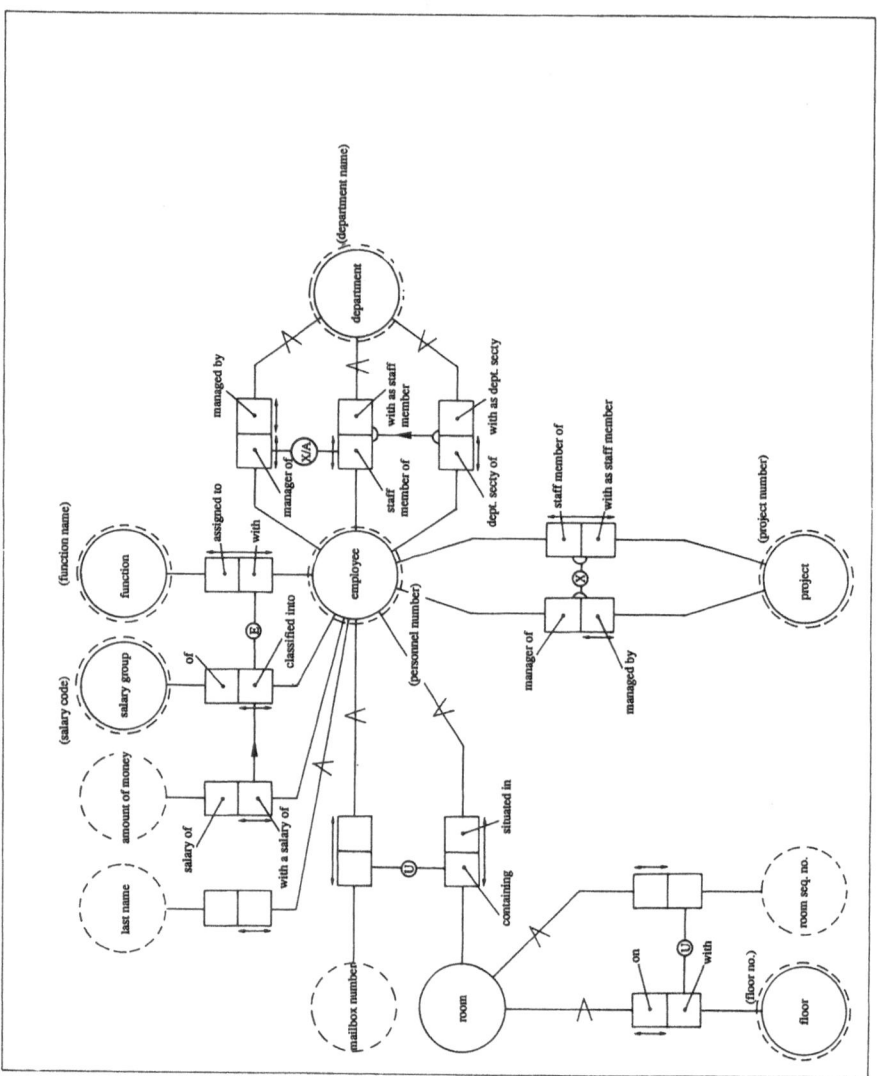

Figure 10.39.

employee	room	
	floor	
personnel number	floor number	room sequence number
situated in	with	of
J683	2	11
P597	0	03
P597	2	11
P597	1	03
F759	2	11

Figure 10.40.

sequence number." This expresses the fact that every combination of a floor and a room sequence number refers to an object of the type "room."

In general, this is how we will express that the combinations of certain objects in population tables refer to objects of another type. In the next chapter, we shall take a look at some other examples of this.

We summarize the most important conclusions in this section below:

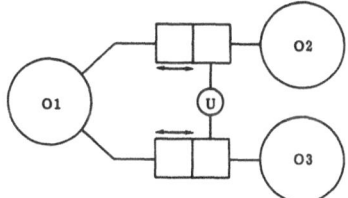

The combinations of objects of type O2 and O3 form one-to-one references to objects of type O1. If the two roles of object type O1 are total, this information structure diagram is referenceable.

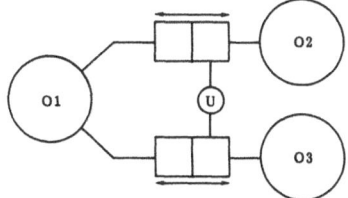

The combinations of objects of type O2 and O3 form synonymous (and thus unique) references to objects of type O1. If the two roles of object type O1 are total, this information structure diagram is referenceable.

The following rule contains a number of conclusions taken from the previous sections.

The compatibility rule:

- Equality constraints must involve individual roles of the same object type.
- Subset and exclusion constraints must involve individual roles of the same object type or combinations of roles of the same object types.
- Totality constraints must involve one or more individual roles of the same object type.
- Uniqueness constraints must involve one or more roles of the same fact type or individual roles of different fact types whose co-roles belong to the same object type.

For example the following situations are not allowed on the basis of this rule:

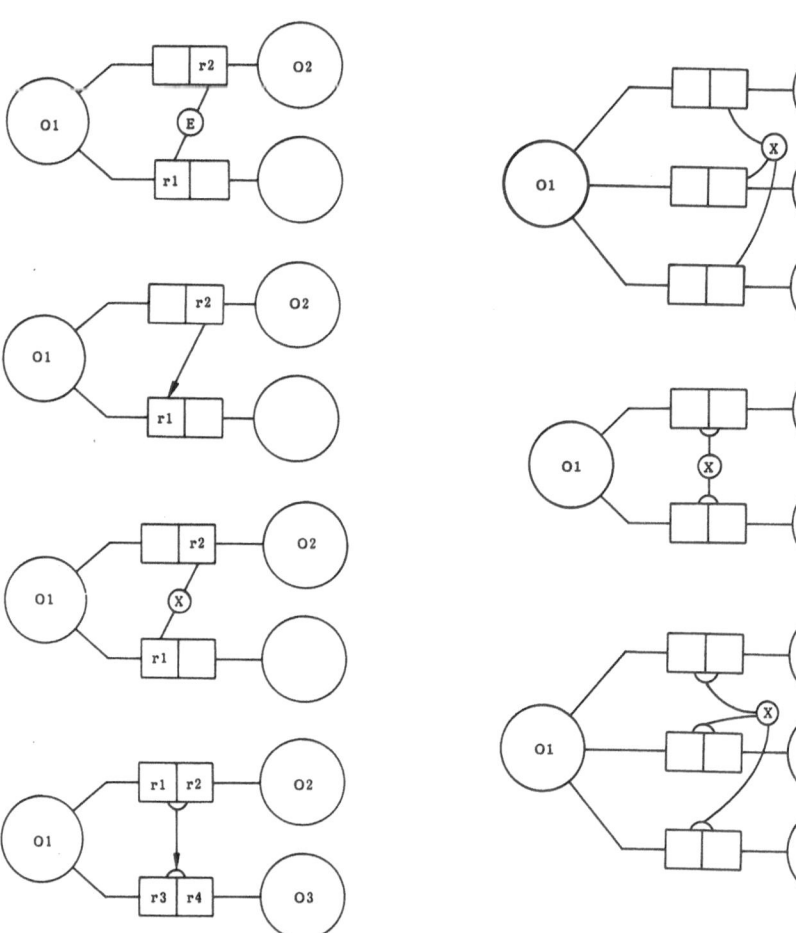

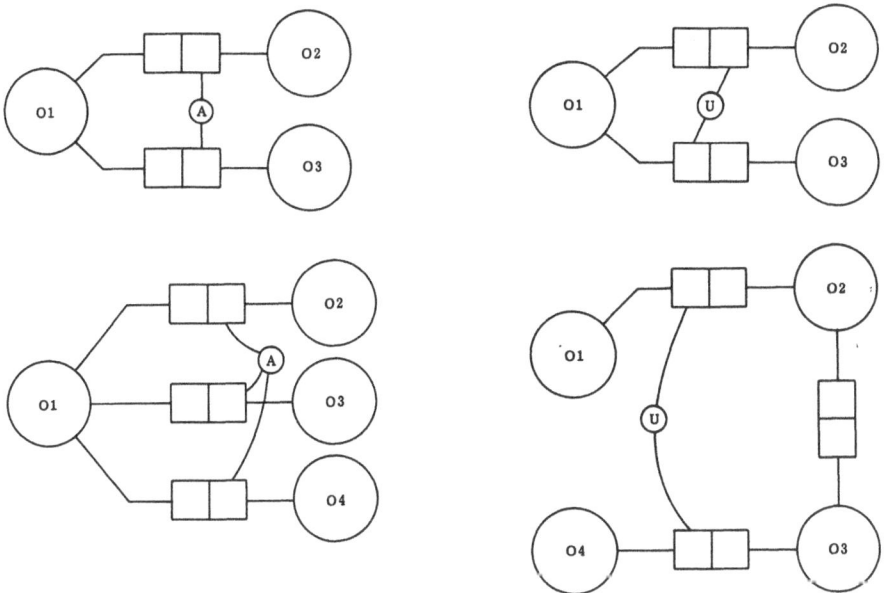

10.6 Idea types involving one object type.

Up to now, we have only come across examples of idea types whose roles belong to **different** object types. It sometimes happens that the roles of an idea type belong to one single object type. We shall show two examples of this by adding just a little bit more to the library case.

The departments in the library are organized as a line organization. Every department in this scheme falls hierarchically under a department that is one step higher. The library's line organization is depicted in Figure 10.41.

The management is seen as one of the departments. We can summarize this in the following rules:

P77: A department can be controlled by another department.
P78: A department may only be controlled by one other department.

These rules are described in the part of the information structure diagram that is depicted in Figure 10.42.

Figure 10.43 depicts a population diagram that is constructed on the basis of the organizational chart in Figure 10.41.

This diagram exemplifies a (binary) idea type in which the roles belong to the same object type. Because the roles of a bridge type always involve, by definition, one lexical and one non-lexical object type, and therefore different object types, these kinds of constructions can only occur for **idea types**.

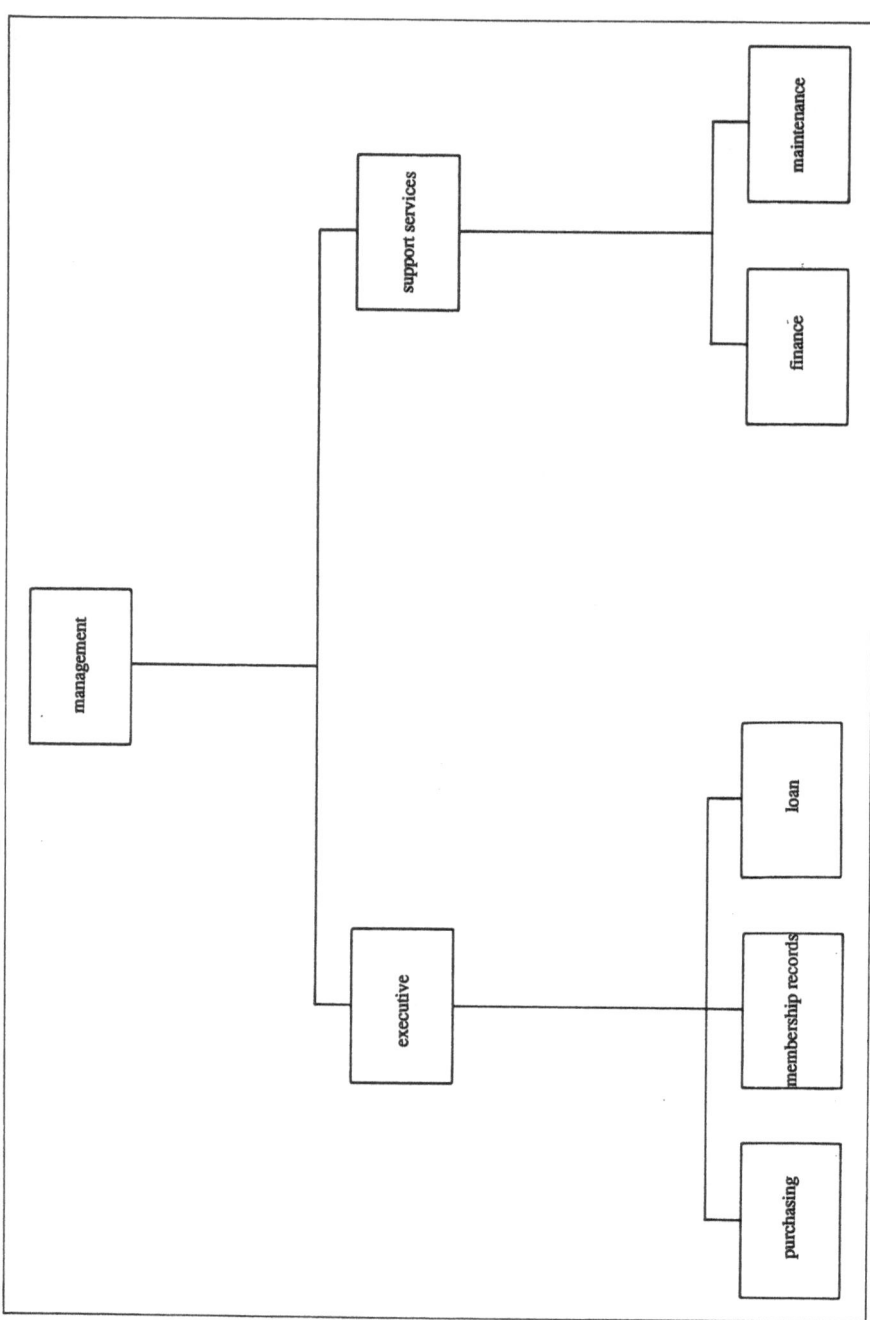

Figure 10.41.

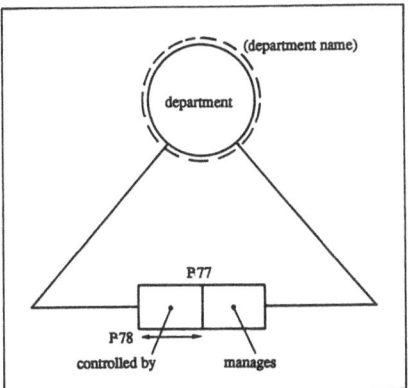

Figure 10.42.

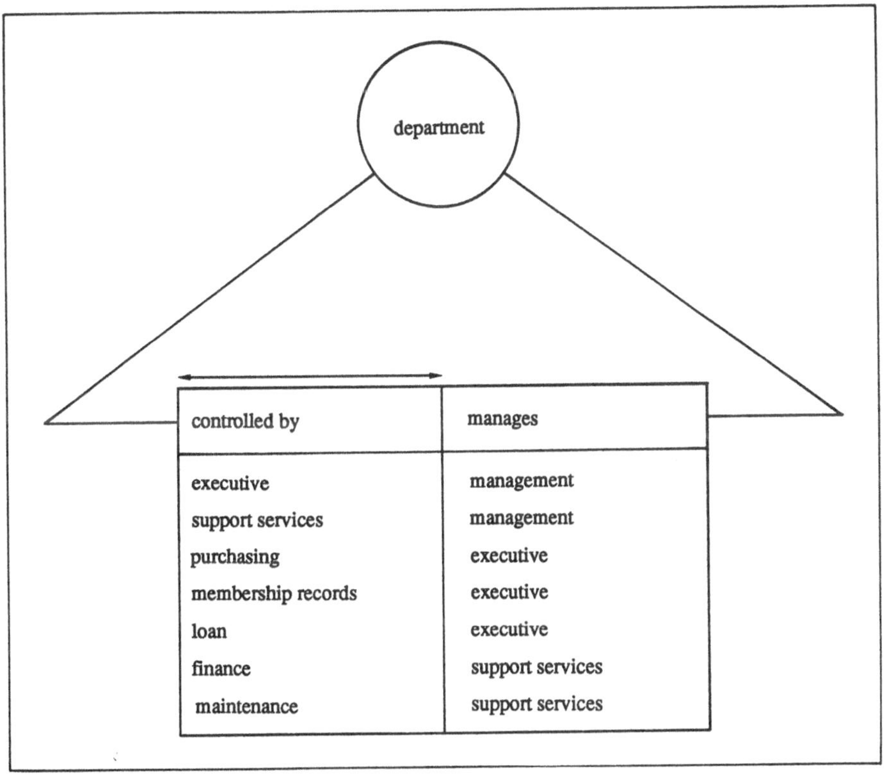

controlled by	manages
executive	management
support services	management
purchasing	executive
membership records	executive
loan	executive
finance	support services
maintenance	support services

Figure 10.43.

Below is another example of an idea type involving one object type.

Some of the library departments are staff departments. A staff department advises one other department. Every department can in turn be advised by only one staff department. In Figure 10.44, we have added the staff departments Personnel and Planning to the organizational chart.

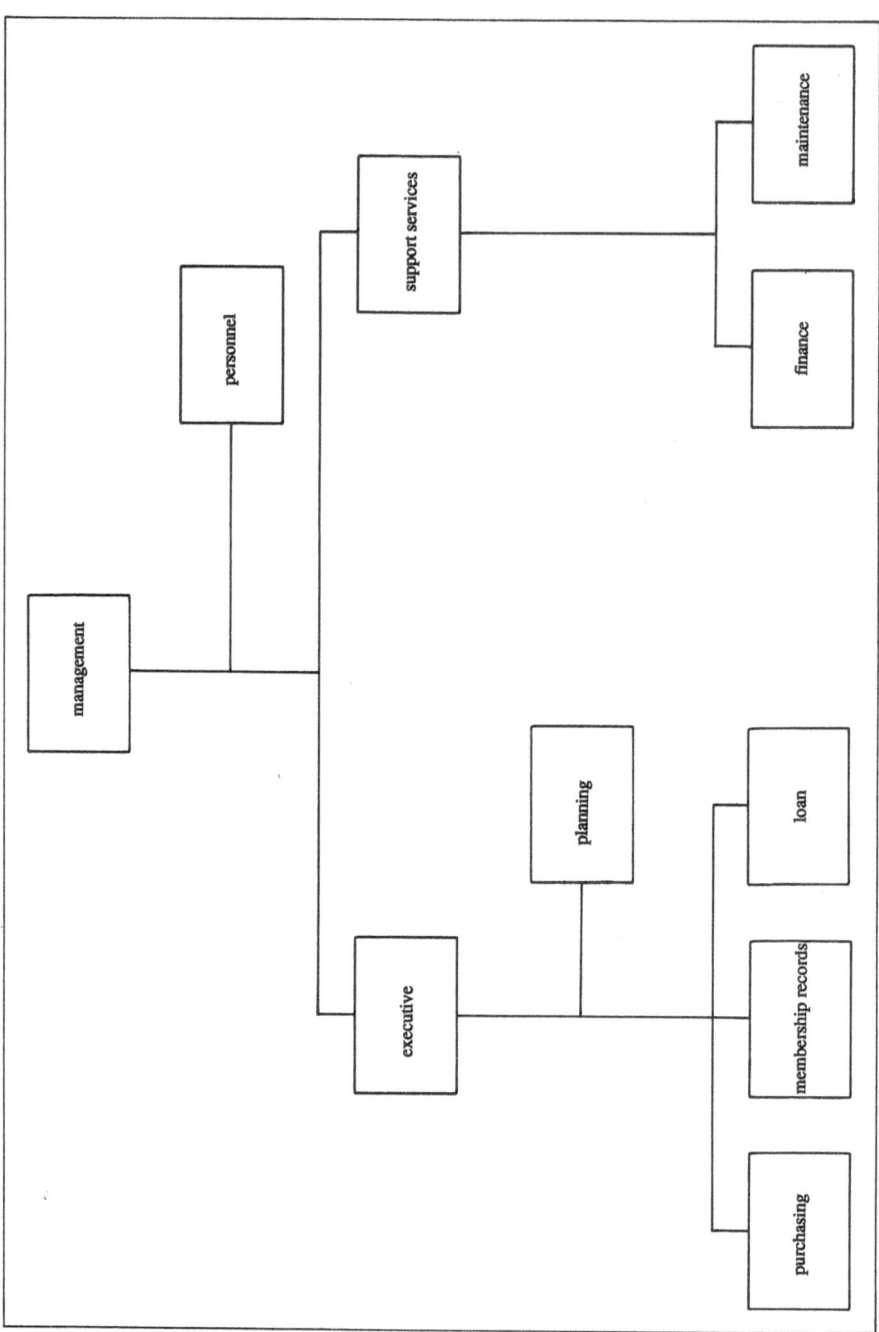

Figure 10.44.

The Personnel Department advises (is a staff department of) Management, and the Planning Department advises (is a staff department of) the Executive Department. The relationship between the Personnel Department and Management is of another type than that between, for example, the Executive Department and Management. Management is **advised** by the Personnel Department, while Management **manages** the Executive Department. From the way this is depicted in Figure 10.44, it appears that there are two different types of relationships between departments. This can be summarized by the following rules:

P79: A department can advise another department.
P80: A department can advise only one other department.
P81: A department may only be advised by one other department.

These rules are described in the part of the information structure diagram that is depicted in Figure 10.45.

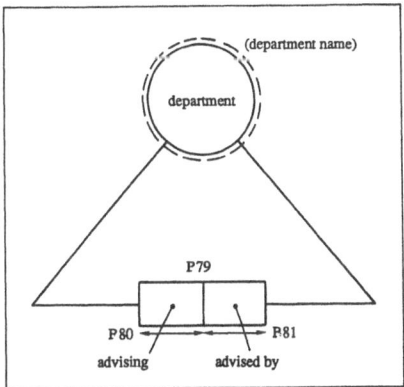

Figure 10.45.

Figure 10.46 contains a population diagram constructed on the basis of the organizational chart of Figure 10.44.

Figure 10.47 is a combination of the diagrams in Figures 10.42 and 10.45.

A department that falls under another department, which is managed by another department, or which is advised by another department (and which is thus a line department) may not itself advise another department (and therefore cannot be a staff department). This can be summarized in the following rules:

P82: A department which is controlled by another department cannot advise another department.

P83: A department that manages another department cannot advise another department.

P84: A department which is advised by another department may not itself advise another department.

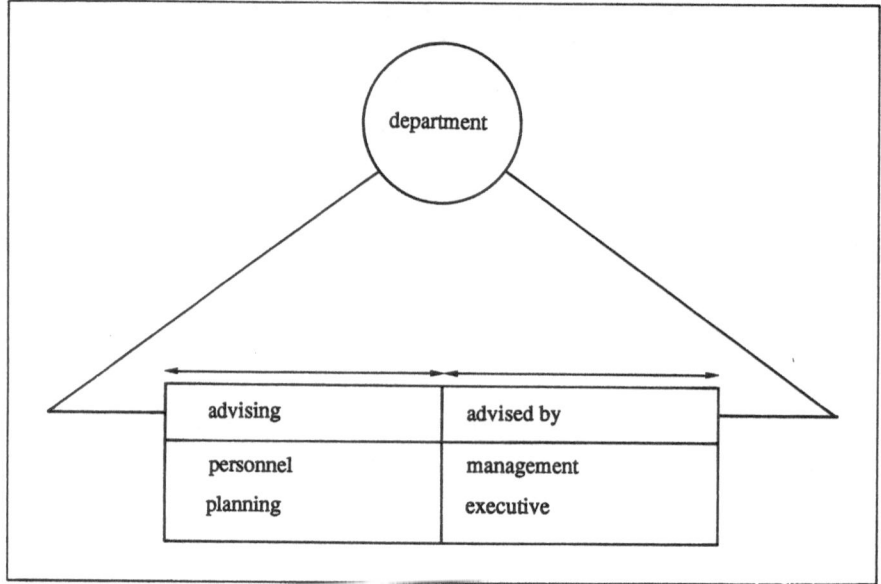

Figure 10.46.

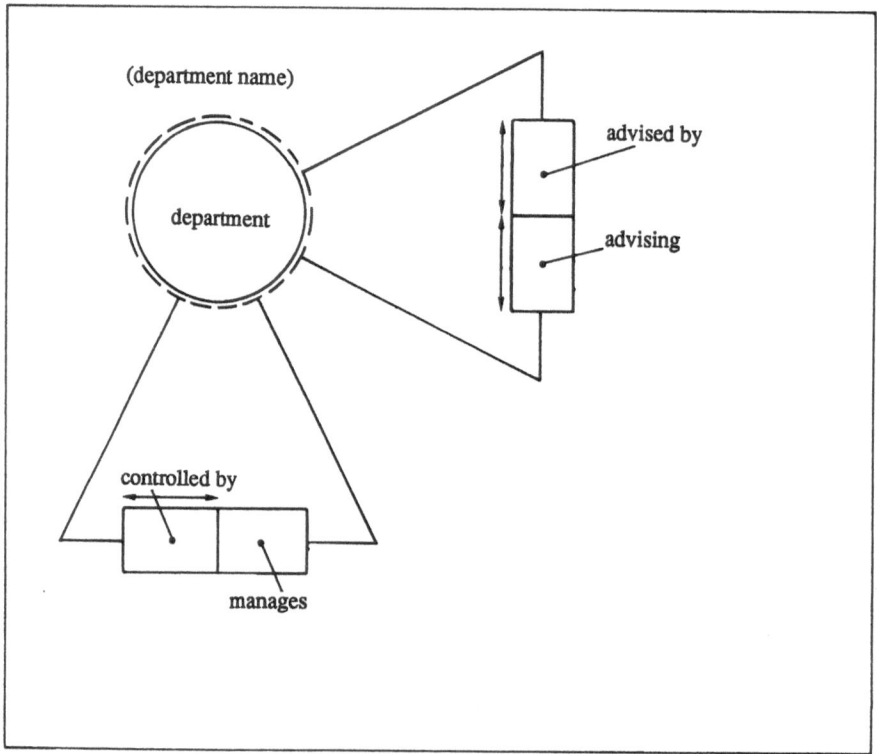

Figure 10.47.

Adding these rules to the diagram of Figure 10.47 results in the diagram of Figure 10.48.

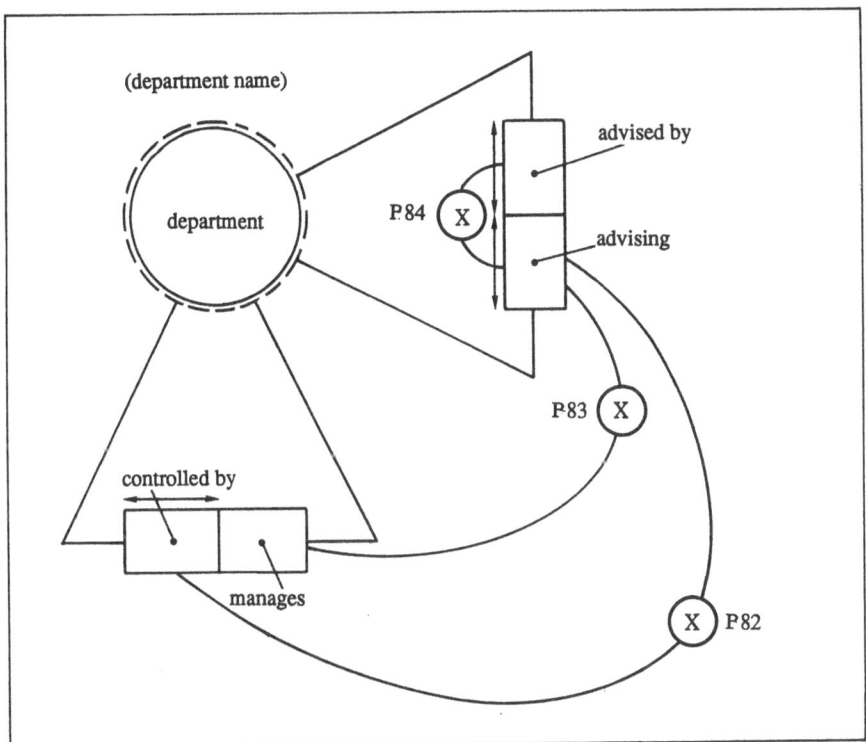

Figure 10.48.

Rule P84 is an exclusion constraint involving the roles of one and the same idea type. Because of the compatibility rule (an exclusion constraint must involve roles of the same object type), this can only occur if both roles of this idea type belong to the same object type, such as is the case here.

Further constraints that hold for the diagram of Figure 10.48 are that a department cannot be controlled by itself and cannot advise itself. Further, there may be only one department that is not controlled by another department. These constraints are, however, non-graphical, and as such, do not belong to the information structure diagram. We will be getting back to these constraints in Chapter 16.

The diagram in Figure 10.48 looks fairly complicated and is not really satisfactory. Intuitively, we feel a need for the individual object types "line department" and "staff department." We shall adapt the information structure diagram in this sense in Chapter 14.

In Figure 10.49, we have added the new fact types and constraints dealt with in this section to the information structure diagram.

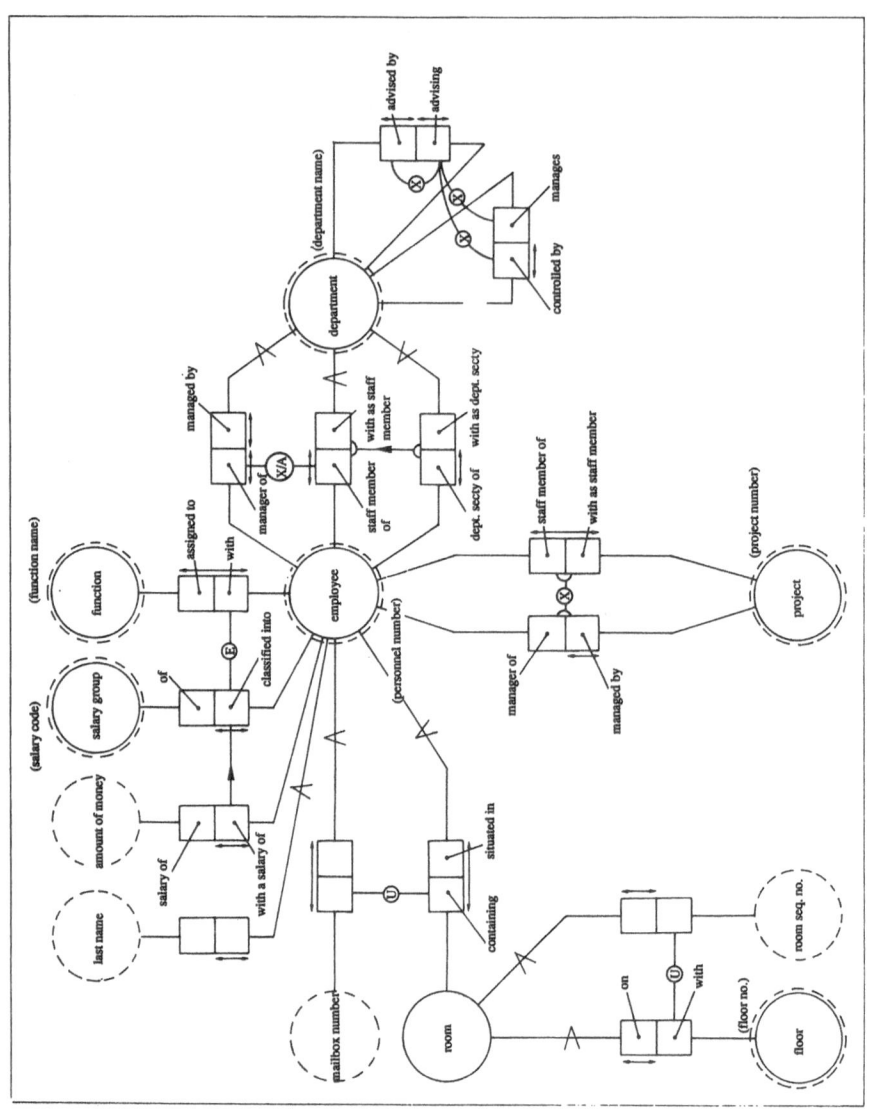

11   THE NIAM METHOD OF INFORMATION ANALYSIS IN PRACTICE - 3

In the previous practical chapters, we dealt with the first six and the eleventh steps of the NIAM process of information analysis. In this chapter, the ninth step comes up for discussion. The intermediate steps 7, 8, and 10 will be treated in subsequent practical chapters.

In step 9, we determine the remaining graphical constraints involving the roles of the fact types which were added to the information structure diagram in step 5.

9. Add the remaining graphical constraints.

This step consists of the following substeps:

– For every pair of non-total roles of one object type, check whether these roles are equal.
– For every pair of non-total roles of one object type, check whether one role is a subset of the other role.
– For every pair of combinations of roles of the same object types, check whether one combination of roles is a subset of the other combination of roles.
– Check whether two or more non-total roles of one object type exclude each other.
– Check whether two or more combinations of roles of the same object types exclude each other.
– Check whether combinations of two or more **co-roles** of one object type are unique.
– Check whether combinations of two or more roles of one object type are total.

We shall draw on a number of examples from the library case in order to illustrate this step, without going into the above substeps one by one.

11.1 The classification system

Figure 11.1 provides an example of a further extended version of the catalog card.

A classification system for books has been added to the catalog card. Below is a verbal description of this classification system.

<u>CATALOG CARD</u>

Johnson, J.H., Peterson, P.   ISBN 90 6233 134 3

Public Library Management

The Publishing Co. - Amsterdam - 1981   1st edition

A practical manual for public library management.

Contains a detailed practical case and several exercises

with answers.

textbook	Eng	category	5.62
			8.07
			6.23

C30960 1981

C43728 1981

C31604 1985

Figure 11.1.

Some books are classified not only into a certain kind, but also into one or more so-called categories. This classification system provides information about the kind of subjects treated in these books. Every book can be classified into one or more main categories, and each of these can be classified into one or more subcategories. A combination of a main and a subcategory is called a category. The classification system is denoted by a code which always consists of three positions. The first position denotes the main category, and the following two positions denote the subcategory. For example, in the catalog card of Figure 11.1, the "5" designates a main category, and is then a so-called main category code, while the "62" designates a subcategory, a so-called subcategory code. The main category generally indicates the subject matter of a particular book. The subcategory gives a more detailed indication of the subject matter. For example, the "5" denotes the main category "business administration/ organization theory," and the "62" denotes the subcategory "administrative organization." The "8" indicates the main category "service organizations," and the "07" the subcategory "libraries." Each main category is not only denoted by a main category code but also by a main category name, and each subcategory not only has a subcategory code but also a subcategory name. Main category names and subcategory names likewise refer unambiguously to main categories and subcategories, respectively. The main category and subcategory names are not listed on the catalog cards, but are provided in a separate list which is available for perusal. The classification system is used to categorize books into certain categories and to be able to look them up according to these categories.

We invite the reader, before reading any further, to try to carry out the analysis steps dealt with thus far (including step 9) on the basis of the catalog card of Figure 11.1, and to add the rules regarding the classification system to the information structure diagram of the library case.

In the above description, four new lexical object types have been mentioned, namely the main category code, the subcategory code, the main category name and the subcategory name. Only the main category codes and the subcategory codes are listed on the catalog card. Because we will initially only be looking at the catalog card, we shall momentarily disregard the lexical object types "main category name" and "subcategory name" in our analysis. In Figure 11.2, we have listed the names of the lexical object types on the catalog card. The designation "category" can be found on every catalog card which contains a classification. This designation concerns only the external representation of the data, and is therefore not relevant for the information represented on the card.

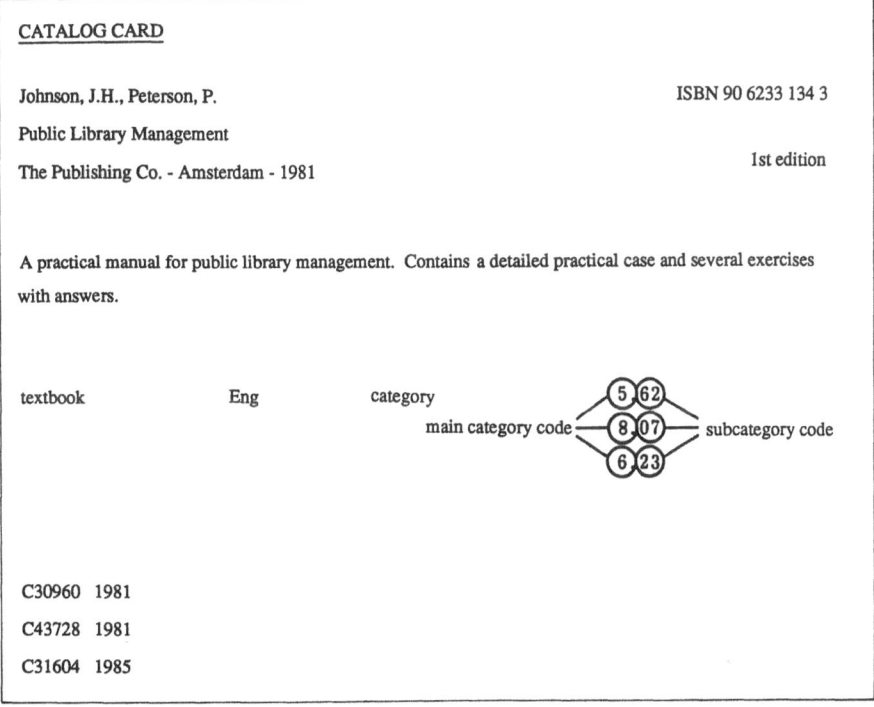

Figure 11.2.

isbn	main category code	subcategory code
90 6233 134 3	5	62
90 6233 134 3	8	07
90 6233 134 3	6	23

Figure 11.3.

In Figure 11.3, we have described the new portion of the catalog card by means of a population table, in which we have listed the names of the lexical objects and of the lexical object types.

As we already know, an ISBN refers to a book. It appears from the above description of the new portion of the catalog card that a main category code refers to a non-lexical object of the type "main category," and a subcategory code to a non-lexical object of the type "subcategory."

book	main category	subcategory
isbn	main category code	subcategory code
90 6233 134 3	5	62
90 6233 134 3	8	07
90 6233 134 3	6	23

Figure 11.4.

In Figure 11.4, we have added the names of these non-lexical object types to the population table.

In the description of this latest addition to the catalog card, "categories" were mentioned. However, the name of this object type has not yet been listed in the population table. A combination of a main category and a subcategory is called a "category" in the description. In other words, a **combination** of a main category and a subcategory refers uniquely to a non-lexical object of the type "category." As we saw in the previous chapter, the name of this non-lexical object type is placed in the population table above the combination of the columns "main category" and "subcategory," as has been done in Figure 11.5

We now see that the population table describes a binary sentence type involving the non-lexical object types "book" and "category." We have added possible role names of this binary sentence type to the population table of Figure 11.6.

The relationship between a book and a category described by this binary

book	category	
	main category	subcategory
isbn	main category code	subcategory code
90 6233 134 3	5	62
90 6233 134 3	8	07
90 6233 134 3	6	23

Figure 11.5.

book	category	
	main category	subcategory
isbn	main category code	subcategory code
classified into	of	
90 6233 134 3	5	62
90 6233 134 3	8	07
90 6233 134 3	6	23

Figure 11.6.

sentence type is depicted in an information structure diagram, as in Figure 11.7.

We must still add to this the "vertical" relationships between the object types **within** the columns (combined or not) of the population table. These cover not only the relationships between "ISBN" and "book," between "main category code" and "main category," and between "subcategory code" and "subcategory," but also the relationships between "category" and "main category" and between "category" and "subcategory," that is, between the object types within the combined columns. Adding these relationships to the information structure diagram of Figure 11.7 results in the diagram of Figure 11.8.

In line with the description of this addition to the catalog card, we have expressed in this figure that each main category is referred to in a one-to-one way by a main category code, and that every subcategory is referred to in a one-to-one way by a subcategory code.

The description mentions that not every book is classified into a category. In concrete terms, this means that the role "book classified into category" is not total. It is further stated in the description that a book can be classified into more than one category. It is natural to assume that one particular category can be related

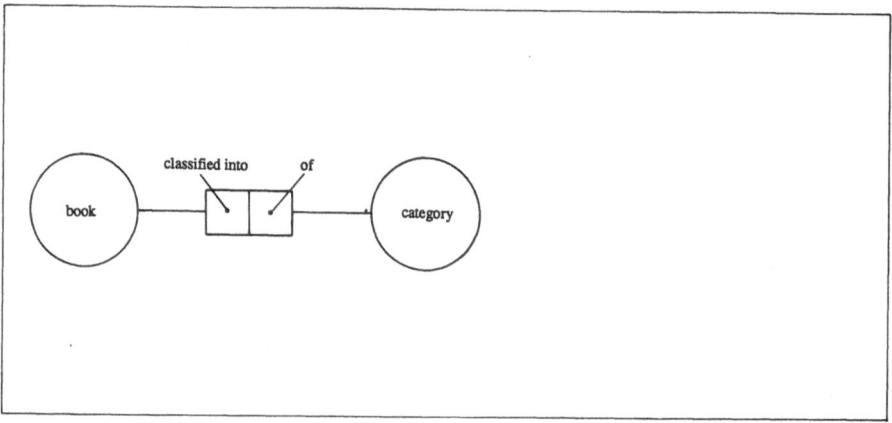

Figure 11.7.

to more than one book. This means that none of the roles of the fact type involving "book" and "category" is unique. Furthermore, it appears from the description that every category consists of one main category and one subcategory. This means that the roles "category consisting of main category" and "category consisting of subcategory" are unique and total. Adding these constraints to the information structure diagram of Figure 11.8 results in the diagram of Figure 11.9.

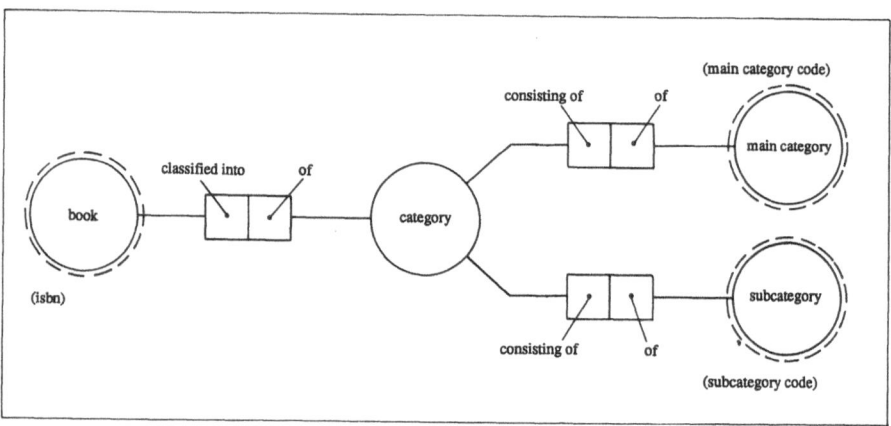

Figure 11.8.

We are now up to step 9 of the NIAM method of information analysis: the addition of the remaining graphical constraints.

It is stated in the description of the new part of the catalog card that the combination of a main category and a subcategory is called a "category." Every category thus consists of (is constructed from) a main category and a subcategory. This means that every combination of a main category and a subcategory belongs to one category, that a category is uniquely referred to by a combination of a main category and a subcategory. In concrete terms this means that in the information

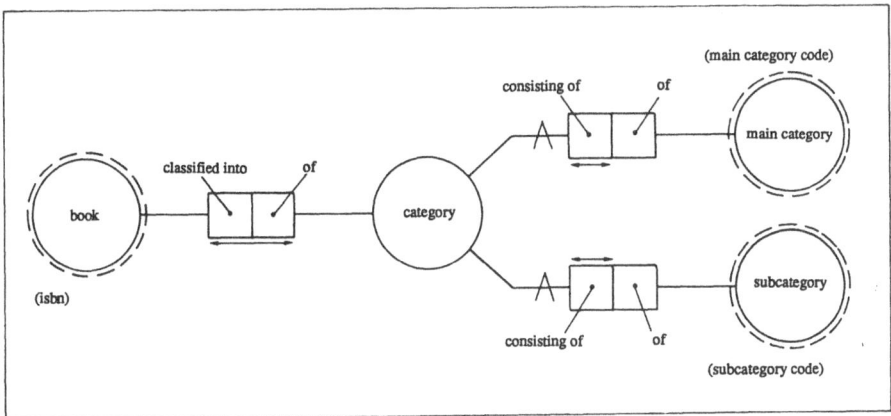

Figure 11.9.

structure diagram the combination of the roles "main category of category" and "subcategory of category" is unique, as we have shown in Figure 11.10.

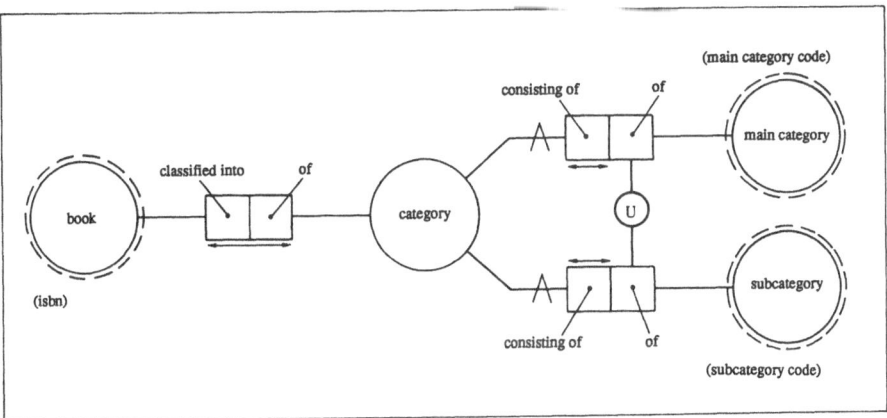

Figure 11.10.

The description of the classification system also mentions main category names and subcategory names. Every main category can be referred to in a one-to-one way by a main category name, and every subcategory can be referred to in a one-to-one way by a subcategory name. We have added the lexical object types "main category name" and "subcategory name" to the information structure diagram of Figure 11.11.

The names of **two** lexical object types, namely "main category code" and "main category name," are now listed in abridged notation for the bridge type belonging to the non-lexical object type "main category." This expresses the fact that there are **two** bridge types belonging to the non-lexical object type "main category" in which the roles of the non-lexical object type are total and in which all the roles are unique, so that both of them can be represented in an abridged notation. These

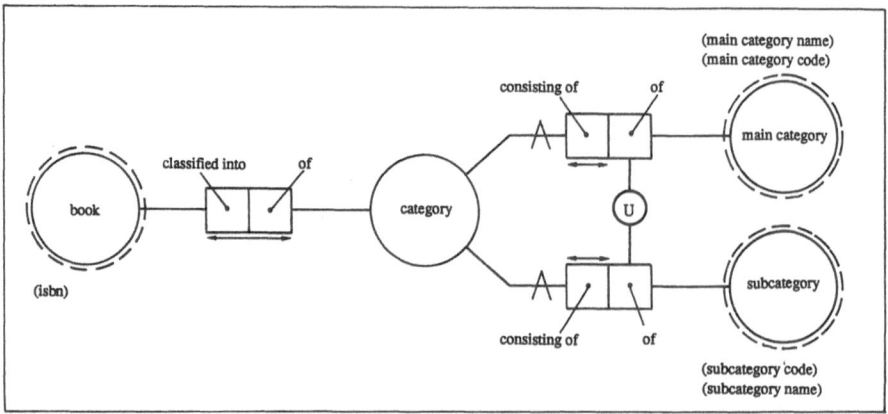

Figure 11.11.

bridge types involve the lexical object types "main category code" and "main category name," respectively. With the agreed-upon abridged notation for bridge types, more than one bridge type can be depicted per non-lexical object. This is also true for the non-lexical object type "subcategory."

In the next section, we shall add more to the example of the classification system.

11.2 Primary and secondary categories

Figure 11.12 contains a yet further extended version of the catalog card.
What follows is a verbal description of what has been added to the catalog card.

A distinction is made between a primary category and a secondary category of a book. The primary category denotes the main subject of the book. The secondary categories denote other likely subjects or subjects related to the book. A book may be classified into only one primary category and one or more secondary categories. A book classified into a primary category does not necessarily have to be classified into a secondary category. However, a book can only be classified into a secondary category if it is also classified into a primary category. A certain subject cannot be both the primary category and a secondary category of **the same** book. However, a certain category may be the primary and a secondary category of **different** books.

Once again, we invite the reader to attempt, before reading any further, to add the rules regarding the primary and the secondary categories of a book to the information structure diagram.

Because a category can function as the primary category **and** as a secondary category of different books, there are two different kinds of relationships between

CATALOG CARD

Johnson, J.H., Peterson, P.   ISBN 90 6233 134 3

Public Library Management

The Publishing Co. - Amsterdam - 1981   1st edition

A practical manual for public library management. Contains a detailed practical case and several exercises with answers.

textbook	Eng	category	primary:	5.62
			secondary:	8.07
				6.23

C30960 1981

C43728 1981

C31604 1985

Figure 11.12.

books and categories. In these relationships, a category can appear in two different roles, namely in the role of a primary category and in the role of a secondary category. We have depicted this in Figure 11.13.

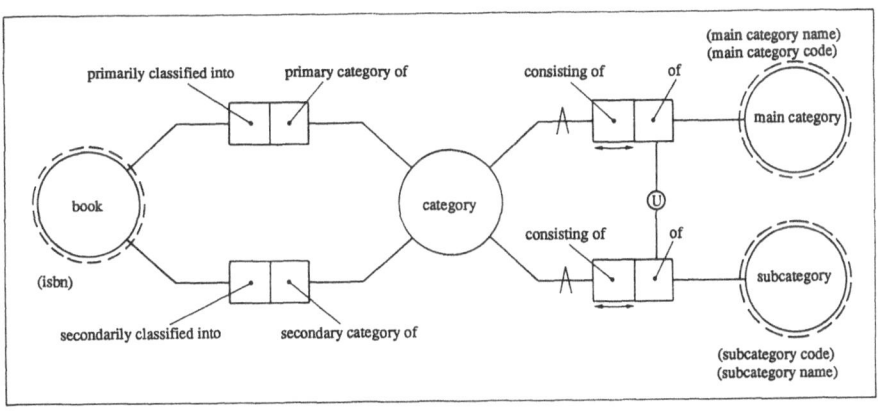

Figure 11.13.

In the above description of the part just added to the catalog card, it is stated that a book may be classified into only one primary category. The role "book primarily classified into category" is therefore unique. Naturally, a certain category can function as a primary category of several books. Furthermore, it is stated in the description that a book can be classified into one or more secondary categories. A certain category can, of course, function as a secondary category of several books. This means that neither the role "book secondarily classified into category" nor the role "category secondary category of book" is unique. We have depicted this in Figure 11.14.

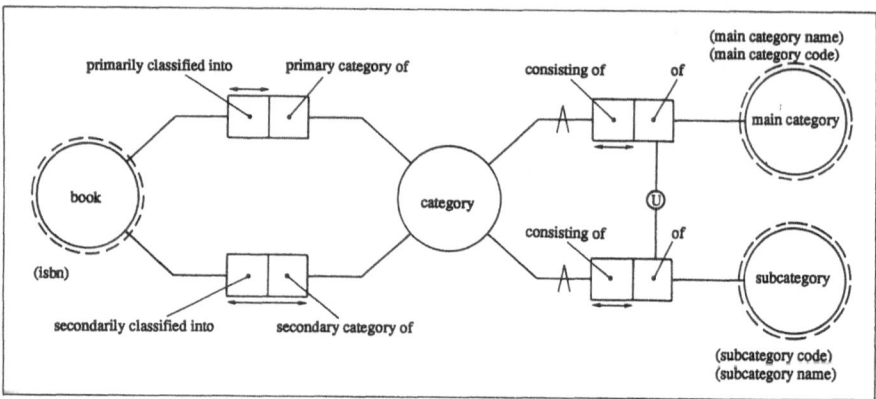

Figure 11.14.

The description of the new part of the catalog card states that a book can only be classified into a secondary category if a primary category of this book is already known. In concrete terms this means that the role "book secondarily classified into category" is a subset of the role "book primarily classified into category." Further, the description states that a certain category can never be both the primary and a secondary category of **the same book**. However, a certain category can be the primary and a secondary category of **different** books. This means that the **combinations** of the roles "book primarily classified into category" and "category primary category of book," on the one hand, and the roles "book secondarily classified into category" and "category secondary category of book," on the other hand, must exclude each other. We have represented these constraints in Figure 11.15.

11.3 Translations

Lastly, we shall make a final addition to the catalog card. The definitive form of the catalog card is as shown in Figure 11.16.

When a book is a translation of another book in the library, the ISBN of the latter book is listed on the catalog card. Therefore, the book to which the catalog card in Figure 11.16 refers is a translation of the book having the ISBN 01 3557 561 1.

The fact that a book is a translation of another book creates a relationship

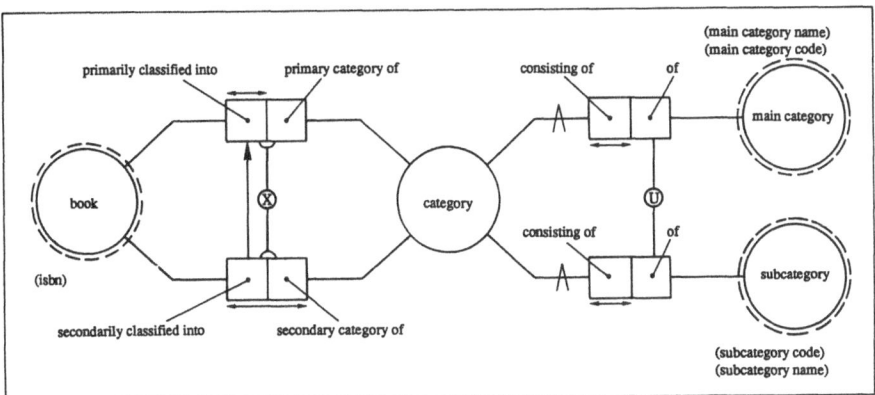

Figure 11.15.

CATALOG CARD

Johnson, J.H., Peterson, P.   ISBN 90 6233 134 3

Public Library Management

The Publishing Co. - Amsterdam - 1981   1st edition

A practical manual for public library management. Contains a detailed practical case and several exercises

with answers.

Translation of: 01 3557 561 1

textbook   Eng   category   primary: 5.62

                                                    secondary: 8.07

                                                                    6.23

C30960 1981

C43728 1981

C31604 1985

Figure 11.16.

---

between the two books. We have represented this relationship in the diagram of Figure 11.17.

A book can naturally only be the translation of one other book, although a certain book can be translated into several different languages. This means that

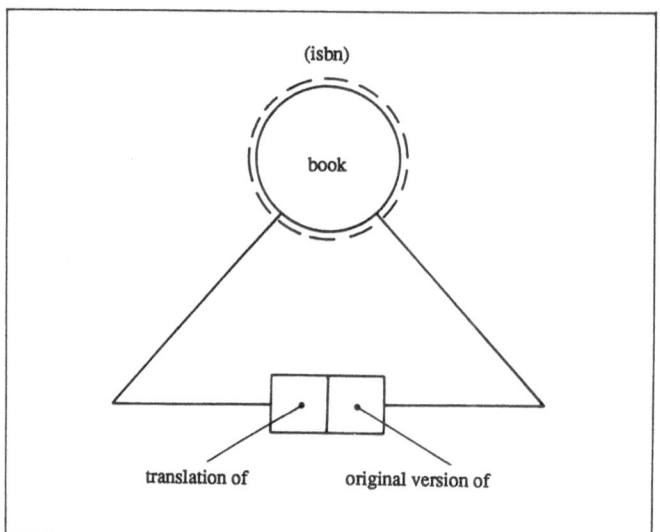

Figure 11.17.

the role "book translation of book" in Figure 11.17 is unique. We have depicted this constraint in Figure 11.18.

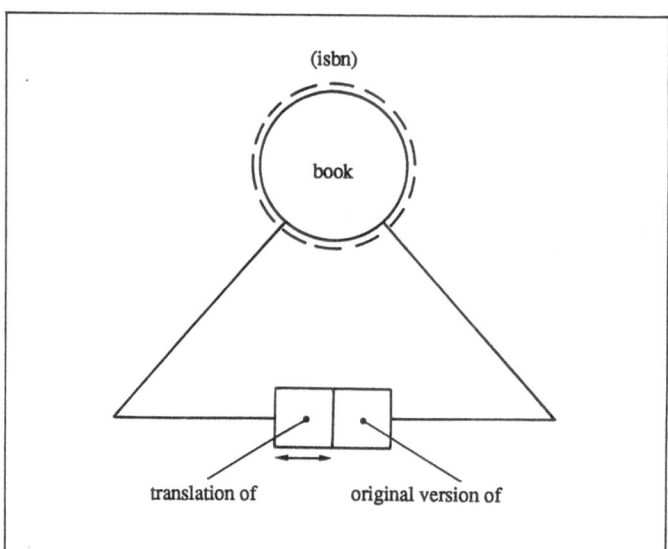

Figure 11.18.

In principle, a book that is a translation of another book can, in turn, be translated into another language. This book would then occur in both the population of the role "book translation of book" and that of the role "book original version of book." Thus, these roles do not exclude each other. For example, in

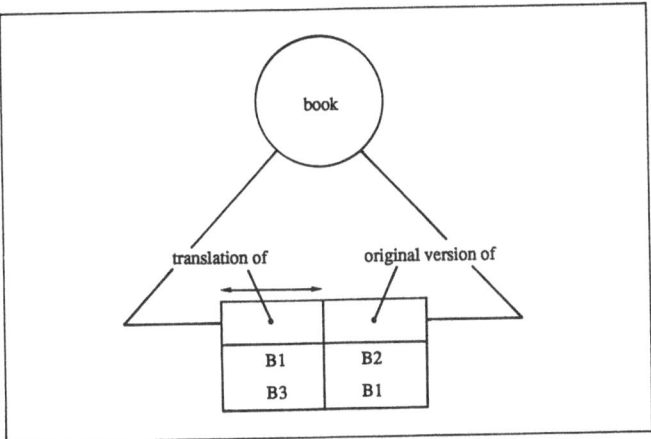

Figure 11.19.

Figure 11.19, book B1 is a translation of book B2, and book B1 is in turn the original version of book B3.

In Figure 11.20, we have added the new object types, fact types, and constraints to the information structure diagram.

11.4 The loan card

The allowable information contents of the information flow "book data" and the constraints which are valid for these have now been described completely. As the last practical example in this chapter, we shall analyze the information contents of the information flow "loan data" (see Figure 6.1). This information flow contains information with respect to the loans of book copies to library members. Figure 11.21 contains a concrete example of the information contents of this information flow.

What follows below is a verbal description of this example.

The data concerning the lending of book copies to library members are listed per member and per borrowed copy on loan cards. The issuing of a book copy to a library member on a particular date is called a loan. Every loan is identified by a sequence number, called the loan number. The loan card lists the loan number, the membership number of the member who is checking out the book copy, the copy number of this copy, and the date on which the loan took place (called the loan date). Further, the latest date by which the borrowed book copy must be brought back (the due date) is filled in on the loan card. This date is always three weeks later than the loan date. A loan can be renewed at the request of the member. In that case, the loan period is always extended three weeks, and the due date is accordingly changed on the loan card. A loan can

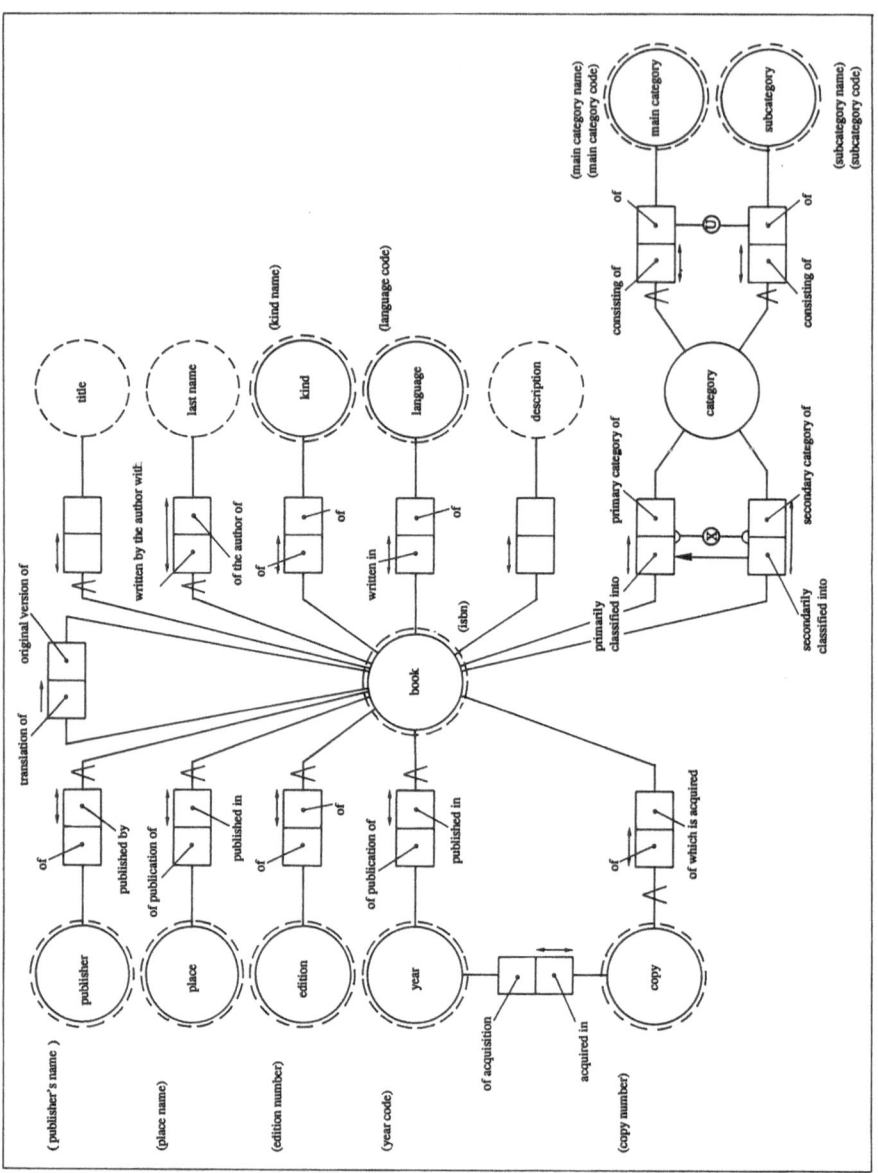

Figure 11.20.

LOAN CARD

loan number	3931 2119091
membership number	2 2 5 7 7 3
copy number	C 3 0 9 6 0
loan date	0 3 0 6 8 5
	d d m m j j
due date	2 4 0 6 8 5
returned on	0 2 0 7 8 5
fine	0 0 , 7 0

Figure 11.21.

be renewed several times. A renewal request is allowed unless the book has been reserved by another member.

When a borrowed copy is returned to the library, the date on which this happens (called the return date) is filled in on the loan card. When the loan period has been exceeded, that is, when the copy is returned after the due date, the member must pay a fine. This amounts to 70 cents a week, or part thereof, beyond the due date. When this happens, the amount of the fine is listed on the loan card.

Of course someone who has borrowed a certain book copy and then returned it can borrow it again. However, one may not borrow the same **copy** twice on the same day, that is, check it out on the same day on which it was brought back.

The loan number, the membership number, the copy number, the loan date, and the due date of a loan must always be known.

The loan cards are stored for a while after the borrowed copy has been returned and the loan "terminated," for the purpose of collecting statistical data. Consequently, the loan date must be listed on the loan card. After all, someone who borrows a book copy can borrow it again after a while. Without the loan date, it would be impossible to distinguish these two loans. The loan is therefore determined by the borrowed book copy, the member borrowing the book, **and** the date on which the loan took place.

Every library member is identified by a membership number.

So far the description of the loan card. We invite the reader once again to attempt, before reading further, to add the rules valid for the information contents of the loan card to the information structure diagram.

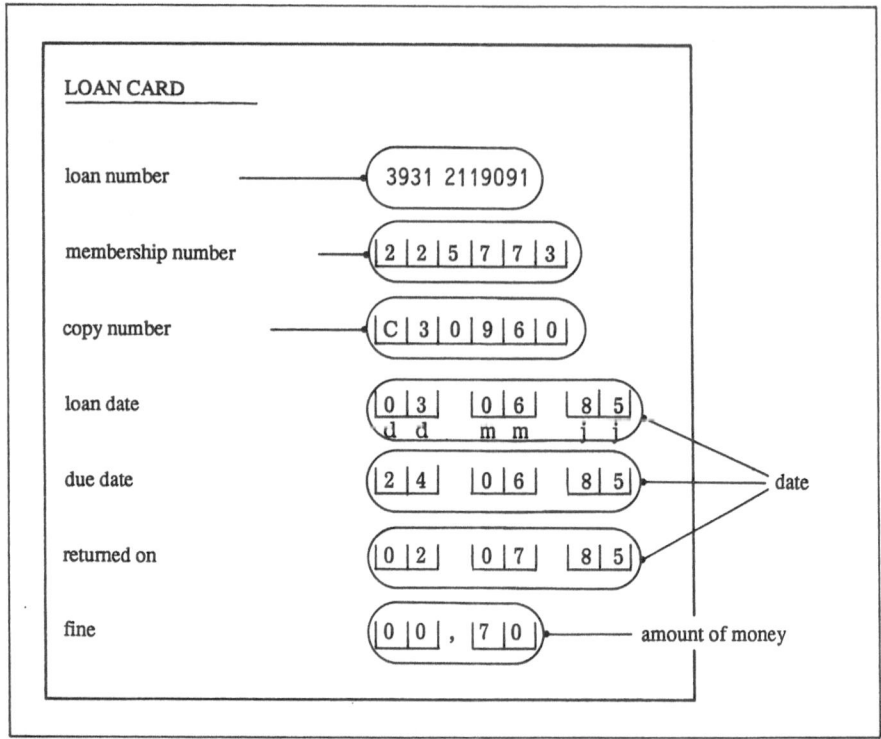

Figure 11.22.

Figure 11.22 lists the object type names of the lexical objects appearing on the loan card. The loan number, the membership number, and the copy number speak for themselves.

The object type "date" appears on the loan card in the roles "loan date," "due date," and "return date." The amount of money appears on the loan card in the role "fine." We have ran into the concept "amount of money" earlier, in the role of the salary of a library employee.

In Figure 11.23, we have described the information contents of the loan card by means of two population tables, in which we have initially only filled in the lexical objects and the names of their lexical object types. We have opted for two population tables only because of space problems.

Clearly, a loan number refers to a loan, a membership number to a member, and, as we already know, a copy number to a (book) copy. The amount of money and the date are independent lexical object types whose objects do not refer to any particular non-lexical objects.

loan number	membership number	copy number	date
39312119091	225773	C 30960	03.06.85

loan number	date	date	amount of money
39312119091	24.06.85	02.07.85	00.70

Figure 11.23.

We have added in Figure 11.24 the names of the non-lexical object types to the population tables.

It follows from the above description of the loan card that:

- a **loan** is made by a **member**
- a **loan** involves a book **copy**
- a **loan** takes place on a loan **date**
- a **loan** involves a **due date**
- a **loan** involves a **return date**
- a **loan** can involve a fine of a certain **amount of money.**

We have denoted these relationships in the population tables of Figure 11.25, and added the role names of the elementary sentence types determined by these relationships.

We have represented these sentence types in Figure 11.26 by means of an information structure diagram.

Adding the bridge types, which correspond to the "vertical" relationships **within** the columns of the population table, results in the diagram of Figure 11.27.

From the way the loan card is arranged together with its description, it appears that only one member can make a loan, that only one book copy is involved, and

loan	member	copy	
loan number	membership number	copy number	date
39312119091	225773	C 30960	06.03.85

loan			
loan number	date	date	amount of money
39312119091	06.24.85	07.02.85	00.70

Figure 11.24.

that a loan takes place on only one date. Because the due date is adjusted for renewals, there is only one due date for a loan. The loan is terminated when the member brings back the book copy. A loan therefore has only one return date. When the loan is terminated a certain amount of money may be levied in fines. There can be only one fine for a loan. All of this means that the following roles in the information structure are unique:

- "loan made by member"
- "loan involving copy"
- "loan made on date"
- "loan due on date"
- "loan terminated on date"
- "loan with a fine of amount of amount of money."

In the description of the loan card, it is stated that "the membership number, the copy number, the loan date, and the due date of a loan must be known at every moment." This means that the following roles in the information structure diagram are total:

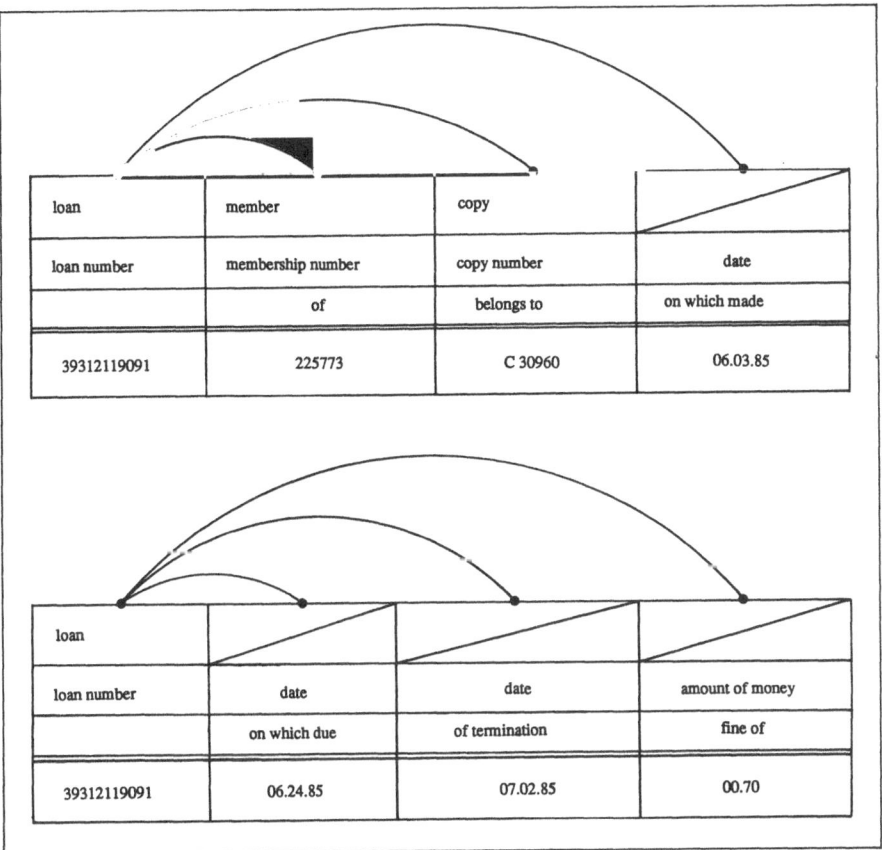

Figure 11.25.

- "loan made by member"
- "loan involving copy"
- "loan made on date"
- "loan due on date."

The return date is only known when the borrowed book copy is brought back. The role "loan terminated on date" is therefore not total. Only in those cases in which the book is brought back after the due date is a fine levied. This means that the role "loan with a fine of amount of money" is not total.

In Figure 11.28, we have added these uniqueness and totality constraints to the information structure diagram.

A possible fine is calculated by comparing the return date to the due date. The fine can thus only be determined if the return date is known. This means that the role "loan with a fine of amount of money" is a subset of the role "loan terminated on date."

It is stated in the description of the loan card that one book copy is provided

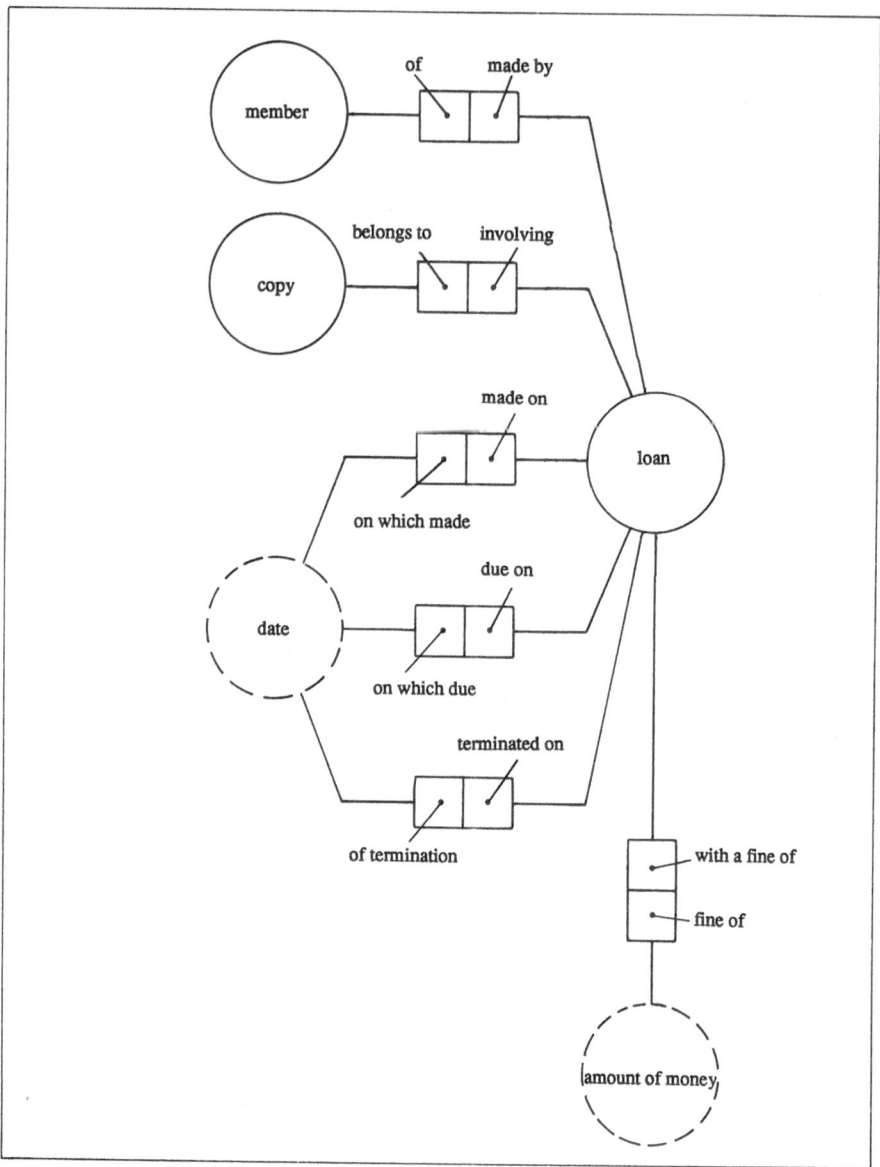

Figure 11.26.

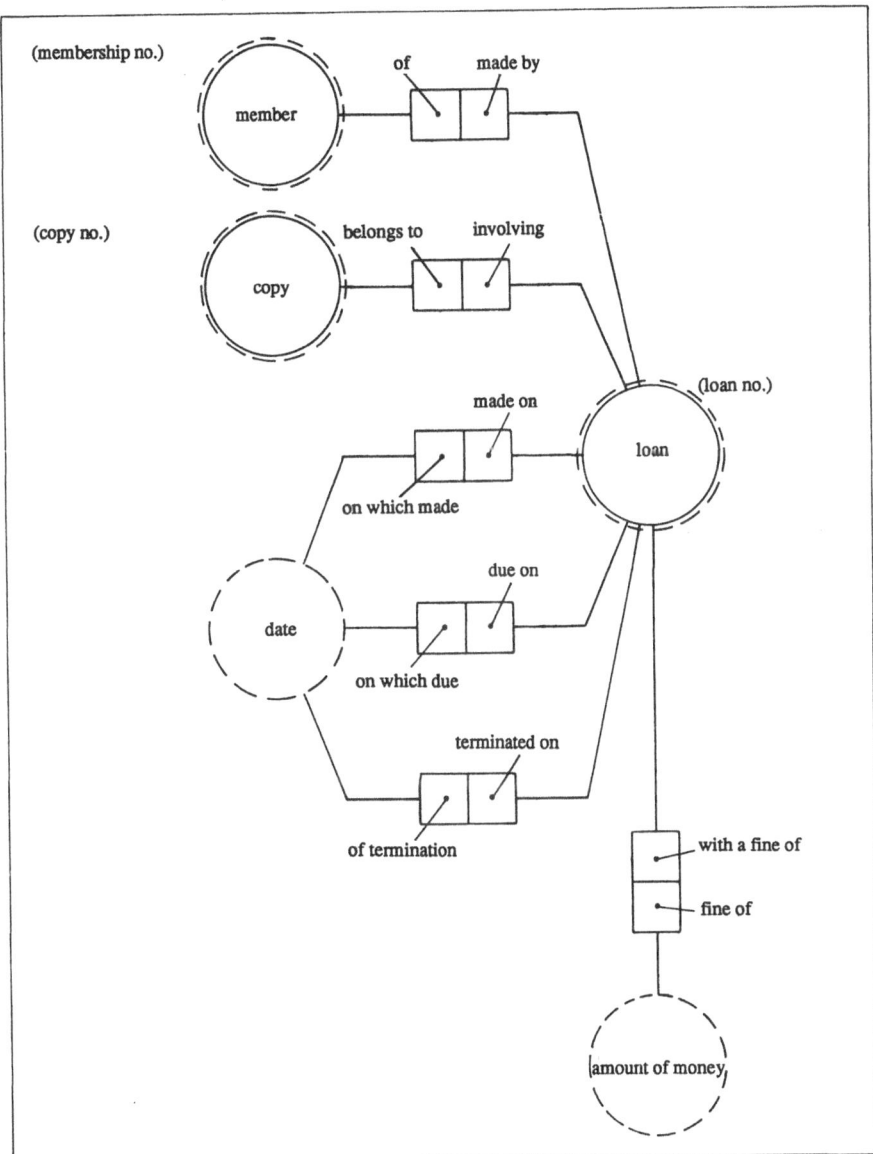

Figure 11.27.

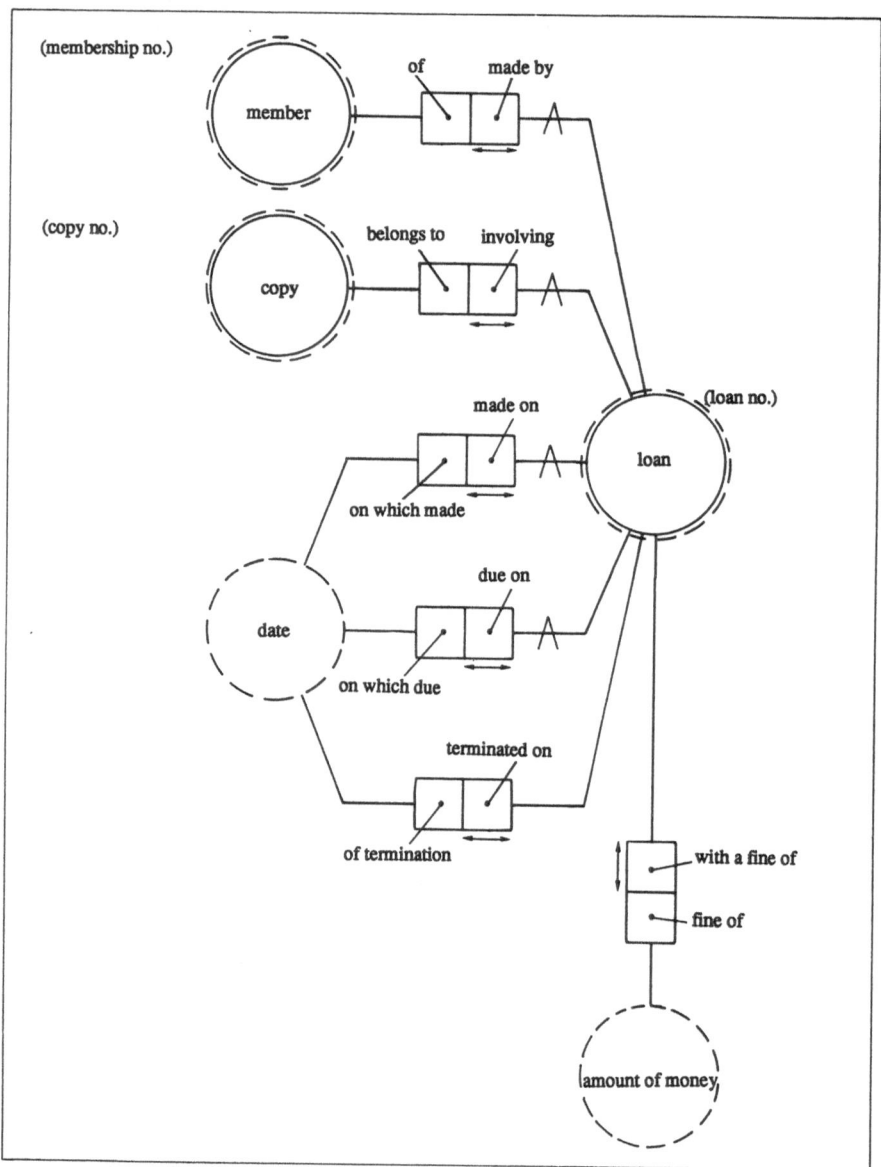

Figure 11.28.

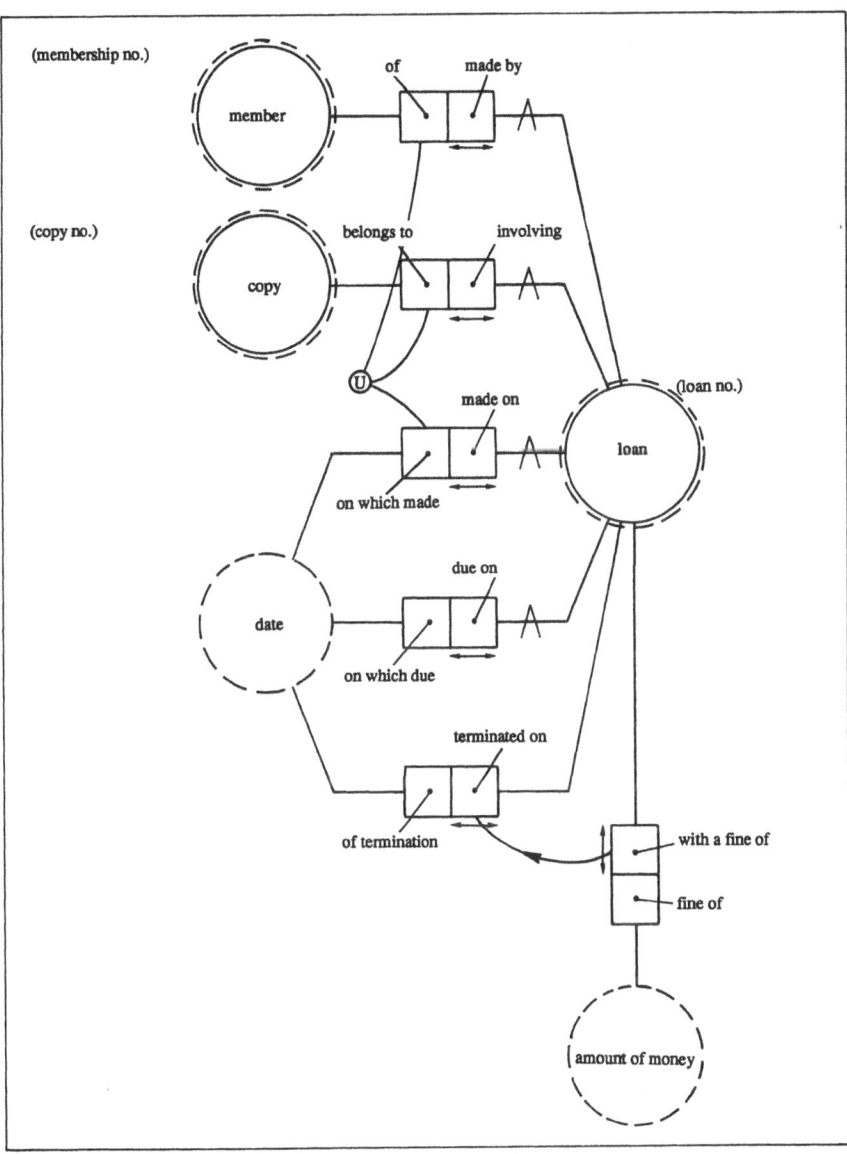

Figure 11.29.

to one library member on one particular date, and that a loan is consequently determined (or stated otherwise, denoted or identified) by a combination of the borrowed book copy, the member borrowing the copy, and the date on which the loan took place. In concrete terms, this means that in the information structure diagram the combination of the roles "copy belongs to loan," "member of loan," and "date on which is made loan" is unique.

In Figure 11.29. we have added the subset constraint and the uniqueness constraint dealt with above to the information structure diagram.

We can see in this diagram that every loan is unambiguously denoted by not only the loan number, but also by a combination of the member, the loan copy, and the loan date.

11.5 Historical information

We have seen earlier that the information base of an information system describes at any moment a certain state of reality. When the current state of reality no longer exists, the users usually delete the information concerning this state from the information base. However, this is not always done. We have seen, for example, that when a borrowed book copy is brought back to the library, the information about that particular loan is not immediately deleted from the information base, although the loan as such no longer exists.

Information which is related to a past state of reality is called *historical information*. Therefore, the information involving "terminated" loans is an example of historical information. Because the loan data has to be stored for a certain period of time, we have explicitly defined a relationship between the object types "loan" and "date" (in the role of loan date) in the information structure diagram.

In this example, we can see how, in general, information which is historical can be described. In such cases, a fact type must *explicitly* be defined with respect to the object type to which this historical information is related (such as the object type "loan") and an object type whose objects are instants in time (such as the object type "date"). These time instants indicate when the relevant historical information was created. The role of the time instants (in our example, the role "date on which is made loan") is always part of a unique combination of roles which identifies the objects to which the historical information is related.

A "time instant" can be a year, a month, a day or any indication of time. Depending on the kind of information processing being analyzed, it may be necessary to know the time periods for some historical information accurately, down to the last hour, minute, second or even fraction of a second.

Track is kept of not only the date on which a loan commenced (the loan date), but also the date on which it ended (the return date). This is often the case for historical information; not only is the time when the historical information came into existence important, but often also the time when this information ceased to

exist. This likewise has to be explicitly indicated in the information structure
diagram, as we have done in our example by means of the role "date of termination
of loan."

11.6 Summary

A summary of the ninth step in the NIAM method of information analysis is given
below.

9. Add   the   remaining   graphical   constraints.

9.1. For every pair of non-total roles
of one object type, check whether
these roles are equal.

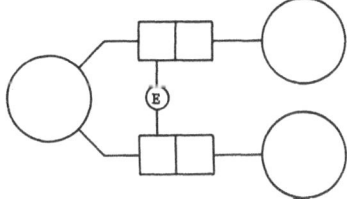

9.2. For every pair of non-total roles
of one object type, check whether
one role is a subset of the other
role.

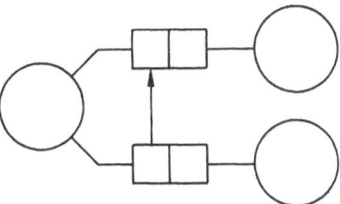

9.3. For every pair of combinations
of roles of the same object types,
check whether one combination
of roles is a subset of the other
combination of roles.

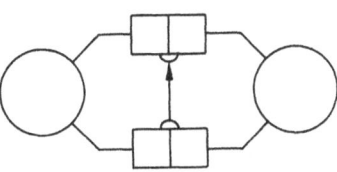

9.4. Check whether two or more non-total roles of one object type exclude each other.

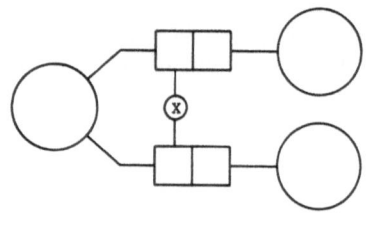

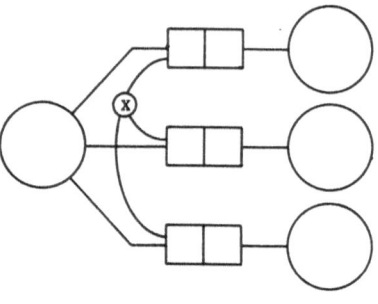

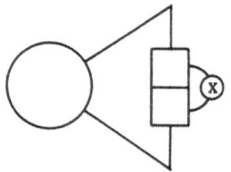

9.5. Check whether two or more combinations of roles of the same object types exclude each other.

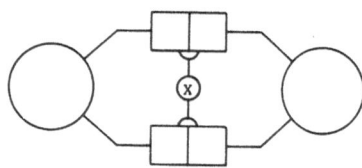

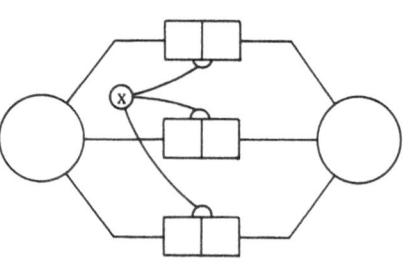

9.6. Check whether combinations of two or more co-roles of one object type are unique.

9.7. Check whether combinations of two or more roles of one object type are total.

12 FACT TYPES CONSISTING OF MORE THAN TWO ROLES

Up to now, we have only considered elementary sentence types and fact types consisting of two roles. In this chapter we will examine elementary sentence types and fact types that consist of more than two roles. We shall see that fact types having more than two roles can always be replaced by binary fact types by introducing an extra object type. As a consequence, an information structure diagram can always be represented such that it contains only binary fact types. This explains why up to this point we have been able to restrict ourselves so specifically to binary fact types.

First of all, we shall look into elementary sentence types and fact types with three roles. Then we shall extend this to elementary sentence types and fact types with an arbitrary number of roles.

12.1 Unique combinations of roles in ternary sentence types

In one of the examples in Chapter 7, we were able to see that the library makes use of a job tracking system. In such a system, the work that the staff members in the various departments have to carry out over a certain period is divided up into activities. Each of these activities is assigned to one or more employees who can be part of different departments. One or more activities can be assigned to one employee. Each activity is referred to in a one-to-one way by an activity number. We shall next assume, as an extension of what we assumed in Chapter 7, that there is a maximum number of working hours which has been determined for every employee, and for every activity assigned to him or her.

Figure 12.1 contains an example of an overview illustrating which activities have been assigned to which employees and the maximum number of hours an employee can work on each activity assigned to him or her.

Employee J683 is assigned activities A21, A48, and A19, for which he may work a maximum of 44, 50, and 44 hours, respectively. Activities A21 and A48 are assigned not only to employee J683, but also to employee P597. Unlike employee J683, employee P597 may work a maximum of 50 hours on activity A21 and a maximum of 44 hours on activity A48. This example can be described by means of the population table of Figure 12.2.

This population table describes a sentence type that consists of three roles. Sentence types consisting of three roles are called *ternary sentence types*. The question is now whether this sentence type is **elementary**. Just as with **binary** sentence types and fact types, roles or combinations of roles of **ternary** sentence types can be unique. We shall demonstrate that there is a relationship between the uniqueness of the roles and of the combinations of roles in ternary sentence types

personnel number	activity number	no. of hours
J683	A21	44
J683	A48	50
P597	A21	50
P597	A48	44
J683	A19	44
K731	A21	44

Figure 12.1.

and the question of whether or not these sentence types are elementary.

It is natural to assume in our example that an employee is assigned only one maximum number of working hours per activity.

employee	activity	
personnel number	activity number	number of hours
who is assigned	assigned to	maximally to be worked
J683	A21	44
J683	A48	50
P597	A21	50
P597	A48	44
J683	A19	44
K731	A21	44

Figure 12.2.

Yet Figure 12.3 contains an example of a population that does not satisfy this assumption. Employee J683 has been assigned two rather than one maximum number of working hours for activity A21 (namely 44 and 45). In this population, the combination of employee J683 and activity A21 occurs twice.

The fact that an employee is assigned only one maximum number of working hours per activity means in concrete terms that in the population table of Figure 12.2, every possible combination of an employee and an activity may occur only once. The fact that every possible combination of an employee and an activity may occur only once in the population table means that the combination of the roles of the object types "employee" and "activity" in the ternary sentence type described by this table is unique. We have represented the uniqueness of this

employee	activity	
personnel number	activity number	number of hours
who is assigned	assigned to	maximally to be worked
J683	A21	44
J683	A21	45
P597	A21	50

Figure 12.3.

employee	activity	
personnel number	activity number	number of hours
who is assigned	assigned to	maximally to be worked
J683	A21	44
J683	A48	50
P597	A21	50
P597	A48	44
J683	A19	44
K731	A21	44

Figure 12.4.

combination of roles in Figure 12.4 by drawing, just as we would do for binary fact types, a uniqueness symbol above the relevant columns.

Every combination of an employee and an activity may only occur once in this population table. On the other hand, a combination of an employee and a number of hours (for example J683 and 44) and of an activity and a number of hours (for example A21 and 44) may occur more than once.

The ternary sentence type described by this population table is elementary if the sentence type cannot be split for all possible populations into smaller, i.e., binary, sentence types without losing information. Or stated otherwise, the ternary sentence type is elementary if information is lost when a possible population table of this sentence type is split into smaller, i.e., binary, tables.

In order to check whether the table in Figure 12.4 is elementary, we have split this table into three binary tables in Figure 12.5.

empl.	activity
pers. no.	act. no.
J683	A21
J683	A48
P597	A21
P597	A48
J683	A19
K731	A21

empl.	
pers. no.	no. hours
J683	44
J683	50
P597	50
P597	44
K731	44

activity	
act. no.	no. hours
A21	44
A48	50
A21	50
A48	44
A19	44

Figure 12.5.

In these binary tables, we can no longer infer in all cases which numbers of hours hold for which assignments of activities. It is not clear, for example, whether employee J683 may now work 44 or 50 hours on activity A21. We can no longer reconstruct from the binary tables the fact that this is 44 hours (as is depicted in the first entry of the table in Figure 12.4). Clearly, information got lost when the table in Figure 12.4 was split up. It follows from this that the ternary sentence type described by this population table is elementary.

We are therefore dealing here with a ternary sentence type that is elementary. In Figure 12.6, this ternary sentence type is described by means of an information structure diagram.

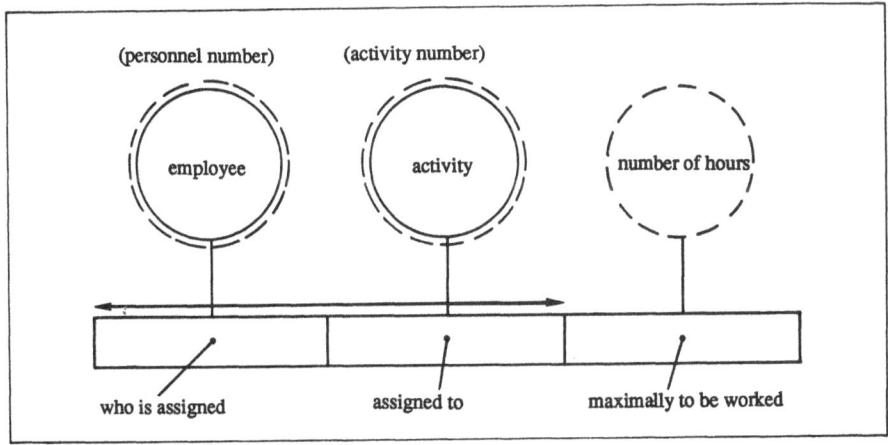

Figure 12.6.

The ternary sentence type is described by two bridge types and (because it is ternary **and** elementary) by a *ternary fact type*. A ternary fact type is a fact type that consists of three roles.

In the remainder of this section, we shall take up all the remaining possibilities with respect to the uniqueness of roles or combinations of roles in ternary sentence types. We shall repeatedly check whether the sentence type described by every population table is elementary by splitting that population table into binary tables and then looking to see whether in doing so information has been lost. After this analysis, we will be in a position to make a connection between the uniqueness of roles, or of combinations of roles in ternary sentence types, and the question of whether or not these sentence types are elementary.

The possibilities still left open to us are given below.

employee	activity	
personnel number	activity number	number of hours
who is assigned	assigned to	maximally to be worked
J683	A21	44
J683	A48	50
P597	A21	50
P597	A48	44
J683	A21	19
J683	A19	44

Figure 12.7.

In Figure 12.7, the combination of the roles of the object types "activity" and "number of hours" is unique. An activity can be assigned in combination with a maximum number of working hours to only one employee. Every combination of an activity and a number of hours may occur only once in the table, while a combination of an employee and an activity (for example J683 and A21) and a combination of an employee and a number of hours (for example J683 and 44) may occur more than once. We have split this population table into three binary tables in Figure 12.8.

We can no longer infer in all cases from these binary tables which numbers of hours hold for which assignments of activities to employees. Thus, it is not clear whether employee J683 may now work 44, 50, or 19 hours on activity A21. We can no longer reconstruct from the binary tables the fact that this is 44 or 19 hours (as is depicted in the first and next to last entries in the population table in Figure 12.7). In splitting the table of Figure 12.7 into binary tables, some information has clearly been lost, so that the sentence type described by the population table in

empl.	activity
pers. no.	act. no.
J683	A21
J683	A48
P597	A21
P597	A48
J683	A21
J683	A19

empl.	
pers. no.	no. hours
J683	44
J683	50
P597	50
P597	44
J683	19

activity	
act. no.	no. hours
A21	44
A48	50
A21	50
A48	44
A21	19
A19	44

Figure 12.8.

Figure 12.7 is elementary. We have depicted this sentence type in Figure 12.9 by means of an information structure diagram.

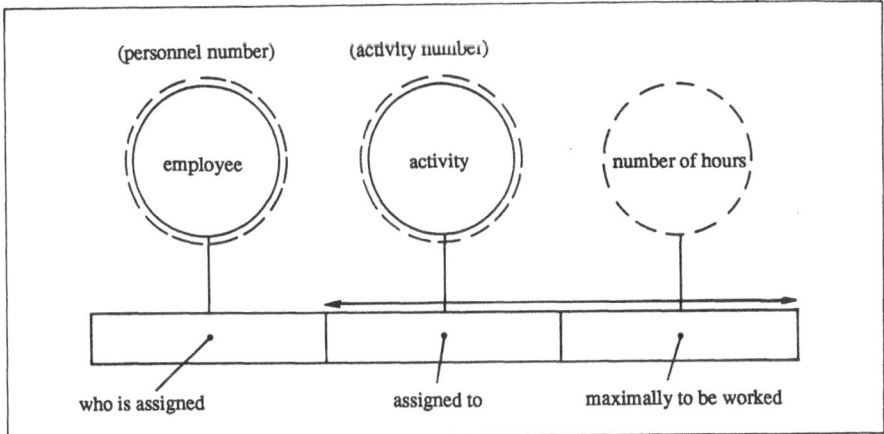

Figure 12.9.

In Figure 12.10, the combination of the roles of the object types "employee" and "number of hours" is unique. An employee can be assigned a certain maximum number of working hours for only one activity. Every combination of an employee and a number of hours may only occur once in the table, while a combination of an employee and an activity (for example J683 and A21) and a combination of an activity and a number of hours (for example A21 and 44) may occur more than once. We have split this population table into three binary tables in Figure 12.11.

One of the things we can no longer infer from these binary tables is whether employee J683 may now work 44, 50, or 19 hours on activity A21. We are unable to reconstruct from the binary tables the fact that this is 44 or 19 hours (as is depicted in the first and next to last entries in the population table of Figure 12.10). As information has clearly been lost when the population table of Figure 12.10 was

employee	activity	
personnel number	activity number	number of hours
who is assigned	assigned to	maximally to be worked
J683	A21	44
J683	A48	50
P597	A21	50
P597	A48	44
J683	A21	19
K731	A21	44

Figure 12.10.

empl.	activity	empl.		activity	
pers. no.	act. no.	pers. no.	no. hours	act. no.	no. hours
J683	A21	J683	44	A21	44
J683	A48	J683	50	A48	50
P597	A21	P597	50	A21	50
P597	A48	P597	44	A48	44
K731	A21	J683	19	A21	19
		K731	44		

Figure 12.11.

split up, the sentence type described by this table is elementary. We have described this ternary sentence type in Figure 12.12 by means of an information structure diagram.

In the above examples, one combination of two roles was unique every time. It is possible in ternary sentence types for more than one combination of two roles to be unique. We will track this possibility below.

In Figure 12.13, the combinations of the roles of the object types "employee" and "activity" and of the object types "activity" and "number of hours" are unique. An employee can be assigned only one maximum number of working hours for a certain activity, and an activity can be assigned in combination with one maximum number of working hours to only one employee. Every combination of an employee and an activity and of an activity and a number of hours may only occur once in this population table. A combination of an employee and a number

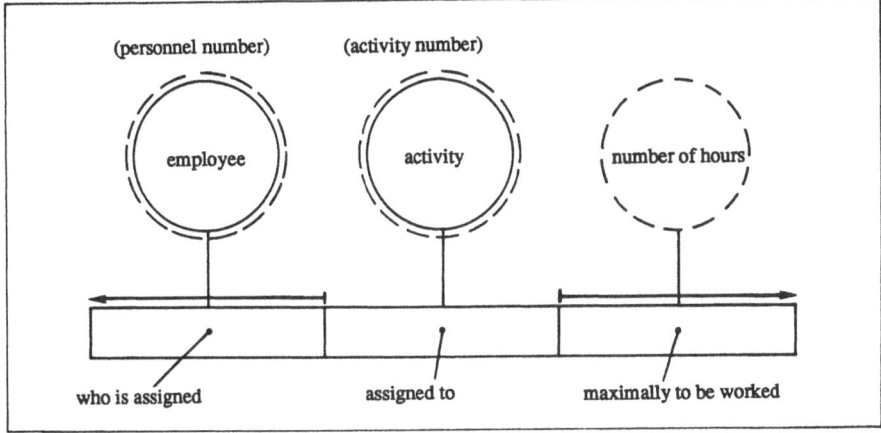

Figure 12.12.

employee	activity	
personnel number	activity number	number of hours
who is assigned	assigned to	maximally to be worked
J683	A21	44
J683	A48	50
P597	A21	50
P597	A48	44
J683	A19	44

Figure 12.13.

of hours (such as J683 and 44), on the other hand, may occur more than once. We have split this population table into three binary tables in Figure 12.14.

One of the things we can no longer infer from these binary tables is whether employee J683 may now work 44 or 50 hours on activity A21. The fact that this is 44 hours (as depicted in the first entry in the population table of Figure 12.13) can no longer be reconstructed from the binary tables. Clearly, in splitting up the table of Figure 12.13, information has been lost, thus making the sentence type described by this table elementary. We have described this elementary sentence type in Figure 12.15 by means of an information structure diagram.

In Figure 12.16, the combinations of the roles of the object types "employee" and "activity" and of the object types "employee" and "number of hours" are

empl.	activity
pers. no.	act. no.
J683	A21
J683	A48
P597	A21
P597	A48
J683	A19

empl.	
pers. no.	no. hours
J683	44
J683	50
P597	50
P597	44

activity	
act. no.	no. hours
A21	44
A48	50
A21	50
A48	44
A19	44

Figure 12.14.

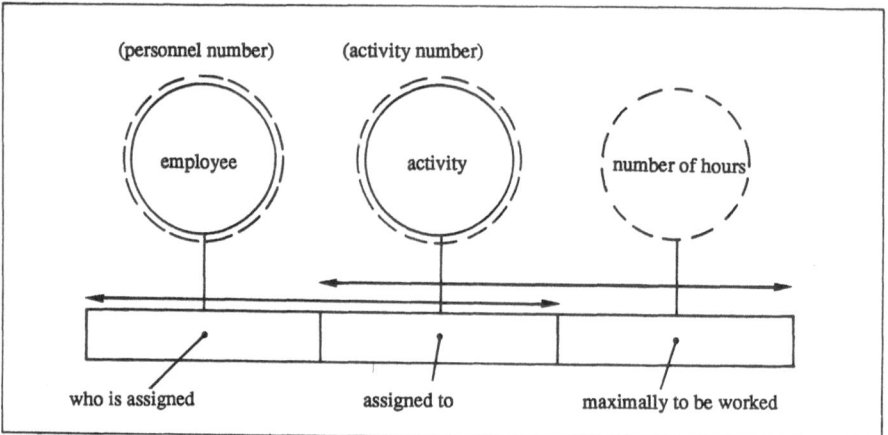

Figure 12.15.

employee	activity	
personnel number	activity number	number of hours
who is assigned	assigned to	maximally to be worked
J683	A21	44
J683	A48	50
P597	A21	50
P597	A48	44
K731	A21	44

Figure 12.16.

unique. An employee can be assigned only one maximum number of working hours for a certain activity, and a certain maximum number of working hours can be assigned to an employee for only one activity. Every combination of an employee and an activity and of an employee and a number of hours may only occur once in the population table. A combination of an activity and a number of hours (such as A21 and 44), on the other hand, may occur more than once. We have split this table into three binary tables in Figure 12.17.

empl.	activity
pers. no.	act. no.
J683	A21
J683	A48
P597	A21
P597	A48
K731	A21

empl.	
pers. no.	no. hours
J683	44
J683	50
P597	50
P597	44
K731	44

activity	
act. no.	no. hours
A21	44
A48	50
A21	50
A48	44

Figure 12.17.

One of the things we can no longer reconstruct from these binary tables is whether employee J683 may now work 44 or 50 hours on activity A21. The fact that this is 44 hours (as is depicted in the first entry in the population table of Figure 12.16) can no longer be reconstructed from the binary tables. Clearly, information was lost when the table in Figure 12.16 was split up, so that the sentence type described by this table is elementary. In Figure 12.18, we have described this elementary sentence type by means of an information structure diagram.

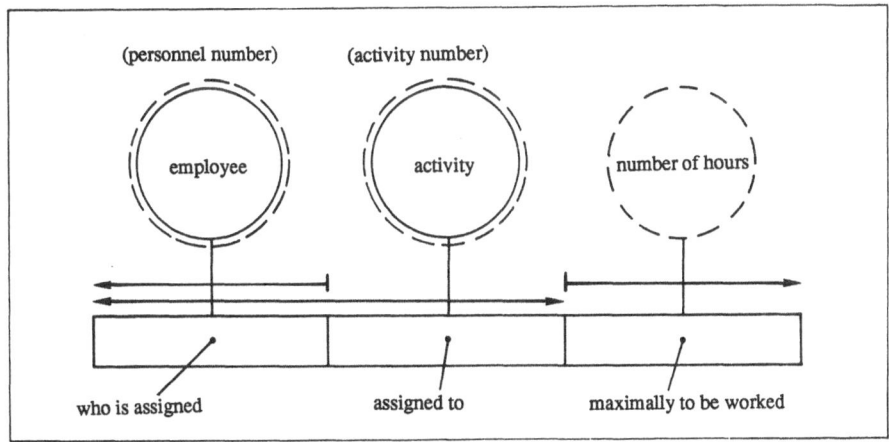

Figure 12.18.

employee	activity	
personnel number	activity number	number of hours
who is assigned	assigned to	maximally to be worked
J683	A21	44
J683	A48	50
P597	A21	50
P597	A48	44
J683	A21	19

Figure 12.19.

In Figure 12.19, the combinations of the roles of the object types "employee" and "number of hours" and of the object types "activity" and "number of hours" are unique. An employee can be assigned a certain maximum number of working hours for only one activity, and an activity can be assigned in combination with a maximum number of working hours to only one employee. Every combination of an employee and a number of hours and of an activity and a number of hours may only occur once in the population table. A combination of an employee and an activity (such as J683 and A21), on the other hand, may occur more than once. In Figure 12.20, we have split this population table into three binary tables.

empl.	activity	empl.		activity	
pers. no.	act. no.	pers. no.	no. hours	act. no.	no. hours
J683	A21	J683	44	A21	44
J683	A48	J683	50	A48	50
P597	A21	P597	50	A21	50
P597	A48	P597	44	A48	44
		J683	19	A21	19

Figure 12.20.

One of the things we can no longer reconstruct from these binary tables is that employee J683 may work 44 or 19 hours on activity A21, as is depicted in the first and last entries in the population table in Figure 12.19. As information was clearly lost when this population table was split up, the sentence type described by this table is elementary. We have described this elementary sentence type in Figure 12.21 by means of an information structure diagram.

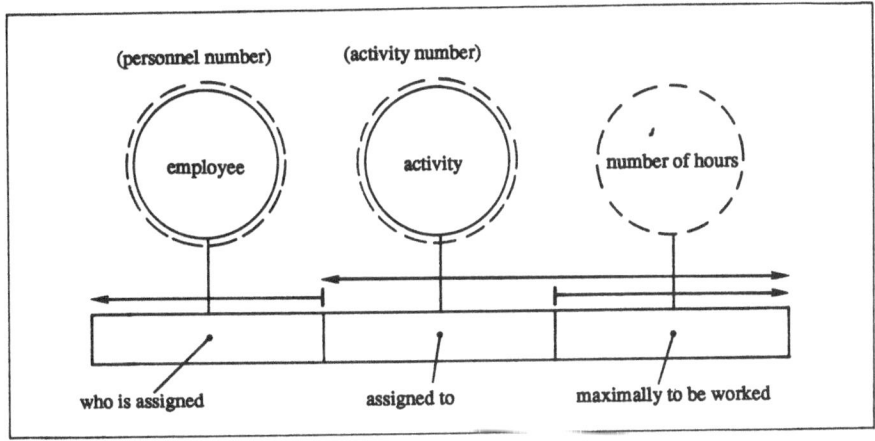

Figure 12.21.

It is possible in ternary sentence types for not only two, but even three, combinations of two roles to be unique, as the example of Figure 12.22 shows.

employee	activity	
personnel number	activity number	number of hours
who is assigned	assigned to	maximally to be worked
J683	A21	44
J683	A48	50
P597	A21	50
P597	A48	44

Figure 12.22.

In Figure 12.22, the combinations of the roles of the object types "employee" and "activity", of the object types "employee" and "number of hours", and of the object types "activity" and "number of hours" are unique. An employee can be assigned only one maximum number of hours for a certain activity. An activity can be assigned in combination with a maximum number of working hours to only one employee. An employee can be assigned a certain maximum number of working hours for only one activity. Every combination of an employee and an activity, of an employee and a number of hours, and of an activity and a number of hours may only occur once in the population table. In Figure 12.23, we have split this population table into binary tables.

empl.	activity
pers. no.	act. no.
J683	A21
J683	A48
P597	A21
P597	A48

empl. .	
pers. no.	no. hours
J683	44
J683	50
P597	50
P597	44

activity	
act. no.	no. hours
A21	44
A48	50
A21	50
A48	44

Figure 12.23.

One of the things we can no longer infer from these binary tables is whether employee J683 may now work 44 or 50 hours on activity A21. We can no longer reconstruct the fact that this is 44 hours (as is depicted in the first entry in the population table of Figure 12.22). Clearly, in splitting up the population table, information has been lost, so that the sentence type described by this table is elementary. In Figure 12.24, we have described this sentence type by means of an information structure diagram.

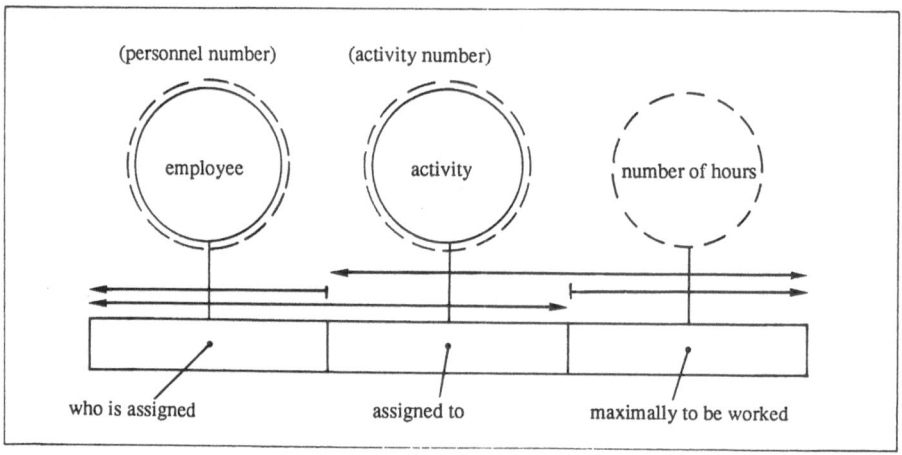

Figure 12.24.

Lastly, let us assume that none of the roles or of the combinations of roles in this ternary sentence type is unique; in other words, that there are no constraints on the populations of the roles of this sentence type. We have depicted this situation in Figure 12.25.

employee	activity	
personnel number	activity number	number of hours
who is assigned	assigned to	maximally to be worked
J683	A21	44
J683	A48	50
J683	A48	44
P597	A21	50
P597	A48	44
P597	A21	44

Figure 12.25.

Every combination of an employee and an activity (such as P597 and A21), of an employee and a number of hours (such as J683 and 44), and of an activity and a number of hours (such as A21 and 44), may occur more than once in this population table. We have depicted the fact that none of the roles or combinations of roles of this sentence type is unique by drawing a uniqueness symbol across **all** of the roles. After all, by virtue of the singularity rule, it holds that every combination of objects is represented only once in the population table. Aside from the question of whether this would be meaningful in practice, we apparently can now assign one or more maximum numbers of working hours to an employee for a certain activity.

We have split this population table up into three binary tables in Figure 12.26. We can no longer infer from these binary tables whether employee J683 may work for 44 or 50 hours on activity A21. We can no longer reconstruct the fact that this is 44 hours (as is depicted in the first entry in the population table of Figure 12.25) from the binary tables. Here as well, information was clearly lost when the population table was split up, so that the sentence type described by the population table of Figure 12.25 is elementary. In Figure 12.27, we have described this elementary sentence type by means of an information structure diagram.

The question now is whether **every** possible population table of a ternary sentence type in which a combination of two or three roles is unique cannot be split into binary tables without loss of information. In other words, does the fact that a combination of two or three roles in a ternary sentence type is unique

empl.	activity
pers. no.	act. no.
J683	A21
J683	A48
P597	A21
P597	A48
P597	A21

empl.	
pers. no.	no. hours
J683	44
J683	50
P597	50
P597	44

activity	
act. no.	no. hours
A21	44
A48	50
A48	44
A21	50

Figure 12.26.

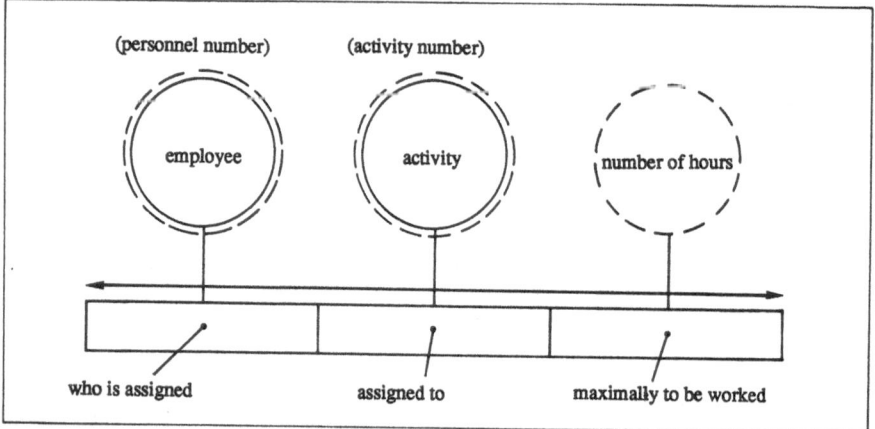

Figure 12.27.

imply that this sentence type is elementary? That this is not the case is demonstrated by the example in Figure 12.28.

In this example, the combination of the object types "employee" and "activity" is unique. Splitting up the population table of Figure 12.28 results in the binary tables of Figure 12.29.

In this case, unlike the previous examples, the population table of Figure 12.28 can **indeed** be reconstructed from these binary tables, as can easily be verified. When the population table of Figure 12.28 was split up, clearly **no** information was lost, so that we cannot determine on the basis of this population table whether the sentence type described by this table is elementary. Our conclusion is that if a combination of two or three roles in an elementary sentence type is unique, we may not automatically conclude that this sentence type is elementary.

We must **proof** that this sentence type is elementary by showing that there is at least one population table which cannot be split into binary tables without loss of information.

employee	activity	
personnel number	activity number.	number of hours
who is assigned	assigned to	maximally to be worked
J683	A21	44
J683	A48	50
P597	A21	44
P597	A48	50
J683	A19	44
K731	A21	44

Figure 12.28.

empl.	activity		empl.			activity	
pers. no.	act. no.		pers. no.	no. hours		act. no.	no. hours
J683	A21		J683	44		A21	44
J683	A48		J683	50		A48	50
P597	A21		P597	44		A19	44
P597	A48		P597	50			
J683	A19		K731	44			
K731	A21						

Figure 12.29.

In the next two sections, we will take a look at the different possibilities with respect to the uniqueness of **individual** roles of a ternary sentence type and see what their consequences are for deciding whether or not the sentence type is elementary. To conclude this section, we repeat below the definitions of a ternary sentence type and a ternary fact type.

A ternary sentence type:
A sentence type that consists of three roles.

A ternary fact type:
A fact type that consists of three roles.

12.2 Implied uniqueness constraints

In ternary sentence types of course not only **combinations** of roles, but also **individual** roles can be unique.

employee	activity	
personnel number	activity number	number of hours
who is assigned	assigned to	maximally to be worked
J683	A21	44
J683	A21	50
J683	A48	44

Figure 12.30.

. In Figure 12.30, the role of the object type "employee" and the combination of the roles of the object types "employee" and "activity" are unique. The population depicted in this figure is in conflict with both constraints; employee J683 and the combination of this employee and activity A21 occur more than once in this population table. If an employee may only occur once in this population table, every **combination** of an employee with another object (for example, an activity) may naturally also only occur once. If an individual role of a sentence type is unique, it follows directly that every combination of this role with another role is also unique. The uniqueness of an individual role is thus a stronger constraint than the uniqueness of a combination of this individual role with one or more roles. Because the role of "employee" is already unique, the uniqueness symbol in Figure 12.30 with respect to the combination of the roles of "employee" and "activity" is redundant. Uniqueness constraints which are implied by stronger uniqueness constraints and which are thereby redundant (such as the uniqueness of the combination of the roles of "employee" and "activity") are, of course, not represented explicitly in an information structure diagram.

We can formulate the foregoing somewhat more generally as follows:

The uniqueness of a combination of roles is always implied by the uniqueness of an individual role or of a combination of roles that are part of the former combination.

As formulated above, this rule is valid for not only ternary sentence types, but also for sentence types (and therefore fact types) which consist of an arbitrary number of roles. A sentence type or a fact type consisting of an arbitrary number of roles, say n, is called an *n-ary sentence type* or an *n-ary fact type*.

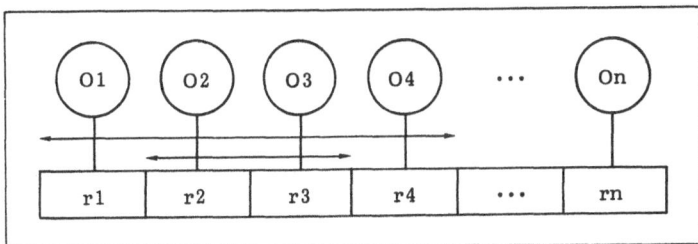

Figure 12.31.

Figure 12.31 shows an example of an n-ary fact type. The uniqueness of the combination of roles r1, r2, r3, and r4 is implied by the uniqueness of the combination of roles r2 and r3. The uniqueness symbol with respect to the combination of roles r1, r2, r3, and r4 is therefore redundant, and consequently should not be drawn explicitly. This holds a fortiori for **binary** sentence types and fact types (these are n-ary sentence types and fact types for which n is equal to 2), such as is shown in Figure 12.32.

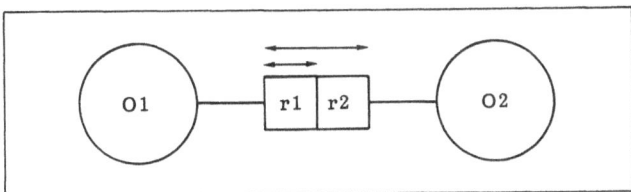

Figure 12.32.

The uniqueness of the combination of roles r1 and r2 is implied by the uniqueness of role r1. The uniqueness symbol with respect to the combination of roles r1 and r2 is therefore redundant and should consequently not be drawn.

We conclude this section with the remark that an n-ary sentence type or fact type must always involve at least one **non-lexical** object type. If not, an n-ary fact type would describe a relationship between only **lexical** objects. We saw earlier that the NIAM method of information analysis does not consider relationships between only lexical objects.

To summarize:

An n-ary sentence type:
A sentence type that consists of an arbitrary, say n, number of roles. When n is equal to 2, we are dealing with a binary sentence type. When n is equal to 3, we

are dealing with a ternary sentence type. An n-ary sentence type must involve at least one non-lexical object type.

An n-ary fact type:
A fact type that consists of an arbitrary, say n, number of roles. When n is equal to 2, we are dealing with a binary fact type. When n is equal to 3, we are dealing with a ternary fact type. An n-ary fact type must involve at least one non-lexical object type.

12.3 Unique roles in ternary sentence types

In this section, we will, as a follow-up to Section 12.1, take up the various possibilities with respect to the uniqueness of **individual** roles in ternary sentence types. We shall make use of the example used in Section 12.1. Here as well, we shall check each time to see whether the sentence type described by each population table is elementary by splitting the population table into binary tables and then verifying whether some information was lost in the process.

We run through the various possibilities below.

employee	activity	
personnel number	activity number	number of hours
who is assigned	assigned to	maximally to be worked
J683	A21	44
P597	A21	44
K731	A48	50

Figure 12.33.

In Figure 12.33, the role of the object type "employee" is unique. An employee can be assigned only one activity and one maximum number of working hours. Every employee may occur only once in this population table. Every activity and every number of hours (such as A21 and 44), on the other hand, may occur more than once. In Figure 12.34, we have split this population table into binary tables.

Of course, the role of "employee" is unique in these binary tables as well.

empl.	activity		empl.			activity	
pers. no.	act. no.		pers. no.	no. hours		act. no.	no. hours
J683	A21		J683	44		A21	44
P597	A21		P597	44		A48	50
K731	A48		K731	50			

Figure 12.34.

Because every employee may occur only once in the binary tables, we can always infer from these tables which activity is assigned to an employee with which maximum number of working hours. We can therefore reconstruct the population of Figure 12.33 from the binary tables of Figure 12.34. It follows from this that the population table of Figure 12.33 can be split into binary tables without information being lost. The population table of Figure 12.33 contains all possible combinations of employees, activities and numbers of hours which are allowed within the sentence type described by this table. It follows from this that this sentence type can be split into binary sentence types without loss of information, and therefore is **not** elementary.

We give below an overview of the remaining possibilities concerning the uniqueness of one or more individual roles of a ternary sentence type. In each of these cases, it can be easily verified that the ternary sentence types are **not** elementary.

empl.	act.		empl.	act.	empl.		act.	
pers. no.	act. no.	no. hours	pers. no.	act. no.	pers. no.	no. hours	act. no.	no. hours.
J683	A21	35	J683	A21	J683	35	A21	35
J683	A48	35	J683	A48			A48	35
P597	A63	25	P597	A63	P597	25	A63	25

An activity can be assigned to only one employee and with only one maximum number of working hours.

empl.	act.		empl.	act.	empl.		act.	
pers. no.	act. no.	no. hours.	pers. no.	act. no.	pers. no.	no. hours	act. no.	no. hours.
J683	A21	44	J683	A21	J683	44	A21	44
J683	A48	50	J683	A48	J683	50	A48	50
P597	A21	32	P597	A21	P597	32	A21	32
P597	A48	65	P597	A48	P597	65	A48	65

A certain maximum number of working hours can be assigned to only one employee and to only one activity.

empl.	act.	
pers. no.	act. no.	no. hours
J683	A21	44
P597	A48	44

empl.	act.
pers. no.	act. no.
J683	A21
P597	A48

empl.	
pers. no.	no. hours.
J683	44
P597	44

act.	
act. no.	no. hours
A21	44
A48	44

An employee can be assigned only one activity and only one maximum number of working hours, and an activity can be assigned to only one employee with only one maximum number of working hours.

empl.	act.	
pers. no.	act. no.	no. hours
J683	A21	44
P597	A48	50

empl.	act.
pers. no.	act. no.
J683	A21
P597	A48

empl.	
pers. no.	no. hours.
J683	44
P597	50

act.	
act. no.	no. hours.
A21	44
A48	50

An activity can be assigned to only one employee and with only one maximum number of working hours, and a certain maximum number of working hours can be assigned to only one employee and to only one activity.

empl.	act.	
pers. no.	act. no.	no. hours
J683	A21	44
P597	A21	50

empl.	act.
pers. no.	act. no.
J683	A21
P597	A21

empl.	
pers. no.	no. hours.
J683	44
P597	50

act.	
act. no.	no. hours
A21	44
A21	50

An employee can be assigned only one activity and only one maximum number of working hours, and a certain maximum number of working hours can be assigned to only one employee and to only one activity.

empl.	act.	
pers. no.	act. no.	no. hours
J683	A21	44
P597	A48	50

empl.	act.
pers. no.	act. no.
J683	A21
P597	A48

empl.	
pers. no.	no. hours.
J683	44
P597	50

act.	
act. no.	no. hours.
A21	44
A48	50

An employee can be assigned only one activity and only one maximum number of working hours. An activity can be assigned to only one employee and with only one maximum number of working hours. A certain maximum number of working hours can be assigned to only one employee and to only one activity.

We conclude that a ternary sentence type in which at least one individual role is unique is always non-elementary.

12.4 The n-1 rule

We have now reached the point where we can draw a few conclusions from the foregoing.

In the previous section, we saw that if at least one individual role in a ternary sentence type is unique, this sentence type is non-elementary. It follows from this that in an elementary ternary sentence type, at least one combination of two roles or the combination of all three roles is always unique. This leads to the following rule:

- In an elementary ternary sentence type, at least one combination of two roles or the combination of all three roles is unique.
- If at least one individual role in a ternary sentence type is unique, this sentence type is not elementary.

This rule for ternary sentence types can easily be extended to cover sentence types with an arbitrary number of roles (n-ary sentence types):

- In an elementary n-ary sentence type, at least one combination of n-1 roles or the combination of all n roles is unique.
- If at least one combination of less than n-1 roles or at least one individual role in an n-ary sentence type is unique, this sentence type is not elementary.

When n is equal to 3, the rule reported above for ternary sentence types is called into existence. The rule holds a fortiori for binary sentence types (in which case n is equal to 2).

NOLOT name 1	NOLOT name 2	· · ·	NOLOT name (n-1)	NOLOT name n
LOT name 1	LOT name 2	· · ·	LOT name (n-1)	LOT name n
role name 1	role name 2	· · ·	role name (n-1)	role name n

Figure 12.35.

NOLOT name 1	NOLOT name 2	・・・	NOLOT name (n-1)	NOLOT name n
LOT name 1	LOT name 2	・・・	LOT name (n-1)	LOT name n
role name 1	role name 2	・・・	role name (n-1)	role name n

Figure 12.36.

Figure 12.35 provides an example of an elementary n-ary sentence type.

In this example, at least one combination of n-1 roles (the uniqueness symbol drawn with a solid line) or the combination of all n roles (the uniqueness symbol drawn with a broken line) is unique.

Figure 12.36 provides an example of a non-elementary n-ary sentence type. In this example, at least one combination of less than n-1 roles is unique.

From now on, we shall call the above rule for n-ary sentence types the *n-1 rule*. This rule is often used in practice to verify whether or not an n-ary sentence type is elementary. However, some caution is called for. The n-1 rule states that **if an n-ary sentence type is elementary**, at least one combination of n-1 roles or the combination of all n roles is unique. The reverse, however, does not generally hold: if a combination of n-1 or n roles in an n-ary sentence type is unique, it does not necessarily follow that this n-ary sentence type is elementary. The fact that an n-ary sentence type is elementary must always be proven by showing that there is at least one population table which cannot be split into smaller tables without loss of information. On the other hand, if at least one combination of less than n-1 roles in an n-ary sentence type is unique, this n-ary sentence type is certainly not elementary.

To summarize:

The n-1 rule:

- If an n-ary sentence type (fact type) is elementary, at least one combination of n-1 roles or the combination of all n roles is unique.
- If at least one combination of less than n-1 roles or at least one individual role of an n-ary sentence type (fact type) is unique, this sentence type (fact type) is not elementary.

In order to continue with the library case, we will assume that an employee can be assigned only one maximum number of working hours for the activities assigned him or her. In the previous section, we saw that the (ternary) fact type that describes these facts is elementary. This is depicted by the part of the information structure diagram represented by Figure 12.37.

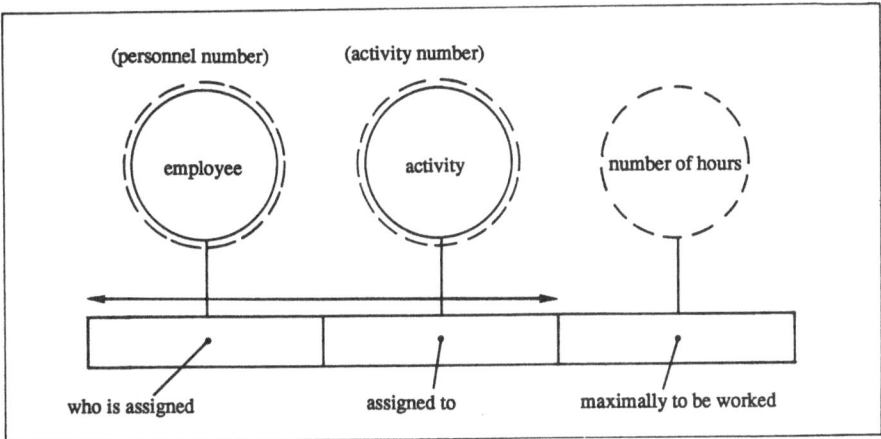

Figure 12.37.

We have added this ternary fact type to the information structure diagram in Figure 12.38.

In the next section, we shall show that an information structure diagram in which a non-binary fact type occurs (such as the diagram of Figure 12.38) is not in agreement with the 100% principle. We shall then show that this is the reason we introduce extra non-lexical object types to replace all non-binary fact types by binary fact types.

12.5 Replacing non-binary fact types by binary fact types

Earlier in this book, we stated that the 100% principle was one of the basic principles of the NIAM method of information analysis. This principle states that the grammar must describe **completely** and **explicitly** all of the rules which are valid for the information exchange with the information system. This means that the grammar, and consequently the information structure diagram as well, may not contain any implicit knowledge which is, as it were, "hidden behind" the rules of the grammar.

We shall now show that the information structure diagram of Figure 12.38 (still) does not completely satisfy this demand. We only have to look at the uniqueness constraint in this figure with respect to the ternary fact type. This uniqueness constraint states that the combination of an employee and an activity is always unique. Actually, this means that every combination of an employee and an activity refers uniquely to "something" that is not explicitly depicted in the diagram; or stated otherwise, that every combination of an employee and an

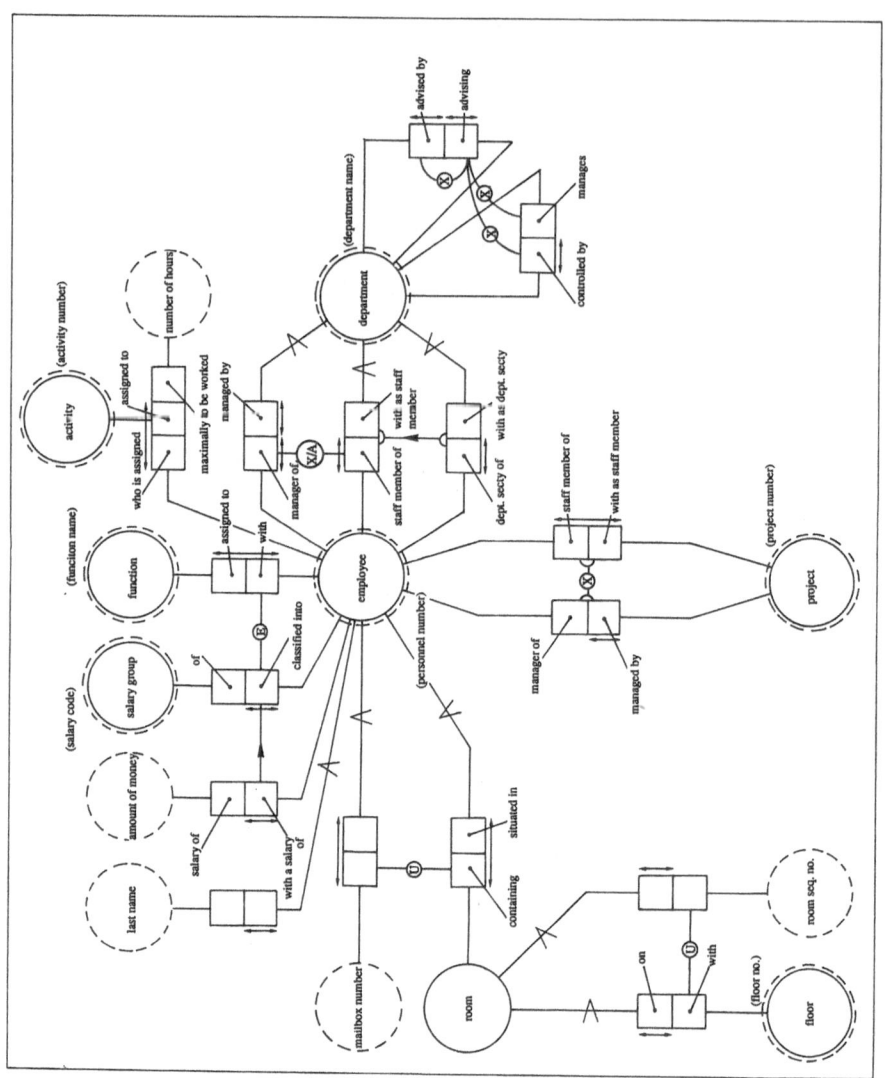

Figure 12.38.

activity refers uniquely to an object whose object type is not represented in the information structure diagram. This object consists of the assignment of an activity to an employee. We could call this a "task." By virtue of the 100% principle, we must include the object type "task" and all the knowledge related to the objects of this type explicitly in the information structure diagram and thus in the grammar.

Every task is related to one employee and one activity. A combination of an employee and an activity refers uniquely to a task. A certain maximum number of hours that the particular employee may work on this task is determined. We can summarize this, and what was stated earlier in Section 12.1, in the following rules:

P85 : There are activities.
P86 : Every activity is referred to in a one-to-one way by an activity number.
P87 : There are tasks.
P88 : A task can involve an employee.
P89 : A task can involve only one employee.
P90 : Every task involves an employee.
P91 : A task can involve an activity.
P92 : A task can involve only one activity.
P93 : Every task involves an activity.
P94 : A maximum number of working hours can belong to a task.
P95 : Only one maximum number of working hours may belong to a task.
P96 : A combination of an employee and an activity belongs to only one task.

These rules are described by the portion of the information structure diagram depicted in Figure 12.39.

The role "task to which is assigned number of hours" is not total. It appears from this that we have assumed that the maximum number of working hours does not have to be known for every task. This makes it possible to define tasks and to include them in the information base, and to determine the maximum number of working hours and register this in the information base at a later moment. The information structure diagram of Figure 12.38 did not lead to these considerations. Introducing the object type "task" forced us to ponder and decide on matters which were still left unresolved in the information structure diagram of Figure 12.38.

The diagram in Figure 12.39 is referenceable because every task can uniquely be referred to by a combination of an employee and an activity. The fact that every task can be referred to by a combination of an employee and an activity follows from totality constraints P90 and P93. That this can be done **in a unique way** follows from uniqueness constraint P96, and that it can even be done **in a one-to-one way** follows from uniqueness constraints P89 and P92.

If we replace the ternary fact type involving employees, activities, and numbers of hours in Figure 12.38 by Figure 12.39, the information structure diagram of Figure 12.40 results.

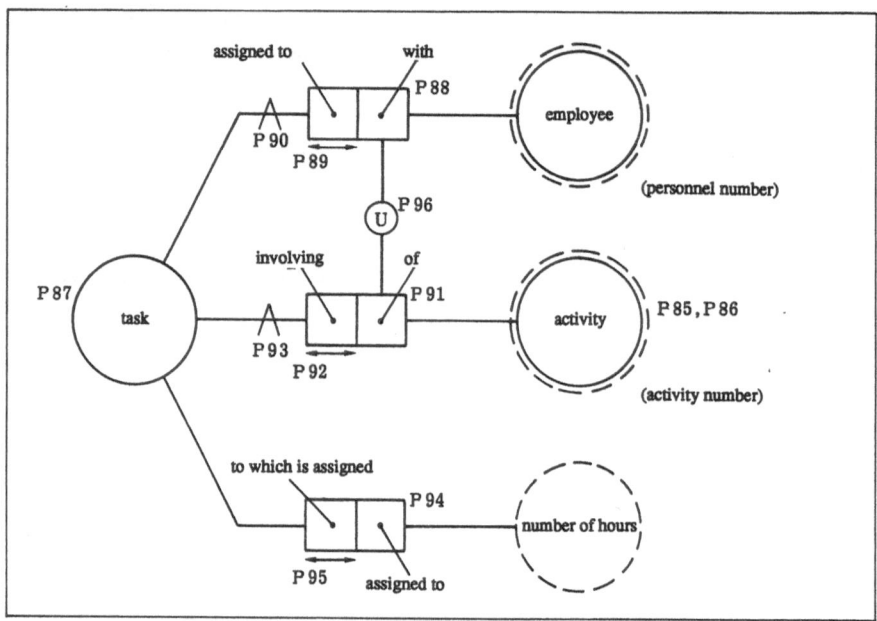

Figure 12.39.

Unlike the previous diagram, this one is in agreement with the 100% principle. In this diagram, all knowledge is represented explicitly. The above rules P87 through P96 were assumed **implicitly** in the diagram of Figure 12.38, and are now depicted **explicitly** in the new diagram. The new information structure diagram, unlike that in Figure 12.38, consists exclusively of **binary fact types**. An information structure diagram that consists exclusively of binary fact types is called a *binary information structure diagram.*

Figure 12.41 demonstrates the relationship between a non-binary information structure diagram and its corresponding binary diagram.

We arrived from the non-binary information structure diagram of figure 12.38 at the binary diagram of Figure 12.40 by means of the following steps:

- We noted in the diagram of Figure 12.38 that the combination of the roles "employee who is assigned activity" and "activity assigned to employee" is unique.
- We defined an object type "task" in which the objects were uniquely referred to by a combination of an employee and an activity.
- We defined binary fact types involving the object types "employee," "activity," and "number of hours" and the object type "task."
- We translated the uniqueness constraint in the non-binary diagram involving the combination of the roles "employee who is assigned activity" and "activity assigned to employee" into a uniqueness constraint in the binary diagram involving the combination of the roles "employee with task" and "activity of task".

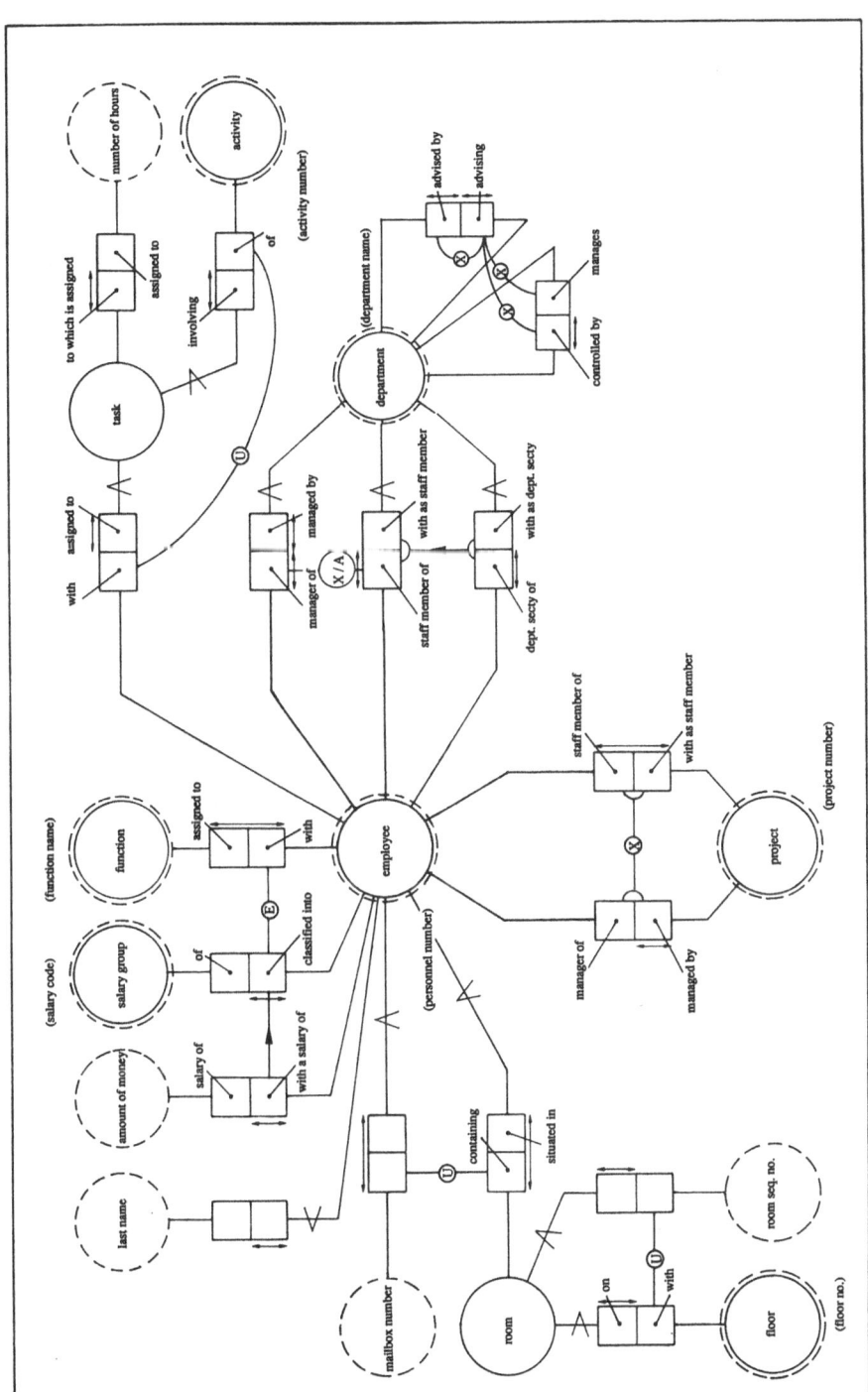

Figure 12.40.

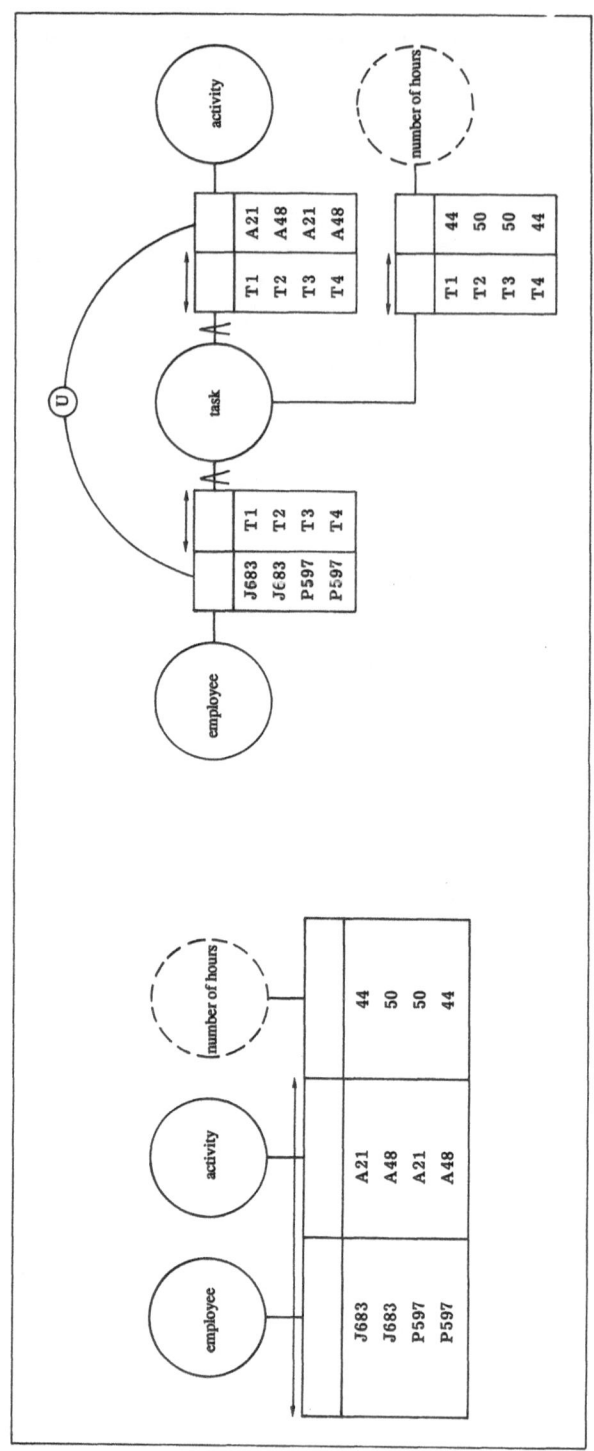

Figure 12.41.

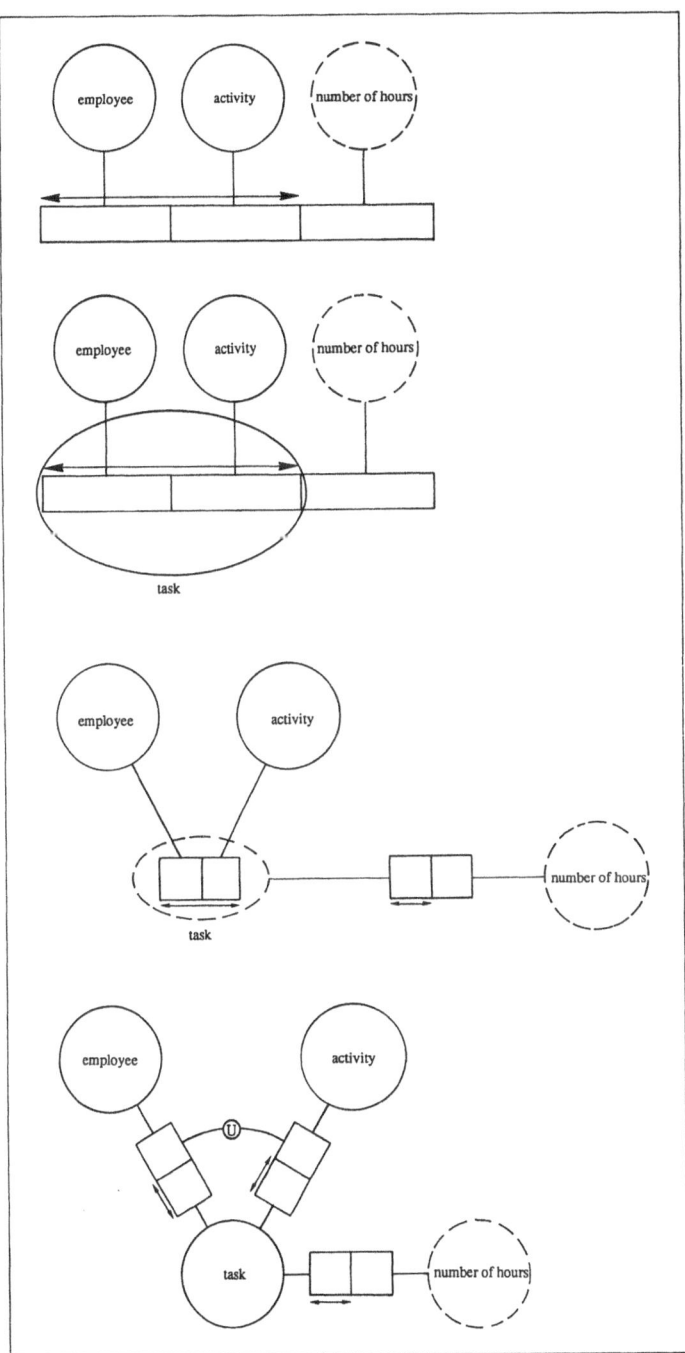

Figure 12.42.

The process described by these steps is symbolically represented in Figure 12.42.

This process, in which a non-binary information structure diagram is converted into a binary diagram, is sometimes called "nesting". We then say, in somewhat less formal terms, that the roles "employee who is assigned activity" and "activity assigned to employee" are "nested" in the non-lexical object type "task". This process always leads to the introduction of a **non-lexical** object type.

The conversion of a non-binary information structure diagram into a binary one is explained here on the basis of a ternary fact type. The same process is obviously generally valid for n-ary fact types. Figure 12.43 provides an example of an arbitrary n-ary fact type.

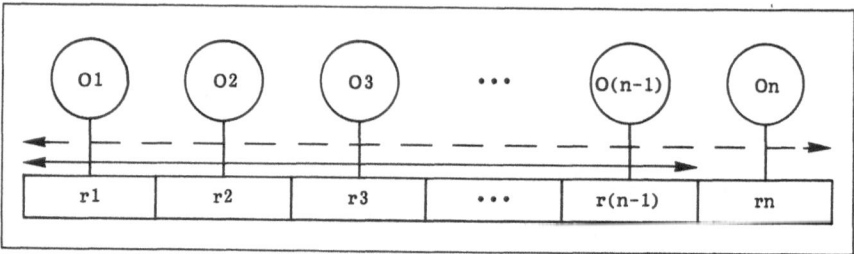

Figure 12.43.

In this example, at least one combination of n-1 roles (the uniqueness symbol drawn in solid lines) or a combination of n roles (the uniqueness symbol drawn in broken lines) is unique. The non-binary diagram is transformed into a binary diagram (Figure 12.44) by introducing a new object type, say O, and defining binary fact types which are related to this new object type and object types O1 through On. The uniqueness constraint in the n-ary fact type involving the combination of roles r1 through r(n-1) and rn, respectively, is translated into a uniqueness constraint in binary fact types involving the combination of the roles r'1 through r'(n-1) and r'n, respectively.

To conclude the matters which have been discussed in this section, we can state that an information structure diagram in which a non-binary fact type occurs is not in agreement with the 100% principle. In such a diagram, certain rules cannot yet be discerned or have been left unresolved. Therefore, a non-binary information structure diagram must be "transformed" into a binary diagram. Consequently, in what follows we will assume that an information structure diagram must always be, by definition, binary. A non-binary diagram, such as that in Figure 12.38, is only acceptable as an intermediate result.

One of the characteristic features of the NIAM method of information analysis is that part of the grammar of an information system is always described by a binary information structure diagram. NIAM therefore falls under the so-called "binary methods". In the field of information analysis, these methods are characterized by the fact that they lead to a so-called "binary information model" or "binary conceptual schema".

"Analysis" is, by definition, the splitting up of a problem into its smallest

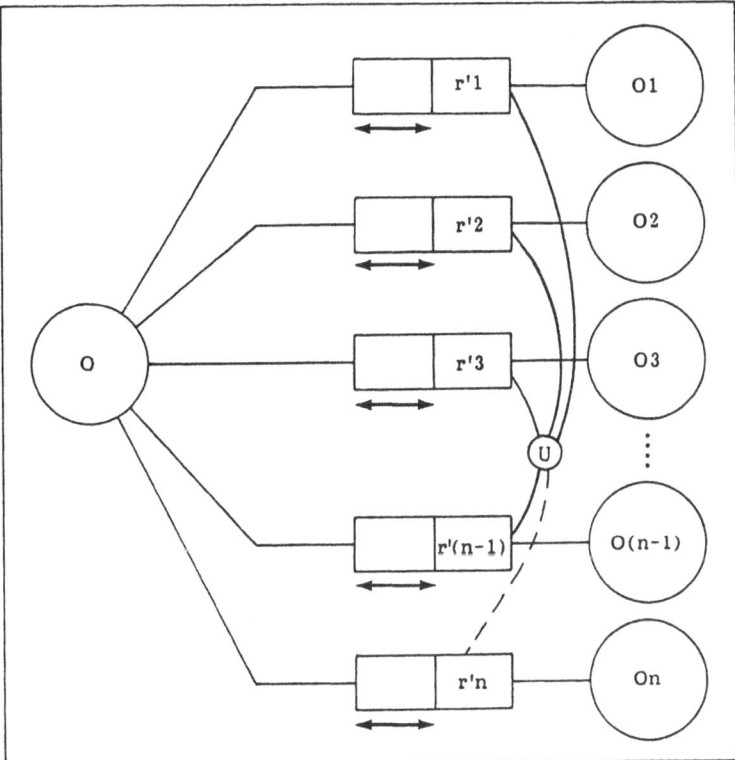

Figure 12.44.

components and examining the possible relationships between them and the rules governing these relationships. The smallest components from which information is constructed are binary relationships between the objects concerned. Obviously, information analysis consists of the analysis of these smallest components, i.e. binary relationships. In describing the grammar of an information system on the basis of a binary information structure diagram, all of the rules which are valid for the information exchange with the system must be described completely and explicitly. The chance that certain rules cannot be distinguished or are left "unresolved" is then small. Or at any rate, it is smaller than when we confine ourselves to a description based on non-binary relationships.

We shall express the fact that, in the NIAM method of information analysis, the grammar of an information system is described on the basis of **binary fact types**, by refining the definition of the natural language principle (one of the main principles in the NIAM method) to its definitive form as follows:

Information can always be described by means of **binary** deep structure sentences in a natural language.

It follows from this principle that information is always built up from binary

facts and that the grammar can consequently always be described on the basis of
binary fact types.

Lastly, we provide below an overview of the way in which each of the ternary
fact types discussed in Section 12.1 can be transformed into binary fact types.
During this process, one must always keep a close watch on the way in which the
uniqueness constraints involving combinations of roles of the n-ary fact types are
translated into uniqueness constraints involving combinations of roles of different
binary fact types.

To summarize:

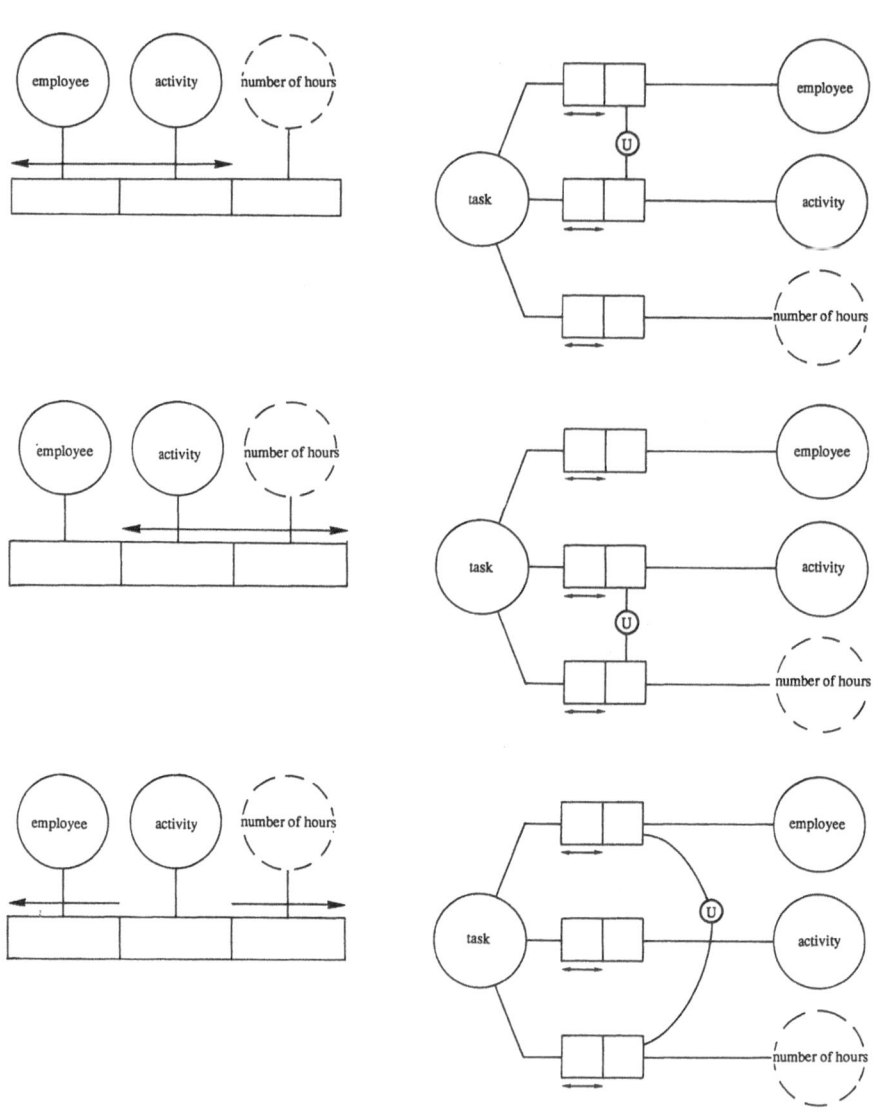

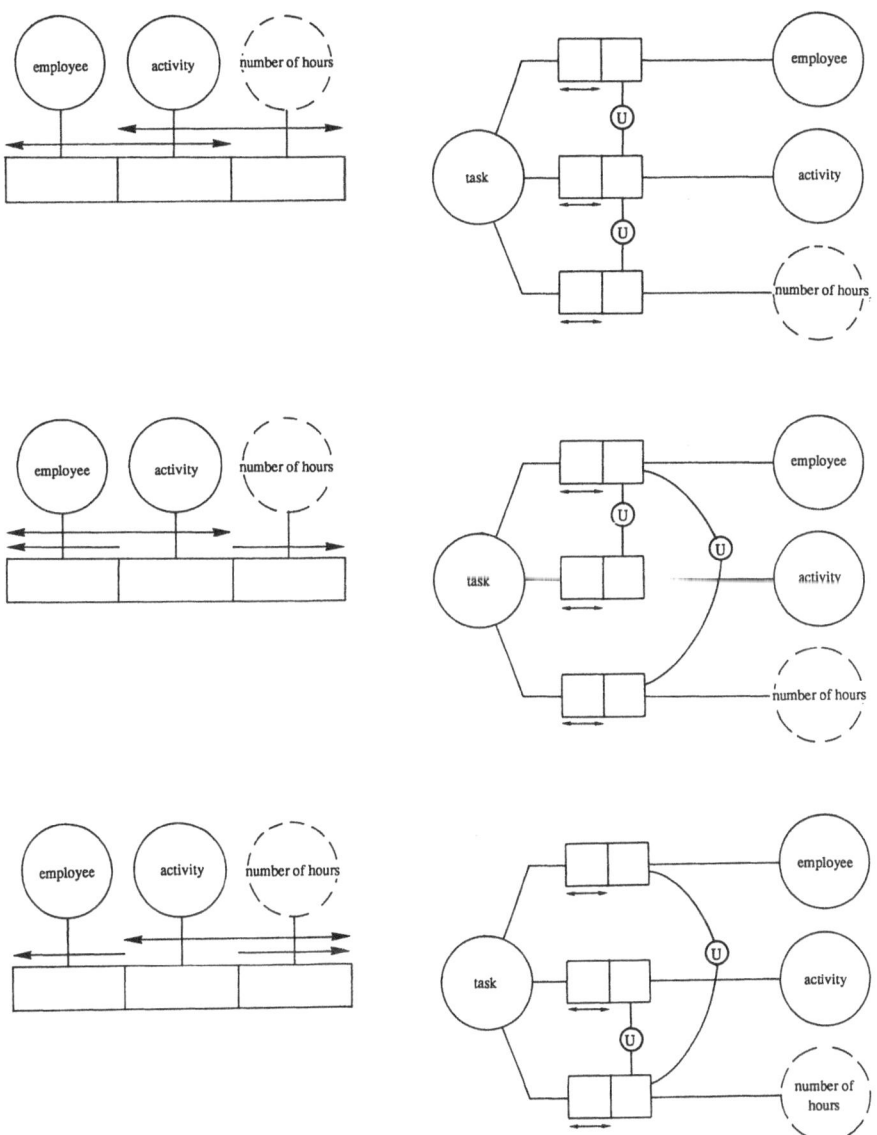

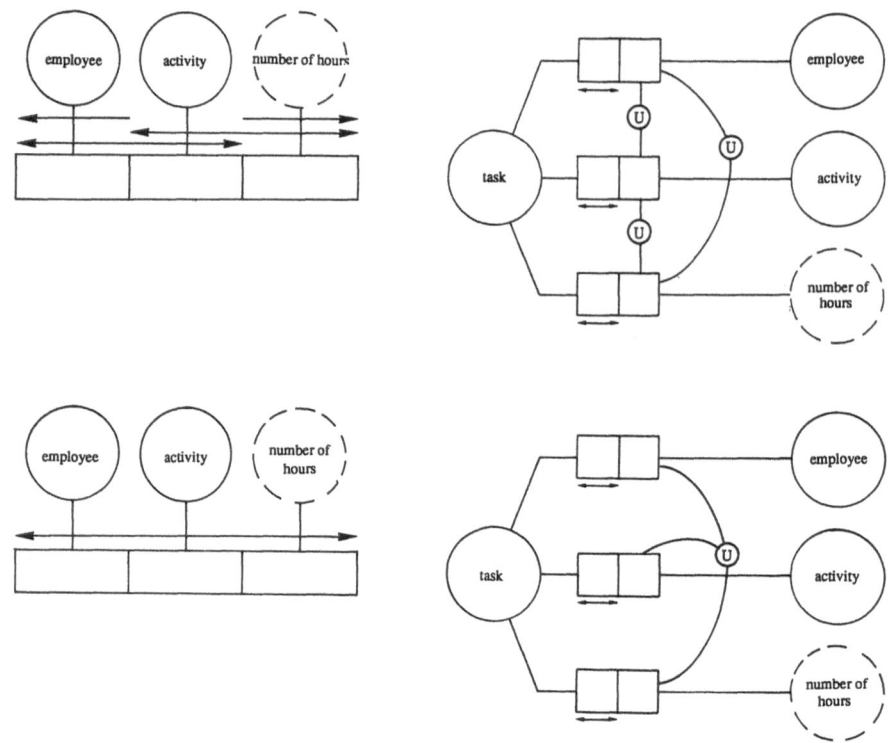

A binary information structure diagram:
An information structure diagram that contains exclusively binary fact types.

The natural language principle:
    Information can always be described by means of binary deep structure sentences in a natural language.

13 THE NIAM METHOD OF INFORMATION ANALYSIS IN PRACTICE - 4

13.1 The reservation card

In this chapter, we will add to the stepwise plan of the NIAM method of information analysis by dealing with non-binary fact types.

To this end, we will describe the allowable information contents of the information flow "reservations data" (see Figure 6.1). This information flow contains data about the reservations of books by library members. This data is noted on "reservation cards." One of these reservation cards is represented in Figure 13.1. We shall use this figure as a concrete example of the contents of the information flow "reservations data."

RESERVATION CARD

membership no. | 2 | 2 | 5 | 7 | 7 | 3 |

ISBN | 9 | 0 | 6 | 2 | 3 | 3 | 1 | 3 | 4 | 3 |

reservation date | 0 | 3 | | 0 | 6 | | 8 | 5 |
 d d m m j j

Figure 13.1.

A description of the reservation card follows below.

If all of the copies of a certain book are loaned out, the book can be reserved by a library member. As soon as a copy of the book is returned, the member who made the reservation is notified. That copy is then held for that member for a maximum of one week. Once a book is reserved, the outstanding loans of copies of it can no longer be renewed.

The reservations data are listed on reservation cards, which are kept by the checkout desk. The membership number of the person making the reservation, the ISBN of the book on reserve, and the date on which the reservation was made are listed on the reservation card. It follows from the fact that an ISBN rather than a copy number is listed on the reservation card that only a **book** and never a certain **copy** of it can be reserved. The first copy of the reserved book which is returned is always loaned out to the person who made the reservation.

A member can reserve more than one book, and it happens that a book is reserved by more than one member. In the latter case, the copy which is returned is loaned out to the person who made the first reservation for that book.

In recording a reservation, the membership number, the ISBN, and the reservation date must always be listed on the reservation card.

A reservation always elapses one week after a borrowed copy of the reserved book is brought back to the library. If the person who first reserved the book does not pick up the copy before that time, the copy is again made available for loan in the normal way.

The reservation cards of expired reservations are kept for a while, for the purpose of collecting statistical data. Consequently, the date of the reservation needs to be listed on the reservation card. After all, it is possible for someone who has reserved a book to reserve it again at a later time. If the reservation dates of these two reservations of the same book by the same member were not listed, it would not be possible to distinguish between them. (We assume that a member may reserve the same book only once on the same day; he or she can reserve however several different books on the same day.)

This takes care of our description of the reservation card. We invite the reader to attempt, before reading any further, to use the stepwise plan of the NIAM method of information analysis to add those rules which are valid for the information contents of the reservation card to the information structure diagram.

The lexical objects which are listed on the reservation card are of the type "membership number," "ISBN," and "date." In Figure 13.2, we have described the data of the reservation card by means of a population table, in which we have inititally listed only the lexical objects and the names of the lexical object types.

membership no.	ISBN	date
225 773	90 6233 134 3	03.06.85

Figure 13.2.

As we already know, a membership number refers to a member, and an ISBN to a book. In Figure 13.3, we have added these non-lexical object types to the population table.

Up to now in these practically oriented chapters, we have only taken binary sentence types into account. However, as of this moment, we also need to take into account the fact that there are elementary sentence types with more than two roles. In practice, binary sentence types occur most often, followed by ternary

member	book	
membership no.	ISBN	date
225 773	90 6233 134 3	03.06.85

Figure 13.3.

sentence types and then sentence types with more than three roles. Consequently, we shall always try to split a sentence type described by a population table into binary sentence types first. If this is not possible without loss of information, we will next try to split this sentence type (or part of it) into ternary sentence types. If this is not possible either, we will then try to split this sentence type (or part of it) into sentence types with four roles, and so on.

We shall now show that the sentence type described by the population table of Figure 13.3 cannot be split into binary sentence types without loss of information, and that it is therefore elementary. To this end, we have filled in the population table in Figure 13.4 such that all the possible combinations of a member, a book, and a date have been included.

member	book		
membership no.	ISBN	date	
225 773	90 6233 134 3	03.06.85	(1)
225 773	10 2952 035 3	05.05.85	(2)
139 524	90 6233 134 3	05.05.85	(3)
139 524	90 6233 134 3	03.06.85	(4)
225 773	90 6233 134 3	08.10.85	(5)
225 773	10 2952 035 3	03.06.85	(6)

Figure 13.4.

In Figure 13.5, we have split this (ternary) population table into binary tables.

We cannot infer from these binary tables whether member 225773 has reserved book 90 6233 134 3 on 03.06.85, on 05.05.85, or on 08.10.85. The information that this was on 03.06.85 and on 08.10.85, as is depicted in the first and next to last entries in the table in Figure 13.4, was lost when the table was split up. Because of this loss of information, the sentence type described by this table is elementary.

member	book		member			book	
membership no.	ISBN		membership no	date		ISBN	date
225 773	90 6233 134 3		225 773	03.06.85		90 6233 134 3	03.06.85
225 773	10 2952 035 3		225 773	05.05.85		10 2952 035 3	05.05.85
139 524	90 6233 134 3		139 524	05.05.85		90 6233 134 3	05.05.85
225 773	10 2952 035 3		139 524	03.06.85		90 6233 134 3	08.10.85
			225 773	08.10.85		10 2952 035 3	03.06.85

Figure 13.5.

If we next determine which combinations of roles of this ternary sentence type are unique, we can use the n-1 rule to verify our conclusion that this sentence type is elementary. The population table of Figure 13.4 contains all possible combinations of a member, a book, and a date. By pointing out the combinations which could never occur, we can directly see which combination (or combinations) of roles is (or are) unique. To help us, we have numbered the entries in the population table of this figure.

In the first and fifth entries, the combination of member 225773 and book 90 6233 134 3 occurs twice with two different reservation dates. This is possible because one member can reserve the same book on two different dates (for example, one or both reservations could have expired in the meantime).

In the first and sixth entries, the combination of member 225773 and the date 03.06.85 appears for two different books. This is possible because one member can reserve more than one book on a certain day.

In the first and fourth entries, the combination of book 90 6233 134 3 and the date 03.06.85 occurs for two different members. This is likewise possible, because different members can reserve the same book on one certain day.

The conclusion to be drawn is apparently that all possible combinations of a member, a book, and a date are allowed and that there are no constraints on the populations of the roles of this sentence type. In Figure 13.6, we have represented this, as agreed, by drawing a uniqueness symbol across all the columns of the population table.

In the previous chapter, we dealt with the n-1 rule, which reads:

- In an elementary n-ary sentence type, at least one combination of n-1 roles or the combination of all n roles is unique.
- If at least one combination of less than n-1 roles or at least one individual role in an n-ary sentence type is unique, this sentence type is not elementary.

If we were therefore to conclude from our analysis of the uniqueness of the roles of the ternary sentence type in Figure 13.4 that, contrary to expectations, one or more individual roles are unique, it would follow directly from the n-1 rule that this sentence type is not elementary.

member	book	
membership no.	ISBN	date
reserving	reserved by	of reservation
225 773	90 6233 134 3	03.06.85
225 773	10 2952 035 3	05.05.85
139 524	90 6233 134 3	05.05.85
139 524	90 6233 134 3	03.06.85
225 773	90 6233 134 3	08.10.85
225 773	10 2952 035 3	03.06.85

Figure 13.6.

Conversely, it does **not** follow from the n-1 rule that an n-ary sentence type is elementary if a combination of at least n-1 or n roles is unique. The proof that an n-ary sentence type is elementary must **always** be provided by showing that there is a population table which cannot be split into smaller tables without loss of information, as we have done above with the aid of the population table in Figure 13.5. In Figure 13.7, we have depicted the elementary sentence type that is described by the population table of Figure 13.6 by means of an information structure diagram.

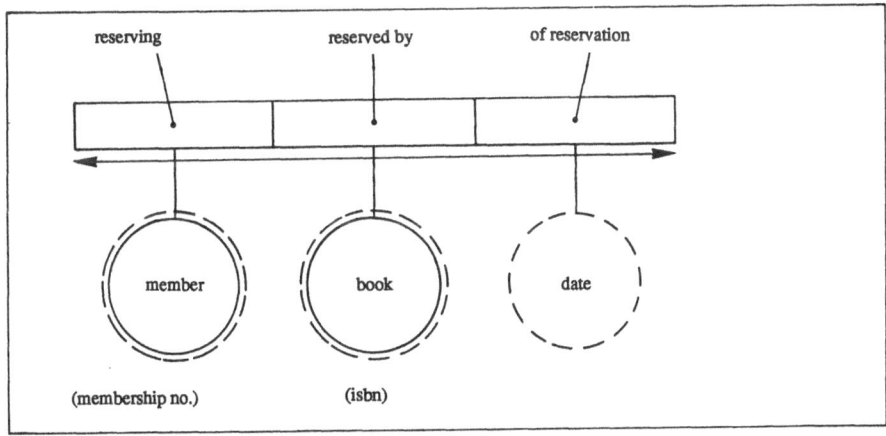

Figure 13.7.

Bearing non-binary sentence types in mind, we shall refine step 4 of the NIAM method of information analysis as follows:

4. Determine the elementary sentence types.

    4.1 First investigate whether the sentence type described by the population table(s) can be split into binary sentence types without loss of information. If this is not possible, investigate whether this sentence type (or part of it) can be split into ternary sentence types without loss of information. If this is not possible either, investigate whether this sentence type (or part of it) can be split into sentence types consisting of four roles, etc. Demonstrate that any non-binary sentence types found this way are elementary by showing that there is a population table in which information gets lost during further splitting. (For this process, use a population table in which all possible combinations of objects occur.)

    4.2 Determine (likewise on the basis of a population table containing all possible combinations of objects) which combinations of roles of any non-binary sentence types found this way are unique. When a combination of less than n-1 roles or an individual role of an n-ary sentence type is unique, this sentence type is not elementary and a mistake has been made in the previous step.

    4.3 Connect the columns of the population table, belonging to one sentence type, to each other.

The part of the information structure diagram depicted by Figure 13.7 contains a non-binary fact type. We saw in the previous chapter that non-binary fact types always need to be replaced by binary fact types. This is done in step 7 of the NIAM method of information analysis.

7. Replace every non-binary fact type by binary fact types.

This step consists of four substeps. We shall now carry out these steps for the information structure diagram of Figure 13.7.

    7.1 "Nest" a unique combination of roles of the non-binary fact type into a new non-lexical object type.

In the ternary fact type in Figure 13.7, the combination of all three roles is unique. In Figure 13.8, we have "nested" the combination of these three roles into a new non-lexical object type.

    The objects of this new object type are referred to uniquely by a combination of a member, a book, and a reservation date. For fairly obvious reasons, we shall call this new object type "reservation."

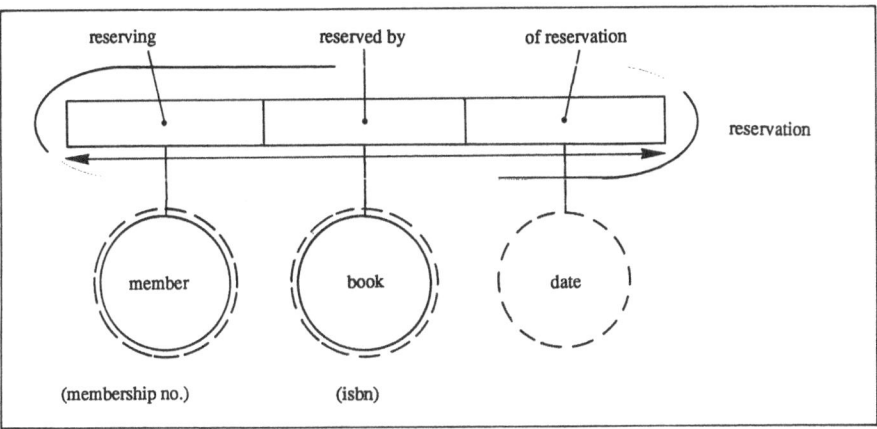

Figure 13.8.

7.2 Define binary fact types, each of which involves one of the object types of the original non-binary fact type and the new object type defined in the previous substep.

In our example this means that we need to define binary fact types involving on the one hand the object types "member," "book," and "date," and on the other hand, the new object type "reservation." We have done this in Figure 13.9.

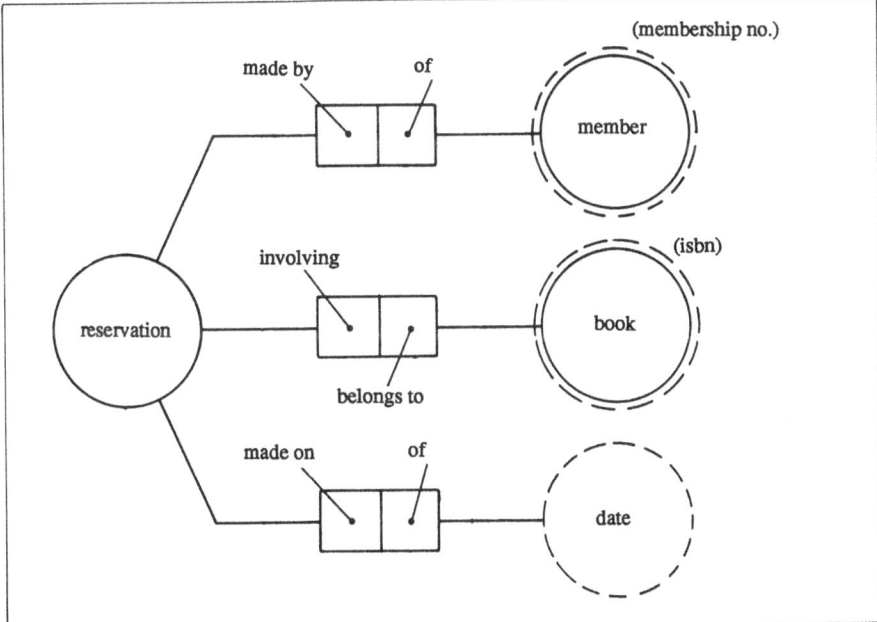

Figure 13.9.

7.3 For every unique combination of roles in the original non-binary fact type, draw a uniqueness symbol with respect to the corresponding roles of the binary fact types defined in the previous substep.

In the ternary fact type in Figure 13.7, the combination of all three roles is unique. These roles correspond to the roles "member of reservation," "book belongs to reservation," and "date of reservation" in the binary diagram (Figure 13.9). The combination of these roles is thus unique. Consequently, in Figure 13.10, we have connected these roles by means of a uniqueness symbol.

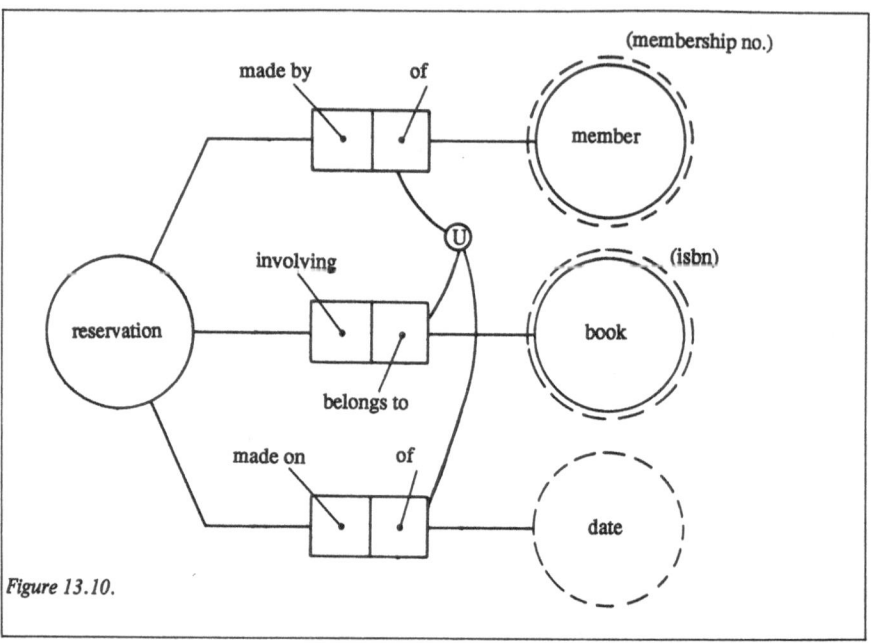

Figure 13.10.

7.4 Determine the uniqueness and the totality of the individual roles of these binary fact types.

It appears from the format of the reservation card and the description of it that a reservation can be made by only one member, for only one book, and on only one date. This means that the roles "reservation made by member," "reservation involving book," and "reservation made on date" are unique. In the description of the reservation card, it is further stated that the member who made the reservation, the book involved, and the date on which the reservation was made must always be known. This means that the roles "reservation made by member," "reservation involving book," and "reservation made on date" are total. We have represented these uniqueness and totality constraints in Figure 13.11.

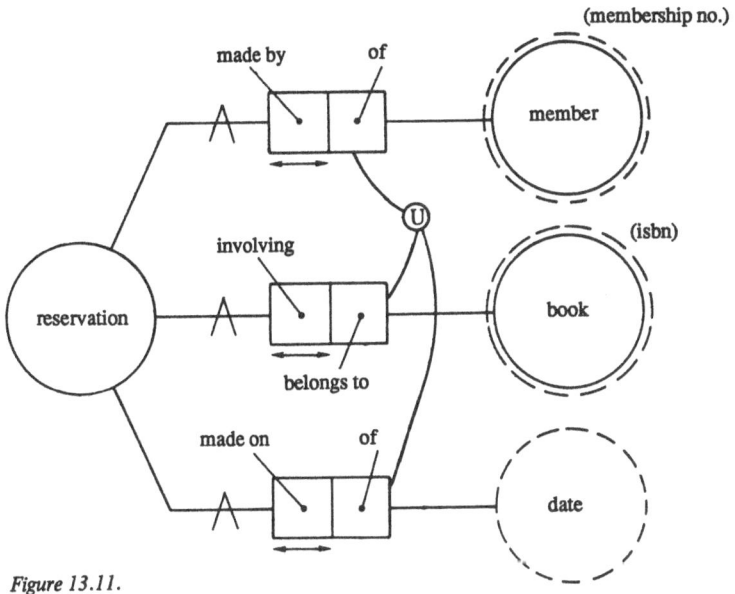

Figure 13.11.

Every reservation can be referred to uniquely and in a one-to-one way by a combination of a member, a book, and a date. The fact that this can be done uniquely follows from the uniqueness of the combination of the roles "member of reservation," "book belongs to reservation," and "date of reservation." The fact that this can be done in a one-to-one way follows from the uniqueness of the roles "reservation made by member," "reservation involving book," and "reservation made on date." And the fact that each reservation can thereby be referred to follows from the totality of these roles. The diagram of Figure 13.11 is thus referenceable.

13.2 The day sequence number

To conclude this chapter, we shall add something more to the example of the reservation card. We reported in the description of the reservation card that as soon as a copy of a book on reserve is brought back, it is loaned out to the first member to have made a reservation for that book. The reservation date is therefore crucial. Yet, we have also seen that it is possible for a book to be reserved by more than one member on the same day. In such cases, it is impossible to see on the reservation card in Figure 13.1 which member reserved that particular book first on that day. Therefore, a so-called "day sequence number" is noted on the reservation card. With the help of this number, the reservations of a certain book made on a same day are numbered consecutively. The reservation card then looks like the one depicted in Figure 13.12.

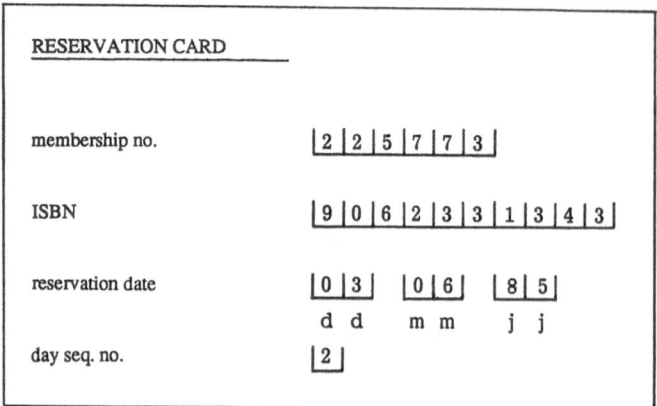

Figure 13.12.

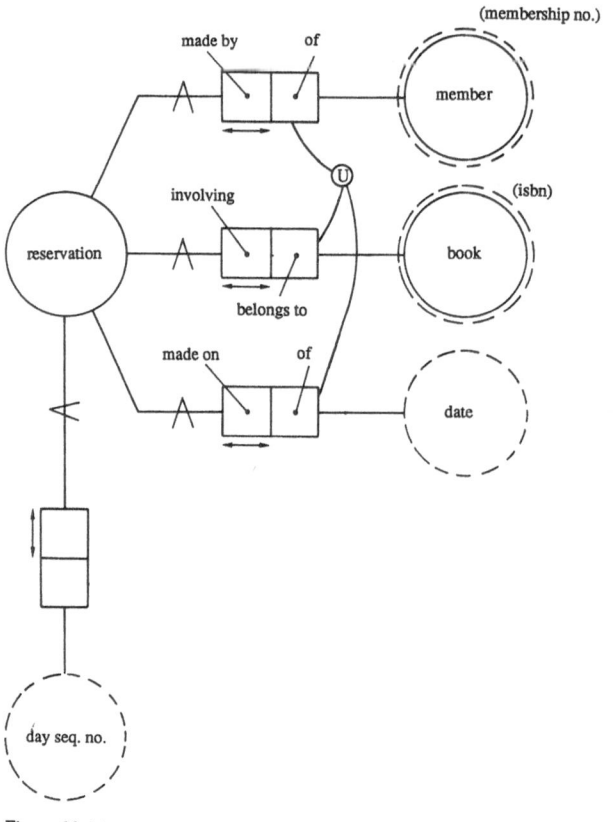

Figure 13.13.

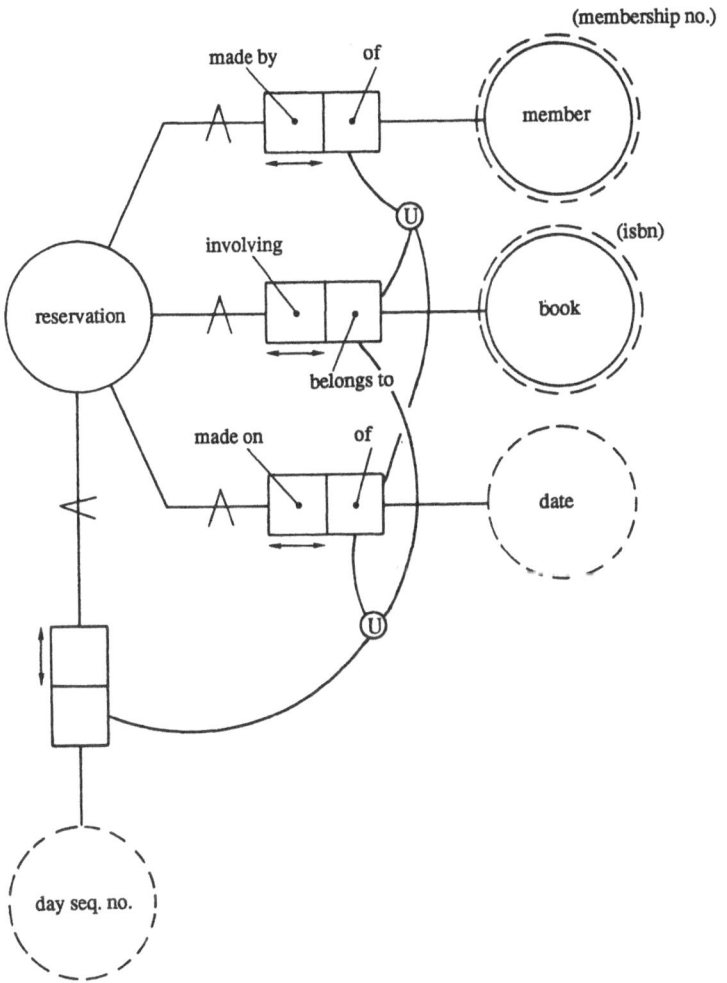

Figure 13.14.

A "1" is always filled in for the day sequence number, except when someone else also has reserved the book on that particular day. In that case, a sequence number which indicates the order of the reservations for this book on that day is filled in. Thus, in the example in Figure 13.12, member 225773 is apparently the second member who has reserved book 90 6233 134 3 on 03.06.85. The lexical object type to which these sequence numbers belong will be called, in analogy to the terminology on the reservation card, a "day sequence number." Every individual reservation has exactly one day sequence number. In Figure 13.13, we have added the lexical object type "day sequence number" to the information structure diagram.

The role "reservation with day sequence number" is unique, because only one

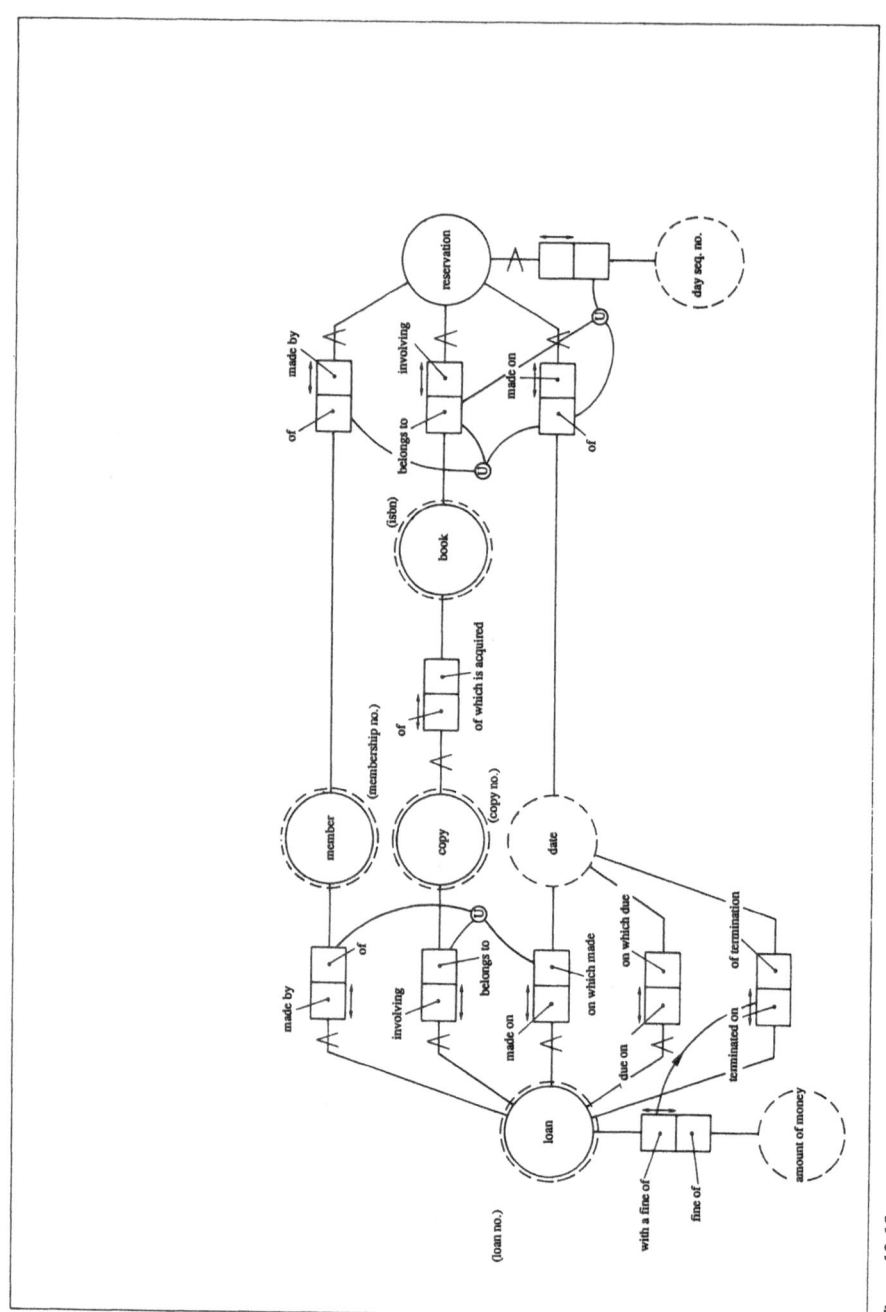

Figure 13.15.

day sequence number can belong to a reservation. This role is total, because every reservation must have a day sequence number.

There is only one combination of a book, a date, and a day sequence number for a reservation. This means that the combination of the roles "book belongs to reservation," "date of reservation," and "day sequence number of reservation" is unique. In Figure 13.14, we have represented this in the customary manner by means of a uniqueness symbol.

Every reservation can now not only be referred to uniquely (and even in a one-to-one way) by a combination of a member, a book, and a date, but also by a combination of a book, a date, and a day sequence number. Therefore, on the reservation card in Figure 13.12, both the combination of member 225773, book 90 6233 134 3, and date 03.06.85 and the combination of this book, the same date, and day sequence number 2 refer to one and the same reservation.

In Figure 13.15, we have added the rules involving the reservations of books to part of the information structure diagram of the library case.

13.3 Summary

Below is a summary of the steps of the NIAM method of information analysis dealt with in this chapter.

4. Determine the elementary sentence types.

   4.1 First investigate whether the sentence type described by the population table(s) can be split into binary sentence types without loss of information. If this is not possible, investigate whether this sentence type (or part of it) can be split into ternary sentence types without loss of information. If this is not possible either, investigate whether this sentence type (or part of it) can be split into sentence types consisting of four roles, etc. Demonstrate that any non-binary sentence types found this way are elementary by showing that there is a population table in which information gets lost during further splitting. (For this process, use a population table in which all possible combinations of objects occur.)

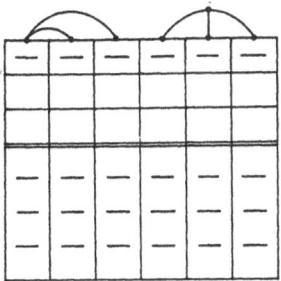

4.2 Determine (likewise on the basis of a population table containing all possible combinations of objects) which combinations of roles of any non-binary sentence types found this way are unique. When a combination of less than n-1 roles or an individual role of an n-ary sentence type is unique, this sentence type is not elementary and a mistake has been made in the previous step.

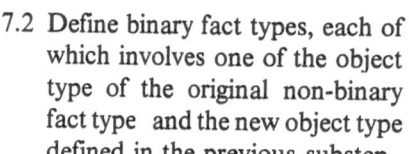

4.3 Connect the columns of the population table which belong to one sentence type to each other.

7. Replace every non-binary fact type by binary fact types.

7.1 "Nest" a unique combination of roles of the non-binary fact type into a new non-lexical object type.

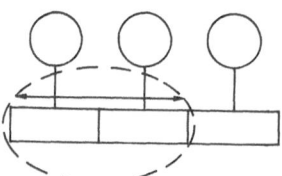

7.2 Define binary fact types, each of which involves one of the object type of the original non-binary fact type and the new object type defined in the previous substep.

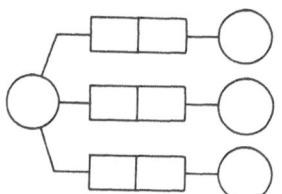

7.3 For every unique combination of roles in the original non-binary fact type, draw a uniqueness symbol with respect to the corresponding roles of the binary fact types defined in the previous substep.

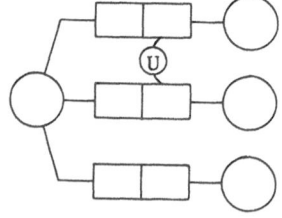

7.4 Determine the uniqueness and
the totality of the individual roles
of these binary fact types.

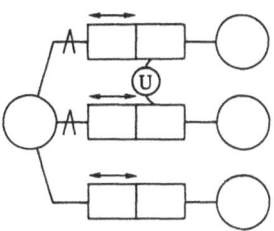

14 FACT TYPES CONSISTING OF ONE ROLE

Up to this point, we have taken a look at fact types that consist of two or more roles. We shall now show that there are also fact types that consist of one single role.

14.1 Unary sentence types and unary fact types

Let us have a look at the following elementary deep structure sentence:

"The employee with personnel number F759 is a department manager."

If we "parse" this sentence with the aid of the general structural formula for elementary deep structure sentences (Figure 5.5), we find for this sentence the structure represented in Figure 14.1:

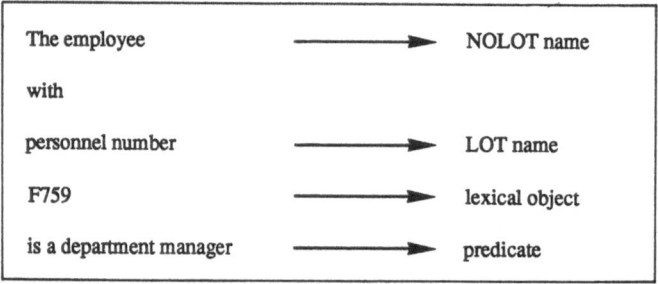

Figure 14.1.

At first glance, we might perhaps expect "department manager" to be the name of a second non-lexical object type. However, the structural formula for elementary deep structure sentences then requires that the name of a second lexical object type and of a second lexical object also be given. Because the above sentence contains the name of only one lexical object type and only one lexical object, "department manager" is necessarily part of the predicate. The above sentence therefore involves only one single object, namely an object of the type "employee."

A second elementary deep structure sentence is depicted in Figure 14.2, and like the above sentence, involves only one single object.

This second sentence involves the same non-lexical object type ("employee"), the same lexical object type ("personnel number"), and contains the same predicate ("is a department manager") as the first sentence. Both sentences therefore belong to the same elementary sentence type. Figure 14.3 contains a population table which describes this sentence type.

Because this population table consists of only one column, the sentence type to which it refers apparently contains only one role. An elementary sentence type that contains only one role is called a *unary sentence type*.

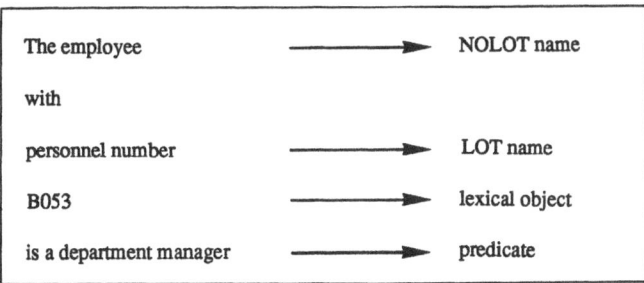

Figure 14.2.

An information structure diagram that describes the sentence type of Figure 14.3 looks like the one depicted in Figure 14.4.

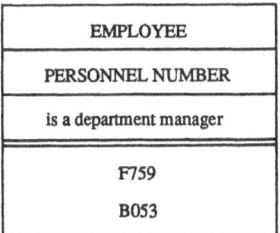

Figure 14.3.

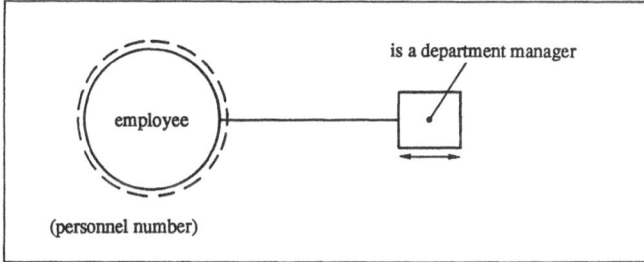

Figure 14.4.

This diagram contains a fact type with one single role, called a *unary fact type*.

A possible population based on this information structure diagram is represented in Figure 14.5.

The uniqueness symbol with respect to the only role of this unary fact type is fairly trivial. It denotes that the (sole) role of a unary fact type is always unique, just as in a binary fact type the combination of both roles is, by virtue of the singularity rule, always unique.

As we know, lexical object types can only involve bridge types, and bridge types are, by definition, always **binary** fact types. **Unary** fact types are therefore necessarily always idea types and only involve non-lexical object types.

To illustrate this, we have added in Figure 14.6 the lexical object type "personnel number," its population, and an associated population of the object type "employee" to the population diagram of Figure 14.5.

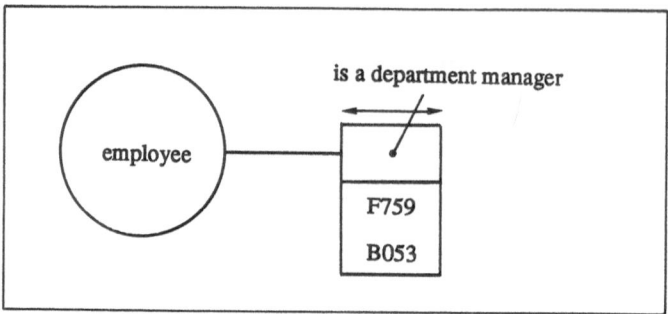

Figure 14.5.

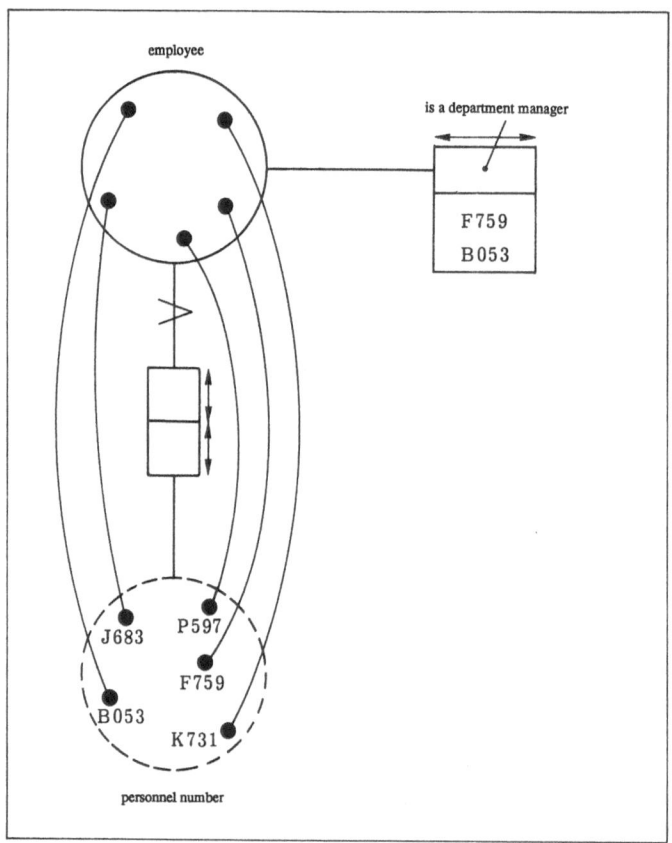

Figure 14.6.

We can see that the population of the role "employee is a department manager" is a subset of the population of the role "employee with personnel number." This follows from the fact that the role "employee with personnel number" is total, while the role "employee is a department manager" is not. The population of the latter role contains all department managers, and this is a subset of all employees.

To summarize:

A unary fact type:
A fact type that consists of only one role. A unary fact type is always an idea type and therefore always involves a non-lexical object type.

14.2 Subtypes

We have seen in Chapter 12 that an information structure diagram in which fact types with more than two roles occur, does not completely satisfy the requirements of the 100% principle. For this reason, every non-binary fact type is replaced, after a new object type has been introduced, by a number of binary fact types. We ended Chapter 12 with the demand that an information structure diagram must, by definition, always be binary; that is, that it must contain only binary fact types.

However, if an information structure diagram may only contain **binary** fact types, any possible **unary** fact types need to be "deleted" from the diagram as well. To do this, we shall use a reasoning process similar to that which we used for fact types with more than two roles.

The part of the information structure diagram that is depicted in Figure 14.4 (still) does not completely satisfy the requirements of the 100% principle, as it contains knowledge which is "hidden behind" the rules of the grammar. The unary fact type in Figure 14.4 expresses the knowledge that some employees are department managers. That is, at any given moment, there is a subset within the set of all employees, consisting of all the employees who are department managers at that moment. In other words, there is an object type, say "department manager," which contains all employees who are department managers.

However, this object type is not explicitly depicted in the diagram of Figure 14.4. The information structure diagram is only in agreement with the 100% principle if this object type is represented explicitly. If we do this, the diagram of Figure 14.7 results.

The object type "department manager" contains all employees who are department managers, and therefore all the employees in the diagram of Figure 14.4 who occur in the population of the unary fact type. We have left out this unary fact type in the above diagram because the fact that an employee belongs to the object type "department manager" represents exactly the same information as the fact that an employee belongs to the population of the unary fact type. Or stated otherwise, we have "replaced" the unary fact type by the object type "department manager."

The objects which belong to the object type "department manager" are employees, and therefore belong to the object type "employee" as well. The objects of the type "department manager" thus form a subset of the objects of the type "employee." This has been represented in the diagram of Figure 14.7 by connecting both object types with an arrow. This symbol is analogous to the subset symbol and points to the set (in this case an object type) which contains the other set (likewise an object type); the arrow points from the "smallest" set to the "largest" set.

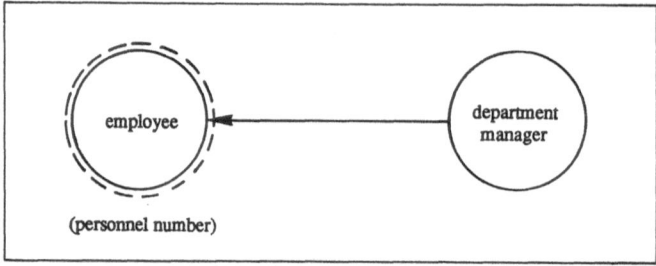

Figure 14.7.

The object type "department manager" is represented explicitly in the diagram of Figure 14.7, unlike Figure 14.4. Any possible attributes that are only valid for department managers can be explicitly described in this diagram (unlike that of Figure 14.4) by means of facts involving objects of the type "department manager." The information structure diagram of Figure 14.7 describes the knowledge regarding the organization of the library more explicitly and more exactly than does the diagram of Figure 14.4, and is therefore more in agreement with the 100% principle.

In analogy to what was said about non-binary fact types in Chapter 12, we can state in somewhat less formal terms that the new object type "department manager" has been created by "nesting" the role of the unary fact type in Figure 14.4. We have depicted this in Figure 14.8.

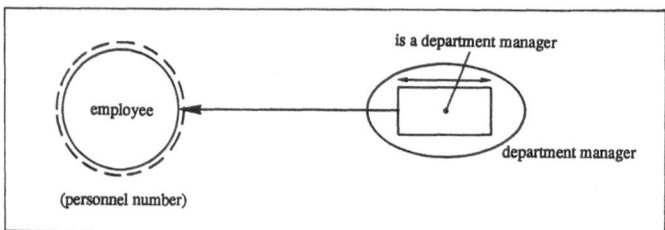

Figure 14.8.

Because unary fact types can only involve non-lexical object types, only non-lexical object types are "created" in this way.

The object type "department manager" introduced in this way is called a *subtype* of the object type "employee." As we have just seen, subtypes can only involve non-lexical object types, and are always non-lexical object types themselves.

Conversely, the object type "employee" is called a *supertype* of the object type "department manager." The arrow pointing from a subtype to its supertype is called a *subtype symbol*.

The objects which belong to a subtype (such as "department manager") always form a subset of the objects which belong to the corresponding supertype (in this case "employee"). Thus, all department managers are also employees. All objects of the type "department manager" therefore also belong to the object type "employee." One of the consequences of this is that every department manager can occur in the populations of all the roles of the object type "employee." Every department manager has, for example, a personnel number, and every department manager can have a function and a salary. It holds in general that:

every object of a subtype can occur in the populations of all of the roles of its supertype.

It is sometimes said in less formal terms that all the "attributes" (i.e., roles) of a supertype are "inherited by" or "are valid for" all the objects of a related subtype. However, the reverse does not generally hold. Not every employee is a department manager. The attributes which hold solely for department managers do not hold for every employee.

Every department manager is an employee and must therefore occur in the populations of all the total roles of the object type "employee." Therefore, every department manager must occur, for example, in the population of the total role "employee with personnel number." In general, it holds that:

every object of a subtype must occur in the populations of every total role of its supertype.

Even though there is no bridge type related to the object type "department manager," the information structure diagram in Figure 14.7 is still referenceable. After all, every department manager must occur in the population of the total role "employee with personnel number" and can therefore be uniquely referred to by a personnel number, just as can the other employees.

From now on, we shall always include subtypes instead of unary fact types in an information structure diagram.

To summarize:

A subtype:
A non-lexical object type whose objects form a (real) subset of the objects of another non-lexical object type.

A supertype:
A non-lexical object type having another non-lexical object type as subtype.

Subtypes are graphically depicted by means of the subtype symbol.

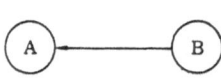

Non-lexical object type B
is a subtype of
non-lexical object type A.
Non-lexical object type A
is a supertype of
non-lexical object type B.

- Every object of a subtype can occur in the populations of all of the roles of its supertype.
- Every object of a subtype must occur in the populations of all of the total roles of its supertype.
- Not every object of a supertype can automatically occur in the populations of the roles of its subtypes.

14.3 Constraints with respect to subtypes

We shall now define a second subtype of the object type "employee" to which all the employees who work for a department as a department staff member (not as a department manager) belong. Figure 14.9 is the result of adding this subtype to the diagram of Figure 14.7.

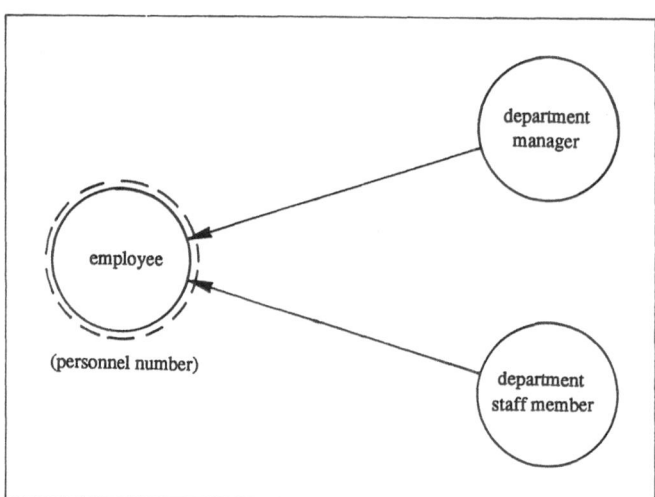

Figure 14.9.

A population of both subtypes is depicted in Figure 14.10. For illustrative purposes, we have represented these subtypes in the form of "nested roles."

Employees who are department managers are not at the same time department staff members and vice versa. The roles "employee is a department manager" and

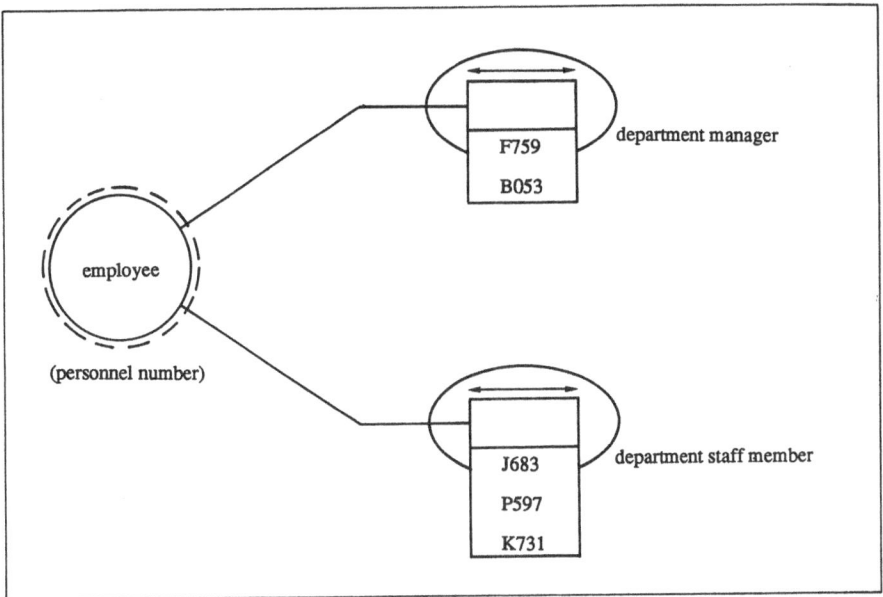

Figure 14.10.

"employee is a department staff member" therefore exclude each other. We have indicated this in the customary way in Figure 14.11 by an exclusion symbol.

Because we have agreed to always replace unary fact types by subtypes, we shall replace exclusion constraints involving roles of unary fact types by exclusion constraints involving subtypes. These are represented as in Figure 14.12.

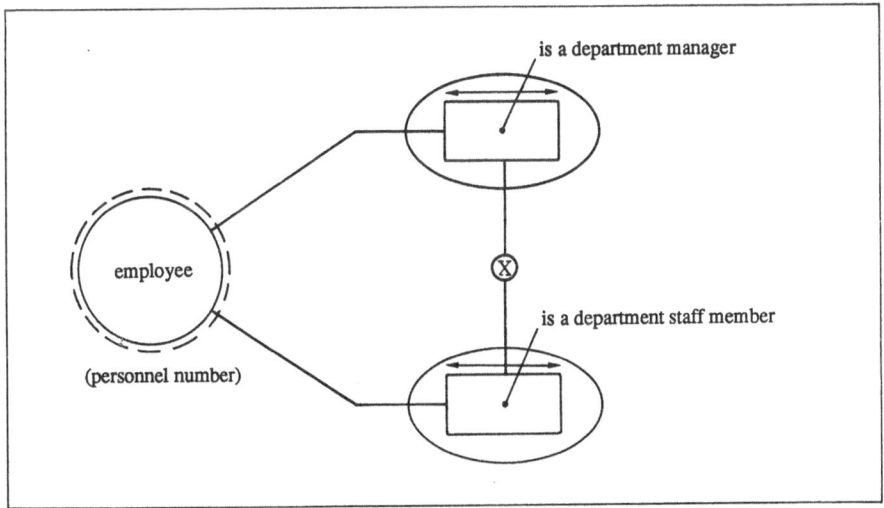

Figure 14.11.

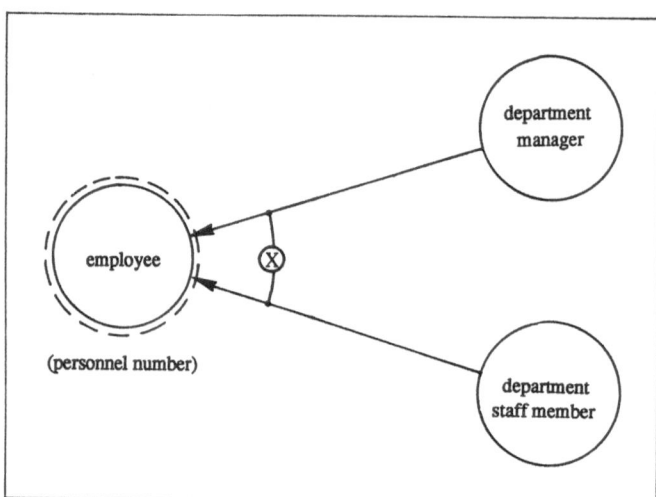

Figure 14.12.

The exclusion symbol now expresses the fact that the objects of the subtypes "department manager" and "department staff member" form sets which exclude each other. We speak in such cases of *exclusive subtypes*. We can represent these in terms of sets, as Figure 14.13 shows.

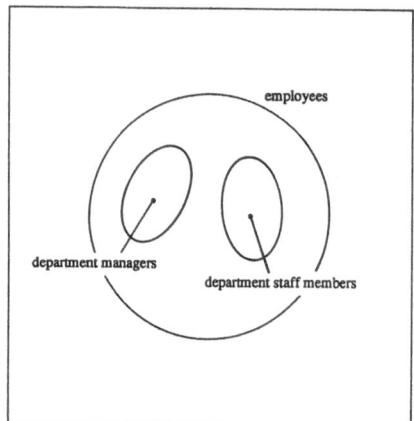

Figure 14.13.

The exclusion symbol is always drawn so as to connect the relevant subtype symbols. We saw earlier that an exclusion constraint can, by virtue of the compatibility rule, only involve objects of the same type. It follows from this that a subtype exclusion constraint can only involve subtypes of the same object type.

Let us now assume that **every** employee must be either a department manager or a department staff member. In the diagram of Figure 14.10, this means that the combination of the roles "employee is a department manager" and "employee is a department staff member" is total. We have represented this in the customary way in Figure 14.14 by a totality symbol.

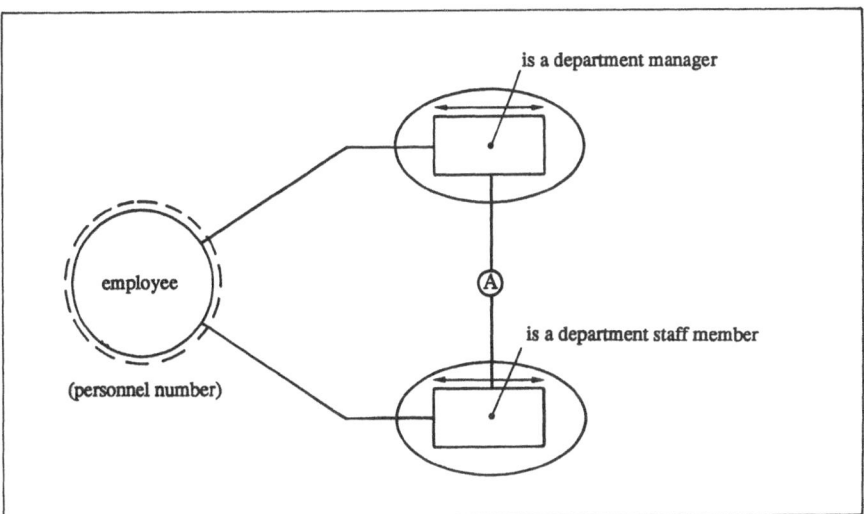

Figure 14.14.

Because we have agreed to always replace unary fact types by subtypes, we shall replace totality constraints involving roles of unary fact types by totality constraints involving subtypes. These are represented as in Figure 14.15.

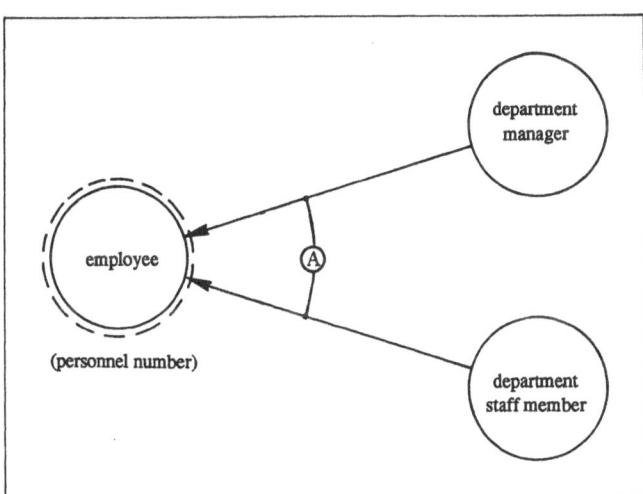

Figure 14.15.

The totality symbol expresses the fact that **every** object of the type "employee" must belong to the subtype "department manager" or to the subtype "department staff member" (or possibly to both). In this case, we say that the **combination** of

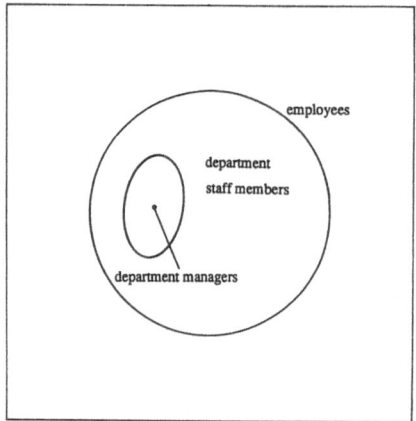

Figure 14.16.

these **subtypes** is **total**. We can represent this in terms of sets, as Figure 14.16 shows.

The totality symbol is always drawn so as to connect the subtype symbols concerned. We have seen earlier that a totality constraint can, by virtue of the compatibility rule, only involve objects of the same type. It follows from this that a subtype totality constraint can only involve subtypes of the same object type.

Let us now assume that every employee must be either a department manager or a department staff member **and** that an employee can never at the same time be both a department manager and a department staff member. This means that the subtypes "department manager" and "department staff member" exclude each other **and** that their combination is total. This is represented as in Figure 14.17.

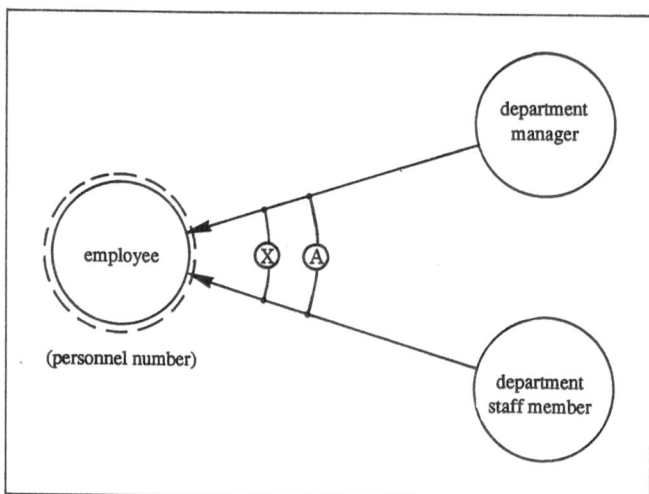

Figure 14.17.

The subtypes "department manager" and "department staff member" exclude each other and their combination is total: every employee is a department manager or a department staff member, but never both a department manager and a department staff member. We can represent this in terms of sets as in Figure 14.18.

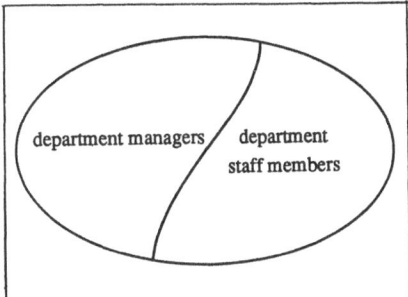

Figure 14.18.

In light of the fact that in practice subtypes often exclude each other while their combination is total, we will frequently represent these kinds of situations in an abridged notation, as has been done in Figure 14.19.

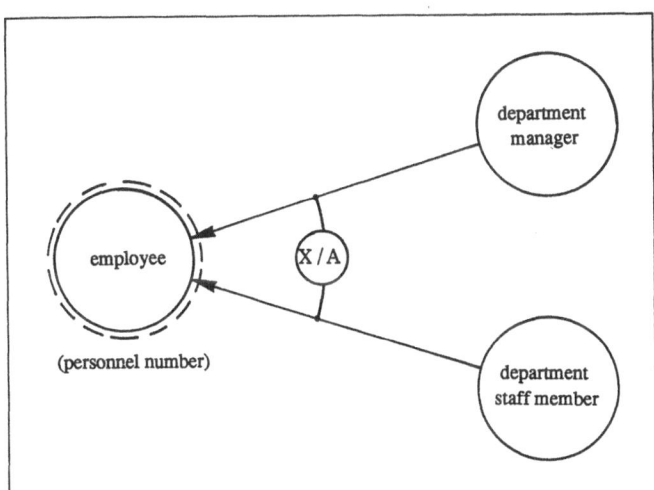

Figure 14.19.

We note that the symbol X/A is a shortcut for drawing **two individual** constraints, an exclusion constraint and a totality constraint, involving the same subtypes. In Chapter 10, we introduced an analogous shortcut for drawing exclusion and totality constraints involving the same combination of roles.

Obviously, exclusion constraints and totality constraints can also involve three or more subtypes, as Figure 14.20 exemplifies.

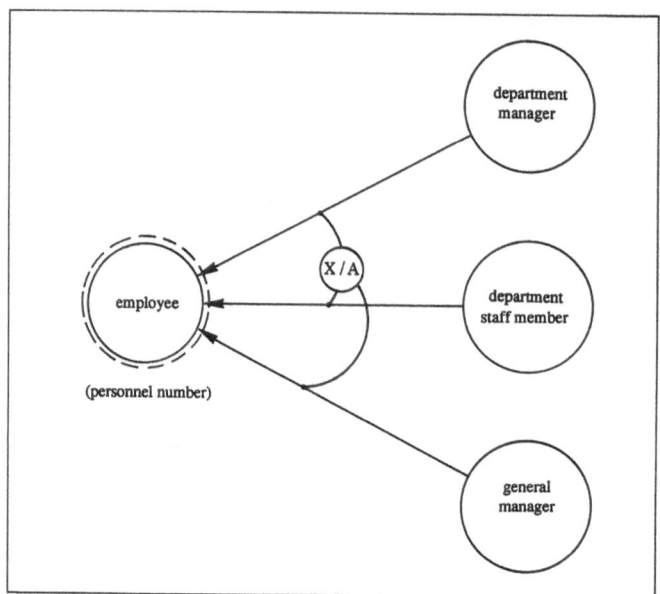

Figure 14.20.

To summarize:

Exclusive subtypes:
Two or more subtypes of the same object type exclude each other if the objects belonging to these subtypes form exclusive or non-overlapping sets.

A subtype exclusion constraint:
A constraint that expresses the fact that two or more subtypes of the same object type exclude each other.

Total subtypes:
A combination of two or more subtypes of the same object type is total if every object of this object type belongs to one or more of the subtypes.

A subtype totality constraint:
A constraint which expresses the totality of a combination of two or more subtypes of the same object type.

The fact that two or more subtypes of the same object type exclude each other is represented by means of the subtype exclusion symbol:

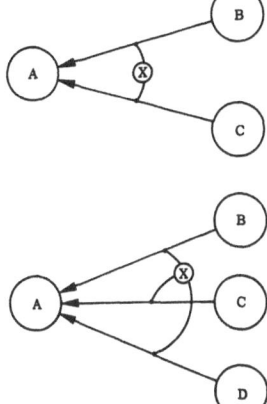

Subtypes B and C of object
type A exclude each other

Subtypes B, C and D of object
type A exclude each other

The fact that the combination of two or more subtypes of the same object type
is total is represented by means of the subtype totality symbol:

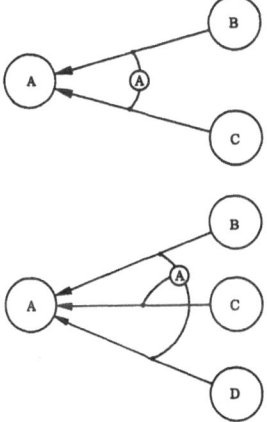

The combination of subtypes
B and C of object type A
is total

The combination of subtypes
B, C and D of object type A
is total

The fact that two or more subtypes of the same object type exclude each other
and that their combination is total can be represented by combining the subtype
exclusion and totality symbols:

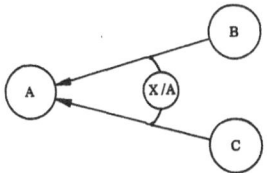

Subtypes B and C of
object type A exclude each
other and their combination
is total

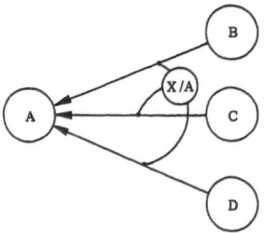

Subtypes B, C and D of object type A exclude each other and their combination is total

In the following section, we will see that a subtype can in turn have one or more subtypes. This creates hierarchical subtype structures.

14.4 Object type families

Object types can form hierarchical structures, called *object type families*. Figure 14.21 is an example of an object type family. The object type "employee" is called the *father* of this object type family. The subtype symbols always point toward the father of the object type family.

We saw earlier that it can only be said with respect to two sets that one set is a subset of the other if the elements of both sets can be compared, that is, if the elements of these sets are of the same kind or type. For this reason, all of the objects in an object type family must ultimately belong to one and the same object type. Consequently, an object type family has, by definition, only one father. When following the direction of the arrows in the subtype symbols, we must always end up with one father.

Subtype families are always cycle-free, which means that when we follow the subtype symbols in the direction of the arrows, we may never end up at our starting point. The structure of Figure 14.22 is impossible and is consequently not allowed.

On the basis of subtype symbol 1, the objects of type A form a subset of the objects of type B. On the basis of subtype symbol 2, the objects of type B form a subset of the objects of type C. And on the basis of subtype symbol 3, these objects would again form a subset of the objects of type A. The impossibility of this is made evident when we attempt to represent these subsets as we have done in Figure 14.23.

We can then point to an element, say x, in set C which does not belong to set A. If C were to be a subset of A (as subtype symbol 3 suggests), **every** element of C would also have to belong to A.

Because a structure such as the one depicted in Figure 14.24 is likewise impossible, it is also rejected.

The reason why it is impossible is made clear when we again attempt to express this structure in terms of sets, as has been done in Figure 14.25.

On the basis of subtype symbols 1 and 2, the objects of types B and C form subsets of the objects of type A. By virtue of the exclusion symbol, subsets B and

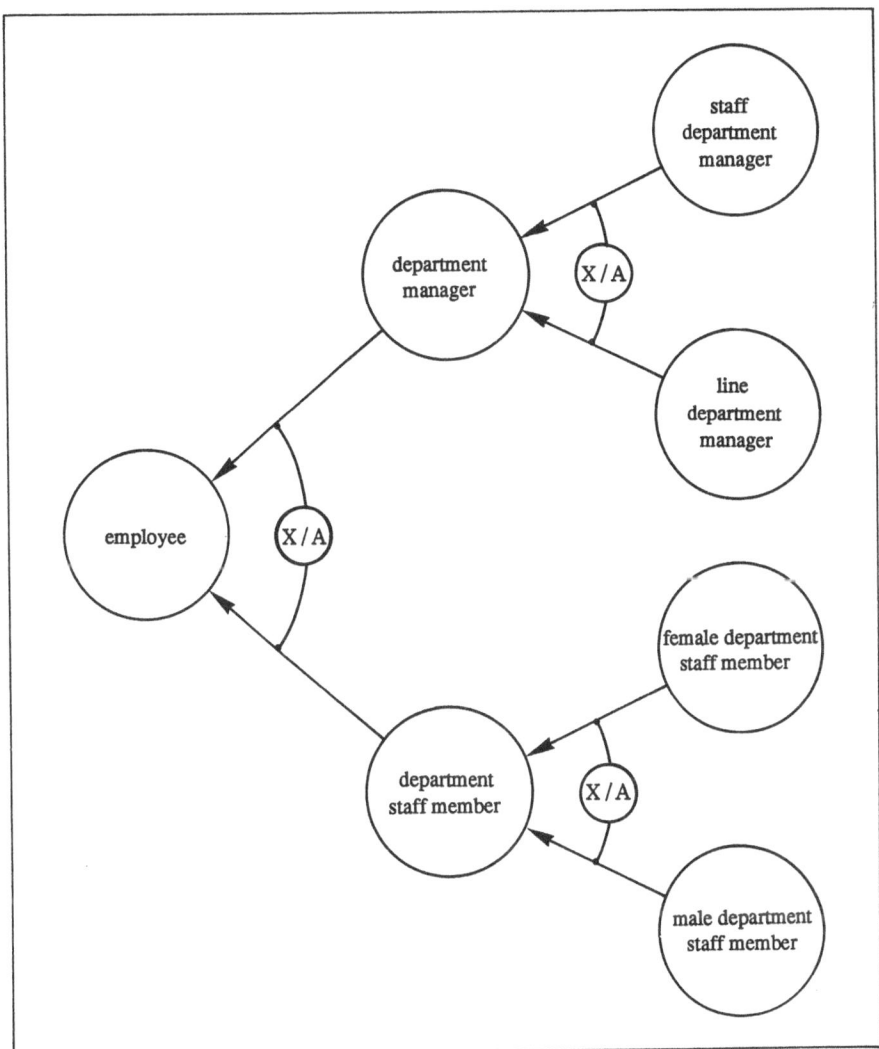

Figure 14.21.

C have no common elements. Because these sets lack common elements, they can of course not have any (non-empty) subsets in common, as subtype symbols 3 and 4 suggest.

We shall not accept a structure such as that depicted in Figure 14.26 in an information structure diagram.

The subtype symbol indicated by an * is redundant. When "department manager" is a subtype of "employee" and "staff department manager" a subtype of "department manager," "staff department manager" is a fortiori a subtype of "employee." The subtype symbol with respect to "employee" and "staff department manager" is therefore implied by the remaining subtype symbols and does

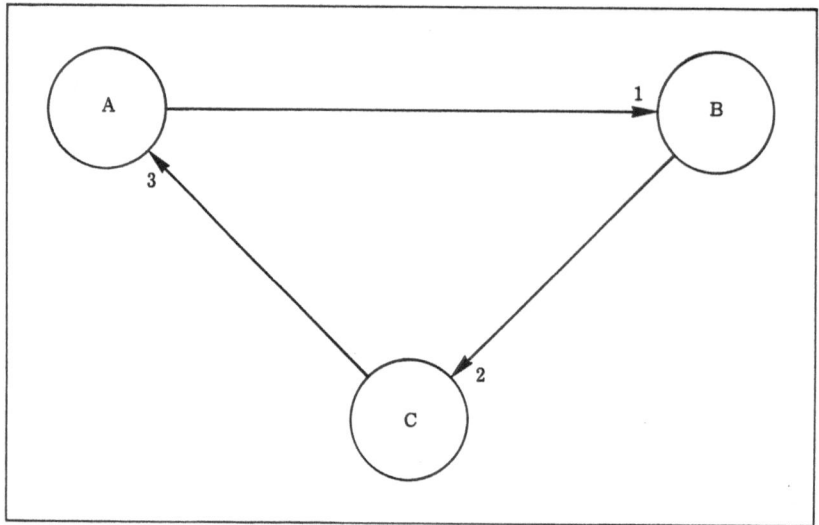

Figure 14.22.

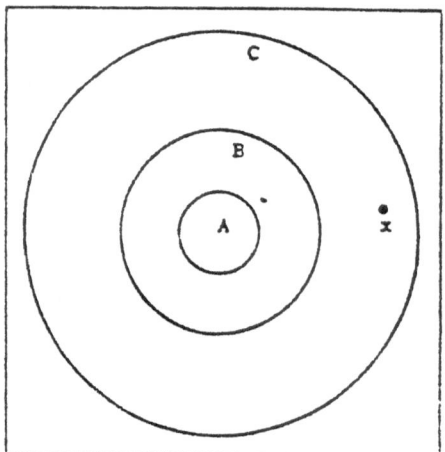

Figure 14.23.

not add any new knowledge to the diagram. We shall not explicitly draw these
kinds of implied, and therefore redundant, subtype symbols.

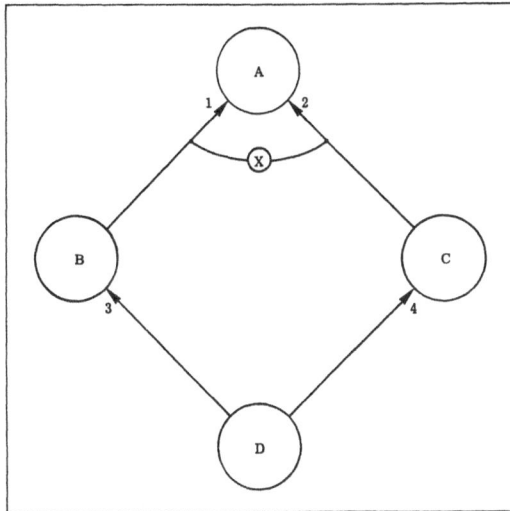

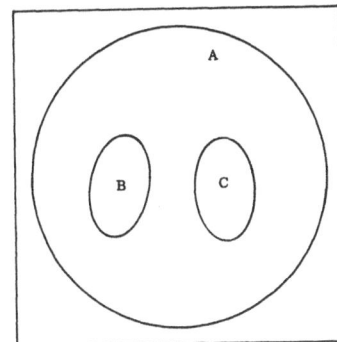

Figure 14.25.

Figure 14.24.

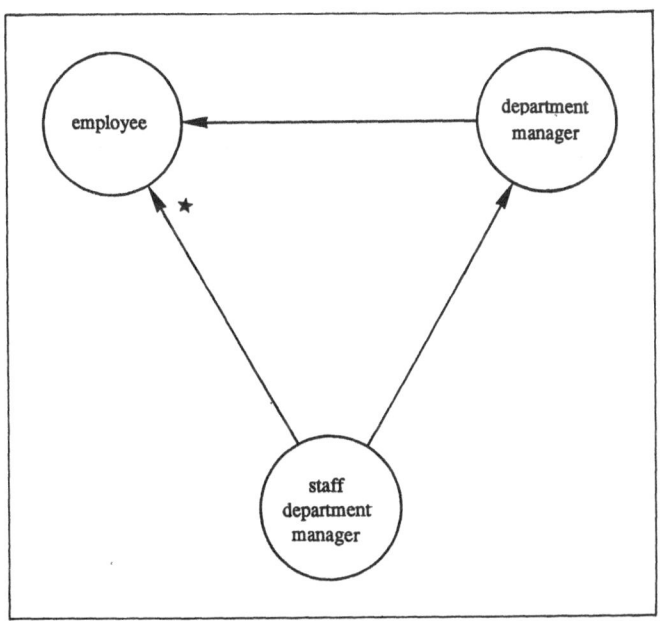

Figure 14.26.

To summarize:

A subtype family:
A hierarchical structure of subtypes.

The father of a subtype family:
An object type that itself has no supertype within the subtype family. A subtype family has only one father. If we follow the subtype symbols in a subtype family in the direction of the arrows, we end up at the father of the subtype family.

The following structures are not allowed:

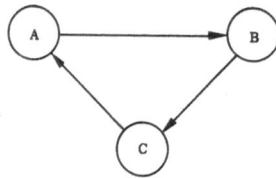

If the objects of type A
form a subset of the objects
of type B and these again form
a subset of the objects of type C,
the objects of type C cannot form
a subset of the objects of type A.

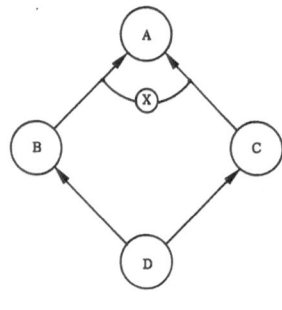

If the objects of types B and C form
exclusive sets, they cannot have any
subsets in common.

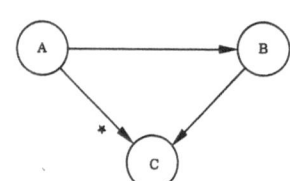

The fact that object type A
is a subtype of object type C
is implied by the fact that
object type A is a subtype
of object type B and that
this object type is again
a subtype of object type C.

Network structures, as the following example illustrates, can occur within subtype families.

From now on, we will call all of the library employees who manage a project "project managers," and all of the employees who work on a project (but who do not manage this project) "project staff members." Hereby, we have defined the subtypes "project manager" and "project staff member."

We agreed earlier that an employee who manages a project can work on **another** project as a project staff member. It follows that the subtypes "project manager" and "project staff member" do not exclude each other.

Because not every employee has to be a project manager or a project staff member, the combination of both subtypes is not total. Figure 14.27 represents a subtype family with the object type "employee" as father. Figure 14.28 contains a combination of Figures 14.19 and 14.27.

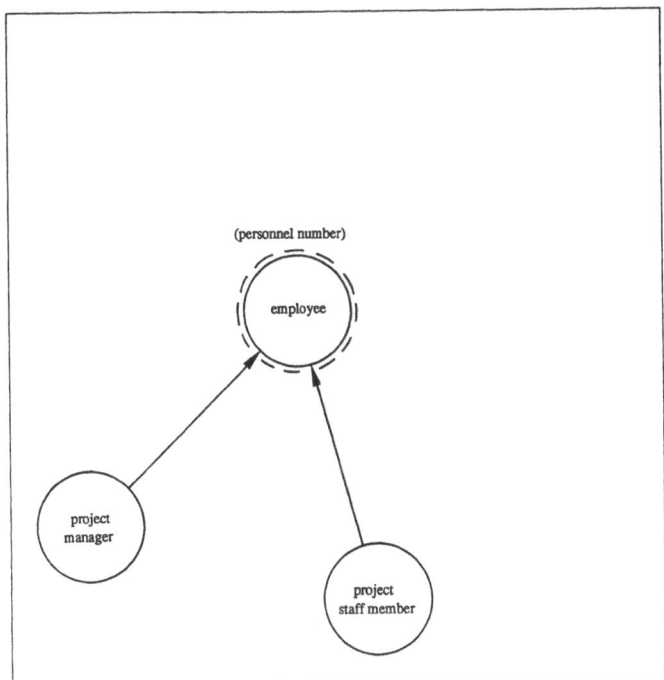

Figure 14.27.

This diagram contains a combination of two subtype families. Together these two subtype families form a larger family with "employee" as father and containing the object types "department manager," "department staff member," "project manager," and "project staff member."

Let us now call those employees who are at a given moment both department managers and project managers "department managers with project responsibility." In this way, we have introduced the object type "department manager with project responsibility."

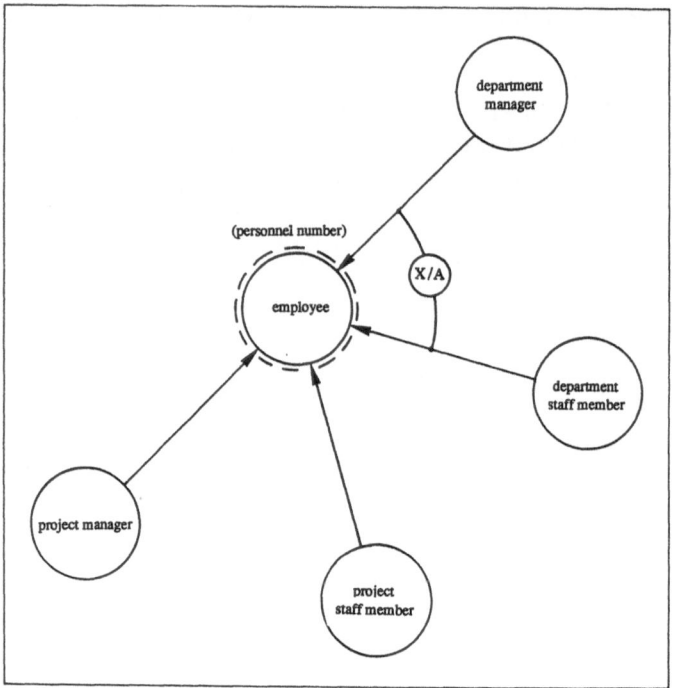

Figure 14.28.

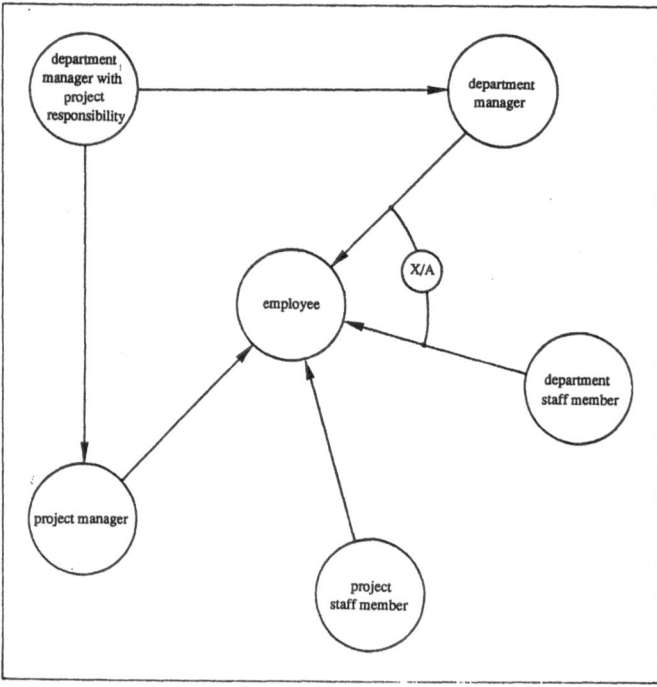

Figure 14.29.

The objects of the type "department manager with project responsibility" belong to both the object type "department manager" and the object type "project manager." The object type "department manager with project responsibility" is therefore a subtype of both "department manager" and "project manager."

14.5 Introducing subtypes into an information structure diagram

We have repeated in Figure 14.30 part of the information structure diagram that was created in the previous chapters.

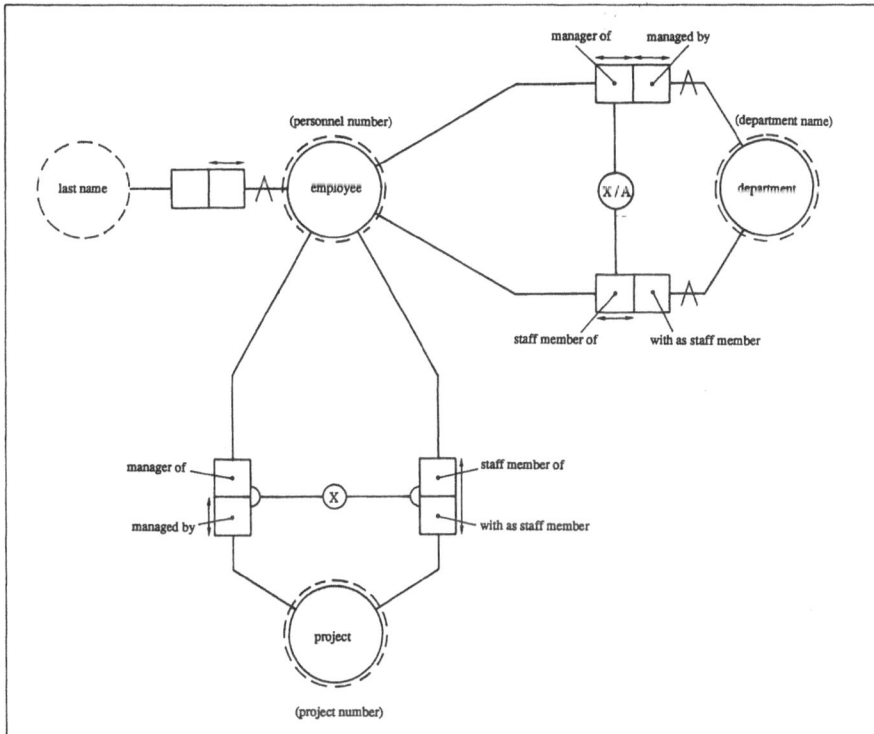

Figure 14.30.

In the preceding section, we defined the subtypes "department manager," "department staff member," "project manager," and "project staff member." Introducing these subtypes to the diagram of Figure 14.30 results in Figure 14.31.

Let us compare these two figures. Only department managers can be put in charge of managing a department. Consequently, the role "employee manager of department" in Figure 14.31 has been assigned to the object type "department manager." Because only department staff members work for a department in the

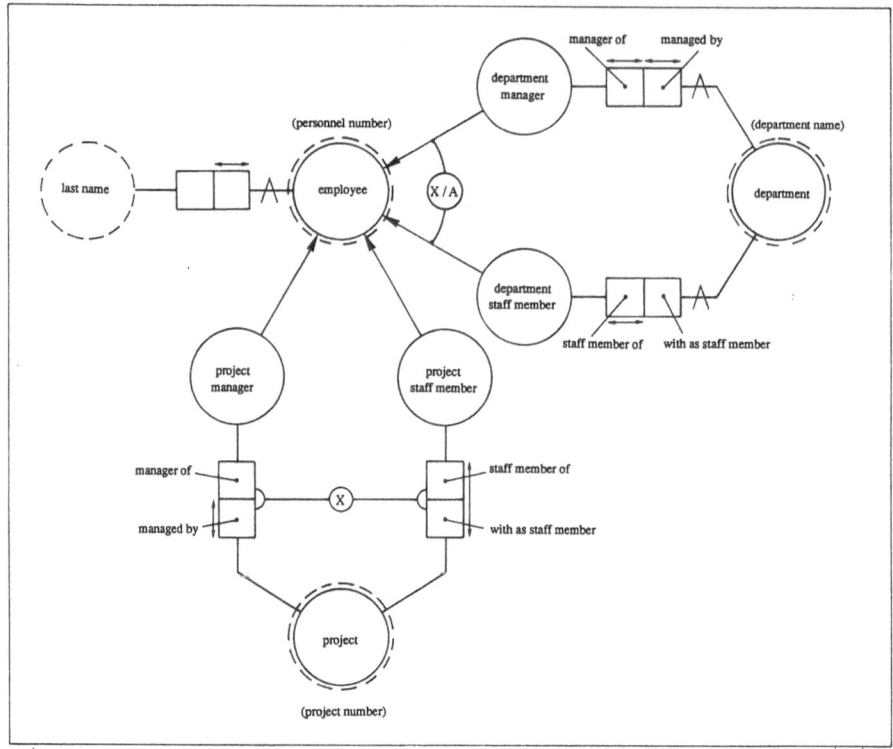

Figure 14.31.

sense in which we have defined it, the role "employee staff member of department" is assigned to the object type "department staff member." Because these two subtypes exclude each other and their combination is total, the exclusion and totality symbol involving the *roles* "employee manager of department" and "employee staff member of department" have been made redundant. As these constraints are now implied by the exclusion and totality constraint involving the two subtypes, they are omitted in the diagram of Figure 14.31. It is sometimes also said less formally that we have "replaced" the exclusion and totality constraint involving the **roles** "employee manager of department" and "employee staff member of department" by an exclusion and totality constraint involving the **object types** "department manager" and "department staff member."

Projects are only managed by project managers. Consequently, the role "employee manager of project" has now been assigned to the object type "project manager." In the sense in which we have defined it, only project staff members work on a project. Consequently, the role "employee staff member of project" has now been assigned to the object type "project staff member."

It still holds that an employee who is a project manager of a project can also be a project staff member of another project, but **never of the same project**. The exclusion constraint involving the combinations of the roles "employee manager of project" and "project managed by employee" on the one hand, and "employee staff member of project" and "project with as staff member employee" on the other hand, stays in force even though the subtypes "project manager" and "project staff member" have been introduced. We can conclude from this that when subtypes are introduced into an information structure diagram:

– totality constraints involving combinations of roles can be "replaced" by totality constraints with respect to subtypes.
– exclusion constraints involving *individual* roles can be "replaced" by totality constraints with respect to subtypes.
– exclusion constraints involving **combinations** of roles cannot be "replaced" by exclusion constraints with respect to subtypes.

As was stated earlier, all of the roles of a supertype also involve all of its subtypes. Therefore, all of the roles involving the object type "employee" also involve the subtypes "department manager," "department staff member," "project manager," and "project staff member." After all, all of the features of the employees are also valid for department managers, department staff members, project managers, and project staff members. So, department managers, department staff members, project managers, and project staff members each have a personnel number and a last name. The reverse is not automatically true. The roles involving a subtype do not automatically involve all of the objects of its supertype. For example, not all of the employees may manage a department; only department managers manage departments.

The diagram in Figure 14.31, with subtypes, is more explicit than the diagram in Figure 14.30, without subtypes. After all, the knowledge which is perhaps implicitly assumed in the diagram without subtypes is explicitly depicted in the diagram with subtypes. Introducing subtypes can lead to a greater in-depth analysis of information. We can then check whether there are any other fact types which exclusively involve a certain subtype, something which might not have occurred to us in a diagram without subtypes.

We have repeated in Figure 14.32 part of the information structure diagram that was created in Chapter 10.

Departments can manage and advise other departments. A department can be controlled by only one department, can advise only one department, and can be advised by only one department. A department which advises another department cannot at the same time be controlled by or manage another department. A department that is advised by a department cannot at the same time advise another department.

In the above diagram and the description of it, it is stated implicitly ("hidden behind the lines") that there are two kinds of departments: line departments, which manage each other and report to each other according to a line organization, and staff departments, which advise line departments. The organizational chart of Figure 3.1 has already expressed the fact that there are two kinds of departments. The line departments in this figure are connected by vertical lines and the

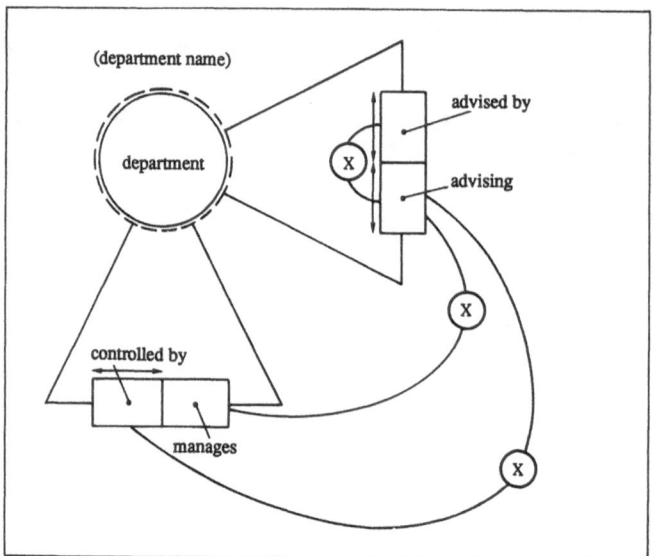

Figure 14.32.

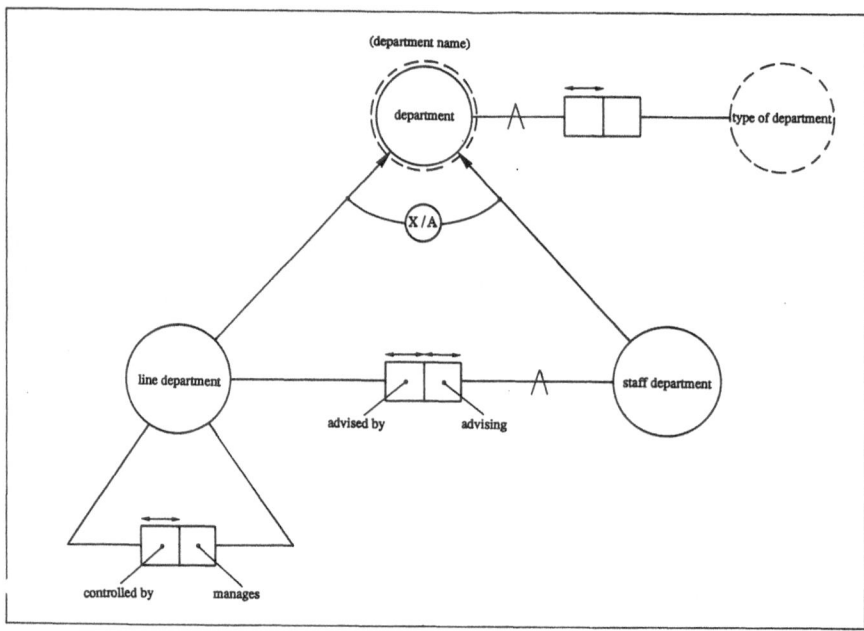

Figure 14.33.

staff departments are connected by horizontal lines to line departments. When we make the distinction between these two types of departments explicit by dividing the object type "department" into the subtypes "line department" and "staff department," the information structure diagram of Figure 14.33 results.

We have now explicitly represented the fact that **every** department is either a line department or a staff department (both type of departments exclude each other and their combination is total), and that **every** staff department must advise a line department (the role "staff department advising line department" is total). In the diagram without subtypes, we would not be able to represent the latter constraint explicitly. Consequently, the diagram with subtypes (Figure 14.33) is more explicit than the one without subtypes (Figure 14.32). All of the exclusion constraints in the diagram of Figure 14.32 have now been replaced by one exclusion constraint involving the subtypes "line department" and "staff department."

In order to be able to distinguish between line and staff departments, we have added the lexical object type "type of department" to the information structure diagram. The type of department indicates whether a certain department is a line department or a staff department.

The subtypes introduced in this chapter have been included in the information structure diagram of Figure 14.34.

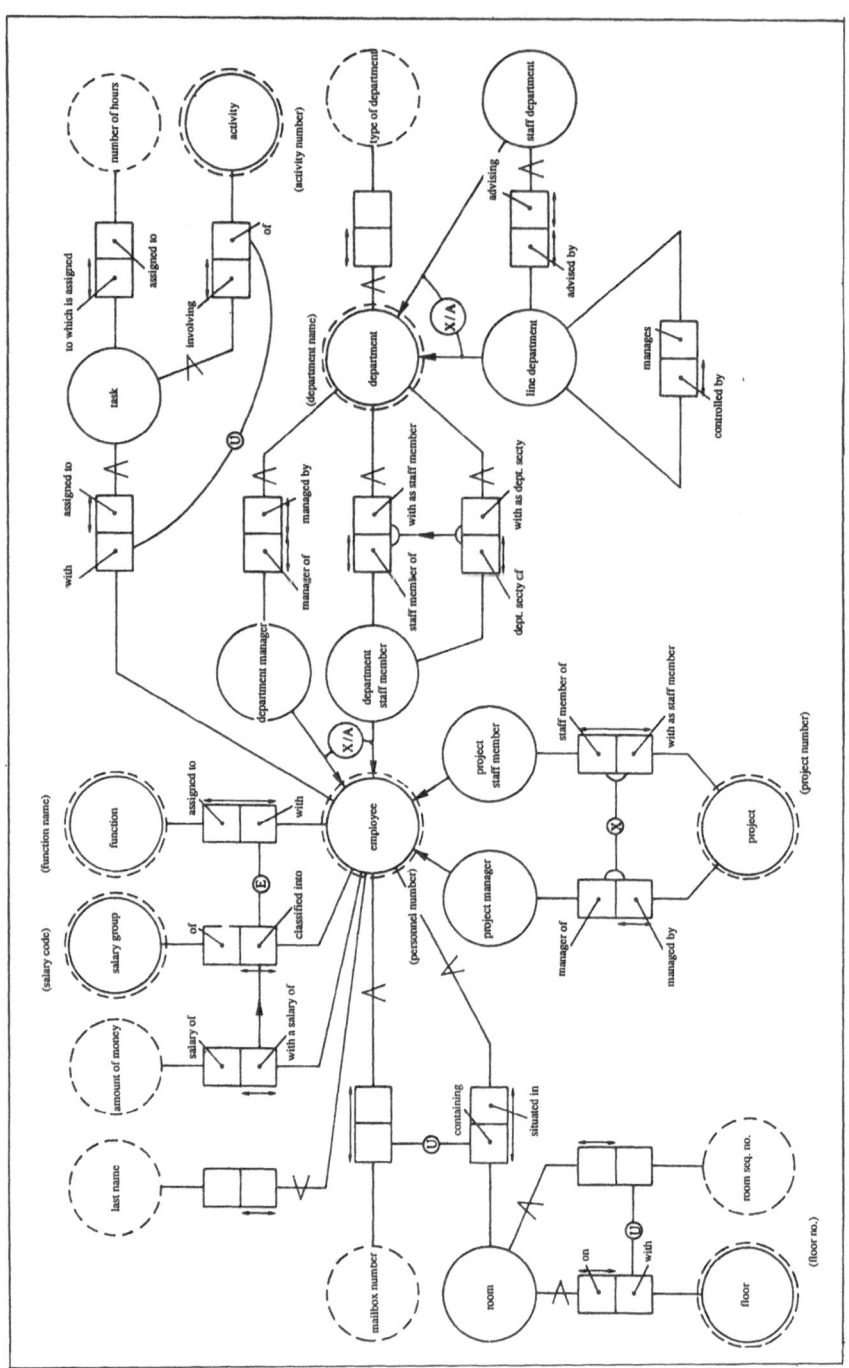

Figure 14.34.

15 THE NIAM METHOD OF INFORMATION ANALYSIS IN PRACTICE - 5

In this chapter, we shall add the treatment of subtypes to the stepwise plan of the NIAM method of information analysis. To this end, we will further expand the information structure diagram of the library case which we constructed in the foregoing practical chapters.

A portion of this information structure diagram is depicted in Figure 15.1.

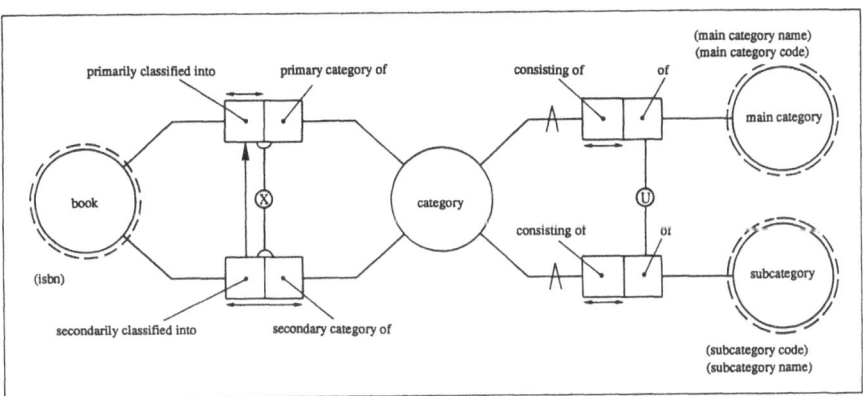

Figure 15.1.

We saw in Chapter 11 that some books are classified according to a system which provides information about the subjects dealt with in a book. A book can be classified into a primary category and one or more secondary categories.

We shall now assume that this is only true for textbooks. Further, we will assume that every textbook **must** be classified into a primary category and that some textbooks **may** be classified into one or more secondary categories.

Therefore, within the set of all books about which something is known in the information base, we can denote a subset whose objects **must** occur in the population of the role "book primarily classified into category" and which **may** occur in the population of the role "book secondarily classified into category". This subset is formed by all textbooks. The books which are not textbooks may not occur in the populations of these roles.

This knowledge has not yet been explicitly represented as such in the information structure diagram. We can represent this knowledge explicitly by defining a subtype "textbook," of the object type "book" consisting of all textbooks. The roles "book primarily classified into category" and "book secondarily classified into category" then exclusively involve this subtype. We have carried this out in Figure 15.2.

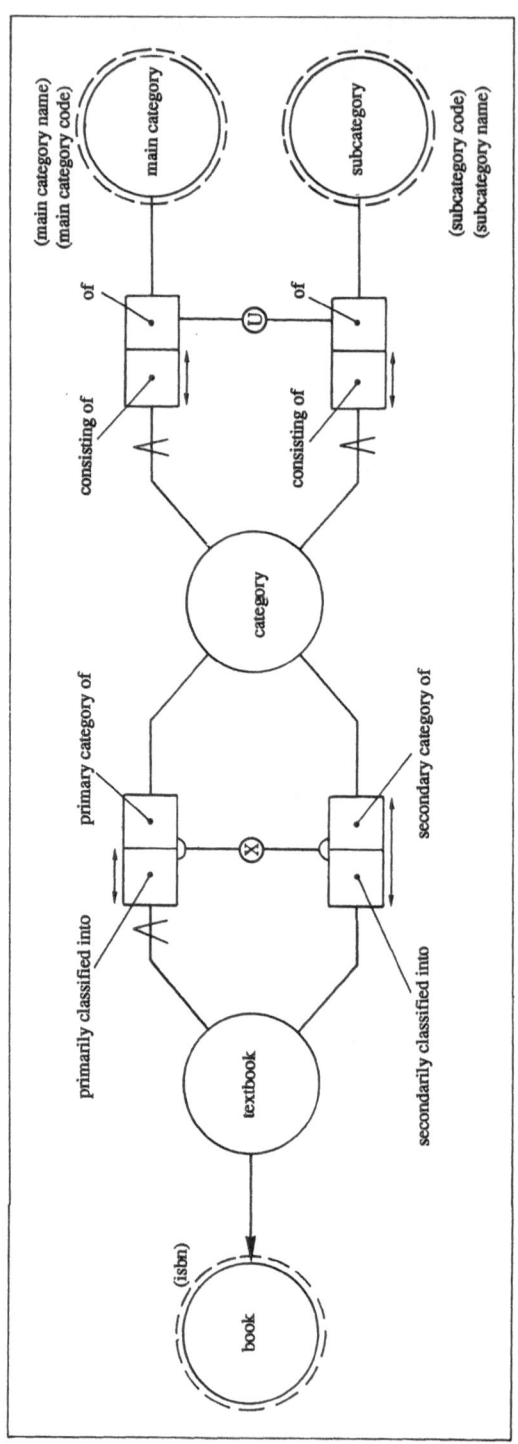

Figure 15.2.

The role "textbook primarily classified into category" is total because, as was stated above, a primary category must be known for each textbook. However, as a secondary category does not have to be known for every textbook, the role "textbook secondarily classified into category" is not total. The diagram as it now stands shows that only the textbooks are classified into categories. Depending on the kind, it can be determined unambiguously whether any book is a textbook.

The definition of the subtypes takes place in step 8 of the NIAM method of information analysis:

8. Where necessary, define subtypes.

This step consists of the following substeps:

8.1 Where necessary, define subtypes.
8.2 Adapt the information structure diagram such that the roles which exclusively involve a subtype, are connected to the subtype rather than to the supertype.
8.3 Determine the uniqueness and totality of the individual roles of the subtypes.

In the above example, substep 8.1 leads to the definition of the subtype "textbook." Substep 8.2 leads to the fact that the roles "book primarily classified into category" and "book secondarily classified into category," are now related solely to this subtype, while substep 8.3 leads to the totality constraint involving the role "textbook primarily classified into category." Of course, the original uniqueness constraints with respect to the roles "book primarily classified into category" and "book secondarily classified into category" continue to remain valid after the subtypes are introduced.

The formulation of substep 8.1 is still too general. To begin with, we will show two more examples of subtypes and then refine the formulation of substep 8.1 on the basis of these examples.

The next example involving subtypes concerns the contents of the information flow "membership data," containing information about the library members. (See Figure 3.5.) This data is recorded on "membership cards." We shall use the membership cards to exemplify the information contents of the information flow "membership data."

There is a membership card for every member of the library. The membership number, the name (including first initials), the address, and the age of the member are listed on the membership card. For junior members, a reference to the type of education this member is undergoing is included, for the purposes of collecting statistical data. Lastly, the card indicates whether the member paid the subscription fee for the current year. Only adult members have to pay a subscription fee. Members up to the age of 18 are considered junior members, while those older than 19 are considered adult members.

The type of education is listed on the membership card by means of an "education code." A "fee indicator" indicates whether or not a member has paid the subscription fee for the current year.

MEMBERSHIP CARD

MEMBERSHIP NUMBER:

NAME:

NUMBER & STREET:

CITY/TOWN:

AGE:

EDUCATION:

FEE PAID:

Figure 15.3.

The rules concerning the information listed on the membership card are described by the portion of the information structure diagram which is represented in Figure 15.4.

The education code is only recorded for junior members. Therefore, only junior members can occur in the population of the role "member with education code." Because only adult members have to pay a subscription fee, only the adult members occur in the population of the role "member with fee indicator." The roles "member with education code" and "member with fee indicator" therefore exclude each other.

It follows from this that within the set of all library members, two subsets exclusively involving respectively the roles "member with education code" and "member with fee indicator" can be denoted. All junior members belong to the former set and all adult members to the latter. It can unambiguously be determined on the basis of the age whether someone is a junior or an adult member. The knowledge concerning junior and adult members can be expressed more explicitly by introducing the subtypes "junior member" and "adult member" in the diagram of Figure 15.4, as has been done in Figure 15.5.

Every member is **either** a junior member **or** an adult member. Consequently, the subtypes "junior member" and "adult member" exclude each other and their combination is total.

To summarize, we can state that:

- The junior members and the adult members form two subsets of the object type "member."
- It can be determined unambiguously on the basis of the age whether a certain member is a junior or an adult member.

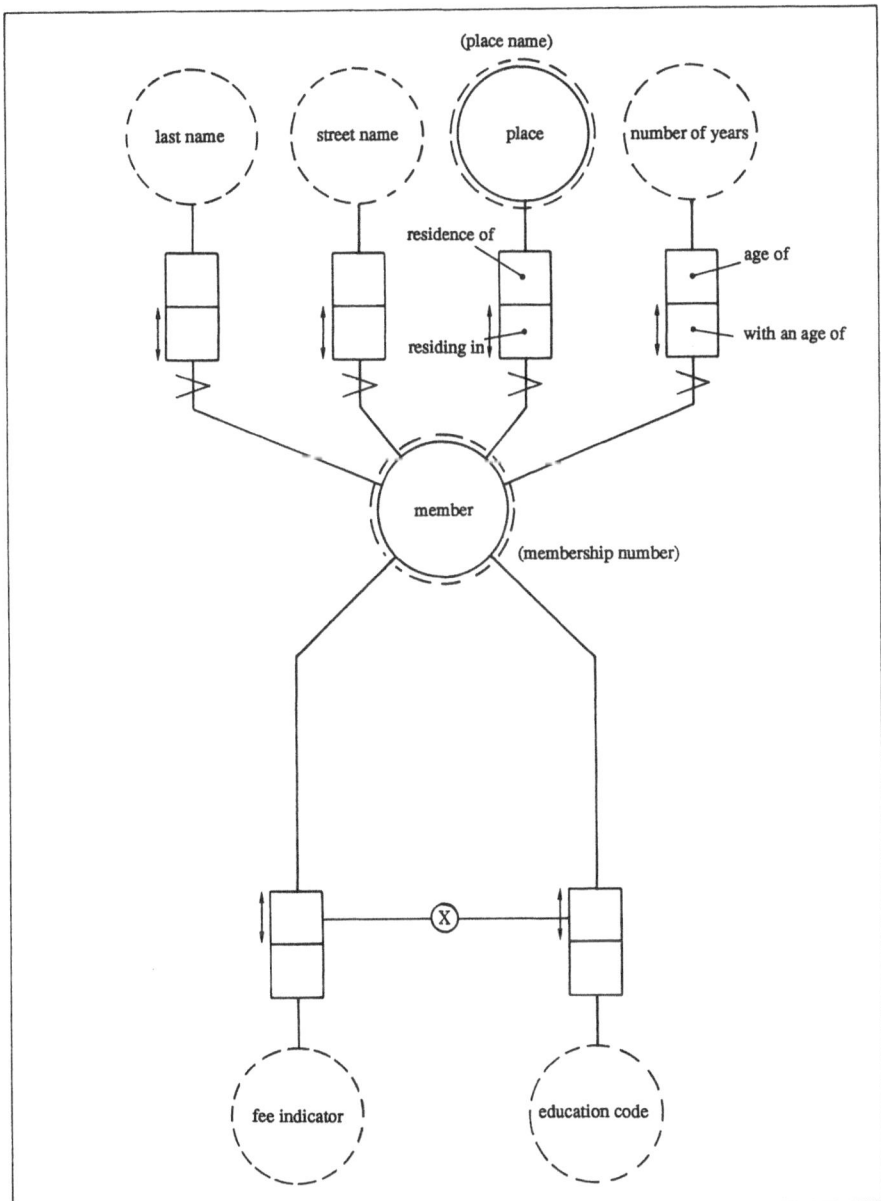

Figure 15.4.

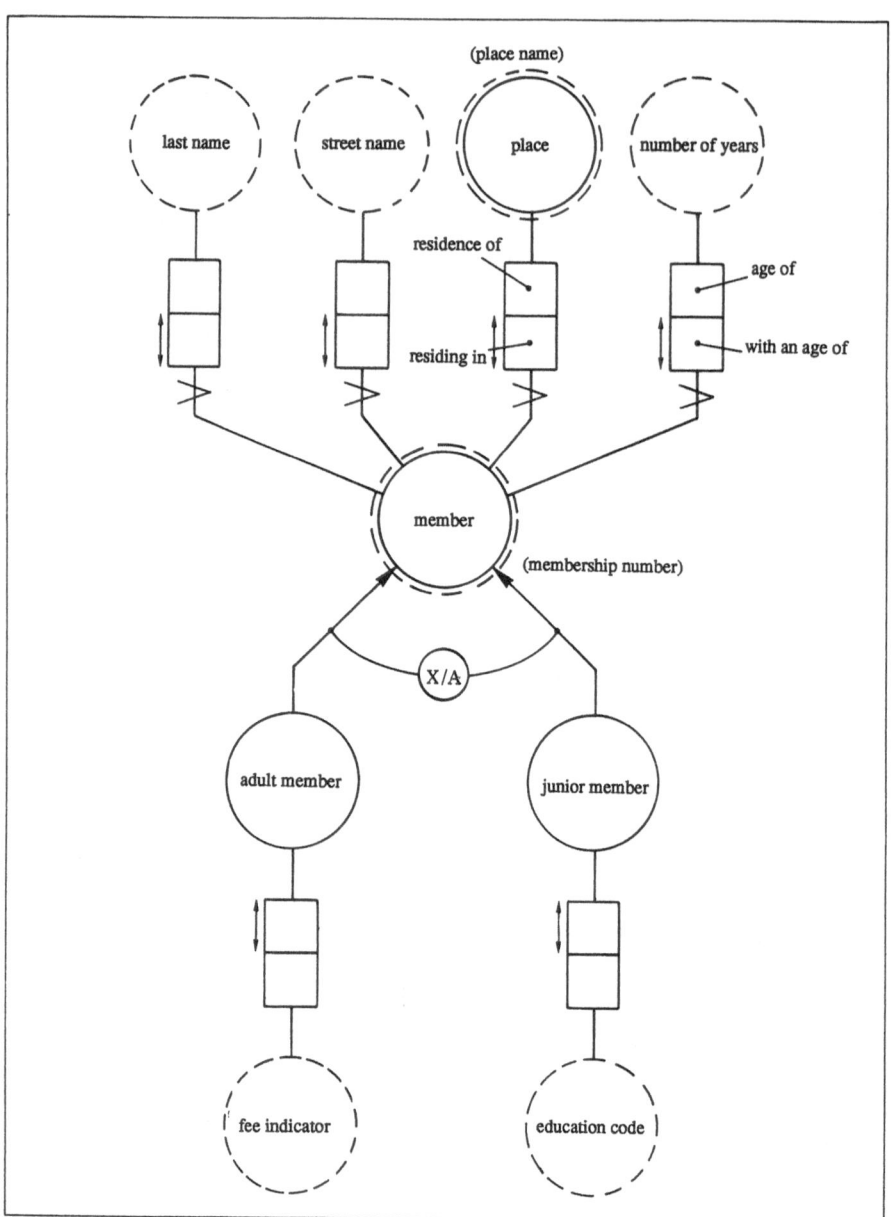

Figure 15.5.

– The role "member with education code" involves only junior members, and the role "member with fee indicator" involves only adult members.

Furthermore, "junior member" and "adult member" appear to be normal concepts commonly in use in the library.

The following and last example of subtypes involves the reservations of books. In Figure 15.6, we have repeated the part of the information structure diagram of the library case involving reservations.

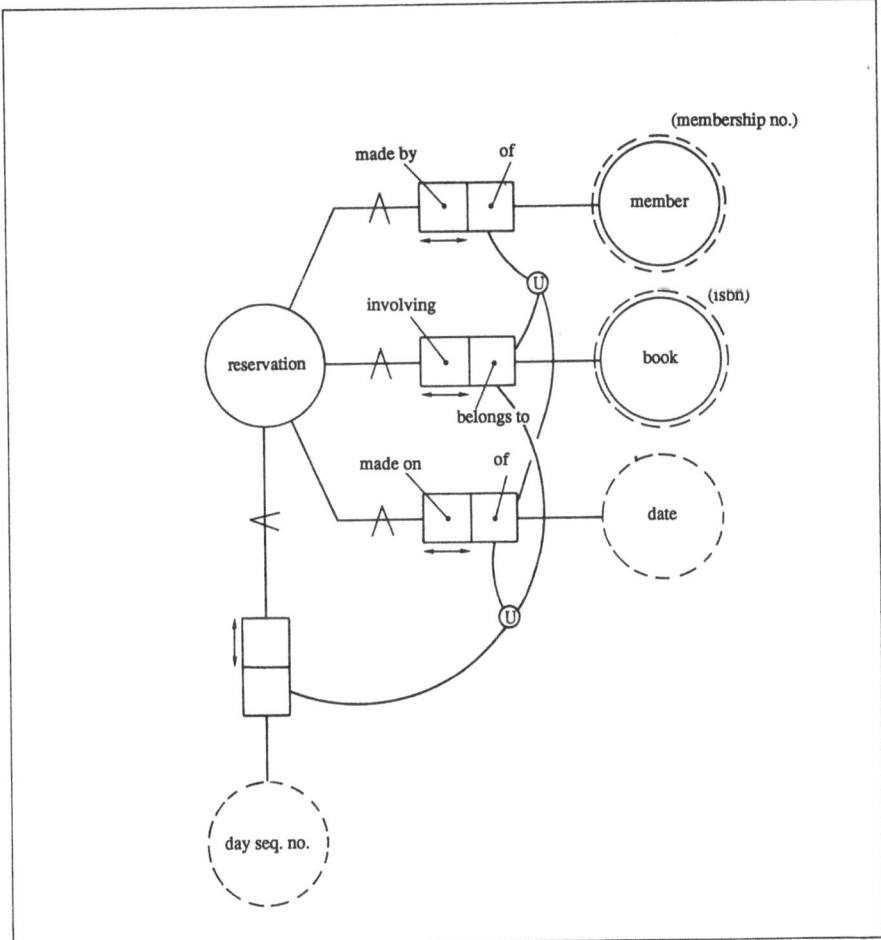

Figure 15.6.

In dealing with reservations in Chapter 13, we saw that when a copy of a reserved book is returned, it is kept for one week for the member who first reserved the book. If this member does not show up within this period to borrow the copy, the reservation lapses and the copy can again be loaned out to someone else.

Therefore, it is assumed in the library that a reservation always expires one week after a copy of the reserved book has been returned, regardless of whether or not the copy has in the meantime been loaned out to the member who first reserved the book.

It is stated in the library regulations that there may never be more than two nonexpired reservations at a time for any one member, and that the loan of a copy of a reserved book may never be renewed unless this reservation has lapsed. These regulations create constraints which restrict the number of nonexpired reservations and loan renewals allowed per member. In Chapter 17, we shall see that in order to express this and other constraints, we will need the object types "expired reservation" and "nonexpired reservation." The expired and nonexpired reservations form two subsets of all of the reservations recorded in the information base. Whether or not a particular reservation has expired on a particular date can be determined unambiguously by comparing the return dates of the borrowed copies of the reserved book with this date. Every reservation is either an expired reservation or a nonexpired reservation. The concepts "expired reservation" and "nonexpired reservation" are in common use in the library.

To summarize:

- The expired and nonexpired reservations are subsets of the objects of the type "reservation."
- By comparing the return dates of borrowed copies of a reserved book with the date on which the reservation is considered, it can be determined whether or not a reservation has expired.
- There are constraints (such as those mentioned above) which involve expired or nonexpired reservations only.
- The concepts "expired reservation" and "nonexpired reservation" are normal terms used daily by the library employees (the future users of the information system).

Based on the above considerations, we have introduced in Figure 15.7 the subtypes "expired reservation" and "nonexpired reservation" to the information structure diagram.

Every reservation is **either** an expired reservation **or** a nonexpired reservation. Consequently, the subtypes "expired reservation" and "nonexpired reservation" exclude each other and their combination is total.

Whether or not a reservation has expired depends on the date on which the reservation is being considered. A certain reservation can belong at a certain period in time to the subtype "nonexpired reservation" and at another period in time (namely one week after a copy of the reserved book has been returned) to the subtype "expired reservation." Subtypes such as these, in which the population is determined by a time period, occur fairly often in practice. Yet there are no fact types which directly involve the subtypes "expired reservation" and "nonexpired reservation," even though these subtypes can explicitly express certain knowledge about the library, namely the fact that the reservations can be classified into

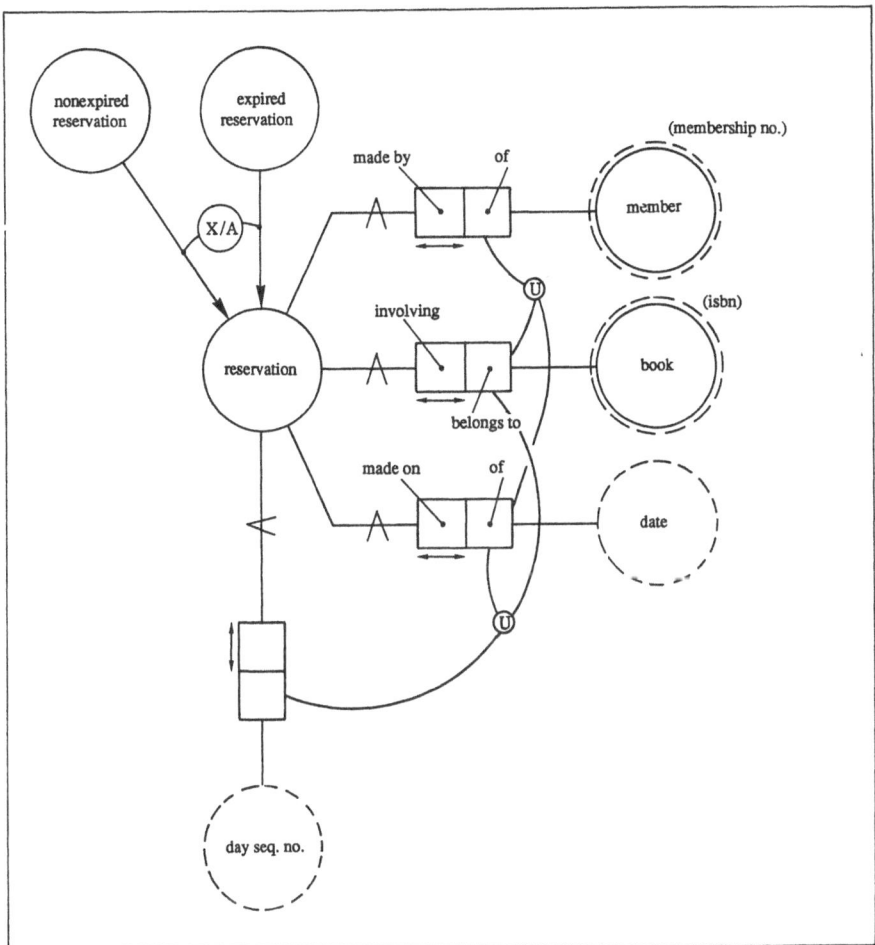

Figure 15.7.

expired or nonexpired reservations and the fact that there are constraints involving expired or nonexpired reservations only.

When should one introduce subtypes and just how far should one go in introducing them? An analysis of the above two examples provides an answer to these questions. In each of these examples it holds that:

- In the object type under consideration, we can denote one or more subsets of objects exclusively involving one or more roles and/or one or more constraints.
- On the basis of one or more facts which involve the objects of the object type under consideration, we can unambiguously determine to which of these subsets a certain object belongs.
- These subsets involve normal concepts commonly in use among the future users of the information system.

In the above examples, we have defined subtypes which correspond to each of the subsets mentioned above.

On the basis of this, we shall refine substep 8.1 into:

8.1 For every object type check whether:

– A subset of objects involving exclusively one or more roles and/or one or more constraints can be denoted in this object type.
– It can be unambiguously determined on the basis of one or more facts involving objects of the object type under consideration, whether or not an object of this object type belongs to this subset.
– This subset concerns a concept that occurs in the (professional) language of the future users of the information system.

When this is the case, define a subtype that corresponds to this subset.

(Note that these are practical rather than formal rules.)

In the diagram of Figure 15.4, the roles "member with education code" and "member with fee indicator" exclude each other. Therefore, in the set of all library members, we can denote two subsets exclusively involving each of these roles. This factor has somewhat influenced the definition of the subtypes "junior member" and "adult member." Constraints involving **individual** roles can therefore lead to the definition of subtypes. Still, as the following example shows, this does not necessarily have to be the case (see Figure 15.8).

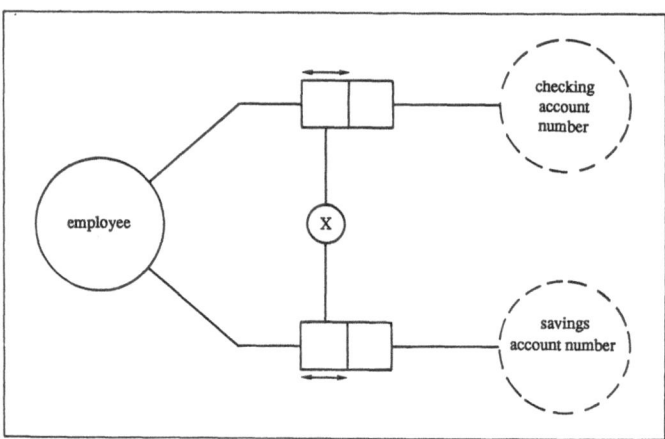

Figure 15.8.

So that salary records can be maintained, the number of a checking account or savings account must be known for every employee. Although an employee may have more than one checking and/or savings account, only one account number, either a checking account number or a savings account number, is recorded for every employee in the information base. Consequently, the roles "employee with checking account number" and "employee with savings account number" exclude each other. In the set of all employees, we can denote two subsets of employees. In these sets, either a checking account number or a savings account number is known in the information base. Even so, it would not be meaningful in this case to introduce the subtypes "employee with checking account number" and "employee with savings account number" because they do not occur in the everyday language of the future users of the information system and are thus not

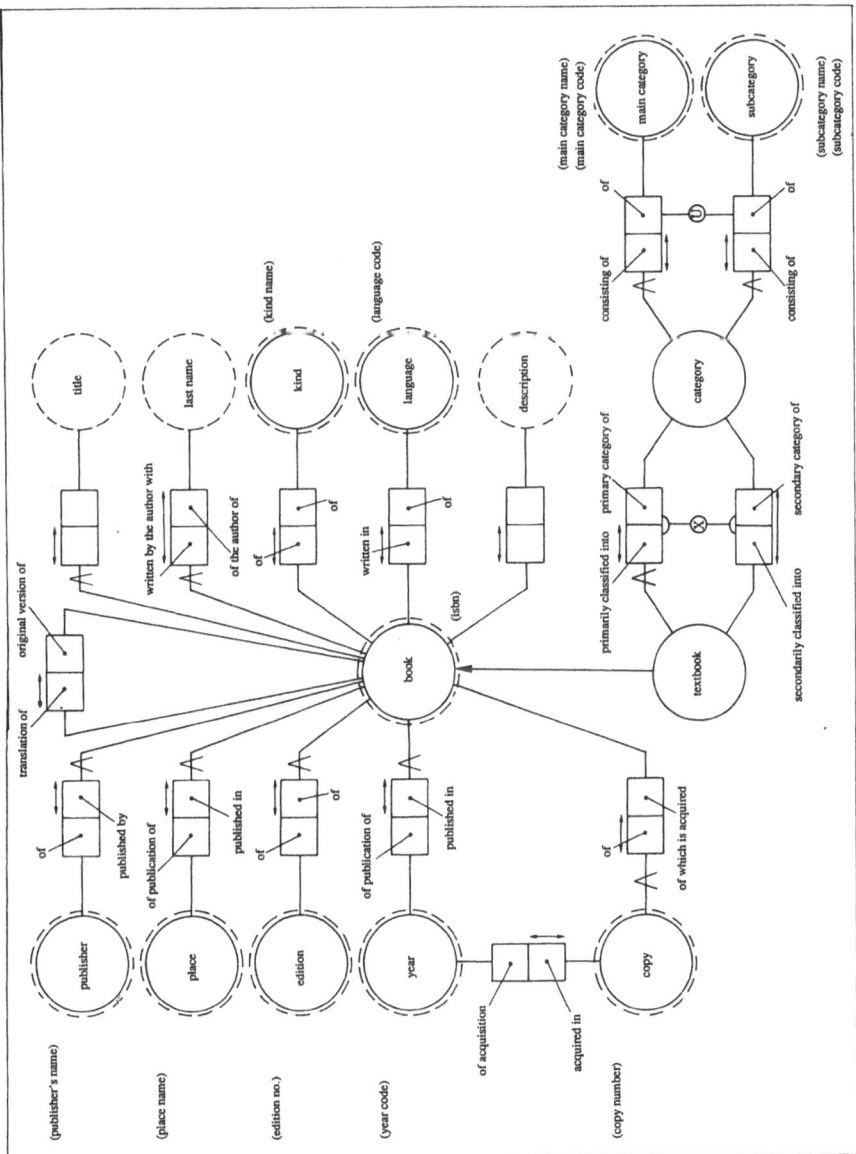

Figure 15.9.

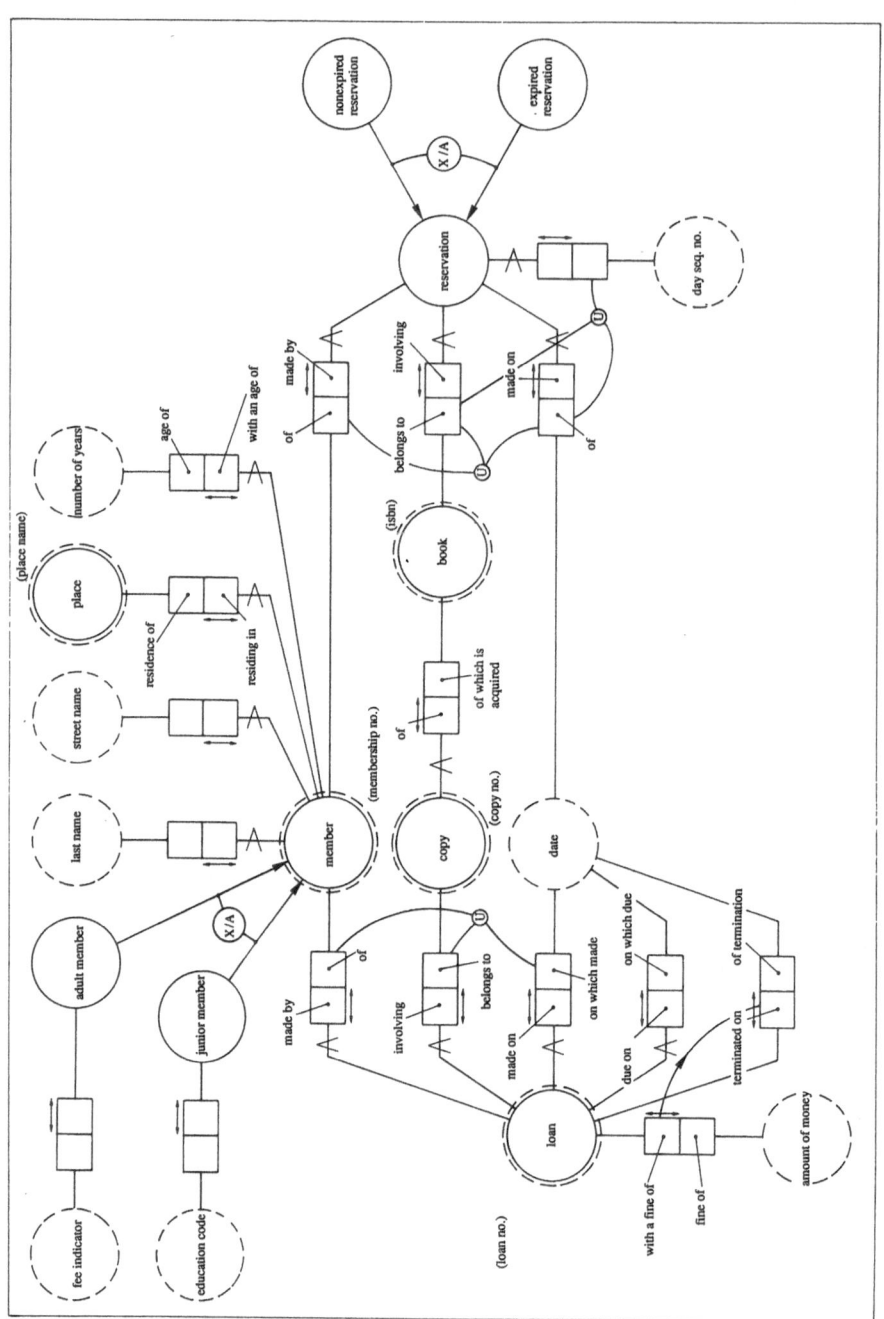

Figure 15.10.

"viable" concepts for these users. Bear in mind that the grammar is not a description of the rules which are valid within **reality**, but of the rules which are valid for the **communication** about this reality via the information system.

Moreover, constraints involving **combinations** of roles never lead directly to subtype definitions. The fact that in the diagram of Figure 14.34 employees can be project managers and project staff members of different projects, is in itself no reason to define the subtypes "project manager" and "project staff member." In the set of all employees, there is not a set exclusively involving the role "employee project manager of project" or "employee project staff member of project," and there are no constraints exclusively involving the project managers or project staff members. Consequently, although introducing these subtypes is not incorrect, it is in this case hardly meaningful in practice. Introducing these subtypes adds no additional knowledge to the original diagram (Figure 12.40).

Summary

Below is a summary of the steps in the NIAM method of information analysis dealt with in this chapter.

8. Where necessary, define subtypes.

8.1 For every object type, check whether:

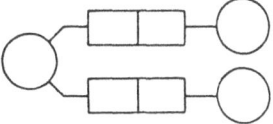

– A subset of objects involving exclusively one or more roles and/or one or more constraints can be denoted in this object type.

– It can be unambiguously determined on the basis of one or more facts involving objects of the object type under consideration, whether or not an object of this object type belongs to this subset.

– This subset concerns a concept that occurs in the (professional) language of the future users of the information system.

When this is the case, define a subtype that corresponds to this subset.

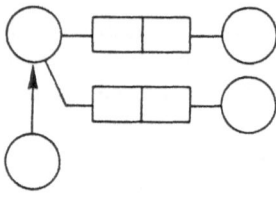

8.2 Adapt the information structure diagram such that the roles which exclusively involve a subtype, are connected to the subtype rather than to the supertype.

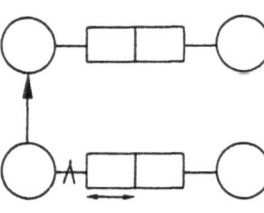

8.3 Determine the uniqueness and totality of the individual roles of the subtypes.

16 NON-GRAPHICAL CONSTRAINTS

Up to now, we have only considered constraints which can be represented in the information structure diagram by means of graphical symbols. We have called these "graphical constraints." In this chapter, we shall consider constraints for which no graphical symbols exist and which consequently cannot be represented in the information structure diagram: **non-graphical** constraints. These have to be described separately apart from the information structure diagram. Together, the specification of the non-graphical constraints and the information structure diagram (which includes the graphical constraints) form a description of the grammar of the information system.

A fairly common misconception is that the grammar is described well enough by the information structure diagram, and that drawing this diagram alone is sufficient during information analysis. However, in the process of information analysis, the non-graphical constraints have to be analyzed as well and described along with the information structure diagram (including the graphical constraints). To accomplish this, we use the information structure diagram as a starting point.

We have remarked earlier that constraints restrict the allowable populations of the object-type roles described in the information structure diagram, and therefore always involve **roles**. Roles can be referred to by the expressions we dealt with in Section 5.12 (the references to role populations). The specifications of non-graphical constraints consist of these types of expressions, to which one or more conditions restricting the populations of these roles are added. On the one hand, the natural language principle makes it possible for everyone to read the resulting expressions, and on the other hand, they constitute descriptions of the non-graphical constraints which are exact enough for the scope of information analysis.

The non-graphical constraints can be classified into a number of types. In the following section, we shall draw a few examples from the library case to demonstrate each of these types. In many cases it will be sufficient merely to quote these examples. The description of non-graphical constraints is so natural in most cases that it is not necessary to formulate rules and guidelines. On the basis of a few examples of the most frequently occurring types of non-graphical constraints, the reader will, in general, be capable of specifying non-graphical constraints in practice.

The constraints dealt with in the following sections are related to the part of the information structure diagram that is depicted in Figure 16.1.

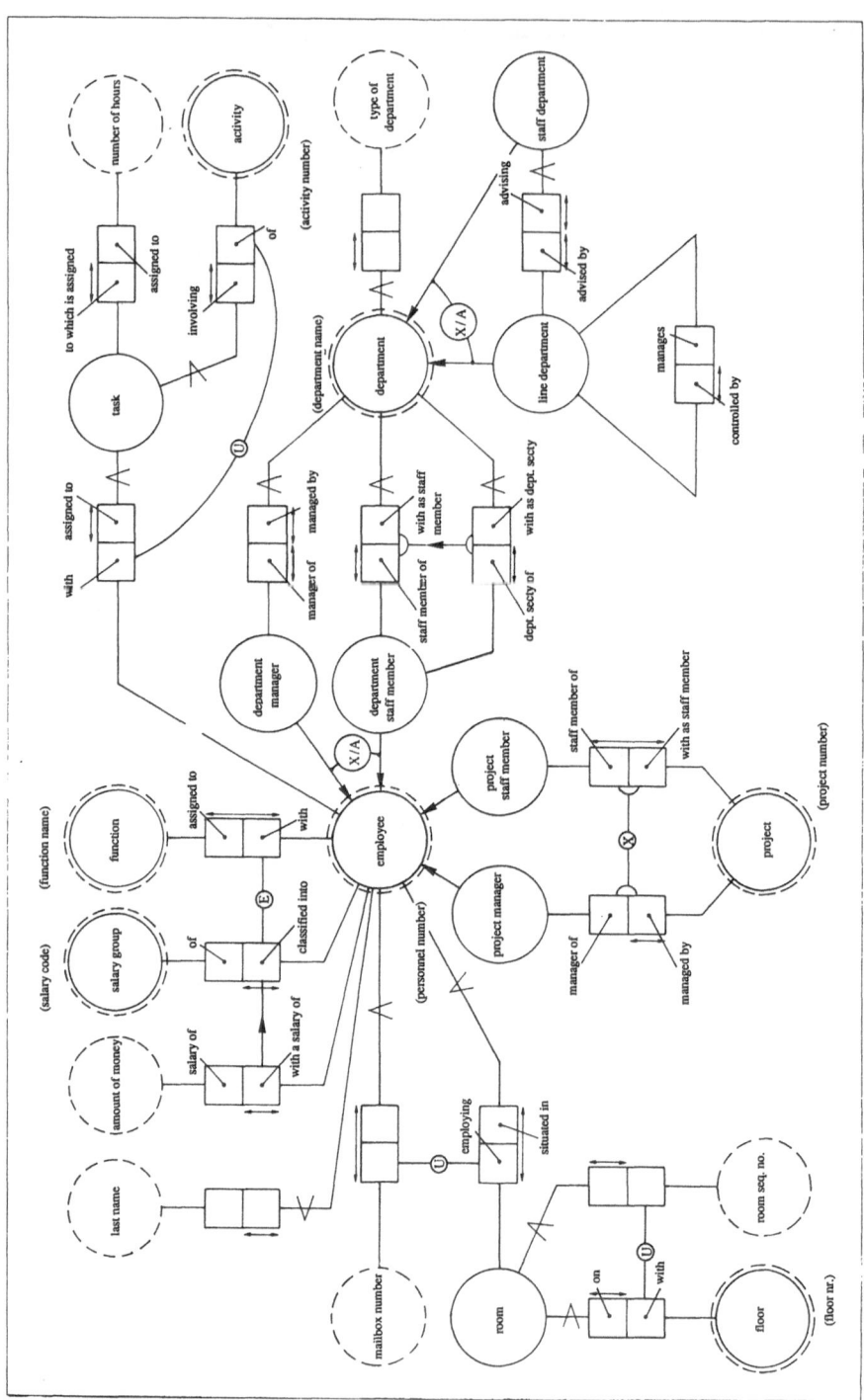

Figure 16.1.

16.1 Value constraints

Value constraints are non-graphical constraints which prescribe which lexical objects may occur in the populations of certain roles of lexical object types.

We shall illustrate this by an example.

In the library, the (annual) salary of an employee may not exceed 75,000 (dollars). Of course, no salary can be less than zero. This constraint forms a restriction on the lexical objects of the type "amount of money" which may occur in the populations of the role "amount of money salary of employee," and is consequently a value constraint. This value constraint is described as follows:

for every amount of money a :
a **salary of employee** $\geqslant$ 0
and
a **salary of employee** $\leqslant$ 75,000.

This can be read as follows:

For every object of the type "amount of money," say a, it holds that in the role of an employee's salary, this amount must be greater than or equal to 0 and always smaller than or equal to 75,000. The expression "a salary of employee" refers to a lexical object a in the role of an employee's salary.

As we saw earlier, it is allowable to add as many fillers to these kinds of expressions as one wishes in order to improve the readability, as has been done in, for instance, the underlying example:

for every amount of money a :
a is as **salary of** an **employee** $\geqslant$ 0
and
a is as **salary of** an **employee** $\leqslant$ 75,000.

The rule stating that when the fillers have been left out, valid references to roles (i.e., expressions which consist of only object type names and role names) is also valid here. Where desirable, plurals may be used in these expressions too. Just as with the references to roles in Chapter 5, we shall from now on print the "required" words in bold and the fillers in normal type when we are specifying non-graphical constraints. This makes it easier to follow these expressions in the information structure diagram.

Moreover, the above expressions may also be written as:

for every amount of money a :
a is as **salary of** an **employee** $\leqslant$ 75,000 **and** $\geqslant$ 0.

or as:

for every amount of money a :
$0 \leqslant$ a as **salary of** an **employee** $\leqslant 75{,}000.$ (1)

The mathematical signs "$\geqslant$" and "$\leqslant$" may be replaced by, respectively, "greater than or equal to" and "less than or equal to," if this improves the readability.

Strictly speaking, the above expression contains the specification of two constraints instead of one constraint:

– The salary of an employee must be greater than or equal to 0.
– The salary of an employee must be less than or equal to 75,000.

The specifications of non-graphical constraints often contain several individual constraints. However, from now on we shall consider, for the sake of convenience, all of the constraints which are specified by one expression as one single constraint.

Like graphical constraints, non-graphical constraints are verified by the information processor. When we address the following request to the information processor:

Add: the **employee with personnel number J683 with a salary of** 76,000

the information processor responds as follows:

Request not executed because of violation of constraint (the salary of an employee must be greater than or equal to 0 and less than or equal to 75,000).

Another example of a value constraint is given below.

The library is housed in a 4-story building. The numbers of the floors can therefore never exceed 4. The ground floor is assigned the number 0. Further, there is a small cellar, which is assigned the number -1. There are therefore no floor numbers less than -1. This leads to the following value constraint:

for every floor number fn :
$-1 \leqslant$ fn **of floor** $\leqslant 4.$

Because the lexical object type "floor number" has only one role, it is not necessary to include this role name in the description of the constraint. The above expression can therefore be written as:

for every floor number fn :
$-1 \leqslant$ fn $\leqslant 4.$

Because the object type "floor number" has only one role, it is absolutely clear that the above constraint concerns only this one role.

Note that a role name may only be omitted in the description of a constraint if the relevant object type has only one role. Therefore, in expression (1) above, the role name "salary of employee" must be explicitly given because the object type "amount of money" has more than one role: the role "salary of employee" and the role "fine of loan." Naturally the value constraint which is described by expression (1) is only valid for salaries and not for fines.

The value involving the floor numbers can also be expressed as follows:

for every floor number fn :
fn **belongs to** {-1,0,1,2,3,4}.

This denotes that the lexical objects of the type "floor number" have to belong to the set {-1,0,1,2,3,4}, which is a set formed by the numbers -1,0,1,2,3 and 4.

The allowable ranges of values of lexical object types which, like the above, consist of a finite number of objects can always be represented in this way.

Some other examples of value constraints are given below.

Every floor contains at least one and never more than 15 rooms. The sequence numbers of the rooms per floor are therefore never less than 1 and never greater than 15:

for every room sequence number rsn :
$1 \leqslant rsn \leqslant 15$.

or:

for every room sequence number rsn :
rsn **belongs to** {1,2,3,4,5,6,7,8,9,10,11,12,13,14,15}.

However, because of the length of the set of allowable sequential room numbers, the first expression is handier and more readable.

At least one hour and at most 160 hours may be assigned to one activity per employee. The number of hours assigned does not have to be a whole number, but may also contain decimal fractions. The lexical objects of the type "number of hours" therefore have to cover a continuous range of values between 1 and 160 hours. This constraint is specified as follows:

for every number of hours h :
$1 \leqslant h \leqslant 160$.

The activity numbers are always greater than 1, and because the activities are numbered consecutively, there is no upper limit for the activity numbers:

for every activity number an :
an $\geqslant 1$.

16.2 Cardinality constraints

One of the first constraints involving the organization of the library which we dealt with in this book read:

"A department may not contain more than 10 (department) staff members."

When a department occurs several times in the population of the role "department with as staff member department staff member," that department necessarily occurs repeatedly with a different department staff member. After all, the fact that a certain department staff member works for a certain department is only included once in the information base. If a department occurs more than 10 times in the population of this role, this department then occurs with more than 10 different staff members. In this case, that department contains more than 10 department staff members, which is in conflict with the above constraint. We have depicted this situation in Figure 16.2.

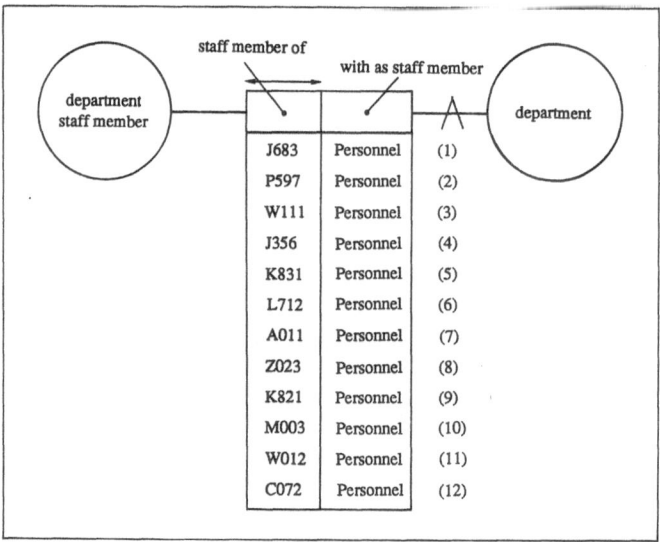

Figure 16.2.

It follows from this that the above constraint is the equivalent of the following proposition:

Every department may occur at most 10 times in the population of the role "department with as staff member department staff member."

Constraints which restrict the number of times an object of a certain object type may occur in the role populations of this object type (such as the above constraint) are called *number constraints* or *cardinality constraints*. (The concept "cardinality" is often used in set theory to mean "the number of times that something occurs in something.")

Because we have not introduced any graphical symbols for these kinds of constraints, they are considered to be non-graphical constraints.

The above constraints can now be described as follows:

for every department d :
number of department staff members staff member of of d ⩽ 10.

This must be read as follows: for every department (thus for every object of the type "department") it holds that the number of department staff members who are staff members of that department must not exceed 10. Or, stated differently, the number of times that an object of the type "department" may occur in the population of the role "department with as staff member department staff member" is at most equal to 10.

Note that a cardinality constraint is specified by means of a reference to the co-role of the role to which this constraint refers. The above expression is therefore the specification of a cardinality constraint involving the role "department with as staff member department staff member." This expression contains a reference to its co-role, i.e. the role "department staff member staff member of department."

Of course, fillers and plurals may be added where desired to the above expression to improve the readability:

for every department d :
the **number of department staff members** who are **staff member of** d ⩽ 10.

The description "less than or equal to" may also be used instead of the mathematical sign "⩽."

Just like all the other constraints, the cardinality constraints are verified by the information processor. Let us suppose that at a given moment 10 department staff members work for the Personnel Department and that we address the following request to the information processor:

Add: department staff member with personnel number C072 is **staff member of** the **department** Personnel.

The information processor would then respond as follows:

Request not executed because of violation of rule P17 (a department may not contain more than 10 department staff members).

We must then either refrain from adding this staff member to the Personnel Department or first delete the fact that another staff member works for this department, so that once the above request has been executed, the total number of staff members in this department is again equal to 10.

Some more examples of cardinality constraints follow below. In most cases, the reader will be be capable of formulating these constraints him- or herself.

Each department can have a maximum of 2 departmental secretaries:

for every department d :
number of department staff members who are **departmental secretary of** d $\leqslant 2$.

Every line department may manage a maximum of 6 other line departments:

for every line department ld :
number of line departments controlled by ld $\leqslant 6$.

An employee may never be assigned more than 2 functions at a time:

for every employee e :
number of functions assigned to e $\leqslant 2$.

A room may never contain more than 4 employees:

for every room r :
number of employees situated in r $\leqslant 4$.

An employee may never be situated in more than 2 rooms:

for every employee e :
number of rooms containing e $\leqslant 2$.

In the previous section, we saw that the room sequence numbers begin with 1 and are never larger than 15. Because these rooms are numbered sequentially, it follows that there may never be more than 15 rooms on each floor:

for every floor f :
number of rooms on f $\leqslant 15$. (1)

Likewise, in the previous section, we saw that the building has 6 floors, including the ground floor and the cellar. Because the rooms are numbered sequentially per floor, in principle only one given room sequence number can occur on each of the 6 floors. That is, every room sequence number can belong to at most 6 different rooms (namely, one on each floor):

for every room sequence number rsn :
number of rooms with rsn $\leqslant 6$.

This constraint is not to be confused with the following one:

for every room sequence number rsn :
$1 \leqslant$ rsn $\leqslant 15.$ (2)

Constraint (2) is a **value** constraint restricting the value of each room sequence number to at most 15. On the contrary, constraint (1) is a **cardinality** constraint which restricts the **number** of rooms on each floor to a maximum of 6.

Note that constraint (1) is implied by constraint (2) and vice versa (bearing in mind the fact that the rooms are numbered sequentially, beginning with number 1). One of these two constraints is therefore redundant. This example illustrates that non-graphical constraints can be implied by other (graphical and non-graphical) constraints. Such constraints are redundant and are therefore not included in the grammar. Consequently, in the above example, either constraint (1) or constraint (2) must be included in the grammar.

Uniqueness and totality constraints which involve individual roles are actually special cases of cardinality constraints. The uniqueness constraint which is depicted in Figure 16.3 states that a room may only be located on one floor.

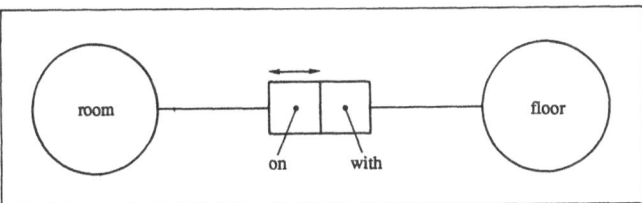

Figure 16.3.

As a consequence, every room can only occur once in the population of the role "room on floor." Because this role, at least in the diagram of Figure 16.3, is not total (the floor does not have to be known for each room), **no** rooms or **at most one** room belong to each floor. Or, stated differently, the number of times that one particular room may occur in the population of the role "room on floor" is maximally equal to 1. This is a cardinality constraint involving the role "room on floor." The uniqueness constraint in Figure 16.3 can therefore also be specified as follows:

for every room r :
number of floors with r $\leqslant$ 1.

In Figure 16.4, a totality constraint involving the same role is depicted instead of a uniqueness constraint. This totality constraint states that the floor must be known for **every** room.

Because the role "room on floor," at least in the diagram of Figure 16.4, is not unique, it holds that every room must be located on **at least one** floor. Or, stated differently, every room must occur at least once in the population of the role "room

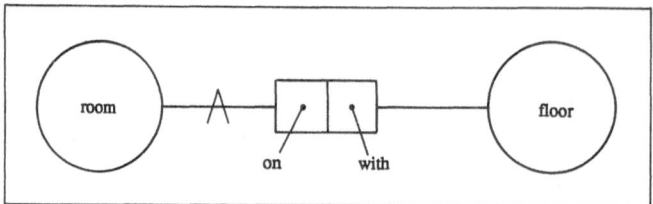

Figure 16.4.

on floor." This is also a cardinality constraint involving the role "room on floor." Therefore, the totality constraint in Figure 16.4 can also be specified as follows:

for every room r :
number of floors with r $\geqslant 1$.

We have depicted the fact that the role "room on floor" is both unique and total in Figure 16.5.

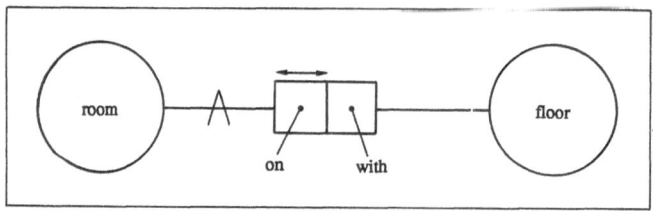

Figure 16.5.

It follows from the above two examples that we can also specify the uniqueness and totality of this role as follows:

for every room r :
number of floors with r $= 1$.

Therefore, uniqueness and totality constraints can always be specified as cardinality constraints. However, while cardinality constraints are not graphical, uniqueness and totality constraints are. In setting up an information structure diagram, we strive to include as many constraints as possible in graphical form. We will therefore always represent uniqueness and totality constraints by means of uniqueness and totality symbols.

16.3 Subtype defining constraints

Let us suppose that the name of the function which is assigned to the department manager is always "manager," and that only employees with the function "manager" can be department managers. This is a constraint which can be described as follows:

for every employee e :
e **is a department manager if and only if**
function name of function assigned to e = "manager."

Because the object type "function" has only one bridge type, the role name "function name of function" may be omitted in this expression:

for every employee e :
e **is a department manager if and only if**
function assigned to e = "manager."

The symbol "⇔" may also be used instead of the words "if and only if":

for every employee e :
e **is a department manager** ⇔
function assigned to e = "manager."

Which objects belong to the type "employee" and which to the subtype "department manager" can be determined with the help of this constraint. Such constraints are called *subtype defining constraints*. A subtype defining constraint always belongs to a certain subtype.

Let us suppose that the type of department of line departments is always equal to "ld" and that of staff departments to "sd." On the basis of the type of department, it can be determined to which of the subtypes "line department" and "staff department" every object of the type "department" belongs. This leads to the following two subtype defining constraints:

for every department d :
d **is a line department if and only if**
the **type of department of** d = "ld." (1)

for every department d :
d **is a staff department if and only if**
the **type of department of** d = "sd." (2)

Because the subtypes "line department" and "staff department" are mutually exclusive and their combination is total, the second subtype defining constraint can also be written as follows:

for every department d :
d **is a staff department if and only if it does not hold that:**
d **is a line department.**

If we leave constraint (2) as it is, we can also describe constraint (1) as follows:

for every department d :
d **is a line department if and only if it does not hold that:**
d **is a staff department.**

As we remarked in the last practically oriented chapter, we must ensure, when setting up an information structure diagram, that there is, as far as possible, a subtype defining constraint for every subtype.

16.4 Other non-graphical constraints

In addition to value constraints, cardinality constraints, and subtype defining constraints, there are many other non-graphical constraints which cannot be classified into a certain type. Several examples are given below.

A line department can manage another department; it can, however, never manage itself. This constraint is described as follows:

for every line department ld **holds** that **not:** ld **manages** ld

or:

for every line department ld **holds** that **not:** ld **controlled by** ld.

Note that this constraint does **not** mean that the roles "line department manages line department" and "line department controlled by line department" exclude each other. After all, a line department which manages another line department and comes under yet another line department occurs in the population of both roles. This is the case, for example, for the Support Services Department in Figure 16.6 (see also the organizational chart in Figure 3.1).

An employee can only be a departmental secretary of a department if he or she has the function of "secretary:"

for every employee e :
if e **is departmental secretary of** a **department**
then e **is with function** "secretary."

The symbol "⇒" may also be used instead of the words "if...then:"

for every employee e :
e **is departmental secretary of** a **department** ⇒
e **is with function** "secretary."

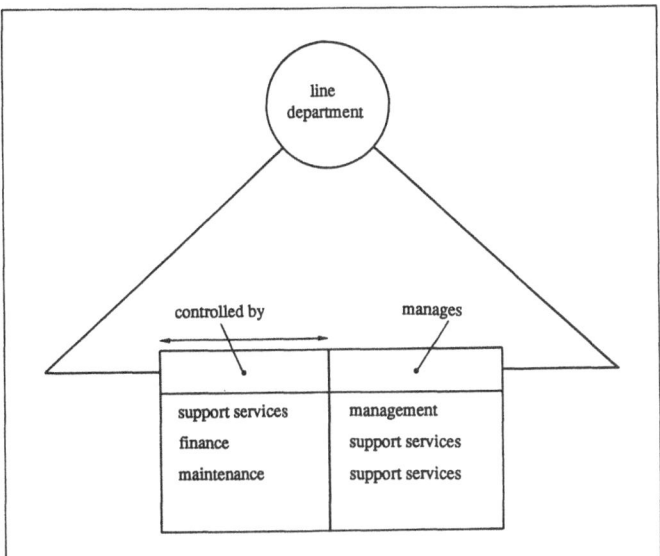

Figure 16.6.

In Figure 16.7, we have added the fact that each department has a budget to the information structure diagram. A department's budget is a role of the lexical object type "amount of money." This lexical object type also occurs in the role of an employee's salary. The obvious constraint is that the total of the salaries of all of the employees who work for a department, including that of the department manager, must be less than the department's budget. This constraint is described as follows:

for every department d :
(the **total of** the **amounts of money** which are the **salaries of** the **department staff members** who are **staff member of** d + the **amount of money** that is the **salary of** the **department manager** who is **manager of** d) ≤ (the **amount of money** that is the **budget of** d).

16.5 Non-graphical descriptions of graphical constraints

In Section 16.2, we saw that uniqueness and totality constraints are actually special cases of cardinality constraints and therefore can be described non-graphically. In general, all graphical constraints can also be described non-graphically. To illustrate this, we shall in this section use concrete examples to provide non-graphical descriptions of all of the types of graphical constraints dealt with in this book. However, in practice, we shall always represent graphical constraints in information diagrams by graphical symbols, as has already been said.

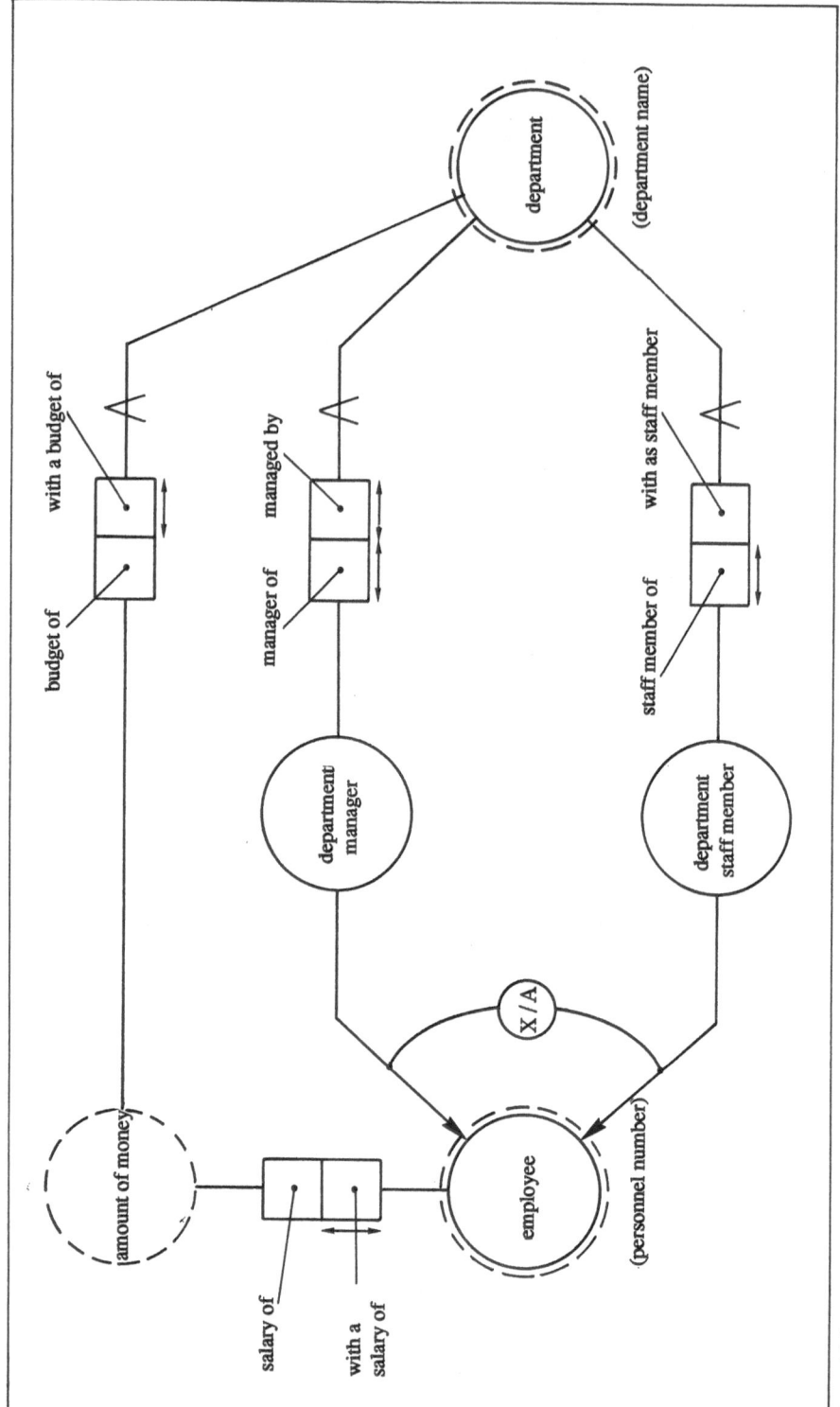

Figure 16.7.

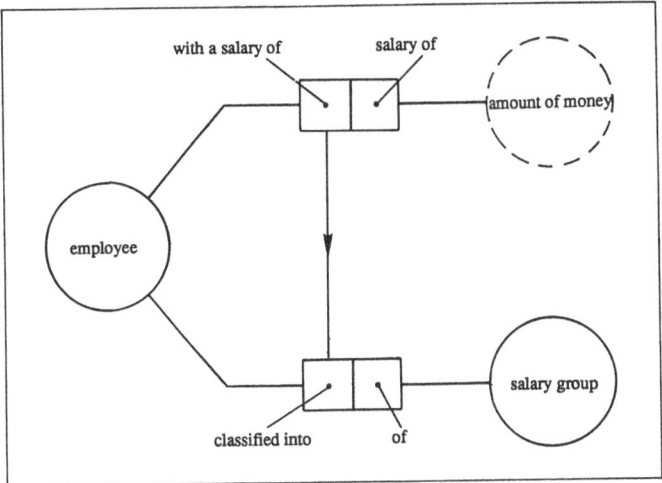

Figure 16.8.

The subset constraint in Figure 16.8 can be described by the following expression:

for every employee e :
if e is **with a salary of** a certain **amount of money**
then e is **classified into** a **salary group.**

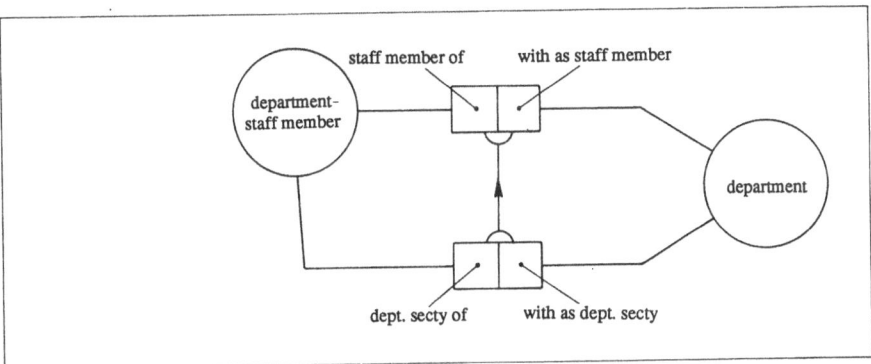

Figure 16.9.

The subset constraint in Figure 16.9 can be described by the following expression:

for every employee e **and for every department** d :
if e is **departmental secretary of** d,
then e is **staff member of** d.

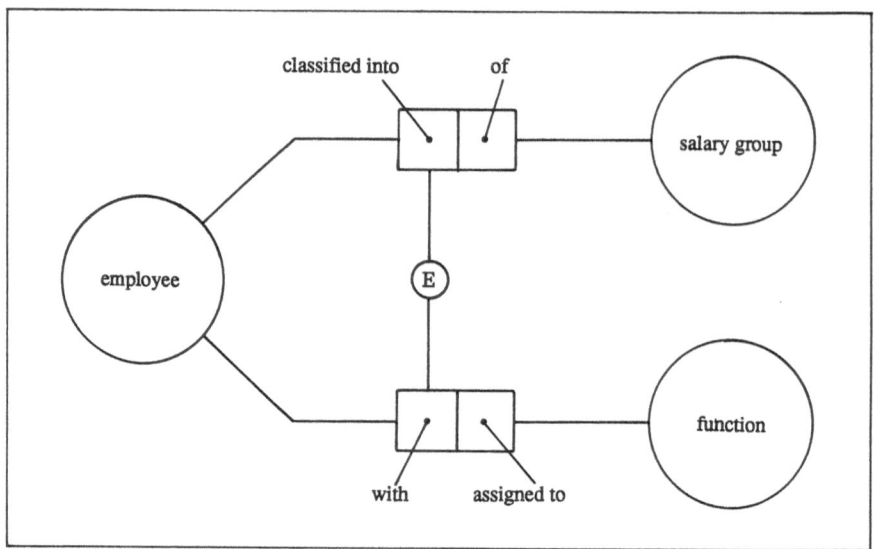

Figure 16.10.

The equality constraint in Figure 16.10 can be described by the following expression:

for every employee e :
. **if** e **is classified into** a **salary group,**
then e **is with** a **function**
and
if e **is with** a **function,**
then e is **classified into** a **salary group.**

The exclusion constraint in Figure 16.11 can be described by the expression:

for every employee e :
if e **is manager of** a **department, then not:**
e **is staff member of** a **department.**

The exclusion constraint in Figure 16.12 can be described by the expression:

for every employee e **and for every project** p :
. **if** e **is manager of** p, **then not:**
e **is staff member of** p.

The totality constraint of Figure 16.13 can be described by the following expression:

for every employee e :
e is **manager of** a **department or**
e is **staff member of** a **department.**

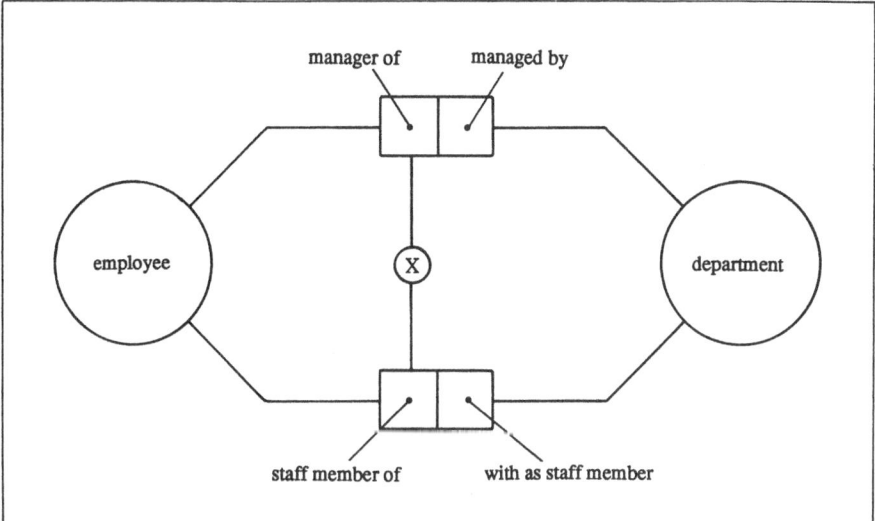

Figure 16.11.

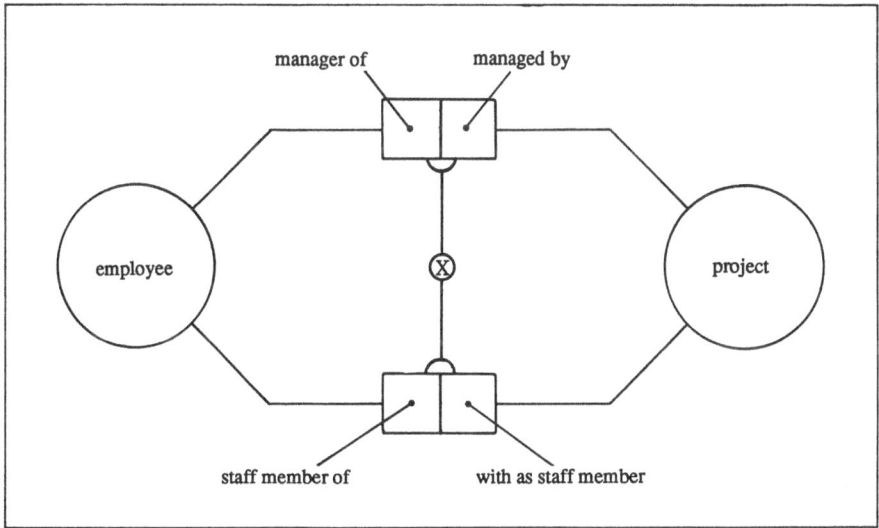

Figure 16.12.

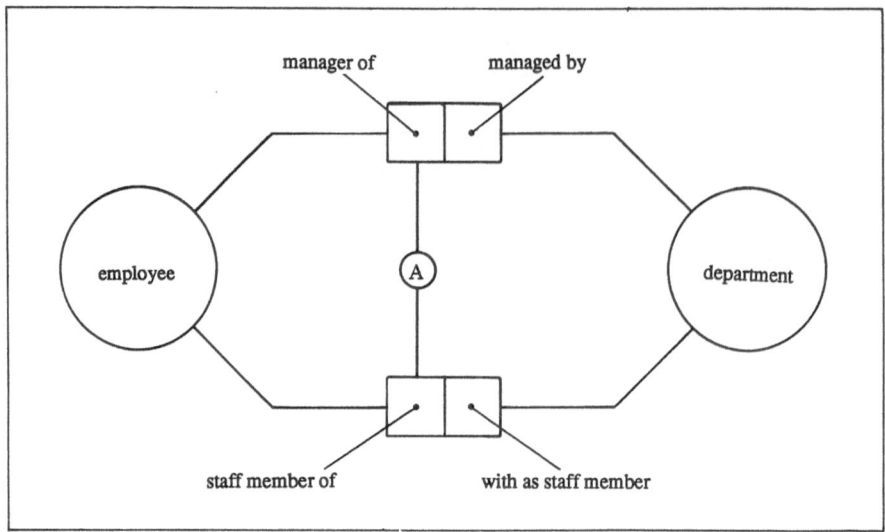

Figure 16.13.

The uniqueness constraint of Figure 16.14 can be described by:

for every floor f and every room sequence number rsn :
number of rooms **on f and with** rsn ≤ 1.

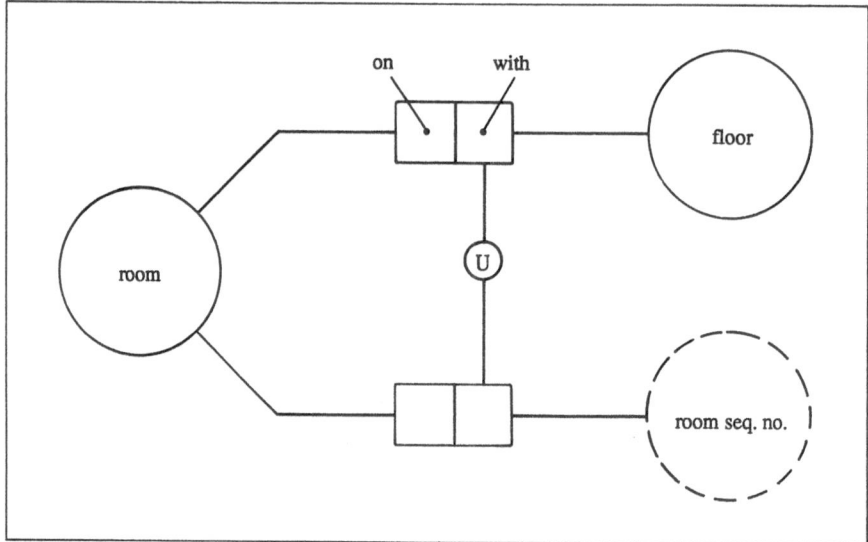

Figure 16.14.

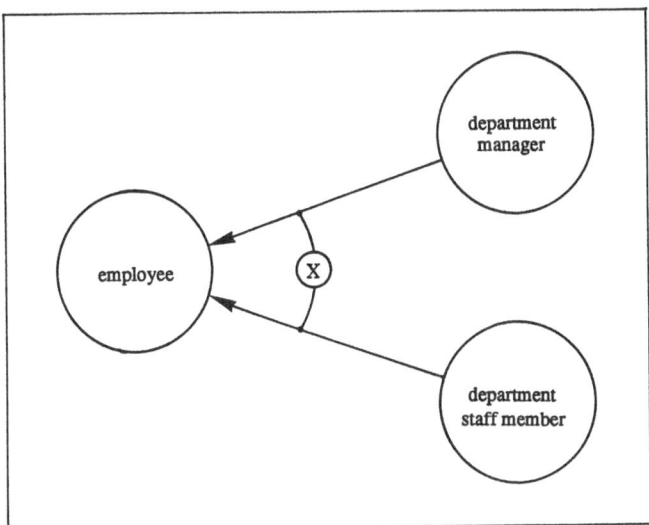

Figure 16.15.

The exclusion constraint in Figure 16.15 can be described by the expression:

for every employee e :
if e **is** a **department manager, then not:**
e **is** a **department staff member.**

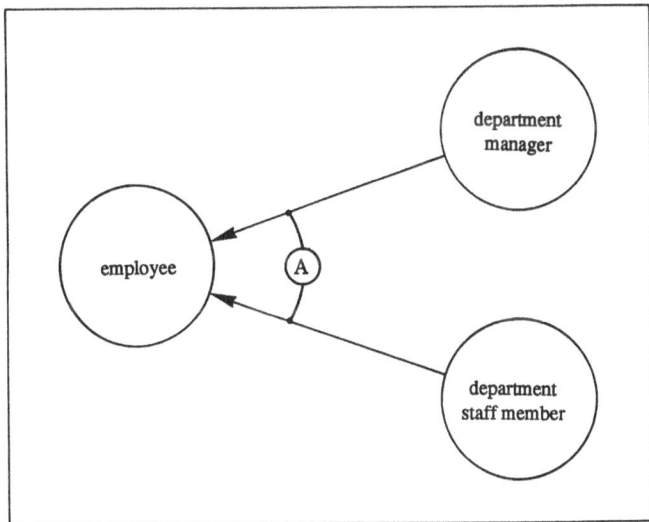

Figure 16.16.

The totality constraint in Figure 16.16 can be described by the following expression:

for every employee e :
e **is a department manager or**
e **is a department staff member.**

16.6 Derivable fact types

We are going to expand the library case once again.

A project has a budget. A project's budget is a role of the lexical object type "amount of money." A project is "assigned" to a department and must be financed from the department's budget. Several projects can be assigned to a department. The total of the budgets of all the projects assigned to a department is called the "project budget."

This has been depicted in Figure 16.17.

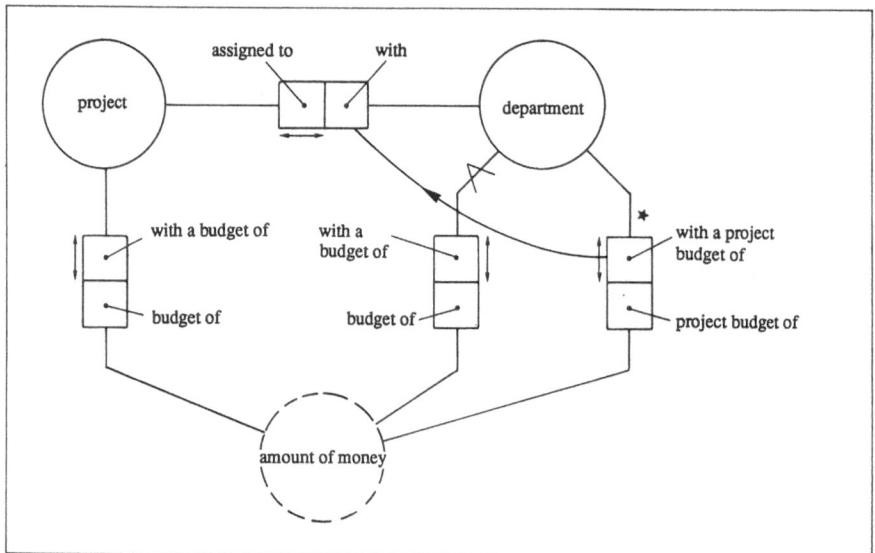

Figure 16.17.

The lexical object type "amount of money" now occurs in the following roles:

– salary of an employee
– budget of a department
– budget of a project
– project budget of a department

as well as in the role of a fine of a loan (in the practically oriented chapters).

Naturally, we can only speak in terms of "the project budget" of a department if at least one project has been assigned to that department. The role "department with a project budget of an amount of money" is consequently a subset of the role "department with project."

As stated above, a department's project budget must equal the total of the budgets of all the projects assigned to that department. This constraint is described as follows:

for every department d :
the **amount of money** that is the **project budget of** d =
the **total** of the **amounts of money** which are the **budget of**
the **project**s which are **assigned to** d.

The project budgets of the various departments, i.e., the populations of the role "amount of money project budget of department," can be derived, on the basis of this constraint, from the budgets of the projects assigned to these departments.

For that reason, we might be tempted to think that the fact type consisting of the roles "amount of money project budget of department" and "department with a project budget of amount of money" is actually redundant.

In the previous chapters, we saw that **constraints** which are implied by other constraints are not included as such in the grammar. On the contrary, **fact types** whose populations can be derived at any moment from the populations of other fact types are explicitly included in the grammar and are therefore represented in the information structure diagram. After all, these fact types "arose," like all other fact types, from the concrete examples of the contents of the information flow being considered. These examples represent the information needs of the future users of the information system. The fact types in the information structure diagram must describe these information needs completely, even when it appears upon further analysis that the populations of a number of these fact types can be derived from the populations of other fact types as a result of one constraint or another.

Therefore, the fact type involving a department's project budget "arose" from the need for information about the project budgets of the various departments. The need for this information is not impeded by the fact that this information can be derived from other information (moreover, it is possible that this is not even known at the time the analysis is begun). Because the information structure diagram must describe the information needs of the future users of the information system completely, this fact type must also be given explicitly.

Fact types whose populations can be derived from the populations of one or more populations as a result of one or more constraints are called *derivable fact types*. The facts belonging to these derivable fact types are called *derivable facts*. The information described by derivable facts is also known as "derivable information." When derivable facts come up during the analysis of examples of the contents of information flows, the corresponding fact types must be explicitly included in the information structure diagram, just as all other fact types are.

Such obvious things as (sub)totals that appear on all kinds of overviews are normally considered as elements which only involve the external data representation and therefore have no role to play in information analysis. In step 3.1 of the NIAM method of information analysis ("Determine the lexical objects and name the lexical object types"), as we have seen, one determines which of the lexical objects that occur in the examples will play a role in the information analysis. Just which of these objects are generally considered to concern only the external data representation depends on the type of information processing being analyzed.

For clarity, derivable fact types are denoted in the information structure diagram by the symbol "*," called the **derivability symbol**. In Figure 16.17, we have used this derivability symbol to denote the fact type involving the project budgets of the departments.

Bear in mind that during information analysis, one has to make an abstraction of all considerations relevant to the way in which the information system will be realized. Therefore, during information analysis, whether or not the facts of a derivable fact type (such as the fact type involving the project budgets in our example) will actually be stored in the information system is not yet important. It is possible that these facts will be stored or that they will be derived from other facts when the information system requests it. The decision of whether or not to store these kinds of facts is determined by technical efficiency factors which have no role to play during information analysis. After all, the information need of the users of the information system does not depend on the question of whether or not these facts will be stored.

We saw earlier that the information processor can, on the basis of a constraint, draw certain conclusions about the populations of the fact types with which the constraint is concerned. In the case of derivable fact types, the information processor can derive the entire population of the derivable fact type from one or more constraints and from the populations of one or more fact types involving these constraints.

Subtypes for which subtype defining constraints are valid are likewise derivable information. Thus, the information processor can, for example, derive the population of the subtype "department manager" from the functions of the employees, given the constraint that all of the employees assigned the function "manager" are department managers.

A second example of a derivable fact type follows below. We assume for this that a project is always assigned to a department having a project manager (see Figure 16.18).

This constraint is described as follows:

for every project p :
p is **assigned to** the **department with as staff member**
the **department staff member** who is **manager of** p
or

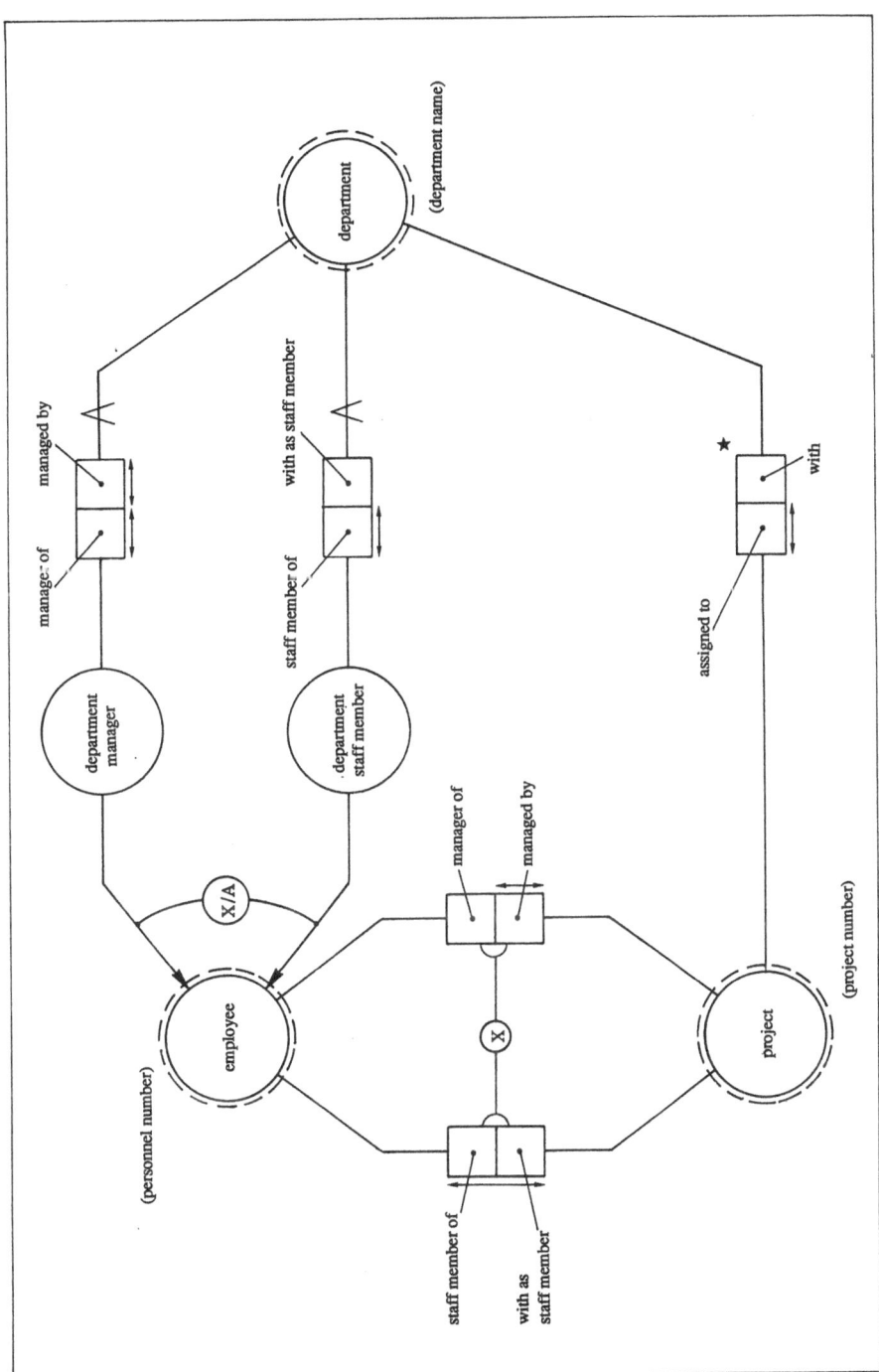

Figure 16.18.

p is **assigned to** the **department** which is **managed by** the **department manager** who is **manager of** p.

On the basis of this constraint, (in Figure 16.18) the population of the fact type involving the object types "project" and "department" can be derived at any moment from the population of the fact types involving the project managers of a project, and the department managers and staff members of a department. The fact type involving the object types "project" and "department" is therefore derivable and is consequently denoted in the information structure diagram by the derivability symbol.

Finally, we will use Figure 16.17 to point out a fairly common error in reasoning. Naturally, a department's project budget (the total of the budgets of all the projects assigned to that department) must be smaller than, or at most equal to, that department's budget. In spoken language, a department's project budget is sometimes said to "be always within" the department's budget. It could be concluded from this general description that the role "amount of money project budget of department" is a subset of the role "amount of money budget of department," as represented in Figure 16.19.

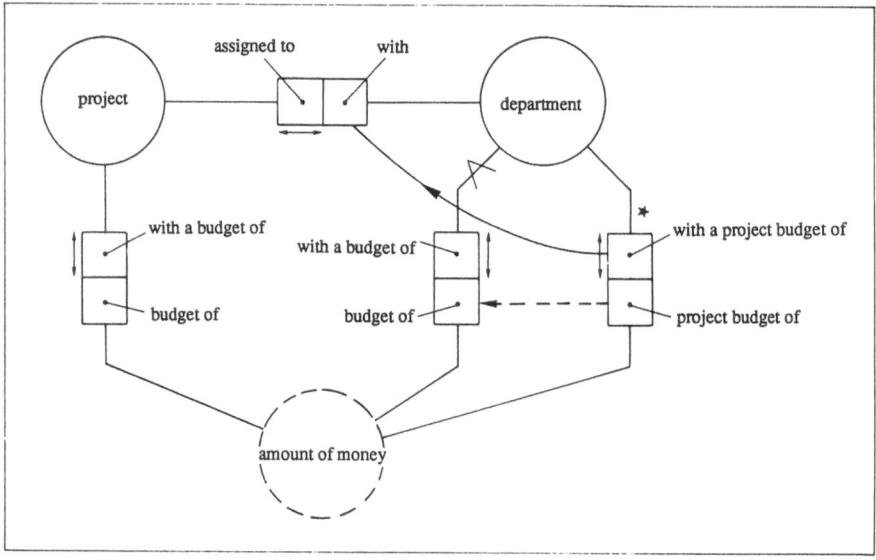

Figure 16.19.

This subset constraint would mean that every money amount that occurs as a department's project budget must also occur as the budget of the same department. Therefore, the Personnel Department could only have a project budget of, say, $50,000, if that department also has a departmental budget of **exactly the same** amount, namely $50,000. This is clearly not a correct representation of the above constraint.

On the contrary, this constraint is a non-graphical constraint which should be described as follows:

for every department d :
the **amount of money** that is the **project budget of** d is $\leqslant$ the **amount of money** that is the **budget of** d.

16.7 Transition constraints

To conclude this chapter, we shall consider one last type of constraint.

We saw earlier in this book that the grammar contains all the constraints which describe the states and state transitions allowed in the information base. Thus far, we have only taken a look at constraints which concern one single information base state, the state constraints. These consist of the specifications of the object types and fact types, and of all graphical and non-graphical state constraints.

The constraints which are discussed in this section, called *transition constraints*, restrict the possible information base state transitions. As we already know, state constraints restrict the populations of object type roles. Transition constraints restrict the *changes* which may occur in these populations. Just like the other constraints, transition constraints always involve object type roles. Because the information structure diagram always involves one single information base state, a transition constraint can never be depicted graphically. Therefore, transition constraints are by definition non-graphical constraints.

From now on, we shall assume that if the users address a request to the information processor to change the information base, the information processor will, when executing this request, temporarily store the old information base state. By "old state" we mean the state of the information base just before it received the request. If the requested change is executed, the information processor verifies, by comparing the old state with the new state, whether any transition constraint has been violated by executing the change. If a transition state has been violated, the information processor restores the old state (which results in the nonexecution of the request), notifies the users that the request has not been executed, and gives the reason why it has not. If no transition constraint has been violated during the change, the information processor deletes the old state (which results in the execution of the request) and notifies the users that the request has been successfully executed.

As we just saw, a transition constraint describes the allowable changes in the populations of one or more roles. It appears from the foregoing that a transition constraint must indicate which populations of the involved roles are allowed in the new information base state, given certain populations in the old state.

A description of a transition constraint must therefore contain two references to the role (or roles) being considered: one reference involving the populations of the role (or roles) in the old information base state and one reference to the populations of the role (or roles) in the new state. In the description of the transition constraint, we shall place the quantifier "old" in front of the reference to a role involving the old state, and the quantifier "new" in front of the reference to a role involving the new state.

Let us now follow an example of a transition constraint. We assume that the salaries of the library employees may never be lowered. This constraint restricts the salary changes which may occur in the information base and is consequently a transition constraint. This constraint is described as follows:

for every employee e :
new amount of money salary of e ⩾ **old amount of money salary of** e.

The following is a second example of a transition constraint.

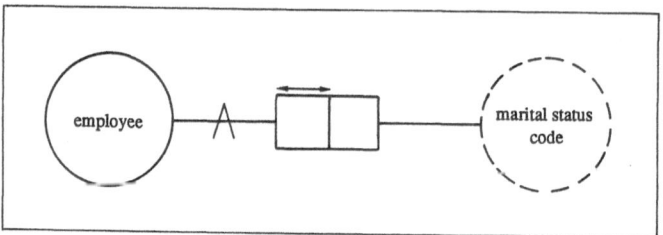

Figure 16.20.

The marital status of every library employee is maintained by means of a so-called "marital status code." The marital status of an employee can be: married, unmarried, widowed, or divorced. This boils down to the following value constraint:

for every marital status code msc :
msc **belongs to**
{unmarried, married, widowed, divorced}.

old \ new	unmarried	married	widowed	divorced
unmarried		X		
married			X	X
widowed		X		
divorced		X		

Figure 16.21.

Not all of the conceivable changes in the marital status code are allowed; the marital status can only be changed from "unmarried," "widowed," or "divorced" into "married" and only from "married" into "widowed" or "divorced". The checks in Figure 16.21 represent the changes allowed in the marital status code.

A table like the one in Figure 16.21 is called a *transition matrix* or *transition table*. These kinds of tables are important tools in analyzing the permissible value changes in lexical objects. The following transition constraint for the marital status code can easily be derived from the transition matrix of Figure 16.21:

for every employee e :
if the **new marital status code of** e = "married"
then the **old marital status code of** e = "unmarried"
or "widowed" **or** "divorced"
and
if the **new marital status code of** e = "widowed"
or "divorced"
then the **old marital status code of** e = "married."

This transition is only valid for **changes** in the marital status code. When the marital status of an employee is **added** for the first time, there is only a new marital status code and no old one, which means that the transition constraint is not applicable. When the marital status code of an employee is merely **deleted**, there is only an old marital status code and no new one, so that the transition constraint is not applicable here either. As we already know, a fact is changed by deleting it and adding an update of it in one single request.

We remarked earlier that the information base is a reflection of the state of the reality at any moment. This state generally changes as a result of events which take place within the reality. In reaction to any change in state occurring within this reality which is relevant for the information system, the information base state is altered at the request of the users, so that the information base then again describes the new state of the reality. The information base state always changes as a result of **events** occurring within the reality. The transition constraints describe which changes in state may occur, **independently of the events** based on these changes. Therefore, the transition constraints do **not** describe the causal relationships between the events within the reality and the resulting changes in the information base state. (For these reasons, moreover, we designate these as "transition constraints" rather than "dynamic constraints," as the concept "dynamic" implies causality.) These causal relationships, that is, the constraints that determine what requests the users may address to the information system as a result of which events, are described outside the information analysis process. Abstractions are made from these events during information analysis and only the changes in state which may occur in the information base are analyzed. The specification of the allowable changes in state is usually more stable (that is, less subject to changes, seen in terms of time) than that of all the relevant events which can occur in the reality.

Just like other constraints, the transition constraints originate from the rules and laws that are valid within the reality.

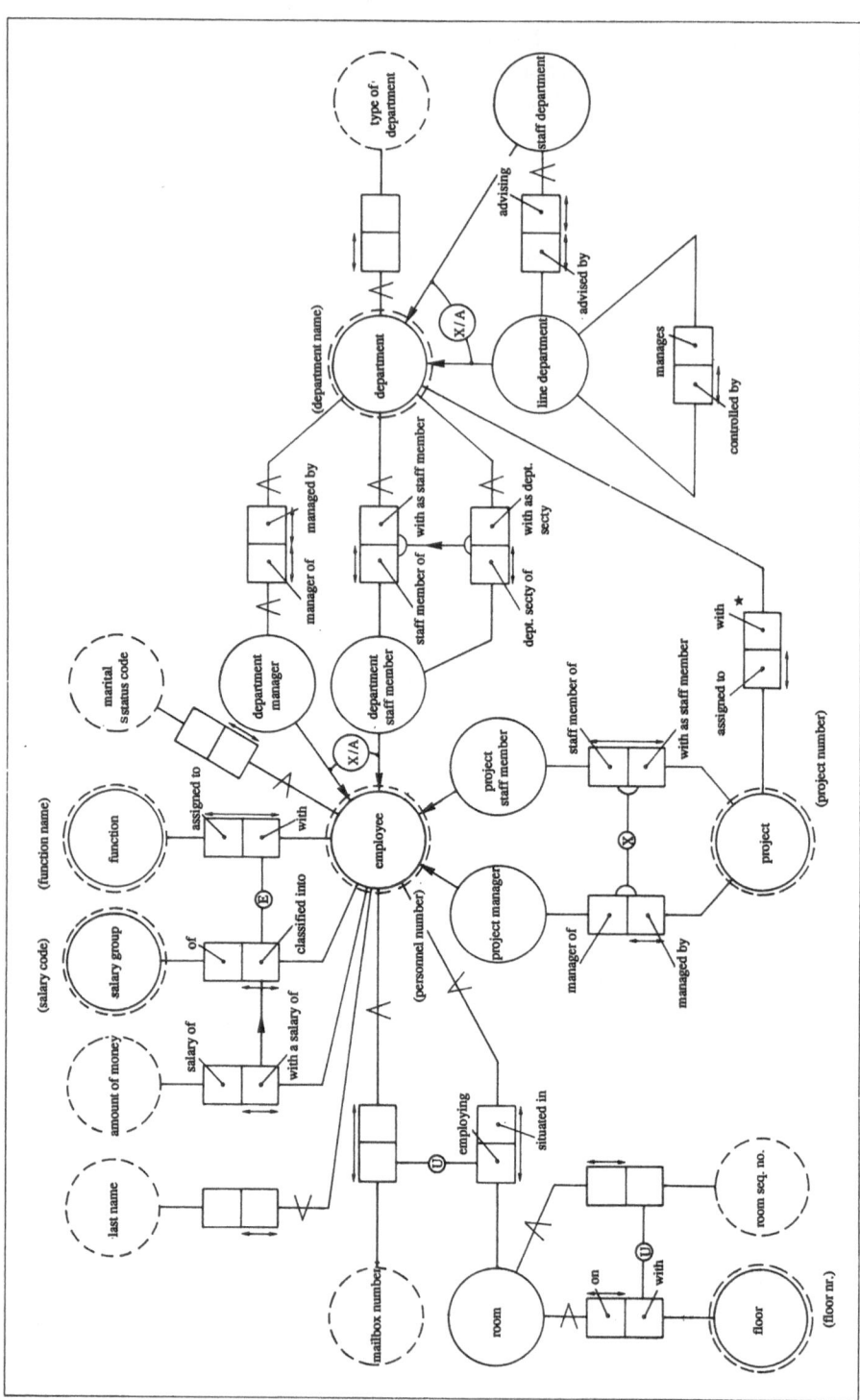

Figure 16.22.

16.8 Summary

A summary of the most important concepts discussed in this chapter is given below.

Value constraint:
A (non-graphical) constraint which prescribes which lexical objects may occur in the role populations of a lexical object type.

Cardinality constraint:
A (non-graphical) constraint which restricts the number of times an object of a certain object type may occur in the role populations of this object type.

Subtype defining constraint:
A (non-graphical) constraint which prescribes when an object of a certain object type belongs to a subtype of it.

Derivable fact type:
A fact type whose population can be derived at any moment from the populations of one or more fact types on the basis of one or more constraints.

Derivable fact:
A fact that belongs to a derivable fact type.

Derivable fact types are denoted in an information structure diagram by the derivability symbol:

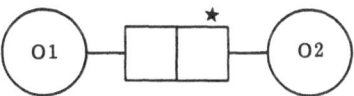

the fact type involving object types
O1 and O2 is derivable.

Transition constraint:
A (non-graphical) constraint which prescribes which changes are allowed within the populations of one or more roles.

17 THE NIAM METHOD OF INFORMATION ANALYSIS IN PRACTICE - 6

We will take up the tenth step in the NIAM method of information analysis in this chapter, which completes the stepwise plan. In step 10, we determine all of the non-graphical constraints involving the fact type roles added to the information structure diagram in the previous steps.

10. Add the non-graphical constraints.

This step consists of the following substeps:

- For every role of a lexical object type, check whether a value constraint applies.
- For every non-unique role, check whether a cardinality constraint applies.
- For every subtype, check whether a subtype defining constraint applies.
- For the roles of every object type, check whether other non-graphical constraints apply.
- For every fact type, check whether a transition constraint applies.

Figures 17.1 and 17.2 contain part of the information structure diagram for the library case, as we have constructed it so far. We shall now go through the above substeps for this part of the information structure diagram. In most cases, we will give the constraint, followed by brief comments. We invite the reader to try to determine the comments on the constraints him- or herself.

10.1 For every role of a lexical object type, check whether a value constraint applies.

The edition numbers of the books are always greater than or equal to 1:

for every edition number en :
en $\geqslant$ 1.

All of the year codes range between 0 and 99:

for every year code yc :
$0 \leqslant yc \leqslant 99$.

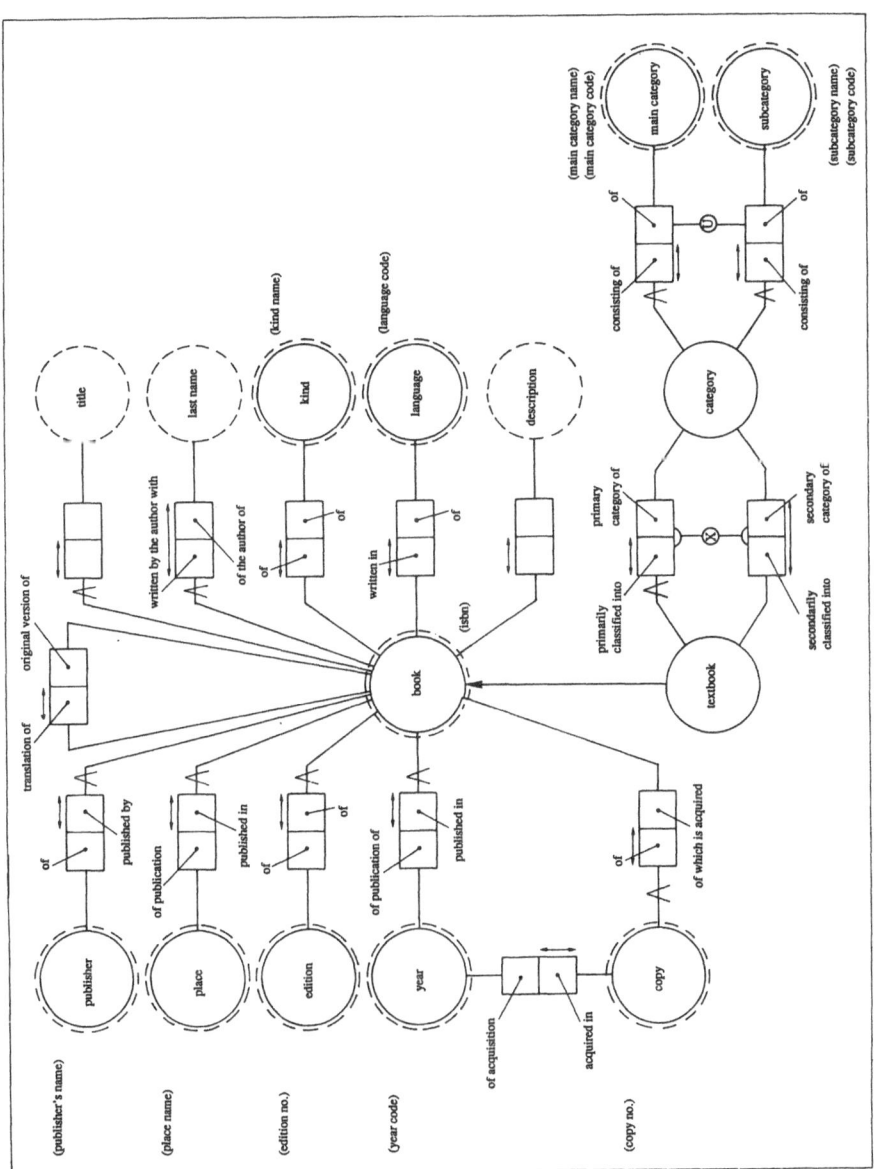

Figure 17.1.

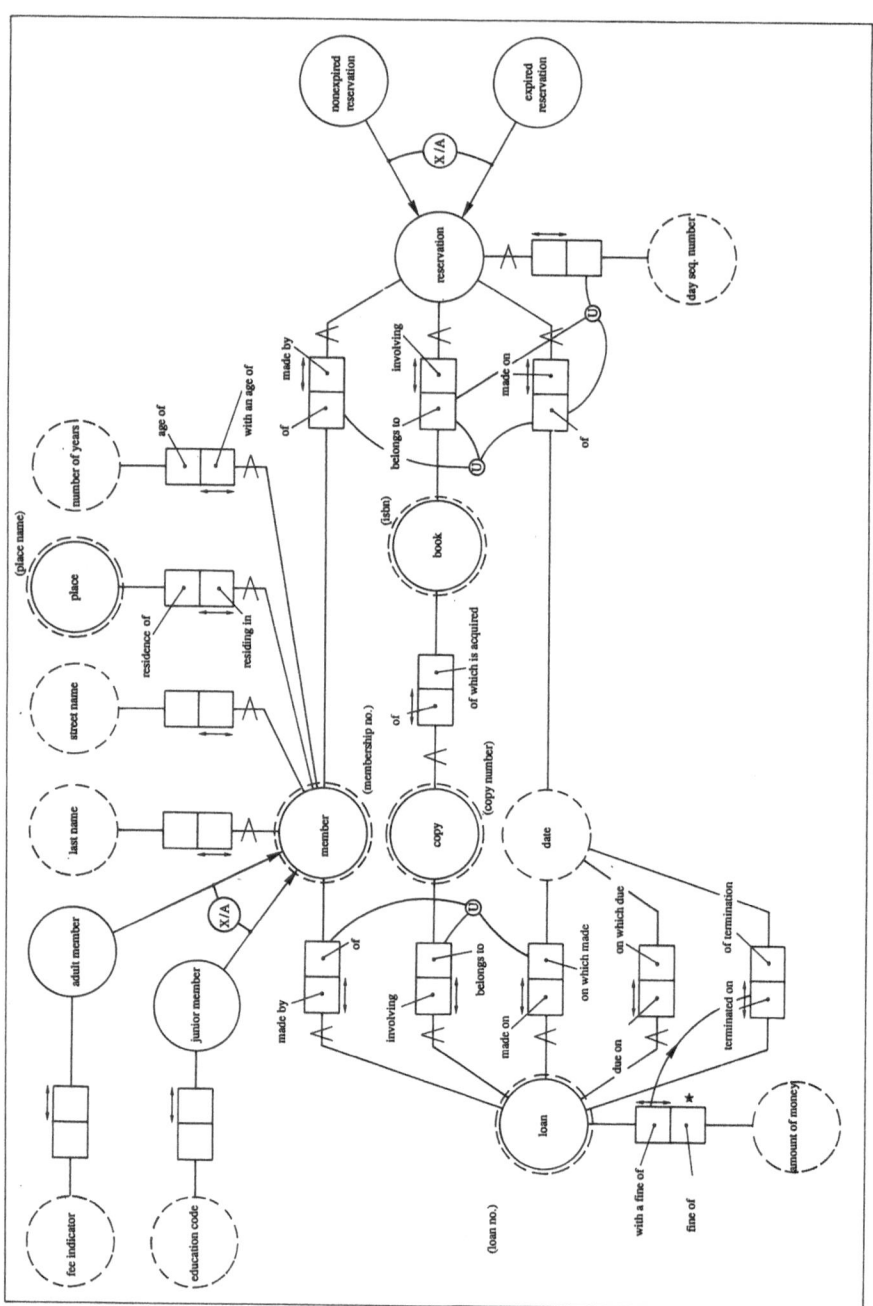

Figure 17.2.

The only language codes used in the library are "Eng" for English, "Fr" for French, and "Ger" for German. We could suppose that this is a general rule in the library, which leads to the following value constraint:

for every language code lc :
lc **belongs to** {Eng,Fr,Ger}.

However, this prevents books which are written in another language from being added to the information base in the future. Therefore, the above value constraint is, from a practical point of view, only meaningful if we are positive that the grammar, and consequently the information system, will not be changed in the future and that the library will not acquire books written in any other language. Since we cannot be sure of this, we should not include this value constraint in the grammar. In that case, we can include all possible language codes in the information system. The totality of the role "language with language code" guarantees that a language code can never be assigned to a book unless it has previously been included in the information base.

We will assume that there are "never" any kinds of books in the library other than textbooks, novels, children's books, and reference books. This leads to the following value constraint:

for every kind name kn :
kn **belongs to** {textbook,novel,children's book, reference book}.

As a consequence, we will be unable to add other kinds of books to the information base in the future, unless the grammar regarding this point is altered.

The main category codes are always greater than or equal to 1 and less than or equal to 9. The subcategory codes are always greater than or equal to 1 and less than or equal to 99:

for every main category code mc :
$1 \leqslant mc \leqslant 9$.

for every subcategory code sc :
$1 \leqslant sc \leqslant 99$.

The fines that have to be paid on overdue books are set at a maximum of 50 dollars. That is, the fine may never be larger than 50. A fine levied on an overdue book is always larger than 0:

for every amount of money a :
$0 < a$ **fine of loan** $\leqslant 50$.

Because the lexical object type "amount of money" has several roles, we have had to include the role name "fine of loan" explicitly in the description of this constraint.

The day sequence number for reservations of a same book on a same day is always greater than 0 and less than or equal to 9:

for every day sequence number dn :
$0 < \text{dn} \leqslant 9.$

The reservations made on a same day for a same book are numbered sequentially, beginning with 1; we have also decided to allow no more than 9 reservations of a book per day.

The fee indicator for an adult library member is equal to "1" if the fee has been paid, and to "0" if it has not been paid:

for every fee indicator fi :
fi **belongs to** $\{0,1\}$.

The education code for a junior library member is equal to "k" for kindergarten, "g" for grammar school, "h" for high school, and "o" for other and special types of education:

for every education code ec :
ec **belongs to** $\{k,g,h,o\}$.

As a consequence of this value constraint, all junior members have to be classified into these 4 types of education. If we wish to make provision for the fact that there could be a change in the educational system in the future and that these types of education might need to be registered in the information base, we should not include this value constraint in the information base. This would mean that any conceivable education code could be assigned to a junior member. Should we nevertheless wish to keep the education codes "under control," it might be advisable to define a **non-lexical** object type "type of education." This allows any type of education to be unambiguously denoted by an education code. We have represented this in Figure 17.3.

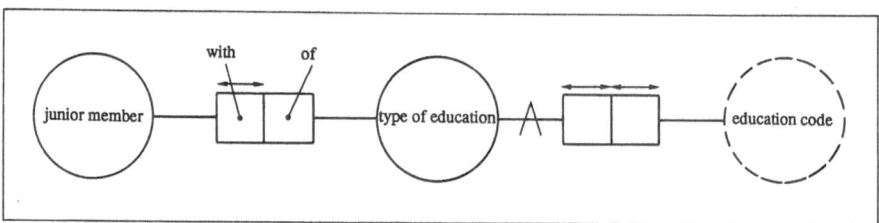

Figure 17.3.

As a consequence of the totality of the role "type of education with education code," a certain type of education can only be assigned to a junior member if that type of education and its corresponding education code have already been put in the information base at an earlier stage. Moreover, the use of education codes can be safeguarded by ensuring that only certain authorized users can add and delete the education codes in the future information system. In such a case, we are faced with deciding between including a value constraint for a lexical object type (i.e., "education code") and adding a non-lexical object type (i.e., "type of education"), whose objects are denoted by the objects of the lexical object type.

10.2 For every non-unique role, check whether a cardinality constraint applies.

One of the library regulations is that no more than 10 copies of a book may be purchased by the library:

> **for every book** b :
> **number of copies of** b $\leqslant$ 10.

For budgetary reasons, no more than 300 copies of new books may be purchased by the library per year:

> **for every year** y :
> **number of copies acquired in** y $\leqslant$ 300.

The following examples demonstrate that the cardinality constraints are generally more complex.

For every member, at most 6 loans can be "outstanding." A loan is considered "outstanding" when the borrowed copy of the book has not yet been returned, that is, when there is no date of termination of a loan.

> **for every member** m :
> **number of loans made by** m **and not terminated on** a date $\leqslant$ 6.

For every member, no more than two loans of novels written in English may be outstanding:

> **for every member** m :
> **number of (loans made by** m **and not terminated on** a **date and involving a copy of a (book of** the kind "novel" **and written in** the **language with language code** "Eng") $\leqslant$ 2.

A member may not have more than 2 nonexpired reservations:

> **for every member** m :
> **number of nonexpired reservations made by** m $\leqslant$ 2.

10.3 For every subtype, check whether a subtype defining constraint applies.

Any book whose kind name is "textbook" is a textbook:

for every book b :
b is a textbook if and only if kind of b = "textbook."

Members older than 18 are adult members and all others are junior members:

for every member m :
m is a junior member if and only if
number of years of age of m ≤ 18.

for every member m :
m is an adult member if and only if
number of years of age of m > 18.

10.4 For the roles of every object type, check whether other non-graphical constraints apply.

The year of acquisition of a copy of a book must always be later than the year of publication of that particular book:

for every copy c :
year code of year of acquisition of c ≥ year code of year of publication of book of which is acquired c.

The date of termination of a loan is always later than the loan date:

for every loan l :
date of termination of l ≥ date on which made l.

The sign "≥" must be interpreted correctly, as dates cannot be compared with each other in the same way as normal numbers.

Because the return date is always 3 weeks later than the loan date and can be extended by 3 weeks, the return date must always be a multiple of 3 weeks later than the loan date:

for every loan l :
(date on which due l − date on which made l) can be divided by 21.

The "-" sign must be interpreted correctly in this case because dates cannot be subtracted from each other in the same way as normal numbers. We assume that the difference between the two dates is expressed in days.

A book can never be a translation of itself:

for every book b **not:**
b is a **translation of** b.

A loan can only be renewed if there are no nonexpired reservations for the borrowed copy of the book:

for every loan 1 :
date on which due 1 > **date on which made** 1 + 21
only if
1 is **involving** a **copy of** a **book** that **does not belong to a nonexpired reservation.**

The expression "date > date on which 1 is made + 21" refers to a date that is 3 weeks later than the loan date. As is already known, the due date is always 3 weeks later than the return date and can be extended by 3 weeks. If the due date is more than 3 weeks later than the loan date, we are dealing with a loan which has been renewed. All of the roles of the supertype "reservation" are also valid for the subtype "nonexpired reservation." This is the reason that the expression "book that does not belong to a nonexpired reservation" is allowed.

A book can only be reserved if all of the loans of the copies of this book are outstanding:

for every book b :
b **belongs to a reservation only if**
for every copy c **of** b :
c **belongs to a loan** that is **not terminated**
on a date.

If a borrowed copy of a book is returned after the due date, a fine of 70 cents is levied for every week or part thereof that the book is overdue:

for every loan 1 :
if date of termination of 1 > **date on which due** 1 **then**
amount of money fine of 1 =
((**date of termination of** 1 - **date on which due** 1) ÷ 7) * 0.7 + 0.7.

Because dates cannot be subtracted from one another in the same way as normal numbers, the symbol "-" must be interpreted correctly as meaning the difference between the two dates in days. The " ÷ " means division, where the remainder is omitted. The fine to be levied on all loans returned after the due date can be calculated on the basis of this constraint. The fact type involving the fine is therefore derivable, so it has been provided with a derivability symbol in Figure 17.2.

10.5 For every fact type, check whether a transition constraint applies.

The date of termination of a loan can only be increased by renewing the loan:

for every loan l :
the **new date on which due** l > the **old date on which due** l.

The "greater than" sign must be interpreted correctly in this case, because dates cannot be compared to each other in the same way as normal numbers.

Summary

A summary of the tenth step in the NIAM method of information analysis follows below.

10. Add the non-graphical constraints.

   10.1 For every role of a lexical object type, check whether a value constraint applies.

   10.2 For every non-unique role, check whether a cardinality constraint applies.

   10.3 For every subtype, check whether a subtype defining constraint applies.

   10.4 For the roles of every object type, check whether other non-graphical constraints apply.

   10.5 For every fact type, check whether a transition constraint applies.

APPENDIX 1   THE DATA MODEL

Table of Contents

1 Introduction

Some of the following items are determined during the design phase:

- how the information which is exchanged with the (automated) information system must be represented internally in the information system.
- how this information must be represented externally for the users.
- how this internal representation must be transformed into the external representation, and vice versa, while preserving the meaning of the data.

In this appendix, we will show how the internal representation of the information can be determined on the basis of the grammar. Because a large part of the information is stored internally in the information system, we will be able to see how the results of the NIAM method of information analysis can be used to design databases and files.

The information system should be realized in such a way that there can only be an exchange of data which is in agreement with all of the rules of the grammar.

Therefore, the data representing the information in the information system must describe only facts which belong to the fact types described in the information structure diagram. The information system may only accept facts which satisfy all of the graphical and non-graphical constraints. Consequently, a logical step would seem to be to derive the description of the internal representation of the information directly from the specification of the grammar. Because the information structure diagram describes a significant portion of the rules of the grammar, we will derive the internal representation of the information as far as possible directly from the information structure diagram.

The fact types described by the information structure diagram can be seen as binary relations. These can be represented directly in the information system, provided the non-lexical objects, which by definition cannot be represented, are represented by lexical objects.

However, the current technology in the field of automated information systems requires that these binary relations be combined into larger groups as much as possible, in order to provide a more efficient representation. As a result, we will combine the fact types described by the information structure diagram into larger relations, which describe the same facts as the original fact types, and represent all of the non-lexical objects by lexical objects. We shall consider the resulting relations to be a description of the representation of the information with which we are concerned.

We shall determine these relations in such a way that all of the graphical constraints which are represented in the information structure diagram can be expressed by the graphical symbols for these relations.

At the beginning of this book, we defined "data" as the "representation of information". Analogously, from now on we shall call the description of the internal representation of information by the abovementioned relations a *data model*.

We will use concepts originating from the environment of relational languages to partially describe the data model. Consequently, the data model is as independent as possible of specific software and implementation technologies, and in this sense is considered to be "neutral".

The process of deriving the data model from the information structure diagram will be called *grouping* fact types. This process can be completely formalized.

In this appendix we will describe the grouping process in general terms. In most of the cases which are not too complex, the process described here yields correct results.

In sum, the following starting points are valid for the grouping process:

- The non-lexical objects must be represented by lexical objects.
- The fact types must be combined into larger relations which describe the same facts as the original fact types.
- These relations should be determined in such a way that the graphical constraints in the information structure diagram can be translated, without loss of meaning, into similar constraints involving these relations.

In Section 2, we will examine the subject of representing the non-lexical objects by lexical objects and the demands this places on the information structure diagram. In Sections 3 through 7, we will show how the fact types described in the information structure diagram must be combined into larger relations. In Sections 8 through 11, we will deal with the topic of translating the graphical constraints in the information structure diagram into similar graphical constraints in these larger relations. In Section 12, we will demonstrate the grouping process for the information structure diagram of the library case. And finally, in Section 14, we will give an informal description of a simple grouping algorithm.

2 Representability

Since, by definition, non-lexical objects cannot be directly represented, they must be represented in the data model by means of lexical objects. Clearly, we must select lexical objects which refer uniquely to the corresponding non-lexical objects.

We saw earlier that an information structure diagram must always be referenceable, which means that **every** non-lexical object must be referred to uniquely by one or more lexical objects.

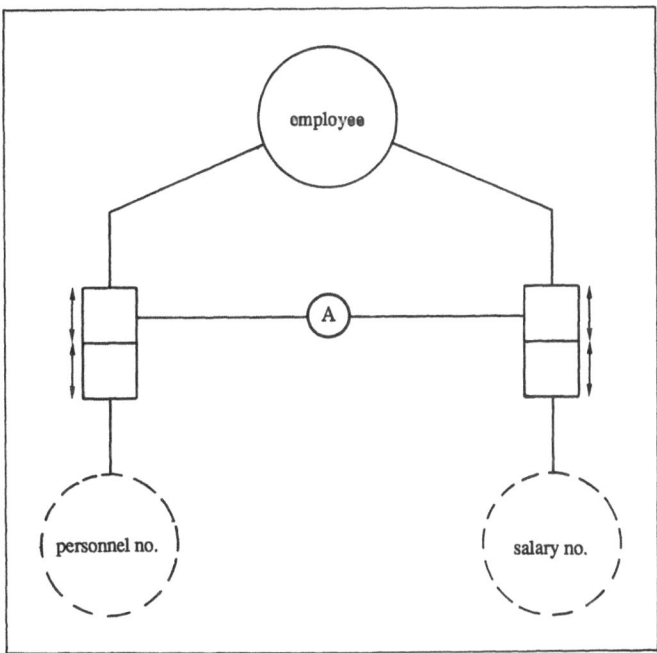

Figure 1.

In the information structure diagram of Figure 1, every employee can be referred to uniquely by means of a personnel number and/or a salary number. This information structure diagram is therefore referenceable. However, it is possible to have employees with only a personnel number and no salary number, and employees with only a salary number and no personnel number. When we wish to represent the information described by this information structure diagram in the information system, we have to represent the employees by personnel numbers or salary numbers; that is, by various kinds of lexical objects. With today's computer technology, this leads to a form of representation which is usually unacceptable, primarily for reasons of efficiency. Instead, the current state of technology requires that all of the non-lexical objects of a certain type be represented by lexical objects of a same type or by combinations of lexical objects of a same type, as is the case in the diagram of Figure 2.

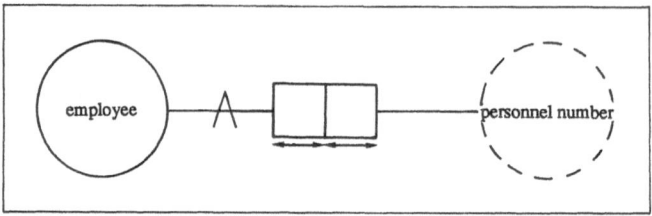

Figure 2.

In this diagram, all of the employees can be uniquely denoted by personnel numbers, and thus by lexical objects of a same type.

In the diagram of Figure 3, all of the rooms can be denoted uniquely by a combination of a floor number and a room sequence number, and thus by a combination of lexical objects of same types.

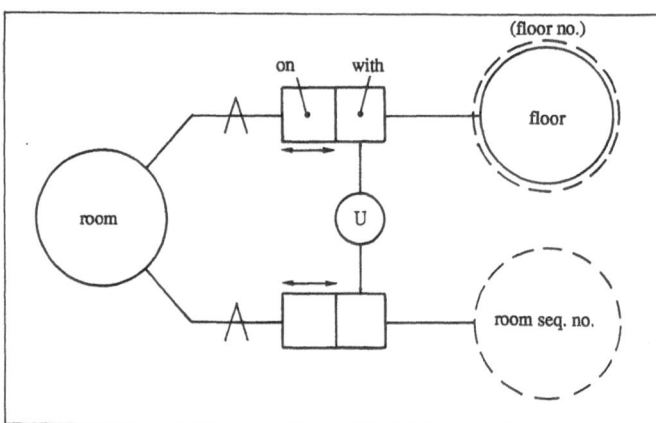

Figure 3.

In the diagram of Figure 4, all of the employees can be denoted uniquely by nicknames, and thus by lexical objects of a same type. However, it is possible for different nicknames to refer to the same employee. When we wish to represent the information described by this information structure diagram in the information system, we must represent every employee by a nickname. It is then possible for an employee to be represented by different nicknames. In today's computer technology, this leads to a method of representation which is usually unacceptable, primarily from the point of view of efficiency. Instead, present day technology requires every non-lexical object to be represented in a one-to-one way by one or more lexical objects.

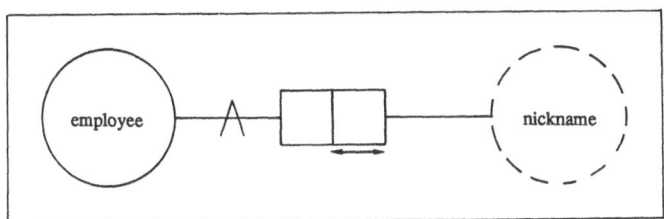

Figure 4.

Consequently, in realizing an automated information system, we require (bearing efficient implementation in mind) that the information structure diagram belonging to the specifications of this information system satisfy the following demand:

All objects of a same non-lexical object type must be referred to in a one-to-one way by lexical objects or combinations of lexical objects, belonging to the same lexical object type(s).

These lexical objects or combinations of lexical objects must then be selected as representations of the corresponding non-lexical objects.

An information structure diagram that satisfies this demand is considered to be *representable*.

The information structure diagrams in Figures 1 and 4 are not representable, while the diagrams in Figures 2 and 3 are. In the diagram of Figure 2, each employee has to be represented by a personnel number, and in the diagram in Figure 3, each room has to be represented by a combination of a floor number and a room sequence number. Likewise, the information structure diagram in Figure 5 is also representable. In this diagram, every employee has to be represented by either a personnel number **or** a combination of a mailbox number, a floor number and a room sequence number. It is possible, as this diagram shows, for the non-lexical objects of a same type to be represented in different ways. In such cases, a selection must be made from these various possible types of representation. We shall return to this point in the next section.

In addition, we note that a non-representable information structure diagram, such as the one in Figure 1 or in Figure 4, can in principle be implemented. However, with today's technology, the efficiency of this implementation will usually be unsatisfactory. Instead of a "representable information structure diagram", we should actually be talking about an "efficiently representable information structure diagram".

The representability demand stems from technological limitations, and is therefore a technical demand which only involves the realization aspects of the information system. As a result, this demand only holds during the realization phase and not during the information analysis phase.

For the purpose of realization, a non-representable information structure diagram must be modified until it becomes representable. This can be done in collaboration with or by those carrying out the information analysis.

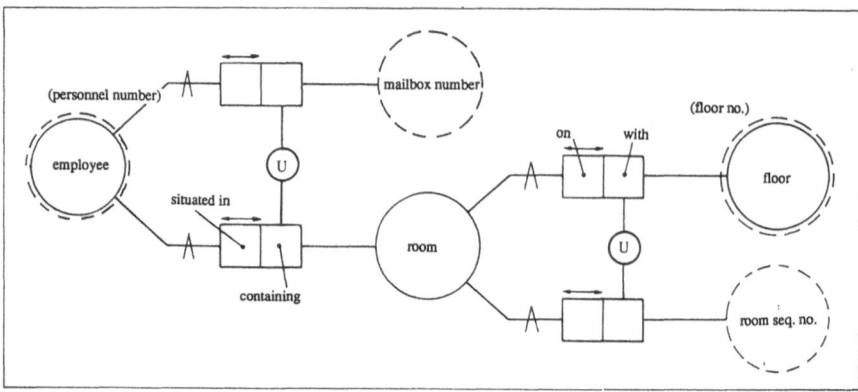

Figure 5.

In this appendix, we shall only discuss the implementation of representable information structure diagrams.

The reader should easily be able to verify whether the information structure diagram for the library case developed in the previous part of this book is representable.

3 Grouping fact types into relations

Part of the library case and a likely population have been depicted in Figure 6.

For the sake of clarity, we have represented in full all of the bridge types in which both roles are unique and in which the role of the non-lexical object type is total, rather than using the abridged notation for bridge types. Likewise, we have explicitly represented a number of subset and equality constraints implied by totality constraints. Since these subset and equality symbols are redundant, they have been depicted with broken lines.

Because the role "language of book" is not total and the role "language with language code" is, the former is a subset of the latter. Similarly, the role "kind of book" is a subset of the role "kind with kind name". Therefore, not every language and every kind which are known in the information base have to occur in the populations of the roles "language of book" and "kind of book". Apparently, language codes and kind names which have not (yet) been assigned to a book can occur.

As appears from the diagram in Figure 6, we assume in this example that the role "year of publication of book" is total. The roles "year of publication of book" and "year with year code" are now both total and are therefore equal. If we assume that the information structure diagram consists only of what is in the diagram in Figure 6, a certain year can only occur in the information base if it is a year of publication of a book.

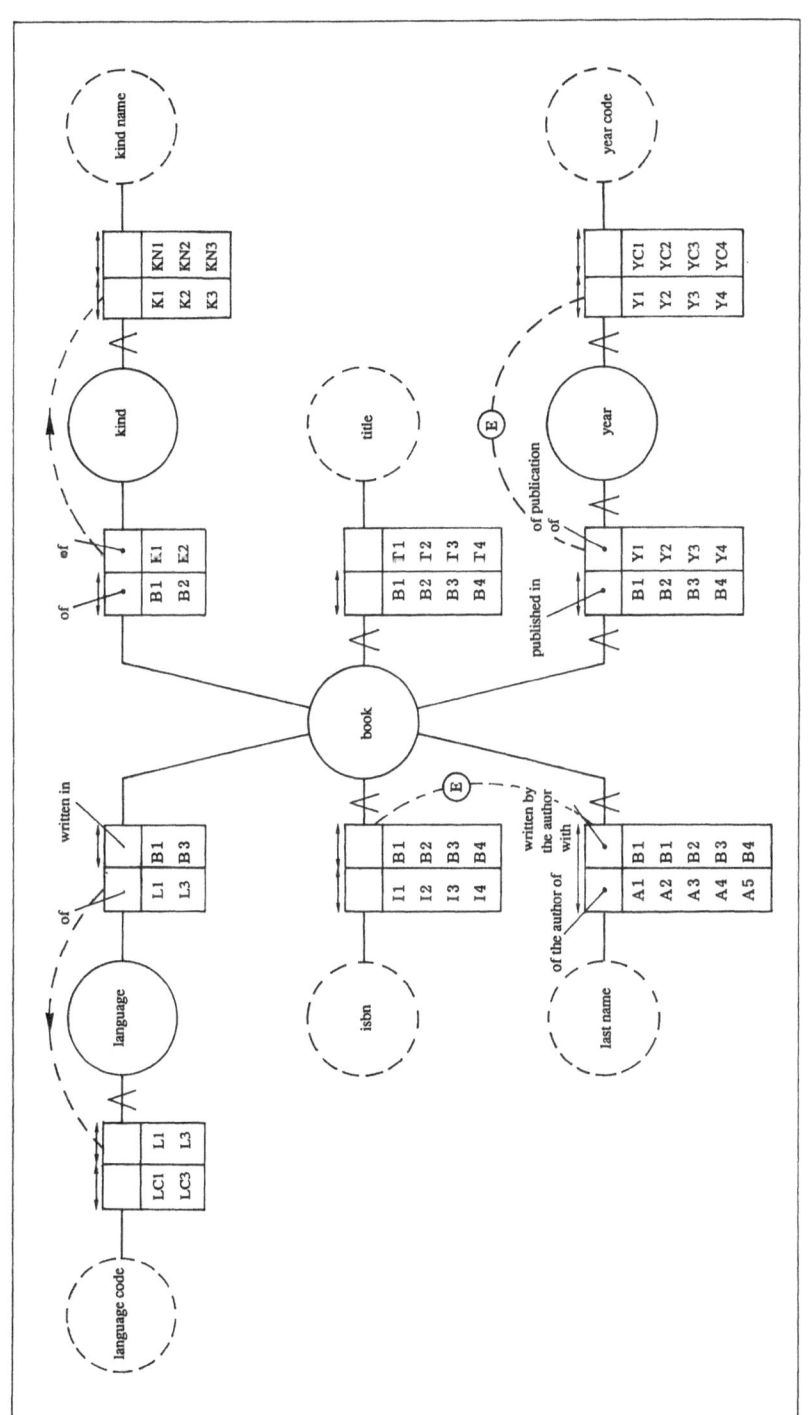

Figure 6.

Because the role "book written by the author with last name" is total, it is equal to all of the other total roles of the object type "book". We have denoted one of these implied equality rules (namely the equality of the roles "book written by the author with last name" and "book with ISBN") by an equality symbol of broken lines.

On the basis of this information structure diagram, the non-lexical object of the types "book", "kind", "language" and "year" must be represented by lexical objects of the types "ISBN", "kind name", "language code" and "year code", respectively.

As remarked in the introduction to this appendix, we shall combine the fact types described in this information structure diagram into larger relations which describe the same facts as the original fact types. We shall then replace the non-lexical objects in these relations by their lexical representations. The resulting relations then form a description of the representation of the information in this information structure diagram.

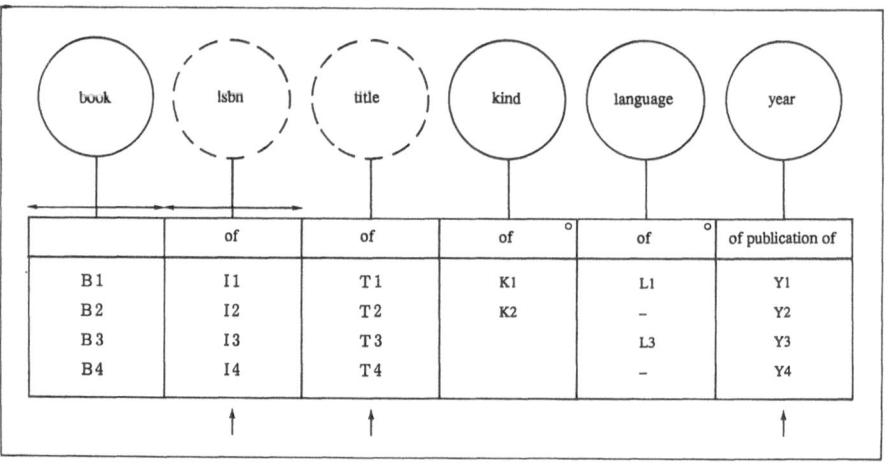

Figure 7.

In Figure 7, we combined all of the fact types of the object type "book" in Figure 6 in which the roles of "book" are unique, into one single non-binary "fact type".

According to the information structure diagram of Figure 6, every book has only one ISBN, one title, one kind and one year of publication and is only written in one language. Therefore, each book may occur only once in the population of Figure 7. This has been represented in the figure in the usual way by a uniqueness symbol involving the "role" of the object type "book".

According to the information structure diagram in Figure 6, every ISBN belongs to only one book. Every book occurs only once in the population of Figure 7. Therefore, every ISBN can likewise occur only once in this population. This has also been represented in this figure by a uniqueness symbol involving the "role" of the object type "ISBN".

By comparing the populations of Figures 6 and 7, we can check whether the non-binary "fact type" in Figure 7 describes exactly the same facts as the fact types in the information structure diagram in Figure 6. Because this non-binary "fact type" was created by combining a number of binary (and therefore elementary) fact types, this "fact type" is clearly not elementary. As we use the concept "fact type" for **elementary associations** only, from now on we will simply refer to combined elementary and non-elementary associations as *relations*. The "roles" involved in a relation will henceforth be referred to as the *attributes* of this relation. This brings us into line with the terminology used in relational languages. This nomenclature eliminates any confusion between the fact type roles and the "roles" which are created when fact types are combined.

For the sake of convenience, from now on we will not make a sharp distinction between a relation and its population and between an attribute and its population. Therefore, a relation can be seen as a table, and an attribute as one of the columns in this table.

Attributes (or combinations of attributes) which are denoted by a uniqueness symbol are called *unique attributes* (or *unique combinations of attributes*).

4 Mandatory and optional attributes

Because the roles "book with ISBN", "book with title" and "book published in year" are total in the information structure diagram of Figure 6, every book must occur with an ISBN, a title and a year of publication in the relation in Figure 7. This means that no empty or blank spaces may occur in these attributes.

In the information structure diagram of Figure 6, the roles "book of kind" and "book written in language" are not total. It follows from this that not every book has to occur in the relation in Figure 7 with a kind and a language. This means that the relevant attributes may contain empty or blank spaces. (We have denoted the empty spaces in Figure 7 by a "-" sign.)

Attributes which may not contain empty or blank spaces are called *mandatory attributes*, and those which may contain empty or blank spaces are called *optional attributes*.

From now on, we will denote the optional attributes by means of the symbol "°", as was done in Figure 7. We shall call this the *null value symbol*. The empty or blank spaces in the optional attributes in a relation are internally represented in the information system by a special and agreed value that may never occur as an actual value of any attribute. This value is called the *null value*.

Since realization demands that the information structure diagram must be representable, every relation contains at least one unique and mandatory attribute or one unique combination of mandatory attributes. This attribute or combination of attributes contains the lexical objects which are representations of the non-lexical objects of the object type around which that relation was formed. Therefore, in our example the relation "book" contains the unique and mandatory attribute

"ISBN". This attribute contains the lexical objects of the type "ISBN", which constitute the representations of the objects of the type "book".

5 Attribute names

Every attribute in the relation of Figure 7 contains objects of one particular object type. We have given every attribute in this figure the same name as the corresponding object type role. The attribute of the object type "book" has not been given a name because it corresponds to more than one object type role. If we add to every attribute, name the name of the object type to which it is related, it is no longer necessary to draw every object type explicitly, as we did in Figure 7. This results in the diagram of Figure 8.

book	isbn of	title of	kind of °	language of °	year of publication
B1	I1	T1	K1	L1	Y1
B2	I2	T2	K2	–	Y2
B3	I3	T3	–	L3	Y3
B4	I4	T4	–	–	Y4

Figure 8.

From now on, we will consider it sufficient to list the name of the object type to which the attribute is related, except when this makes the attribute name less clear. We have done this in Figure 9.

book	isbn	title	kind °	language °	year of publication
B1	I1	T1	K1	L1	Y1
B2	I2	T2	K2	–	Y2
B3	I3	T3	–	L3	Y3
B4	I4	T4	–	–	Y4

Figure 9.

Because the object types are not drawn explicitly, the graphical representation no longer shows which attributes contain non-lexical objects and which contain lexical objects. In order to be able to make this distinction, we have underlined the names of the attributes containing non-lexical objects. The attributes "book", "kind", "language" and "year of publication" contain non-lexical objects of the types "book", "kind", "language" and "year", respectively, and the attributes "ISBN" and "title" contain lexical objects of the types "ISBN" and "title".

Henceforth, we shall call attributes that contain non-lexical objects *non-lexical attributes*, and attributes that contain lexical objects *lexical attributes*.

How we arrived at Figure 9 from the fact types in the information structure diagram of Figure 6 is summarized below.

- We combined the fact types in which the roles of a same object type are unique into one relation.
- We included the unique roles of this object type only once in this relation.
- We gave each attribute the same name as the object type to which it is related.
- Where we felt it would enhance the clarity, we added the name of the role corresponding to this attribute to the attribute name.
- We underlined the names of the attributes of non-lexical object types (the non-lexical attributes).
- We denoted the attributes corresponding to unique roles, or combinations of attributes corresponding to unique combinations of roles, by the uniqueness symbol.
- We denoted the attributes corresponding to non-total roles (the optional attributes) by the null value symbol.

(This process of grouping fact types into relations corresponds to what is termed a "natural outer join" in relational languages.)

6 Binary relations

We saw above that the fact types in which the roles of a same object type are unique, form one relation. In the information structure diagram of Figure 6, neither of the fact type roles involving the object types "book" and "last name" is unique. Consequently, this fact type can never form a relation with other fact types. After grouping, fact types in which neither role is unique continue to exist as separate binary relations, as is depicted in Figure 10.

The fact that none of the attributes of this binary relation is unique has been, as usual, represented by a uniqueness symbol involving the combination of these attributes. A binary relation always corresponds to only one single fact type; every entry in the binary relation in Figure 10 describes one single fact. Consequently, there may never be any empty or blank spaces in a binary relation. If the last name of an author of a certain book is not known, this would be represented by not including this book in the binary relation of Figure 10. For this reason, the attributes in a binary relation may never be denoted by the null value symbol.

To summarize:

- Fact types in which neither of the roles is unique form separate binary relations.
- These are given a uniqueness symbol involving the combination of both attributes.

book	isbn	title	kind °	language °	year of publication
B1	I1	T1	K1	L1	Y1
B2	I2	T2	K2	–	Y2
B3	I3	T3	–	L3	Y3
B4	I4	T4	–	–	Y4

book	last name of the author of
B1	A1
B1	A2
B2	A3
B3	A4
B4	A5

Figure 10.

– The attributes of a binary relation may never contain empty or blank spaces and may consequently never be denoted by the null value symbol.

7 Replacing non-lexical attributes by lexical attributes

If we wish to represent the information described by the information structure diagram of Figure 6 by means of the relations in Figure 10, we must replace the non-lexical objects in these relations by their representations.

The non-lexical objects in the relations in Figure 10 are books, kinds, languages and years. It appears from the information structure diagram of Figure 6 that every book must be represented by an ISBN, every kind by a kind name, every language by a language code and every year by a year code.

Replacing all the non-lexical objects in the relations of Figure 10 by their representations results in the relations of Figure 11.

Every non-lexical attribute has now been replaced by a lexical attribute that contains the representations of the non-lexical objects. We have given these lexical attributes the same names as the lexical object types to which they are related. We shall agree to add the role names and non-lexical object type names from the information structure diagram to each of these attribute names when this enhances the clarity. This is exemplified by the attribute of the object type "year" in Figure 11.

The first relation in Figure 11 contains two attributes whose objects belong to the same object type, namely to the object type "ISBN". Moreover, both attributes

isbn	isbn	title	kind name °	language code °	year code of year of publication
I1	I1	T1	KN1	LC1	YC1
I2	I2	T2	KN2	–	YC2
I3	I3	T3	–	LC3	YC3
I4	I4	T4	–	–	YC4

isbn	last name of the author of
I1	A1
I1	A2
I2	A3
I3	A4
I4	A5

Figure 11.

are unique and mandatory. Consequently, these two attributes always contain exactly the same objects. It is clearly sufficient to include these attributes only once in this relation, as we did in Figure 12.

The way in which we arrived at the relations in Figure 12 from those in Figure 10 is summarized below.

isbn	title	kind name °	language code °	year code of year of publication
I1	T1	KN1	LC1	YC1
I2	T2	KN2	–	YC2
I3	T3	–	LC3	YC3
I4	T4	–	–	YC4

isbn	last name of the author of
I1	A1
I1	A2
I2	A3
I3	A4
I4	A5

Figure 12.

- We replaced every non-lexical attribute by a lexical attribute containing the representations of the non-lexical objects.
- We gave the lexical attributes the same names as the lexical object types to which these attributes are related.
- Where we felt it was necessary for clarity, we added role names and non-lexical object type names from the information structure diagram to these attributes.
- We included the attributes which involve the same lexical object types and which are unique and mandatory only once in every relation.

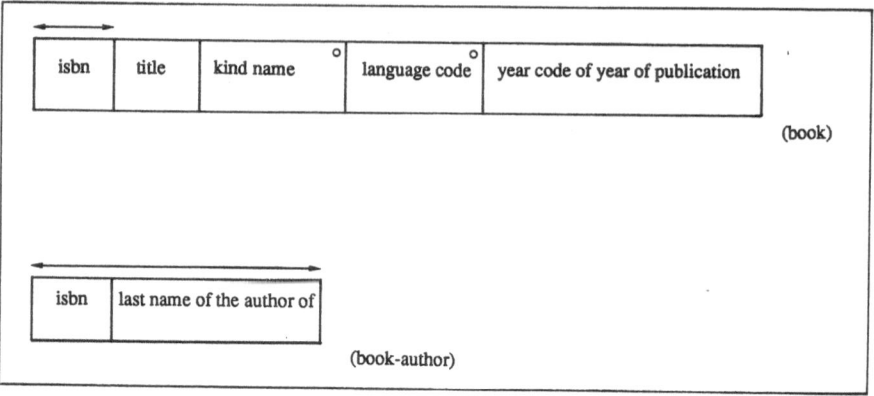

Figure 13.

Omitting the population in Figure 12 results in Figure 13.

This is a graphical representation of the relations, without any populations. We can consider these to be "abridged notations" for the relations.

As appears from Figure 13, we have given every relation a name that is as clear as possible.

8 Translating the remaining graphical constraints

In the information structure diagram of Figure 6, the roles "book with ISBN" and "book written by the author with last name" are total and therefore equal. In the data model of Figure 13, these roles correspond to the attributes "ISBN" of the relations "book" and "book-author", respectively. Because the roles corresponding to these attributes are equal, both attributes must always contain the same lexical objects (the same ISBN's). We have depicted this in Figure 14 by drawing an equality symbol between these attributes. We will call such attributes *equal attributes*.

This equality symbol is a translation of the equality constraint implied by the totality of the roles "book with ISBN" and "book written by the author with last name".

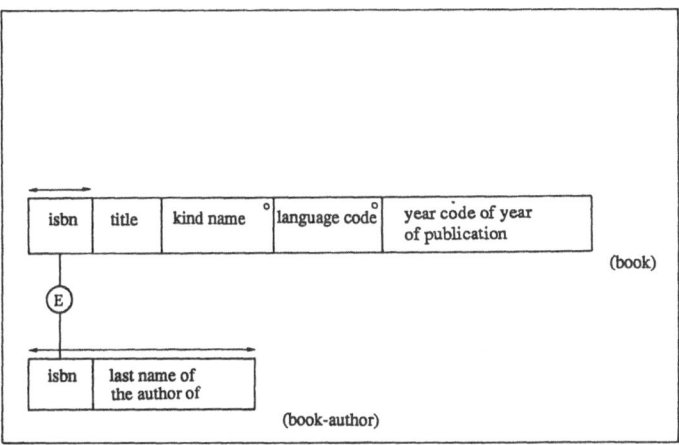

Figure 14.

All of the graphical constraints in the information structure diagram must be similarly translated into corresponding graphical constraints involving the attributes of the relations in the data model. In this process, the equality and subset constraints implied by totality constraints must not be overlooked.

9 Unary relations

We have now grouped the fact types involving the object types "book", "ISBN", "title", "language", "kind", "year" and "last name" in the information structure diagram of Figure 6 into two relations. However, the bridge types involving the object types "language" and "language code", "kind" and "kind name" and "year" and "year code" have been left out of consideration. Bridge types, in particular, are often overlooked, because the abridged notation for some of them makes them less conspicuous. Carrying out the grouping process for the three remaining bridge types in the information structure diagram of Figure 6 results in the three relations depicted in Figure 15.

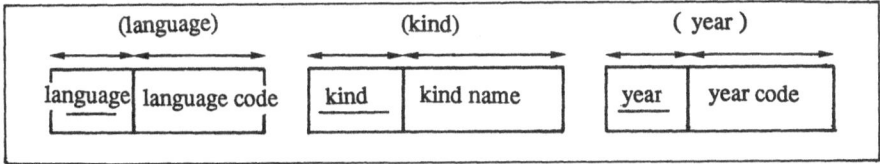

Figure 15.

Because both roles of these bridge types are unique, both attributes of these three relations are unique. Replacing the non-lexical attributes by lexical attributes (as described in Section 6) leads to the three relations of Figure 16.

We have now created three relations containing only one attribute. Relations which contain only one attribute are called *unary relations*.

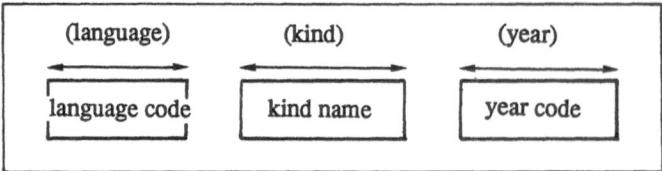

Figure 16.

Of course no empty or blank spaces can occur in a unary relation, so that the only attribute of a unary relation may never be denoted by the null value symbol.

Further, it can be observed that these relations contain only the representations of non-lexical objects of one single object type. After all, a language code is the representation of a non-lexical object of the type "language", the kind name is the representation of a kind, and the year code is the representation of a year.

The result of adding the three unary relations in Figure 16 along with the remaining graphical constraints in the information structure diagram to the data model of Figure 14 is depicted in the diagram of Figure 17.

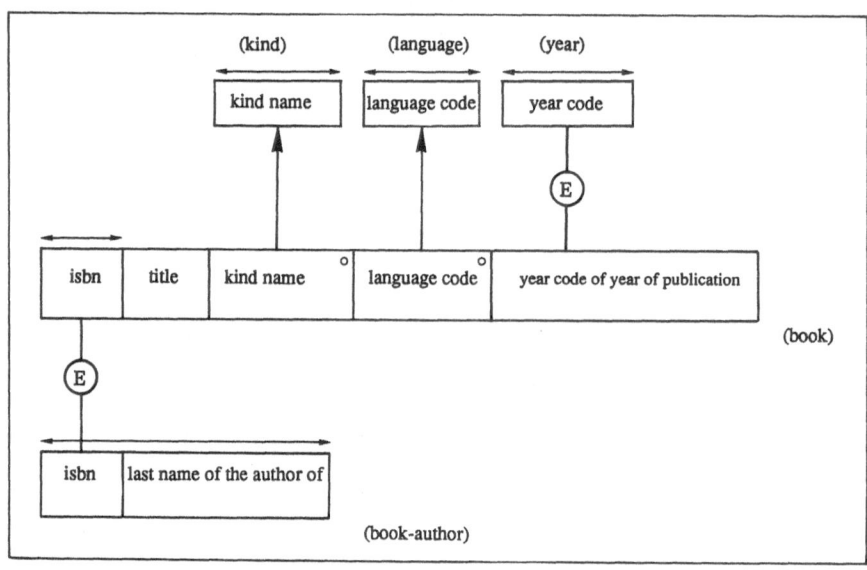

Figure 17.

In the information structure diagram of Figure 6, the role "kind of book" is not total, while the role "kind with kind name" is. Consequently, the role "kind of book" is a subset of the role "kind with kind name". In the data model, these roles correspond to the attributes "kind name" of the relations "book" and "kind", respectively. Because the role "kind of book" is a subset of the role "kind with kind name", every kind name which occurs in the relation "book" (naturally excluding the empty or blank spaces) must also occur in the relation "kind". The reverse is not necessarily true; not every kind name which occurs in the relation "kind" must also occur in the relation "book". This has been depicted in Figure 17 by means of a subset symbol.

In such a case, we say that the attribute "kind name" of the relation "book" is a **subset** of the attribute "kind name" of the relation "kind". The subset symbol for these attributes is a translation of the subset constraint implied in the information structure diagram by the totality of the role "kind with kind name". The relation "kind" contains all valid or usable kind names. It is not necessary for every one of these kind names to occur as a name of a kind of one of the books.

For the same reason, the attribute "language code" of the relation "book" is a subset of the attribute "language code" of the relation "language". Every language code which occurs in the relation "book" (naturally excluding the empty or blank spaces) must also occur in the relation "language". This relation contains all valid or usable language codes. It is not necessary for every one of these language codes to occur as a language code in one of the books.

The relation "year" is a slightly different case. In the information structure diagram of Figure 6, both of the roles "year of publication of book" and "year with year code" are total and therefore equal. Consequently, the attribute "year code of year of publication" of the relation "book" is equal to the attribute "year code" of the relation "year", as the equality symbol in Figure 17 indicates. Every "year code" that occurs in the relation "book" must also occur in the relation "year". And, vice versa, year codes may only occur in the relation "year" if they also occur in the relation "book". Therefore, the relation "year" contains only those numbers of years which occur as the year of publication of a book in the relation "book". It appears from this that the relation "year" can be deleted from the data model, without harming the specifications expressed by the information structure diagram. The diagram in Figure 18 represents the data model with the relation "year" deleted. Moreover, this is the final result of grouping the information structure diagram of Figure 6.

It goes without saying that every constraint in the data model must involve (by virtue of the compability rule) attributes or combinations of attributes which contain lexical objects of the same type. The names of the attributes indicate the lexical object types to which the attributes are related.

How we arrived at the diagram of Figure 18 is summarized below:

- We translated every graphical constraint in the information structure diagram into a similar constraint involving the attributes corresponding to the roles on which these constraints are based.
- In doing this we ensured that every constraint in the data model involves only attributes or combinations of attributes which contain objects of the same type.
- We deleted from the data model those relations which only contain the representations of the objects of one single lexical object type and which are only connected by means of one or more equality symbols to one or more relations.

(We note in addition that in the data model, the subset symbols have another meaning than the so-called "sets" which are defined in the CODASYL standards for databse languages.)

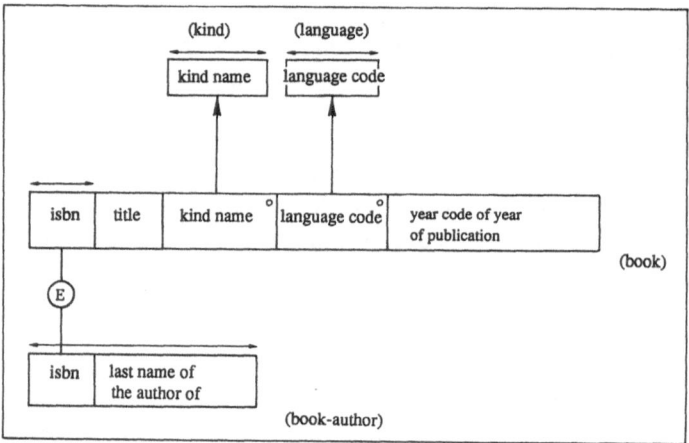

Figure 18.

10 Translating totality constraints involving combinations of roles

In Figure 19, we have modified the information structure diagram of the previous sections somewhat and added the object type "copy". A copy belongs to a certain book and is acquired in a certain year. As a supplement to the analysis performed in the previous part of this book, we assume that the **combination** of the roles "year of publication of book" and "year of acquisition of copy" is total. This totality constraint expresses the fact that every year occurring in the information base must either be a year of publication of a book or a year of acquisition of a copy. Consequently, the information base does not contain any numbers of years which are not the year of publication of a certain book and/or the year of acquisition of a certain copy.

In the fact types involving the object type "copy", the roles of the object type "copy" are unique. This results in a separate relation for copies, which has been represented in Figure 20.

A copy is represented by a copy number, a book by an ISBN and a year by a year code. After the non-lexical objects are replaced by their representations, the relation in Figure 21 results.

Grouping the remaining fact types in the information structure diagram of Figure 19 into relations and then translating all of the graphical constraints, results in the data model of Figure 22.

In this case, too, the unary relation "year" contains only the representations of the non-lexical objects of one object type (namely the object type "year"). In the information structure diagram of Figure 19, the role "book of which is acquired copy" is not total, so that it is a subset of one of the total roles of the object type "book". This is expressed in the data model of Figure 22 by indicating that the attribute "ISBN of book of which is acquired" is a subset of the attribute "ISBN" of the relation "book".

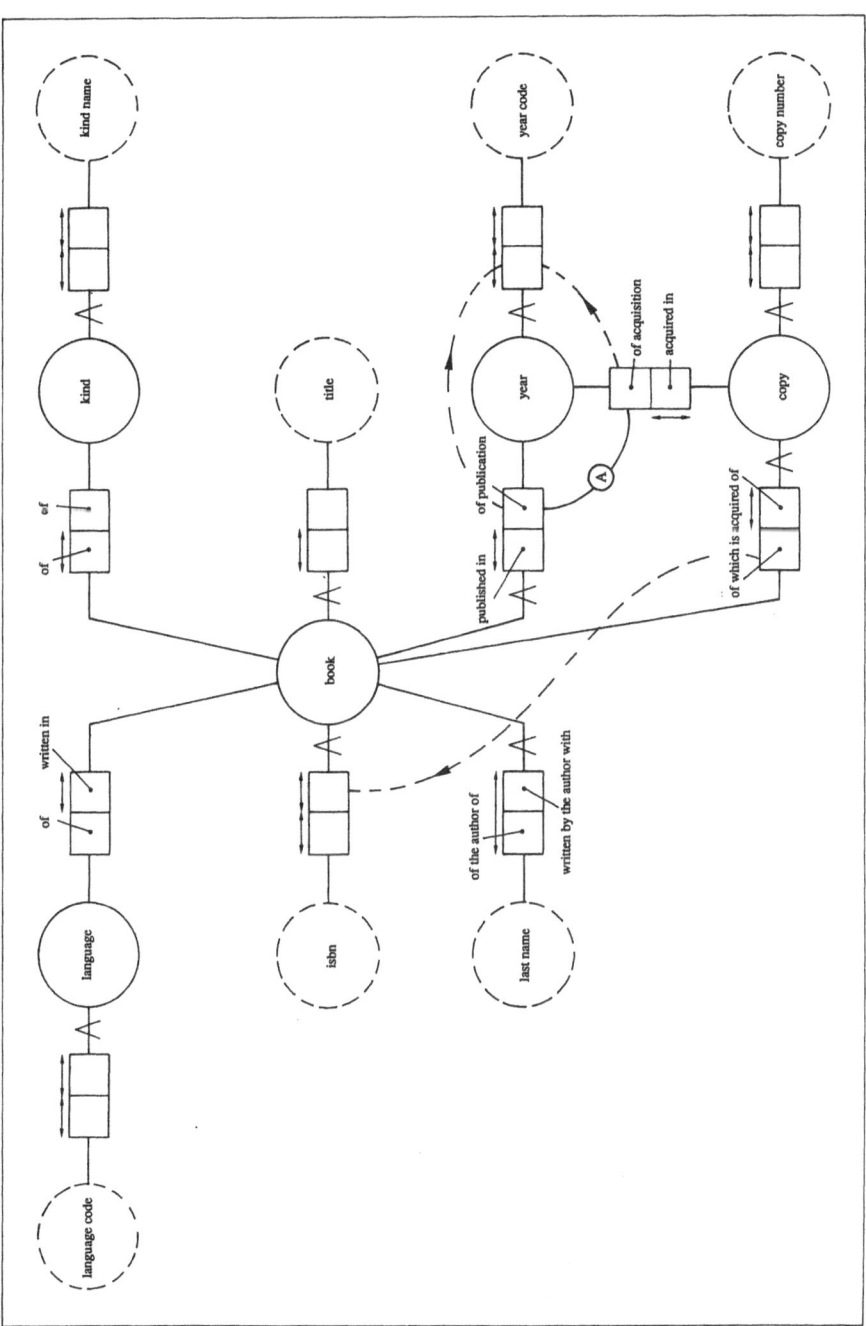

Figure 19.

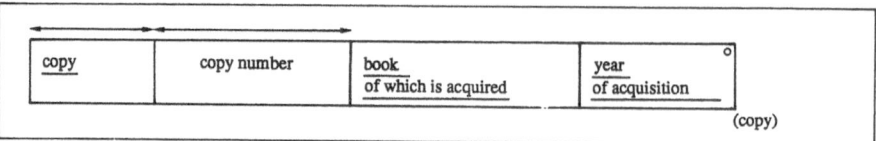

Figure 20.

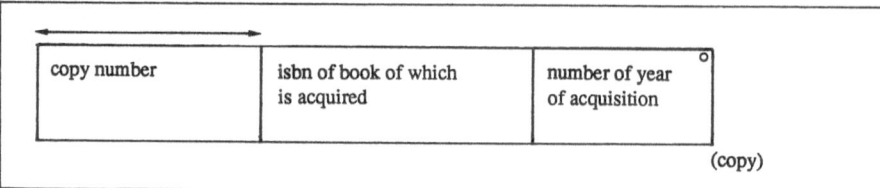

Figure 21.

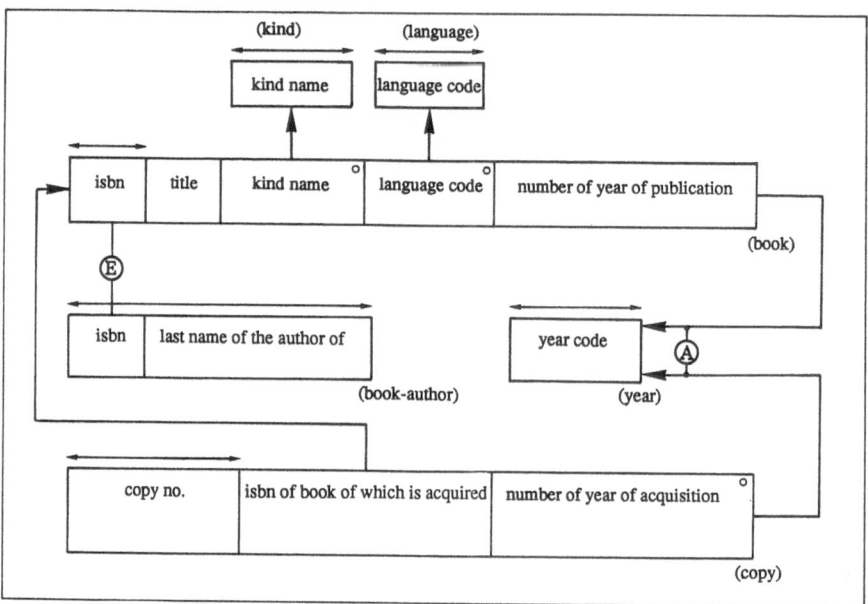

Figure 22.

The individual roles "year of publication of book" and "year of acquisition of copy" are not total, although the role "year with year code" is. Consequently, these roles are subsets of the role "year with year code". The roles "year of publication of book" and "year of acquisition of copy" correspond in the data model to the attributes "year code of year of publication" of the relation "book" and "year code of year of acquisition" of the relation "copy", respectively. The role "year with year code" corresponds to the attribute "year code" of the unary relation "year". The fact that this last role is total is expressed in the data model by indicating that the attributes "year code of year of publication" of the relation "book" and "year code of year of acquisition" of the relation "copy" are subsets of the attribute "year code" of the relation "year".

The fact that the **combination** of the roles "year of publication of book" and "year of acquisition of copy" is total is represented in the data model by a totality symbol involving the **subset symbols** connecting the relations "book" and "copy" to the relation "year". This expresses the fact that every year code occurring in one of the relations "book" and "copy" must also occur in the relation "year" **and** that every year code that occurs in the relation "year" must also occur in the relations "book" or "copy". Therefore, the relation "year" contains only year codes which occur as the year of publication of a book and/or as the year of acquisition of a copy in the relations "book" and "copy". Consequently, we can delete the relation "year" from the data model without harming the specifications expressed in the information structure diagram. Deleting the relation "year" from the data model results in the diagram of Figure 23. Moreover, this is the final result of grouping the information structure diagram of Figure 19.

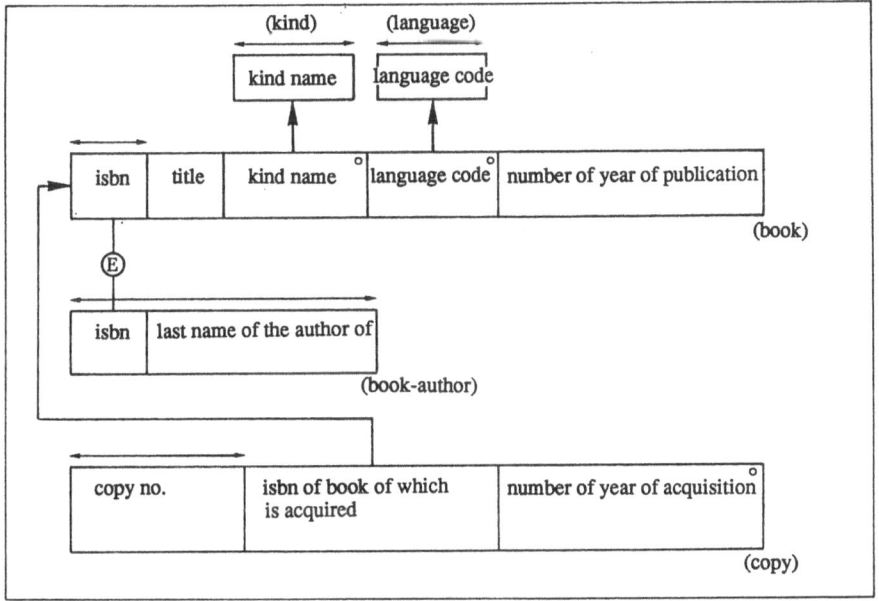

Figure 23.

To summarize:

We deleted from the data model those relations which only contain representations of the objects of one single non-lexical object type and which are connected to one or more relations by means of one or more equality or totality constraints.

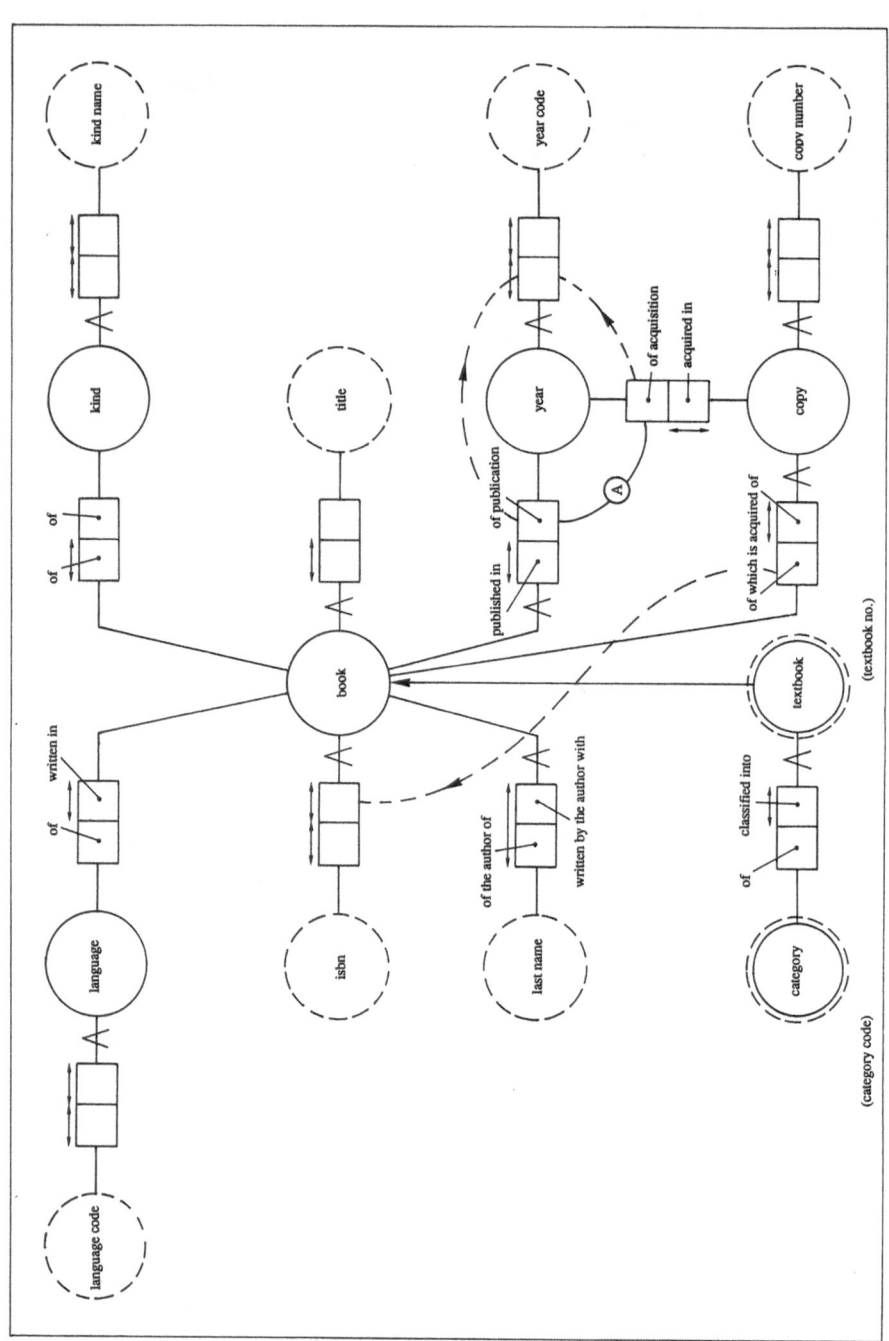

Figure 24.

11 Representing subtypes in a data model

In the previous section, we added the subtype "textbook" to the information structure diagram in Figure 24. In this section only, we will assume that every textbook has not only an ISBN, but also a unique so-called "textbook number". Only textbooks have a textbook number and a category. Every category is denoted in a one-to-one way by a category code. For the purposes of illustration, in this section, we will disregard the fact that earlier in this book we constructed a category code consisting of a main category and a subcategory code.

Although the object type "textbook" is a subtype of "book", it is a separate object type with characteristics which are only valid for the objects of this type (such as a textbook number and a category). Therefore, the fact types involving the object type "textbook" and having unique roles for this object type, form a separate relation. We have represented this in Figure 25.

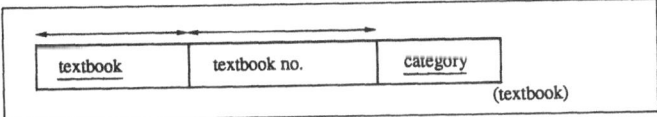

Figure 25.

Each textbook can be represented by a textbook number and, because textbooks belong to the object type "book", they can be represented by an ISBN as well. For reasons which we will explain further on in this section, we propose always to represent the objects of a subtype by representations of the objects of their supertype. On the basis of this, we will represent every textbook by an ISBN. Replacing the non-lexical attributes in Figure 25 by lexical attributes results in the diagram of Figure 26.

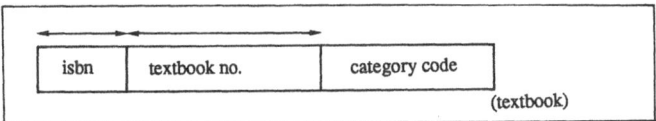

Figure 26.

In Figure 27, we have added this relation to the data model of Figure 23.

Subtypes such as the subtype "textbook" in our example are always represented by separate relations. This expresses the fact that a subtype is a subset of objects of a certain object type. The relation "textbook" contains all textbooks and the relation "book" all books. The characteristics which are only valid for textbooks are included in the relation "textbook". The characteristics valid for all books, and therefore for textbooks as well, are included in the relation "book".

The fact that the object type "textbook" is a subtype of the object type "book" is represented in the diagram of Figure 27 by the subset symbol connecting the

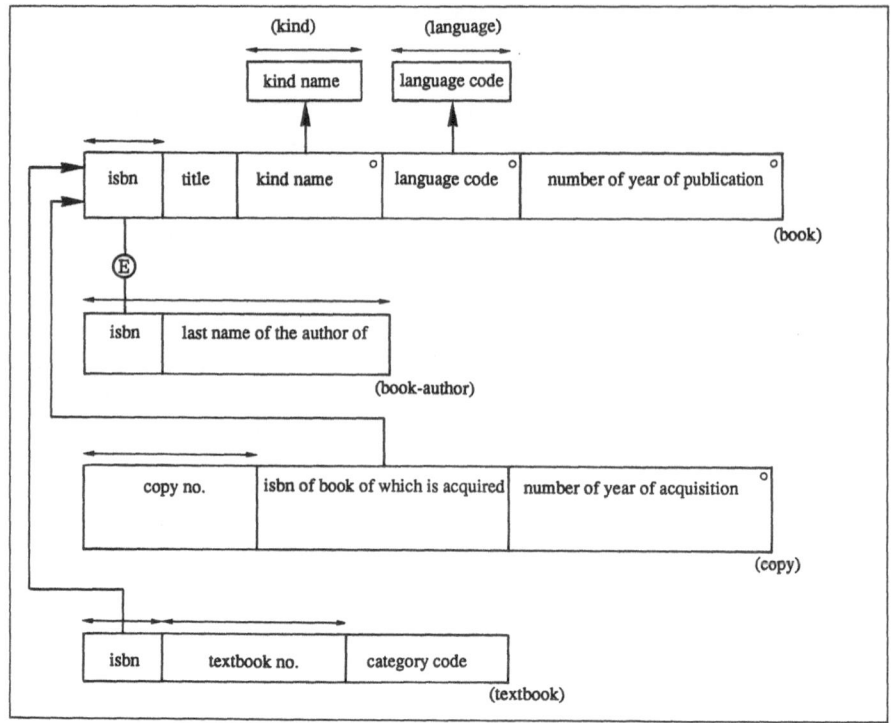

Figure 27.

relations "textbook" and "book". This expresses the fact that every ISBN which occurs in the relation "textbook" must also occur in the relation "book". In other words, the characteristics which are valid for books are also valid for textbooks.

Subtype symbols are always translated in a data model by subset symbols. These subset symbols must always be related to attributes containing lexical objects of the same type. By representing textbooks by objects of the type "ISBN" (the representations of the objects of the supertype), the lexical objects of this type occur in both the relation "book" and the relation "textbook". The fact that the object type "textbook" is a subtype of the object type "book" is then represented by a subset symbol involving the attributes of the object type "ISBN".

To summarize:

- The objects of a subtype must always be represented by representations of the objects of their supertype.
- The fact that an object type is a subtype of another object type must be represented by a subset symbol involving the attributes containing the representations of the objects of its supertype and pointing from the relation of the subtype to the relation of the supertype.

Lastly, the non-graphical constraints must be translated into expressions involving the attributes of the relations in the data model. The **data model** then consists of these translations of the non-graphical constraints, the translations of the graphical constraints and the graphical representation of the relations. In this book, we will not elaborate on the description of non-graphical constraints in a data model.

12 A practical example

We shall now derive the data model for the entire information structure diagram of the library case. To this end, we shall add a few hitherto neglected details to the description of the grouping process. We have depicted part of the information structure diagram of the library case in Figure 18. Initially, we will not consider the fact types involving the object types "textbook", "category", "main category" and "subcategory".

As a supplement to the analysis performed in the previous part of this book, we will assume that the role "edition of book" is total. Consequently, the information base contains only edition numbers which occur as edition numbers of books.

Figure 29 contains the relations which result from the process of grouping the fact types (except those involving the object types "textbook", "category", "main category" and "subcategory").

The binary relations "kind", "language", "year", "edition", "place" and "publisher" have all arisen out of bridge types represented in abridged notation. This illustrates once again how important it is not to overlook these kinds of bridge types when grouping.

Figure 30 is the result of replacing the non-lexical attributes by lexical attributes and translating the graphical constraints.

The relation "edition" contains only the representations of the non-lexical objects of the type "edition" and is only connected to another relation by an equality symbol. As a consequence, we will delete this relation from the data model.

The relation "year" contains only the representations of non-lexical objects of the type "year" and is only connected to other relations by a totality symbol. Consequently, we will delete this relation from the data model, as we decided to do earlier.

Once the relations "edition" and "year" have been deleted, the diagram of Figure 31 results.

Grouping the remaining fact types in the diagram of Figure 28 yields the relations in Figure 32.

The uniqueness symbol involving the combination of the attributes "main category" and "subcategory" of the relation "category" is a translation of the uniqueness symbol involving the combination of the roles "main category of category" and "subcategory of category". There are two bridge types involving the

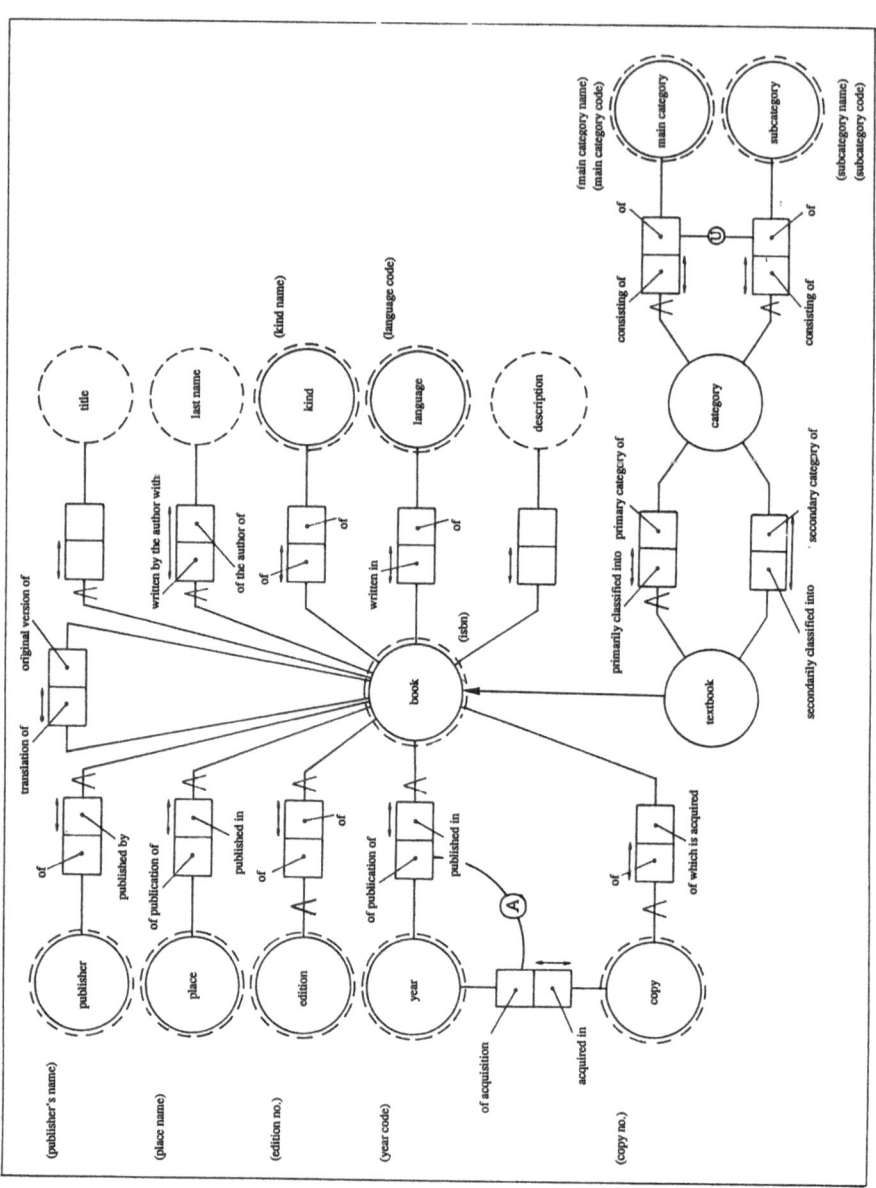

Figure 28.

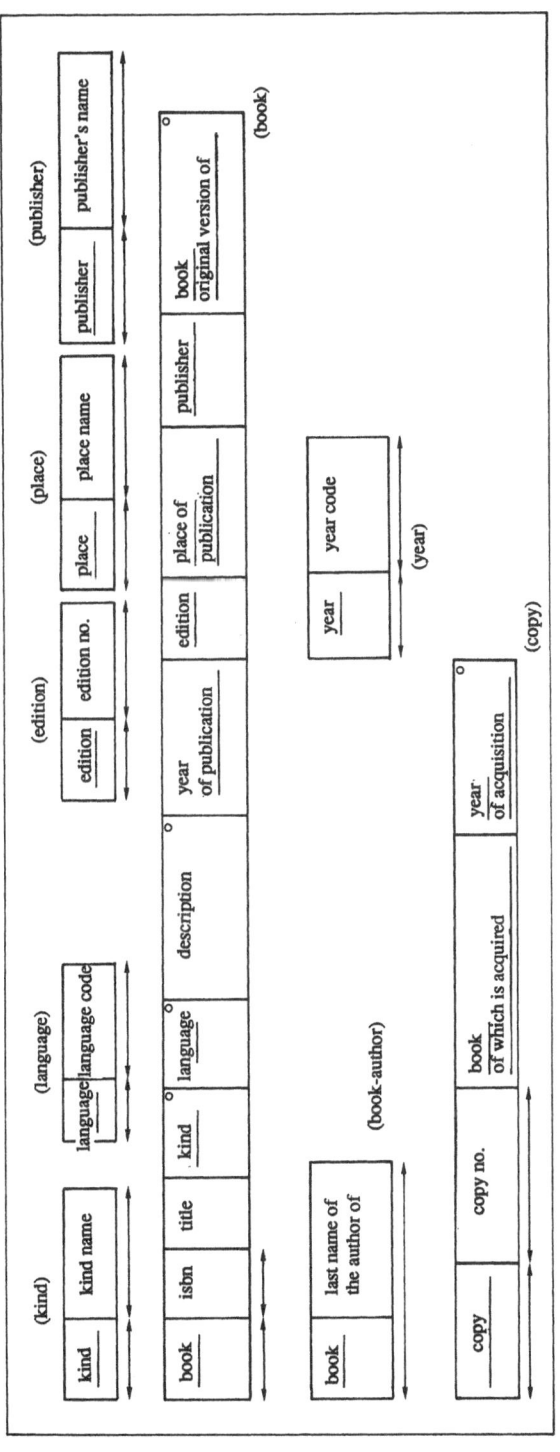

Figure 29.

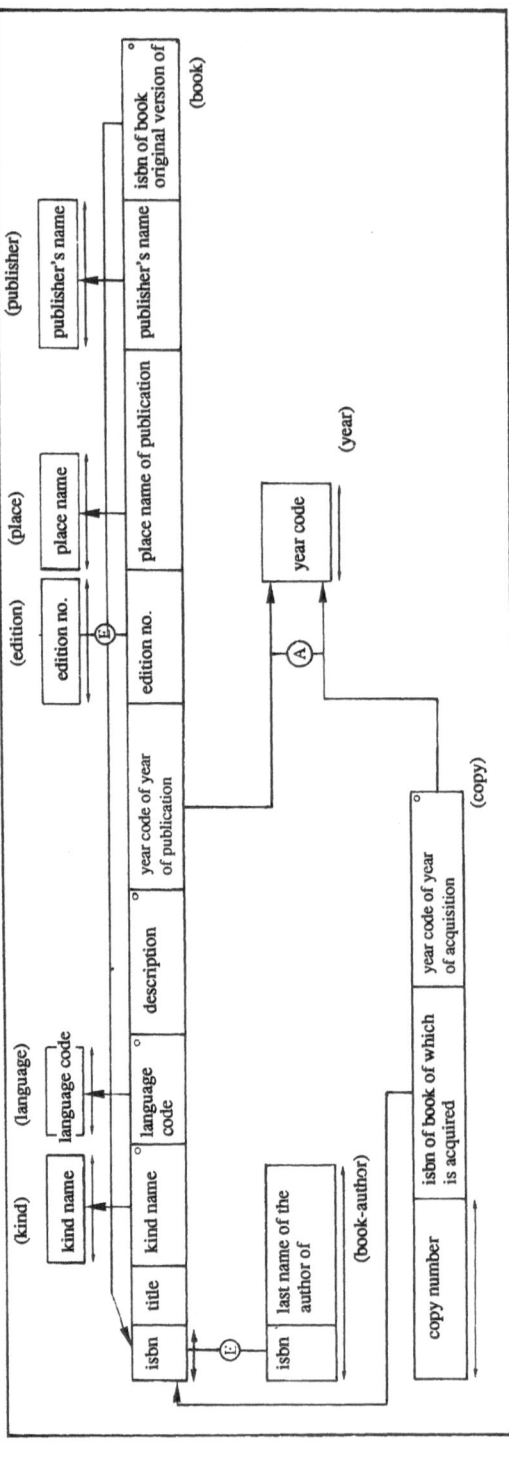

Figure 30.

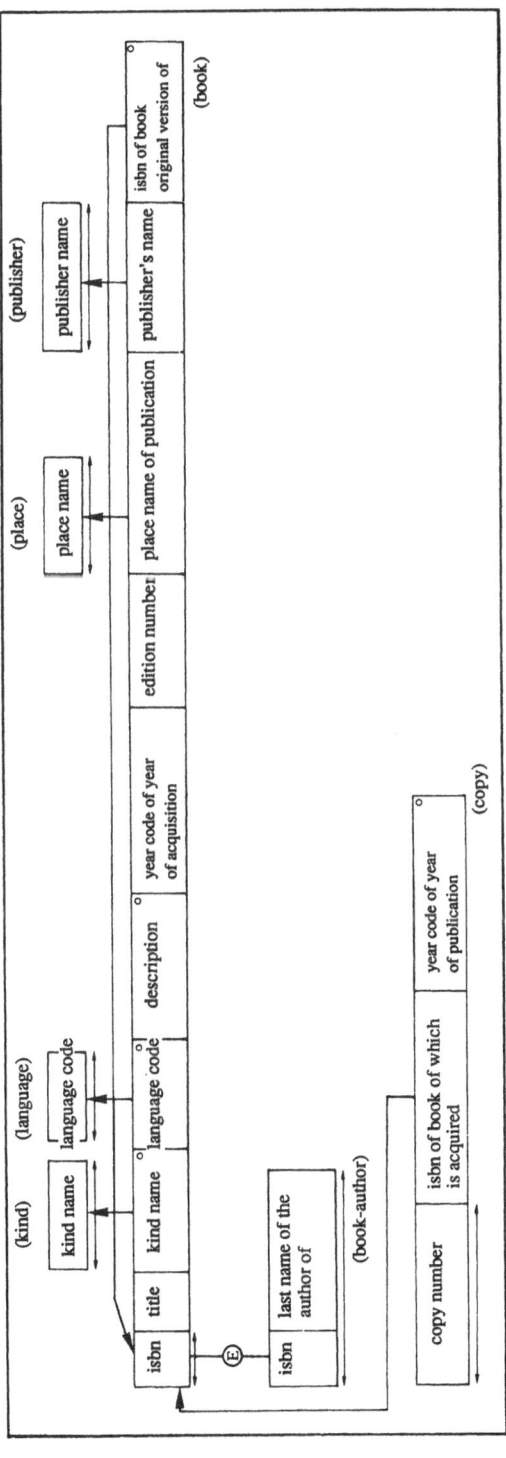

Figure 31.

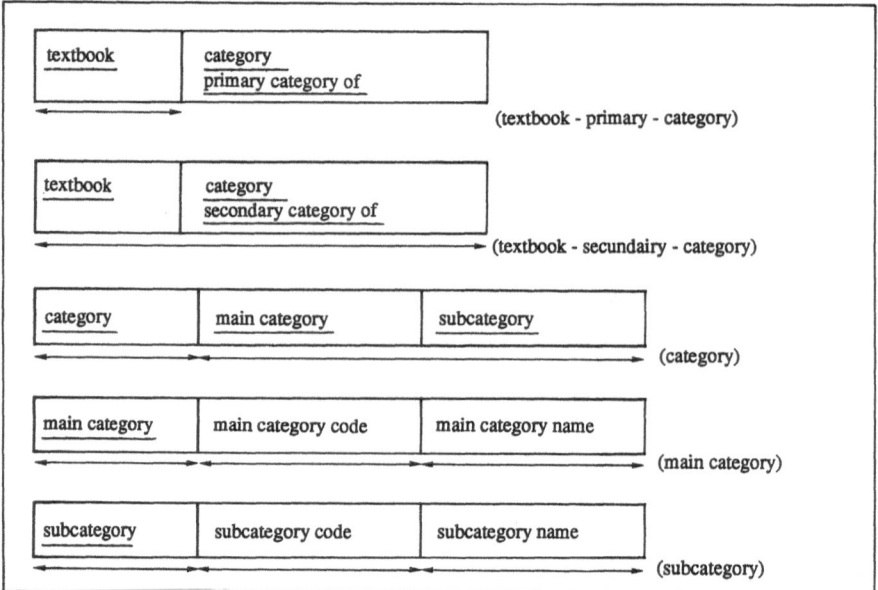

Figure 32.

object type "main category" and two involving the object type "subcategory", both of which are represented in abridged notation. All the roles of these bridge types are therefore unique. These bridge types (in abridged form) are grouped into the relations "main category" and "subcategory" whose attributes are, as a consequence of the uniqueness of all of the roles, unique.

It appears from the information structure diagram that a main category can be represented by either a main category code **or** a main category name, and that a subcategory can be represented by either a subcategory code **or** a subcategory name. Therefore, for the main and subcategories, we can choose from two possible representations.

If the non-lexical objects of a certain type can be represented in different ways, as is the case here, we must choose one form of representation for every relation in which such objects occur. This choice is usually based on technical considerations (i.e. efficiency). For all of the relations in Figure 32, we will represent the main categories by main category codes and the subcategories by subcategory codes.

Due to the uniqueness constraint involving the combination of the roles "main category of category" and "subcategory of category" and the uniqueness of the roles of the object type "category", every category can be unambiguously denoted by a combination of a main category and a subcategory. It follows from this that a category can be represented by a combination of a main category code and a subcategory code, or by a combination of a main category name and a subcategory name, or any other likely combinations of these. We shall represent the categories here by combinations of a main category code and a subcategory code. This means

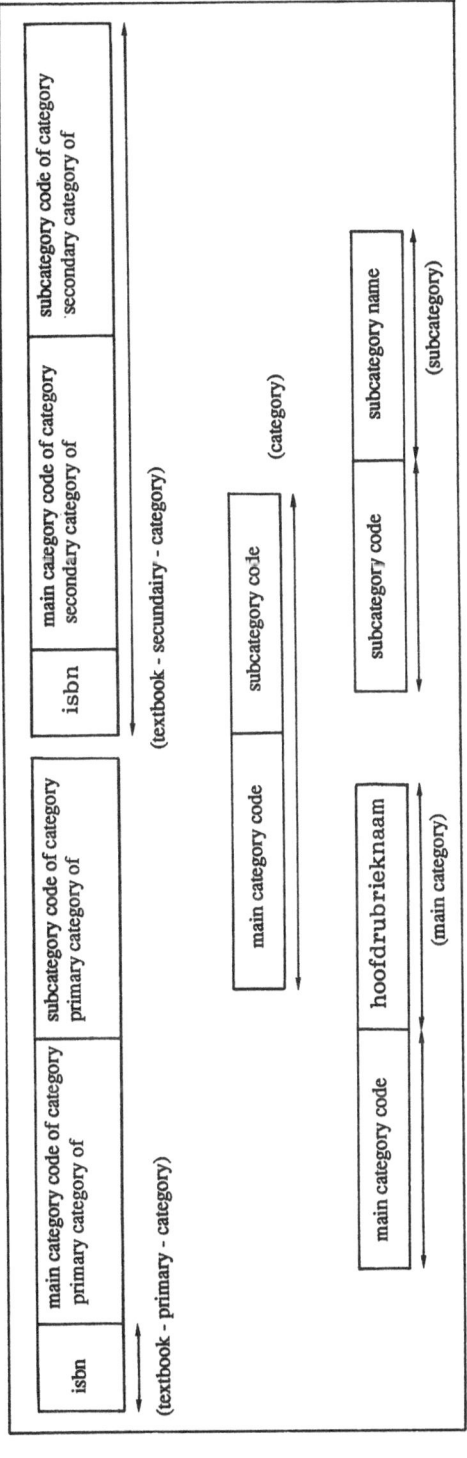

Figure 33.

here by combinations of a main category code and a subcategory code. This means that the non-lexical attributes "category primary category of" and "category secondary category of" and the non-lexical attribute "category" of the relation "category" can each be replaced by a **combination** of two lexical attributes containing main category codes and subcategory codes, respectively.

The diagram in Figure 33 is the result of having thus replaced the non-lexical attributes by lexical attributes.

The attributes "category primary category of" and "category secondary category of" are each replaced by a combination of a main category code and a subcategory code. After the attribute "category" in the relation "category" has been replaced by a combination of a main category and a subcategory, this relation contains the combination of a main and a subcategory twice. As both combinations of attributes are unique and mandatory, they both contain the same combinations of objects. As a result, these combinations only have to be included once in this relation.

The diagram in Figure 34 illustrates the result of translating the graphical constraints in the information structure diagram.

Subset symbol (1) is a translation of the subset constraint implied by the fact that the role "category primary category of textbook" is not total, while the role "category consisting of main category" is. Subset symbol (2) is a translation of the subset constraint resulting from the fact that the role "main category of category" is not total, while the roles "main category with main category code" and "main category with main category name" are. The remaining subset symbols are translations of similar totality constraints implied by subset constraints.

The relations "main category" and "subcategory" contain any valid or usable main and subcategory codes, along with their main and subcategory names. The relation "category" contains any valid or usable combinations of main and subcategory codes.

Figure 35 is a combination of Figures 31 and 34, in which the subtype symbol involving the object types "textbook" and "book" has been translated by means of a subset symbol involving the relations "textbook" and "book".

Figure 36 depicts another part of the information structure diagram of the library case. In Figure 37, the result of the grouping process has been added to the data model of Figure 35.

It appears from the information structure diagram of Figure 36 that a loan can be represented by either a loan number or a combination of a membership number, a copy number and a loan date. We have represented the loans here by loan numbers. According to the information structure diagram, a reservation can be represented by either a combination of a membership number, an ISBN and a reservation date, or a combination of an ISBN, a reservation date and a day number. As appears from the diagram in Figure 37, we have represented the reservations by combinations of a membership number, an ISBN and a reservation date.

The subset constraint involving the roles "loan with a fine of amount of money" and "loan terminated on date" can only be represented graphically in the data model by placing the attributes "date of termination" and "amount of money fine

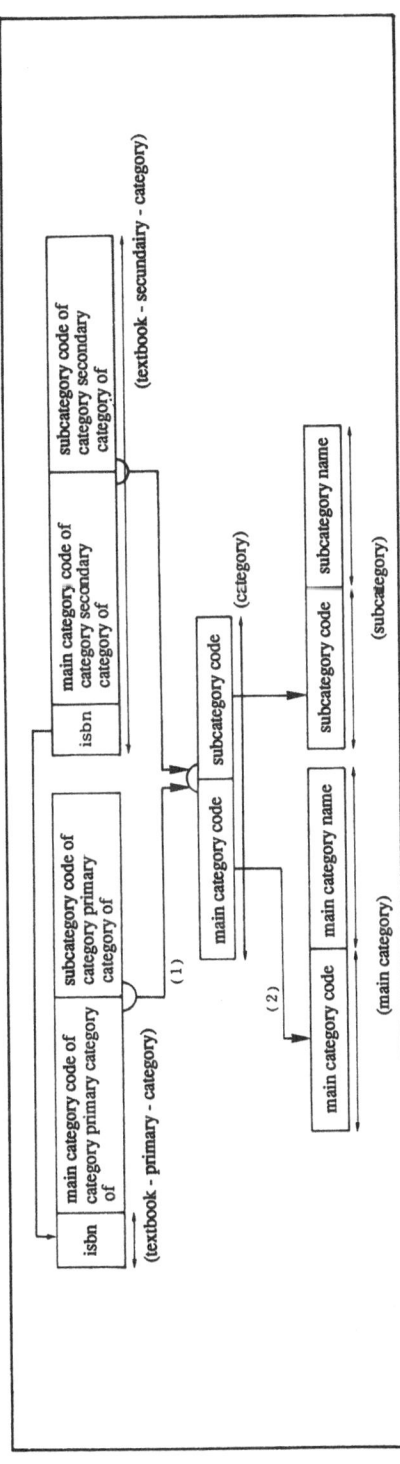

Figure 34.

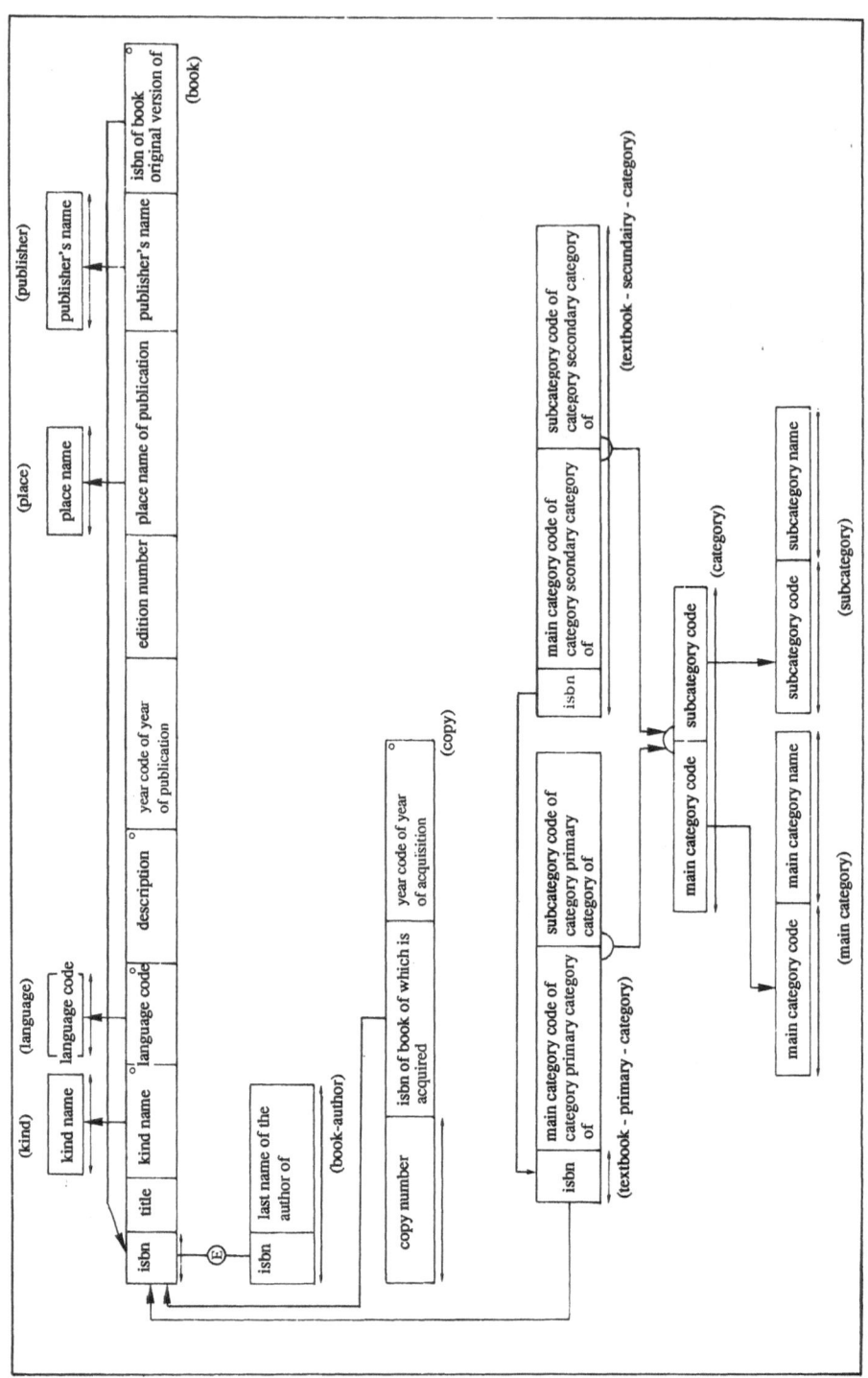

Figure 35.

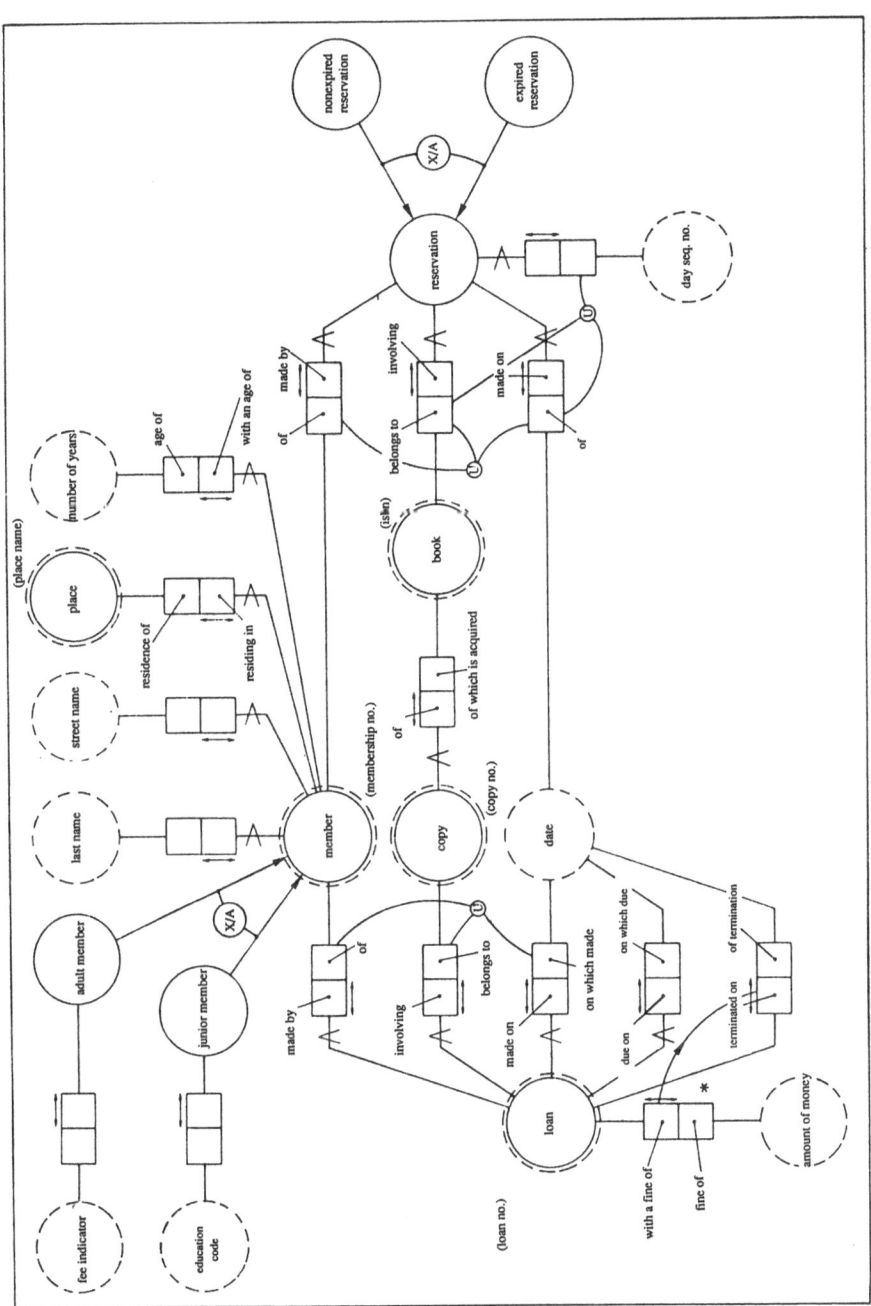

Figure 36.

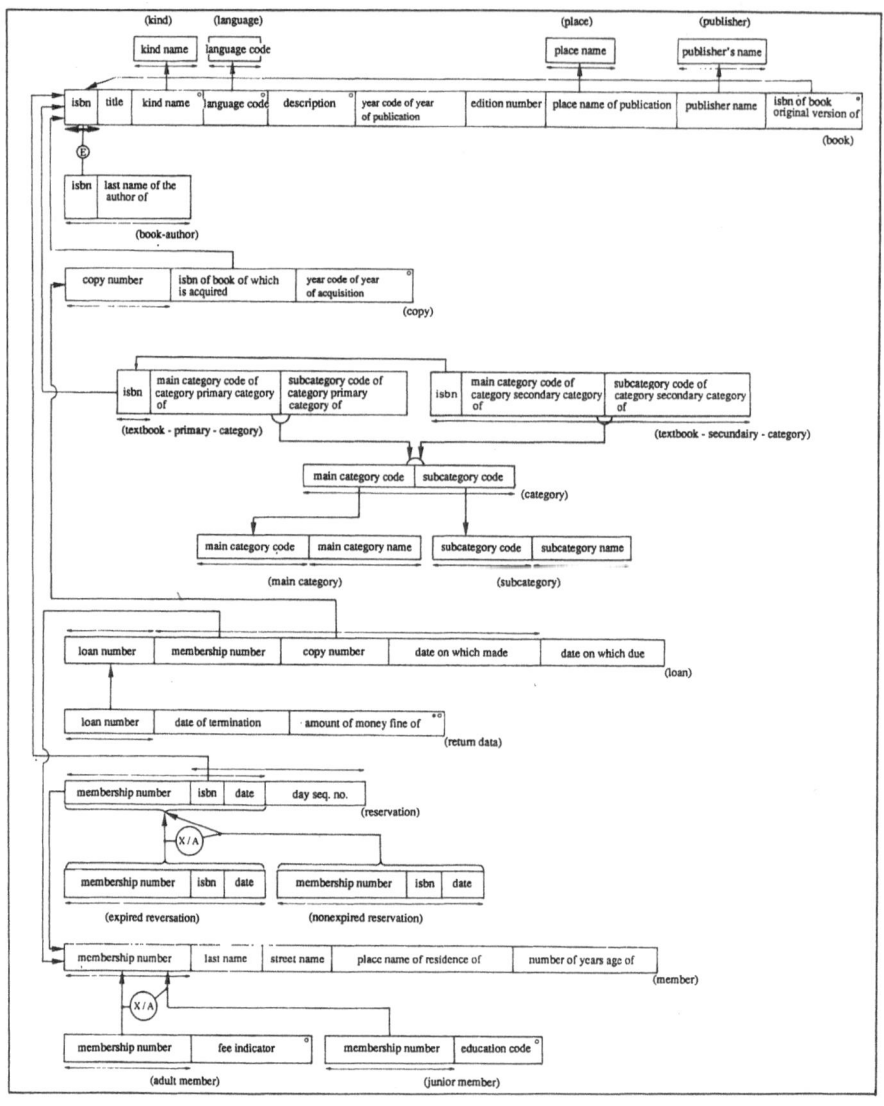

Figure 37.

of", together with the loan number (or the membership number, the copy number and the loan date), in a separate relation. In Figure 37, we have called this separate relation "return data". The subset symbol involving the loan numbers of the relations "loan" and "return data" then express the fact that a date of termination can only concern a loan registered at an earlier date. This is a translation of the fact that the role "loan terminated on date" in the information structure diagram is not total.

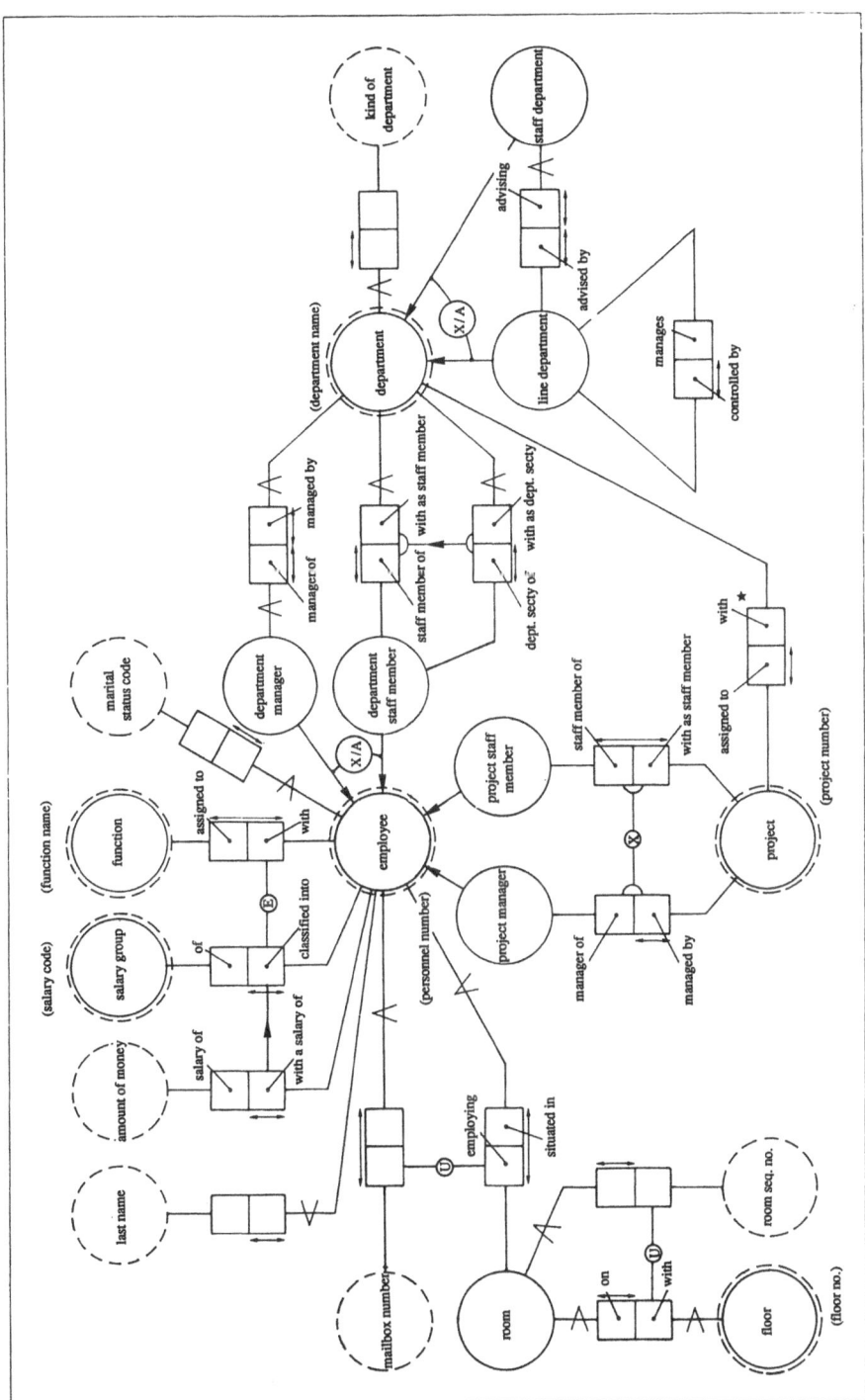

Figure 38.

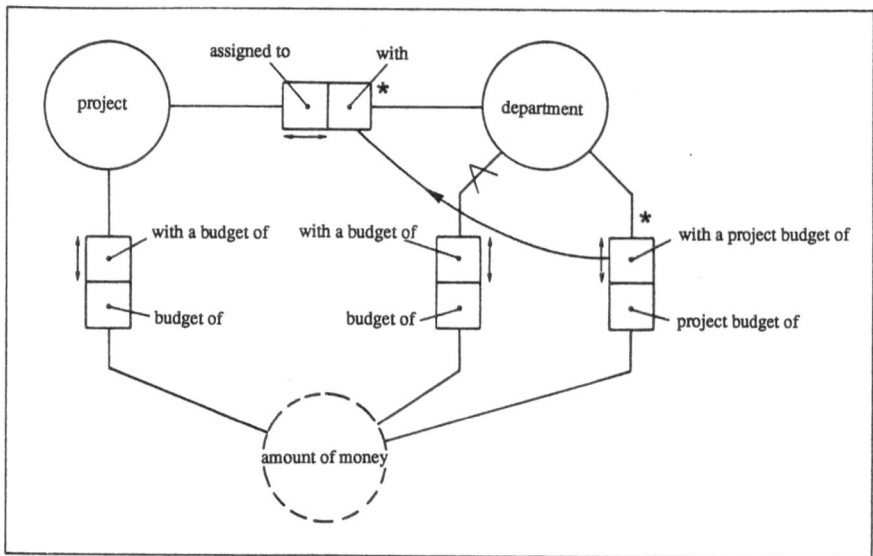

Figure 39.

The derivability symbol involving the fact type belonging to the object types "loan" and "amount of money" have been represented by a derivability symbol involving the corresponding attribute "amount of money fine of" of the relation "return data". This expresses the fact that the (lexical) objects of this attribute can be derived or calculated from the objects of other attributes on the basis of one or more non-graphical constraints. Later on in the design phase, a decision must be made as to whether this attribute will actually be stored physically or derived through software.

The exclusion and totality symbols connecting the subset symbols involving the relations "expired reservation", "nonexpired reservation" and "reservation" express the fact that every reservation must be either expired or nonexpired. This is depicted in the information structure diagram by the exclusion and totality constraints involving the subtypes "nonexpired reservation" and "expired reservation". This is similarly valid for the exclusion and totality constraints involving the relations "adult member" and "junior member".

Figures 38 and 39 depict yet another part of the information structure diagram of the library case. As a supplement to what we determined in the previous part of this book, we shall assume that the roles "floor with room" and "department manager manager of department" are total. Figure 40 illustrates the data model resulting from this part of the information structure diagram.

The fact type involving the object types "department manager" and "department" is grouped in the relation "department manager". Because **both** roles of this fact type are unique, it could also have been grouped in the relation "department".

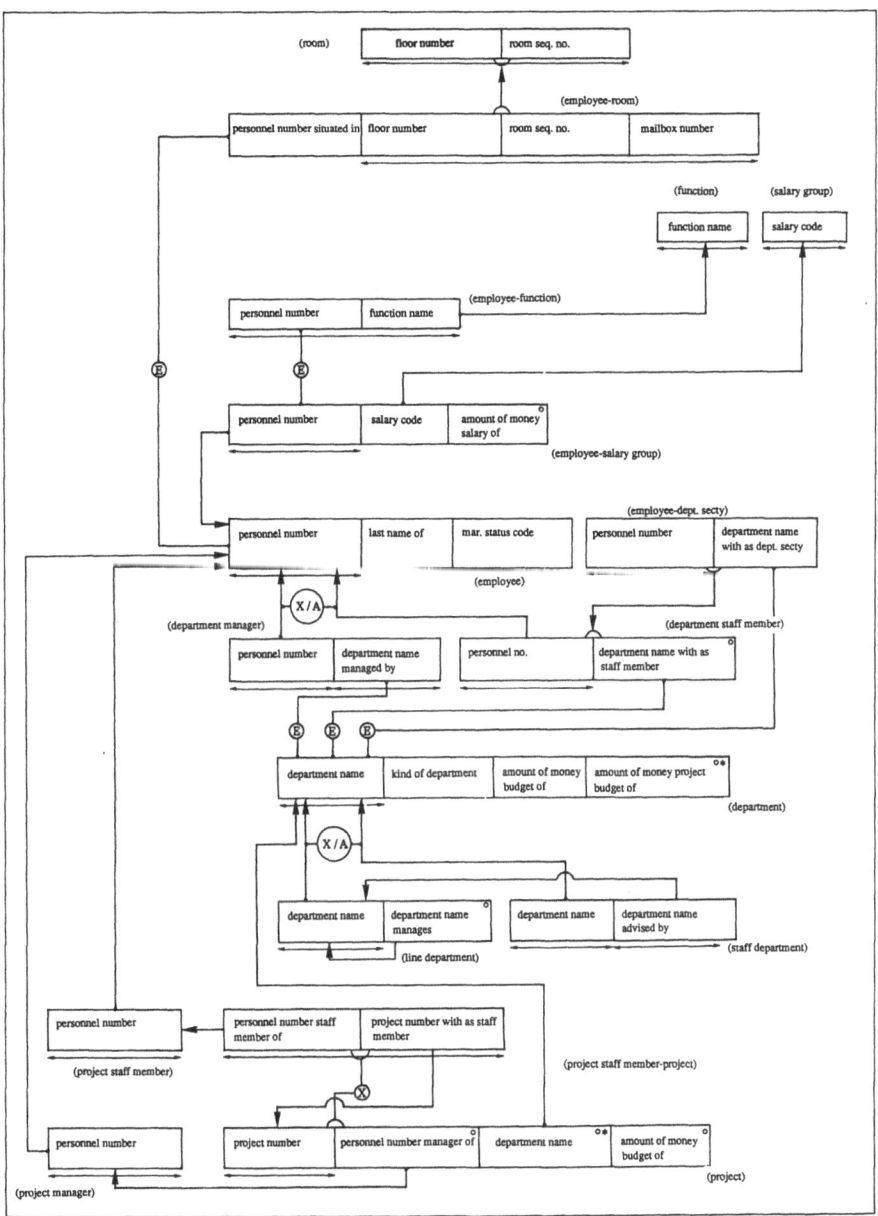

Figure 40.

Generally speaking, the choice between the two possible relations to which a fact type with two unique and total roles is added, is an arbitrary one. In such cases, the choice usually falls on the solution offering the greatest efficiency with respect to the internal data representation.

Because of the totality of the role "department manager manager of depart-

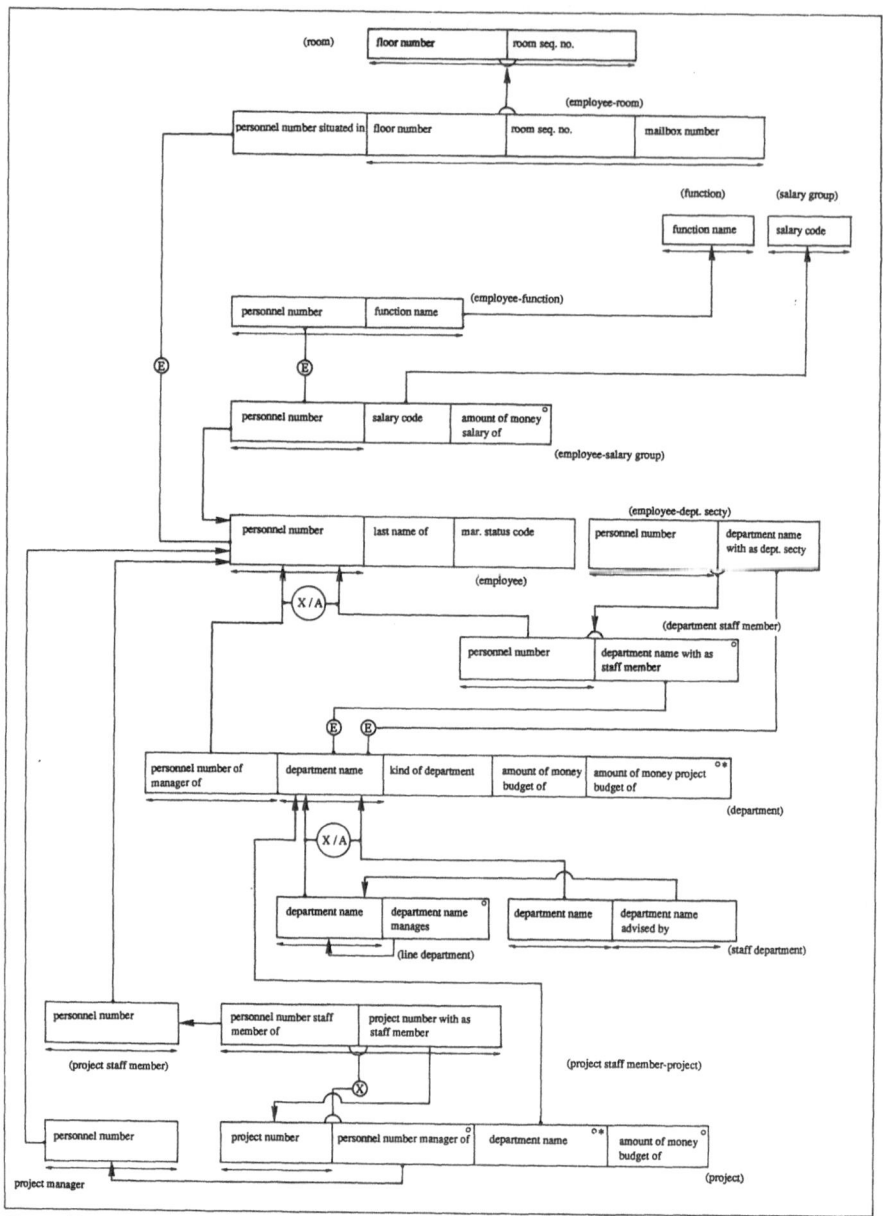

Figure 41.

ment", the attribute "department name managed by" of the relation "department manager" is a mandatory attribute. As a result of the totality of the role "department managed by department manager", this attribute is equal to the attribute "department name" of the relation "department". As both attributes are equal, unique and mandatory, they always contain the same objects.

Consequently, the relations "department manager" and "department" are combined into one relation, in which the attribute "department name" will, of course, only be included once, as shown in Figure 41.

If two unique and mandatory attributes of two relations or two unique combinations of mandatory attributes are equal, these two relations are always combined, so that the equal attributes or the equal combinations of attributes are included only once.

Finally, we note that empty spaces in optional attributes may not be "taken into account" when verifying constraints. After all, there are no lexical objects in empty spaces (an empty space has no value). Therefore, the population of Figure 42, for example, satisfies the uniqueness constraint depicted there.

a	b	c	d
a1	b1	c1	d1
–	b1	c1	d2
–	–	c1	d3

Figure 42.

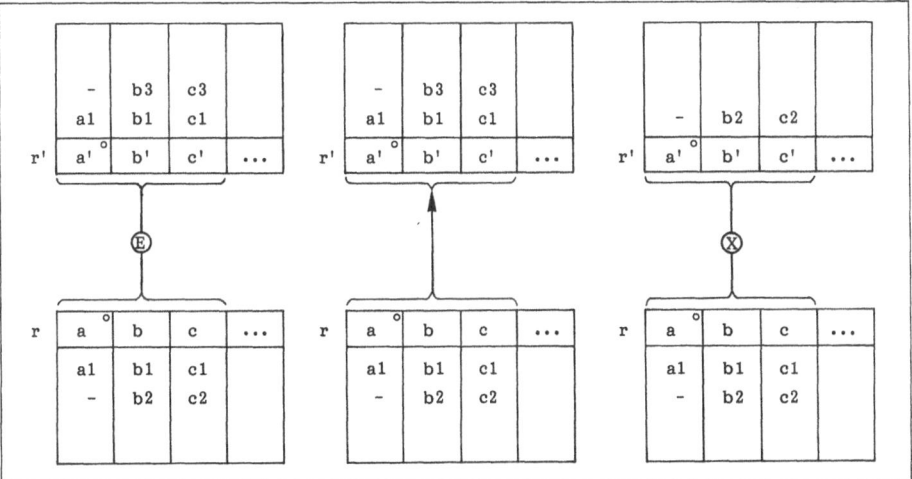

Figure 43.

Because of the uniqueness constraint involving the combination of attributes a, b and c, every **combination** of lexical objects (values) may occur only once in the populations of these attributes. Hence, the combination of lexical objects a1, b1 and c1 occurs only once. By contrast, in the population of the combination of attributes b and c, every combination may occur more than once. By the same token, all of the populations in Figure 43 satisfy the constraints depicted there.

13 The data model

The data model serves as a link between information analysis and design. The data model describes which data may be exchanged with the information system, how it needs to be represented in the information system, and what rules are valid for this data. All of the rules which are specified during information analysis are represented graphically or non-graphically in the data model.

As far as the data to be processed by the system is concerned, the information analysts and the designers of an information system integrate their work in terms of the data model.

The majority of the data described by the data model is stored in data files and/or databases. Consequently, the data model is the basis and the starting point for the definition of files and databases.

During the design phase, care must be taken to implement all of the rules which are expressed in the data model (including the non-graphical constraints) in the information system. While some of the graphical constraints can be implemented via the definitions of data files and databases, others may require implementation through software.

A decision has to be made as whether to physically store derivable attributes (those attributes corresponding to the roles of derivable facts and consequently provided with a derivability symbol) or whether to use software to derive them.

14 The grouping process

We have summarized below the steps in the process of grouping fact types into relations which were described in the foregoing sections.

1. **Group the fact types into relations**
   - Put all of the fact types in which the roles of same object type are unique together into one relation. Include these unique roles only once in this relation. (Be careful to add each of the fact types to only one relation and do not forget the bridge types represented in abridged notation.)
   - In every relation, assign the attributes the same names as the object types to which they are related. If it enhances the clarity, add the names of the roles that correspond to these attributes.
   - To enhance the clarity, underline the names of the non-lexical attributes (i.e. those attributes which contain non-lexical objects).
   - Denote every attribute or every combination of attributes corresponding to a unique role or a unique combination of roles by a uniqueness symbol.
   - Denote every attribute corresponding to a non-total role (every optional attribute) by a null value symbol ("0").
   - Denote every attribute corresponding to a role of a derivable fact type by a derivability symbol ("*").

- Fact types in which neither role is unique form separate binary relations, which are given a uniqueness symbol involving the combination of both attributes.
- The attributes of unary and binary relations may not contain any empty spaces and may consequently never be denoted by a null value symbol.
- Assign a name which is as clear as possible to every relation.
- Subtypes always form separate relations.

2. **Replace the non-lexical attributes by lexical attributes**
   - Replace every non-lexical attribute by a lexical attribute or by a combination of lexical attributes which contain representations of the corresponding non-lexical objects.
   - Assign to these lexical attributes the same names as the lexical object types to which these attributes refer.
   - If it enhances the clarity, add the role names and non-lexical object type names from the information structure diagram to these names.
   - The objects of a subtype must always be represented by the representations of the objects of the corresponding supertypes.
   - Include attributes or combinations of attributes which involve the same object types and which are unique and mandatory, only once in every relation.

3. **Translate the remaining graphical constraints**
   - Translate the remaining graphical constraints into similar constraints involving the attributes corresponding to the roles to which the constraints are related. (Do not forget the equality and subset constraints implied by totality constraints.)
   - Split a relation into several relations if that is necessary to graphically express a constraint in the data model. The relations resulting from the split must each contain the same unique and mandatory attribute or the same unique combination of mandatory attributes as the original relation.
   - Translate every subtype symbol by using a subset symbol which points from the relation of the subtype to the relation of the supertype and which connects the attributes containing the representations of the objects of the supertype.
   - Be sure that every constraint in the data model only involves attributes containing objects of the same type.
   - Delete relations which only contain the representations of non-lexical objects of one single non-lexical object type and which are only connected to one or more other relations by one or more equality and/or totality symbols.
   - Combine relations that contain equal and mandatory attributes or equal unique combinations of mandatory attributes into one relation. Include these attributes or combinations of attributes once only.

4. **Translate the non-graphical constraints**
   - Translate the specifications of the non-graphical constraints into similar expressions involving the attributes of the data model.

In most cases and disregarding null values, the relations resulting from this grouping process satisfy the demands known as the "fifth normal form".

The grouping process has been described here in very general terms and is certainly not complete. In order to be applicable in all situations, the description of this process must be refined. In this appendix, it has simply been our intention to give a reasonable impression of how the specification of the internal representation of information can be derived from the information structure diagram; we therefore consider this general description of the grouping process to be sufficient for our purposes.

The grouping process can be formalized and refined into an algorithm. Most of the available computerized support tools for NIAM implement this algorithm and automatically generate definitions of databases.

Although grouping fact types and constraints into a data model is not difficult, it is a fairly complex and multi-facetted process, and mistakes can therefore easily occur. Moreover, grouping extensive information structure diagrams, such as those which occur in actual practical situations, is very time consuming. In practice, the use of automated aids containing an implementation of a grouping algorithm is practically unavoidable. Such support tools also offer the opportunity of quickly verifying the specifications at various times in the analysis by using a prototype database.

APPENDIX 2   DEFINITIONS, SYMBOLS, PRINCIPLES, RULES AND ANALYSIS STEPS

This appendix contains a listing of the concepts, graphical symbols, principles, rules and analysis steps used in this book. The number of the page on which they were first mentioned or are redefined in the text is given for easy reference.

This appendix is to be used as an index.

Table of Contents

1 DEFINITIONS

Activity diagram: 32
A graphical representation of how information and/or goods are exchanged in an object system.

Analysis: 9
The phase in the development of an information system in which the specifications of the information system are formulated. These are exclusively concerned with the conceptual aspects of the information system.

Binary fact: 47
A fact that involves exactly two objects.

Binary fact type: 58
A fact type that involves exactly two object types.

Binary idea: 48
An idea that involves exactly two non-lexical objects.

Binary information structure diagram: 288
An information structure diagram that contains exclusively binary fact types.

Binary sentence type: 79
An elementary sentence type that involves exactly two object types.

Bridge: 47
A fact that concerns one non-lexical and one lexical object. A bridge indicates how a lexical object refers to a non-lexical object or which lexical object represents a certain characteristic of which non-lexical object. A bridge is by definition a binary fact.

Bridge type: 58
A fact type that involves one non-lexical object type and one lexical object type and whose populations thus consist of bridges.

Cardinality constraint: 358
A (non-graphical) constraint which restricts the number of times an object of a certain object type may occur in the role populations of this object type.

Communication: 1
Exchange or transfer of information.

Compound request: 101
A request from the users to the information processor to add or delete more than one fact to or from the information base. A compound request consists of two or more elementary requests. The information processor first executes these elementary requests and then verifies whether the resulting state transition and the new information base state are in agreement with the rules of the grammar.

Conceptual aspects of an information system: 9
Everything concerned with what the information system must do and the non-technical demands it must meet.

Constraints: 61
Rules which are not specifications of object types and fact types. Constraints restrict the facts which are allowed on the basis of the definitions of object types and fact types.

Construction: 11
The realization phase in which the automated part of the information system is realized on the basis of the design.

Controlled process: 4
A process from a real or an abstract world which is controlled and executed by one or more persons and/or equipment.

Co-role: 79
The other role in a binary sentence type or in a binary fact type.

Data: 1
The representation of information in a communication medium.

Derivable (inferable) fact: 372
A fact that belongs to a derivable fact type.

Derivable (inferable) fact type: 372
A fact type whose population can be derived at any moment from the populations of one or more fact types on the basis of one or more constraints.

Design: 11
The realization phase of the automated part of an information system in which it is determined:
   – how the data to be exchanged with the information system must be represented externally for the users.
   – how these data are to be represented internally to ensure efficient processing in the information system.
   – how these data are to be processed in order to transform the internal data representation into the external data representation and vice versa.

Elementary deep structure sentence: 72
An elementary sentence which is formulated such that it completely and explicitly represents all the knowledge which is necessary to understand this sentence.

Elementary proposition: 42
A proposition that expresses one single fact. Elementary propositions cannot be split into smaller propositions, without having the facts expressed by them get lost.

Elementary request: 101
A request from the users to the information processor to add or delete one single fact to or from the information base.

Elementary sentence: 68
A sentence in a natural language which forms the description of one elementary proposition.

Elementary sentence type: 75
A set or class of elementary deep structure sentences which describe the same type of information.

Elementary sentence type population: 75
The elementary deep structure sentences which belong at a given moment to an elementary sentence type.

Elementary sentence type role: 78
A column in a population table of an elementary sentence type.

Environment: 7
That which does not belong to the information system and which exchanges information with the information system. The environment can be considered as the set of all of the users of the information system. Unlike the behavior of an information system, the behavior of the environment is not by definition deterministic.

Equal roles: 168
Roles of the same object type whose populations are always equal.

Equality constraint: 168
A constraint which expresses the equality of two roles of a same object type

Exclusion constraint: 182, 197
A constraint which expresses the fact that roles of the same object type or combinations of roles of the same object types exclude each other.

Exclusive roles: 182, 197
Roles of the same object type or combinations of roles of the same object types whose populations exclude each other.

Exclusive subtypes: 320
Two or more subtypes of the same object type exclude each other if the objects belonging to these subtypes form exclusive or non-overlapping sets.

Fact: 46
An elementary proposition that expresses a relationship between objects in a certain reality. A fact expresses the proposition or supposition that this relation exists at a certain moment in the reality.

Fact type: 54
A set or class of facts which express the same kind of information.

Fact type population: 54
The facts which belong at a given moment to a fact type.

Father of a subtype family: 326
An object type that itself has no supertype within the subtype family. A subtype family has only one father. If we follow the subtype symbols in a subtype family in the direction of the arrows, we end up at the father of the subtype family.

Function: 36
A functional part of an information system.

Grammar: 2, 5, 20, 63, 85
The description of all the rules which prescribe which information base states and
information base state transitions may occur and the meaning of the data stored
in the information base. The grammar consists of a specification of:
- the elementary sentence types to which the elementary deep structure
  sentences describing the contents of the information base must belong.
- the constraints.

Graphical constraint: 96
A constraint which is represented by a graphical symbol in the information
structure diagram.

Idea: 48
A fact that involves only non-lexical objects.

Idea type: 58
A fact type that exclusively involves non-lexical object types and whose populations thus consist of ideas.

Information, communicable knowledge: 1, 40
Elementary propositions about objects in reality which we know or assume to be
true at a particular moment.

Information analysis: 10
The analysis phase in which the information that is to be exchanged with the
information system, is analyzed and described. During information analysis, the
data which may be exchanged with the information system and their meanings
(i.e., how these data are to be interpreted by the users) are described. This
description is the grammar of the information system.

Information base: 5, 36, 63
The description of all the facts which belong at a certain moment to the communicable knowledge or information about a certain reality, in so far as this
knowledge is to be registered by the information system.

Information base state: 20
The contents of the information base at a certain moment.

Information base state transition: 20
A change in the contents of the information base.

Information flow diagram: 36
A graphical representation of the information exchange between the functions and the environment of an information system.

Information processor: 22
The active component of an information system which:
- interprets and executes the questions and requests of the users.
- addresses questions and answers to the users.
- sees to it in carrying out these operations that the rules of the grammar are not violated.

Information structure diagram (ISD):   85
A graphical representation of elementary sentence types and thus of part of the grammar of an information system. Together, the information structure diagram and the specifications of the constraints describe the grammar of an information system.

Information system: 4
An information processing system that:
- receives information and requests for information from its environment and provides information and answers to requests to its environment.
- can store information in time.
- can derive new information from given information.

Knowledge: 1
Everything that someone knows about a certain subject or a certain area.

Lexical object (label):   44
An object in a certain reality which can be uttered, written down, or otherwise represented. Lexical objects always consist of letters, numbers, symbols and/or other characters. Lexical objects can be used as names for or references to other objects.

Lexical object type (label category), LOT: 51
A set or class of equivalent lexical objects.

Messages:
The information exchange between the users and the information system is accomplished by means of messages. These messages involve:
- questions the users have about the information described by the information base or the grammar.
- requests from the users to change the information base.
- answers and questions from the information system in response to the questions and requests of the users.

N-ary fact type: 279
A fact type that consists of an arbitrary, say n, number of roles. When n is equal to 2, we are dealing with a binary fact type. When n is equal to 3, we are dealing with a ternary fact type. An n-ary fact type must involve at least one non-lexical object type.

N-ary sentence type: 279
A sentence type that consists of an arbitrary, say n, number of roles. When n is equal to 2, we are dealing with a binary sentence type. When n is equal to 3, we are dealing with a ternary sentence type. An n-ary sentence must involve at least one non-lexical object type.

Non-elementary proposition: 42
A proposition that can be split into elementary propositions. These elementary propositions express the same information as the original proposition.

Non-graphical constraint: 96
A constraint which cannot be graphically represented in the information structure diagram and which must therefore be described separately from the information structure diagram.

Non-lexical object (entity):   44
An object in a certain reality which cannot be uttered, written down, or otherwise represented. Non-lexical objects must be named by lexical objects or referred to by means of lexical objects.

Non-lexical object type (entity category), NOLOT: 49
A set or class of equivalent non-lexical objects.

Object: 40
A matter or object from a real or an abstract world or part of one.

Object system: 8
The entity formed by the controlled process, the information system, and its environment.

Object system analysis: 10
The analysis phase in which the object system as a whole (which encompasses the controlled process, and the information system and its environment) is analyzed and described. During object system analysis the following items are defined and described:
  - the controlled process.
  - the controlling and executing activities being carried out for this process.
  - the type of information that the users exchange while performing these activities.
  - the type of information which, in support of the controlling and executing activities, must be exchanged with the information system.

Object type population: 52
The objects which belong at a given moment to an object type.

Population diagram: 55
A graphical representation of a fact type and one of its possible populations.

Population table: 77
A representation in table form of an elementary sentence type and one of its possible populations.

Predicate of an elementary sentence: 69
A name for the relation between the objects in a certain reality which are described by the elementary sentence.

Reality(universe of discourse):   2, 40
That part and those aspects of a real or an abstract world to which the information exchanged during communication is related.

Realization: 9

The phase in the development of an information system in which the information is realized according to its specifications. During the realization phase, only the realization aspects of the information system are considered. Not only the automated part of the information system, but also the nonautomated part, is realized during the realization phase by specifying manual administrative procedures, relevant organizational measures and any other solutions.

Realization aspects of an information system: 9

Everything concerned with how the information system must be realized and the technical demands it must meet.

Reference to a role: 88

An array of object type names and role names, where the name of the object type of each role appears to the left of the role name, and the name of the object type of its co-role to the right of the role name. A reference to a role determines a connected path of object types and fact types in the information structure diagram and refers to a role and its population. "Fillers" can be added to references to a role where this is thought desirable and plurals can be used.

Referenceable information structure diagram: 149

An information structure diagram in which every non-lexical object can always be referred to uniquely.

Role: 57

A column in a population diagram of a fact type.

Rules: 60

Elementary propositions which are not facts. **Together** facts and rules constitute communicable knowledge or information about a certain reality.

State constraints: 66

Constraints which involve one single information base state. State constraints prescribe which facts may be found at any moment in the fact type populations.

Subset: 175, 191
A role of an object type or a combination of roles of object types is a subset of another role of the same object type or of another combination of roles of the same object types, if the population of the first role or the first combination of roles always forms a subset of the population of the second role or the second combination of roles.

Subset constraint: 175, 191
A constraint which expresses the fact that a role of an object type or a combination of roles of object types is a subset of another role of the same object type or of another combination of roles of the same object types.

Subtype: 316
A non-lexical object type whose objects form a (real) subset of the objects of another non-lexical object type.

Subtype defining constraint: 362
A (non-graphical) constraint which presribes when an object of a certain object type belongs to a subtype of it.

Subtype exclusion constraint: 320
A constraint that expresses the fact that two or more subtypes of the same object type exclude each other.

Subtype family: 326
A hierarchical structure of subtypes.

Subtype totality constraint: 213
A constraint which expresses the totality of a combination of two or more subtypes of the same object type.

Supertype: 316
A non-lexical object type having another non-lexical object type as subtype.

Ternary fact type: 266
A fact type that consists of three roles.

Ternary sentence type: 262
A sentence type that consists of three roles.

Total role(s):   144, 213
A role or a combination of roles of one object type with the characteristic that each
object of this object type must occur in the population of this role or in the
population of at least one of the roles of this combination.

Total subtypes: 322
A combination of two or more subtypes of the same object type is total if every
object of this object type belongs to one or more of the subtypes.

Totality constraint: 144, 213
A constraint which expresses the totality of a role or of a combination of roles.

Transition constraint: 66, 377
A (non-graphical) constraint which presribes which changes are allowed within
the populations of one or more roles.

Unary fact type: 313
A fact type that consists of only one role. A unary fact type is always an idea type
and therefore always involves a non-lexical object type.

Unique role(s):   131, 205
A role or a combination of roles in every population of which every object or every
possible combination of objects may occur only once.

Uniqueness constraint: 131, 205
A constraint which expresses the uniqueness of a role or of a combination of roles.

Universe of discourse: 2, 40
See Reality.

Value constraint: 355
A (non-graphical) constraint which prescribes which lexical objects may occur in
the role populations of a lexical object type.

2 GRAPHICAL SYMBOLS

Derivability symbol: 372

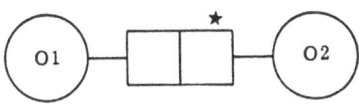

The fact type involving object types O1
and O2 is derivable.

Subset symbol: 175, 191

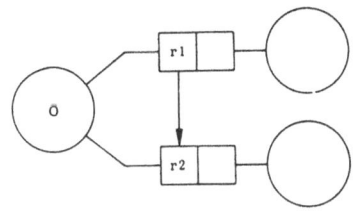

Role r1 of object type O is a subset of
role r2 of this object type.

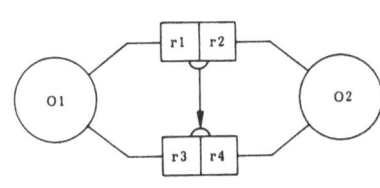

The combination of roles r1 and r2 of
object types O1 and O2 is a subset of
the combination of roles r3 and r4 of
these object types.

Fact type symbol: 54

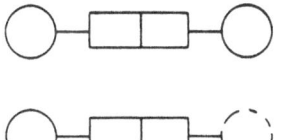

idea type

bridge type

Equality symbol   168

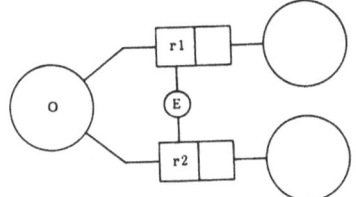

Roles r1 and r2
of object type O are equal.

Object type symbol: 50, 52

non-lexical object type

lexical object type

Population diagram: 55

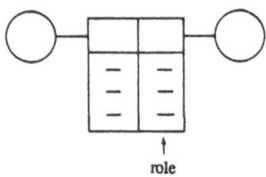

role

Population table: 76

NOLOT name 1	• • •	• • •
LOT name 1	• • •	• • •
role name 1	• • •	• • •
lexical object 1	• • •	• • •
• • •	• • •	• • •
• • •	• • •	• • •

role

Subtype symbol: 316

Non-lexical object type B
is a subtype of
non-lexical object type A.

Non-lexical object type A
is a supertype of
non-lexical object type B.

Totality symbol: 144, 213, 322

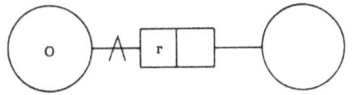

Role r of object type O is total.

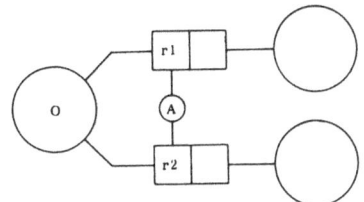

The combination of roles r1 and r2
of object type O is total.

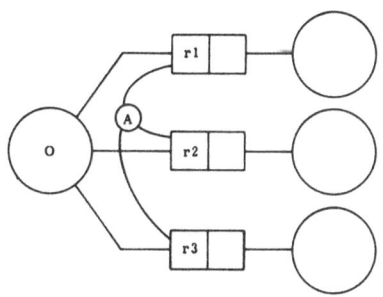

The combination of roles r1, r2 and r3
of object type O is total.

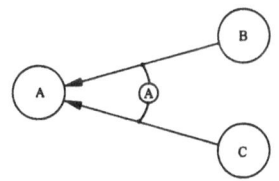

The combination of subtypes B and C
of object type A is total.

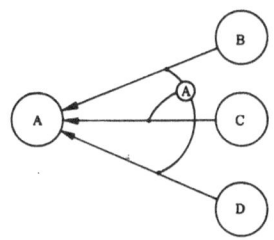

The combination of subtypes B, C and
D of object type A is total.

Exclusion symbol: 182, 197, 320

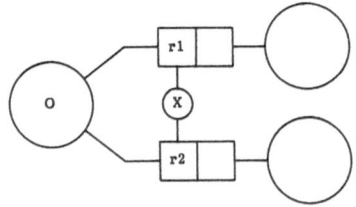

Roles r1 and r2 of object type O exclude each other.

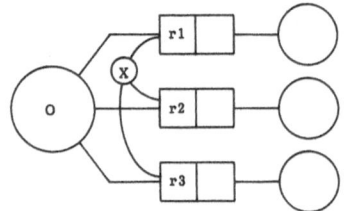

Roles r1, r2 and r3 of object type O exclude each other.

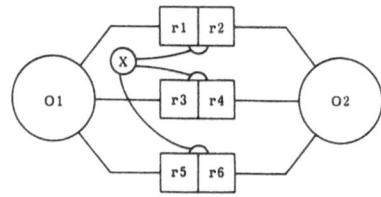

The combinations of roles r1 and r2 and r3 and r4 of object types O1 and O2 exclude each other.

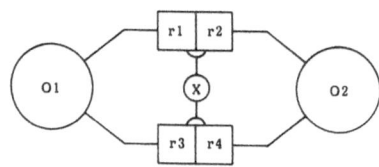

The combinations of roles r1 and r2, r3 and r4 and r5 and r6 of object types O1 and O2 exclude each other.

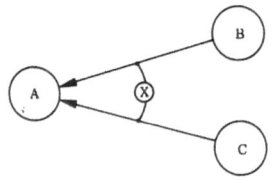

Subtypes B and C of object type A exclude each other.

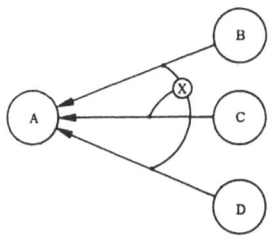

Subtypes B, C and D of object type A
exclude each other.

Uniqueness symbol: 131, 205

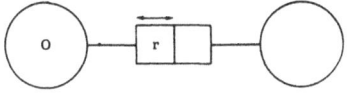

Role r of object type O is unique.

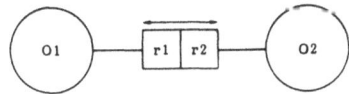

The combination of roles r1 of object
type O1 and r2 of object type O2 is
unique.

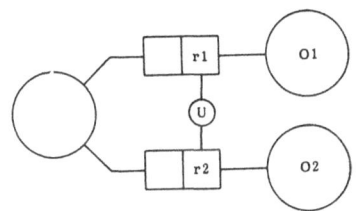

The combination of roles r1 of object
type O1 and r2 of object type O2 is
unique.

The four possible uniqueness constraints in binary fact types: 138

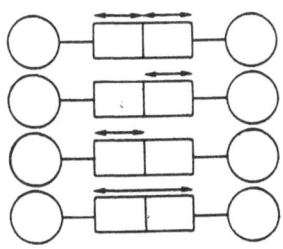

Uniqueness constraints involving bridge types: 139, 218

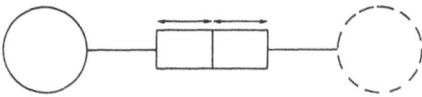

The lexical objects of this lexical object type refer unambiguously (and thus uniquely) via the bridge type to the non-lexical objects of the non-lexical object type.

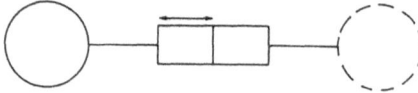

The lexical objects of this lexical object type refer non-uniquely via the bridge type to the non-lexical objects of the non-lexical object type.

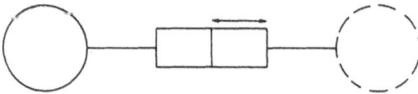

The lexical objects of this lexial object type refer uniquely via the bridge type to the non-lexical objects of the non-lexical object type.

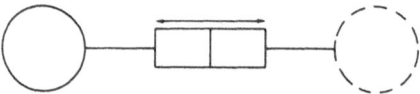

The lexical objects of this lexical object type refer non-uniquely via the bridge type to the non-lexical objects of the non-lexical object type.

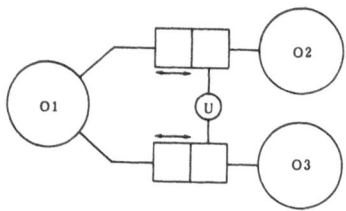

The combinations of objects of types O2 and O3 form one-to-one references to objects of type O1.

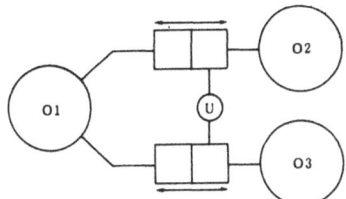

The combinations of the objects of types O2 and O3 form unique references to objects of type O1.

The abridged notation for bridge types: 153

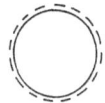

The combined exclusion and totality symbol: 214, 323

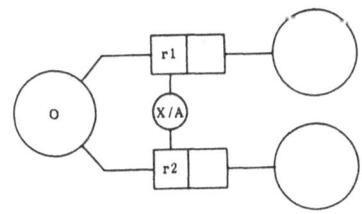

Roles r1 and r2 of object type O exclude each other and their combination is total.

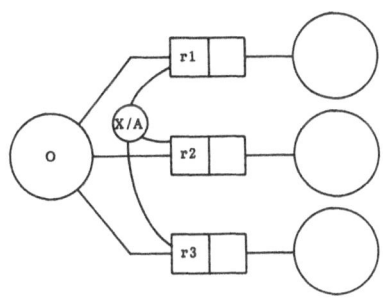

Roles r1, r2 and r3 of object type O exclude each other and their combination is total.

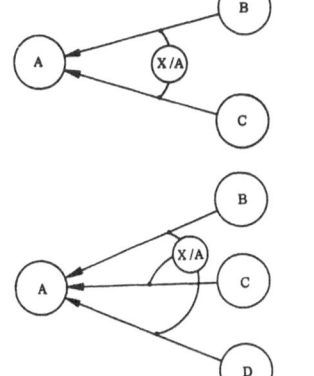

Subtypes B and C of object type A exclude each other and their combination is total.

Subtypes B, C and D of object type A exclude each other and their combination is total.

The following situations are not allowed:

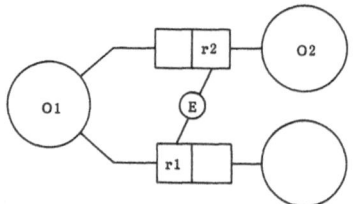

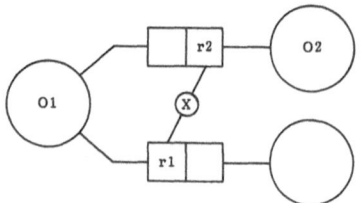

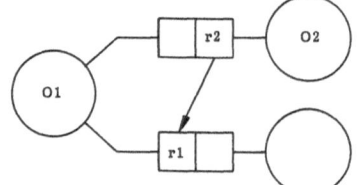

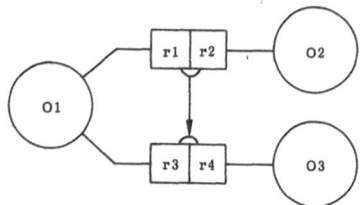

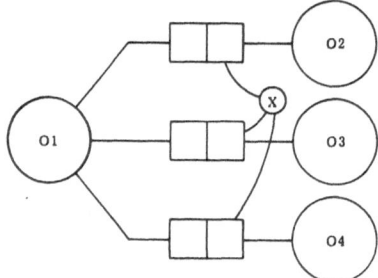

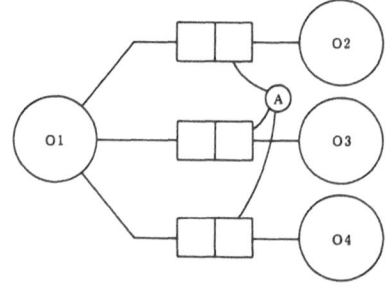

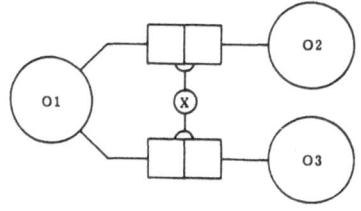

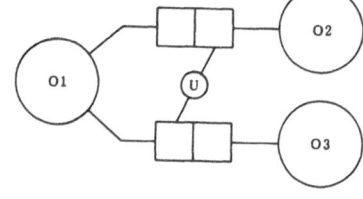

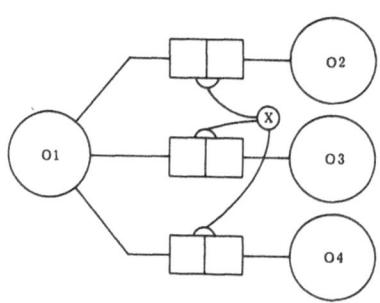

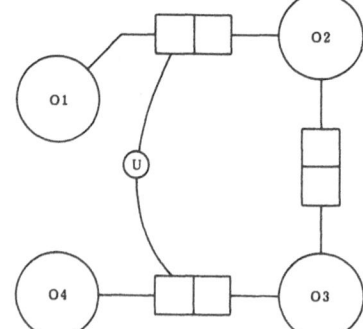

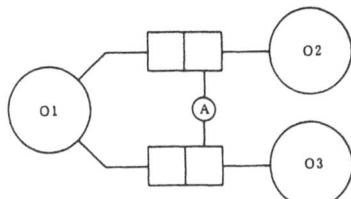

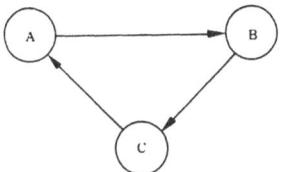

If the objects of type A form a subset of the objects of type B and these again form a subset of the objects of type C, the objects of type C cannot form a subset of the objects of type A.

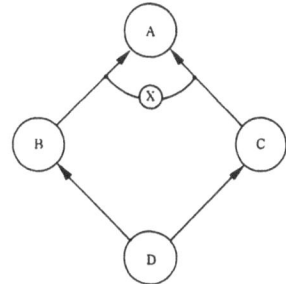

If the objects of types B and C form exclusive sets, they cannot have any (non-empty) sets in common.

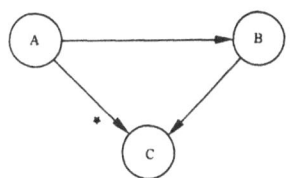

The fact that object type A is a subtype of object type C is implied by the fact that object type A is a subtype of object type B and that this object type is again a subtype of object type C.

3 PRINCIPLES

Conceptual principle: 15

The grammar exclusively describes the conceptual aspects of the information exchange with the information system.

100% principle: 15

The grammar describes all of the conceptual aspects of the information exchange with the information system.

Natural language principle: 68, 293

Information can always be described by means of binary deep structure sentences in a natural language.

4 RULES

Singularity rule: 55, 137

The combination of all roles of a fact type is always unique.

N-1 rule: 284

– If an n-ary sentence type (fact type) is elementary, at least one combination of n-1 roles or the combination of all n roles is unique.
– If at least one combination of less than n-1 roles or at least one individual role of an n-ary sentence type (fact type) is unique, this sentence type (fact type) is not elementary.

Referenceability rule: 149

An information structure diagram must be referenceable.

The with/of rule: 87

If no role name is listed by a bridge type, it is assumed that the role of the non-lexical object type has the standard name "with", and that the role of the lexical object type has the standard name "of".

Role identification rule: 87

A role of a binary fact type is uniquely denoted by combining the name of the object type of that role, the role name itself, and the name of the object type of the other role (the co-role) of that fact type.

Role name rule: 86

The name of a role of an object type is one of the predicates of the elementary sentences which begin with an object of this object type and which belong to the elementary sentence type that describes the fact type belonging to that role.

Subtype rule: 317

- Every object of a subtype can occur in the populations of all of the roles of the supertype.
- Every object of a subtype must occur in the populations of all of the total roles of its supertype.
- Not every object of a supertype can automatically occur in the populations of the roles of its subtypes.

Compatibility rule: 226

- Equality constraints must involve individual roles of the same object type.
- Subset and exclusion constraints must involve individual roles of the same object type or combinations of roles of the same object types.
- Totality constraints must involve one or more individual roles of the same object type.
- Uniqueness constraints must involve one or more roles of the same fact type or individual roles of different fact types whose co-roles belong to the same object type.

Rules for references to role populations: 91

A subset of a role can be referred to by adding a restrictive condition to the reference to that role directly after the name of a lexical object type. The restrictive condition consists of a mathematical sign and a lexical object (a "value") to which the objects of the lexical object type must be compared.

The following mathematical signs are allowed:

$=$ or : "equal to"
$>$ or : "greater than"
$<$ or : "smaller than"
$\geq$ or : "greater than or equal to"
$\leq$ or : "smaller than or equal to"
$\neq$ or : "not equal to"

The " = " sign may be left out, if so desired.

When a non-lexical object type has only one bridge type, the name of the role of the non-lexical object type of this bridge type and the name of the lexical object type can be omitted in expressions using the equal sign (" = ").

In a reference to a role, several restrictive conditions can be combined by means of "and" and "or".

References to roles can be combined by means of "and" and "or". This creates expressions which refer to the union or to the intersection of several role populations.

A reference which consists of only the name of an object type refers to the union of the populations of all roles of this object type.

A reference which consists of only the name of a subtype refers to all of the objects which belong to this subtype.

5 THE STEPS IN THE NIAM METHOD OF INFORMATION ANALYSIS

Begin with an activity diagram or a comparable description of the object system. On the basis of this, draw up (when necessary) an information flow diagram.

Repeat the following steps for one or more information flows which begin or end in the information system or part of it.

1. Select or devise an example of the contents of the information flow(s) to be analyzed.

2. Describe the example in natural language.

3. Describe the example by means of one or more population tables.

   3.1 Determine the lexical objects and name the lexical object types.

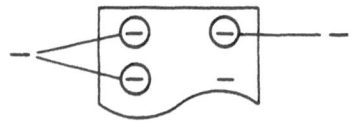

3.2 Create one or more population tables listing the lexical objects and the names of the lexical object types.

3.3 Determine the non-lexical object types and note their names in the population table(s).

4. Determine the elementary sentence types.

4.1 First investigate whether the sentence type described by population tables can be split into binary sentence types without loss of information. If this is not possible, investigate whether this sentence type (or part of it) can be split into ternary sentence types without loss of information. If this is not possible either, investigate whether this sentence type (or part of it) can be split into sentence types consisting of four roles, etc. Demonstrate that any non-binary sentence types found this way are elementary by showing that there is a population table in which information gets lost during further splitting. (For this process, use a population table in which all possible combinations of objects occur.)

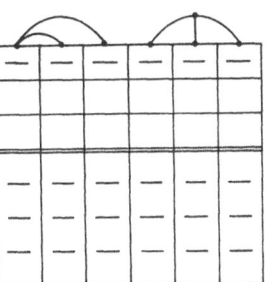

4.2 Determine (likewise on the basis of a population table containing all possible combinations of objects) which combinations of roles of any non-binary sentence types found this way are unique. When a combination of less than n-1 roles or an individual role of an n-ary sentence type is unique, this sentence type is not elementary and a mistake has been made in the previous step.

4.3 Connect the columns of the population table which belong to one sentence type to each other.

5. Add the fact types which are described by these sentence types to the information structure diagram.

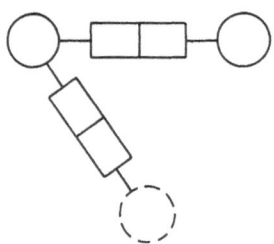

6. Determine the uniqueness constraints and totality constraints with respect to the individual fact types.

6.1 Determine the uniqueness constraints with respect to the individual fact types.

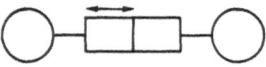

6.2 Determine the totality constraints with respect to the individual fact types.

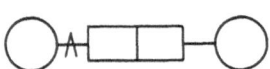

7. Replace every non-binary fact type by
    binary fact types.

    7.1 "Nest" a unique combination of
    roles of the non-binary fact type
    into a new non-lexical object
    type.

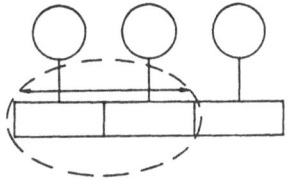

    7.2 Define binary fact types, each of
    which involves one of the object
    types of the original non-binary
    fact type and the new object type
    defined in the previous substep.

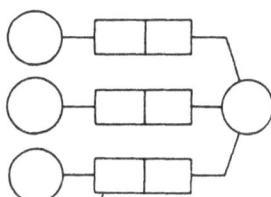

    7.3 For every unique combination of
    roles in the original non-binary
    fact type, draw a uniqueness sym-
    bol with respect to the corre-
    sponding roles of the binary fact
    types defined in the previous sub-
    step.

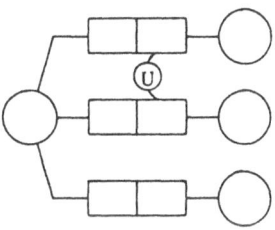

    7.4 Determine the uniqueness and
    the totality of the individual roles
    of these binary fact types.

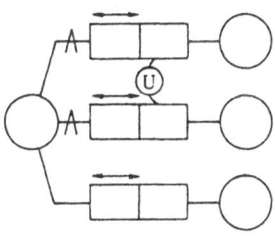

8. Where necessary, define subtypes.

    8.1 For every object type check whether:

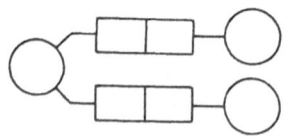

        – a subset of objects involving exclusively one or more roles and/or one or more constraints can be denoted in this object type.

        – it can be unambiguously determined on the basis of one or more facts involving objects of the object type under consideration, whether or not an object of this object type belongs to this subset.

        – this subset concerns a concept that occurs in the (professional) language of the future users of the information system.

       When this is the case, define a subtype that corresponds to this subset.

    8.2 Adapt the information structure diagram such that the roles which exclusively involve a subtype, are connected to the subtype rather than to the supertype.

    8.3 Determine the uniqueness and totality of the individual roles of the subtypes.

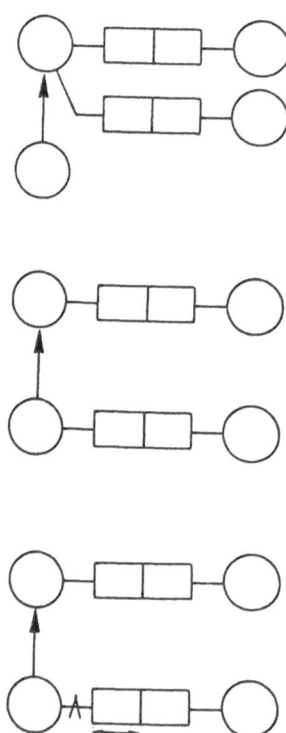

9. Add the remaining graphical constraints.

9.1 For every pair of non-total roles of one object type, check whether these roles are equal.

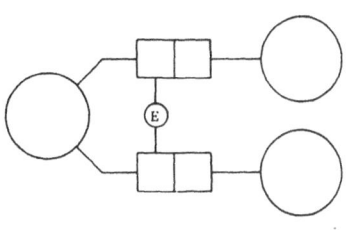

9.2 For every pair of non-total roles of one object type, check whether one role is a subset of the other role.

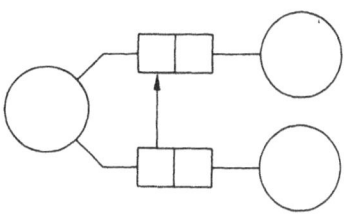

9.3 For every pair of combinations of roles of the same object types, check whether one combination of roles is a subset of the other combination of roles.

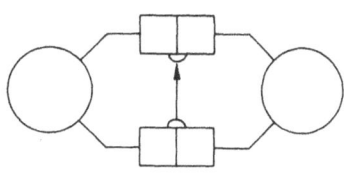

9.4 Check whether two or more non-total roles of one object type exclude each other.

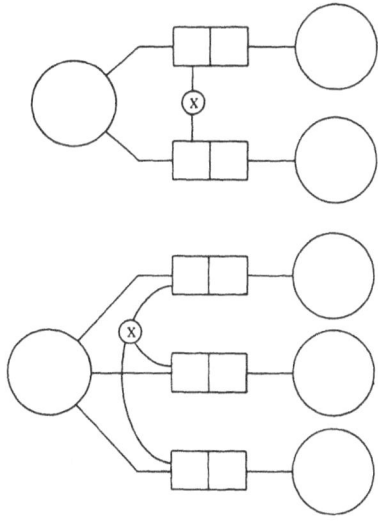

9.5 Check whether two or more combinations of roles of the same object types exclude each other.

9.6 Check whether combinations of two or more co-roles of one object type are unique.

9.7 Check whether combinations of two or more roles of one object type are total.

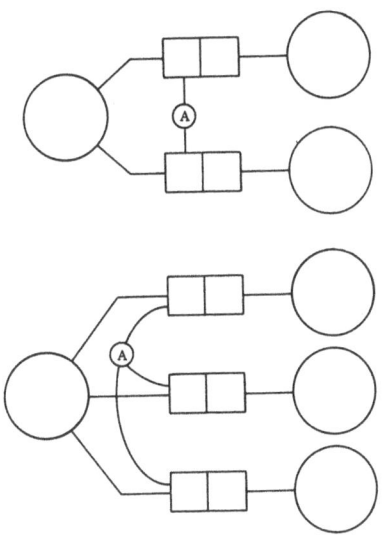

10. Add the non-graphical constraints.

   10.1 For every role of a lexical object type, check whether a value constraint applies.

   10.2 For every non-unique role, check whether a cardinality constraint applies.

   10.3 For every subtype, check whether a subtype defining constraint applies.

   10.4 For the roles of every object type, check whether other non-graphical constraints apply.

   10.5 For every fact type, check whether a transition constraint applies.

11. Verify the information structure diagram.

    11.1 Verify the information structure.

        – Verify, with all due consideration of the constraints, whether (imaginary) tables, each corresponding to one fact type in the information structure diagram, can be "filled" with the contents of the original population tables.

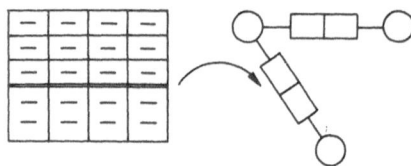

        – Verify, with all due consideration of the constraints, whether the original population tables can be reconstructed from (imaginary) tables, each one corresponding to one fact type in the information structure diagram.

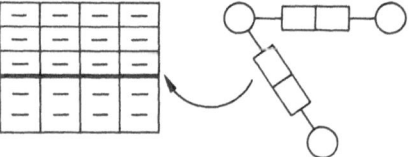

    11.2 Verify the constraints.

        – Have all of the necessary constraints been specified completely?

        – Are there any constraints which are implied by other constraints and which are therefore redundant?

        – Are there constraints which are in conflict with each other?

11.3 Verify the referenceability.

- Can every non-lexical object
  be referred to uniquely by a
  lexical object or by a combination of lexical objects?

REFERENCES AND BIBLIOGRAPHY

1 J.J. Van Griethuysen (ed.), "Concepts and Terminology for the Conceptual Schema and the Information Base", ISO Report, publication number ISO/TC97/SC5-N695, 1982.
2 M. Lundeberg, G. Goldkuhl and A. Nilson, "Systeemontwikkeling volgens ISAC – de ISAC-methodiek", Samson: Alphen aan den Rijn, 1981.
3 M.F. Connor, "Structured Analysis and Design Technique (SADT) Introduction", SofTech Report nr. 9595-7, SofTech Inc.: Waltham Mass, U.S.A.
4 G.F. Hice, W.S. Turner and L.F. Cashwell, "System Development Methodology (SDM)", North-Holland: Amsterdam, 1978.
   H.B. Eilers, "Systeemontwikkeling volgens S.D.M.", Academic Service: The Hague, 1985.
5 Text and course material from the course "Nijssen Information Analysis Method", Control Data, Rijswijk, 1983.
6 G.M. Nijssen, "Information Analysis", Seminar text, Control Data, 1980.
7 P.S. Thompson, "Information Analysis – Concepts and Methodology", Control Data, Data Management Technology Center, 1981.
8 G.M.A. Verheijen and J. Van Bekkum, "NIAM: An Information Analysis Method", Proceedings of the IFIP WG 8.1 Working Conference on Comparative Review of Information Systems Design Methodologies, Noordwijkerhout, 1982, in: Olle, Sol and Verrijn-Stuart (eds.), "Information Systems Design Methodologies", North Holland: Amsterdam, 1982 (pp. 537-590).
9 G.M. Nijssen, "An Architecture for Knowledge Base Software", J. of Australian Computer Society, Nov. 1981.
10 R. Meersman and G.M. Nijssen, "From data bases to knowledge bases", Infotech State of the Art Review, Pergamon Press: London, 1983.
11 F. Van Assche and R. Meersman, "Modelling and Manipulating Data Bases in Terms of Semantic Nets", 8th International Joint Conference on Artificial Intelligence, Karlsruhe, 1983.
12 R. Meersman, "The High-Level End-User", in: "Data Base: The 2nd Generation", Infotech State of the Art Report, series 10, nr. 7, Pergamon Press: London, 1982.
13 F.J.M. Van Assche, "A System Development System for Data Management", Symposium on Application Systems Development of ACM, Nuremberg, 1983, B.G. Teubner: Stuttgart, 1983.
14 F. Van Assche, D. Simons and M. Vanhoednaghe, "The Automated Mapping From a Binary Conceptual Schema to a 5th NF Data Base Schema", Control Data, International Center for Information Analysis Services, Brussels, 1983.
15 D. Vermeir and N. Prabhakaran, "On the Generation of Database Schemata", Research Report, Department of Computer Science, University of Queensland, Australia, 1982.

16 M.J. Carkeet and G.M. Nijssen, "A Comparison of Conceptualisation and Normalisation", Research Report, Department of Computer Science, University of Queensland, Australia, 1982

17 E. Falkenberg and G.M. Nijssen et al., "Feature Analysis of ACM/PCM, CIAM, ISAC and NIAM", Proceedings of IFIP WG 8.1 Working Conference on Information Systems Design Methodologies: A Feature Analysis, York, 1983.